Business in Latin America

Business in Latin America provides readers with a comprehensive overview of the business environment of this dynamic and challenging region. The book begins with an overview of the most important macroenvironments shaping the region's opportunities and risks, while the second part focuses on the business strategies that respond to those opportunities and risks. Capturing the dynamism of this region, this new edition provides a thorough and nuanced understanding of the commonalities and differences within the multifaceted business environments of Latin America.

The second edition has been thoroughly revised and updated to include:

- The sources of economic, political, and natural risks, including the impact of COVID-19.
- The endemic role of corruption in institutions, the economy, and society.
- The region's cultural and social diversity and resilience.
- The role of technology and digitalization on corporate and marketing strategies.
- The challenges of managing local and regional supply chains.

The book includes examples and cases from across the region on corporate strategies, marketing, entrepreneurship, leadership, human resource management, and social and environmental sustainability. An ideal resource for anyone considering a business venture in the region, the book will especially appeal to practitioners and students who have a particular interest in Latin America.

Fernando Robles is an Emeritus Professor of International Business and International Relations at the School of Business of the George Washington University. A native of Peru, Robles received a bachelor's degree in Civil Engineering at the National University of Engineering, Lima, Peru and a master's degree from the Graduate School of Business Administration (ESAN) in Lima, Peru. He has an MBA degree from Georgia State University and a PhD in Business Administration from the Pennsylvania State University.

Nila M. Wiese is a Professor of International Business and Marketing in the School of Business and Leadership at the University of Puget Sound in Tacoma, Washington. A native of Honduras, she received a dual BS degree in Marketing and Management from Oklahoma State University, a master's in International Management from Baylor University, and a PhD in Marketing from University of Oregon.

Business in Latin America

Strategic Opportunities and Risks

Second Edition

Fernando Robles and Nila M. Wiese

Routledge
Taylor & Francis Group

NEW YORK AND LONDON

Designed cover image: © Reinier Snijders / EyeEm / Getty Images

Second edition published 2023
by Routledge
605 Third Avenue, New York, NY 10158

and by Routledge
4 Park Square, Milton Park, Abingdon, Oxon, OX14 4RN

Routledge is an imprint of the Taylor & Francis Group, an informa business

© 2023 Fernando Robles and Nila M. Wiese

First edition published by Willan 2014

ISBN: 978-1-032-02278-9 (hbk)
ISBN: 978-1-032-02277-2 (pbk)
ISBN: 978-1-003-18267-2 (ebk)

DOI: 10.4324/9781003182672

Typeset in Minion
by Deanta Global Publishing Services, Chennai, India

To Carol and Natalie for their quest for clarity of my ideas. F.R.

To my parents, Adalberto and Gloria, for their love and support. N.W.

Contents

Figures

Tables

Introduction

This second edition updates the business conditions in Latin America as it enters the second decade of the twenty-first century. The timing of the update finds the world and the region at a turning point due to the disruptions of the 2020 health pandemic on societies and economies. Businesses everywhere adjusted to the upheaval by reformulating their models and operations to survive the shifting trends in markets and consumption styles. Writing the update was a challenge as conditions and strategies continued to change during the period of writing. We found that certain structural conditions of the region, such as corruption and cultural norms, were constant, whereas others were fluid, such as migration flows and challenges to democratic processes. Sorting the enduring from the changing conditions was a challenge. We understood that, in many cases, these events will be resolved over time, and companies will find solutions to the current challenges. In that sense, the aim of the book is to set a baseline that would help the reader advance knowledge of business conditions in the region. In writing this edition, we were guided by the following objectives:

1. To provide a comprehensive overview of the business environment in Latin America.
2. To identify the major drivers of market opportunities and risks in Latin America.
3. To assess the characteristics and behaviors of Latin American consumers and the implications for marketing strategies in the region.
4. To determine the most relevant business drivers and critical success factors for effective strategies in Latin American markets for companies from within and outside the region.
5. To assess effective managerial and leadership practices for the region.

Organization and Content

We have reorganized and condensed the structure of the previous edition to improve the flow of topics. This second edition is organized in two major parts; the first begins with a macro perspective on the Latin American market, focusing on the region's economic, geopolitical, legal, sociocultural, technological, and competitive environments. A new chapter describing population dynamics and demographic transitions in the region sets the stage for later discussions about strategies for the region. The chapter on culture has also been reorganized and updated to include a description of national cultures, followed by an analysis of the impact of culture on organizational culture, leadership, and talent management. This first part closes with a new chapter focusing on the sources of internal and external risks in the region and countries' and firms' resilience in managing these risks. In this chapter, we explore the impact of COVID-19 on fragile Latin American economies and study the nature of corruption and environmental degradation. Part II of the book moves the reader from

DOI: 10.4324/9781003182672-1

context to the practice of business. We begin this second half of the book by taking a closer look at the Latin American consumer and consumer markets; identifying new trends, values, and behaviors; and discussing effective ways to reach them. The following three chapters provide a discussion of strategies for diverse types of companies: large multinationals from outside the region, Latin American multinationals, and small and entrepreneurial firms. A new chapter analyzes the participation of Latin America in global value chains and the creation of regional ones. The final chapter captures the key strategic opportunities and risks discussed throughout the book and provides an outlook for the future of the region.

A brief description of each chapter follows.

The first chapter, 'The Economic Environment of Latin America,' sets the stage for the rest of the book by assessing the region's macroeconomic situation during the past two decades, its current economic situation, and attempts to emerge from the health and economic crisis caused by the COVID-19 virus. Countries in the region continue to share a legacy of issues that include poor educational and health systems, income inequality, weak infrastructure, a large informal sector, corruption, and obsolete legal and regulatory frameworks. The onset of the global pandemic in early 2020 further exposed these institutional voids and inefficiencies and accentuated the economic, political, and social problems that had been brewing in the region for several years. The chapter is organized into four sections. The first section provides an overview of Latin America's macroeconomic growth in the twenty-first century, focusing on key indicators of growth and development. The next two sections assess trade and investment patterns, highlighting the region's position in the global economic order. The fourth section presents a discussion of the effects of the COVID-19 pandemic on the region's economic situation and prospects. The chapter closes with a review of the region's need for a new approach to growth and development that centers on issues of social equality and inclusion as well as environmental sustainability.

Chapter 2, 'The Political and Legal Environment of Latin America,' reviews Latin America's political progress in the past four decades, with most countries experiencing a period of relatively democratic regimes beginning in the early 1990s. In 2021, most countries have electoral democracies in place, but democracy in the region remains fragile. The regulatory environment in Latin America has also seen improvements, with reductions of regulations and streamlining of bureaucratic procedures. However, law enforcement and the judicial system remain weak and riddled with corruption. The first section of this chapter provides a snapshot of Latin America's political environment, followed by discussions on the weakening of democracy and the rise of populism and authoritarianism across the region. The following two sections highlight some of the main areas of institutional weakness and current corruption trends in the region. The final section summarizes key aspects of the region's regulatory environment. The chapter ends with a synthesis of positive and negative trends in the political and legal environments of the region.

Chapter 3, 'The Competitive Environment of Latin America,' provides an understanding of the degree of competitiveness and the competitive structure in Latin America. The competitive landscape in Latin America has evolved significantly over the past few decades. A stronger presence of multinational corporations (MNCs) from developed and emerging economies; established, large family-controlled domestic conglomerates; and a vibrant sector of small- and medium-size businesses have contributed to shaping a more dynamic competitive environment. The chapter is organized into four sections. The first section describes the factors that explain the levels, drivers, and barriers of competitiveness in Latin America. The second section focuses on the role Latin American countries play in global supply chains, focusing on how countries in the region can leverage and enhance their positions in global value chains in the medium and long term. The next section describes the current structure of competition in the region, highlighting the various types of organizational players and their defining characteristics. A summary of the main issues related to competition and competitiveness in the region closes the chapter.

Chapter 4, 'Demographic Transitions and Population Dynamics in Latin America,' is a new chapter that provides a comprehensive review of the Latin American population. The chapter starts with the region's transition from a young, rural population into an older, urban population and the drivers and stages of this evolution. The following section accounts for the powerful force of migration from and within the region and the motivations driving these trends. The third section focuses on race and ethnicity and explains how ethnic and racial groups in the region are reclaiming their ancestry and civic rights, particularly those of African and Indigenous roots. The next section covers education in Latin America, with a particular focus on the learning outcomes of their youth. The following section centers on urbanization; Latin America is one of the most urbanized regions in the world with megalopolises that rival the populations and economic power of entire countries. The next section reviews housing conditions and provides an assessment of household economic power and differences in household income wealth distribution. The last section of the chapter addresses health and healthcare systems with an emphasis on identifying countries with resilient health systems. The chapter closes with an assessment of the pandemic's effect on economic contraction and population dynamics.

Chapter 5, 'The Sociocultural Environment of Latin America,' explores the region's national and business cultures. Latin America has been characterized as conservative in terms of moral values, but the increase of non-religious affiliations has moved countries into more liberal and tolerant views on abortion, contraception, divorce, and sexual preferences. Latin American business culture is rooted in its European colonial heritage; this legacy has created long-term organizational and decision-making styles characterized by concentration of power, multilevel hierarchical structures, strong networks of relationships, and paternalism. The first part of the chapter discusses key components of Latin American culture with an emphasis on values and the influence of religion and beliefs. The second part provides a description of business culture under the perspective of four well-known business cultural frameworks. The next section identifies the idiosyncratic manifestation of particular national cultures. The fourth section focuses on the influence of cultural norms and values on leadership styles. The fifth section centers on the status and roles of women as leaders in business organizations. The last section focuses on the important role of talent development as a significant source of competitive advantage. We argue that adopting culturally appropriate practices will have a direct impact on organizational performance.

High uncertainty and risk are omnipresent, and their economic and social consequences for society drive business decisions.

Chapter 6, 'Business Risks and Uncertainty in Latin America,' closes Part I by providing a summary analysis of the nature and types of risks in Latin America. First, we review a well-known framework to understand uncertainty and risks and develop scenarios for companies to prepare and respond. In the following sections, we identify, define, and assess different types of risks: economic, political, corruption, crime and violence, societal, and natural and climate. In each section, we identify the drivers of risks, provide an assessment of their level across Latin America, identify the vulnerability of countries, and determine their adaptive capacity and resilience. It is important to note that the level of risks may have dissipated by the time of your reading, whereas new risks may have emerged after this publication. As you read, keep in mind that drivers of risk may be the same for the region but may manifest in different forms, creating a high degree of heterogeneity across countries in the region. The chapter concludes with a discussion on the need to have a solid framework to understand uncertainty and risks to prepare for the future.

Chapter 7, 'Marketing Strategies for Latin American Consumer Markets,' describes how consumer markets have grown in size and purchasing power, becoming increasingly segmented, more sophisticated and discerning, and less frugal while remaining distinctive. This chapter begins with an overview of the size, characteristics, and evolving values and consumption patterns of consumer markets in the region. The chapter covers key strategic marketing decisions, including value creation, segmentation, branding and positioning, and pricing. The chapter then presents an overview of communication strategies to effectively reach Latin American consumers, particularly in the context of consumers' high levels of connectivity. The chapter concludes with an assessment of retailing and omnichannel strategies used by firms in the region.

Chapter 8, 'Corporate Strategies for Firms from Outside the Region,' reviews the strategies of MNCs in Latin America. MNCs assess opportunities and risks in relation to other emerging markets. The chapter is organized in four sections. The first section discusses the challenges for strategy formulation in regional markets and elaborates on the advantages and disadvantages of MNCs in Latin America. The next section introduces a framework for a regional strategy for MNCs within the context of a global strategy and describes a path of regional expansion for these companies. The following section describes the extent of replication and adaptation of MNCs in the region. The fourth section is a case study of a regional strategy from the premier global retailer: Walmart. The chapter ends with a critical summary of key aspects of non-regional MNCs in Latin America.

Chapter 9 focuses on the 'Strategic Approaches of Multilatinas and Global Latinas.' During the past three decades, firms native to Latin America successfully internationalized to other countries in the region (Multilatinas) and to countries across the globe (Global Latinas). The majority of Multilatinas and Global Latinas are privately owned, many by large, family-owned or family-controlled conglomerates, yet many are still wholly or partially owned by the state. This chapter defines and describes Multilatinas and Global Latinas, providing an assessment of their competitive strengths and weaknesses in their national, regional, and global markets. The chapter also identifies the various paths to internationalization Latin American firms have followed and their most common strategic approaches. The chapter highlights the relative dominance of Mexico, Brazil, and Chile as the countries with the largest number of Latin American multinationals; the diversity of sectors in which Latin American multinationals operate; their preference for internationalization through acquisitions and strategic alliances; and the resilience and innovation they have demonstrated to survive and thrive during the present health and economic crisis.

Chapter 10, 'The Entrepreneurial Environment of Latin America,' focuses on innovation and entrepreneurship in Latin America. Promotion and access to entrepreneurial opportunities are considered main drivers of innovation, employment, income generation, poverty eradication, and social inclusion. In this context, new ventures and the formalization and growth of micro, small-, and medium-size enterprises are critical for prosperity in Latin America. This chapter starts by providing a brief discussion of factors that facilitate or hinder innovation in Latin America. The second and third sections of the chapter provide an overview of the state of entrepreneurship in Latin America, rates of entrepreneurial activity, and insights on attitudes toward entrepreneurship in the region, followed by an analysis of the entrepreneurial ecosystem in select countries and in the region as a whole. The next section takes a more in-depth look at specific types of entrepreneurs in the region, including technology, women, and social entrepreneurs. The final section focuses on small- and medium-size businesses, presenting a discussion of their competitive strengths and weaknesses as well their strategic choices to compete both domestically and internationally. The chapter closes with a summary assessment of opportunities and challenges faced by Latin American entrepreneurs and small- and medium-size businesses.

Chapter 11, 'Global and Regional Value Chains in Latin America,' reviews Latin America's participation in global and regional value chains. Global value chains (GVCs) are the engines of the global economy. Their emergence has been driven by a combination of increased fragmentation and dispersion of production, as many countries have upgraded their capabilities and invested in supporting infrastructure that has lowered transportation and communication costs. Latin America has been largely at the edges of GVCs, mostly supplying raw materials and commodities based on its natural resources. The chapter is organized in four parts. The first part introduces basic concepts of value chains. The second part analyzes Latin America's participation in GVCs. The third section focuses on regional value chains and sectorial differences. The last section focuses on the multinational firm's perspective and logic to configure value chains and assess the attractiveness of Latin American countries based on MNC's considerations. We conclude the chapter with an assessment of Latin America's potential for deeper participation in GVCs.

The final chapter, 'Strategic Opportunities and Risks in Latin America: A Summary,' aims to provide the reader with an overview of the main strategic opportunities and risks in Latin America. The chapter is comprised of four sections. The first section summarizes key elements of the region's economic, political, competitive, and sociocultural environments to set a baseline for understanding the business conditions in the region. The next section provides a summary of strategic approaches to the region, from marketing approaches to capture Latin American consumers to corporate strategies for foreign and domestic firms of all sizes. The third section identifies key sources of risk and uncertainty facing the region in the present and in the near future as well as highlights the most important business opportunities for firms interested in Latin America. The chapter's concluding thoughts present a brief speculation about the future of business in the region.

Uniqueness

The book is unique in several ways:

1. It is grounded in *strategic thinking*, presenting an assessment of opportunities and risks and discussing various strategic frameworks for firms operating in the region. As such, it seemed appropriate to embed concepts and examples of product, process, management, and business-model innovations throughout.
2. It approaches business in Latin America from a *triple bottom results perspective*, focusing not only on financial goals but also social and environmental outcomes.
3. *Innovation* is a running theme throughout the book, from discussing product, process, and management innovations to highlighting innovative entrepreneurial activity in the region.
4. It focuses on *risk analysis and risk management*. Coping with volatility and uncertainty must be a key strategic consideration for companies operating in the region. Recent events show that all world regions are vulnerable to pandemics, catastrophes, and crises. The preparedness and resilience of different countries (and companies) may ameliorate the impact of these negative macro events. On the contrary, the lack of political leadership or poor infrastructure may amplify the negative consequences of global or regional events.

The book captured real-time events and data that illustrate how these important events can shape the future of the region.

5. It provides an analysis of the consequences derived from the COVID-19 pandemic on the economic, political, and social conditions of the region and its implications for business.

6. The book incorporates issues related to diversity and inclusion, sustainable environmental practices, social-driven business models, and ethical considerations for doing business in the region.

Latin America is a mosaic of countries with distinct cultures and political economies, and diverse environments. This book provides a comprehensive analysis of the business environment in Latin America and makes an important contribution to understanding the various strategic approaches that may enable success in the region.

Acknowledgments

In closing, we would like to recognize the support provided by our own institutions for the research and preparation of this book. Special thanks go to Carol Robles for her valuable editorial assistance and to Ryan Wiese and Sophia Ciserella for their research and editorial support. We also acknowledge the encouragement and support received from Routledge, particularly our editorial team, Terry Clague, Ella McFarlane and Alexandra McGregor. Finally, we appreciate the effort of Shelley Strelluf at Taylor and Francis and Vijay Bose at Deanta Global who guided us to the final stage of manuscript production preparation.

Finally, we acknowledge the immense support of our families during the process of manuscript preparation.

Part 1

The Business Environment in Latin America

1 The Economic Environment of Latin America

Introduction

This chapter reviews the macroeconomic situation of Latin America as it attempts to emerge from the health and economic crisis caused by the COVID-19 virus. The chapter 'sets the stage' for the rest of the book by assessing the region's economic growth during the past two decades, its current economic situation, and the prospects for future growth and development. In our first edition (Robles, Wiese, & Torres-Baumgarten, 2015), we questioned the degree to which the growth that the region had experienced during the first decade of the twenty-first century was sustainable. At the time, the region had successfully emerged from the 2008 recession with growth similar to or higher than before the financial collapse. But by 2014, concerns for the sustainability of such economic growth into the future loomed due in part to an overreliance on natural resource exports, realignment of countries in the region into two geographic clusters, continued social inequalities, and increasing warning about irreversible climate change. In 2020 and 2021, those concerns have been exacerbated by the health and economic crisis that enveloped the globe with the spread of the coronavirus.

The new global economic order of stagnation or slow growth in advanced, developed economies, as well as growth and rising affluence in emerging countries, was mirrored in Latin America, especially between the early 1990s through 2014. In the following five-year period (2015–2019), the region's growth began to slow down, and its political stability also began to falter (see Chapter 2 for a discussion of the region's political environment). Countries in the region continue to share a legacy of issues that include poor educational and health systems, income inequality, weak infrastructure, a large informal sector, corruption, and obsolete legal and regulatory frameworks. The onset of the global COVID-19 pandemic in early 2020 simply made these institutional voids and inefficiencies visible and accentuated the economic, political, and social problems that had been brewing in the region for several years.

The chapter is organized into four sections. The first section provides an overview of macroeconomic growth in the twenty-first century—for the region overall and for select countries. This section focuses on key indicators of growth and development, including a discussion of the effects of the COVID-19 pandemic on the region's economies. The next two sections offer a brief assessment of trade and investment patterns which highlight the region's position in the global economic order. The fourth section presents a discussion of the effects of the COVID-19 pandemic on the region's economic situation and prospects. The chapter closes with an assessment of the opportunities the region offers and the challenges it faces at present and into the future, focusing on the region's need for a new approach to growth and development that centers on issues of social equality and inclusion as well as environmental sustainability.

DOI: 10.4324/9781003182672-3

Latin America's Economic Performance from 2000 to Present

In 2021, Latin America and the Caribbean is a region of approximately 650 million people and expected to reach 700 million by 2030. Latin America's total gross domestic product (GDP) in 2020 was US$4.84 trillion (versus US$5.79 trillion in 2019), representing about 5% of the total world GDP (World Bank, 2021a). According to the International Monetary Fund (IMF), the Economic Commission for Latin America and the Caribbean (ECLAC), and the World Bank (WB), the region's GDP in 2020 contracted 6.8%–7.7%; this was much larger than the estimated decreases to world GDP of 3.3%–4.4% and the worst performance of any other developing region (ECLAC, 2021c; Maurizio, 2021; World Bank, 2021a). Latin America's average per capita gross national income (GNI, PPP) in 2020 was US$15,363, down from US$16,355 in 2019. However, intra-regional differences in GNI per capita are significant, ranging from a high of US$24,000 in Chile to a low of US$5,000 in Honduras (World Bank, 2021a). Brazil is by far the largest economy; Mexico, Argentina, Colombia, Chile, and Peru are the next most important markets in terms of total GDP (throughout the book, we refer to these countries as the 'LAC-6'). Composition of the region's GDP in 2020 was 60% services, 24% manufacturing, and 6% agriculture. Although the percentage contribution of each sector varies from country to country, the relative importance of these three components remains the same, with services being the largest contributor to GDP for all countries in the region (CIA World Factbook, 2021).

From 2003 to 2008, Latin America experienced average GDP growth rates per year of about 6.6%, prompting some to refer to this prosperous time as the region's 'Golden Years' (Talvi & Munyo, 2013). Growth did not return to the pace preceding the 2008–2009 crisis, but most countries in the region recovered relatively quickly, with the region experiencing average GDP growth rates of 5.84% and 4.37% in 2010 and 2011, respectively. Growth slowed down in 2012–2013 with an average regional GDP growth rate of 2.78% for both years; it fell sharply in 2016 (−0.39%), recovered in 2017 (1.78%), but remained low through 2019 (World Bank, 2021a). In 2020, driven by the economic collapse caused by the global COVID-19 pandemic, Latin America's GDP growth rate was −6.3% (World Bank, 2021a). Current projections estimate a GDP growth rate for the region of about 6% in 2021 and 3% in 2022. These growth expectations will bring the GDP of 14 of the 33 countries in the region back to 2019 levels by the end of 2022. By the first half of 2021, about 40% of the economic activity that had been lost in 2020 had been recovered. In the LAC-6, recovery of the economy in 2021 was being driven by a resilient services sector and robust commodities exports. In addition, strong domestic demand and an increase in remittances from abroad were also contributing to economic growth across the region (ECLAC, 2021c; Oliveros-Rosen, 2021).

The region's sustained growth during the period from 2003 to 2013 is most evident in the rise of average GDP per capita for the region, which increased steadily from a low of US$3,787 in 2003 to a high of US$10,433 in 2014. Since then, GDP per capita has steadily decreased with the most significant drop happening in 2020 (US$7,417) as a result of the COVID-19 pandemic (World Bank, 2021a). GDP per capita figures, of course, obscure persistent income distribution inequalities in the region, even after the undeniable growth of the middle class during the past two decades. The pandemic will deepen these inequalities, as low- and middle-income households have been the hardest hit (Oliveros-Rosen, 2021).

The growth seen of the past two decades was fueled by several factors: (a) the rapid rise in demand for Latin America's natural and agricultural resources, along with corresponding price increases of these commodities; (b) the growth of the middle class and parallel increases in consumption of durable and non-durable goods; (c) the effectiveness of social programs that resulted in poverty alleviation and related increases to consumption levels; and (d) greater access to capital because of higher investment flows into the region. These conditions contributed to sustained GDP growth in the region, the lifting of millions from poverty, and the enhanced competitiveness of many Latin American firms.

As pointed out above, however, growth levels were uneven across Latin American countries, and these disparities are expected to continue into the new decade. What accounts for this heterogeneity in performance across individual Latin American countries? Economic policies pursued by each country, the makeup of their economies, and their trade and investment relationships with the rest of the world help explain these differences. For instance, while some countries have pursued more free-market oriented policies (e.g., Chile) that have led to better performance, others have adopted state-directed capitalism with a pivotal role for government in identifying and directing key industrial policies (e.g., Brazil), leading to mixed performance; still others have pursued populist experiments (e.g., Venezuela) that have led to lower performance. These different experiences also highlight the impact of political instability on economic performance in the region. The countries in the region also differ in terms of their attractiveness to domestic and foreign investors, with some remaining attractive options (e.g., Chile, Panama), others showing signs of slow growth or instability (e.g., Brazil, Peru), and others representing an increasingly challenging business environment (e.g., Venezuela, Nicaragua). Table 1.1 and Figure 1.1 summarize key economic indicators for select Latin American countries.

As mentioned above, from 2000 to 2014, the region experienced sustained growth driven by favorable economic conditions, including high demand and prices for the region's commodities, a consolidation of democratic regimes, and the region's insertion into the global economy through liberalization and integration policies. This period of high economic growth was paralleled by social reforms in the region that led to poverty alleviation (Beccaria et al., 2013) and the growth of the middle class. During this period, the gap between rich and poor in Latin America narrowed. The proportion of Latin Americans living in poverty (income below US$5.50 per day) fell from 44% to 26% over that same period with more than 75 million people rising out of poverty. In addition, Latin America's middle class (income of US$13–US$70 per day) grew by 50% (50 million) to about 150 million people; by 2012—and for the first time in the region's history—the middle class exceeded the number of people living in poverty (regional average of 30%). By 2018, the gains were even more significant: the average size of the middle class in the region was 37% of the total population, with some variations across countries, (e.g., 31% in Colombia versus 55% in Chile). The middle class and the vulnerable class (those with income of US$5.50–$13 per day) combined made up almost 70% of the region's total population (Ferreira, et al., 2013; Raineri & Benoit, 2020; World Bank, 2013a; World Bank, 2021c). These more affluent individuals not only spent heavily on durable and non-durable goods but also became more active citizens, expecting and demanding from the region's governments an increasingly larger share of their countries' riches. These empowered groups seek greater access to education, health, and job opportunities. They have also grown tired of corruption and government inefficiency and more concerned with persistent social inequalities and worsening climate change. Starting in 2015, as the region's economic growth slowed (an annual growth rate of 3.2% from 2000 to 2014 was replaced by a growth rate of less than 0.5% from 2015 to 2019), countries in the region chose to manage deficits by cutting spending on education, health, and other social programs (Raineri & Benoit, 2020).

Table 1.1 Population, GDP, GDP p/c, GDP Growth Rates

Country	Population (Millions) 2020	GDP (US$ Billions) 2020	GDP p/ Capita (US$) 2020	GNI p/ Capita PPP (US$) 2020	GDP Growth Rate % 2020	GDP Growth Rate % 2021 (est.)
Argentina	45.38	383.07	8,441.9	20,210	−10.5	4.9
Bolivia	11.67	36.69	3,143.0	8,250	−8.0	5.1
Brazil	212.56	1,444.73	6,796.8	14,550	−5.3	3.2
Chile	19.12	252.94	13,231.7	23,980	−6.0	5.0
Colombia	50.88	271.35	5,332.8	14,280	−7.0	5.0
Costa Rica	5.09	61.52	12,076.8	19,840	−4.8	3.0
Cuba	11.33	103.13 (2019)	9,099.7 (2019)	—	−8.5	3.0
Dominican Republic	10.85	78.84	7,268.2	17,060	−5.5	5.0
Ecuador	17.64	98.81	5,600.4	10,580	−9.0	1.0
El Salvador	6.49	24.64	3,798.6	8,050	−8.6	3.5
Guatemala	16.86	77.60	4,603.3	8,690	−2.5	3.5
Honduras	9.90	23.83	2,405.7	5,050	−8.0	4.5
Mexico	128.93	1,076.16	8,346.7	18,170	−9.0	3.8
Nicaragua	6.62	12.62	1,905.3	5,410	−4.0	1.3
Panama	4.31	52.94	12,269.0	25,010	−11.0	5.5
Paraguay	7.13	35.61	4,949.7	12,590	−1.6	3.5
Peru	32.97	202.01	6,126.9	11,490	−12.9	9.0
Uruguay	3.47	55.71	15,438.4	21,630	−4.5	4.0
Venezuela	28.44	482.36 (2014)	16,055.6 (2014)	—	−30.0	−7.0
Total LAC	652.28	4,838.00	15,868.4	15,363	−7.7	3.7
China	1,402	14,722.84	16,117	17,200	2.3	8.5
US	329.48	20,936.60	62,530	66,060	−3.5	6.3

Sources: ECLAC (2021b). *Preliminary Overview of the Economies of Latin America and the Caribbean 2020*. https://www.cepal.org/en/publications/type/preliminary-overview-economies-latin-america-and-caribbean;
World Bank Databank https://data.worldbank.org/;
Bureau of Economic Analysis (2021), US Department of Commerce https://www.bea.gov

The failure of governments across the region to meet the expectations of this more affluent and empowered citizenry led to protests and other forms of activism in 2019, and although the COVID-19 pandemic tempered social unrest in 2020, it did not stop it. The pandemic has, in fact, made more evident the fragility and deep divisions of Latin American societies. The losses in employment and income caused by the health pandemic have pushed many people into lower income brackets, reversing the social and economic gains of the past two decades. Moreover, some groups have been more vulnerable than others regarding losses of jobs, income, and life (i.e., the poor in general, those living in rural areas or on the margins of urban centers; the youth, women, and Indigenous communities). As the region emerges from the pandemic, social discontent will likely surface again. We address issues of political and social instability in Chapters 2 and 6; issues related to the middle class and social inequality are explored in greater detail in Chapter 4. In the closing section of this chapter, we summarize current perspectives on a human-centered vision for the future growth and development of the region.

Latin America is one of the regions of the world that has been most severely affected by the COVID-19 pandemic and is expected to be one of the slowest to recover (Oliveros-Rosen, 2021; World Bank, 2021b). In 2020, the emergence of the COVID-19 pandemic laid bare downward trends that had become evident in the region for at least the past five years. The

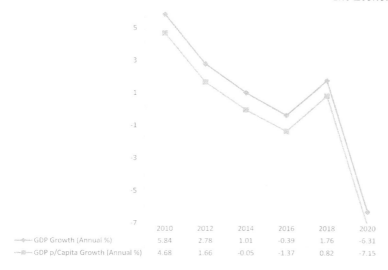

	2010	2012	2014	2016	2018	2020
GDP Growth (Annual %)	5.84	2.78	1.01	-0.39	1.76	-6.31
GDP p/Capita Growth (Annual %)	4.68	1.66	-0.05	-1.37	0.82	-7.15

Figure 1.1 Trends in GDP and GDP per capita growth rates, 2000–2020. Source: Authors' elaboration with data from the World Bank Databank. https://data.worldbank.org

region had been experiencing an economic slowdown since 2014, which led to higher unemployment and income losses during the 2015–2019 period. Since the onset of the pandemic in March 2020, the economic outlook of the region has been discouraging, with almost 30 million people losing their jobs and more than two million companies disappearing (Raineri & Benoit, 2020; World Bank, 2021a). In 2020, the pandemic pushed almost five million people out of the middle class and into the ranks of the poor and the vulnerable. If the offsetting effects of Brazil's temporary social transfer program were excluded from this analysis, these statistics would be even more discouraging, with an estimated 12 million people exiting the middle class and 20 million people falling into poverty. In total, the middle class shrunk to 37.3%, the vulnerable rose to 38.5%, and the poor made up 21.8% of the population in the region (World Bank, 2021c).

Structural challenges already present in the region only worsened the effects of the global pandemic on the region's economies. Among the most important structural challenges facing the region are the high level of informality, productivity lags, low incomes and widening income gaps, and lack of investment in health, infrastructure, and education (Part I of the book explores these challenges in depth). To a large extent, it is the effect of these structural challenges (e.g., informality, poorly funded and inefficient health and education systems, persistent income inequalities, etc.), in addition to ineffective political leadership, that has made the ongoing pandemic so difficult to manage.

The region must manage its fiscal stability if it is to retain the confidence of domestic and foreign investors. Fiscal balances as a percentage of GDP worsened in 2020 because of the COVID-19 pandemic with some minor recovery expected in 2021. Fiscal deficits in 2020 ranged from 15% in Brazil to 6% in Mexico, compared to deficits in 2019, which ranged from 1.5% to 6%. In 2021, a minor recovery is expected with deficits ranging from 9% to 4% (Price, 2020). To manage their economic woes in 2020, countries assumed record levels of debt, but responses varied widely among countries in the region. In Brazil, Peru, and Chile, governments provided significant assistance to small businesses to keep them afloat. In Mexico, Colombia, and Argentina, on the other hand, government help was minimal because of choice (i.e., Mexico) or lack of funds (i.e., Argentina and Colombia). The overall effect of government help, however, was also impacted by accompanying governmental measures instituted across the region, such as limited business closures, lockdowns, and infusions of capital to their respective public health systems. Policy decisions made by central banks regarding interest rates, currency values, and inflation have also been critical during the pandemic (Price, 2020; World Bank, 2021b). Yet, starting in mid-2021, Latin America's central banks were feeling increasing pressure to raise interest rates in order to keep inflation low (e.g., Chile and Mexico both set 3% inflation targets +/– 1%). In mid- to late 2021, Brazil, Chile, and Mexico were all considering interest rate hikes in order to counter rising consumer prices on transportation, food, and housing, among other consumer services (Capurro, 2021; Gonzalez & Campos, 2021). Keeping interest rates low long enough to allow the region's economies to fully recover and avoiding overreactions to higher inflation will continue to be important, at least through the end of 2022. Maintaining liquidity will likely need to be prioritized over shoring up currency values in order to allow the private sector, especially small- and medium-size businesses, enough time to rebuild. See Table 1.2 for inflation and unemployment rates for select Latin American countries.

One of the main effects of the COVID-19 pandemic has been the rise in unemployment across the region, with some sectors being more negatively affected than others. Latin

Table 1.2 Inflation and Unemployment Rates

Country	CPI Inflation (Annual %) 2020	Unemployment Rates (%) 2020
Argentina	36.1*	11.7
Bolivia	0.9	5.6
Brazil	3.2	13.7
Chile	3.0	11.5
Colombia	2.5	15.4
Costa Rica	0.7	17.1
Cuba	—	3.9
Dominican Republic	3.8	8.9
Ecuador	−0.3	6.2
El Salvador	−0.4	7.0
Guatemala	3.2	4.7
Honduras	3.5	9.4
Mexico	3.4	4.7
Nicaragua	3.7	5.8
Panama	−1.6	10.2
Paraguay	1.8	7.6
Peru	1.8	6.2
Uruguay	9.8	12.7
Venezuela	254.9	9.1

Sources:
Swiss Re Institute (2021).
The World Bank https://data.worldbank.org/indicator/FP.CPI.TOTL.ZG?locations=ZJ.
* Data from S&P Global Ratings: https://www.spglobal.com/ratings/en/research/articles/210624-economic-outlook-latin-america-q3-2021-despite-a-stronger-2021-long-term-growth-obstacles-abound-12013558

America has been the most heavily impacted region in the world in terms of loss of earnings and hours worked (Maurizio, 2021). The International Labor Organization (ILO, 2020) estimates that the losses in working hours in 2020 from 2019 (16.2%) were four times those experienced during the recession in 2009 and almost double the estimated losses at the global level (8.8%). Working hour losses for the two main economies in the region were significant, with Brazil at 15% and Mexico at 12.5%. The largest losses to employment were observed between April and June of 2020, with economic activity and employment falling between 10% and 40% since January 2020. Although, by December 2020, employment levels had almost recovered to January 2020 levels, more than 28 million people lost their jobs that year, reflecting a regional unemployment rate of 10.6% compared to 8.3% in 2019 and a contraction in the labor force participation from 63% in 2019 to 58% in 2020. Across countries, unemployment rates in the fourth quarter of 2020 ranged from 4% to 20%, indicating marked differences in the effect of the pandemic on the region's employment (Maurizio, 2021).

Employment losses had a disproportionate impact on certain population segments and sectors, such as the services and informal sectors. The service sector, such as retailing, hospitality, and tourism, suffered significant employment losses. It is estimated that in the second quarter of 2020, 45% of jobs in the restaurant and hotel sectors had been lost compared to a loss of about 25% for the region as a whole (ILO, 2021). Tourism is a particularly important sector in the region, accounting for 26% of total GDP in the Caribbean in 2019 and 10% in the rest of Latin America. The sector has a multiplier effect, generating income for both the government and the private sector across a range of products and services as well as jobs and foreign currency. More than 50% of Latin America's workers are informally employed, and 90% of those living in poverty are informal workers (World Bank, 2021c). The pandemic had a significantly negative effect on the informal sector, with employment losses at the height of the pandemic being more than 20% higher than those in the formal sector (ILO, 2020; Maurizio, 2021). In 2021, the recovery of employment losses is being led by the informal sector as micro and small businesses and the self-employed are able to resume their economic activities. By the end of 2020, formal employment had not yet recovered the losses from the year, and whether these losses are ever recovered will depend on labor dynamics in the region over the short and medium term.

The effects of the COVID-19 pandemic on employment have also differed by gender, age, and skill level. Globally, employment and job income losses have been greater for women than for men; in Latin America, the gender gap was also evident. By the end of 2020, the unemployment rate was 9.3% for men and 11.9% for women (compared to 6.9% and 9.3% for 2019, respectively). Moreover, an estimated 13 million women exited the labor force versus 10 million men. Women's labor force participation fell to 46.9% in 2020 (from 51.4% in 2019), about a 9% decline; the male labor force participation dropped from 74.7% to 69.6% (a decline of about 7%). These figures indicate that by the end of 2020, female labor force participation had receded to 2001 levels (ECLAC, 2021c; ILO, 2020). One of the reasons women's employment was more severely affected by the pandemic was the concentration of women's employment in sectors that were subject to closures or contraction, such as retailing and hospitality. Second, more women tend to be employed in the informal sector, which was more severely impacted than the formal sector. In Latin America, one in two women work in the informal sector; in certain occupations, such as domestic service, 80%–90% of employment can be informal. During the pandemic, job losses for those in the informal sector were significant and subject to gender differentials. For instance, in Mexico, the number of women employed in the informal sector declined by 40%, 10% higher than the decline for men in the informal sector. Similar differentials were observed in Peru, Costa

Rica, and other countries of the region. Third, women reduced hours or exited the workforce to attend to family responsibilities, especially those related with caring for family members or children's education. The longer the pandemic continues to affect economic activity in the region, the more likely women's employment losses will be exacerbated, thus widening the existing gender gap (ILO. 2020; Maurizio, 2021). Employment losses for young workers (15–24 years old) and for those with lower skill levels were also greater than those for adults and higher skilled workers. Equally significant were the more acute job income losses suffered by vulnerable populations, namely women, the self-employed, youth, and low-skilled workers (Maurizio, 2021).

The globalization wave that began in the 1990s led to an increase in trade and investment. Countries around the world sought to create opportunities for growth through regional integration initiatives, bilateral and multilateral trade agreements, investment incentives, and macroeconomic stabilization policies. Companies also sought to leverage the opportunities offered by this global interconnectedness. For businesses, globalization meant access to inputs (e.g., natural resources, labor, technology, capital) anywhere in the world and the possibility of establishing production facilities and accessing consumers in multiple markets. The result of these transformations was the emergence of geographically dispersed global value chains connected through trade, foreign direct investment, and offshore production. (The role and position of Latin America in global value chains is explored further in Chapters 3 and 11.) In this context, Latin America entered the new century in a favorable position: (a) China and other developed markets had a seemingly endless demand for the region's mining and agricultural resources, which supported the region's export-led economic strategy and attracted record amounts of foreign direct investment; (b) the region's increasingly affluent consumers had a voracious appetite for goods and services, which led to a demand for domestic and foreign goods that range from foodstuffs and automobiles to financial and telecommunication services; and (c) many of the region's firms grew enough to pursue opportunities abroad for market- or efficiency-seeking purposes. These global networks of producers and consumers translated into dynamic trade and investment relationships for Latin America.

Until late in the twentieth century, Latin America was known for its policies of import substitution and protectionist measures; yet, from 1980 to the present, the region underwent a transformation that led to liberalization of trade and investment and the region's integration with the world economy. In the past 30 years especially, the region embarked on a series of changes that included reduction or elimination of trade barriers, strengthening of regional integration schemes, the formation of new trade alliances, the implementation of regional integration initiatives, and the liberalization of investment, all of which contributed to unprecedented growth in international trade and foreign direct investment. The next section provides an overview of Latin America's trade relationships with other regions of the world.

Latin America's International Trade

World trade in 2020 reached US$22.5 trillion, a contraction of 12% from total world trade in 2019 (US$24.9 trillion). Merchandise trade declined 7.6% in value terms and 5.3% in volume from 2019 to reach US$17.7 trillion. This indicates a continuation of the decline in world merchandise trade registered in 2019, down from 2018 by 0.1% in volume and 3.0% in value—the first decline registered since the 2008–2009 financial crisis. Trade in services declined by 21% in value terms from 2019 to US$4.75 trillion (WTO, 2020; WTO, 2021). In Latin America, merchandise trade in 2020 declined by 6.9% in volume terms and by 12.2% in value terms from 2019 to reach US$936 billion. Trade in commercial services declined by 35% from 2019 to reach US$136 billion (ECLAC, 2021a; WTO, 2021). In 2020, Latin America accounted for only 4.8% of global trade, and while this is much lower than other world regions, it points to significant opportunities for expansion. Table 1.3 shows imports and exports for select countries in Latin America.

Latin American countries' export-oriented economies have proved resilient, having weathered domestic and global crises over the past two decades. Compared to 2019, all countries in the region saw a decline in exports in 2020, but most of them are expected to fully recover to 2019 levels by the end of 2021 (Price, 2020). In fact, in the first quarter of 2021, the region's exports, in value terms, grew 8.9% compared to the same period in 2019. The sustainability of this recovery throughout the rest of 2021 is, of course, fragile, with the improvements to the value of exports due to higher prices that counteracted a drop in volume of about 2.2% (IADB, 2021). A continuation of stable or increasing prices on precious minerals and metals, oil, food, and some manufactured goods will aid in export recovery as will depreciated currencies. A return of tourists to the region will also be critical for export recovery. Although imports have not yet recovered, as the global and regional economies return to a growth path, higher demand and favorable prices for Latin America's products will improve its overall trade prospects.

International Trade Patterns and Trends

Latin American countries differ in terms of their key trading partners and their main import and export products. Mexico and the Central American countries trade more heavily with the United States than with any other major economic power. As a result, the economic performance of these countries is closely linked to US economic performance (it has been said that when the US economy catches a cold, Mexico's economy sneezes). On the other hand, South American economies have solidified their trade and investment ties with Asian countries, particularly China.

In 2020, exports of services declined more than those of goods. Exports fell across all service categories, but travel and transport were the most affected sectors, with container trade contracting, primarily because of a reduction of exports via maritime routes to North America and the rest of the Latin American region. Tourism to the region, especially via air travel, was severely impacted by lockdowns and travel restrictions. During the first half of 2020, the value of the region's travel account shrank by 53%. Imports of services were also affected. During the first half of 2020, the value of travel from the region fell by 55%. In terms of exports of goods, all products, with the exception of agricultural and livestock (+5%), declined during the first half of 2020. Exports of mining and oil alone dropped 25%. Imports of goods also declined, with fuels (−36%) and consumer goods (−20%) being the hardest hit. Imports of intermediate (−14%) and capital goods (−14%) also declined, which is likely to have a direct impact on the region's production capacity, which is heavily reliant on imported inputs (ECLAC, 2021a).

In terms of geographic destination, exports intra-regionally as well as to the United States and Europe all declined during the first half of 2020 (27%, 20%, and 15%, respectively). Trade with China has been more resilient, with exports to China increasing by 1% during the first half of 2020 and by about 35% year on year during the first quarter of 2021. Exports to the rest of the world also recovered at the start of 2021, with exports to the United States, Europe, and the rest of the Latin American region also recovering at the start of 2021 but at a slower pace (3.9%, 4.0%, and 11.6%, respectively) (IADB, 2021).

Shifts of the region's export destinations were already evident during the first decade of the twenty-first century. Three export market destinations, the United States, China, and Latin

Table 1.3 Imports and Exports of Merchandise and Services 2020 for Select LAC Countries

Country	Merchandise Exports (US$ Billions) 2020)	Services Exports (US$ Billions) 2020	Top Three Export Markets (% Total) 2019	Main Exports 2019–2021	Merchandise Imports (US$ Billions) 2020	Services Imports (US$ Billions) 2020	Top Three Sources of Imports (% Total) 2019
Argentina	54.88	9.24	Brazil (16) China (11) US (7)	Food, energy, autos	42.35	11.60	Brazil (21) China (18) US (14)
Belize	0.32	0.38	—	—	0.79	0.16	—
Bolivia, Plurinational State of	7.02	0.60	Argentina (16) Brazil (15) United Arab Emirates (UAE) (12)	Energy, precious and industrial metals, food	7.08	1.74	Brazil (22) Chile (15) China (13) (2017)
Brazil	209.88	27.86	China (28) US (13) Netherlands (5)	Aviation, iron ore, food, consumer goods	166.28	47.36	China (21) US (18) Argentina Germany (6)
Chile	71.73	6.32	China (32) US (14) Japan (9)	Copper, food, tourism	59.03	11.32	China (24) US (20) Brazil (8)
Colombia	31.01	4.90	US (31) China (11) Panama (6)	Energy, minerals, flowers	43.49	9.09	US (27) China (20) Mexico (7)
Costa Rica	12.17	6.81	US (38) Netherlands (6) Belgium (5)	—	14.94	3.41	US (41) China (13) Mexico (7)
Cuba	2.18	—	China (38) Spain (11) Netherlands (5)	—	8.04	—	Spain (19) China 915) Italy (6)
Dominican Republic	10.36	3.83	US (54) Switzerland (8) Canada (5)	Gold, medical instruments, cigars	17.09	3.00	US (50) China (13) Brazil (4)
Ecuador	20.23	1.65	US (30) China (13) Panama (8)	Energy, food, flowers, tourism	17.96	2.69	US (22) China (18) Colombia (9)
El Salvador	5.03	2.03	US (40) Guatemala (15) Honduras (15)	—	10.59	1.43	US (30) China (14) Guatemala (13)
Guatemala	11.57	2.53	US (33) El Salvador (8) Guatemala (5)	Food, clothing, furniture, precious metals	18.20	2.75	US (36) China (12) Mexico (11)
Honduras	7.73	1.94	US (54) El Salvador (8) Guatemala (5)	—	9.87	1.82	US (42) China (10) Guatemala (8)

Country							
Mexico	417.67	16.80	US (78) Canada (3) Germany (2)	Industrial and consumer products, energy	393.25	25.04	US (45) China (18) Japan (4)
Nicaragua	5.19	0.88	US (60) El Salvador (5) Mexico (5)	—	6.71	0.59	US (27) Mexico (12) China (11)
Panama	10.36	8.50	Ecuador (20) Guatemala (14) China (8)	Logistics, banking, tourism, copper	15.36	3.01	China (21) US (19) Japan (16)
Paraguay	8.53	0.66	Brazil (32) US (12) Canada (5)	Food, electricity	10.22	0.87	Brazil (24) US (22) China (17)
Peru	42.41	3.24	China (29) US (12) Canada (50)	Industrial metals, precious metals, food	36.10	7.32	China (24) US (22) Brazil (6)
Uruguay	6.85	3.45	—	Food, tourism, logistics	7.56	3.43	—
Venezuela	5.02	—	India (34) Chile (28) US (12)	—	6.55	—	China (28) US (22) Brazil (8)
China	2,599.12	278.08	US (17) Hong Kong (10) Japan (6)	—	2,055.75	377.53	South Korea (9) Japan (8) Australia (7)
US	1,431.64	684.00	Canada (17) Mexico (16) China (70)	—	2,407.55	435.75	China (18) Mexico (15) Canada (13)

Sources: *WTO Statistical Review* 2020 and 2021;
CIA World Factbook, https://www.cia.gov/the-world-factbook/countries/;
World Integrated Trade Solution, https://wits.worldbank.org/countrysnapshot/en

America itself, accounted for the bulk of the shift of Latin American exports. The most significant change was the decline in exports to the US, which accounted for 61.3% in 2000 and only 24% 2011. Exports to Asia increased to 23% in 2011 from 5.8% in 2000. Intra-regional exports also increased during this period, jumping to 27% in 2011 vs. 17.3% in 2000 (WTO, 2012). The last decade saw a consolidation of these trade relationships, with only minor variations year to year. See Table 1.4 for the region's top export and import partners in 2019.

The increased demand for Latin American primary commodities (agricultural and mining products) by emerging economies in Asia—in particular, China—has been an important contributor to the economic growth of Latin American commodity exporters during the past two decades. This reliance on commodity exports presents the risks of dependence on low value-added exports, commodity price volatility, and the assumption that there will be sustainable imports of commodities by countries such as China. Thus, any economic growth slowdown in the main buyers of these exports can have a significant adverse effect on Latin American exporters. Latin American countries with more diversified export markets and products are likely to be less vulnerable to lower demand and/or lower prices in the world commodity markets.

Brazil and Mexico remain the two largest exporters and importers in the region (see Table 1.3). We compare both countries using 2019 data, which is less likely to be distorted by the effects of the global pandemic in 2020. In 2019, about 28% of Brazil's exports were to China, with the US accounting for only 13% of its exports. The Netherlands, Argentina, and Japan were the next three largest export markets (4.5%, 4.3%, and 2.4%, respectively). China and the United States were Brazil's two main sources of imports (20% and 17%, respectively). Brazil's main exports are raw materials (e.g., soya, corn, lumber, metals and minerals, and oil), which account for almost 50% of all its exports. Intermediate and capital goods make up about 65% of Brazil's imports (e.g., machinery, component parts). In contrast, 78% of Mexico's exports were to the United States, with Canada, Germany, and China the next major markets, making up only 3.1%, 1.5%, and 1.5%, respectively. The United States, China, and Japan were the three main sources of imports (45%, 18%, and 4%, respectively). Mexico's main exports are manufactured goods (e.g., automobiles and electronics) and oil. Its main imports are primarily capital goods (45%) and consumer goods (25%), as well as intermediate goods, such as component parts for automobiles and electronics. Commodities make up only 10% of Mexico's total exports. As is evident, Brazil and Mexico are both export-oriented, but

Table 1.4 Region's Top Export and Import Partners

	% Share of Total
Top Export Markets	
United States	44.53
China	12.40
Brazil	2.61
Canada	2.36
Others	2.18
Top Import Partners	
United States	32.28
China	18.79
Brazil	4.40
Germany	3.99
Japan	3.10

Source: World Bank – World Integrated Trade Solution https://wits.worldbank.org/countrysnapshot/en/

they have pursued different trade strategies with trade representing 78% of Mexico's GDP but only 30% of Brazil's (2019 figures). Mexico focuses on manufactured good exports to advanced economies, primarily the United States. Brazil, on the other hand, pursues a strategy of commodity exports to a more diversified mix of markets, with China being an important trading partner (WITS, 2021).

Importance of Intra-regional Trade in Latin America

For almost six decades, Latin American countries have attempted, with varying degrees of success, to integrate their economies. The five main integration agreements/groups in the region are:

- The Central American Integration System (SICA – https://www.sica.int/sica/vista_en .aspx): Belize, Costa Rica, El Salvador, Guatemala, Honduras, Nicaragua, Panama, and the Dominican Republic (associate member).
- The Andean Community (CAN – www.comunidadandina.org): Bolivia, Colombia, Ecuador, and Peru.
- The Southern Common Market (MERCOSUR – https://www.mercosur.int/en/): Argentina, Brazil, Paraguay, Uruguay, and Venezuela (Bolivia is in the process of joining).
- The Caribbean Community (CARICOM – https://www.caricom.org). Members: Antigua and Barbuda, Bahamas, Barbados, Belize, Dominica, Grenada, Guyana, Haiti, Jamaica, Montserrat, St. Lucia, St. Kitts and Nevis, St. Vincent and the Grenadines, Suriname, and Trinidad and Tobago. Associate member states: Anguilla, Bermuda, British Virgin Islands, Turks and Caicos Islands, and Cayman Islands.
- The Pacific Alliance (https://alianzapacifico.net/en/): Chile, Colombia, Mexico, and Peru.

In addition, Mexico is a member country of the USMCA (United States, Mexico, Canada Free Trade Agreement, formerly known as NAFTA).

As the region enters this new decade, regional integration will play a critical role in Latin Americas' growth and development. Regional integration can help the region's economies leverage their complementarities in production, especially manufacturing of goods; collaborate to improve their trade and investment environments; build scale by having access to larger regional markets; and open internationalization opportunities for small- and medium-size businesses.

Intra-regional trade across the various integration schemes has had many ups and downs. It reached historical peaks of about 21% during the second half of the 1990s, fueled by the creation of MERCOSUR and the relaunch of the Andean and Central American integration regimes. It saw highs again during the 'golden years' between 2006 and 2013 but has been steadily declining since 2014. In 2019, it reached 14%, similar to the levels registered in the early 1990s, and was expected to fall to 12% in 2020 as a result of the global economic crisis caused by the COVID-19 pandemic (ECLAC, 2019; ECLAC, 2021a).

In 2020, the Central American Common Market showed the best trade performance overall (value of exports declined 2%, and value of imports declined 15% from 2019, compared to declines of 13%–16% in exports and 18%–28% in imports in all other sub-regions). Central America's relatively positive performance was, in part, because of the large share represented by intra-regional trade (i.e., 25% of its exports). Central America is the bloc with the most trade links within the region; the Pacific Alliance has the least. In terms of products sold within the region, automobiles have the largest share of intra-regional trade (17%), with other consumer and industrial goods also dominating intra-regional trade transactions (e.g., food and beverages, textiles and clothing, chemicals and petrochemicals, pharmaceuticals, wood and paper). Latin America was also an important destination for the region's exports based on the number of exporting firms, which ranged from 31%–84% of all exporting firms in eight select Latin American countries. More than 90% of firms exporting to the regional market were micro, small-, and medium-size firms (MSMEs) (ECLAC, 2021a). For some countries, the regional market is the most important destination for their exports (e.g., Argentina, Bolivia, the Dominican Republic, Paraguay, Uruguay, and all the Central American countries). For others, the US market was more important than their regional markets (e.g., Colombia, Ecuador, Mexico, Venezuela). Yet for others, Asia is more important as an export market than countries in the region (e.g., Brazil, Chile, Peru). The sectors with the highest share of intra-regional imports were agriculture, fishing, and food and beverages (see Table 1.5a, b) (ECLAC, 2021a).

Foreign Direct Investment in Latin America

Global foreign direct investment (FDI) in 2019 totaled US$1.54 trillion, representing a 3% increase from 2018. This represented a 5% increase for the developed economies and a decrease of 2% for the developing economies. Developed economies attracted 52% of total world investment, while developing economies attracted 44%. Latin America and the Caribbean accounted for 10% of total global investment flows compared to 31% for the developing economies in Asia (ECLAC, 2020). The decade ending in 2019 saw the highest inflows of FDI into the region, which reached its peak in 2012 (US$173 billion; 14% of global FDI flows). This was in keeping with global patterns of investment, with 2012 being considered a landmark year for developing markets, in that it was the first time that developing market FDI inflows surpassed developed market inflows (ECLAC, 2013). Starting in 2013, investment into the region began to fall steadily. In 2019, inward FDI (IFDI) to Latin America reached US$160.7 billion, representing 3.2% of the region's GDP and a drop of 7.8% from 2018. The economic collapse of 2020 led to a drop in investment into Latin America of 45% from 2019. Although the COVID-19 pandemic is partially to blame, this drop in investment flows is in line with current trends that have shown a steady decline in FDI inflows since they peaked in 2012 (Price, 2020; ECLAC, 2020). Although portfolio investments (e.g., debt securities, mutual fund holdings) are also important to consider, they have fallen sharply during the second half of the past decade, registering their lowest level in 2019. Other types of investment (e.g., trade credits, loans) have also been falling since 2015, registering a negative value in 2019. Our discussion in this section focuses exclusively on FDI inflows and outflows (IFDI and OFDI). In the following sections, we review FDI patterns in the region during the last two decades, with a special emphasis on the period 2010–2019. We then provide an overview of investment flows in 2020 with a view into the near future.

Investment Flows 2010–2019

As mentioned above, investment flows into Latin America during the 2010–2019 period were some of the highest in recent history, averaging 3.4% of the region's GDP (ECLAC, 2020). Investment flows during the first half of the decade (2010–2014) were certainly more

Table 1.5a Merchandise and Services Trade by Regional Integration Schemes (2010, 2014, 2020)

Regional Integration Schemes	Merchandise Exports (Billions US$)			Merchandise Imports (Billions US$)			Services Exports (Billions US$)			Services Imports (Billions US$)		
	2010	2014	2020	2010	2014	2020	2010	2014	2020	2010	2014	2020
Andean Community (CAN)	99.4	132.4	100.7	96.7	144.6	104.6	10.6	16.3	10.4	19.5	28.5	20.8
Central American Common Market (CACM)	42.9	53.6	52.1	66.3	88.7	75.7	17.9	27.5	22.7	9.9	14.4	13.0
Caribbean Community (CARICOM)	17.8	22.6	12.6	24.9	33.0	23.0	9.8	12.8	7.1	6.1	11.2	8.1
Southern Common Market (MERCOSUR)	349.1	387.0	285.2	306.0	371.7	233.0	46.6	59.7	41.6	88.2	126.1	66.2

WTO (2021). World Statistical Review 2021.
ECLAC (2021). International Trade Outlook for Latin America and the Caribbean 2020.

Table 1.5b Share of the LAC Region of Imports and Exports by Main Integration Schemes

Regional Integration Schemes	Exports (%)	Imports (%)
Pacific Alliance	9.2	8.7
Southern Common Market (MERCOSUR)	21.5	21.3
Caribbean Community (CARICOM)	22.1	25.3
Andean Community (CAN)	22.8	26.7
Central American Common Market (CACM)	30.8	35.4
Latin America and the Caribbean	14.8	15.4
Latin America and the Caribbean (excluding Mexico)	21.5	24.7
United States*	42.1	32.5
European Union*	10.7	13.5
China*	12.5	18.3

Sources: ECLAC (2021). *International Trade Outlook for Latin America and the Caribbean 2020*;
WTO (2021). *World Statistical Review 2021*.
* Shares for the United States, the European Union, and China are presented for comparison.

robust than in the second half (2015–2019), with investment falling by an average of 13.9% during that period. This decline during the second half of the decade was not limited to Latin America but, rather, reflected a slowdown of the global economy, including contractions to foreign investment in both developed and developing countries (ECLAC, 2020).

In 2008, Latin America's share of the world's total IFDI was 9.3%; ten years later, it was 10.4%. That level of investment inflow was sustained in 2019 (10.5%) with the accumulated stock of capital over the last decade reaching nearly US$2.5 trillion (ECLAC, 2020).

Whereas annual flows of FDI capture the more recent activity by foreign firms, the stock of FDI measures the value of all of the investment commitments accumulated by firms historically. Thus, this value indicates the extent of the holdings of regional assets by foreign investors in a region. In contrast to annual flows, the FDI stocks adjust to trends at a much slower pace, as they reflect not only the annual increments of investments but also decisions of multinational firms to liquidate and disinvest from their historical positions.

In terms of FDI outflows, the region's share in 2008 was 2.2% of the world's total, and although that share fell to 0.2% in 2018, the region's OFDI represented 3.9% of the world's total in 2019. A large proportion of capital outflows was in the form of income generated by IFDI, and the ratio of those outflows to the capital stock can be used as an indicator of FDI profitability. Average return on FDI peaked at the start of the decade, dropped in 2015, and recovered during the second half of the decade, even if it never reached the levels of 2010–2011. This trend mirrored what was experienced in the rest of the world. In 2019, average profitability of FDI was 5.6%, 0.2% lower than in 2018. In fact, in 2019, compared to 2018, no country in the region saw an increase in FDI profitability except for minimal increases in Brazil and Costa Rica. The most significant losses to FDI profitability during the second half of the decade were experienced in countries highly reliant on extractive industries, which were more severely affected by commodities demand and prices. Capital outflows can have a negative effect on countries' balance of payments. In 2019, the region experienced a current account deficit of 1.8% of GDP, with FDI income contributing a negative 1.9% of GDP to that deficit (ECLAC, 2020; UNCTAD, 2021).

IFDI Distribution by Country

During the 2010–2019 period, there were marked differences in the distribution of total FDI entering the region. The South American sub-region was the main recipient of investment, with 64% of the accumulated US$2.5 trillion capital stock being captured by countries in South America. The 'LAC-6' captured 85% of total capital stocks (see Figure 1.2 for country distribution of capital stock). Still, investments into South American countries fell during the second half of the decade. Mexico, Central America, and the Caribbean, on the other hand, saw either no changes or minor increases to investment inflows. In 2019, compared to 2018, only nine countries in the region registered increases to their investment inflows (Chile,

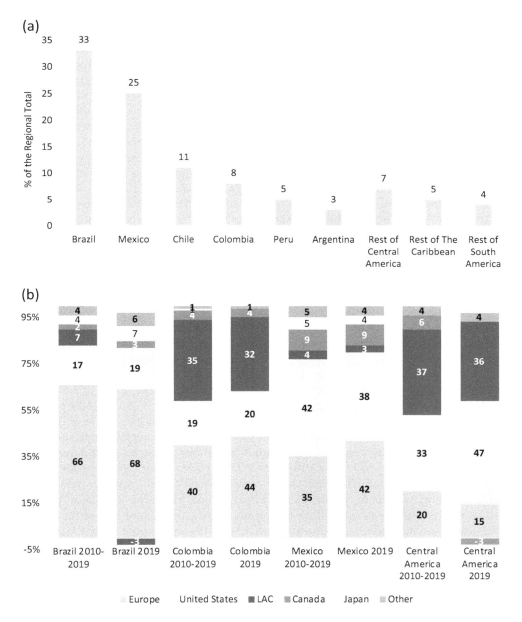

Figure 1.2 FDI patterns (a) % share of total accumulated FDI stock by country and sub-region; (b) IFDI distribution by country and sub-region, 2019/2020. (a) Source: Authors' elaboration with data from ECLAC (2020). *Foreign Direct Investment in Latin America and the Caribbean 2020*

Colombia, Dominican Republic, Guatemala, Guyana, Panama, Paraguay, Peru, and Trinidad and Tobago). In 2019, the main recipients of investment were Brazil (43%), Mexico (18%), Colombia (9%), Chile (7%), and Peru (6%). Most of the FDI in 2019 was equity investments (48% of the total) or reinvested earnings (41%), thus indicating confidence in the region by both new investors and established companies (ECLAC, 2020).

IFDI Source Countries

The previous section identified the key recipients of FDI in Latin America, but which countries are the primary providers of direct investment in Latin America? During the five years between 2007 and 2011, the US was the primary single source of FDI into the region, accounting for 22% of Latin American FDI inflows (ECLAC, 2012). The Netherlands and Spain each accounted for 10% of these inflows, with Latin American countries not far behind (9%). Canada and Japan were also sources for FDI into Latin America, each accounting for about 4% of total FDI inflows. However, 40% of the inward flows from 2007 to 2011 were attributed to 'other countries' (see Figure 1.2). These flows came from locations such as Switzerland, Panama, Bermuda, the Cayman Islands, the Virgin Islands, other Caribbean islands, and Luxembourg. Some of the FDI derived from these source countries, such as Switzerland, is due to FDI undertaken by large multinational companies (MNCs) (e.g., Nestle, Roche); but some of the flows originating in smaller locations may be related to MNCs seeking to establish corporate domiciles for taxation or other reasons in intermediate countries prior to the FDI reaching its final destination. In cases such as this, it is difficult to determine what the original source of FDI is. This is further complicated by the fact that there are other countries in the region that either do not disclose information on this practice or the data is incomplete. For example, ECLAC estimates that much of the FDI originating from China into Latin America is, in fact, funneled through Peru and Venezuela, yet these countries do not report on this practice (ECLAC, 2012).

Despite the fact that it may, at times, be difficult to determine the original source of FDI, the main investors into Latin America have remained fairly stable over the past two decades. However, the proportion accounted for by each of these source countries can shift slightly. During the first half of the last decade (2010–2014), the main sources of investment inflows were Europe (51%), the United States (22%), and Latin America (12%) (ECLAC, 2020).

The US accounted for a slightly greater portion of FDI inflows in 2012 versus the previous five years (24% versus 22%, respectively). Intra-regional FDI increased to 14% in 2012 (from 9% in the previous five years), signaling greater investments by the region's multinationals. The other notable shift is with regard to Spanish investment in the region. Between 2007 and 2011, Spain was responsible for 10% of the FDI into Latin America, in contrast to only 5% in 2012. This decrease might reflect the economic difficulties that Spain was facing at the time, prompting its firms to refrain or curtail international expansion into Latin America or even to divest assets already within the region. During the second half of the decade (2015–2019), the main sources of investment flows into the region were Europe (52%), the United States (25%), and Latin America (10%) (ECLAC, 2020). Some of the increases in foreign investment by the United States during the last five years might reflect a growing trend in favor of nearshoring. The increases in manufacturing costs in historically low-cost production sites, such as China, and the growing volatility in transportation costs over the past decade has prompted producers to locate in slightly higher cost production sites that are closer to their customers. Increases in labor costs resulting from nearshoring can be offset by lower transportation costs and labor automation, and the reduction in the physical and cultural distance between a manufacturer and its customer base offers added market advantages. The practice of nearshoring has boded well for the Mexican economy as well as for other Latin American economies with close trade and investment linkages to the United States, especially in light of the current tensions between the United States and China and the strains on supply chains brought about by the COVID-19 pandemic.

Sectoral Concentration of FDI

Analysis of FDI flows into Latin America reveals that investments are still concentrated in sectors that have historically attracted FDI, yet the relative importance of each sector varies over time, country, and sub-region (see Figure 1.3).

As the main manufacturing hubs in the region, Brazil and Mexico attract the bulk of manufacturing investment. During the first half of the past decade (2010–2014), the five main sectors receiving investment were oil and carbon-based products, beverages and tobacco, base metals, foodstuffs, and transport equipment, in that order. The sectoral composition of manufacturing investment changed slightly during the 2015–2019 period, with the five main sectors receiving investment being transport equipment, oil and carbon-based products, paper

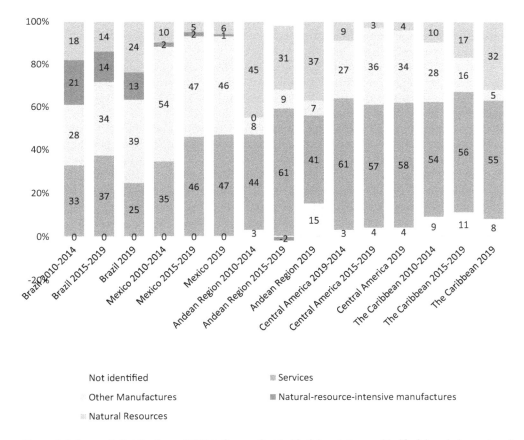

Figure 1.3 Sectoral distribution of FDI inflows—first half of decade/second half of decade by regional bloc. Source: Authors' elaboration with data from ECLAC (2020). *Foreign Direct Investment in Latin America and the Caribbean 2020*

products, foodstuffs, and chemicals, in that order. Overall, taking manufacturing invest-ments in these two countries together, transport equipment, extractive-related products, and basic consumer goods (e.g., beverages and foodstuffs) captured most of the investment dur-ing the past decade (ECLAC, 2020). In 2019, the largest declines in investment occurred in select industries: in the primary sector, mining; in the services sector, construction, financial services, and information and communication services; and in manufacturing, electronics and computers, chemicals, metallurgy, and automobiles (ECLAC, 2020).

The changes in the sectoral composition of FDI into the region are made evident by the differences in cross-border mergers and acquisitions (CBMAs) during the first and second halves of the past decade. CBMAs grew consistently between 2010 and 2014, peaking in number of operations in 2012 and in terms of value in 2014. Mergers and acquisitions fell sharply in 2015, in both value and number of operations, and never fully recovered to the levels seen in the first half of the decade, with the weakest result being observed in 2019 (number of CBMAs in 2019 fell 44% compared to 2010). The active patterns of CBMAs during the first half of the decade coincided with the region's economic boom and favorable external conditions, with investments flowing primarily into manufacturing, mining, financial services, and transport. The second half of the decade saw a contraction of economic activity in the region (and the world), with investment falling in almost all sectors, except for tourism and energy and water supply. In 2019, investments were concentrated in the renewable and non-renewable energy sectors (primarily in the 'LAC-6') and telecommunications (primarily in Central America) (ECLAC, 2020)

Greenfield investments in the region also reflect sectoral differences. Greenfield investments have shown a consistently upward trend over the past 15 years, especially from 2008 to 2014. The total value of these investments in the 2015–2019 period, although still positive, was 18% lower than the total investment in the first half of the decade. In 2019, the value of investments rose by 35% from the previous year, with renewable energies capturing the largest share of investors' attention for the past five years. The transport and logistics and tourism sectors have also received increased investments during this period. On the other hand, the metals, automotive, and telecommunications sectors, the three most attractive sectors in the first half of the decade, have seen declining investment (ECLAC, 2020).

Sectoral distributions and shifts not only indicate global demand conditions, national economic policies, and investors' outlooks, but they are also significant because of the implications on host-country employment. Labor-intensive sectors typically generate a greater number of jobs than those that are either non-labor intensive or those in which technologies can replace the need for labor. For instance, commerce, construction, call centers, and tourism are likely to generate more jobs per dollar invested than manufacturing, mining, or large-scale agriculture.

Outward FDI

An indication that traditional patterns of FDI flows are changing with the world economic rea-lignment is the increase of foreign investment originating in Latin America. The strong long-term growth in the region during the past two decades gave rise to strong national companies with increasing financial resources and liquidity to invest not only in their domestic mar-kets but also abroad (see Figure 1.4). This process of internationalization of Latin American companies led to a surge of investment outflows from Latin America, which grew from an average of $10 billion before 2005 to $30 billion after 2005, reaching a high of $48 billion in 2011 (ECLAC, 2013). In 2019, investment outflows from Latin America reached US$44.5

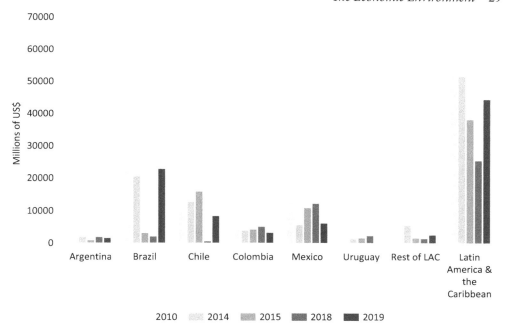

Figure 1.4 Outward FDI for select countries (2010, 2014, 2018, 2019). Source: Authors' elaboration with data from ECLAC (2020). *Foreign Direct Investment in Latin America and the Caribbean 2020*

billion, 75% higher than in 2018, with Brazil, Chile, Colombia, and Mexico accounting for 91% of the total OFDI that year. The largest investor abroad was Brazil with $22.8 billion and investments that spanned the rest of Latin America, the United States, Europe, and Asia. Chilean investments were second (US$8.4 billion), while Mexico came third (US$6.2 billion) (ECLAC, 2020). In 2020, the top three investors abroad were Chile ($11.6 billion, +24.8%), Mexico (US$6.5, −40.6%), and Colombia (US$2.0 billion, −38.9%) (UNCTAD, 2021).

Investment Flows 2020–2021

In 2020, IFDI into Latin America dropped by 45.4% (US$87.6 billion), representing 8.8% of total world investment inflows. CBMAs fell sharply by 67% to US$7.8 billion. The losses in FDI experienced by the region were the most severe among developing countries (UNCTAD, 2021). The top five recipients of FDI were Brazil (US$24.8 billion, −62.1%), Mexico (US$29.1 billion, −14.7%), Chile (US$8.4 billion, −33%), Colombia (US$ 7.7 billion, −46.3%), and Argentina (US$4.1 billion, −38.1%). The five main sources of investment were the United States, Spain, the Netherlands, Luxembourg, and Canada. Other important investing countries in the region were Chile, France, Germany, South Korea, and Italy.

In 2020, drops in investment levels varied by country and sector. Investment into the South American sub-region decreased by half to US$52 billion, with countries such as Brazil (−62% to US$25 billion), Chile (−33% to US$8.4 billion), and Peru (88% to US$982 million) registering their lowest levels of FDI in 20 years. In Central America, FDI inflows declined by 24% to US$33 billion, partly due to reinvesting of earnings in Mexico, where losses were only 15%. IFDI into Costa Rica and Panama shrunk considerably (38% to US$1.7 billion and 86% to less than US$1 billion, respectively). Finally, in the Caribbean countries, excluding offshore financial centers, investment flows dropped by 36%, primarily due to lack of investment in the tourism sector. Among the most affected countries were the Dominican Republic (US$2.6 billion), Haiti (drop of 60% to $30 million), and Trinidad and Tobago (–US$439 million). Inflows in hydrocarbons, manufacturing, and tourism contracted severely, while inflows in minerals and metals remained somewhat stable thanks to a recovery of global commodity prices during the last two quarters of 2020 (UNCTAD, 2021).

Intra-regional investment flows were deeply impacted as well, with outflows of investment by Latin American multinationals turning negative (–US$3.5 billion), largely due to negative outflows registered in Colombia (–39%), Mexico (–41%), and Peru (–47%). The exception was Chile, which saw an increase of its outward investment flows of 24.8% to US$11.6 billion. Greenfield announcements by Latin American multinationals in 2020 decreased by 57% to US$7.9 billion, primarily due to retrenchment by firms in Mexico (–71%), Colombia (–65%), Brazil (–39%), and Chile (–37%). Together, Chile, Colombia, and Mexico generated almost all outward investment in the region (UNCTAD, 2021).

In 2019 and 2020, FDI in the region was predominantly in the form of greenfield projects, which amounted to US$112.3 billion and $56.5 billion, respectively, versus CBMAs, which amounted to US$23.6 billion and US$7.8 billion, respectively. In 2019, the services sector attracted most of the investment (42%), with manufacturing and primary sectors accounting for 39% and 22%, respectively. Greenfield investments by value during the 2019–2020 period were primarily in energy, automotive, information and communication, and the hospitality industries. CBMAs were concentrated in extractive industries, information and communication, and finance and insurance. Announcements of international project finance deals during 2019–2020 period were primarily in renewable energy, mining, oil and gas, and transportation infrastructure. Investments aligned with the sustainable development goals were concentrated in the areas of infrastructure, renewable energy, food and agriculture, and health (UNCTAD, 2020; UNCTAD, 2021).

In Latin America, domestic investment typically outstrips FDI. In particular, large holding groups that are well positioned financially tend to acquire available assets from both other private investors and state-owned companies (e.g., energy, utilities, transportation). Moreover, the strains of lower revenues and new debt commitments affecting businesses in 2020–2021 will likely lead to consolidation in certain sectors. Maintaining low interest rates will facilitate the ability of domestic investors to engage in acquisitions and greenfield investments (Price, 2020). But, as we mentioned earlier, recovery will be asymmetrical, and this will be evident in investment trends as well. Energy and mining have always attracted large amounts of investment, with retail, agricultural production, and consumer goods rounding up the list for most attractive investment sectors. Whether these sectors will continue to attract investors in 2022 and beyond remains a question (Price, 2020).

In summary, the rebalancing of the global economy and the various global crises of the past two decades have had a differential impact on the trade and investment patterns of Latin American countries. Strong demand from growing Asian economies has favored Latin American countries, which are exporters of mining and food commodities. On the other hand, countries that have mostly relied on manufacturing exports and services have faced stiff Asian competition in global markets. Cycles of economic growth and recession in the United States, the European Union, China, and the rest of the world have also impacted Latin American countries' trade balances and investment flows. These dynamics and the competing visions and development strategies pursued by countries in the region, especially its two most important economies—Brazil and Mexico—have led to regional polarization and clustering, as the discussion above illustrates.

Latin America's Recovery Post-COVID: Toward a Socially Inclusive and Environmentally Responsible Growth Model

Any optimistic prospects for recovery after the region and the world emerge from the COVID-19 pandemic will depend, to a large extent, on how each country fared during the pandemic in terms of social and economic losses and on the policies each country adopted to manage the pandemic and prepare for the recovery.

As the region looks to the future, recovering from the devastating effects of the COVID-19 pandemic, and the political, social, and environmental crises the region faced in 2020–2021, will be a slow and uneven process. By the end of 2021, almost all countries in the region are expected to reach GDP growth rates similar to or higher than those from 2019. Yet, this growth will not be sufficient to recover from the significant losses of 2020. The recovery will also be uneven, reflecting larger losses in some countries as evidenced by the differing recovery paths across countries in the region. For instance, Chile's GDP drop in 2020 was one of the smallest among the big six, and Chile's high vaccination rate, among other reasons, is already leading to a fast recovery in 2021, with GDP expected to exceed 2019 levels by 2022. Argentina, on the other hand, saw a significant drop in its GDP in 2020, and the country's slow recovery through 2022 will keep GDP well below its 2019 levels (Price, 2020; Swiss Re Institute, 2021).

What will drive recovery in the region? The answer is a combination of domestic policies and external factors. At the domestic level, the success of governments in achieving high rates of vaccination and adopting safety measures will drive economic activity, lower unemployment, and the revitalization of key sectors, such as tourism (ILO, 2021). In addition, maintaining low interest rates (and avoiding hawkish responses to rising inflation) will make it possible for firms to borrow capital and for consumers to increase spending on large ticket items. Governments' prioritization of reforms and investments in the health and education sectors, as well as support for micro and small businesses, will be critical in recovering losses to human talent pools and productivity. Small businesses tend to have a large impact on local development, thus supporting these businesses, including initiatives to stimulate formalization, are likely to have a positive effect on the economy as a whole (ILO, 2021). Finally, how governments across the region address social and political instability (to be discussed further in Chapter 2) will be an important signal to both domestic and foreign investors.

External factors will also be critical to the region's recovery. First, imported capital is expected to return to the region (approximately US$350 billion by the end of 2020). How much of this capital each country attracts will depend on investors' assessment of how well each country managed the pandemic (Price, 2020). Second, as global trade recovers, the region's commodity exports will drive economic growth, just as they have done in the past two decades.

Short-term recovery is critically important, but medium and long-term growth will be even more so. The bleak prospects that the region faces due to the pandemic can also present immense opportunities. During times of economic hardship, governments and societies can adopt isolationist, xenophobic, and nationalistic attitudes that might seem appealing in the short term but which can have devastating effects in the long term. The region must fight against these tendencies and, instead, embrace openness, cooperation, and integration. However, new growth and development strategies must also seek to correct the failures of the 'free-market' model that has dominated the global scene for the past three decades. Embracing liberalization and globalization had undeniable positive effects in the Latin American region: it generated sustained positive economic growth that helped to lift millions of people from poverty and increased the size of the middle class, opened access to a wide range of goods and services (e.g., communication, health, education), and created many opportunities for jobs and new business formation. It also led to relative political stability, even if that stability remains fragile. Nevertheless, the economic progress of the past 30 years also produced negative outcomes. The two most important challenges are the social and environmental gaps that have emerged not only in Latin America but also in most of the world (CEPAL, 2020). The current economic model has concentrated the gains from globalization among an increasingly smaller elite that controls economic and political power. Those in lower- and middle-income brackets continue to be vulnerable to any external shock or change in their personal lives, and to feel their civil rights and liberties threatened by increasingly authoritarian governments. The pandemic made this clear.

For Latin America, long-term growth and development strategies will need to address these challenges by finding spaces for innovation and transformation. For starters, the threat of climate change opens opportunities for technology-intensive solutions that will lead to improvements to the region's competitiveness and the diversification of the region's economies. Similarly, social inequality is a source of inefficiencies and a barrier to productivity and competitiveness (CEPAL, 2016; CEPAL, 2018; CEPAL, 2020), yet correcting social inequalities and facilitating social inclusion can have positive effects on the region's economy. Policies and investments that incorporate marginalized populations (e.g., Indigenous and Afro-descendant communities, women, and the poor and extreme poor) by opening economic opportunities and eliminating structural barriers can lead to a higher skilled labor force, faster adoption of technology, productivity gains, and greater resiliency to external shocks. (See Chapter 3 for a more in-depth discussion of these challenges and opportunities.) Countries in Latin America and the Caribbean have a window of opportunity to not only recover from the worst economic and social crisis in recent history but to transform themselves into socially inclusive and environmentally responsible societies.

Summary

After a relatively sustained period of macroeconomic stability and growth during the first 15 years of the twenty-first century, Latin America experienced steady declines of economic prosperity and growing social inequality during the second half of the past decade. In 2020, the COVID-19 pandemic brought with it an economic collapse that only made evident the structural challenges the region was already facing. The optimism derived from the economic gains experienced through 2013 has been tempered by slower growth of late and the ongoing health and economic crisis of 2020–2021. At this juncture, Latin American economies will need to imagine and adopt new models of development that are human centered, addressing not only stark social inequalities, but the real threats of climate change. Public and private investments in the region, domestic and foreign, should seek to close the economic, social, and environmental gaps that the 'old model' produced. Each country is likely to forge its own path to reignite their economies for the next decade, but any reengineering effort will also require deeper integration within the region and with the rest of the world.

References

Beccaria, L., Maurizio, R., Fernández, A. L., Monslavo, P., & Álvarez, M. (2013). Urban poverty and labor markets dynamics in five Latin American countries: 2003–2008. *Journal of Economic Inequality, 11*, 555–580.

Bureau of Economic Analysis, U.S. Department of Commerce. (2021, July 29). *Gross domestic product, second quarter 2021 (advance estimate) and annual update.* https://www.bea.gov/news/2021/gross -domestic-product-second-quarter-2021-advance-estimate-and-annual-update

Capurro, M. E. (2021, July 8). Latin America rate hikes are coming on relentless core inflation. Bloomberg. http://www.bloomberg.com/news/articles/2021-07-08/latin-america-rate-hikes-on-tap-as-core-inflation-shows-no-mercy

CEPAL-U.N. Comisión Económica para América Latina. (2016, May). *Horizontes 2030-La igualdad en el centro del desarrollo sostenible*. Ciudad de México: Trigésimo sexto período de sesiones de la CEPAL. https://www.cepal.org/es/publicaciones/40159-horizontes-2030-la-igualdad-centro-desarrollo-sostenible

CEPAL-U.N. Comisión Económica para América Latina. (2018, May). *La ineficiencia de la desigualdad*. La Habana, Cuba: Trigésimo Séptimo Período de Sesiones de la CEPAL. https://repositorio.cepal.org/bitstream/handle/11362/43566/4/S1800302_es.pdf

CEPAL-U.N. Comisión Económica para América Latina y el Caribe. (2020, October). *Construir un nuevo futuro: Una recuperación transformadora con igualdad y sostenibilidad*. Trigésimo octavo período de sesiones de la CEPAL. https://www.cepal.org/es/publicaciones/46227-construir-un-nuevo-futuro-recuperacion-transformadora-igualdad-sostenibilidad

CIA World Factbook. (2021). *The world factbook*. https://www.cia.gov/the-world-factbook/

ECLAC-U.N. Economic Commission for Latin America and the Caribbean. (2012). *Foreign direct investment in Latin America and the Caribbean 2011*. https://www.cepal.org/en/publications/1147-foreign-direct-investment-latin-america-and-caribbean-2011

ECLAC-U.N. Economic Commission for Latin America and the Caribbean. (2013). *Foreign direct investment in Latin America and the Caribbean*. http://www.eclac.org/noticias/paginas/1/33941/2013-371_PPT_FDI-2013.pdf.

ECLAC-U.N. Economic Commission for Latin America and the Caribbean. (2019). *ECLAC contributions to integration in Central America*. https://www.cepal.org/sites/default/files/wysiwyg/eclacs_contributions_to_central_americas_integration.pdf

ECLAC-U.N. Economic Commission for Latin America and the Caribbean. (2020). *Foreign direct investment in Latin America and the Caribbean 2020*. https://www.cepal.org/en/publications/46541-foreign-direct-investment-latin-america-and-caribbean-2020.

ECLAC-U.N. Economic Commission for Latin America and the Caribbean. (2021a). *International trade outlook for Latin American and the Caribbean 2020*. https://www.cepal.org/en/publications/46614-international-trade-outlook-latin-america-and-caribbean-2020-regional-integration

ECLAC-U.N. Economic Commission for Latin America and the Caribbean. (2021b). *Preliminary overview of the economies of Latin America and the Caribbean 2020*. https://www.cepal.org/en/publications/type/preliminary-overview-economies-latin-america-and-caribbean

ECLAC-U.N. Economic Commission for Latin America and the Caribbean. (2021c). *Economic Survey of Latin America and the Caribbean 2021*. LC/PUB.2021/10-P/Rev.1. Santiago, Chile. https://www.cepal.org/en/publications/47193-economic-survey-latin-america-and-caribbean-2021-labour-dynamics-and-employment

Ferreira, F. H. G., Messina, J., Rigolini, J., López-Calva, L.-F., Lugo, M. A., & Renos Vakis, R. (2013). *Economic mobility and the rise of the Latin American middle class*. Washington, DC: World Bank. https://openknowledge.worldbank.org/bitstream/handle/10986/11858/9780821396346.pdf?sequence=5&isAllowed=y

Gonzalez, A., & Campos, R. (2021, July 1). Latam central banks look past COVID as inflation phantoms loom. Reuters. https://www.reuters.com/world/americas/latam-central-banks-look-past-covid-inflation-phantoms-loom-2021-07-02/

IADB-Inter-American Development Bank. (2021, June 3). *Latin America trade recovers from pandemic impacts*. https://www.iadb.org/en/news/latin-america-trade-recovers-pandemic-impacts

ILO-International Labor Organization. (2020). *ILO monitor: COVID 19 and the world of work*. 7th ed. Geneva. https://www.ilo.org/wcmsp5/groups/public/---dgreports/---dcomm/documents/briefingnote/wcms_767028.pdf

ILO-International Labor Organization. (2021, June 30). *Tourism recovery is key to overcoming COVID-19 labour crisis in Latin America and the Caribbean*. Labour Overview Series for Latin America and the Caribbean 2021. https://www.ilo.org/caribbean/newsroom/WCMS_809331/lang--en/index.htm

Maurizio, R. (2021, April). The employment crisis in the pandemic: Towards a human-centred job recovery. *International Labour Organization-Labour Overview Services Latin America and the Caribbean 2021*. https://www.ilo.org/wcmsp5/groups/public/---americas/---ro-lima/documents/publication/wcms_779118.pdf

Oliveros-Rosen, E. (2021, June 24). Economic outlook Latin America Q3 2021: Despite a stronger 2021, long-term growth obstacles abound. *S&P Global*. https://www.spglobal.com/ratings/en/research/articles/210624-economic-outlook-latin-america-q3-2021-despite-a-stronger-2021-long-term-growth-obstacles-abound-12013558

Price, J. (2020, December 21). 2021 *Latin America forecast: An uneven recovery awaits (part I)*. Americas Market Intelligence. https://americasmi.com/insights/2021-latin-america-forecast-an-uneven-recovery-awaits-part-i/

Raineri, R., & Benoit, P. (2020, August 7). As Latin America looks to a COVID recovery, it will need to tackle its growing middle-class angst. Inter Press Service. http://www.ipsnews.net/2020/08/%e2%80%8bas-latin-america-looks-covid-recovery-will-need-tackle-growing-middle-class-angst/

Robles, F., Wiese, N. M. & Torres-Baumgarten, G. (2015). *Business in emerging Latin America*. New York, NY: Routledge.

Swiss Re Institute. (2021, June). *Latin America market report 2021: A long road to recovery*. https://www.swissre.com/institute/research/topics-and-risk-dialogues/economy-and-insurance-outlook/expertise-publication-latin-america-market-report-2021.html

Talvi, E., & Munyo, I. (2013). *Latin America macroeconomic outlook, a global perspective: Are the golden years for Latin America over?* Brookings Global-CERES Economic & Social Policy in Latin America Initiative 2013 Latin America Macroeconomic Outlook. http://www.brookings.edu/research/opinions/2013/11/07-latin-america-growth-rate-talvi-munyo.

UNCTAD. (2020). *World investment report 2020*. Geneva. https://unctad.org/system/files/official-document/wir2020_en.pdf

UNCTAD. (2021). *World investment report 2021*. Geneva. https://unctad.org/system/files/official-document/wir2021_en.pdf

WITS-World Integrated Trade Solution. (2021). *Latin America and Caribbean trade*. https://wits.worldbank.org/countrysnapshot/en/LCN

World Bank. (2013). Growth in Latin America's middle classes. http://www.worldbank.org/en/news/feature/2012/11/13/crecimiento-clase-media-america-latina

World Bank. (2021a). Databank. http://data.worldbank.org/

World Bank. (2021b). *Global economic prospects, January 2021*. Washington, DC. https://doi.org/10.1596/978-1-4648-1612-3

World Bank. (2021c). Pandemic crisis fuels decline of middle class in Latin America and the Caribbean. Press release No: 2021/182/LAC https://www.worldbank.org/en/news/press-release/2021/06/24/pandemic-crisis-fuels-decline-of-middle-class-LAC

WTO. (2012). *World trade report 2012*. http://www.wto.org/english/res_e/statis_e/its2001_e/its01_toc_e.htm

WTO. (2020). *World trade statistical review 2020*. https://www.wto.org/english/res_e/statis_e/wts2020_e/wts2020_e.pdf

WTO. (2021). *World trade statistical review 2021*. https://www.wto.org/english/res_e/statis_e/wts2021_e/wts2021_e.pdf

2 The Political and Legal Environment of Latin America

Introduction

Latin America has made a lot of political progress in the past four decades, with most countries in the region experiencing a period of relatively democratic regimes that began in the early 1990s. In 2021, all countries in the region, except for Cuba, had electoral democracies in place (even if some were more legitimate than others). Yet democracy in the region has always been fragile, but the past five years seem to indicate that democracy in the region is in an especially precarious state. The regulatory environment in Latin America has also seen improvements with reductions of regulations and streamlining of bureaucratic procedures. However, law enforcement and the judicial system remain weak and riddled with corruption. In this chapter, we first provide a snapshot of Latin America's political environment, followed by discussions on the weakening of democracy and the rise of populism and authoritarianism across the region. The next sections highlight some of the main areas of institutional weakness and current corruption trends in the region. The next section provides a summary discussion of Latin America's regulatory environment. The chapter ends with a synthesis of positive and negative trends in the political and legal environments of the region.

A Snapshot of the Political Environment in Latin America

During the 1980s through the mid-1990s, Latin America became a notable example of what has been referred to as the third wave of democratization. During this period, Latin America replaced three decades of dictatorships and military rule with democratically elected governments. In 2001, the Organization of American States adopted the Inter-American Democratic Charter, whereby country members made a commitment to preserve democracy (Feinberg & Gedan, 2021; Zovatto, 2020). Over the next 30 years, power alternated among governments of the left, right, and center. The end of the Cold War and the painful and unequal effects of the neoliberalization policies of the 1980s (i.e., privatization, spending cuts, liberalization of trade and investment), led to a backlash against right-leaning parties, resulting in the so-called 'pink tide,' which began with the election of Hugo Chavez in Venezuela in 1998. The first decade of the twenty-first century saw the ascension to power of several left and left-center presidents, including Luiz Inacio Lula da Silva (2003), Evo Morales (2006), and Cristina Fernandez de Kirchner, Daniel Ortega, and Rafael Correa (2007). This movement to the left was supported by those who had been most hurt by the neoliberal model or had failed to receive any of the gains of economic liberalization and were, thus, seeking fairer redistribution of wealth (e.g., Indigenous communities, farmers, those employed in the informal sector) (Dannefjord, 2021).

DOI: 10.4324/9781003182672-4

The staying power of these left-center governments coincided with the commodity boom that supported high levels of economic growth in the region through 2014. Healthy public budgets allowed these governments to fund social programs and provide subsidies that were popular among certain segments of the population. These programs had positive, measurable results: at least 20 million people were lifted out of poverty in Brazil during da Silva's presidency and 30 million during Hugo Chavez's early years as president of Venezuela. As commodity prices started to fall, it became more difficult for left-leaning governments to fund the social programs that had earned them popular support. In addition, the increased revenues of the booming years had not been invested in areas of long-term return, such as education, health, and infrastructure. As government coffers dried up, so did support for left-leaning governments (EIU-The Economist Intelligence Unit, 2019). In addition, and as we relate later in this chapter, many of these left-leaning presidents had begun to show authoritarian tendencies, seeking to grab power at the expense of the rule of law. Between 2015 and 2018, a counter trend resulted in the election of right and right-center candidates, including Mauricio Macri in Argentina (2015), Jair Bolsonaro in Brazil, Ivan Duque in Colombia, and Sebastian Piñera in Chile (all in 2018). The pendulum seems to be swinging left again, with the region experiencing a new pink tide, as shown by the elections of Manuel Lopez Obrador in Mexico (2018), Alejandro Fernandez in Argentina (2019), Luis Arce in Bolivia (2020), and Pedro Castillo in Peru (2021). The new swing to the left is being fueled by anger at the political and economic elite, rising poverty, continued social inequalities, and feelings of exclusion by certain segments of the population (Aquino, 2021; Dannefjord, 2021; Ward, 2020; World Politics Review, 2021; Zovatto, 2014).

As mentioned in Chapter 1, in the 2014–2020 period, the region registered some of its lowest economic growth rates in decades. Dissatisfaction with economic growth and increasing discontent with the lack of progress in the closing of social gaps has only been exacerbated by the economic crisis caused by the COVID-19 pandemic. The COVID-19 pandemic has had painfully negative effects on the region's economies and societies. What the effects on the region's political environment and democratic regimes will be is still uncertain and likely will vary among countries in the region. How far right or far left the pendulum will swing also remains a question which the 2021–2022 electoral cycle will help to answer (Arnson, 2020; Dannefjord, 2021).

As the rest of this chapter will make clear, countries in the region differ in terms of their institutional strength, levels of corruption, governance effectiveness, economic growth and stability, and quality of their social safety nets. By mid-2021, it was clear that some countries, such as Chile, Costa Rica, and Uruguay, were outperforming others, such as Brazil, Honduras, and Venezuela, in their handling of the pandemic on a wide range of metrics, ranging from funding adequate responses by their respective health systems and providing safety nets to coordinating effective and accelerated vaccination programs. The perceptions of each country's population on the diligence and effectiveness with which their respective governments have managed the pandemic and the post-pandemic recovery will have a direct effect on whether these fragile democracies are able to weather the crisis (Arnson, 2020).

The current scenario is mixed at best, and forecasts on long-term effects are difficult to predict. For one, many governments in the region have tried to use the pandemic to quash social discontent and protests that had risen prior to the pandemic. Curtailing civil rights will not be received favorably, nor tolerated, by populations that have experienced greater openness and engagement in political decision making over the past two decades. The opposite, in fact, may happen. In Colombia, President Ivan Duque responded to the 2019 and 2020 protests against the government's social and economic policies and plans to reform the country's pension and labor systems with police repression. This led to the death and injury of many Colombians and fueled even more protests. Politicians of the opposition have joined the protesters, raising their voices to call for reforms to the military and the police (Colombia politics, 2020). The importance of the right to protest, in the street or in the ballot box, will be especially true for the middle classes in the region, which are less tolerant of corruption and more vocal about demanding protection of their civil rights. Second, governments in the region will face real difficulties in providing the kinds of economic growth and public services that their societies expect. The economic losses from the pandemic are real and, thus, depleted public budgets will greatly limit the ability of governments in the region to provide the higher standard of living or greater access to quality public services their populations demand (Arnson, 2020). These pressures on the government are also likely to escalate, as those who have suffered losses to their incomes and wealth, especially those in the lower and middle-income brackets, seek to recover what they have lost. This would make for a very difficult scenario for countries with good governance; the challenge will be even greater for countries in the region that are poorly governed. This brings us to another factor that may further weaken the region's democratic regimes. Corruption, already a problem in the region, has been grotesquely evident during the pandemic (more on this later in the chapter). The wave of scandals related to the management of the pandemic has stoked the flames of indignation seen during other corruption scandals that plagued the region in the last decade (e.g., Odebrecht and Lava Jato). This widespread indignation has led to mass protests, the resignations and jailing of government officials, and more. The fragile democracies in Latin America may not be able to withstand much more.

Democracy at Risk

Even before the COVID-19 pandemic hit the region, Latin America was already experiencing a democracy deficit with weak institutions, mass protests, questionable electoral processes, and the emergence of authoritarian leaders (Feinberg & Gedan, 2021; Sheridan, 2019; Zechmeister & Lupu, 2019). Since 2018, support and satisfaction with democracy has been weakening in the region. Latinobarómetro found that by the end of 2018, support for democracy had fallen to 48% of the region's population, down 5% from 2017, and a decrease of 13% from 2010. About a third of those polled indicated indifference between having a democratic or authoritarian government, with those between 16–26 years of age being even more apathetic. Most worrisome of all, less than one-fourth of those polled indicated being satisfied with democracy, the lowest percentage since 1995. It follows that Latin Americans will choose leaders that promise to address their social and economic needs and will not much care if those promises are sincere or if those leaders lack democratic credentials (Arnson, 2020; Corporación Latinobarómetro, 2018; Zovatto, 2019). These findings were supported by the Latin American Public Opinion Project (LAPOP), which reported that in 2018/19, support for democracy in the 18 countries included in their study (LAC-18) was at its lowest level (58% compared to 69% in 2008). The region's average satisfaction with democracy stood at less than 40%, a drop of almost 20% from 2010. LAPOP's analysis determined that Latin Americans have a high tolerance for military and legislative coups under circumstances of high crime and high corruption. Although tolerance for military coups under high crime (39%) and high corruption (37%) were lower in 2018/19 when compared to a decade earlier (52% and 46%, respectively), these levels of tolerance are significant. Tolerance for executive coups (i.e., shutting down of legislative bodies) is lower than for military coups, but this tolerance has been increasing over time (24% in 2018/19 up from 15% in 2010). There are significant differences across countries and demographics as shown in Figure 2.1, with countries such as Uruguay and Argentina scoring consistently high on support for democracy and intolerance of military and legislative coups and countries such as Honduras and Peru scoring low on support of democracy and high on tolerance of coups (Arnson, 2020; Zechmeister & Lupu, 2019).

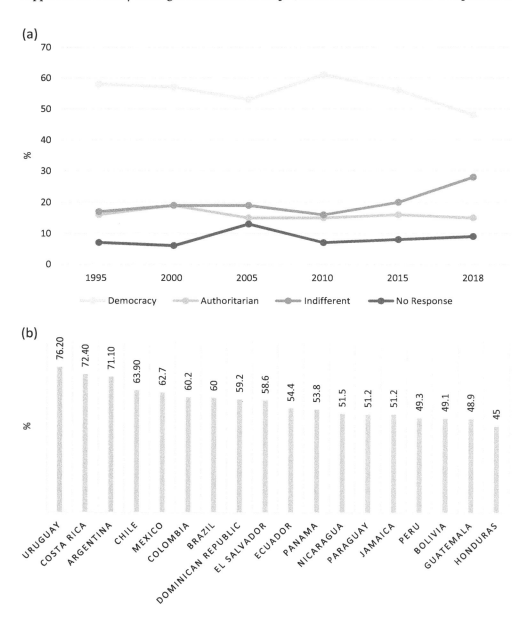

Figure 2.1 (a) Support for Democracy in the Region on a Decline (Source: Corporación Latinobarómetro (2018). Informe 2018.) (b) Support for Democracy by Country (2018/19) (Source: Zechmeister, E. J., & Lupu, N. (Eds.). (2019). *Pulse of democracy*. Nashville, TN: LAPOP.) (c) Support for Democracy by Education Level (2018) (Source: Corporación Latinobarómetro (2018). Informe 2018.) (d) Support for Democracy by Socioeconomic Status (2018) (Source: Corporación Latinobarómetro (2018). Informe 2018.)

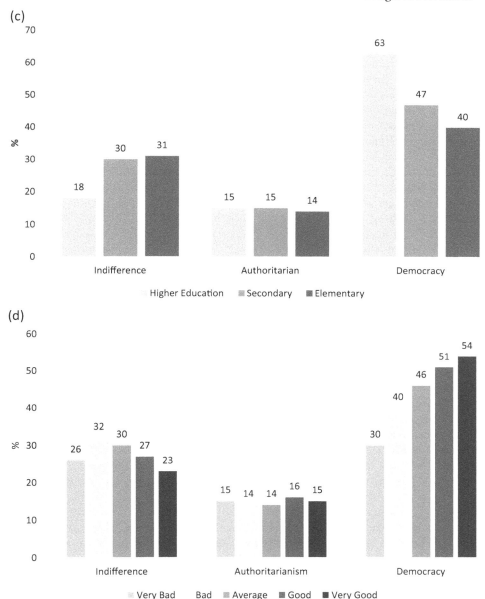

Figure 2.1 (Continued)

Why is support for democracy declining in Latin America? The trend toward democratic backsliding (and the corresponding wave of autocratization underway is discussed below) can be explained by looking at people's support for democracy as a regime in the abstract and in practice. The political attitudes of citizens toward democracy are a strong determinant of the resilience and stability of a democratic system. LAPOP finds that support for democracy is higher in those countries with more stable democracies (e.g., Uruguay and Costa Rica), while support is lowest in those countries where democracy is weakest or lacking legitimacy (e.g., Guatemala, Honduras, Nicaragua) (Zechmeister & Lupu, 2019). So, what do Latin Americans feel and think about democracy? First, Latin Americans are dissatisfied with the outcomes and performance of their democratic governments, which has led to disillusionment with democratic regimes and institutions. As Linde and Ekman (2003, p. 399) stated, satisfaction with democracy 'is an indicator of support for the performance of the democratic regime.' Lack of progress by the region's governments in providing better and more equal access to social services and economic opportunities, paired with scandalous and rampant corruption at the highest levels of government are mainly to blame for these negative attitudes. Satisfaction with democracy in their own countries ranges from 26% in Panama to 60% in Uruguay, with most countries in the region scoring in the 30%–40% range (Zechmeister & Lupu, 2019). In fact, disillusionment with the performance of their democracies is such that some citizens do not believe their countries to be real democracies.

Less than 60% of the population in Honduras, Nicaragua, and El Salvador believe their countries are democracies, and even the highest scoring countries (i.e., Paraguay, Peru, and Mexico) are considered democracies by no more than 66%–67% of the population. After three decades of uninterrupted democratic governments, these numbers are hardly something to cheer about. Dissatisfaction with democracy is highest among women, urban citizens, and those of working age (26–55) and with higher levels of wealth and education. These demographics, with the exception of the gender variable, are consistent with those of the people who do not believe their countries are democratic. This profile also shares similarities to those who indicated greater support for democracy in the abstract, which tend to be more educated, more affluent, and urban. Thus, more highly educated, wealthier, urban citizens support democracy as a regime but tend to be more critical of it when the system fails to deliver the outcomes expected by its citizens. One could assume that these citizens are those more likely to benefit from the status quo and are also those who have come to expect and demand more from their governments. The only inconsistency was seen in terms of gender and age; while men and older citizens were more supportive of democracy as a regime, they were less likely to express dissatisfaction with poor performance by their democratic governments (Zechmeister & Lupu, 2019).

A contrary position to the notion of democratic backsliding is that the Latin American democracies have, in fact, proven resilient (Feinberg & Gedan, 2021; López-Calva, 2021, Zovatto, 2020). The last decade handed Latin America economic shocks, debt crises, social unrest, health and environmental crises, and the emergence of authoritarianism; however, democracy, albeit imperfect, remains in place throughout the region with some exceptions such as Cuba, Nicaragua, and Venezuela (see current heads of state in Table 2.1). Moreover, 'elections are popularly accepted as the only legitimate means of coming to power—and the region has the highest levels of election participation in the world, with a regional average of 67%' (Zovatto, 2020). The Chileans who protested en masse in 2019 demanded more democracy not less, including greater protection of civil rights. The protests forced the president, Sebastian Piñera, to change his staunch position against constitutional changes and, ultimately, led to a landslide plebiscite vote in favor of constitutional reform, which is to take place in 2022 (Feinberg & Gedan, 2021; Ward, 2020). In Peru, massive street demonstrations (before and during the pandemic) showed that people were engaged in the political process and were willing to make their voices heard. Similar mass protests have occurred in Bolivia, Colombia, Ecuador, and Guatemala (Dannefjord, 2021). Even when some governments have responded to these demonstrations in more repressive ways than others, the mere fact that Latin Americans can and have demonstrated against elected officials to demand more equitable opportunities should be considered an enduring gain from the last 30–40 years of democracy. Gains in transparency and accountability are also evident. Impeachment, indictments,

Table 2.1 Heads of State in Select Latin American Countries

Country	Current President/Head of State	Current Term Ends	Political Ideology (Left, Center, Right)
Mexico and Central America			
Belize	Johnny Briceño	2025	Center-Left
Costa Rica	Rodrigo Chavez	2026	Center-Right
El Salvador	Nayib Armando Bukele Ortez	2024	Right
Guatemala	Alejandro Giammattei	2023	Right
Honduras	Xiomara Castro	2025	Left
Mexico	Andreas Manuel Lopez Obrador	2024	Left
Nicaragua	Jose Daniel Ortega Saavedra	2025	Left
Panama	Laurentino 'Nito' Cortizo Cohen	2024	Left
South America			
Argentina	Alberto Angel Fernandez	2023	Left
Bolivia, PS	Luis Alberto Arce Catacora	2025	Left
Brazil	Luiz Inácio Lula da Silva	2026	Left
Chile	Gabriel Boric	2025	Left
Colombia	Gustavo Petro	2026	Left
Ecuador	Guillermo Lasso Mendoza	2025	Right
Guyana	Mohamed Irfann Ali	2025	Center-Left
Paraguay	Mario Abdo Benitez	2023	Right
Peru	Pedro Castillo	2026	Left
Suriname	Chandrikapersad (Chan) Santokhi	2025	Center-left
Uruguay	Luis Alberto Lacalle Pou	2024	Right
Venezuela, BR	Nicolas Maduro Moros	2024	Left
The Caribbean			
Antigua and Barbuda	Gaston Browne	2023	Center-Left
Barbados	Mia Mottley	2027	Center-Left
The Bahamas	Philip Davis	2026	Left
Cuba	Miguel Diaz-Canel	2023	Left
Dominica	Roosevelt Skerrit	2025	Center-Left
Dominican Republic	Luis Rodolfo Abinader Corona	2024	Center-Left
Grenada	Dickon Mitchell	2027	Center-Left
Haiti	Ariel Henry (Acting)	2023	Right
Jamaica	Andrew Holness	2025	Center-Right
St. Kitts and Nevis	Terrance Drew	2027	Center-Left
St. Lucia	Philip Pierre	2026	Center-Left
St. Vincent and the Grenadines	Ralph Gonsalves	2025	Left
Trinidad and Tobago	Keith Rowley	2025	Center-Left

Source: Author.

and calls for resignations of politicians and current and former government officials (e.g., those involved in the Odebrecht bribery scandal) would have been unimaginable in the late 1980s. Finally, transitions of power continue to occur relatively smoothly, even in cases of extreme polarization and discontent about the results of an election (e.g., Argentina in 2019 and Peru in 2021). Remarkably, 14 elections were held in the region during the pandemic, all amid significant logistical difficulties and without reliable mail-in voting. Compared to historical averages and results from the previous election, turnout was higher in some cases and lower in others (Feinberg & Gedan 2021; López-Calva, 2021); however, in general, the many barriers to mobility and safety that the COVID-19 pandemic presented did not seem to have a shattering effect on Latin Americans' exercising their right to vote.

The declining belief in and commitment to democratic systems of governance in Latin America by the region's citizens is a concerning trend. Yet, the institutional voids and poor governance exposed by the pandemic are likely to have positive long-term effects on democracy, especially if they lead to much needed improvements to electoral procedures and logistics. In Chapter 6, we explore the risks related to this weakening of democratic traditions in the region as well as the counterforces that may prevent further erosion of democratic regimes and institutions.

Renewed Populism and Authoritarianism

As Latin American countries adopted democratic regimes in the mid and late 1980s, most countries in the region did not allow a president to be reelected for a consecutive term. In the mid-1990s, this began to change, with Alberto Fujimori in Peru (1993) and Carlos Menem in Argentina (1994) successfully changing their countries' constitutions in order to seek a second consecutive term. Soon after, Brazil (1998) and Venezuela (1999) followed suit. The trend continued into the first decade of the twenty-first century, with Rafael Correa of Ecuador, Evo Morales of Bolivia, and Cristina Fernandez-Kirchner of Argentina, all serving multiple terms. The most egregious of these instances occurred in Venezuela (2009) and Nicaragua (2014), which passed legislation allowing for indefinite presidential reelections, with Daniel Ortega currently serving his fourth term as Nicaragua's president (Cachanosky & Padilla, 2018). (In November 2021, Ortega won reelection for a fifth term amidst an election process riddled with accusations of fraud and repression of opposition candidates.) Most of these countries were also part of the Alliance for the Peoples of Our America (ALBA) group and part of the pink tide that characterized this period (Zovatto, 2014). More recently, Juan Orlando Hernández, president of Honduras, used a controversial 2015 ruling by the country's Supreme Court to seek reelection in 2017, and in September 2021, Nayib Bukele replaced the magistrates in El Salvador's Supreme Court with his supporters who have now granted him the right to seek reelection in the next electoral cycle ("Corte de El Salvador," 2021; Sandoval, 2016). In all these cases, the actions of incumbent leaders manipulating their countries' laws to seek consecutive reelection have been received negatively by most of these countries' citizens who see these actions as unconstitutional and as corrupt attempts by politicians to entrench themselves in the highest executive office. Moreover, there is a real risk of countries in the region adopting 'democratic dictatorships,' as is the case of Venezuela and Nicaragua (Zovatto, 2014). These events explain, in great part, the erosion of Latin Americans' trust in the electoral process and in democracy itself.

In addition to heads of state seeking reelection, populism of right and left tendencies is returning to Latin America (Corrales, 2018). Examples of right-leaning populist leaders include Jair Bolsonaro of Brazil and Nayib Bukele of El Salvador; left-leaning populist leaders include Luis Arce of Bolivia and Manuel Lopez Obrador of Mexico. Populism has two main characteristics: (a) it advocates for uneven inclusion, by promoting the inclusion of previously excluded groups of the population while creating obstacles and hardships for groups seen as opponents. Populist movements embrace an 'us vs. them' ideology, sowing internal divisions by pitting segments of the population against each other. (b) Populism also leads to the weakening, and even elimination, of institutions that may question or restrain the powers of the presidency. Checks and balances are not welcome in countries led by populist heads of state, and populist leaders of the left and right are known to use the power of the state to control dissent among citizens. Take the example of Brazil's Bolsonaro, who, in September 2021, issued a decree limiting the power of tech companies to censor content. Bolsonaro's decree is aimed at combating what he sees as the arbitrary removal of content and accounts from social media platforms (BBC News, 2021). Although Bolsonaro claims the new bill is aimed at protecting free speech, it should be noted that over the past year and a half, Twitter, YouTube, and Facebook have removed content shared by the president and his supporters that was considered misinformation (about COVID-19, federal judges, etc.). And the decree preceded planned demonstrations by Bolsonaro's followers to protest against Brazil's Congress and Supreme Court which have placed the president on a list of people being investigated for spreading misinformation (BBC News, 2021).

Right-wing 'toughness' can be inflexible, removed from the social and economic challenges faced by their societies, and perceived as elitist; leftist anger is too contemptuous of the value of institutions and the positive effects of market-driven regimes. Both can be prone to corruption. Latin America has a long history of supporting, or at least tolerating, 'caudillismo' (i.e., strongmen as political leaders) and 'hyper-presidentialism' (i.e., personal and hegemonic leaders who use 'separation of powers' as an argument to justify their abuse of the executive office and the rejection of checks and balances). This trend toward populism is not unfamiliar to people in the region and is very likely to take hold if allowed to flourish (Corrales, 2018; Political risk, 2020; Rose-Ackerman et al, 2011; Zovatto, 2014). Support for populist leaders is not surprising when one considers the weak institutional environment of most Latin American countries, a topic we explore in the next section.

The Institutional Environment

One of Latin America's main challenges is its weak institutional environment. If the region is to avoid falling into the trap of supporting 'saviors' at the expense of democracy again, then it must solidify and strengthen its social and political institutions. Doing so will be difficult when faced with the region's almost cynical attitude toward institutions. In this section, we briefly describe perceptions of trust and legitimacy toward institutions such as political parties, the executive, legislative bodies, the judiciary, and the media. We also summarize findings on key governance indicators that shed additional light on the strengths and weaknesses of Latin America's political institutions.

The Latin American Public Opinion Project (2019) found that citizens in Latin America largely distrust their countries' political systems and institutions (see Figure 2.2). About 60% of the region's population respect their countries' political institutions, and less than half indicated feeling proud of their political systems (a drop of almost 7% since 2010). Moreover, only about 40% of people in the 18 countries surveyed believe courts in their countries can guarantee fair trials or feel their rights are protected. Regarding trust in specific institutions, the institution least trusted among Latin Americans is political parties (28%, a drop of 7% since 2010), with trust in legislatures a close second (39% vs. 46% a decade ago). Trust in the executive and in elections were also low (43% and 46%, respectively), with trust in the executive registering the largest erosion in 2018/19 as compared to 2010 (−12.4%). There are marked intra-regional differences, with 60% of Costa Ricans believing they should support their country's political systems, while only 42% of Peruvians felt the same way. In addition, Nicaragua and Honduras experienced the largest declines across all four indicators of institutional strength (trust in political parties, national legislatures, the executive, and elections) (Zechmeister & Lupu, 2019; Zovatto, 2019).

The lack of trust in political parties and in legislatures is not surprising. People in Latin America do not have much confidence in the motivations, integrity, or competence of political candidates who are put forth by parties that have long been entrenched in power but have, thus far, failed to provide real solutions to the problems afflicting the region.

(a)

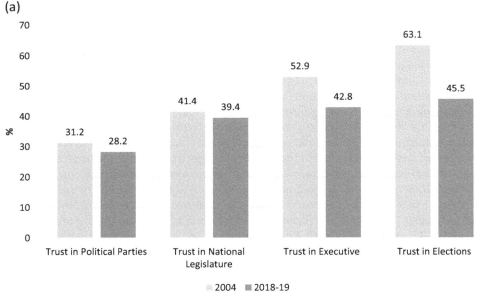

(b)

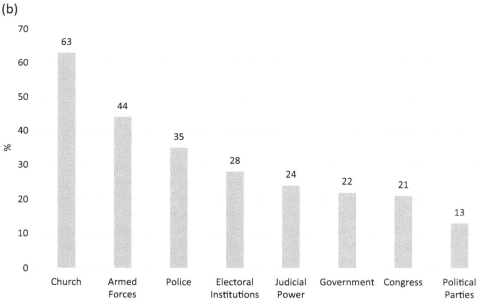

Figure 2.2 (a) Latin Americans' Trust in Key Political Institutions (Source: Zechmeister, E. J., & Lupu, N. (Eds.). (2019). *Pulse of democracy*. Nashville, TN: LAPOP.) (b) Latin Americans' Trust in Institutions (Source: Corporación Latinobarómetro (2018). Informe 2018.)

There is a sense that political parties are controlled by a minority of elite traditionalists who simply recycle the same individuals for elections at all levels (e.g., presidents, governors, mayors, representatives, etc.). It is not uncommon in Latin America, for instance, to see spouses and relatives of incumbent government officials run for the same offices or be placed in positions of power because of their family connections. Why, then, would people have any trust or hope that these individuals will govern effectively and honestly when they are not even willing to welcome new voices and perspectives into their political parties (Zovatto, 2014)?

Latinobarómetro reported similar findings. Trust in institutions, except for the church (63%), is low across the board with citizens' trust not reaching 50%: the armed forces (44%), police (35%), electoral organisms (28%), judicial branch (24%), the executive (22%), legislatures (21%), and political parties (13%) (Corporación Latinobarómetro, 2018).

The existence of weak institutions leads to low levels of trust among citizens, which, in turn, leads to dissatisfaction with democracy as a regime. The result is a social and political environment characterized by fragmentation, polarization, and a lack of integration. This is fertile terrain for the emergence of populist and authoritarian leaders. Thus, in countries where institutions are strong, where there is a free press, independence between the executive, legislative and judiciary branches of government, and respect for civil rights, the risk of authoritarianism will be lower; where institutions are weak, the risk will be higher (Corporación Latinobarómetro, 2018; Zovatto, 2014).

Corruption in Latin America

Corruption is one of Latin America's most serious woes. The Corruption Perception Index shows that corruption continues to be perceived as a serious problem across the region. Latin American countries' corruption perception scores have remained mostly unchanged since 2015, with a few exceptions (see Table 2.2 and Figure 2.3 for corruption indicators for selected Latin American countries). Uruguay, Chile, and Costa Rica show some of the lowest levels of perceived corruption. Among the Caribbean countries, Barbados, the Bahamas, and St. Vincent and the Grenadines were the strongest performers. At the bottom of the rankings are Venezuela, Haiti, Honduras, and Guatemala. In the past decade, the countries that recorded the most improvements in corruption perceptions were Argentina, Ecuador, Jamaica, and Guyana. The countries with perceived worsening corruption were Nicaragua, Guatemala, Honduras, and the Bahamas (Transparency International, 2020).

The World Bank's Worldwide Governance Indicators (WGI), which uses a wide range of sources to measure views and experiences of corruption, also reports that control of corruption has remained low for the past decade (2009, 58.61 percentile rank; 2019, 52.86 percentile) (World Bank, 2021b). The Rule of Law Index measures 'three forms of corruption: bribery, improper influence by public or private interests, and misappropriations of public funds or other resources' (p. 23). Significant differences were found among countries' scores on the Absence of Corruption factor, with Uruguay, St. Vincent and the Grenadines, Barbados, Chile, and Costa Rica all scoring between 0.66–0.73, and Peru, Honduras, Venezuela, Mexico, and Bolivia scoring the lowest (0.27–0.33) (WJP, 2020).

Corruption in Latin America is, of course, not only a perception but a reality. For instance, graft and profiteering have been all too common during the COVID pandemic. Here are some examples (Kitroeff & Taj, 2020):

- In Ecuador, a criminal ring colluded with health officials to sell body bags to hospitals for 13 times their real price ($148 vs. $11). The ring seemed to have involved a former president and members of his family, among others.
- The former Bolivian health minister was arrested on corruption charges for paying a Spanish firm millions for 170 ventilators priced at almost twice the price offered by another seller and three times the price charged by the manufacturer. The ventilators turned out to be unsuitable to treat seriously ill coronavirus patients.

Table 2.2 Corruption in Latin America

Country	Transparency International Corruption Perceptions Index 2020		WJP Rule of Law Index 2020* Absence of Corruption		Corruption Barometer 2019**
	Score (0–100)	Rank 1/180	Score (0.00–1.00)	Global Rank 1/128	%
Antigua and Barbuda	—	—	0.61	38	—
Argentina	42	78	0.52	52	93
The Bahamas	63	30	0.63	37	80
Barbados	64	29	0.70	25	53
Belize	—	—	0.43	75	—
Bolivia, PS	31	124	0.27	124	—
Brazil	38	94	0.45	69	90
Chile	67	25	0.69	26	85
Colombia	39	92	0.39	95	94
Costa Rica	57	42	0.66	30	82
Dominica	55	48	0.6	40	—
Dominican Republic	28	137	0.39	94	93
Ecuador	39	92	0.42	86	—
El Salvador	36	104	0.38	98	93
Grenada	53	52	0.65	32	—
Guatemala	25	149	0.34	108	90
Guyana	41	83	0.46	66	59
Haiti	18	170	—	—	—
Honduras	24	157	0.32	114	91
Jamaica	44	69	0.55	47	78
Mexico	31	124	0.27	121	90
Nicaragua	22	159	0.34	105	—
Panama	35	111	0.42	82	90
Peru	38	94	0.33	111	96
St. Kitts and Nevis	—	—	0.64	33	—
St Lucia	56	45	0.64	34	—
St. Vincent and the Grenadines	59	40	0.70	24	—
Trinidad and Tobago	40	86	0.49	55	85
Uruguay	71	21	0.73	22	—
Venezuela, RB	15	176	0.31	117	93

Sources:
Transparency International, Corruption Perception Index 2020.
*WJP Rule of Law Index, 2020. The table reports only the 'Absence of Corruption' factor.
**Transparency International, Global Corruption Barometer 2019 (Table reports only the 'percentage of people who think corruption in the government is a big problem' for LAC-18: Argentina, the Bahamas, Barbados, Brazil, Colombia, Costa Rica, Chile, the Dominican Republic, El Salvador, Guatemala, Guyana, Honduras, Jamaica, Mexico, Panama, Peru, Trinidad and Tobago, and Venezuela.)

- In Brazil, government officials in at least seven states were being investigated for malfeasance in the use of more than US$200 million of public funds for the pandemic.
- In Colombia, dozens of political campaign donors received lucrative contracts to provide emergency supplies during the health crisis.
- In Peru, the police chief and interior minister resigned over claims that their subordinates had used public funds to purchase diluted sanitizer and flimsy masks that were given to police officers who later became infected and died. After an investigation into wrongdoing was initiated by prosecutors, boxes of evidence went missing.

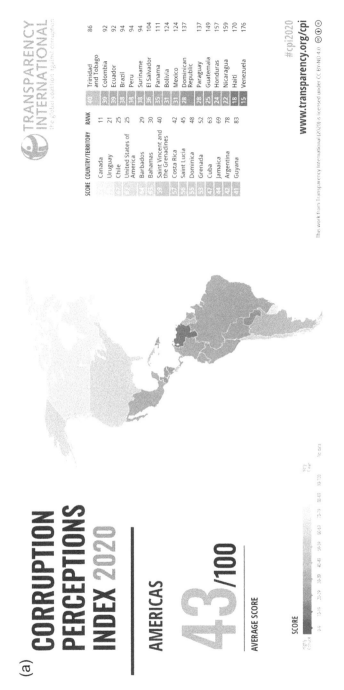

Figure 2.3 (a) Corruption in Latin America (Source: Transparency International. (2020). The Corruption Perception Index. https://www.transparency.org/en/cpi/2020/index/tto).

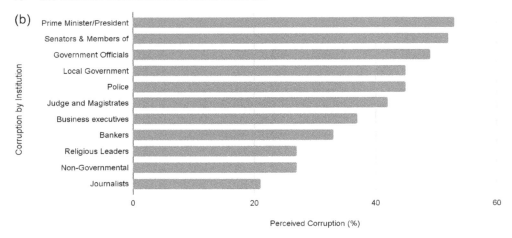

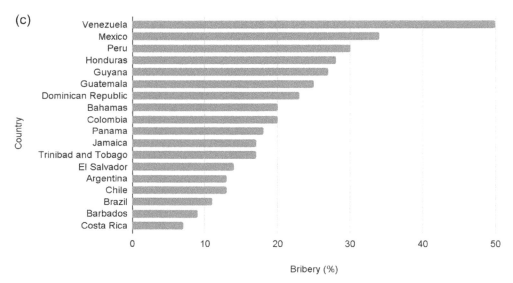

Figures 2.3 (Continued) (b) Perceived Corruption by Institution (Source: Authors' elaboration with data from Global Corruption Barometer 2019 Report) (c) Bribery in Latin America (Source: Authors' elaboration with data from *Global Corruption Barometer, Latin America & The Caribbean 2019*. Transparency International)

- In Mexico, faulty ventilators purchased from the son of the head of the federal electricity commission were returned after it was reported that the federal hospital system had paid 85% more than the lowest priced option.
- In Honduras, several mobile hospitals were purchased at higher than market prices without a proper bidding process or warranties. The hospitals were unsuitable to treat coronavirus patients.

The pandemic has allowed governments in the region to use 'emergency powers' to suspend rules and protocols for public contracts, transparency and access to information requirements, and reviews by their legislative bodies. In this context, it has been easier for government officials and politicians to engage in acts of corruption (Kitroeff & Taj, 2020).

Although perceptions of corruption and actual corruption have not changed much over the past decade, tolerance for corruption has been declining across Latin America and the Caribbean.

> High-level politicians have been found guilty of corruption in Guatemala and Brazil, and a wave of legal action against the perpetrators of grand corruption swept across the continent, including the Lava Jato investigation, or 'Operation Car Wash', in Brazil. This presents a real opportunity for anti-corruption in the region.
>
> (Pring & Vrushi, 2019, p. 2)

Citizens across the region are more aware of incidences of corruption (and criminal activities) by those in power thanks in part to more access to information, activism by civic and social groups, and, in some cases, a more independent judiciary (Sheridan, 2019). These factors have contributed to Latin Americans being better informed and more willing to express their frustration and anger with their voices and their votes. People's increasing intolerance of corruption, especially in the public sector, is associated with their low levels of support for and satisfaction with democratic regimes. In 2018, the region's average government approval was 32%, down from 60% in 2009, and the lowest average registered since 1995 (Corporación Latinobarómetro, 2018). The countries with the highest levels of government approval were the Dominican Republic and Costa Rica (both at 53%); those with the lowest levels of government approval were Brazil (6%), Mexico (18%), El Salvador (22%), and Argentina, Nicaragua, and Paraguay (23%). Although these figures do not align exactly with the Corruption Perception Index and Rule of Law Index scores, in general, countries with low government approval ratings also ranked high in corruption.

The Regulatory Environment of Latin America

Regulatory bureaucracies with complex, outdated, and inefficient legal systems characterize Latin American countries. Business-oriented regulations also tend to offer less protection than those received in more developed countries. One example of this is the weak protection of property rights in the region. In this type of environment,

> an individual or a business and their assets are invisible to the law and so do not exist in a legal sense. Because they and their property have no rights under the law, they cannot be subject to binding legal contracts. This decreases the value of assets and limits the efficiency of markets.
>
> (Schaefer & Schaefer, 2008, p. 199)

To better understand how the regulatory system hinders firms' competitiveness and the region's attractiveness to investors, we review Latin America's ratings and rankings on two legal indices. We first summarize the information provided by the World Bank's Ease of Doing Business Index and then look at the Rule of Law Index for other measures of the region's regulatory environment.

Ease of Doing Business Index

At its core, regulation is about freedom to do business. Regulation aims to prevent worker mistreatment by greedy employers (regulation of labor), to ensure that roads and bridges do not collapse (regulation of public procurement), and to protect one's investments (minority shareholder protections).

(World Bank, 2020, p. 2)

The Ease of Doing Business Index assesses the quality of a country's business environment by tracking regulations in 12 areas of business: 'processes for business incorporation, getting a building permit, obtaining an electricity connection, transferring property, getting access to credit, protecting minority investors, paying taxes, engaging in international trade, enforcing contracts, and resolving insolvency.' It also tracks employment regulations and government contracting (World Bank, 2020—written report). In the following paragraphs, we focus our discussion on the first ten regulatory areas.

The 2020 Ease of Doing Business (EDB) scores and rankings for the region are shown in Table 2.3 (World Bank, 2021a). Although the scores for some Latin American countries have improved over the past few years, much remains to be done to reduce the regulatory obstacles faced by businesses.

Table 2.3 Ease of Doing Business 2020 Rankings and Scores

Country	Score 0–100	Global Rank 1/190	Regional Rank 1/33
Chile	72.6	59	1
Mexico	72.4	60	2
Puerto Rico	70.1	65	3
Colombia	70.1	67	4
Jamaica	69.7	71	5
Costa Rica	69.2	74	6
Peru	68.7	76	7
Panama	66.6	86	8
El Salvador	65.3	91	9
St. Lucia	63.7	93	10
Guatemala	62.6	96	11
Uruguay	61.5	101	12
Trinidad and Tobago	61.3	105	13
Dominica	60.5	111	14
Antigua and Barbuda	60.3	113	15
Dominican Republic	60	115	16
The Bahamas	59.9	119	17
Brazil	59.1	124	18
Paraguay	59.1	125	19
Argentina	59	126	20
Barbados	57.9	128	21
Ecuador	57.7	129	22
St. Vincent and the Grenadines	57.1	130	23
Honduras	56.3	133	24
Guyana	55.5	134	25
Belize	55.5	135	26
St. Kitts and Nevis	54.6	139	27
Nicaragua	55.5	142	28
Grenada	53.4	146	29
Bolivia, PS	51.7	150	30
Suriname	47.5	162	31
Haiti	40.7	179	32
Venezuela, BR	30.2	188	33

Sources: World Bank (2021a). Ease of Doing Business Rankings. https://www.doingbusiness.org/en/rankings?region=latin-america-and-caribbean

In terms of regional averages, Latin America's best score is in the area of starting a business (79.6), followed by the ability to get an electricity connection (71.7), and trading across borders (69.1). The worst regional averages are in the areas of resolving insolvency (39.2), protecting minority investors (47.3), and getting credit (52.0). Yet, compared to the 190 countries included in the index, the region ranked lowest in the areas of paying taxes (128), registering property (122), and starting a business (119). Its highest rankings were in the areas of getting electricity (96), getting credit (98), and trading across borders (106). In terms of specific countries in the region, Chile, Mexico, and Colombia are the top three ranked countries in the region (59, 60, and 67 out of 190, respectively); Suriname, Haiti, and Venezuela rank lowest in the region (162, 179, 188 out of 190, respectively) (World Bank, 2020).

Starting a business in Latin America takes more procedures, time, and money than in any other region of the world (regional averages of eight procedures, 29 days, and 31% of per capita income). Over the past decade, some reforms have been implemented to improve the process of starting a business in the region, including establishing one-stop shops (Guatemala, Paraguay, and Mexico) or online platforms for business registration (Colombia, Panama, Mexico, and Ecuador) and simplifying procedures (Honduras, Brazil, and Peru). A similar situation is evident when analyzing the other indicators. Dealing with construction permits, getting electricity, registering property, paying taxes, trading across borders, and enforcing contracts all require a significant number of procedures and time and money, with Latin America being one of the worst performers when compared to other regions of the world (World Bank, 2020).

Clearly, Latin American countries must seek to implement reforms that increase efficiencies in all the regulatory areas mentioned. For instance, simplifying taxation systems, allowing electronic filing and payment of taxes, and streamlining import and export regulations would create a regulatory environment that is more attractive to domestic and foreign businesses.

The Rule of Law Index

'The World Justice Project defines the rule of law as a durable system of laws, institutions, norms, and commitment that delivers': accountability, just laws, open government, and accessible and impartial dispute resolution (WJP, 2020, p. 1). These four principles are assessed through eight factors: constraints on government powers, absence of corruption, open government, fundamental rights, order and security, regulatory enforcement, civil justice, and criminal justice. The scores across these eight factors show significant differences between countries regarding adherence to the rule of law (see Figure 2.4). Uruguay, Costa Rica, and Chile are the top performers in the region, while Nicaragua, Bolivia, and Venezuela ranked the lowest. The range of scores across the eight factors assessed is significant. For instance, on Constraints on Government Powers, scores ranged from 0.76 (Costa Rica) to 0.17 (Venezuela); on Order and Security, scores ranged from 0.78 (Antigua and Barbuda) to 0.50 (Venezuela); and on Regulatory Enforcement, scores ranged from 0.71 (Uruguay) to 0.19 (Venezuela). In terms of sub-regions, the Caribbean countries received higher scores overall, while Mexico and the Central American countries received lower scores.

Understanding the kinds of laws that regulate business activity in a country matter, but enforcement and equal treatment under the law are also important considerations when assessing a country's legal environment. Even if laws exist on the books, they may not be followed in practice, and violations may not be prosecuted. A case in point is labor laws. The 2021 International Trade Union Confederation Global Rights Index ranks 149 countries on protection of workers' rights. The index looks at reported violations of workers' rights and analyzes each country's laws and practices against almost 100 indicators derived from International Labor Organization

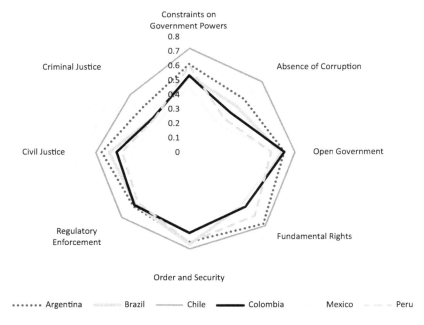

Figure 2.4 Rule of Law Index for LAC-6 (Source: Authors' elaboration with data from the World Justice
        Project Rule of Law Index 2020)

conventions (ITUC, 2021). Among the top ten offenders in the world are three Latin American
countries—Brazil, Colombia, and Honduras—which earned their places because of violence
against workers, including murders; undermining of collective bargaining; and union busting
and dismissals. On a scale of 1 (sporadic violations) to 5+ (no guarantees of rights), the Americas
(including the US and Canada) scored an average of 3.48 (compared to Europe's score of 2.50),
with Brazil, Colombia, Ecuador, Guatemala, and Honduras being the worst offenders. Uruguay
and Costa Rica were the best performers, with sporadic violations (ITUC, 2021).

Summary

Latin America has come a long way in adopting democracy as the predominant governmental
system in the region. Yet, Latin American democracies remain fragile. The failure of national
governments in enacting and implementing the kinds of policies and development programs
needed to eradicate poverty, reduce inequality, and move the region out of its current economic growth slump is driving the democratic fatigue currently afflicting Latin American
citizens. Lack of progress controlling crime and corruption round-up the list of citizens' frustrations with their current governments. Weak governance and institutional voids have led
to a lack of trust on major political institutions (e.g., all branches of government, the police,
electoral systems, etc.), and increasing protests and demonstrations by segments of the population most affected (e.g., those in lower and middle-income brackets, vulnerable minorities).
In the midst of growing citizen discontent and anger (Bremmer & Kupchan, 2020), populist
and autocratic leaders seem to be making a comeback, and the region is at risk of these individuals succeeding in their efforts to entrench themselves in positions of power.

The scenario described above is a negative one, with real prospects for ongoing instability,
citizen discontent, and democratic backsliding. Yet, there are reasons for optimism. Civilian

protests and demonstrations, uninterrupted transitions of power via democratic processes, lower tolerance for corruption, and greater activism across the region are all positive signs. Latin Americans may have taken a few steps back on the road to solidifying democracy and achieving stability, but they are unlikely to renounce their hard-won civil rights and political freedoms to give way to the dictatorial aspirations of a handful of politicians.

On the regulatory context, Latin America seems to have stagnated, making little progress over the past five years to establish a regulatory environment that encourages investment and productivity while protecting consumers, minority investors, and other stakeholders. Red tape and inefficient systems of taxation, business registration, and the like will need to be corrected if the region is to overcome its record as the region with the worst ease of doing business environment among all regions of the world.

In Chapter 6, we explore the risks to firms doing business in Latin America that emerge from the political and regulatory realities discussed in this chapter, as well as risk management and mitigation strategies that firms can pursue to reduce their risk exposure.

References

Aquino, M. (2021, June 21). Another pink tide? Latin America's left galvanized by rising star in Peru. Reuters. https://www.reuters.com/world/americas/another-pink-tide-latin-americas-left-galvanized-by-rising-star-peru-2021-06-21/

Arnson, C. J. (2020). Democracy at risk. *Latin Trade* (August/October), 28–29.

BBC News. (2021, September 6). Bolsonaro: New bill will limit tech giants' power to remove content. https://www.bbc.com/news/world-latin-america-58470093

Bremmer, I., & Kupchan, C. (2020, March 19). Risk 9: Discontent in Latin America. Eurasia Group. https://www.eurasiagroup.net/live-post/risk-9-discontent-in-latin-america

Cachanosky, N., & Padilla, A. (2018, December 24). Latin American populism in the twenty-first century. *The Independent Review*, 24(2), 209–226 . https://ssrn.com/abstract=3147096

Colombia politics: New protest wave signals a possible return of mass unrest. (2020, September 24). EIU ViewsWire, New York. https://login.ezproxy.ups.edu:2443/login?url=https://www-proquest-com.ezproxy.ups.edu:2443/wire-feeds/colombia-politics-new-protest-wave-signals/docview/2446603450/se-2?accountid=1627

Corporación Latinobarómetro. (2018). Informe 2018. https://www.latinobarometro.org/latContents.jsp

Corrales, J. (2018, June 25). Opinion: The return of populism, Latin America style. *The New York Times*. https://www.nytimes.com/2018/06/25/opinion/mexico-colombia-populism.html?auth=link-dismiss-google1tap&referringSource=articleShare

Corte de El Salvador avala reelección del presidente Nayib Bukele. (2021, September 3). *La Prensa* https://www.laprensa.hn/mundo/1490469-410/corte-el-salvador-avala-reeleccion-presidente-nayib-bukele

Dannefjord, J. (2021, March 9). Is there a new Pink Tide on Latin America's horizon? *The Perspective*. https://www.theperspective.se/is-there-a-new-pink-tide-on-latin-americas-horizon/

EIU-The Economist Intelligence Unit. (2019). Where next and what next for Latin America? https://www.eiu.com/public/topical_report.aspx?campaignid=latinamerica2019

Feinberg, R. E., & Gedan, B. N. (2021, April 12). Latin America's surprisingly resilient democracies. *World Politics Review*. https://www.worldpoliticsreview.com/articles/29561/across-latin-america-democracy-proves-surprisingly-resilient

ITUC-International Trade Union Confederation. (2021). 2021 ITUC global rights index. Brussels, Belgium. https://files.mutualcdn.com/ituc/files/ITUC_GlobalRightsIndex_2021_EN_Final.pdf

Kitroeff, N., & Taj, M. (2020, June 21). Latin America also confronts graft epidemic. *New York Times*, Late Edition. https://www.nytimes.com/2020/06/20/todayspaper/quotation-of-the-day-latin-america-also-confronts-graft-epidemic.html

Linde, J., & Ekman, J. (2003, May). Satisfaction with democracy: A note on a frequently used indicator in comparative politics. *European Journal of Political Research, 42*(3), 391–408. https://doi.org/10.1111/1475-6765.00089

López-Calva, L. F. (2021, February 17). The virus and the votes: How is COVID-19 changing voter turnout in LAC? UNDP in Latin America and the Caribbean. https://www.latinamerica.undp.org/content/rblac/en/home/presscenter/director-s-graph-for-thought/the-virus-and-the-votes--how-is-covid-19-changing-voter-turnout-.html

Political risk in Latin America. (2020, December 28). CE Noticias Financieras. Miami, FL. https://login.ezproxy.ups.edu:2443/login?url=https://www-proquest-com.ezproxy.ups.edu:2443/wire-feeds/political-risk-latin-america/docview/2473731473/se-2?accountid=1627

Pring, C., & Vrushi, J. (2019). Global corruption barometer Latin America & The Caribbean 2019: Citizens' views and experiences of corruption. Transparency International. https://images.transparencycdn.org/images/2019_GCB_LAC_Report_EN1.pdf

Rose-Ackerman, S., Desierto, D. A., & Volosin, N. (2011). Hyper-presidentialism: Separation of powers without checks and balances in Argentina and the Philippines. *Berkeley Journal of International Law, 29*(1), 246–333.

Sandoval, E. (2016, Noviembre 11). Polémica en Honduras: Juan Orlando Hernández busca reelección basado en fallo. CNN en Español. https://cnnespanol.cnn.com/2016/11/11/polemica-en-honduras-juan-orlando-hernandez-busca-reeleccion-basado-en-fallo/

Schaefer, P. F., & Schaefer, P. C. (2008). Property, the rule of law, and development in the Americas. In J. Haar and J. Price (Eds.), *Can Latin America compete? Confronting the challenges of globalization.* New York: Palgrave Macmillan.

Sheridan, M. B. (2019, October 10). Why political turmoil is erupting across Latin America. *The Washington Post.* https://www.washingtonpost.com/world/the_americas/why-political-turmoil-is-erupting-across-latin-america/2019/10/10/a459cc96-eab9-11e9-a329-7378fbfa1b63_story.html

Transparency International. (2020). The corruption perception index. https://www.transparency.org/en/cpi/2020/index/tto

Ward, A. (2020, October 26). Chileans want a more equal society. They're about to rewrite their constitution to have it. Vox. https://www.vox.com/21534338/chile-constitution-plebiscite-vote-pinochet

World Bank. (2020). Doing business 2020. Washington, DC: World Bank. https://openknowledge.worldbank.org/bitstream/handle/10986/32436/9781464814402.pdf

World Bank. (2021a). Ease of doing business rankings. https://www.doingbusiness.org/en/rankings?region=latin-america-and-caribbean

World Bank. (2021b). Worldwide governance indicators. https://info.worldbank.org/governance/wgi/Home/Reports

World Justice Project (WJP). (2020). The rule of law index. https://www.worldjusticeproject.org/rule-of-law-index/

World Politics Review-The Editors. (2021, June 29). After the end of the 'Pink Tide.' What's next for South America? *World Politics Review.* https://www.worldpoliticsreview.com/insights/27904/after-the-end-of-the-pink-tide-what-s-next-for-south-america

Zechmeister, E. J., & Lupu, N. (Eds.). (2019). *Pulse of democracy.* Nashville, TN: LAPOP.

Zovatto, D. (2014). Reelection, continuity, and hyper-presidentialism in Latin America. Brookings. https://www.brookings.edu/opinions/reelection-continuity-and-hyper-presidentialism-in-latin-america/

Zovatto, D. (2019, September 17). Latin America: Political change in volatile and uncertain times. IDEA International. https://www.idea.int/news-media/news/latin-america-political-change-volatile-and-uncertain-times

Zovatto, D. (2020, February 28). The rapidly deteriorating quality of democracy in Latin America. Brookings. https://www.brookings.edu/blog/order-from-chaos/2020/02/28/the-rapidly-deteriorating-quality-of-democracy-in-latin-america/

3 The Competitive Environment of Latin America

Introduction

The competitive landscape in Latin America has evolved significantly over the last few decades. Formerly protected markets, which were dominated by a few large family groups and state-owned enterprises, have been replaced by open markets and more diverse competition. Although large family-controlled domestic conglomerates still play a dominant role, there is now a stronger presence of multinational corporations from developed and emerging economies and a more vibrant small- and medium-size business sector. This dynamic competitive environment will require firms doing business in Latin America to leverage the unique opportunities offered by the region's macroenvironment (e.g., abundant natural resources, a growing consumer market) while managing its many risks (e.g., unstable political climate, regulatory bureaucracy, crime). This chapter provides a better understanding of the degree of competitiveness for select countries in Latin America and of the competitive structure in the region.

The chapter is organized in four sections. The first section describes the factors that explain the level of competitiveness of countries in Latin America, including drivers of and barriers to competitiveness vis-à-vis other regions of the world. The second section focuses on the role Latin American countries play in global supply chains, focusing on how countries in the region can leverage and enhance their positions in global value chains in the medium and long term. The next section describes the current structure of competition in the region, highlighting the various types of organizational players and their defining characteristics. A summary of the main issues related to competition and competitiveness in the region closes the chapter.

The Global Competitiveness of Latin America

The success of firms operating in Latin America depends, to a large extent, on the conditions for competitiveness at the country level. In this section, we explore the various factors that explain the level of competitiveness of Latin American countries vis-à-vis other regions of the world.

As noted in the opening chapter of the book, the region experienced steady economic growth from the late-1990s through 2014. During the 2015–2021 period, economic growth in the region has slowed, and progress in areas such as productivity gains and technology adoption has stagnated. Even if challenges remain, overall, the last two decades have resulted in increased competitiveness of several countries in the region. This section describes the competitiveness of select Latin American countries and of the region as a whole, primarily

DOI: 10.4324/9781003182672-5

using information from the *World Economic Forum's 2019 Global Competitiveness Report.*
This allows us to compare Latin America to other regions of the world and to assess
competitiveness improvements over time. We focus our discussion especially on those
factors that point to enhanced competitiveness and those that indicate areas of improvement
for the region and for specific countries. First, a short explanation about what the index
measures.

The Global Competitiveness Index (GCI) 4.0, introduced in 2018, relies on a new
framework for evaluating country competitiveness; thus, the information in the 2019 report
is not directly comparable to the information presented in the first edition of this book. The
GCI 4.0 framework assesses the attributes and qualities of a country's economy that lead to
more efficient use of its factors of production. The index measures total factor productivity,
under the assumption that productivity gains are the main determinant of long-term
economic growth. The GCI considers '12 pillars of productivity,' which are organized into
four categories: enabling environment, human capital, markets, and innovation ecosystem.
This framework emphasizes four factors that are believed to be the most significant for
productivity and long-term growth as the world advances toward its fourth industrial
revolution, namely, agility, resilience, human capital, and innovation (Schwab, 2019). It
is important to note that, although the index ranks countries and presents comparative
information, it does not assume competitiveness to be a zero-sum game. Rather, the index
aims to provide information about a country's progress in reaching an ideal state on a scale
of 0 to 100 (i.e., the closer to 100 a country performs on any single pillar, the more that issue
has stopped being a constraint to productivity growth).

Latin America and the Caribbean (LAC), just like other emerging regions, has experienced
improvements to its competitiveness, but these improvements are not yet sufficient to reach
what the GCI refers to as the 'frontier.' Table 3.1 summarizes the 2019 GCI competitiveness
scores and rankings for the region as a whole and for selected Latin American countries
(Schwab, 2019). The regional performance averages across the 12 pillars indicate that smaller
competitiveness gaps are observed in macroeconomic stability, health, financial systems, and
infrastructure. The larger gaps are in innovation capability, institutions, information and
communication technology (ICT) adoption, and market size. The main factors hindering
competitiveness across the region are a weak innovation ecosystem, especially in terms
of a lack of innovation capability, and a weak enabling environment, driven primarily
by institutional voids and low ICT adoption. Market size and product market are also
deterrents of productivity for some countries in the region. In terms of gains and losses to
competitiveness from 2018 to 2019, the most important gain was in the area of ICT adoption,
followed by business dynamism and skills. Losses were most evident in the areas of product
markets, market size, and institutions.

At the country level, the 2019 Index reveals that the five most competitive countries in
the region are Chile, Mexico, Uruguay, Colombia, and Costa Rica, in that order. The least
competitive are El Salvador, Bolivia, Nicaragua, Venezuela, and Haiti (Schwab, 2019). Chile
is the most competitive country in the region, ranking 33 in the world primarily because
of its macroeconomic stability, well-developed infrastructure, strong financial system, open
markets, and investments in human capital development. Mexico, the second most competitive country in the region (48th in the world), owes its strong position to its stable macro-
economics, well-developed infrastructure, and large market size. Brazil, the largest economy
in Latin America, ranks eighth in the region (71st worldwide) because of low scores on the
pillars of institutions, ICT adoption, product and labor markets, and innovative capability.
For the three lowest ranked countries—Nicaragua, Venezuela, and Haiti—weak institutional

Table 3.1 Summary of GCI Scores for LAC

Country	Rank	Score (out of 141)	Enabling Environment				Human Capital		Markets				Innovation Ecosystem	
			Institutions	Infrastructure	ICT Adoption	Macroeconomic Stability	Health	Skills	Product Market	Labor Market	Financial System	Market Size	Business Dynamism	Innovation Capability
Chile	33	70.5	64	76	63	100	90	70	68	63	82	63	65	42
Mexico	48	64.9	48	72	55	98	82	58	58	56	62	81	66	44
Uruguay	54	63.5	62	69	80	86	85	67	55	59	58	45	58	38
Colombia	57	62.7	49	64	50	90	95	60	53	59	65	67	64	36
Costa Rica	62	62	57	69	60	74	93	69	59	59	60	47	56	36
Peru	65	61.7	49	62	46	100	95	60	57	59	61	62	56	40
Panama	66	61.6	51	69	50	90	92	58	59	56	68	49	59	63
Brazil	71		48	65	58	69	79	56	46	53	65	81	60	37
Barbados	77	60.9	55	58	76	70	87	65	44	62	71	19	60	49
Dominican Republic	78	58.9	50	65	52	75	76	59	54	63	60	54	57	39
Trinidad and Tobago	79	58.3	48	58	60	89	78	61	46	59	68	41	57	35
Jamaica	80	58.3	49	63	48	70	80	63	52	67	67	36	68	34
Argentina	83	57.2	50	68	58	34	84	72	47	52	53	69	58	35
Ecuador	90	55.7	48	69	48	74	85	61	43	52	56	54	46	42
Paraguay	97	53.6	44	60	46	75	81	51	55	55	56	47	51	33
Guatemala	98	53.5	42	56	38	75	74	51	59	51	58	51	56	22
Honduras	101	52.7	44	57	30	75	78	50	55	56	60	42	54	32
El Salvador	103	52.6	40	61	41	70	78	48	54	53	62	43	53	31
Bolivia	107	51.8	38	57	51	74	74	58	44	46	58	46	47	28
Nicaragua	109	51.5	42	56	36	74	90	47	51	53	53	39	50	28
Venezuela	133	41.8	26	46	47	0	82	64	36	46	39	57	29	31
Haiti	138	36.3	31	27	28	60	51	41	38	49	44	34	14	19
LAC Avg			47.1	61.3	50.9	73.7	82.2	58.7	51.6	55.9	60.3	51.2	53.8	34.3
% Change from 2018			-1.4	0.2	9.8	-0.5	-0.6	2.2	-4.3	1.1	1.4	-2.5	2.8	1.8

Source: Schwab, K. (2019). The Global Competitiveness Report 2019. *World Economic Forum – WEF.*

environments, small market size, and lack of innovation capabilities account for their low competitiveness positioning (Schwab, 2019).

Next, we explore in greater detail each of the sets of factors driving competitiveness— enabling environment, human capital, markets, and innovation ecosystem— while highlighting select indicators and countries to illustrate specific areas of productivity gains and areas in need of further improvement.

Enabling Environment

In terms of the enabling environment, the performance of countries in the region is mixed and widely dispersed. The region, as a whole, performs relatively high on infrastructure (61.3) and macroeconomic stability (73.7) but performs lower on institutions (47.1) and ICT adoption (50.9); these performance levels hold across countries as well. Yet, the gaps between the best and worst performers indicate significant intra-regional variations; for institutions, that gap is 38; for infrastructure, 70; for ICT adoption, 52; and for macroeconomic stability, 100 (Schwab, 2019).

Institutions

The region scored 47.1, the second lowest score among all world regions, which is a reduction of 1.4 from 2018. The gap between Latin America's score and that of the highest performing region, Europe and North America, was 17.6. The country scores ranged from 26–64, but the majority of countries scored between 40–55 (Schwab, 2019). The issue of weak institutional environments and institutional voids is widespread in Latin America, a topic that we address in detail in Chapter 2. Suffice it to say that increasing crime rates, excessive red tape, inefficiencies and corruption in the public sector, a lack of checks and balances between governmental branches, and policymaking that has failed to address present and future needs all continue to be barriers to enhanced productivity across the region.

Infrastructure

The existence of a well-developed infrastructure is critical to a country's competitiveness, as it influences where economic activity is located, what type of economic activity can flourish in a region, and access to domestic and international markets. An extensive and efficient infrastructure also impacts an organization's logistical costs and constraints as well as the ability of firms to reach rural and low-income markets, thus increasing the size of a market (Schwab & Sala-i-Martin, 2013). Essential to a well-developed infrastructure are high quality and reliable systems of transportation (roads, ports, etc.) and utilities (electricity and water). Looking into the future, infrastructure that allows countries to prepare for and to respond with resilience and agility to increasing climate change threats will be of paramount importance. Equally important is the need for countries in the region to invest in digital infrastructure that may result in the productivity gains needed to move Latin America forward post-pandemic. Table 3.2 summarizes some key infrastructure indicators.

In general, Latin America lags behind other regions of the world in terms of infrastructure. The 2019 GCI gives the region a score of 61.3 (+0.2% from 2018), placing the region as the third lowest, just above the regions of sub-Saharan Africa and South Asia. The gap between Latin America's score and that of the highest performing region (Europe and North America, 79.7) is 18.4. Most countries in the region scored between 55 and 70, with a

Table 3.2 Select Indicators of Infrastructure and ICT Adoption for Select Latin American Countries (2019)

Country	Investment in Infrastructure as % of GDP 2019	Efficiency of Seaport Services (Scale 1–7)	Electricity Access % of Population	Exposure to Unsafe Drinking Water % of Population	Mobile Broadband Subscriptions per/100 People	Internet Users % of Adult Population
Argentina	0.60	3.9	98.8	8.2	80.7	74.3
Bolivia	5.30	2.0	88.1	18.2	79.9	43.8
Brazil	0.40	3.2	99.7	9.7	88.1	67.5
Chile	1.20	4.9	100.0	3.7	91.6	82.3
Colombia	1.40	4.1	97.0	19.5	52.3	62.3
Costa Rica	2.50	3.9	99.3	6.5	97.2	74.1
Dominican Republic	0.70	4.9	97.1	62.4	60.8	74.8
Ecuador	1.80 (2017)	4.5	97.3	16.4	54.7	57.3
El Salvador	1.10	3.4	96.0	23.6	55.8	33.8
Guatemala	0.90	3.9	92.0	43.0	16.5	65.0
Honduras	1.00 (2018)	4.4	75.0	23.6	32.1	31.7
Mexico	0.80	4.3	100.0	6.8	70.0	65.8
Nicaragua	3.90	3.2	90.0	30.1	29.6	27.9
Panama	2.60	5.7	92.4	17.2	70.3	57.9
Paraguay	1.70	3.5	99.0	18.7	57.7	65.0
Peru	2.10	3.8	95.0	18.5	65.7	52.5
Uruguay	1.40	4.8	99.7	5.7	123.8	68.3
Venezuela	—	2.1	98.9	14.7	54.5	72.0

Sources: WEF Global Competitiveness Report, 2019; http://infralatam.info/en/home/

few exceptions (Schwab, 2019). Although the GCI score seems high when compared to the region's scores on the other three pillars that make up the enabling environment, physical infrastructure and related infrastructure services in Latin America are insufficient, inefficient, outdated, and poorly maintained. One has simply to step into any major airport in Latin America to appreciate how these facilities have insufficient capacity and outdated technology. Insufficient capacity and poor maintenance of road and railway systems also create inefficiencies in the movement of people and products, from traffic congestions to road closures. Moreover, water and power shortages are common across the region, with power outages and lack of access to safe drinking water and adequate sanitation being especially problematic in the lower-income sectors of overpopulated urban centers and for rural communities (Fay et al., 2017). Climate change is creating further strains on the region's infrastructure such as reducing access to energy and water (The Climate Reality Project, 2021). Therefore, improvements to physical infrastructure and related infrastructure services (e.g., energy, water, sanitation) are necessary to begin to correct the structural barriers which help explain the region's poorly diversified production systems, innovation lags, high levels of socioeconomic inequality, exclusion of marginalized population groups, and growing vulnerability to climate change (ECLAC, 2016; Fay et al., 2017; Jaimurzina & Sanchez, 2017; Perez, 2020).

Investments in infrastructure development have been insufficient. In 2005, Latin American investment in infrastructure was about 2% of regional GDP (Fay & Morrison, 2005); in 2011, spending in infrastructure was 2%–3% of regional GDP, which was three times less than China's spending and two times less than India's (CAF, 2013). In 2017, infrastructure spending remained at about the same level (2.8% of GDP), the lowest among all regions of the world with the exception of sub-Saharan Africa. For comparison, infrastructure spending by other regions ranged from 4%–7.7% of GDP (Fay et al., 2017). The ECLAC estimates that, in order to close the existing gaps in infrastructure development, Latin America will need to raise its spending by between 2% and 8% of GDP over current spending levels (Fields, 2013; Jaimurzina & Sanchez, 2017; Ramos Suarez & Perez, 2018).

Deficiencies exist in almost all infrastructure areas. Road density in Latin America lags behind other regions of the world (156 km per 1000 km^2 of land area vs. a world average of 241 km). Moreover, it is estimated that only between 16% and 25% of the road network in the region is paved, with stretches of the secondary and tertiary networks in rural and remote areas—representing 85% of the region's total road network—being particularly neglected (Field, 2013; Jaimurzina & Sánchez, 2017; OECD, 2018b). Rural roads play an important role in the competitiveness of the region, as these roads represent key routes of market connectivity, facilitating almost 90% of the region's natural resource-related exports (Perez, 2020). Inland waterways are virtually unexplored and underdeveloped. For example, in 1997, a plan was formulated by the governments of Argentina, Bolivia, Brazil, Paraguay, and Uruguay to develop the Paraguay and Parana waterways into a shipping channel (the Hidrovia project); however, the legal framework required to implement the project was never enacted by these governments (OECD, 2018b). Seaports have seen some improvements because of private companies' investments, but bottlenecks and poor maintenance of ports remain a problem. The lack of intermodal infrastructure linking seaports to land transportation is also a major weakness throughout the region (OECD, 2018b). These weaknesses translate into low performance measures for the region's logistics (see Figure 3.1). Investments in infrastructure vary widely across the region in terms of amounts of investment, main sectors of spending (roads, ports, etc.), and source of the investment (private or public). The largest percentage of projects tend to be national, with few cross-country initiatives seeking to integrate transport infrastructure to enhance

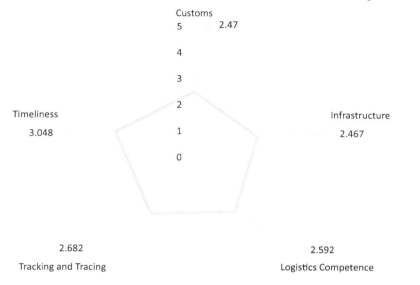

Figure 3.1 Latin America's Logistics Performance Index

regional connectivity. In addition to under investment, the region performs poorly in terms of efficiency and quality of infrastructure spending. Common in the region are project completion delays, unfinished projects, and overspending (Fay et al., 2017).

Climate change will likely create further infrastructure challenges for Latin America. The signs of climate change are visible throughout the region, from fires in the Amazon and melting glaciers in Patagonia to ongoing droughts in South America and more frequent and devastating hurricanes in Central America and the Caribbean. These changes to the natural environment have real consequences for the region's infrastructure. For instance, floods and landslides can destroy roads and bridges, leaving communities without access to markets and basic services; hurricanes can damage electrical grids and water systems, which then need to be rebuilt; and droughts and melting glaciers can lead to water scarcity, both for human consumption and for the generation of hydroelectric power. Examples of the latter are already evident in Argentina, Brazil, Bolivia, Colombia, and Peru, among other countries. For instance, in 2014, droughts and heat waves drew down Sao Paulo's main water reservoir to less than 10% of its capacity, forcing the government to limit water consumption. In the Peruvian Andes, glaciers shrank by about one-third between 2000 and 2016, hurting the communities that depend on glacier runoff for their drinking water supply and energy needs (Coda, 2021; Rodrigues, 2020; The Climate Reality Project, 2021; UNOPS, n.d.).

In addition to more and better investments in physical infrastructure, the region needs to invest more on digital infrastructure. For instance, increasing digitalization of public services such as water, energy, and telecommunications could have a direct impact on generating economic growth (as much as 5.7% GDP growth over ten years, according to the Inter-American Development Bank). Using ICT technologies to design, operate, and maintain roads, ports, electrical and water grids, and other types of physical infrastructures could improve affordability and access by both businesses and individuals, especially those in lower-income communities (Bocanegra, 2020; Cavallo, Powell, & Serebrisky, 2020).

ICT Adoption

In the area of ICT adoption, Latin America received a score of 50.9, the third lowest among all regions. This score reflects a positive change of 9.8 from 2018, almost twice the increase registered by the four best performing regions. In fact, Latin America's improved performance on this pillar mirrored the trend observed in the other two regions with the lowest scores (sub-Saharan Africa, 34.3 and South Asia, 35.1), which also saw the largest increases from 2018 (15.8 and 6.4, respectively). Uruguay, Barbados, Chile, Costa Rica, and Trinidad and Tobago were the best performers (60+); Haiti, Honduras, Nicaragua, and Guatemala were the worst performers (>40) (Schwab, 2019).

Latin America has made significant progress in the area of ICT adoption. In 2020, there were more than 430 million unique mobile subscribers, a penetration rate of almost 70%. There were also 640 million SIM connections (102% penetration rate), and 72% penetration of smartphone connections (ranging from 62% in Peru to 84% in Brazil). Over the next five years, it is expected that half of all new mobile subscribers will come from the two largest countries, Mexico and Brazil. The number of mobile internet users reached 358 million, a 57% penetration rate. By 2025, the adoption rate of smartphone connections is expected to reach 81%, while the penetration rate for mobile internet users will reach 64%. It is estimated that the mobile industry contributed 7% to the region's GDP (US$340 billion) in 2020, and almost 1.5 million jobs were directly or indirectly linked to the mobile ecosystems in the region (GSMA Latin America, 2021). See Table 3.2 for some indicators of ICT adoption for select Latin American countries.

Macroeconomic Stability

Latin America's score on macroeconomic stability was 73.7 (−0.5 from 2018), the third lowest among all regions, compared to 92.6 for the best performing region (Europe and North America). The economic stability of the region is addressed in detail in Chapter 1, and the connections between the regulatory environment and business activity are discussed in Chapter 2. In this section, we highlight some examples of macroeconomic issues constraining productivity growth across the region.

Chile has a very stable macroeconomic context (ranking first alongside 32 other top performing countries) thanks to low inflation (2.25%) and low public debt (25.56%). Mexico's main challenge in terms of its macroeconomic stability is relatively high inflation (5.5%, 111th). Argentina's economy has been in a recession since 2018 (GDP declined by 2.5% in 2018; 1.2% in 2019), leading to an increase in the unemployment rate (9.9%) and in the number of people falling into poverty (31.3%). The country has also seen very high inflation (29.9%, 138th) and increasing deficits, which have led to a less stable macroeconomic context (139th). This has resulted in lower investor confidence and capital flights, with local and foreign investors moving more than $35 billion out of the country since 2018. This, in turn, led the government to reintroduce capital controls, which is likely to further undermine investor confidence (Schwab, 2019). In 2021, the macroeconomic stability of the entire region remains uncertain, and this will remain the case until the COVID-19 pandemic is controlled and economic activity in the region returns to something resembling 'normal.'

In assessing the enabling environment of countries in the region, the challenge for many is their mixed performance. Take the case of Mexico, the second-best performer in the region overall. In 2019, Mexico experienced improvements from the previous year in the areas of institutions (+0.6 points) and ICT adoption (+3.7), but the improvements were not sufficient to close the gap with more competitive economies. Improvements to institutions have been concentrated in the public sector's administrative efficiency (+4.5 points), but security (138th) and transparency (116th) remain extremely problematic. In terms of its macroeconomic stability, Mexico's high inflation rate (5.5%, 111th) is a constraint to its productivity growth (Schwab, 2019). Yet opportunities to develop stronger competitiveness may lay at the intersection of these various factors. For instance, integrating the use of ICT technologies in the design and maintenance of climate change-resilient infrastructure can lead to higher quality infrastructure services, greater efficiencies, and less disruptions, all of which translate into higher economic growth and stability (Coda, 2021).

Human Capital

Human capital is a direct driver of competitiveness, which the GCI assesses using indicators of health and skills. A healthy and well-educated workforce is an important resource for countries, and one that must be developed and supported on an ongoing basis. People's skills and capabilities create economic value through efficiency-driven productivity and the generation of innovations. We present a demographic profile of Latin America, including issues related to health and diversity in Chapter 4. Issues related to talent management are discussed in Chapter 5. Below, we highlight the performance of the region and select countries on the pillars of health and skills.

Health

Latin America scored 82.2 on this pillar (−0.6 from 2018), by far the best regional performance across all pillars (and the third highest after the regions of Europe and North America and East Asia and the Pacific). Yet, the index relies on a single measure: healthy life expectancy (Schwab, 2019). On this measure, the region is doing relatively well (see Table 3.3 for some key indicators of human development).

Encouraging as this high score is, the COVID-19 crisis has shown that the Latin American health sector requires significant structural changes and more robust investments (see Chapter 1 for a longer discussion on the effects of the COVID-19 pandemic). Life expectancy in countries with low levels of human development is much lower than in those with higher levels of human development. In Latin America, for instance, Chile's life expectancy in 2019 was 80, while Haiti's was 64. Life expectancy can also vary within countries. Findings from a study of 363 cities in nine Latin American countries revealed significant differences in life expectancy not only between cities but also between sub-sectors of those cities. In general, gaps in life expectancy ranged from 8 to 14 years, with higher life expectancy being associated with higher levels of education, access to water and sanitation, and less overcrowding. Higher life expectancies were observed in cities in Panama, Chile, and Costa Rica, while cities in Mexico, Brazil, Peru, and El Salvador had the shortest life expectancies. The largest gaps in life expectancy were found in Brazil and Peru for women (6.4 and 6.6 years) and in Brazil and Mexico for men (8.6 and 10.4 years) (Bilal et al., 2019; Bilal, Hessel, Perez-Ferrer et al., 2021).

A workforce that has no access to quality health services or lives in conditions that preclude a healthy lifestyle (lack of sanitation, clean drinking water, etc.) will be more prone to absenteeism and lower productivity. In addition to infrastructure-related improvements that may enhance healthy life expectancy, countries in Latin America should also allocate resources and enact policies that ensure more equal access to high quality health services.

Table 3.3 Select Indicators of Human Development for Select Latin American Countries

Country	Life Expectancy at Birth 2019	Healthy Life Expectancy % 2019	Average Rate of School Enrollment (Ratio of Women to Men) 2013–2018		% of Women from Total STEM Graduates at the Tertiary Level 2008–2018	Average Years of Schooling 2018
			Primary	Secondary		
Argentina	77	66.8	1.00	1.04	46.5	11.4
Belize	75	—	0.95	1.05	41.8	—
Bolivia, PS	72	63.6	0.98	0.97	—	8.9
Brazil	76	65.4	0.97	1.05	36.6	7.6
Chile	80	68.7	0.97	1.01	18.8	10.3
Colombia	77	70.4	0.97	1.06	32.8	8.3
Costa Rica	80	69.8	1.01	1.05	33.4	8.6
Cuba	79	—	0.95	1.03	39.9	—
Dominican Republic	74	64.2	0.93	1.08	40.0	7.8
Ecuador	77	67.2	1.01	1.03	29.2	9.0
El Salvador	73	65.0	0.97	0.99	23.5	6.9
Guatemala	74	63.7	0.97	0.95	34.7	6.4
Haiti	64	56.3	—	—	—	5.6
Honduras	75	64.9	1.00	1.14	37.5	6.5
Mexico	75	66.2	1.01	1.09	31.1	8.6
Nicaragua	74	68.8	—	—	—	6.3
Panama	79	69.4	0.98	1.03	49.0	9.8
Paraguay	74	66.0	—	—	—	8.4
Peru	77	70.3	1.00	1.00	32.9	9.2
Trinidad and Tobago	74	65.0	—	—	—	9.9
Uruguay	78	67.2	0.98	—	44.6	8.7
Venezuela, RB	72	66.2	0.97	1.08	—	10.3
LAC	76		0.99	1.05	33.6	

Sources: World Bank Data Center; PNUD 2019 – Human Development Report 2019, WEF 2019 Global Competitiveness Report.

Skills

The region's score on skills was 58.7 (+2.2 from 2018), with Chile as the best performer (70) and Haiti as the worst performer (41). In general, most countries scored in the 50–65 range (Schwab, 2019). Investing in human capital is an important driver of productivity. In the 2010–2019 period, Latin Americas' labor productivity grew an average of only 0.5%, the lowest performing region after the Middle East and North Africa (compare this to the 3.2% average growth in labor productivity for all emerging and developing economies) (CEPAL, 2020).

In many Latin American countries, the quality of education is poor. Curricula are outdated across levels, from elementary to higher education, and the education is, in many cases, of poor quality or does not reflect the educational needs of the workplaces of the future (e.g., Mexico ranked 99th on digital skills and 103rd on critical thinking; Bolivia ranked 103rd on quality of vocational training and 130th on critical thinking) (Schwab, 2019). Social exclusion and inequality in Latin America also hinder the region's ability to make any progress on skills building.

Latin America has a large pool of low-skilled workers but a shortage of workers with higher skills. In the current environment of hyper-competitiveness among firms from all over the world, increased access to global talent pools, and existent skills gaps in less advanced economies, it is especially important for both governments and firms to invest in skills and capability building. Low wages will no longer be sufficient to compete in global markets, as cost efficiencies can be found in many locations around the world, and automation technology is likely to reduce the need for human labor in certain industries. Moreover, talent adaptability is critical to a well-functioning labor market in which public and private actors must seek to leverage technological advancements (e.g., digitization and automation of production) while protecting the social well-being of workers (Maurizio, 2021; Schwab, 2019). This implies adaptability and flexibility to reimagine the nature of work and of traditional jobs and to envision the jobs of the future. Countries that can translate this vision of the 'future of work' into their educational systems will be in the best position to develop the skill base needed to drive productivity and remain competitive vis-à-vis other countries. Programs that promote lifelong learning (i.e., retraining and reskilling) will also facilitate people's ability to make necessary transitions within the labor market (Maurizio, 2021). For instance, if Latin America is to continue to play an important role in global value chains, it will need to invest in its people. An increasingly knowledge-based economy means more sophisticated processes and cutting-edge technologies will be used throughout global value chains in the years to come. Adequate investments in education and training will ensure Latin Americans can develop or upgrade the skills needed to participate in these global networks.

In the short term, countries in Latin America will need to address any skills lost because of the COVID-19 pandemic. Since March 2020, an estimated 17 million students have had their education interrupted due to lockdowns; in some countries (e.g., Peru), schools remained closed into 2021. There is a real risk that school closures and suspension of schooling may have long-lasting effects on the skill base of the younger generation and negatively impact their ability to enter the labor market in the near future (CEPAL, 2020).

The skills pillar is closely connected to the pillars of innovation capability, ICT adoption, and business dynamism. A country that invests in high quality, state of the art primary, secondary, tertiary, and vocational education will create a deep and adaptable talent pool. This depth in skills, in turn, will energize the country's business environment, driving diversification of economic activity, ideally toward more knowledge-based industries. Such a dynamic business environment should be complemented with resources and policies that facilitate technology adoption and capacity building. More dynamic, diversified, and technologically intense economies tend to produce more formal employment, higher quality jobs, and more negotiating power for workers to ensure fair compensation and social protections (CEPAL, 2020).

Markets

The following set of competitiveness factors measures the size of a country's market and the openness, stability, and/or quality of the country's product market, labor market, and financial system. Productivity, and thus competitiveness, is expected to be higher for countries with large and growing economies; open and competitive product markets; deep, inclusionary, and stable financial systems; and highly skilled, flexible labor markets.

Product Market

This pillar assesses the degree of domestic market competition and trade openness. Latin America scored 51.6 on this pillar (-4.3 from 2018), the third lowest among all regions after South Asia and sub-Saharan Africa. Recent movements toward protectionism may explain some of this loss. In general, Latin American markets are less open and competitive than other regions of the world, with large companies (domestic and foreign) typically dominating domestic markets. In addition, product markets can be negatively affected by global events or changes to trade relationships. Take the case of Mexico. The Trump administration's pressures to replace NAFTA with the revised USMCA (effective July 1, 2020) led to uncertainty and trade tensions among both government officials and business leaders, slowing down development-oriented policymaking and reducing investor confidence. Strengthening regional integration efforts and diversifying trading relationships could lead to an improvement of Latin America's performance on this pillar.

Labor Market

Latin America's score was 55.9 (+1.1 from 2018), the fourth highest among all eight regions. This pillar assesses the flexibility of a country's labor market and the systems and processes aimed at incentivizing productivity. In terms of flexibility, the index focuses on costs, policies, and regulations that affect the hiring and firing of workers. In terms of incentivizing employees, the index uses measures of professional management, pay and productivity, and gender pay gaps (Schwab, 2019).

Labor markets in the region have long been considered rigid and costly. This rigidity emanates from the laws that control employer–employee relations, which usually fall into one of three categories: laws that regulate the hiring and dismissal of employees; government mandated employer contributions to social security, pensions, and health insurance; and collective bargaining. This complicated set of labor regulations makes it difficult for firms to allocate and reallocate human capital in a manner that is most conducive to achieving productivity and competitiveness (Sabatini, 2008; Schwab & Sala-i-Martin, 2013). Some of the labor regulations that companies find rigid and burdensome include a firm's inability to dismiss workers without providing—or paying for—advance notice (ranging from two weeks to three months depending on years of employment) and obligations to pay seniority bonuses and severance payments based on wages and years of employment upon dismissal.

Of course, these regulations counterbalance the lack of protections and safety nets for workers who lose their jobs. The constraints imposed on firms regarding hiring and firing have also led to a large number of workers being employed in the informal sector—especially women and youth—where they have few legal and social protections. Some Latin American countries undertook reforms to labor regulations in the 1990s and early 2000s, primarily relating to the formal hiring of temporary workers; however, the impact of these reforms was not significant enough to reduce the inflexibility of Latin American labor markets or the degree of informal employment. Thus, governments must find a way to meet the flexibility needs of companies (and workers) while protecting the rights of workers ('Brazil's Dilemma,' 2007; Maurizio, 2021; Sabatini, 2008).

Recent demographic trends indicate Latin America is aging, and thus the size of the labor force will gradually shrink. Migration patterns may enlarge or decrease the size of a country's labor pool. In Latin America, economic vulnerability and lack of public safety, among other reasons, drive talent from the region, not only among low-skilled workers but also among those with medium and higher skill levels (i.e., brain drain). These same factors also drive intra-regional migration. In this scenario, Latin America would benefit from more flexible labor markets that allow organizations and individuals to move in and out of the labor market, as opportunities emerge, transform, or disappear.

Financial System

This pillar measures the depth and stability of a country's financial system. The average score for the region was 60.3 (+1.4 from 2018), the fourth highest among all eight regions. Chile was the best performer, while Venezuela was the worst performer, with the majority of countries in the region scoring in the 50–60 range (Schwab, 2019). A well-functioning financial system should capture the savings and investments of individuals and organizations and reallocate them to serve two economic purposes: access to money by consumers willing to spend and access to working capital by entrepreneurs and private sector businesses seeking growth and expansion. 'Resilient, complex, and deep (in the sense of reaching across all income levels, including the working poor) banking systems are synonymous with advanced economies, higher growth, and income equality' (Smith, Juhn, & Humphrey, 2008, p. 79). In relative terms, the Latin American countries' financial systems are relatively well developed, diversified, and stable. Yet the region's financial systems have been notoriously exclusionary, favoring credit to large companies and affluent individuals and excluding micro and small businesses and people from historically disadvantaged groups (e.g., women, Indigenous and Afro-descendant populations, and low-income consumers) (Chironga et al., 2012; Ferraz & Ramos, 2018; Smith, Juhn, & Humphrey, 2008). In 2010, it was estimated that only 21% of the adult population used the financial system for savings, and only 12% used it for credit (Chironga et al., 2012). By 2014, some improvements to access were apparent, but this access remained unequal: 51% of all adults over 15 years of age had at least one account in a formal banking institution, but only 48% of women, 41% of those in the bottom 40% of the income distribution, and 37% of youth (15–24) did (Perez Caldentey & Titelman, 2018). In 2018, the low and uneven access to financial markets by consumer households and small businesses persisted. On average, only 46% of all adults (15 y/o+) had access to the financial system, compared to the world average of 61% and well below the average for high-income economies, such as Western Europe and North America (93%). The Latin American average is also lower than that of other emerging economies in Eastern Europe, East Asia, and the Pacific (72%), Eastern Europe and Central Asia (58%), and the Middle East and North Africa

(53%). Access by those in the top 60% of the income distribution have 1.5 times the levels of access to financial systems as those in the bottom 40% (Perez Candeltey & Titelman, 2018). Furthermore, lack of access to financing has long been one of the main obstacles to growth cited by Latin American entrepreneurs and small- and medium-size businesses (SMEs). In 2010, 30% of SMEs identified access to financing as a major barrier to growth, and while 91% had a checking or savings account, only 45% had a loan or line of credit. Unequal access to banking services by SMEs persisted through the end of the past decade. In 2018, about 94% of SMEs had checking and/or savings accounts, but only 37% had lines of credit, and 23% had long-term loans (Ferraz & Ramos, 2018; Perez Caldentey & Titelman, 2018).

Until recently, the region's financial systems also excluded middle-class consumers and medium-size businesses. However, the rise of the middle class as an important consumer segment, the entrance of foreign-owned banks to the region, and the adoption of technologies by financial institutions (i.e., fin-tech) have all contributed to greater access to and higher quality of financial services. These improvements to access and quality have also benefited lower-income consumers and micro and small businesses, though to a lesser degree. Finally, transparency and sound regulations are essential for inspiring trust in the financial market of a country (Schwab & Sala-i-Martin, 2013); both of these conditions have been missing in the region's financial systems and represent threats to the region's competitiveness.

Market Size

This pillar is measured based on a country's total GDP (PPP) and the total value of its goods and services imports. The average score for Latin America was 51.2 (−2.5 from 2018), the third lowest regional score after sub-Saharan Africa and Eurasia. The range across countries in the region was 19 (Barbados) to 80 (Brazil and Mexico) (Schwab, 2019). As was evident in our discussion in Chapter 1, countries and sub-regions in Latin America differ greatly in terms of the size and composition of their economies, thus the large score differences are not necessarily surprising. In addition, as our prior discussion noted, most Latin American economies experienced lower growth rates over the second half of the past decade. To this economic contraction, or at the very least stagnation, one must add the devastating effects of the COVID-19 pandemic on the region's economies. Depending on the policies that Latin American countries choose to implement to stimulate growth, diversify their economies, and reverse any losses to the middle class, their performance on this pillar will improve or worsen over the next couple of years.

Innovation Ecosystem

A country's innovation ecosystem is assessed by evaluating the pillars of business dynamism and innovation capability. The indicators used to measure these two pillars capture information on issues such as ease of business formation, entrepreneurial climate, diversity of the workforce, and investments in research and development (R&D). Thus, an innovative ecosystem drives productivity by creating the conditions necessary for agility, human capital formation, and innovation.

Business Dynamism

This pillar measures the administrative requirements for starting and running a business and the overall entrepreneurial culture in a country. Latin America's score on business dynamism was 53.8 (+2.8 from 2018), the second lowest among all regions after sub-Saharan Africa, and 14.5 points away from the best performing region (Europe and North America, 68.3). Notwithstanding the minor gains achieved in 2019, this is clearly an area in which countries in the region need to take more aggressive measures to improve the conditions in their business ecosystems. Intra-regional differences are significant with scores ranging from 66 to 14 (Mexico and Chile were the best performers, while Haiti and Venezuela were the worst). This reflects the differences in policies and investments pursued by countries in the region. In 2019, Argentina and Brazil improved their business dynamism scores (+2.9 and +7.8, respectively) mainly due to a reduction or simplification of regulations to start and/or close a business. The regulatory environment of Latin America was discussed at some length in Chapter 2. The entrepreneurial ecosystem of the region is the focus of Chapter 10.

Innovation Capability

'Companies achieve competitive advantage through acts of innovation' (Porter, 1990, 75), and thus, a country's innovative capacity will either support or hinder its firms' abilities to become world competitors. This pillar considers how diverse, collaborative, and innovative a country's talent base is; the country's investments in research and development; and the level of consumers' sophistication (i.e., willingness to buy innovative goods and services). The GCI 4.0 framework identifies innovation capability as the weakest pillar in all Latin American countries, with an average regional score of 34.3, ranging from a low score of 19 (Haiti) to a high of 63 (Panama). The region registered a minor gain in this score (+1.8 from 2018), but progress is neither sufficient nor is it occurring fast enough. Compare, for instance, the improvements registered by two other low performing regions: sub-Saharan Africa (score of 29.4, change from 2018 of +3.6) and the Middle East and North Africa (score of 41.3, change from 2018 of +4.3) (Schwab, 2019). Most of the countries in the region scored in the 30–40 range, primarily because of their meager investments in R&D. The social inequalities that exist in Latin American societies and organizations (e.g., gender gaps) also contribute to the region's low performance on the pillar of innovation capability.

The Global Talent Competitiveness Index (GTIC) focuses on the relationship between human capital and competitiveness. In 2021, the GTIC assessed 134 countries along 70 variables that measure competitiveness inputs and outputs. In terms of inputs, it measures talent enabling (regulatory, market, and business and labor landscapes), talent attraction (external and internal openness), talent growth (formal education, lifelong learning, access to growth opportunities), and talent retention (sustainability and lifestyle). In terms of outputs, it measures vocational and technical skills (mid-level skills and employability) and global knowledge skills (high-level skills and talent impact) (Lanvin & Monteiro, 2021). The 2021 GTIC report indicated that Chile (33rd) and Costa Rica (39th) were the strongest performers in the region. Costa Rica's talent competitiveness is balanced across all input pillars (enable, attract, grow and retain), ranking especially high on the dimensions of internal and external openness. Chile is also strong all-round, especially on the attract and retain pillars, as well as the grow pillar, mainly through firm-sponsored training and access to growth opportunities. Improving gender equality would boost Chile's performance on the pillar of internal openness. Mexico and Brazil, the two economic powerhouses in the region, ranked 65 and 75, respectively. Mexico's ability to attract talent is challenged by its low level of external openness (i.e., lack of opportunities for foreign talent) as well as internal openness (i.e., lack of social inclusion and gender equality). Brazil is strong in the growth pillar, primarily through the training offered by firms, which translate into greater access to growth opportunities. The country's main weaknesses are its regulatory and business and labor landscapes as well as its low level of external openness, which hurts its ability to attract talent (Lanvin & Monteiro, 2021). As mentioned above, attracting and nurturing a diverse, collaborative, and innovative talent base is essential to building a country's competitiveness; thus, countries in the region will need to remove some of the barriers that impact their ability to attract, grow, and retain talent.

The Global Innovation Index (GII) assesses innovation inputs (institutions, human capital and research, infrastructure, market sophistication, and business sophistication) and innovation outputs (creative outputs and knowledge and technology outputs). In line with prior years, the 2021 GII showed that Latin America and the Caribbean lags behind other regions in the world (see Table 3.4). No country in the region made it into the top 50 most innovating economies, and only four countries ranked in the top 60 (Chile was 53rd, Mexico 55th, Costa Rica 56th, and Brazil 57th). Five other countries ranked in the top 80 (Uruguay, Colombia, Peru, Argentina, and Jamaica). The lowest ranked countries were Guatemala (101), Bolivia (104), and Honduras (108). Chile showed the most balanced innovation system, showing particular strengths in institutions and infrastructure. Mexico lagged in both of these pillars, while Costa Rica and Brazil lagged in infrastructure and market sophistication. Brazil was the only country in the region investing more than 1% of GDP in R&D. Of the second tier of countries previously mentioned, Colombia and Peru have steadily improved their rankings and had relatively strong performance in both market and business sophistication (Dutta et al., 2021).

Innovation will be an essential driver of enhanced competitiveness for Latin America as it emerges from the current health pandemic. Undeniably, the majority of Latin American countries have a long way to go in achieving the levels of innovative capability needed to increase productivity, but opportunities to correct this underinvestment abound. A case in point is innovation in environmental sustainability. Between 2000 and 2007, Latin America accounted for only 0.3% of the total average number of environmental patents per million inhabitants, which represented 8.7% of the total number of patents registered by the region. The 2008–2016 period showed a minor improvement, with the percentage contribution by Latin America to the world average number of environmental patents reaching 0.9% (10.6% of all Latin American patents in that period), though this is still below the world average number of environmental patents during the latter period (8.6%) and the percentage for OECD countries (43.5%). Costa Rica's strong performance on the GII provides another example of the potential that environmental innovations offer countries in the region. Over the past few years, Costa Rica has been investing in renewable energy sources—hydro, geothermal, and wind—in order to free itself from dependence on fossil fuels. The country has also invested in smart grids and micro grids that rely on solar energy. By 2016, 98% of the country's electricity came from renewable energy sources (Lanvin, 2018).

The analysis above indicates that there are immense opportunities for Latin American countries to build innovative capabilities that increase their competitiveness in sectors such as energy and natural resource-based industries. Such innovations could help address the effect of frequent droughts on agriculture, expand the renewable energies sector to increase access for local users and to generate exports, and improve the quality of water and sewage treatment, among others (CEPAL, 2020). An added bonus is that these types of innovations are likely to have a positive effect on achieving greater social equality in a region where Indigenous, Afro-descendant, and low-income communities tend to bear the brunt of environmental degradation.

Table 3.4 Global Innovation Index 2021 for Select Latin American Countries

Country	Rank (1/132)	GII Index Score 0–100	Innovation Input Sub-index					Innovation Output Sub-index	
			Institutions	Human Capital and Research	Infrastructure	Market Sophistication	Business Sophistication	Knowledge and Technology Inputs	Creative Outputs
Chile	53	35.1	72.7	35.2	47.4	48.4	30.6	22.3	25.3
Mexico	55	34.5							
Costa Rica	56	34.5	63.1	32.4	40.7	43.0	30.0	22.9	31.3
Brazil	57	34.2	60.6	37.5	41.2	44.9	36.0	25.3	23.5
Uruguay	65	32.2	70.3	31.7	45.4	37.6	22.4	21.4	24.5
Colombia	67	31.7	66.2	28.4	44.9	50.8	29.4	19.2	19.8
Peru	70	31.2							
Argentina	73	29.8	52.8	37.0	42.5	37.5	26.7	18.7	21.9
Jamaica	74	29.6	71.6	25.0	29.9	36.0	26.0	13.5	29.6
Panama	83	28.0	62.8	19.5	46.8	40.7	18.6	10.9	25.8
Paraguay	88	26.4	50.9	19.8	38.9	42.0	25.4	10.0	24.8
Ecuador	91	25.4	44.1	20.5	39.6	50.3	19.9	13.2	18.5
Dominican Republic	93	25.1	55.1	18.5	39.6	39.5	21.8	11.7	19.0
El Salvador	96	25.0	54.5	18.1	30.5	39.1	22.4	8.3	26.0
Trinidad and Tobago	97	24.8	62.0	19.2	33.8	35.8	18.3	15.8	15.6
Guatemala	101	24.1	48.3	12.2	23.7	44.4	22.9	14.2	21.7
Bolivia, PS	104	23.4	37.8	34.0	29.1	48.4	23.7	11.1	13.4
Honduras	108	22.8	45.8	20.7	25.8	47.9	24.0	9.8	15.6

Source: Dutta et al. (Eds.), (2021). *Global Innovation Index 2021.* Geneva: World Intellectual Property Organization.

Latin America's Role in Global Supply Chains

This chapter has highlighted some key areas where Latin American countries are at a competitive disadvantage, namely a weak institutional environment, inadequate infrastructure, lack of innovation capabilities, and poor ICT adoption. Yet Latin America must remain competitive if it is to secure a stronger position in global value chains. The post-COVID-19 scenario points to some changing dynamics in the structure of global chains. To ensure increasing integration into global value chains, countries in Latin America will need to reduce or eliminate their competitiveness weaknesses, while developing additional competitive strengths.

The globalization wave that began in the early 1990s made it possible for companies (especially large firms from the more developed countries) to internationalize their value chains. The lowering of trade and investment barriers, political stabilization, harmonization and streamlining of regulations, and advances in transportation and information technology that both drove and resulted from globalization led to reductions in operational and transaction costs and easier access to inputs and markets. It was this global scenario that allowed companies—initially those from developed markets and later those from emerging economies—to disaggregate their value chains, dispersing value chain activities throughout the globe that led to the formation of integrated global production networks. Companies were now able to seek inputs (e.g., raw materials, labor, capital) anywhere in the world, manufacture products in multiple countries, and sell their products and services to customers near and far (ECLAC, 2020). The emergence and consolidation of global value chains had, and continues to have, a direct impact on global trade and investment patterns. In 2019, about 70%–80% of international trade was linked to global production networks led by large multinationals. In fact, multinational activity accounted for one-third of global production and about half of total world trade (OECD, 2018a; UNCTAD, 2020). Participation in global value chains can have positive effects on countries by generating income through job creation, exports, and taxes. Moreover, the linkages established among companies from various countries can result in knowledge and technology transfers. Thus, the opportunities that can derive from these global value chains have prompted countries around the world to leverage their natural and acquired advantages, pursue different specialization paths, and establish trade and investment alliances with other countries.

A country's participation in global value chains can happen in two ways:

Backward participation, which reflects the local value-added content of exports using imported inputs (i.e., a country uses imported inputs to produce goods and services that will be exported to other countries).

Forward participation, which reflects the domestic value added exported to other countries for additional processing (i.e., a country exports raw materials or intermediate goods and services that will undergo additional processing and then be exported by other countries).

Countries in Latin America participate in global value chains through both backward and forward linkages. In the case of Mexico, for example, backward participation is prevalent. Mexico, especially after the creation of NAFTA, became a manufacturing base for many US-based companies that exported raw materials and machinery to subsidiaries or independent firms in Mexico for final processing (e.g., automobiles, clothing, electronics). Countries in South America, such as Peru, Argentina, and Chile, became integrated into global value chains primarily through forward linkages. Raw materials or intermediate goods (e.g., minerals, metals, component parts) were exported to 'hub' economies (e.g., the United States, China, Japan, Germany) to be further processed into finished products that were then sold to other foreign markets. Countries such as Brazil, with more diversified economies, have been able to participate in global value chains through both forward and backward linkages (e.g., importing machinery, raw materials, and components to be used in the manufacturing of automobiles, electronics, etc., while exporting oil, minerals and metals, and agricultural products to China and the United States for the production of consumer and industrial goods).

As the global economy has changed and transformed over the past two decades, trade and investment patterns have also changed (see Chapter 1). Latin American countries have chosen to specialize in specific activities or components of the value chain. Mexico has become an important production location, with manufacture of low-tech, intermediate-tech, and high-tech products accounting for 75% of its 2018 exports. South American countries, on the other hand, have specialized in the procurement of raw materials (e.g., minerals, metals, agricultural products), with 75% of their 2018 exports being primary commodities and natural-resource-based manufacturing. Central American countries' productive activities are more mixed, with about 50% of their 2018 exports being primary commodities and natural-resource-based manufacturing and about 30% being low and intermediate technology manufacturing. More recently, Central American countries have also become home to call centers that support multinationals' customers all over the world. In some cases, countries have also specialized by industry, based on their skill base and the sophistication of their business ecosystems. For example, Mexico, Argentina, and Brazil manufacture automobiles and other industrial goods, Honduras and El Salvador have robust textiles and clothing sectors, and Panama specializes in logistics and financial services (ECLAC, 2020). In general, Latin American countries are mainly integrated into simpler value chains through forward linkages. Only Mexico, and to a lesser extent Brazil and Costa Rica, have successfully integrated their countries into more complex global chains via backward linkages (ECLAC, 2020).

In general, global value chains have been resilient, weathering the various shocks of the past two decades. The roles played by hub countries and their partners have remained largely unchanged during this time. Yet, the COVID-19 pandemic may cause countries to question their overdependence on global value chains or force them to restructure because of business closures (ECLAC, 2021). Any transformations toward localization of value chains will likely impact Latin America's economies, albeit in different ways. Any moves by trading partners to replace imported inputs with locally sourced ones could reduce demand for Latin America's natural resources. This will hurt those countries in the region that have relied on commodity exports for their growth (Raineri & Benoit, 2020). On the other hand, countries such as Mexico and those in the Central American region would benefit from any decisions by trading partners to reshore their production operations (firms moving production away from Asia and closer to the United States, for example). Nearshoring decisions may also be driven by rising trade tensions between the United States and China and volatile transportation costs. An in-depth discussion of Latin American global value chains is presented in Chapter 11.

The country-level conditions for productivity growth discussed previously can translate into firm-level competitive advantages for companies operating in the region. The competitiveness of firms in the region, especially domestic firms, is often grounded on their intimate knowledge of the domestic consumer markets' needs and wants, business systems, and regulatory frameworks as well as on their organizational flexibility in adapting to uncertain and unstable economic and business environments. Latin American firms' competitive disadvantages can also be linked to some of the country-level conditions noted, such as institutional voids, closed markets, lack of dynamism of the business environment, and low levels of ICT adoption and innovation capability. In the next section, we describe the various organizational players in the region and describe their main organizational strengths and weaknesses. Each of these organizational players is devoted a longer discussion in Part II of the book.

The Structure of Competition in Latin America

The competitiveness of a country is directly connected to the competitiveness of firms operating in it (and vice versa). As Porter (1990, p. 73) stated,

> A nation's competitiveness depends on the capacity of its industry to innovate and upgrade. Companies gain advantage against the world's best competitors because of pressure and challenge. They benefit from having strong domestic rivals, aggressive home-based suppliers, and demanding local customers.

Competition is 'good' because it pressures companies into constant improvement, as no competitive advantage is enduring. A national business environment characterized by dynamic and open competition from diverse organizations is then a source of sustainable competitive advantage for firms in the country. Latin America has been notorious for the lack of competition and a tradition for tolerating monopolies. Yet, starting with the liberalization of the 1990s, attitudes toward competition have slowly changed, and Latin Americans are now more likely to embrace a vibrant competitive environment as beneficial to their countries, companies, and consumers alike.

In this section, we explore the five types of organizations that shape the Latin American competitive landscape: large domestic firms, foreign multinational companies, state-owned enterprises, small- and medium-size businesses, and firms in the informal sector (see Figure 3.2). We describe the role each of these types of organizations plays in the region's business environment, their main organizational characteristics, strengths and weaknesses, and their predominant strategic approaches.

In general, the majority of companies in the region are owned by domestic private investors, with an average of only 9% of firms having at least 10% foreign ownership (range 2.5%–25%) and an average of 0.3% having at least 10% state ownership. Firms tend to be small and medium size (ranging from 66% to 85% of all firms), and about a third are sole proprietorships. Most firms are well-established with an average firm age of 23 years (range 15–27 years), and many of the largest domestic firms have been in business for decades. In some

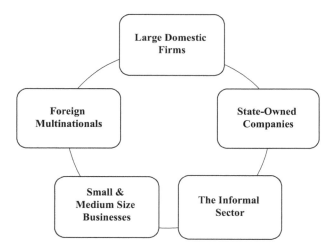

Figure 3.2 Five types of business organizations in Latin America (Source: Authors' elaboration)

countries of the region, especially the smaller economies, firms are primarily engaged in the service sector. However, in the larger countries (Argentina, Brazil, Colombia, Chile, Mexico, and Peru), firms can be equally engaged in the manufacturing sector. Extractive industries and agriculture capture a smaller number of firms, even if those sectors are not necessarily small in value terms. Firms in the formal and informal sector compete side by side, as the size of the informal sector, depending on the industry, can range from 30% to 50% (Francis, Rodriguez Mesa, & Yang, 2013; Ohnsorge & Yu, 2021).

Large Domestic Firms

Large domestic firms refer to large, locally owned or locally controlled companies in the form of single firms or holding groups operating at the national, regional, or global level. What qualifies as 'large' can vary from country to country, but here we use ECLAC's classification and refer to large companies as those that employ more than 250 individuals. In this section, we focus on three types of large domestic firms: national champions, Multilatinas, and Global Latinas. The term 'national champions' refers to locally owned or locally controlled firms that have a dominant position in their domestic market (i.e., control a large share of the market). These firms could be independent companies or conglomerates. National champions that have internationalized by seeking opportunities in other Latin American countries will be referred to as Multilatinas. Finally, large domestic firms that have a presence in markets outside the region are referred to as Global Latinas. We recognize that there are also large domestic firms that occupy non-dominant positions in their respective markets, either because they are not competitive enough or because their markets or industries are highly fragmented. In this book, we focus on the largest, more dominant domestic firms, those referred to above as national champions, Multilatinas, and Global Latinas. We briefly discuss the leading roles of these large domestic firms in the competitive landscape of Latin America.

Many of the large domestic firms are conglomerates ('*grupos economicos*' in Spanish). These conglomerates, which also tend to be family-owned or family-controlled, were founded in the 1950s and 1960s, during the period of import substitution in the region, with some dating back to the beginning of the twentieth century. According to Robles, Simon, and Haar (2003), the origin of many domestic conglomerates centered on three strategic pillars: expansion based on the development of natural resources, growth based on diversification of an industrial base, and the acquisition of financial, construction, and service firms. The liberalization and privatization reforms of the 1990s gave rise to a second wave of formation of large domestic conglomerates that leveraged the opportunities created by the disappearance of older domestic groups, the opening of economic sectors, the influx of capital, and the overall growth of consumer markets.

The growth and stability of large domestic conglomerates over several decades points to specific strategic capabilities of these firms. First, their horizontal and vertical diversification gives them a certain level of protection against market instability. Their broad scope and scale allow them to overcome the limitation of weak domestic capital markets by (a) generating internal revenues and profits that can be reallocated throughout the conglomerate, (b) incorporating a financial services division that can provide easier access to funding, and/or (c) giving them the competitive standing needed to access global capital markets. Second, large domestic firms have a deep understanding of the local markets and of non-market conditions, which results in organizational agility, allowing them to identify and respond quickly to new opportunities and threats. Moreover, their superior distribution networks give them wide and extensive access to markets.

As mentioned previously, a significant number of large domestic conglomerates are family owned or controlled. This ownership arrangement gives domestic conglomerates more control over resource allocation, flexibility, and the ability to make strategic decisions for the long term without having to respond to the short-term performance expectations of publicly traded companies. In general, family owners have grown up knowing the business 'upside-down and inside-out.' The conflicts of interest one usually sees between managers and owners is also minimized, as the success of the firm is tied to the reputation of the family name (Aguilera, Crespi-Cladera, & Kabbach de Castro, 2019; Becker, 2011). Although some patriarchs (and they are predominantly patriarchs) have been less careful about implementing succession plans, in general, large family-owned firms are handed over to the next generation smoothly. This younger generation of leaders tends to be educated abroad, more technologically savvy, and globally minded. Thus, large family groups which tended to be more reactive and more vulnerable to changes in their external environment are now more able to cope and adapt to a dynamic competitive global environment.

Large domestic firms enjoy additional competitive advantages. Their importance to the local economy in terms of job creation and income generation and their strong connections to local governments yield some degree of protection from political risk and some degree of support in the face of foreign competition (although less so now than was the case in the past).

Over the past 20 years, many large domestic firms which had become national (or regional) champions have looked to the rest of the world for growth opportunities. Latin American firms which have sought internationalization are known as Multilatinas and Global Latinas. The competitive advantages of these two types of firms in global markets include lower costs of production, ties to existing clients, connections to cultural and country diasporas, and a diversified product portfolio. Outflows of investments, especially during the second half of the past decade, have been led by Multilatinas and Global Latinas from the larger economies (e.g., Argentina, Brazil, Chile, Colombia, Mexico, and Peru). We expect this internationalization to continue as Multilatinas and Global Latinas seek to strengthen their innovative, operational, and branding capabilities in order to consolidate their market positions. In Chapter 9, we present a more in-depth discussion of Multilatinas and Global Latinas.

In summary, large domestic firms tend to be old and experienced and have demonstrated an ability to survive and thrive through the various economic and political crises suffered by the region. This demonstrates large domestic firms' long-term strategic commitment to their national and regional markets and their ability for allocating and reallocating resources to adapt to cycles in the business environment. Large domestic firms, especially conglomerates, are highly diversified, horizontally and/or vertically, and in the past few years, have shown a keen eye for dying market sectors and emerging latent markets, divesting from the former and securing early mover advantages in the latter. Finally, their ownership structures give them flexibility and agility, and with the new generations taking the helm, a more innovative and globally minded leadership to face their future. Although access to capital and technology and closed management structures continue to be strategic weaknesses, large domestic firms will continue to dominate the competitive landscape in Latin America.

Foreign Multinationals

The liberalization waves of the 1990s attracted many multinational enterprises (MNEs) to the region motivated by a growing and more affluent consumer market, the abundance of natural resources, and the opening of opportunities in previously closed sectors. Between 1991 and 2001, the ownership of the 500 largest companies in Latin America changed dramatically, with ownership by non-Latin multinationals growing from 27% to 39% in a ten-year span. This ownership shift was due primarily to the wave of privatizations of state-owned enterprises during the same period (i.e., the share of government ownership dropped from 20% to 9%) (Martinez, De Souza, and Liu, 2003). Yet, over the next decade, the total percentage of foreign ownership in Latin America remained modest compared to other regions of the world (average of 9% foreign ownership stake as compared to 15% in sub-Saharan Africa and 11% in East Asia). Ownership by non-Latin multinationals is concentrated in large firms and less so in small- and medium-size businesses (20% vs. 6%). In addition, 87% of all firms in the region have no foreign ownership and only 6% are fully owned by foreign investors (Francis, Rodriguez Meza, & Yang, 2013).

The competitive advantages of MNEs over domestic firms include their abundant resources, competencies, and capabilities and their global scale and scope. In addition, MNEs may be more experienced in international markets and understand the need to balance cost pressures with market needs better than a large domestic firm (except for the Multilatinas and Global Latinas). Yet, challenges remain, especially regarding MNEs' ability to adapt to local market needs and rigid and bureaucratic legal business environments as well as the political and social risks still present in the region. We discuss strategies for foreign multinationals operating in Latin America in Chapter 8.

State-Owned Enterprises

State-owned enterprises (SOEs) once dominated Latin American economies, but the adoption of neoliberal policies in the early 1990s resulted in a wave of privatizations meant to improve the fiscal health of governments throughout the region. The rounds of privatization of SOEs that characterized the 1990s had mixed results, with privatizations being more successful in countries such as Chile and Colombia, and less so in Argentina, Mexico, and some of the Central American countries. In many cases, failures were caused by governments' unwillingness to give up a 'cash cow,' a strong sense of nationalism, or the SOEs not being financially attractive to private investors (Robles, Simon, & Haar, 2003).

Nevertheless, SOEs still play a role in the competitive landscape of Latin America and are an important source of revenue and foreign currency for countries in the region. Throughout the region, SOEs are present primarily in the natural resource extraction and energy sectors, as well as in the utilities sector (e.g., waste management, water supply). The largest SOEs are located in Brazil (Petrobras), Chile (Codelco), Colombia (Ecopetrol), and Mexico (PEMEX). The concentration of SOEs in the commodities sector means that these companies are subject to the volatility caused by global changes in demand and prices, as some of the Latin American SOEs experienced during the 2014–2016 commodity slump (Bejar & Yepez, 2019; Kowalski et al., 2013).

Over the past two decades, many of the larger Latin American SOEs sought growth through internationalization. This required them to adopt more professional management and operational processes aimed at increasing efficiencies and productivity. The four largest SOEs mentioned above have performed relatively well in the past decade thanks, in part, to efficiency-driven improvements that have strengthened their financial positions (Bejar & Yepez, 2019). As they enter a new decade, SOEs in the natural resource extraction sector have an opportunity to pursue innovation-intensive strategies that address the environmental challenges currently facing the region.

Small- and Medium-Size Businesses

Small- and medium-size businesses (SMEs), those with fewer than 250 employees, range from 89% to 94% of private sector activity and employment in the region. Micro, small-, and medium-size businesses (MSMEs) represent 99% of all businesses in the region; nine out of ten of these firms are microbusinesses, which operate primarily in the informal sector (we address the informal sector in the next section). There are an estimated 1.5 million SMEs in Latin America that generate 60% of formal employment and 25% of total GDP (Francis, Rodriguez Meza, & Yang, 2013; OECD/CAF, 2019). Most SMEs—referred to in Spanish as PYMES, or MPYMES for micro, small-, and medium-size businesses—are concentrated in the domestic market, particularly in small-scale agriculture and services (e.g., wholesale and retail trade, food, accommodations). The main challenges faced by SMEs are their limited access to financing and technology and their overreliance on the intuition and experience of a manager or founder for most decision making. Some SMEs may also lack well-structured organizational procedures and processes. Faced with increasing competition, SMEs have strategic choices to make to stay relevant in the competitive landscape: they may specialize in a niche market through a customized product offering, internationalize, or insert themselves into a global value chain, acting as suppliers of inputs or services, for example.

The perceived value of SMEs for the continued development of Latin America is evident by the various stimulus measures and programs directed at enhancing the growth and competitiveness of SMEs in the region. These programs usually provide basic business training, funding, or trade assistance. They can also focus on specific populations (e.g., women-owned businesses). Chapter 10 provides a lengthier discussion on small- and medium-size businesses in the region.

The Informal Sector

The informal sector refers to enterprises that operate outside a country's tax and regulatory systems, either fully or partially. In some cases, these enterprises are also responsible for informal employment, which refers to workers employed by companies operating in the informal sector (Boyce, 2020). Thus, the informal sector can include businesses which are not legally registered at inception, become informal over time (not renewing registrations, paying taxes, etc.), or that are legally registered but engage in informal practices. References to the 'informal sector' or the 'informal economy' are not to be confused with references to the black market or to illegal businesses (Boyce, 2020). Even though businesses operating in the informal sector may not follow all regulations, pay all their taxes, or offer their workers all the mandated social protections, they typically engage in a variety of economic activities that are legal in every other respect and are more closely equated with those of independent workers and microbusinesses. There are an estimated 26.2 million microbusinesses in Latin America, which contribute 3.2% to the region's GDP (IDB Invest, 2021; OECD/CAF, 2019). Those operating in the informal sector include small artisans and tradespeople (e.g., seamstresses, mechanics, carpenters), street vendors, and subsistence farmers, among others. They may also include small businesses that follow some, but not all, regulations.

This fluidity and ambiguousness makes estimating the size of the informal sector in Latin America a difficult task, with estimates ranging from 30% to 60%. A 2013 report by the World Bank indicated that among the firms surveyed, 64% indicated having to compete with firms in the informal sector; this applied to firms of all sizes. Although only 10% of all firms seem to start and remain as informal (i.e., not registered legally), a larger percentage reportedly engage in informal business practices (e.g., selling without receipts, hiring unreported workers), with about half of the firms surveyed indicating they compete with firms that are engaged in these informal practices. This was especially the case for SMEs in the larger and medium size countries in the region (Francis, Rodriguez Meza, & Yang, 2013).

Operating in the informal sector can have negative implications for firms. First, micro and small businesses in the informal sector lack legal identity and legal protections, which raises their business risks and operational costs. It also limits their ability to grow because of a lack of access to financing sources in the formal sector. The inability of businesses in the informal sector to contribute more fully to a country's economy reduces a country's competitiveness by creating business conditions that stimulate low productivity and growth. The good news is that the size of the informal economy has been shrinking in Latin America and the rest of the world for the past 30 years. Among the many reasons for the decline is the success of public initiatives aimed at reducing barriers to business formation (e.g., registering a business) (Boyce, 2020; La Informacion, 2013). Yet, unless deliberate efforts are made to avoid it, one of the potential effects of the COVID-19 pandemic could be a recovery period that pushes businesses into greater informality.

Summary

In this chapter, we identified factors that drive and hinder competitiveness in Latin America and described the competitive structure and dynamics in the region. The main drivers of competitiveness in Latin America are its relative macroeconomic stability, a relatively healthy labor market, and a stable (though less than inclusive) financial system. The main barriers to competitiveness for countries in the region are weak institutional environments, inadequate infrastructure, low and slow ICT adoption, and lack of innovation capabilities.

The region's competitiveness has significant room for improvement; however, Latin America has been successful in integrating itself into global value chains, albeit through different mechanisms and geographic hubs. While countries such as Mexico have specialized in manufacturing of consumer and industrial goods, countries such as Peru and Chile have specialized as suppliers of raw materials and intermediate goods. Others, such as Panama and countries in the Caribbean sub-region have specialized in logistics and other supporting services. The structure of global value chains may evolve after the world recovers from the COVID-19 pandemic, and Latin American countries must seek opportunities to deepen and diversify their forward and backward linkages in these global chains.

The competitive landscape in Latin America is composed of large domestic firms, foreign multinationals, state-owned enterprises, small- and medium-size businesses, and firms in the informal sector. Each of these organizational types is the object of in-depth discussions in Part II of the book. In those chapters, we explore the main competitive strengths and weaknesses of these types of companies and their strategic choices.

As Latin America emerges from the current health and economic crisis, countries in the region must seize the opportunity to rebuild and transform their economies through substantial investments in infrastructure, skill building, and research and development. There are also clear opportunities to generate real gains to productivity by closing inequality gaps, promoting inclusivity, and addressing climate change. Integrating solutions to these challenges into policies and programs aimed at increasing economic output has the potential to create a virtuous cycle of growth, productivity, and human development.

References

Aguilera, R. V., Crespi-Cladera, R., & Kabbach de Castro, L. R. (2019). Corporate governance in Latin America: Towards shareholder democracy. *AIB Insights*, *19*(2), 13–17.

Becker, T. H. (2011). *Doing business in the New Latin America*. 2nd ed. California: Praeger.

Bejar, P., & Yepez, J. F. (2019, June 26). How four of the largest state-owned enterprises in Latin America weathered the aftermath of the 2014–2016 commodity price slump. FMI Blog-Dialogo a Fondo. https://blog-dialogoafondo.imf.org/?page_id=11441

Bilal, U., Hessel, P., Perez-Ferrer, C., et al. (2021). Life expectancy and mortality in 363 cities of Latin America. *Nature Medicine*, *27*, 463–470. https://doi.org/10.1038/s41591-020-01214-4

Bilal, U., et al. (2019, December 10). Inequalities in life expectancy in six large Latin American cities from the SALURBAL study: An ecological analysis. *Lancet Planet Health*, *3*, e503–510. https://doi.org/10.1016/S2542-5196(19)30235-9

Bocanegra, N. (2020, July 30). *Pasar de los ladrillos a lo digital, clave para recuperación pospandemia en América Latina: BID*. Infobae. https://www.infobae.com/america/agencias/2020/07/30/pasar-de-los-ladrillos-a-lo-digital-clave-para-recuperacion-pospandemia-en-america-latina-bid/?outputType=amp-type

Boyce, S. (2020, April 16). 9 facts about the informal economy in Latin America. *The Borgen*. https://borgenproject.org/informal-economy-in-latin-america/

Brazil's dilemma: How to make its labor market more flexible. (2007, May 16). Universia Knowledge@Wharton.   https://knowledge.wharton.upenn.edu/article/brazils-dilemma-how-to-make-its-labor-market-more-flexible/

CAF-Development Bank of Latin America (2013). *La infraestructura en el desarrollo integral de America Latina*. http://publicaciones.caf.com/publicaciones.

Cavallo, E., Powell, A., & Serebrisky, T. (Eds.). (2020). *From structures to services. The path to better infrastructure in Latin America and the Caribbean*. Inter-American Development Bank. https://flagships.iadb.org/en/DIA2020/from-structures-to-services

CEPAL-La Comisión Económica para América Latina. (2020, October). *Construir un nuevo futuro. Una recuperación transformadora con igualdad y sostenibilidad*. Trigésimo octavo período de sesiones de la CEPAL. (LC/SES.38/3-P/Rev.1). Santiago, Chile.

Chironga, M., Dahl, J., Goland, T., Pinshaw, G., & Sonnekus, M. (2012). *Micro-, small, and medium-size enterprises in emerging economies: How banks can grasp a $350 billion opportunity*. McKinsey Company.   https://www.mckinsey.com/~/media/mckinsey/industries/financial%20services/our%20insights/tapping%20the%20next%20big%20thing%20in%20emerging%20market%20banking/micro_small_and_med_sized_enterprises_in_emerging_markets_full_report.pdf

Coda, J. I. (2021, April 14). Promoting climate change action in Latin America and the Caribbean. World Bank. https://www.worldbank.org/en/results/2021/04/14/promoting-climate-change-action-in-latin-america-and-the-caribbean

Dutta, S., Lanvin, B., Rivera Leon, L., & Wunsch-Vincent, S. (Eds.). (2021). *Global innovation index 2021-tracking innovation through the COVID-19 crisis*. Geneva: World Intellectual Property Organization.

ECLAC-Economic Commission for Latin America and the Caribbean. (2016). *Horizons 2030: Equality at the centre of sustainable development* (LC/G.2660/Rev.1). Santiago, Chile. https://repositorio.cepal.org/bitstream/handle/11362/40160/S1600652_en.pdf?sequence=4&isAllowed=y

ECLAC-Economic Commission for Latin America and the Caribbean. (2020). *Foreign direct investment in Latin America and the Caribbean 2020*. (LC/PUB.2020/15-P). Santiago, Chile.

ECLAC-Economic Commission for Latin America and the Caribbean. (2021). *International trade outlook for Latin American and the Caribbean 2020*. (LC/PUB.2020/21-P). Santiago, Chile.

Fay, M., Andres, L. A., Fox, C., Narloch, U., Straub, S., & Slawson, M. (2017). *Rethinking infrastructure in Latin America and the Caribbean: Spending better to achieve more*. Washington, DC: IBRD/The World Bank.

Fay, M., & Morrison, M. (2005). Infrastructure in Latin America and the Caribbean: Recent developments and key challenges. *The World Bank*, Report #32640-LCR.

Ferraz, J. C., & Ramos, L. (2018). *Inclusión financiera para la inserción productiva de las empresas de menor tamaño en América Latina*. Santiago, Chile: La Comisión Económica para América Latina y el Caribe (CEPAL), LC/TS.2018/22.

Field, A. M. (2013, March 19). Infrastructure in South America: Fits and starts. *The Journal of Commerce Online*. https://www.joc.com/international-trade-news/infrastructure-news/south -america/infrastructure-south-america-fits-and-starts_20130319.html

Francis, D. C., Rodriguez Meza, J. L., & Yang, J. (2013). Mapping enterprises in Latin America and the Caribbean. *The World Bank Group, Latin America and the Caribbean Series, Note No. 1. Enterprise Surveys*. https://www.enterprisesurveys.org/content/dam/enterprisesurveys/documents/research/ Mapping-Enterprises-LAC-Note.pdf

GSMA Intelligence. (2021). *The mobile economy Latin America 2021*. https://www.gsma.com/ mobileeconomy/wp-content/uploads/2021/11/GSMA_ME_LATAM_2021.pdf

IDB Invest. (2021). *Micro, small, and medium size enterprises*. https://idbinvest.org/en/solutions/ advisory-services/micro-small-and-medium-sized-enterprises

Jaimurzina, A., & Sánchez R. J. (2017). Governance of infrastructure for sustainable development in Latin America and the Caribbean: An initial premise. *FAL Bulletin, 354*(2), 1–13. Santiago, Chile: Economic Commission for Latin America and the Caribbean (ECLAC).

Kowalski, P., et al. (2013). State-owned enterprises: Trade effects and policy implications. *OECD Trade Policy Papers, No. 147*, OECD Publishing, Paris. https://doi.org/10.1787/5k4869ckqk7l-en

La Informacion. (2013, October 25). *Ministro apuesta por reducir de 180 a 5 días la apertura de pymes en Brasil*. https://www.lainformacion.com/economia-negocios-y-finanzas/ministro-apuesta-por -reducir-de-180-a-5-dias-la-apertura-de-pymes-en-brasil_71rVu05kDDvj2YzhlSfIk/

Lanvin, B. (2018, July 10). The world's most innovative countries, 2018. *INSEAD Knowledge*. https:// knowledge.insead.edu/entrepreneurship/the-worlds-most-innovative-countries-2018-9666

Lanvin, B., & Monteiro, F. (Eds.). (2021). *The global talent competitiveness index 2021: Talent competitiveness in times of COVID*. Fontainebleau, France: INSEAD.

Martinez, A., De Souza, I., & Liu, F. (2003). Multinationals vs. mulilatinas: Latin America's great race. *Strategy + Business, 32*. https://www.strategy-business.com/article/03307?pg=0

Maurizio, R. (2021, April). *The employment crisis in the pandemic: Towards a human-centred job recovery*. International Labor Organization. https://www.ilo.org/wcmsp5/groups/public/-- -americas/---ro-lima/documents/publication/wcms_779118.pdf

OECD/CAF-Organization for Economic Cooperation and Development & The Central American Development Bank. (2019). *SME policy index: Latin America and the Caribbean 2019*. https://www .oecd.org/industry/latin-america-and-the-caribbean-2019-d9e1e5f0-en.htm

OECD-Organization for Economic Cooperation and Development. (2018a). *Multinational enterprises in the global economy: Heavily debated but hardly measured*. Policy Note. https://www.oecd.org/ industry/ind/MNEs-in-the-global-economy-policy-note.pdf

OECD-Organization for Economic Cooperation and Development. (2018b). *Enhancing connectivity through transport infrastructure. The role of official development finance and private investment*. Paris: The Development Dimension, OECD Publishing. https://doi.org/10 .1787/9789264304505-en

Ohnsorge, F., & Yu, S. (Eds.) (2021). *The long shadow of informality: Challenges and policies*. Advance Edition. License: Creative Commons Attribution. CC BY 3.0 IGO. World Bank Group.

Perez, G. (2020). Rural roads: Key routes for production, connectivity and territorial development. *FAL, 377*(1), 1–17.

Perez Caldentey, E., & Titelman, D. (Eds.). (2018). *La inclusión financiera para la inserción productiva y el papel de la banca de desarrollo*. Santiago, Chile: CEPAL-La Comisión Económica para América Latina, No. 153 (LC/PUB.2018/18-P). file:///I:/Biz%20LatAm-Book%20Project%202020/Compe titiveness/CEPAL%202018%20Report%20on%20Financial%20Inclusion%20in%20Latin%20Ame rica.pdf

PNUD-Programa de las Naciones Unidas para el Desarrollo. (2019). *Informe sobre Desarrollo Humano 2019*. file:///I:/Biz%20LatAm-Book%20Project%202020/Competitiveness/PNUD%202019%20Infor me%20sobre%20Desarrollo%20Humano.pdf

Porter, M. E. (1990). The competitive advantage of nations. *Harvard Business Review* (March–April), 73–91.

Raineri, R., & Benoit, P. (2020, August 7). *As Latin America looks to a COVID recovery, it will need to tackle its growing middle-class angst.* http://www.ipsnews.net/2020/08/%e2%80%8bas-latin-america -looks-covid-recovery-will-need-tackle-growing-middle-class-angst/

Ramos Suarez, E., & Perez, G. (2018). Development and conflicts linked to infrastructure construction. *FAL Bulletin*, *361*(1), 1–7. Economic Commission for Latin America and the Caribbean (ECLAC).

Robles, F., Simon, F., & Haar, J. (2003). *Winning strategies for the new Latin markets.* Upper Saddle River: Financial Times Prentice Hall.

Rodrigues, M. (2020, December 11). Coastal Brazil is likely to face more heat waves and droughts. *EOS*, *101*. https://doi.org/10.1029/2020EO152124

Sabatini, C. (2008). Labor reform: Undercompetitive economies and unprotected workforce. In Haar, J., and Price, J. (Eds.), *Can Latin America compete? Confronting the challenges of globalization.* New York: Palgrave Macmillan.

Schwab, K. (2019). *The global competitiveness report 2019.* World Economic Forum - WEF. www .weforum.org/gcr

Schwab, K., & Sala-i-Martin, X. (Eds.). (2013). *The global competitiveness report 2012–2013.* World Economic Forum. Geneva, Switzerland.

Smith, J., Juhn, T., & Humphrey, C. (2008). Consumer and small business credit: Building blocks of the middle class. In Haar, J., and Price, J. (Eds.), *Can Latin America compete? Confronting the challenges of globalization.* New York: Palgrave Macmillan.

The Climate Reality Project. (2021, April 28). How is the climate crisis impacting South America? https://www.climaterealityproject.org/blog/how-climate-crisis-impacting-south-america

UNCTAD-United Nations Conference on Trade and Development. (2020). *World investment report 2020: International production beyond the pandemic.* Geneva.

UNOPS. (n.d.). *Combating water scarcity in Peru.* https://www.unops.org/news-and-stories/stories/ combating-water-scarcity-in-peru

4   Demographic Transitions and Population Dynamics in Latin America

Introduction

A population can be described in many ways; we have chosen the dimensions that best describe Latin America (see Figure 4.1). We start the chapter with a description of demographic transition in the region, population drivers, and different stages of its evolution. There are regional variations of this process and groups of countries in each of these stages. The second section focuses on migration. Latin America is a large source of migration to the rest of the world. Certain sub-regions of Latin America, in particular, are sending their young and uneducated people to other countries. As a result, both cities and rural areas are emptying out and are now populated mostly with older people. Most recently, violence and political chaos are driving Latin Americans to seek economic and political refuge in neighboring countries. The next section focuses on race and ethnicity in Latin America. This is a challenging topic given the rise of racially driven movements elsewhere in the world. Ethnic and racial groups in the region are becoming proud of their ancestry and roots. The fourth section describes education in Latin America with a particular focus on the learning outcomes of Latin American youth. In the next section, we focus on the urbanization of Latin America. Latin America is one of the most urbanized regions in the world; this concentration of Latin Americans in cities has resulted in the formation of megalopolis that rival the populations and economic power of entire countries. This is followed by a discussion of Latin American households and their buying power. As part of the process of demographic transformation and modernization, the traditional typical family structure is evolving and creating other types of living arrangements. Another important aspect of this section is the assessment of household economic power. The vast differences of economic power concentration make the region one of the most unequal in the world in terms of income and wealth distribution. The last section centers on Latin Americans' health and lifestyles. The way that Latin Americans go about their daily lives affect their health. The section provides a somber look at the main causes of death in the region and the most important drivers of health risks. The section also includes a very brief assessment of the state of the health systems throughout the region. We conclude this section and the chapter with a snapshot review of the impact of the COVID-19 pandemic ravaging the world at the time of this writing. It will take years for the region to immunize its population and thus regain momentum and recover from the economic contraction generated by the pandemic.

DOI: 10.4324/9781003182672-6

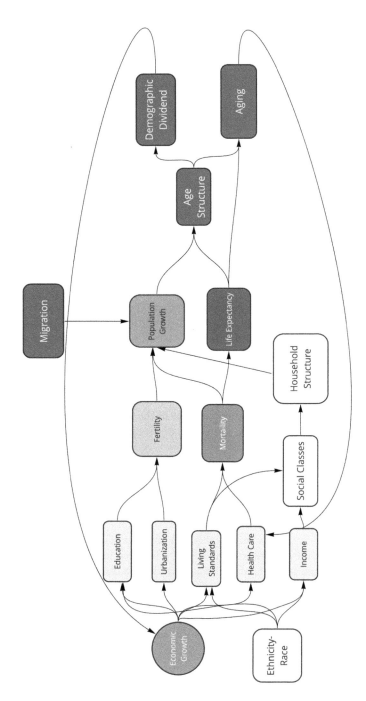

Figure 4.1 Demographic model of Latin America

Latin America's Demographic Transition

The region's population is in transition to an older population. Some countries in the region have a demographic profile similar to European societies, whereas others are younger. At one time, Latin America had one of the world's fastest population growth rates with an annual rate of 2.7% from 1950 to 1955. In 2020, the region's total population was 654 million (8.92% of the world's population) and growing at the slow rate of 0.9% per year (ECLAC, 2020a).

The slowdown of the region's population growth is principally due to falling fertility rates, increased life expectancy, and reduction of overall mortality (see Table 4.1). Assuming that these trends continue, Latin America's population will reach a peak of 707.5 million in 2058, followed by negative growth (ECLAC, 2019).

Stages of Demographic Transition

Latin America has closely followed the demographic transition of mature regions in which a population goes through distinct stages of population change (Brea, 2003). Latin America was in Stage 1 from the 1800s to the early 1900s. During this period, Latin America was a traditional agrarian society characterized by high birth and mortality rates. During Stage 2 of demographic transition until the early 1960s, the region experienced a decline in mortality rates mostly due to urbanization, better access to health services, and improved living conditions. The birth rates at this stage continued to be high, as families were slow to adjust to urban conditions, and there was still a large rural component. Stage 3 started in the early 1960s and continues to the present. At this stage, the region's continued high urbanization and economic development demanded an industrial workforce with more regimented hours. As a result, the lifestyles of many Latin Americans adjusted to a modern work to home commute. As women joined the workforce, they postponed their childbearing decisions, and housing conditions influenced a trend toward smaller families. The region continues its relentless process of urbanization (82.9% in 2019) with declining fertility rates. The number of births per woman has been declining steadily from a high of 3.45 in 1990 to 2.04 in 2020, very close to the population replacement rate (2.01). The births per 1,000 people in 2020 was 16.5, almost half the rate of 1990. These trends will continue in the long term. On the other hand, the mean age of childbearing has remained constant over the years at about 27 years, suggesting that families tend to have fewer children but at the same age (United Nations, 2019a). At the same time, life expectancy has increased gradually to 75.2 years. Better nutrition and access to basic health services has led to declining mortality rates, particularly the infant mortality of previous demographic stages from a high of 126 deaths per 1,000 people in the 1950s to 48 per 1,000 in 1990 to 16.5 per 1,000 in 2020 (United Nations, 2019a). This trend reflects the improvements in treating infection and communicable diseases such as malaria and improvements in health systems in the region. These changes in mortality rates were more intense in certain countries than others.

One major difference between Latin America and demographically mature regions like Europe is out-migration. As a result, over the years, the region has exhibited a net negative migration that has had an impact on population transition, as most Latin American migrants are young. With older populations left behind, the region is increasingly older.

Latin America is bound to reach Stage 4 of demographic transition by 2050, and its demographic profile will resemble that of demographically advanced countries such as Japan and those in Europe. Stage 4 is characterized by low fertility rates, lower mortality, and high stable life expectancy. Latin America seems to be on track to follow this pattern. By 2030, life expectancy in the region will reach 77 years and 80.5 years in 2050. Birth rates per 1,000 of population will continue to decrease and reach a low of 11.2 in 2050. The number of births

Table 4.1 Latin American Population Profile

		1990	2000	2005	2010	2015	2020	2030	2050
Population	Total (mm)	442.8	521.8	557.5	591.3	623.9	653.9	706.2	762.4
	Median Age	21.8	24.3	25.8	27.4	29.1	31.0	34.5	40.8
	% Under 15	36.3	32.2	29.9	27.7	25.6	23.9	21.2	17.1
	% Aged 15–24	19.7	19.2	18.8	18.2	17.5	16.5	14.7	12.3
	% Aged 25–64	39.2	42.9	45.1	47.2	49.1	50.7	52.2	51.6
	% Aged 65+	4.8	5.7	6.2	6.9	7.8	9.0	12	19
	Annual Change Rate (%)	1.9	1.6	1.3	1.2	1.1	0.9	0.7	0.2
Dependency per (1,000)	Young+Old/Working Age	70.3	61.3	57.1	53.1	50.4	4-8.9	49.6	64.4
Support Ratio	Support Ratio	8.1	7.6	7.2	6.9	6.3	5.7	4.4	2.7
Life Expectancy at Birth	Years	67.2	70.7	72.3	73.5	74.4	75.2	77.0	80.5
Fertility	Birth Rate per 1,000	28.2	23.4	21.1	19.0	17.7	16.5	14.1	11.2
	Live Births per Woman	3.45	2.77	2.49	2.26	2.14	2.04	1.89	1.75
	Childbearing Age (Years)	28	27.2	27	27	27.2	27.3	27.7	28.5
Mortality	Death Rate per 1,000	7.0	6.1	5.9	5.9	6.0	6.3	6.9	8.8
	Infant Mortality per 1,000 Births (1yr)	48.0	31	25	20	17	15	12	7
Urbanization	% Urban	70.6	75.5	77.1	78.5	79.8	80.8	83.6	87.8
Net Migration	% Population	-1.9	-1.9	-2.0	-1.3	-0.9	-0.8	-0.2	-0.3

Sources:
United Nations, World Population Prospects 2019a. Volume I, Comprehensive Tables and Volume II, Demographic Profiles, 2019
United Nations, ECLAC, Statistical Yearbook for Latin American and The Caribbean, 2020
United Nations, World Urbanization Prospects, 2018

per woman is expected to be 1.89 in 2030, a rate below the minimum level of population replacement (2.1). At this stage, the gap between birth and mortality rates will continue to decrease from 10.2 (16.5–6.3) to 7.2 (14.1–6.9) in 2030, and only 2.4 (11.2–8.8) in 2050. A country's population ceases to increase when it reaches a negative gap—a situation typical of countries in the advanced stage of demographic transition.

Age Structure and Dependency Ratios

The impact of demographic transformation shapes the age structure of the Latin American population. In 2020, about 67% of the region's population was aged 15–64. This core segment is the main working age population contributing to Latin American economies. The population under 15 years was 39.2% in 1990 and is only 16.5% in 2020—a consistent decline. On the contrary, the older population (65+) has doubled from 4.8% to 9% in 2020 and is expected to reach 19% in 2050 (United Nations, 2019a).

The dependency ratio measures the number of non-working people who are supported by 100 working people. A demographic dividend refers to the period when the working population is increasing and contributing to economic growth and supporting younger and older populations. Such a dividend translates into lower ratios, as the working people are able to support greater numbers of younger and older people. The dependency ratio for Latin America reached a peak of 89% in 1965, but the population dividend experienced by the region during its transition to Stage 3, led to a drop of the dependency ratio to 48.9% in 2020 (United Nations-ECLAC, 2020a). Thus, the demographic dividend that has fueled the economic growth of many regions, particularly Asia, has long been subsiding in Latin America.

As Latin America has moved to Stage 3 and begins its transition into Stage 4 of demographic transformation, its older population will increase, and the younger population will decrease, while the working age population will gradually decrease. The net effect of these trends is a reversal of the dependency ratio, with the ratio expected to increase to 49.6% by 2030 and to 64.4% by 2050.

The Graying of Latin America

As mentioned, the lower fertility rates and improvements in healthcare have increased the size of the older population in Latin America. In 1990, the population of those 65 and older accounted for 4.8% of the total. Two decades later, this segment has doubled to 9%. By 2050, one in five Latin Americans will be a senior citizen. The aging of the population does not bode well for Latin America; the region is not prepared for the challenges of aging (IMF, 2018). As the population ages, the mortality rate of this segment increases due to a higher incidence of chronic diseases related to age such as heart disease. The broad mortality rate in the region in 2050 will be 40% higher than that of 2020. Providing healthcare, economic support, and housing for the elderly will be a challenge to all countries in the region. More on these trends and challenges will be discussed later in the section on health.

Regional Variations of Demographic Transition

Although the region as a whole is in Stage 3 of demographic transformation, there are significant variations in the population dynamics across countries. Some countries, such as Uruguay and Chile, show advanced stages of transformation with low levels of fertility, high life expectancy, older populations, and high levels of urbanization. By contrast, other countries (e.g., Honduras, Guatemala) exhibit younger populations, with high levels of fertility, and substantial rural populations. We will discuss these regional demographic variations next.

Table 4.2 shows the demographic profiles of key Latin American countries and Spain, a reference to a European country already in Stage 4 of demographic transformation.

Figure 4.2 provides a visual dispersion of these countries on the plot of fertility defined as the number of birth rates per 1,000 women and average childbearing age against population growth. Based on these indicators, we grouped Latin American countries into four clusters that define younger and older populations. It should be noted that Spain is included in the plot (far left of Figure 4.2) to depict the demographic destination of Latin American countries. In Table 4.2, countries are grouped by the cluster to which they belong. We discuss these clusters next.

The first group of countries is in *Advanced Demographic Transition*. These countries include Chile, Uruguay, Cuba, and Costa Rica. The group exhibits the lowest population growth and the highest life expectancy. These results are attributed to low fertility rates (births per woman range from 1.62 to 1.98) and a higher median age of childbearing from 26.4 to 28.8 years. Countries in this group are highly urbanized except for Cuba (from 80.7% to 95.1%). Life expectancy ranges from 80 to 81.3 years, making it the oldest group of countries in Latin America. This group is demographically closest to Spain with birth rates per woman at 1.34, median age of childbearing at 31 years, and life expectancy of 84 years of age.

The second group of countries are at a stage of *Moderate Demographic Transition*: Brazil, Colombia, Peru, and Argentina. These countries have large populations and, therefore, more variance in the indicators; however, as a whole, this group exhibits slightly higher births per woman (from 1.74 to 2.27) and similar childbearing age (27–28.6 years). The life expectancy in this group is substantially lower than the first group (76.4–77 years). The main difference between this group and the advanced demographic transition group is their higher infant mortality (10–13 per 1,000 people) and smaller older population (8.7%–11.4%). Thus, this group seems to be in the middle of Stage 3 demographic transition. It is interesting to note the slightly larger contribution of the working age population in Peru and Argentina in supporting the younger and older populations as evidenced by their higher dependency ratios (50.2% and 55.8%, respectively).

The third group of countries is in the *Incipient Demographic Stage*. This group comprises Mexico, Panama, El Salvador, Ecuador, the Dominican Republic, and Venezuela. Fertility rates are higher both in terms of births per 1000 (18–19.9) and younger childbearing age (25.8–26.9 years). Infant mortality is high (14–26 per 1,000 births). These countries are also younger than the first two groups and have a smaller older population (7.5%–8.7%). It is also notable that all these countries have similar population growth except for Venezuela. The current massive migration flow from Venezuela is the main reason for this negative growth and will be analyzed in our review of migration flows in the region in the next section.

The final group is in a stage of *Young Demographic Transition*. These countries are Paraguay, Nicaragua, Bolivia, Honduras, Haiti, and Guatemala. This group exhibits strong population growth (1.3%–2.0%), high number of births per 1000 (20.7–24.8), and similar childbearing age (26.9–29.8 years) to the third group. The group has lower life expectancy (63.5–75 years) and much higher infant mortality (19–54 per 1,000 births). Their populations are the youngest in the region with people under 15 ranging from 28.9% to 33.3%, above the mean for the region of 23.9%. A particular characteristic for this group is a much lower urban population (51.8%–70.1%) suggesting a large rural component of their populations.

Table 4.2 Stages of Demographic Transition in Latin America

Country	Pop Growth %	Births per 1,000	Births per Woman	Mean Age Childbearing years	Death per 1,000	Infant Mortality 1st year per 1,000	Life Expectancy at Birth years	Median Age years	Dependency Ratio %	% Under 15	% 65 and older	% Urban
Spain	0.3	8.4	1.34	31	9.1	2.28	84	44.9	52	15	18.5	80
Latin America	0.9	16.5	2.04	27.3	6.3	15	75.2	31	48.9	23.9	9.0	80.8
Group 1												
Chile	1.2	12.5	1.65	28.8	6.1	7	80	35.3	45.9	19.2	12.2	82.7
Uruguay	0.4	13.9	1.98	27.8	9.4	10	81.3	35.8	54.9	20.3	15.1	95.1
Cuba	0.0	10.2	1.62	26.4	8.9	4	80.7	42.2	46.7	15.9	15.9	77.1
Costa Rica	1.0	14.1	1.76	27.2	5.1	7	80.0	33.5	45.1	20.8	10.3	80.7
Group 2												
Brazil	0.8	14.1	1.74	27.1	6.4	13	75.6	33.5	43.5	20.7	9.6	82.1
Colombia	1.4	15.0	1.82	27	5.5	13	77.0	31.3	45.4	22.2	9.1	81.4
Peru	1.6	18.1	2.27	28.6	5.5	13	76.4	31	50.2	24.7	8.7	78.3
Argentina	0.9	17.1	2.27	28.2	7.6	10	76.5	31.5	55.8	24.4	11.4	92.1
Group 3												
Mexico	1.1	17.7	2.14	26.9	6.0	14	75.0	29.2	50.3	25.8	7.6	80.7
Panama	1.7	19.1	2.47	26.7	5.1	14	78.2	29.7	53.9	26.5	8.5	68.4
El Salvador	0.5	18.4	2.05	26.8	7.0	15	73	27.6	54.4	26.6	8.7	73.4
Venezuela	−1.1	18.0	2.28	26.4	7.0	26	72.1	29.6	54.4	27.3	8.0	88.3
Ecuador	1.7	19.9	2.44	27.4	5.1	14	76.7	27.9	53.8	27.4	7.6	65.9
The Dominican Republic	1.1	19.7	2.36	25.8	6.1	26	73.8	28	53.8	27.4	7.5	82.5
Group 4												
Paraguay	1.3	20.7	2.45	27.9	5.5	19	74.1	26.3	55.5	28.9	6.8	62.2
Nicaragua	1.3	20.9	2.42	26.9	5.1	17	74.2	26.5	54.3	29.5	5.7	59.0
Bolivia	1.4	21.9	2.75	28.6	6.8	30	71.1	25.6	60.5	30.2	7.5	70.1
Honduras	1.7	21.8	2.49	27.7	4.4	15	75	24.3	55.2	30.6	5.0	53.8
Haiti	1.3	24.5	2.96	29.8	8.6	54	63.5	24	60.4	32.5	5.2	55.2
Guatemala	2.0	24.8	2.90	28.6	4.8	21	73.9	22.9	62.3	33.3	5.0	51.8

Sources:
United Nations, World Population Prospects 2019. Volume I, Comprehensive Tables and Volume II, Demographic Profiles, 2019
United Nations (2019b), World Urbanization Prospects: The 2018 Revision, 2019
United Nations, ECLAC, Statistical Yearbook for Latin American and the Caribbean, 2020

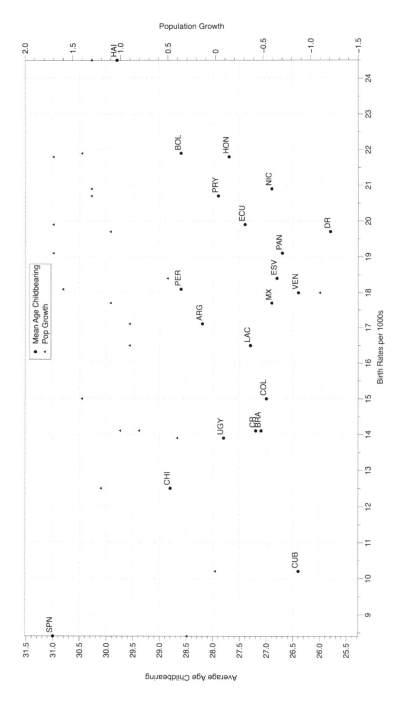

Figure 4.2 Childbearing age and birth rates against population growth

Migration Flows

Migration flows add to or reduce an existing population. Out migration has a number of drivers. Economic migrants leave their home countries for better economic opportunities. Younger people typically take this route when there are not enough jobs in their local economies. Political and asylum seekers leave their homes as a result of repression. This flow has been very important in the region at different times. In the 1970s and 1980s, the military regimes of the Southern Cone and Andean countries experienced out migration from those who espoused more liberal and leftist views than those of the right wing and authoritarian leaders in charge. These migrants went to countries that became havens for political refugees at the time such as Canada, Denmark, Spain, and Mexico. In the 1980s and 1990s, political upheaval impacted Central American countries such as Nicaragua and El Salvador. These political refugees sought refuge in closer destinations such as Costa Rica, Panama, and Mexico. More recently, political instability has been centered in Venezuela, and a large contingent of Venezuelans has left the country for both economic and political reasons. A third type of migrant is fleeing due to drug trafficking, skyrocketing crime rates, and domestic violence. This chaotic situation has displaced people internally (within a country) and externally (out of the region). Colombia went through a period that combined internal warfare and the violence of drug trafficking in the 1980s and 1990s. In the past two decades, large flows of Central American migrants have been arriving at the border of the US and Mexico, driven by the instability in Honduras, Guatemala, and El Salvador. Clearly, the migration flows from Latin America to other regions reduces the populations of countries where these flows originate. On the other hand, immigration to Latin America will add to the populations of countries receiving these flows. These immigration flows may originate from outside the region (global migration) or within the region (intra-regional migration). We account for these three types of migration flows next (i.e., global immigrants, out-migrants, and intra-regional migrants) (Migration Policy Institute, 2020; Council on Foreign Relations, 2019; Americas Quarterly, 2020).

Immigration to Latin America

Immigration to the region began with the discovery of the Americas in 1491. From discovery to independence in the 1880s, Spain and Portugal and the emerging slave trade from Africa provided the historical inflows of people into the region. With independence, a new era of economic expansion, industrialization, and infrastructure building brought other waves of immigration from non-European countries. Examples include immigrants from China brought to build railroads, and those from Japan who were brought in to work in agriculture settlements in Brazil and Peru. Later in the 1880s and early 1900s, the region's open borders led to waves of immigrants from Italy, France, and England particularly to Argentina, Brazil, and Uruguay and, to a lesser extent, to Chile and Venezuela. After World War II, immigration to the region continued from other countries such as Russia, East Asia (Japan and Korea), the Middle East, and India. After the 1970s, the region has experienced renewed immigration from China and Africa. Another stream of immigration is a population of retirees from the US and Europe seeking lower costs of living and warm climates, particularly in Mexico, Ecuador, Costa Rica, Panama, and the Dominican Republic.

The stock of immigrants from historical and recent immigration flows represents only a small percentage of the population of Latin American countries (see Table 4.3). The countries with relatively higher percentages are Costa Rica (10.2%), Chile (8.6%), and Panama (7.3%)

(United Nations Population Division, 2020). Thus, the real impact on the region's population comes from the other two flows discussed next.

Emigration from Latin America

In recent years, Latin America has experienced a net outflow of migration. The peak net outflow was reached in 2005 with a 2% net flow. This trend has been declining, and lately the net outflows have seen a minor reversal, with 0.8% net inflows in 2020 and an expected net inflow of 0.3% in 2050 (UN Population Division, 2020).

The type and motivation to emigrate has changed over time. People escaping endemic violence in the 1980s and 1990s replaced the political asylum seekers of the 1960s and 1970s followed by economic migrants in the 2000s. The first wave of political refugees included older and educated professionals in what was termed as a brain drain from the region. Violence impacted all sorts of people in the 1980s, but only those who could afford it emigrated to regions and countries that provided a safer place for their families. These were mostly people with sufficient wealth and ability to adapt and work in other regions. The most recent wave of economic migrants represents a group of both young and educated professionals seeking a better future and less skilled workers with no future in their own countries.

The destination of the waves of migrants is different. The early political migrants favored European countries that offered political asylum, such as Spain and Denmark. Some political migrants also moved intra-regionally to economically and politically stable countries that offered greater political freedom such as Mexico and Costa Rica. The source of political refugees was from politically repressive regimes in Argentina, Chile, Uruguay, and Peru. Economic migrants favored European countries that allowed long-term residency status because of their family backgrounds. For instance, Argentines sought double nationality and residence in Italy. Others pursued residence in Spain, Portugal, or the United Kingdom (UK) based on their ancestry. The US was also a preferred destination. The most recent wave of both younger skilled and unskilled migrants favors the US but also includes destinations such as Canada, Australia, and European countries that allow migrants to stay after entering illegally or overstaying their visa periods. Because of distance and proximity, the majority of the unskilled and illegal immigrants come to the US from Central America from what has been referred to as the turbulent northern triangle (Guatemala, Honduras, and El Salvador). Despite the distance, unskilled migrants to the US have also come from Brazil, Colombia, Peru, and Ecuador (Pew Research, 2020b).

The US is the largest and preferred destination for Latin Americans by far. The share of immigrants from Latin America into the US has increased from 20% in the 1970s to 50% in 2018 (America's Quarterly, 2020) in terms of annual flows. The peak year of the share of immigration into the US was 2010 when it reached 53%. Mexicans are the largest group among Latin Americans immigrating into the US at 11%, Central Americans are second at 8%, and South Americans represent 7% (Pew Research, 2020).

In terms of migration stocks (accumulated migration), Latin Americans represent 31% of all US immigrants in contrast to 38% from Asian countries. Of the Latin American share, Mexicans represent the largest share of immigrants from Latin America at 25% in 2018. In 2019, 97% of Mexicans living abroad were in the US. In contrast, only 19.4% of Argentines living abroad were in the US (Pew Research, 2020b). A related perspective is to compare the percentage of people from a Latin American country living abroad with the percentage of immigrants from their preferred destination living in their home country (see Table 4.3). For example, about 97% of Mexicans living abroad are in the

Table 4.3 Migration Stocks in Latin America

Country	Outflows		Inflows				
	International Migrants (1,000)	Migrants in US (1,000)	Immigrants in Country Stock	Immigrants as % Population	Immigrants from US (1,000)	Immigrants from Latin America %	Main Country of Source Immigration
Argentina	1,103	215	2,281	5.0	5	84.1	Paraguay
Bolivia	927	93	164	1.4	5	77.0	Argentina
Brazil	1,897	460	1,079	0.5	24	31.3	Paraguay
Chile	643	115	1,645	8.6	20	73.2	Peru
Colombia	3,024	798	1,905	3.7	20	95.7	Venezuela
Costa Rica	150	99	520	10.2	13	92.3	Nicaragua
Cuba	1757	1,344	3	0.0			
The Dominican Republic	1,608	1,174	604	5.6	14	92.3	Haiti
Ecuador	1,127	516	784	4.4	26	78.9	Colombia
El Salvador	1,599	1,429	43	0.7	5	81.3	Honduras
Guatemala	1,368	1,071	84	0.5	9	79.3	El Salvador
Haiti	1,769	737	19	0.2	2	59.3	The Dominican Republic
Honduras	985	656	39	0.4	7	74.2	El Salvador
Mexico	11,796	11,490	1,197	0.9	762	17.2	US
Nicaragua	718	303	42	0.6	4	82.4	Honduras
Panama	139	125	313	7.3	15	65.8	Colombia
Paraguay	896	34	169	2.4	2	90.7	Brazil
Peru	1,519	526	1,224	3.7	26	87.9	Venezuela
Uruguay	367	56	108	3.1	1	59.9	Brazil
Venezuela	5,415	255	1,324	4.8	11	81.7	Colombia
Latin America	42,890	6.5	14,794	2.3	—	—	

Sources:
UN Population Division – 2020 International Migration Highlights https://www.un.org/development/desa/pd/sites/www.un.org.development.desa.pd/files/undesa_pd_2020_international_migration_highlights.pdf
CEPAL – Observatorio Demográfico 2018: Migración InternacionalMigration Data Portal (2021)

US, while 62% of immigrants to Mexico are from the US. In contrast, only 19.4% of Argentines living abroad are in the US, while only 0.2% of immigrants in Argentina come from the US (Pew Research Center, 2018).

Intra-regional Migration

Intra-regional migration is a consequence of relative economic differences and proximity of neighboring countries. Countries with solid economies and better educational and health systems have been the preferred destinations of neighboring populations. At times, it is seasonal workers, and other times it draws permanent residents. For example, Argentina's rich natural resources and excellent educational institutions and healthcare have been a magnet for seasonal work in the agriculture and service sectors. These flows have been tapered by the volatility of the Argentinean economy and its political instability in the 1990s. Global immigrants to Argentina account for 5% of its population—a much larger percentage than the average for the region of only 2.3%. Of the total immigration flows in Argentina, about 84% come from within the region. A large percentage of the intra-regional migrants, 74%, are from neighboring countries (Paraguay, Uruguay, Chile, Bolivia, and Peru) (United Nations Population Division, 2020).

Across the region, intra-regional migration patterns are similar to those of Argentina. For instance, intra-regional migration is high in Paraguay (90.7%), Colombia (95.7%), Costa Rica (92.3%), and the Dominican Republic (92.3%) (see Table 4.3). The exceptions to this trend are the two largest countries in the region. Mexico has a low rate of intra-regional migration (17.2%). Mexico's unique situation of bordering the US may suggest that most migrants pass through its territory to reach its giant neighbor. Brazil, which borders seven South American countries, has only 31.3% of its immigrant population come from the region (United Nations Population Division, 2020). A language barrier can explain lower regional emigration rates to Brazil; not being able to speak Portuguese to work may be a handicap for these migrants. Another barrier is the natural border of Amazonia, which makes Brazil difficult to reach.

The most recent trends of intra-regional migration emanate from the collapse of the Venezuelan and Haitian societies from 2015 to 2020. We focus on the larger migration of Venezuelans after the collapse of their economy and political upheaval. Conditions in Venezuela are dire with 89% of their population in poverty, infant mortality reaching 26% per 100,000 live births, and its economy clocking 500,000% annual inflation (International Monetary Fund- IMF, 2020). Through 2019, about 5.4 million Venezuelans (19% of its population) decided to leave their country (Migration Policy Institute, 2020). About 4.6 million Venezuelans have migrated to other Latin American countries (World Bank, 2019). Most migrants are young professionals with no expectations of a stable future in Venezuela.

Proximity is the main factor guiding where Venezuelans are heading. About 74% go to nearby South American countries, including Colombia, Peru, Ecuador, and Brazil and as far as Argentina, Chile, and Uruguay (Council on Foreign Relations, 2019). Traveling by road and on foot in many cases requires excellent physical condition, a young age, and a good level of education to sort out the complexity of traveling. National surveys of Venezuelan migrants in the Southern Cone countries and Costa Rica indicate that 19% of them have a professional degree (Migration Policy Institute, 2020). Such an influx of qualified migrants offers a promising economic return to their host countries. With precarious legal status, most Venezuelan migrants are forced to join the informal sector of their host economies. A negative attitude toward Venezuelan migrants has been a challenge to their assimilation and ability to contribute to their host countries (Corrales, 2019). These attitudes are shaped by fiscal challenges for local governments that have to assume the additional public expenditures associated with the housing, health, food, and education needs of the arriving population. Some local governments are procuring and receiving financial support from global refugee organizations (UN Population Division, 2020). Therefore, the ability of these highly skilled migrants to make a positive economic and social contribution to their host countries will depend on the receiving countries' ability to find solutions to these assimilation and integration challenges.

Race and Ethnicity in Latin America

Contemporary race relations in Latin America are the product of the region's historical roots, modernization, integration with world events, and its particular mix of ethnic and racial groups. This unique context has produced a distinct set of racial hierarchies and perceptions of race and, most importantly, national identities centered on racial and ethnic origins. As such, race relations in Latin America have developed around very different evolutionary paths from the US experience (Graham, 1990; Wallace, 2020).

Latin America was colonized by Spanish and Portuguese adventurers who arrived in the new world without families and found highly organized and developed Indigenous groups. Miscegenation with the Indigenous populations and later African slaves resulted in a new social hierarchy of mixed-race individuals. In later periods, nation-building efforts used the rationale of racial mixing (Europeanization) as a way to achieve a multiethnic society, leading to the argument that Latin America was a racial democracy (Freyre, 1951). Others have argued that such an egalitarian myth never existed, and race-based hierarchies and racism are the legacy of efforts of European Whites in Latin America to preserve advantages in education, income, and political power under nuanced methods of racial exclusion (Wase, 2021). In contrast to Latin America, race relations in the US are based on its different historical evolution (Degler, 1986; Marx, 1998). Northern European colonizers brought their families to the US. Also, they did not encounter the large concentrations of developed civilizations found, for instance, in Mexico and Peru, and thus did not produce the large mestizo populations present in Latin America. In contrast to Catholicism, the Northern European colonizers espoused Puritan doctrines of Protestantism and Calvinism. The sad legacy of the slave trade in the US led to institutionalized segregation and race-based violence. The broad based racial social movements that have emerged in the US to protest discrimination, racism, and equal rights have emerged only recently in Latin America. As a result, some argue that racial prejudice is not as widespread in Latin America. In this section, we explore this argument further.

The subjective perception of phenotypes by oneself and others makes racial classification fluid, as racial categorization may vary with the social context of the country. Each country has a unique set of historical and social structures that have defined their particular racial identification processes. Such ambiguity creates major issues in census counts of race and self-identity based on race. The following discussion attempts to elaborate on how racial and ethnic relations evolved historically from the colonial period in Latin America to today. The purpose of this overview is to provide some foundation to this complex and controversial topic and provide perspective on how race and ethnicity is one more component of the Latin American population.

Historical Evolution

Native Americans populated the region for thousands of years before the arrival of European colonizers. Advanced civilizations thrived in Mexico and Peru, developing state-of-the art knowledge about math, architecture, and astronomy as well as sophisticated political empires. Colonization by the Europeans brought disease and violence that decimated many of these Indigenous populations, but Indigenous communities have persisted, and their descendants have continued to form thriving communities across the continent.

During the colonial period (1492–1810), both Spanish and Portuguese colonizers used African slaves for plantation agriculture, mining, and other labor needs. About 4–5 million Africans were forcibly brought from Africa in this period as part of the slave trade, concentrating especially in the plantation regions of the Caribbean and northeastern Brazil. These slaves are the ancestors of the current Afro-descendants in Latin America (Wade, 2010).

Over time, widespread miscegenation among White Europeans, slaves, and Indigenous communities generated a complex racial landscape. Today, Latin America hosts a variety of racial designations and ethnic affiliations reflecting the region's diverse roots and ancestry. These varied identifications are expressed in food preferences, music, and lifestyles. Immigrants from Asia and the Middle East have also contributed to the region's ethnic mix but with more limited impact in terms of overall numbers and recipient countries.

Ethnicity, Race, and National Identity

Race is a social construct that groups people arbitrarily based on their distinctive physical and inherited biological traits such as skin color. Ethnicity refers to human groups that share a belief of a common descent. Ethnicity is linked to cultural expressions and self-identification into a particular group. These cultural expressions are traditions, language, religious beliefs, and origin among other shared social foundations. Both concepts are social constructs, as genetics cannot be used to determine race or ethnicity (Wade, 2010).

Miscegenation has been a long and deep process for Latin American societies. Given the voluntary and forced immigration of people from so many racial backgrounds, this process has been complex. Countries with greater and more diverse immigration have achieved a great deal of racial mixing. Countries with less racial diversity had small Indigenous native populations and/or slave trades and were mostly populated by European immigrants. These countries followed nation-building strategies to keep racial mixing to a minimum. In both cases, race and ethnicity have shaped the national character of Latin American countries today.

Two countries that have experienced high levels of miscegenation and have been celebrated for their inclusive and egalitarian ideologies are Brazil and Mexico (Moraes and Saldivar, 2018). Fifty percent of Brazilians are Afro-descendants with the rest of the population being of either European, Asian, or Indigenous groups. Earlier scholarship proclaimed that Brazil achieved a racial democracy after its African residents survived a tortuous journey from slavery to freedom and integration to mainstream society (Freyre, 1956, 1970). During colonial times, five million Africans arrived in Brazil as slaves. Brazil was the last Latin American country to abolish slavery in 1888. The embrace of African heritage as a central part of Brazilian identity was proposed by intellectual leaders such as Gilberto Freyre, who crafted the vision of Brazil as a harmonious multiracial society (Freyre, 1966; Souza and Vinder, 2005). Despite the inclusive rhetoric, a color hierarchy and racism define everyday life in Brazil, with huge economic and political representation gaps for Black citizens. In acknowledgment of this fact, the Cardoso and Da Silva administrations implemented ambitious social programs, including some affirmative actions, particularly in education, with race-based quotas for public universities (Mead, 2004).

Mexico is another example of a country that constructed a national identity on the blending of its Indigenous and European roots through a process known as Mestizaje. The Great Mexican Revolution of 1910–1917 mobilized large Indigenous groups to power and recognition of their rights in a new constitution. Architects of the post-revolutionary government identified a mestizo identity as representing the best of all worlds, or a '*raza cosmica,*' that would erase racial differences. This single national identity, 'we are all mestizos,' was a way of relegating Indigenous tradition to the past and looking forward to a modern nation.

Mexico and Brazil illustrate the interaction between deep racial mixing processes and national identity. Racial and ethnic barriers have not been eliminated fully and real discrimination based on race persists in their societies. Other countries in the region with substantial Indigenous and or Black populations have tried to resolve these differences not through celebrating mestizaje but by creating areas of Indigenous (Chile and Bolivia) or Black autonomy (Nicaragua and Panama). However, the challenges are numerous, and the resolutions have significant impacts on social policies.

Recognition of ethnic and race identity today is important because it is associated with claims of legal rights and protection of patrimony, culture, and language. In many cases, this identity allows members to receive or access social benefits. There has been some progress to accurately count ethnic and racial groups, but much more needs to be done. For instance, the national census of some countries have introduced efforts to use multiple questions to capture languages, lineage, and even family traditions to gauge identity IBGE (2020), INEGI (2021), INEI (2018, 2021). We will use data based on these efforts to describe two population groups (i.e., Indigenous and Afro-descendants) more accurately.

The identity and quantification of other ethnic and racial groups, however, is limited, ambiguous, and fluid (Nobles, 2000). For instance, it is controversial and challenging to identify and quantify European or Asian groups on skin tone. The mixing of these groups, in what has been referred as 'mestizaje,' has resulted in a mélange of skin colors, traditions, and identities. Mixed-race categories have been coined under different terms such as mestizos, criollos, mulattos, and others. Figure 4.3 provides a schematic visual of the different combinations, including one category of arrivals from Asia.

Although there are many different races and ethnicities in Latin America, we focus on two important ones based on their role in nation-building among countries in the region: Indigenous or Native Americans and descendants from the African slaves that arrived during the colonial period, referred to here as Afro-descendants.

Indigenous and Afro-descendant Populations

The challenge of identifying and quantifying race in Latin America is further exacerbated by the fact that, historically, it has not been included in national census data. If racial identification is elicited, the method of identification has been based on a variety of forms. For instance, Mexico included a Black or Afro-American category in 2015 and started using a more comprehensive race option in their census in 2020 (Pew Research, 2016). The country identifies race based on language spoken. Brazil introduced a race question in the 2020 census, and the identification was based on the skin color of the respondent. Such practices

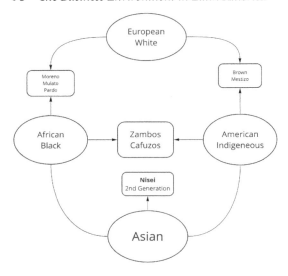

Figure 4.3 Mixed races in Latin America

have been criticized and modified, leading to a more multidimensional categorization based on ethnicity and language aspects. Although there is no consistent practice throughout the region about race identification on census data, we used data from these official sources to estimate the population of two different groups: Indigenous and Afro-descendants.

Indigenous Population

The Indigenous population in the region was estimated at 41.8 million in 2015 or 6.4% of the region's population. This population group is concentrated in Brazil, Mexico, and the Andean Region—a reflection of their pre-colonial origins (see Table 4.4).

The number of ethnic groups and languages manifests the diversity of the Indigenous population. One source puts this diversity at 720 different ethnicities and 560 languages spoken (US Congressional Research Service, 2020). Brazil is host to the most diverse Indigenous population with 241 ethnic groups and 186 different languages spoken. Other countries with substantial and diverse Indigenous populations are Colombia, Mexico, Peru, and Ecuador. Countries with small Indigenous populations with some diversity are Argentina, Paraguay, and Venezuela. On the other hand, countries with small Indigenous populations and low diversity are Chile, El Salvador, Panama, and Uruguay. The later countries were sparsely populated before colonial times and did not attract European colonization because of their lack of mineral resources. Countries with small Indigenous populations such as Chile and Argentina displaced Indigenous groups during the period of the Republic (1800s) under the pretext of nation-building efforts and Europeanization.

Despite this rich heritage, identifying the nature and size of the Indigenous population remains a challenge. A novel study of two countries with large Indigenous populations, Mexico and Peru, addressed these questions (Telles and Torch, 2019). This study used 12 different indicators to assess Indigenous background, among them native language spoken by parents and grandparents and respondent's ability to speak and understand the native language. In addition, the study included the interviewers' identification and phenotype characteristics of

Table 4.4 Race and Ethnicity in Latin America

Country	Native Indigenous						Afro-descendants	
	Year	*Population Million*	*% Total Population*	*% Urban*	*Ethnic Groups*	*Languages*	*Population Million*	*% Total Population*
Argentina	—	0.95	2.4	—	30	15	0.17	0.4
Bolivia	2012	4.12	41	48	114	33	0.27	0.2
Brazil	2010	0.82	0.5	29	29	241	108.3	50.9
Chile	2002	0.79	4.6	65	9	6	0.01	0.1
Colombia	2018	1.90	4.4	22	83	65	3.48	6.8
Costa Rica	2011	0.10	2.4	41	8	7	0.39	7.8
Cuba	—	—	—	—	—	—	4.06	35.9
The Dominican Republic	—	2.26	24	—	—	—	0.93	8.6
Ecuador	2010	1.02	7.0	21	32	13	1.26	7.2
El Salvador	2007	0.01	0.2	51	3	1	0.08	0.1
Guatemala	2002	5.8	41	—	24	24	0.57	0.3
Haiti	—	—	—	—	—	—	10.9	95.5
Honduras	2001	0.55	2.2	15	7	6	0.14	1.4
Mexico	2010	16.8	15	54	67	67	2.57	2
Nicaragua	2005	0.35	6.0	38	9	6	0.31	0.5
Panama	2010	0.42	12.2	24	7	7	0.38	8.8
Paraguay	2012	0.11	1.7	—	20	20	0.04	0.1
Peru	2007	7.6	26.0	53	52	47	1.18	3.6
Uruguay	2014	0.08	2.4	—	—	—	0.16	4.6
Venezuela	2011	0.72	2.8	—	50	37	0.98	3.4
Latin America	2015	41.8	7.8	49	720	560	134	21

Sources:
World Bank, Indigenous Latin America in the Twenty-First Century, 2015
US Congressional Research Service, Indigenous People in Latin America: Statistical Information, 2020.
CEPAL/CELADE: https://www.cepal.org/en/topics/redatam/about-redatam
UN ECLAC, Afro-descendants and the matrix of social inequality in Latin America, 2020

respondents. The study's results indicate that the size of the Indigenous population depends on the criteria used to assess Indigeneity. For instance, based on self-reported ancestors and customs, the Indigenous population is estimated to be 22.2% in Mexico and 23.5% in Peru. Based on fluency in the native language, the estimates are 16.2% in Mexico and 23.4% in Peru. When the indicator is the ability to understand the language, the population increases to 20.9% in Mexico and 42.5% in Peru. Based on the interviewer's independent assessment of respondents, the size of the Indigenous population is 8.8% in Mexico and 6.3% in Peru. As a reference, self-identification questions in their national censuses yield an Indigenous population of 15% in Mexico (2010) and 26% in Peru (2007) (Telles & Torche, 2019).

Using data from the 12 indicators in the study, Telles and Torche (2019) classified the Indigenous population in three groups: Indigenous mestizos, traditional mestizos, and new Indigenous.

Indigenous Mestizos

People in this group tended to have parents and grandparents that spoke an Indigenous language that they themselves understood. About 70% identified themselves as mestizo in Mexico and 88% in Peru. On the other hand, the interviewer identified 23% as Indigenous in Mexico and 5% in Peru in this group. This group had lower educational levels and seemed fully socially assimilated in urban areas. They tended to reject Indigenous lifestyles and adopt the mestizo self-concept. This group is particularly large in Peru (Telles & Torche, 2019).

Traditional Mestizos

People in this group tended to be dark-skinned and speak an Indigenous language. They came from a lower socioeconomic background and were less educated. They lived in rural areas and fit the conventional thinking of the Indigenous population who remain in rural areas and provincial cities.

New Indigenous

People in this group were more likely to be prosperous, younger, educated, and live in urban areas. They tended to be lighter skinned, were less likely to have grandparents who spoke an Indigenous language, and did not speak an Indigenous language themselves. However, they were more likely to identify themselves as Indigenous and were willing to affirm their ancestry. Ideologically, they were also supportive of Indigenous rights.

The results of this study seem to capture the dynamics of rural migration to urban areas by Indigenous populations and their degree of assimilation into the larger societies of their countries. The exponent of this group is the Indigenous mestizo. What is revealing is the rise of a new Indigenous identity—proud of their past and ancestry in a process that could be referred to as reversed assimilation or a revindication or revitalization of their Indigenous roots, even as these populations increasingly reside in urban spaces. This new Indigenous Mexican or Peruvian derives his or her identity from strong Indigenous values and roots despite their inability to speak an Indigenous language.

Afro-Descendants

The Afro-descendant population is concentrated in countries where the European colonizers brought African slaves to work in agriculture. These countries are Brazil, Colombia, Cuba,

Haiti, Ecuador, and to a lesser extent, Mexico. As a distinct ethnic group, Afro-descendants have contributed to the culture, food, and identity of these countries. By far, the majority of the Afro-descendants are in Brazil—80% of the region's Afro-descendant population is in Brazil alone, and they account for 50% of Brazil's population. In Haiti, Afro-descendants account for 90% of the population (ECLAC, 2020b).

The majority of Afro-descendants live in poverty. About 30% are considered poor. In Brazil, 25.6% of Afro-descendants are considered poor based on per capita income (less than $2.50 per day) compared to 11.5% of the general population. In Colombia, 40.9% are poor in contrast to 27.8% of the general population. The same situation is observed in Ecuador with 31.4% of this population considered poor compared to only 19.5% of the general population. Only in Peru do the poverty rate of Afro-descendants reflect that of the general population (about 20%). Afro-descendants also experience greater violence. For instance, Brazilian Afro-descendants suffer death by violence at four times the rate of the general population (ECLAC, 2020b).

In sum, Afro-descendants in Latin America remain marginalized and more vulnerable than other groups. Given this fact, how might we reconcile ongoing racial inequality with the argument that Latin America is a racial democracy?

A novel multicountry study that focused on the extent of the ambiguity of race identification in Latin America may help answer this question. In this study, interviewers independently evaluated the skin color of a respondent based on a skin color chart. The skin color categorization was translated to a scale of skin tones ranging from 1 = lightest to 11 = darkest. The interviewer gauged other phenotype characteristics of the respondents, such as hair type, and questions related to language use, ancestry of parents and family, education, wealth, age, gender, and urban/rural residency. Respondents were also asked to self-identify their race based on census questions.

The results of the study for four countries with substantial Afro-descendant populations (Brazil, Colombia, Panama, and the Dominican Republic) served to assess the extent of Blackness of their populations. Table 4.5 shows the results of the respondents' self-reported race and the interviewers' assessment of the respondents' skin color. The percentage of respondents self-identifying as Black was somewhat similar in the four countries ranging from 8% to 14%. The results also showed a similar percent of self-reported White populations in all countries ranging from 31% to 35%. There seemed to be more of a discrepancy in the mixed-race categories (i.e., pardo and mestizo), as the percentages ranged from 44% in Panama to 64% in the Dominican Republic.

Table 4.5 Self-Reported Racial Identification and Skin Color in Latin America

Race	Brazil	Colombia	Panama	Dominican Republic
White	35	31	31	11
Mestizo	—	52	44	64
Pardo (Brazil)	48	—	—	—
Mulato	—	3	3	11
Black	11	8	14	13
Indigenous	2	4	8	—
Other	4	2	—	1
Mean Skin Color	4.58	4.20	5.14	5.16
Standard Deviation Skin Color	2.18	1.75	1.91	1.92

Source: Telles and Paschell (2014).

The results of the interviewer's assessment of the respondents' skin color revealed a discrepancy between self-racial perception and that of the interviewer. It should be noted that, in contrast to the US, where race identification tends to be based on a 'one-drop of Black' ideology, the idea of Whiteness or Blackness is a relative term in Latin America, where a 'one-drop of White' ideology seems to be more prevalent for race identification. According to the study, the majority of respondents (70%–80%) were in the mid-range of skin color category (3–6). A minority of respondents was either very light or very dark. In all countries, there was a wide discrepancy between the self-reported racial category and the interviewer's independent assessment of their skin color. The interviewer gave a narrow range of skin colors (9–11 in the scale) to those who self-identified as Black. This was the case of 90% in this group in Panama, 80% in Brazil, and 60% in the Dominican Republic. On the other side of the skin color scale, those who identified themselves as White were classified in a narrow scale range of 1 to 3 by the interviewer. This is the case of 80% of those in Brazil and Panama, 60% in Colombia, and 40% in the Dominican Republic. This result suggests a greater ambiguity in who identifies as White in the last two countries (Telles, 2014; 2015).

In the case of Brazil, the average skin color was perceived to be 4.58, with a large dispersion in the interviewer's ratings (standard deviation = 2.18). The interviewer rated skin colors ranging from 1 to 7 to those who self-classified as Whites. Those who self-classified as Blacks had skin color ranging from 2–11 by the interviewer. The interviewer used a distribution of skin color ranging from 4–6 for those who identified themselves as pardos.

Using other social and demographic indicators gathered by the study, the results revealed that wealth was a significant predictor of how one self-reports race in Brazil. The greater the wealth, the greater the respondent's self-classification as pardo or White, regardless of the respondent's skin color. With respect to education, light-skinned people had higher levels of education. Education was also a strong predictor of Black self-identification in some countries. The higher the education level, the more likely that a respondent would self-identify as Black in Brazil and Panama. In Colombia and the Dominican Republic, the results were the opposite: the higher the educational level, the more likely that the respondent would self-classify as White. These results led the authors to conclude that wealth status is a polarizing factor in Brazil just as education is in Colombia and the Dominican Republic.

The conclusion of this novel study is that there is a great deal of ambiguity pertaining to race identity in Latin America, drawing into consideration language, history, skin color, class status, and self-identification (Pew Research, 2016). Affirmative action programs and increased wealth and education of the Afro-descendant population may lead to a stronger appreciation of Black identity and heritage.

An Institutional Perspective of Race in Latin America

Given how people use external physical appearance to classify racial groups, race becomes an organizing principle of social relationships. Racism is the prejudice and belief of superiority of one racial group vis-à-vis others. When a racial group has a dominant impact on all aspects of society, then racism can become institutionalized at all levels and become systematic (i.e., society formalizes some sort of hierarchical designation of superiority among different racial groups). Such institutionalization can be overt and highly developed or covert and loosely structured and provides the rationalization for social, political, and economic stratification of privileges of different racially based groups (Bonilla-Silva, 1997).

The institutionalization of racially based relations allows the dominant group to receive greater economic rewards, access to better education, better prospects in labor markets, and primary positions in the political system. Thus, the preservation of such privileges is an important drive of social relationships and provides the rationalization of social relationships based on race alone. Such rationalization is the basis of systematic racism and the organized map that guides actions of racial actors. Over time, such racial structures become normalized. It is the dispute of such privileges and the drive to recognize the rights of other racial groups that generates racially based conflicts in society (Bonilla-Silva, 1997).

In sum, Latin America has lost its innocence in terms of the long-term assumption that it is a region of racial and ethnic harmony. The historical effort to achieve racial mixture under the guise of nation-building has resulted in masked racism and discrimination. The invisibility of racism has now been unmasked. The rejection of and pressure to end the violence and brutality against Afro-descendants and Indigenous groups by police or drug traffickers through street protests and more militant groups have raised the awareness of the plight of these minorities among all levels of society. The current social discourse calls for inclusiveness, justice, dignity, and tolerance. There is hope that the future will bring more equal representation and fair distribution of equal access to opportunities to all racial and ethnic groups in Latin America.

Education

Latin America has made substantial progress in education. The region enjoys almost universal literacy and attendance. The region's literacy rate is 98.5%—greater than the world average of 86.3% in 2018. Countries with the highest literacy rates are Argentina (99%), Uruguay (98.7%), and Costa Rica (97.9%); those with the lowest literacy rates are Guatemala (81.5%), Honduras (87.2%), and El Salvador (88.5%) (World Population Review, 2020).

The region also performs well in school attendance. Enrollment in primary education is 93.7% compared to the world average of 89.4%. The attendance ratio for secondary school drops to 77.5% but still exceeded the world average of 75.3% in 2018. In terms of gender parity in enrollment, the region enjoys parity up to secondary education, at which point females are more likely than males to complete school (UNESCO, 2020).

Public expenditures in education are an indication of resources available for the educational systems. In this regard, Latin America is behind the world's average of 4.59% of GDP with only 4%. The countries with higher investments in education are Cuba (12.8%), Costa Rica (7%), and Brazil (6.32%). The countries with the lowest investments in education are Paraguay (3.4%), Panama (3.2%), Guatemala (3.2%), and El Salvador (3.6%) (see Table 4.6).

The gap in investments in education creates different educational opportunities within the region and with the rest of the world. One such indicator of gaps is the number of students per teacher. For primary education, the 2018 ratio for the region is 21, whereas the world's is 23.5; for secondary education, the ratio for the region is 16 compared to18 for the world.

Higher investments in education have paid off for countries such as Cuba and Costa Rica. These countries exhibit small student–teacher ratios in primary and secondary levels (9 and 12 respectively). Despite its high expenditure in education, Brazil has not accomplished low student–teacher ratios (ratio of 20). It may be that Brazilian investment is not proportionate to its large population. It is not a surprise to find that countries with the largest student–teacher ratios are also those with the lowest investments in education: Paraguay (24) and El Salvador (27). Other countries with high ratios are Mexico (27) and Venezuela (26).

The 2018 Organization for Economic Cooperation and Development (OECD) PISA project on learning outcomes in reading, math, and science, which included several Latin American

Table 4.6 Student–Teacher Ratios and Proficiency Achievement in Latin America

Country	Investment in Education		Student–Teacher Ratio		Proficiency ECLAC (2017) % Passing		OECD PISA (2019) Score		
	% GDP Primary	Per Student $ Primary	Primary	Secondary	Reading	Math	Reading	Math	Science
Argentina	5.5	3131	17	12	—	—	402	379	404
Bolivia	7.3	—	18	18	—	—	—	—	—
Brazil	6.32	2955	20	17	—	—	413	384	404
Chile	5.42	4358	18	18	69.7	75.4	452	417	444
Colombia	4.50	2981	23	26	—	—	412	391	413
Costa Rica	7.05	4342	12	12	—	—	426	402	416
Cuba	12.8	—	9	10	74.8	77.4	—	—	—
The Dominican Republic	2.0	—	19	19	—	—	342	325	336
Ecuador	5.0	—	24.5	21	—	—	—	—	—
El Salvador	3.59	1347	27	28	—	—	—	—	—
Guatemala	3.21	1160	20.3	10.5	—	—	—	—	—
Haiti	2.8	—	33	24	—	—	—	—	—
Honduras	6.07	—	25.6	16.7	—	—	—	—	—
Mexico	4.52	2602	27	17	57.5	69.4	420	409	419
Nicaragua	4.36	—	30	31	—	—	—	—	—
Panama	3.2	—	22	14	—	—	317	353	365
Paraguay	3.44	1392	24	18	—	—	—	—	—
Peru	3.85	1479	17	14	58.6	68.2	401	400	404
Uruguay	5.05	2965	11	13	—	—	427	418	426
Venezuela	6.9	—	26	18	—	—	—	—	—
Latin America	4.5	—	21.3	16.5	—	—	—	—	—
OECD	5.0	8296	16	14	—	—	487	489	489

Sources:
UNESCO: http://uis.unesco.org
World Bank (2020a): https://data.worldbank.org/indicator/SE.PRM.ENRL.TC.ZS?locations=Z]
World Bank (2020b): https://data.worldbank.org/indicator/SE.XPD.TOTL.GD.ZS
ECLAC: Statistical Yearbook for Latin America and the Caribbean, 2019
OECD: PISA 2018 Results

countries, provides additional insights on the region's education. None of the Latin American students scored above the OECD countries' average on all subjects (OECD, 2020). The highest scores were from Chile, Uruguay, and Costa Rica. The worst performer was the Dominican Republic. Moreover, the PISA project found that expenditures per student account for 49% of the variation in reading performance among all countries in the sample.

What is more telling about the PISA project is the percentage of students who scored at the top and bottom within a given country. The top achievers among Latin American countries were 0.1%–3.5% of all of the students in the sample of students from their respective country. What is worrisome is the percentage of poor performers, which ranged from 23.5% in Chile to a high of 75% in the Dominican Republic.

The PISA project also captured the discrepancy of access to and availability of internet connectivity between the Latin American and OECD students. The study found that 61% of Latin American students taking the test had a computer at home compared to 82% for OECD homes. The gap was even larger in terms of internet access from home—79% of Latin American students reported access, whereas 92% of OECD students did. Moreover, these results may not be representative of all Latin American students, given that it is likely students participating in the PISA project came from privileged homes. Another comprehensive study of 14 countries found that only 42% of students in urban area homes have access to the internet, and the level drops to 14% for rural homes (ECLAC, 2019b, 2020a). The digital handicap of Latin American students suggests the challenge of utilizing remote learning for rural students, particularly. In most Latin American countries, the academic year was just starting when most governments suspended schools due to the COVID-19 pandemic. The shift to remote learning revealed the huge discrepancies of technology readiness for learning across countries, social classes, and urban/rural populations as well as teacher training and preparation. Most reports of the educational situation during the pandemic conclude that students lost the full academic year of 2020 in Latin America (ECLAC, 2020d; UNICEF-UNDP, 2020).

Another study of learning outcome assessments in reading and mathematics included more countries from the region (UNESCO, 2019). The study showed that proficiency in these two subjects was higher in Cuba and Chile followed by Mexico and Uruguay. The worst performers were the Dominican Republic, Nicaragua, and Panama. What was remarkable about this study is that only 30% of students achieved a minimum standard in reading and mathematics. The prospects for the future of youth in the region are at risk.

Other discrepancies in educational performance are explained by differences in socioeconomic and ethno-racial factors. One clear socioeconomic factor is wealth and income differences— students from the wealthiest 20% group are five times more likely to complete secondary school than those from the bottom 20% socioeconomic bracket (UNESCO, 2019). Another study showed that the attendance from students from self-identified Indigenous families was 15% lower than the national average (UNESCO, 2020). Furthermore, in Peru and Mexico, with substantial Indigenous populations, attendance drops 6%–10% when the children and family speak their native language. Similarly, another seven-country study of attendance by children from Afro-descendant families found that their attendance was lower than their peers (World Bank, 2018). Both studies suggested the need for bilingual education in Latin America.

Urbanization

Latin America is the most urbanized world region; 55% of the world is urban and Latin America is 81%. By 2050, it is estimated that 68% of the world and 88% of Latin America will be urbanized (United Nations, 2019c).

In Latin America, the process of urban agglomeration is long and deep. In the 1950s, the rural population in the region was 99 million larger than the 70 million living in cities. In 2018, the urban population of the region was four times larger than the rural one—526 million urban to 126 million rural (UN World Urbanization Prospects, 2018). The annual increase of the urban population has ranged from 4.8% in the period of 1950–1970 to 7.8% in 1990–2018. The pace of urbanization is expected to slow down to an annual rate of 6.2% in the period of 2018–2030 and 4.2% in 2030–2050. The share of the urban population is expected to increase gradually to reach 83.6% in 2030 and 87.8% in 2050.

Urbanization in Latin America is related to lower fertility rates, late childbearing age, and an increase of the older population. In some cases, regional migration has contributed to the growth of cities. In other cases, migration has accelerated the depopulation of rural and small cities, particularly in Central America where people left cities plagued with violence and overpopulation.

Latin American countries fall into two extremes: highly urbanized or predominantly rural. Highly urbanized countries include Argentina, Uruguay, Chile, Brazil, and Venezuela (see Table 4.7). All these countries will have levels of more than 90% urbanization by 2050, with Uruguay leading the pack with 97%. Two other countries that will join this group because of their current rate of annual urbanization are Costa Rica and Colombia. On the other extreme, a few Latin American countries are and will remain mostly rural. These countries are Ecuador, Guatemala, Honduras, and Paraguay. The rest of the countries, including Mexico and Peru, are in between. These two countries have substantial Indigenous populations that remain rural.

Cities are the hubs of urban populations and come in many different sizes and shapes. In 2018, there were six megacities with populations of 10 million, three cities with populations

Table 4.7 Urbanization in Latin America

Country	1990	2018	2030	2050	Average Rate of Change 2015–2020
Argentina	87	92	93	95	1.1
Bolivia	56	69	74	81	2.0
Brazil	74	87	89	92	1.1
Chile	83	88	89	92	0.9
Colombia	69	81	84	89	1.2
Costa Rica	—	80.8	—	—	—
Cuba	73	77	79	84	0.1
The Dominican Republic	—	82.5	—	—	—
Ecuador	55	64	67	75	1.7
El Salvador	49	72	79	86	1.6
Guatemala	42	51	56	67	2.7
Haiti	—	—	—	—	—
Honduras	40	57	64	74	2.8
Mexico	71	80	84	88	1.6
Nicaragua	—	—	—	—	—
Panama	54	68	72	80	2.1
Paraguay	49	62	66	74	1.7
Peru	69	78	81	86	1.4
Uruguay	89	95	96	97	0.5
Venezuela	84	88	89	92	1.3
Latin America	78.5	81.5	84	88	1.3
World	43	55	60	68	1.9

Source: United Nations – World Urbanization Prospects 2018.

of 5–10 million, 63 cities with populations of 1–5 million, and 138 cities with populations of less than 1 million (United Nations, 2018b).

Six megacities account for 18% of the region's urban population. Of these, Mexico City and Sao Paulo, Brazil, with 22 million each, are among the world's ten largest urban agglomerations. Mexico City ranks fourth and Sao Paulo is fifth. These cities will continue to expand in the future, albeit at a slower rate, as they are reaching the limits of sustainability; Sao Paulo's annual growth will drop from 1.3% in the period from 2000 to 2018 to 0.8% from 2018 to 2030. Other megacities in Latin America are Buenos Aires (14.9 million), Rio de Janeiro (13.3 million), Bogota (12.3 million), and Lima (12.2 million). All these cities will exhibit slower growth in the future.

In some countries, the largest city accounts for a high proportion of the country's urban population, a situation that geographers called the 'primacy of the city.' Typically, such a city is also the capital and center of government activities. This situation is particularly true in countries with smaller populations. In Latin America, primacy cities include Asuncion, Paraguay, which accounts for 61.3% of the country's urban population; Santiago de Chile with 87.5%; Montevideo, Uruguay, with 95.2%; and Lima, Peru, with 77.7% (United Nations, 2018a).

Latin American cities suffer from sprawl, poor transportation systems, and high levels of crime among other failures (Muggah, 2018). Based on a colonial design, these cities were designed to have a central square surrounded by a grid system. As cities grew, industrial, business, and residential settlements grew around the periphery. In most cases, a ring of squatter settlements created outer circles further away. In recent years, residents have abandoned the inner residential areas for more distant new developments providing better infrastructure, services, and safety. These new residential areas also attracted new commercial, businesses, and entertainment, eliminating the need for these residents to go back to the central core of the city. This process of unplanned growth has created concentric zones of residential and commercial hubs around the major central core of a Latin American city in what has been referred to as a commercial spine and elite residential sector (Griffin & Ford, 1980). We discuss the structure of families and individuals living in these cities next.

Housing and Households

The household is the living central unit in Latin America. In 2020, the average size of a Latin American household was 3.4 persons, a drop from the average of 3.9 persons in 2010 (PRB, 2020). A number of factors impact the size of a Latin American household. One key factor is income. In 2018, the average family size of the top high-income quintile was 2.6 persons and 4.4 persons in the lowest quintile. Household sizes in the in-between quintiles ranged from 3.2 to 3.9.

The composition of a typical Latin American household depends on whether the people sharing the same house are related or not. If all members of the household are related, a typical Latin American family is multigenerational. It is common to find several generations and extended family members under one roof. Based on national censuses, this type of household accounts for 32% of all households. The more standard household of two parents and siblings living together accounts for 39% of all households. The empty nest household of couples without children at home accounts for 6%, whereas the household with a single parent living with children accounts for 10%. Households of a single person represent 3% of all. The remaining 10% include all other types of household sharing arrangements (Pew Research Center, 2020).

Another factor that is an important determinant of household structure in Latin America is the gender of the head of the family. In a typical family of two-parents living with their children, a man was the head of the family in 32% of households. In families with a single parent living with children, a woman was the head of the household in 11.1% of all households. In contrast, a man was the head of the household in only 1.7% of all households with a single parent. Thus, single women raising children in single-parent households in Latin America is a common phenomenon (Pew Research Center, 2020).

Access to basic household services provides another view of Latin American households. Access to power is almost universal (95.1%). Access to water is more limited at 86.5% of households, and access to sewage and wastewater treatment reaches only 62.4% of Latin American households. The urban–rural divide is clear when it comes to basic household services. About 89.5% of urban households have access to water compared to 74.6% of rural households. The contrast is even larger with respect to sanitation. This basic service is available in about 66.3% of urban households but only 54.1% of rural ones (WHO, 2020).

With an average household size of 3.4 and a population of 653.9 million in 2020, the total number of households in Latin America can be estimated at 192.3 million. Using this approach, Table 4.8 shows the estimates of the number of households by country, with the aggregate of all households in the region being 190.63 million (excluding Caribbean countries). The larger countries of Brazil and Mexico have 67.27 and 35.42 million households, respectively. Medium-size countries such as Colombia and Argentina have 16.22 and 14.68 million households, respectively. Small countries such as Uruguay and Costa Rica have 1.23 and 1.6 million households, respectively. Thus, the variation of household concentrations in

Table 4.8 Households in Latin America

Country	Population	Persons per Household	Households
Argentina	44.78	3.05	14.68
Bolivia	11.5	3.3	3.48
Brazil	212.58	3.16	67.28
Chile	18.9	3.1	6.1
Colombia	50.3	3.1	16.22
Costa Rica	5.11	3.18	1.60
Cuba	11.32	3.1	3.65
The Dominican Republic	10.80	3.21	3.36
Ecuador	17.4	3.12	5.57
El Salvador	6.45	3.6	1.79
Guatemala	17.6	4.55	3.87
Haiti	11.26	4.3	2.62
Honduras	9.74	4.2	2.32
Mexico	127.5	3.6	35.42
Nicaragua	6.54	3.50	1.86
Panama	4.24	3.7	1.14
Paraguay	7.0	3.9	1.79
Peru	32.5	3.8	8.55
Uruguay	3.46	2.8	1.23
Venezuela	28.50	3.52	8.10
Total			190.63
Latin America*	653.9	3.4	192.3

* Average for Latin America
Elaboration by authors with data from the United Nations Database Household Size and Composition (2019c). https://population.un.org/Household/index.html#/countries/840 and United Nations, ECLAC. (2020b). https://www.cepal.org/en/topics/redatam/about-redatam

cities is large. In fact, five countries account for 78% of all households in the region (Brazil, Mexico, Colombia, Argentina, and Peru). These five countries comprise the bulk of markets for all types of goods and services.

A different perspective to assess the distribution of households in the region is the distinction between demographically advanced and younger countries. Countries in an advanced stage of demographic transition (Group 1 in Table 4.2) are urban and affluent with smaller households. For instance, Chile, with 3.1 million households, is affluent and has a higher life expectancy and a larger older population. Countries in the young stages of demographic transition (Group 4 in Table 4.2) have younger populations, are more rural and poorer, and have larger household sizes. For instance, Guatemala and Honduras have average household sizes of 4.55 and 4.2 members, respectively, and their total households are 3.87 and 2.32 million, respectively.

Households can also be grouped by income. Because income is one of the determinant factors of social class, we will use this indicator as a first approximation of social classes in Latin America. (See Chapter 7 for a more detailed discussion.)

A study of households reports on the income of the heads of households (ECLAC, 2020a). Using this indicator as a basis to approximate household income, one can estimate the total income potential in each income-based social class. The study reports that in 2017, 3% of individuals were in the highest income class. The annual household income for this group was estimated at $54,100 (see Table 4.9). The next group comprised individuals with a per capita income considered to be middle income. This group was divided into high-middle class (4.5% of population), middle-middle class (15.7% of population), and low-middle class (25.8% of population). The annual household income for these groups was $22,600, $13,700, and $8,600, respectively. About 25.8% of the population was poor and 19.6 at poverty level with an average annual household income of $4,230 for the combined low-income group. Further, at the bottom of the income pyramid was the population in extreme poverty (10.5%). According to this study, these individuals earned less than $51.20 annually—that is less than one US dollar per week (ECLAC, 2020a).

From 2002 to 2017, the middle-class groups have grown consistently at a rate of 6% annually. This sustained expansion has been the driving force of economic growth in many Latin American countries until recently. In the same period, the poor classes have declined consistently at the rate of 10%. Both trends are indications of social mobility for many Latin Americans. However, with economic stagnation after 2017 and the large impact of the 2020 pandemic, this process is reversing.

According to the same study, the average size of households is small in the upper income groups (2.2) and larger in the lower income groups (4.28). Using the reported average household sizes, we can calculate the number of households for each of the income groups mentioned above. These numbers are reported in Table 4.10. The total number of households using this method is 190.5 million (ECLAC, 2020a).

We use average income per household (as a proxy of buying power) and the number of households in each of the major household income groups to estimate total potential buying power of each income class. The high-income group has a buying power of US$471 million. The mass middle class has a buying power of US$1.16 billion. The low-income (poor) households have a buying power of US$377 million. The total market power of all classes is an estimated US$2.01 trillion. It is remarkable that the 3% of high-income households account for 23.5% of buying power. It is also notable that the middle-class accounts for the bulk of buying power in the region with 57.7% of the total. The low-income (poor) households account for 18.8% of total buying power and 45.4% of the population (25.8 + 19.6). The 10.5% of the population in extreme poverty is not included in this estimate.

Table 4.9 Household Income Classes in Latin America

Class	Annual Income Per Capita US$	Annual % Change 2002–2017	% of Total Population 2017	Population (Millions)	Households (Millions)	Average Household Size	Annual Income per Household US$ (1,000)	Total Buying Power by Class US$ (Millions)
High	>1,096	0.8	3	19.1	8.7	2.2	54.1	471
Middle-High	657.5–1,096	1.4	4.5	29.0	12.1	2.4	22.6	274
Middle-Middle	328.7–657.5	6.2	15.7	100.0	37.2	2.69	13.7	511
Middle-Low	197–328.7	6.6	20.9	133.0	43.5	3.09	8.6	375
Low	109.6–197.2	0.3	25.8	164.1	43.8	3.75	4.23	377
Poverty	51.2–109.6	−13.6	19.6	124.0	29.0	4.28		
Extreme Poverty	<51.2	−1.7	10.5	67.0	16.2	4.14	Negligible	Negligible
Total				636.2	190.5			2,008

Sources:
SEDLAC Socio-economic database for Latin America and the Caribbean
https://www.cedlas.econo.unlp.edu.ar/wp/en/estadisticas/sedlac/estadisticas/
UN CEPAL: Social Panorama of Latin America, 2020

Table 4.10 Household Income Classes by Country (% of Total)

Country	Income Group	GINI Coefficient 2018	High Income	Middle-High	Middle-Middle	Middle-Low	Low—No Poverty	Poverty	Extreme Poverty
Uruguay	High Income	0.40	7.4	14.8	36.7	23.8	14.6	0.1	2.6
Panama		0.49	6.1	10.5	26.9	22.2	17.7	9.1	7.6
Chile		0.44	4.4	6.1	22.5	29.8	26.5	9.3	1.4
Costa Rica		0.48	6.2	9.2	22.5	23.5	23.5	11.8	3.3
Brazil		0.54	4.6	6.9	21.1	23.7	22.3	14.8	5.5
Paraguay	Mid Income	0.46	2.8	4.6	20.2	23.9	26.9	15.6	6.0
Peru		0.43	2.1	4.7	21.0	26.3	27.0	13.9	5.0
Colombia		0.50	2.6	3.9	14.4	21.2	28.1	18.9	10.9
Ecuador		0.45	1.7	3.8	16.8	24.0	30.0	16.7	7.0
Venezuela		0.47	1.5	3.3	13.9	22.5	33.7	18.6	6.4
Argentina		0.41	1.1	3.6	17.5	26.4	32.6	15.9	2.8
Mexico		0.46	1.1	2.2	8.7	15.3	29.0	32.1	11.7
Guatemala	Low Income	0.48	1.0	1.8	7.9	13.0	25.8	35.1	15.4
Nicaragua		0.46	1.0	1.5	6.5	14.3	30.3	28.0	18.3
Bolivia		0.42	0.7	2.8	12.8	21.3	27.4	18.8	16.4
The Dominican Republic		0.44	0.4	1.8	11.8	24.3	33.5	16.3	11.9
El Salvador		0.38	0.4	1.2	7.8	18.8	33.9	29.5	8.3
Haiti	Poor	—	—	—	—	—	—	—	—
Latin America		0.46	3.0	4.5	15.7	20.9	25.8	19.6	10.5

Source: Economic Commission for Latin America and the Caribbean – ECLAC. (2020a). *Social Panorama of Latin America, 2020*. https://www.cepal.org/en/publications/46688
-social-panorama-latin-america-2020

The results above vividly illustrate the inequality of income in Latin America—one of the starkest gaps in the world, as was discussed in Chapter 1. The Gini index of inequality for the region was 0.46 in 2019. The analysis of household incomes by country provides a more refined picture of income inequality (see Table 4.10). The countries with greater concentration of high-income households are Uruguay, Panama, Chile, Costa Rica, and Brazil. Most of these countries, except Brazil, have small populations. Countries with dominant middle classes are Peru, Paraguay, Argentina, Ecuador, Colombia, and Venezuela. These countries have affluent households but not as many as the shares of the first group of countries. The rest of the Latin American countries have reasonable middle-income classes, but the share of the lower income households is higher. For example, in Mexico, 26.2% of households are middle income, but 61% are low income. Most of these countries also have substantial rural populations.

In terms of income distribution measured by the GINI coefficient, the countries with the worst inequality are Brazil, Honduras, Colombia, and Panama. The rest of the countries converge to the region's mean of 0.46, with El Salvador well below that mean (0.38).

Health Status of Latin America

The health status of the region is mixed. On the positive side, life expectancy has been rising and infant mortality declining. On the negative side, gross mortality for all causes has remained high. The gross mortality rate measured by the total number of deaths per year per thousand of population remains stubbornly high at 6.7% (not including the deaths from the 2020 pandemic) (see Table 4.11). In this section, we examine the region's health conditions further.

Causes of Death

Worldwide, the main causes of death before the 2020 pandemic were cardiovascular (31.8%), cancers (17%), and respiratory diseases (7%). Latin America is no different and non-communicable diseases are the dominant cause of death. Expressed in cases per 100,000 people, cardiovascular diseases are the number one cause at 83.5 per 100,000, followed by cerebrovascular diseases at 35.8 per 100,000, and diabetes with 32.9 per 100,000 (see Table 4.11).

The cause of death by country reveals both similarities and differences (see Table 4.11). Cardiovascular disease is the number one cause of death in all Latin American countries except for Peru and Guatemala, where it is number two. Stroke is the second cause of death in a number of countries: Chile, Costa Rica, Cuba, the Dominican Republic, Panama, and Paraguay. Stroke is the third source in Argentina, Bolivia, Brazil, Colombia, and Peru. Lower respiratory disease is the number two source in Argentina, Bolivia, Brazil, Honduras, Uruguay, and Venezuela, and it is number one in Peru and third in Cuba and Ecuador. The predominance of these three large causes of death suggests common drivers of health risks and conditions in the region that will be explained later.

The other top ten causes of death are more particular for each country and may be the result of local environmental conditions, population characteristics, and lifestyles. For instance, cancer seems to have a greater incidence in Argentina, Cuba, and Uruguay. Diabetes has a higher incidence in the Dominican Republic, Guatemala, Honduras, Panama, Paraguay, and Venezuela. Chronic kidney disease is high in Chile, Costa Rica, Ecuador, El Salvador, Honduras, Mexico, Paraguay, and Peru. Other diseases seem to be unique to one

Table 4.11 Top Ten Causes of Death in Latin America

Cause	Arg.	Bol.	Bra.	Chile	Col.	Costa Rica	Cuba	Dom. Rep.	Ecua.	El Salv.	Guat.	Haiti	Hond.	Mex.	Pan.	Parag.	Peru	Uru.	Ven.
Ischemic Heart D.	1	2	1	1	1	1	1	1	1	1	2	1	1	1	1	1	2	1	1
Lower Respiratory Infection	2	1	2	6	7	10	3	8	4	4	1	3	2	9	6	6	1	2	2
Stroke	3	3	3	2	3	2	2	2	3	6	7	2	—	5	2	2	3	5	—
COPD	4	9	4	7	4	5	6	—	9	10	—	—	6	6	7	8	—	3	7
Chronic Kidney D.	5	4	9	4	6	3	10	7	2	2	5	10	4	3	—	4	4	8	5
Lung Cancer	6	—	—	9	—	9	4	—	—	—	—	—	8	—	—	9	—	4	10
Colorectal Cancer	7	—	7	5	5	4	8	4	5	7	—	—	—	8	5	7	5	6	6
Alzheimer	8	7	6	—	9	—	5	—	—	5	3	6	—	—	3	3	8	7	4
Diabetes	9	6	—	10	—	—	—	—	—	—	—	—	—	2	4	—	—	10	—
Breast Cancer	10	—	—	—	—	—	—	—	—	—	—	—	—	—	—	—	—	—	—
Cirrhosis	—	—	10	3	—	7	—	5	7	8	6	5	5	4	—	—	6	—	—
Neonatal D.	—	5	—	—	—	—	—	3	—	—	10	—	7	—	—	—	10	—	—
Stomach Cancer	—	8	8	8	10	6	—	—	8	—	8	—	—	—	—	—	7	—	—
Road Injuries	—	10	—	—	8	8	—	6	6	9	—	—	10	10	10	5	9	—	8
Interpersonal Violence	—	—	5	—	2	—	—	9	—	3	4	9	3	7	8	—	—	—	3
Falls	—	—	—	—	—	—	7	—	—	—	—	—	—	—	—	—	—	—	—
Prostate Cancer	—	—	—	—	—	—	9	—	—	—	—	—	—	—	—	—	—	9	—
Hypertensive Heart D.	—	—	—	—	—	—	—	10	10	—	9	—	—	—	—	10	—	—	9
Diarrheal D.	—	—	—	—	—	—	—	—	—	—	—	7	9	—	—	—	—	—	—
HIV	—	—	—	—	—	—	—	—	—	—	—	4	—	—	9	—	—	—	—
Congenital Defects	—	—	—	—	—	—	—	—	—	—	—	8	—	—	—	—	—	—	—

Source: Institute for Health Metrics and Evaluation – IHME. www.healthdata.org

or two countries. For instance, HIV in Panama (9th), breast cancer in Argentina (10th) and prostate cancer in Cuba (7th). Notably, interpersonal violence is a major cause of death in Colombia (2nd), El Salvador (3rd), Honduras (3rd) and Venezuela (3rd), Honduras (4th) and Guatemala (4th), and to a lesser extent Brazil (5th).

Road traffic homicides are an important cause of death in the region. Traffic accidents are high in Brazil, Ecuador, El Salvador, Paraguay, the Dominican Republic, and Venezuela. We will explore the drivers of this cause later, but one possible culprit is alcohol consumption. Homicides and violence are also a major problem in Central American countries; three countries in the region rank among the most violent in the world: El Salvador (1), Venezuela (3), and Honduras (4). Other countries with violent profiles are Venezuela, Brazil, Colombia, and Mexico. All these countries suffer from endemic problems of drug traffic, the presence of drug cartels, and seemingly intractable armed conflicts. Suicide in the region is not a major problem compared to the other sources of death. The gross rate of suicide per 100,000 in the region was 9.8%, which is low compared to that of Europe at 15.4% (PAHO, 2019), with the higher incidence found in Uruguay, Cuba, and El Salvador.

Health Risks

Lifestyles of Latin Americans are, to a great extent, the drivers of the diseases mentioned above. Other drivers are external but impact the health of Latin Americans, such as access to basic services of water and sanitation and the poor environmental conditions of Latin American cities (Global Health Intelligence, 2021). We summarize lifestyles and drivers of diseases in Table 4.12.

Obesity is an indication of poor diets, sedentary lifestyles, and large intake of calories. Infant obesity is an early indication of a family environment supporting lifestyle choices, particularly the consumption of sugars and fats. The WHO estimates that 18% of children under five are obese worldwide (WHO, 2020a). This obesity epidemic is associated with the high consumption of soft drinks, fast food, and processed foods. In the region, obesity in children under 5 years of age is high in Argentina, Bolivia, Chile, Paraguay, and Panama. Their obesity levels are much higher than the 7.5% average for the region (PAHO, 2019). By the time children reach the age of 5–19 years old, other countries also show high obesity levels among their youth: Costa Rica, the Dominican Republic, Mexico, Peru, and Uruguay. Adult obesity follows the youth epidemic; consistently, countries with obesity among the young also show obesity among adults except for Colombia, El Salvador, and Nicaragua. For the latter countries, their children and youth are not obese, but adults have increased their levels of obesity on par with the rest of the region.

In terms of soft drink consumption, Mexico has the sad record of having the highest consumption per capita in the world. Unfortunately for the region, Brazil ranks third, and Chile and Argentina are in the top ten (Statista, 2020). In addition, the consumption of fruits and vegetables per capita in these countries is low in comparison with other countries in the region. Thus, it seems that a combination of poor diets and sedentary styles may lead to higher obesity levels in the countries mentioned above. The connection between obesity and cardiovascular diseases and diabetes is well supported in the literature (Basu et.al, 2013). It is worth highlighting the 'leaner' countries in the region: Brazil, Colombia, and Cuba. These countries seem to enjoy higher consumption of fruits and vegetables and likely more active lifestyles.

Alcohol consumption is another driver of disease risk. Alcohol consumption in Argentina, Chile, Uruguay, and Panama is higher than the average for the region of 7.8 liters per year

Table 4.12 Drivers of Health Risks

Risk	Arg	Bol	Bra	Chile	Col	Costa Rica	Cuba	Dom Rep	Ecu	El Sal	Guat	Haiti	Hond	Mex	Pan	Par	Peru	Uru	Ven
Tobacco	1	9	3	3	5	5	1	6	8	10	10	—	8	8	8	4	—	1	5
High BP	2	5	2	2	3	1	4	2	3	3	6	3	1	3	3	3	4	2	2
Dietary Risks	3	6	5	6	4	4	5	5	5	6	8	6	6	5	5	5	6	3	4
Obesity	4	2	1	1	2	2	3	3	1	2	5	8	4	2	2	1	2	4	3
High Glucose	5	3	4	4	1	3	2	4	2	1	2	4	2	1	1	2	3	5	1
Alcohol Use	6	8	6	5	7	7	7	8	7	5	3	9	9	6	7	6	7	6	8
Malnutrition	7	1	7	—	6	9	—	1	4	7	1	1	3	7	4	7	1	10	7
High LDL	8	10	8	9	10	8	6	7	10	9	—	10	10	10	10	10	—	7	10
Kidney Dysfunction	9	7	9	8	9	6	9	10	6	4	7	—	7	4	6	8	8	9	6
Occupational Risk	10	—	—	10	—	—	8	—	—	—	—	—	—	—	—	—	9	8	—
Air Pollution	—	4	10	7	8	10	10	9	9	8	4	2	5	9	—	9	5	—	9
Water Sanitation and Hygiene	—	—	—	—	—	—	—	—	—	9	—	5	—	—	—	—	—	—	—
Unsafe Sex	—	—	—	—	—	—	—	—	—	—	—	7	—	—	9	—	10	—	—

Source: Institute for Health Metrics and Evaluation, www.healthdata.org

in 2018. Alcohol consumption has been associated with high blood pressure, heart disease, stroke, liver disease, and digestive problems as well as impaired driving.

Health Systems and Infrastructure

The readiness of Latin American countries to handle health risks was put to the test with the pandemic of 2020. Prior to the pandemic, the countries with higher investments in health measured as a percent of GDP were Argentina, Brazil, Chile, Uruguay, and Costa Rica (see Table 4.13). A second tier of countries with high investments included Mexico, Cuba, and Panama. On the other end of the scale, countries with low investments in health were the Dominican Republic, Venezuela, and Haiti. Another metric to gauge the robustness of a health system is health expenditures per capita. This indicator removes the size of the country and allows the true comparison of small and large countries under the same standard. Using this second proxy, Chile with $2.305 per capita and Cuba with $2.519 are the countries committing greater resources to health in the region. These countries invest 16.1 and 17.6 times more than the poorest country in the region, Haiti with $143 per capita. Other countries with high expenditures per capita are Uruguay ($2,169) and Argentina ($1,989). Using both approaches, we conclude that Argentina, Brazil, Chile, Uruguay, Cuba, Mexico, and Panama are better prepared to deal with health crises.

In terms of health infrastructure, the countries with higher investments in health also have more hospital beds, doctors, and nurses. Density of hospital beds is higher in Cuba with

Table 4.13 Health Systems in Latin America

Country	Health Expenditures		Universal Health Coverage	Doctors per 10,000	Nurses per 10,000	Hospital Beds per 10,000
	% of GDP	US$ Per Capita				
Argentina	9.6	1,929.6	76	39.9	26.0	5.0
Bolivia	6.3	496.0	64	15.9	15.6	1.3
Brazil	9.5	1550.8	78	21.6	101.2	2.1
Chile	9.1	2305.7	66	25.9	133.2	2.1
Colombia	7.6	1155.4	76	21.8	13.3	1.7
Costa Rica	7.6	1336.5	76	28.9	34.1	1.1
Cuba	11.2	2519.3	81	84.2	75.6	5.3
The Dominican Republic	2.8	—	74	15.3	13.8	0.9
Ecuador	8.1	954.8	76	20.4	25.1	1.4
El Salvador	7.1	542.3	75	15.7	18.3	1.2
Guatemala	5.7	483.0	57	3.5	0.7	0.4
Haiti	7.7	143.6	47	2.3	6.8	0.7*
Honduras	7.0	362.3	66	3.1	7.4	0.6
Mexico	5.4	1066.0	76	23.8	24.0	1.0
Nicaragua	8.6	473.9	71	9.8	15.3	0.9
Panama	7.3	1856.7	76	15.7	30.7	2.3
Paraguay	6.7	935.3	68	13.5	16.6	0.8
Peru	5.2	766.6	77	13.0	24.4	1.6
Uruguay	9.2	2169.3	79	50.8	19.0	2.4
Venezuela	3.6	383.5	73	77	9.4	0.9
Latin America	8.0	473.9	—	24.0	5.1	1.9

Source: Pan American Health Organization (PAHO): Health Trends in the Americas – Core Indicators, 2019.

5.3 beds per 10,000. Other countries with high densities but with only one-half the density of Cuba are Argentina (5.0), Brazil (2.1), Chile (2.1), Uruguay (2.4), and Panama (2.3). The rest of the region has a low density of hospital beds with the lowest being in Honduras (0.6) and Mexico (0.7). With respect to the density of doctors, Cuba is far ahead of any country in the region with 84.2 doctors per 10,000 people. Despite its low investments in health, Venezuela also shows a high density of doctors (77 per 10,000 people). Other countries with high densities are Uruguay (50.8) and Argentina (39.9). The rest of Latin America had much lower densities of doctors. Haiti and Honduras have 2.3 and 3.1 doctors per 10,000 people, respectively. Brazil and Chile have an advantage to the rest of the region with respect to the density of nurses with 133.2 and 101.2 nurses per 10,000 people, respectively (OECD, 2020; World Health Organization -WHO, 2020).

In terms of health coverage, Cuba reaches 84% of its population. Coverage for the rest of the region ranges from 47%–78% of the population. Thus, between 25% and 53% of Latin Americans do not count on some form of health protection. Central America has the most acute coverage deficit.

This brief analysis of the health infrastructure of Latin America shows that the countries with greater preparedness to deal with a health crisis, such as the pandemic of 2020, were Argentina, Brazil, Chile, Uruguay, Cuba, Mexico, and Panama. The large disruption created by the 2020 pandemic tested this assumption. The rapid spread of the COVID-19 virus pushed the regional health systems to the brink of collapse, as all countries implemented drastic health measures to contain the infection and its deadly consequences. The human and economic impacts were catastrophic. Countries with greater urban densities and large informal economic systems were particularly vulnerable, such as Peru and Colombia. The multigenerational housing conditions as well as shantytowns with no access to clean water and lack of sewage offered the perfect conditions for the spread of the virus. Furthermore, the need to generate daily earnings pushed many Latin Americans to leave their homes on a daily basis, using public transportation, exposing themselves to the virus on a daily basis. Poor people, unable to afford proper food refrigeration, were forced to frequent informal food markets on a daily basis; these unregulated markets became prime centers of infection. The health systems in Latin America were overtasked with the surge of sick people looking for treatment and unable to control the spread.

The impact of the COVID-19 pandemic of 2020–2021 was catastrophic for Latin America. Table 4.14 provides a snapshot of the impact. This assessment is not a full picture of the situation as the data changes on a daily basis. Adjusting cases and mortality by the size of the population, we can group the Latin American countries in the following impact groups (insufficient data to include Nicaragua):

High infection–high mortality: Brazil, Argentina, Chile, Colombia, and Peru
High infection–low mortality: Uruguay, Panama, Paraguay, and Costa Rica
Low infection–high mortality: Mexico and Ecuador
Low infection–low mortality: Cuba, El Salvador, Guatemala, Venezuela, the Dominican
   Republic, Haiti, Bolivia, and Honduras

It is interesting to note that the countries with better readiness to sustain a health crisis were also the most impacted and had higher mortality rates except for Cuba. Countries with the highest mortality rates were Peru and Brazil. An additional factor to observe was the weak response from public leaders in Brazil that translated into denial of the pandemic and a weak public health response to curtail the infections. Brazil became one of the worst cases in the

Table 4.14 Impact of COVID-19 Pandemic in Latin America

Country	Total Cases (Thousands)	Total Deaths (Thousands)	Cases per 1 Million Population	Deaths per Million	Vaccines per 100 People	% Population Fully Vaccinated	ICU Beds**	ICUs per 100,000	Ventilators**	Ventilators per 100,000**	Economic Contraction 2020 (% of GDP)***
Argentina	3,977	81.9	87,263	1,798	17.0	2.8	8,444	19.2	9,000	20.4	(10.9)
Bolivia	389.9	15	32,991	1,276	5.5	2.1	—	—	—	—	(8.0)
Brazil	16,984	474	79,385	8,318	22	7.2	55,000	26	65,411	31	(5.3)
Chile	1,440	30.1	47,882	3,265	82	37	2,300	12.1	1,520	8	(6.0)
Colombia	3,593	92.5	69,919	1,800	6.9	3.5	5,349	10.7	5,500	11	(7.0)
Costa Rica	331.9	4.2	64,608	823	12	6.8	140	2.74	450	8.8	(4.8)
Cuba	151.2	1	13,362	91	—	—	1,183	2.7	663	3.8	(8.5)
The Dominican Republic	302.9	3.6	27,672	335	14	7.5	—	—	—	—	(5.5)
Ecuador	432.7	20.8	24,186	1,163	5.3	1.5	—	—	—	—	(9.6)
El Salvador	74	2.2	11,377	350	15	2.4	—	—	—	—	(8.6)
Guatemala	262.2	8.3	14,391	456	1.1	<0.1	—	—	—	—	(2.5)
Haiti	15.9	0.3	1,378	29	—	—	—	—	—	—	—
Honduras	242.3	6.4	24,115	646	—	<0.1	—	—	—	—	(8.0)
Mexico	2,434	228	18,669	1,758	11	7.1	4,291	3.37	6,175	4.86	(8.5)
Nicaragua	—	—	—	—	2.1	—	—	—	—	—	(4.0)
Panama	382.8	6.4	87,450	1,463	12	5.9	—	—	—	—	(11.0)
Paraguay	375.9	10	52,120	1,387	1.9	0.2	—	—	—	—	(0.6)
Peru	1,984	186.7	59,433	5,592	4.0	2.0	820	2.64	900	2.90	(12.9)
Uruguay	318.7	4.6	91,474	1,346	52	22	—	—	—	—	(4.5)
Venezuela	243.6	2.7	8,590	96	0.9	—	—	—	—	—	(30.0)
Latin America	174,000	3,740	—	—	—	—	—	—	—	—	—
World	173,738	3,739	—	—	—	—	—	—	—	—	—

Sources:
Worldometers – https://www.worldometers.info/coronavirus/ accessed on June 8, 2021.
John Hopkins, coronavirus resource center. https://coronavirus.jhu.edu/map.html, accessed on June 8, 2021.
New York Times, Coronavirus World Map, accessed on April 9, 2021.
WHO: https://www.who.int/data/gho/data/indicators
World Bank: https://databank.worldbank.org/home.aspx

world in terms of total infections and a source of a virus variance that spread throughout their neighboring countries and the world. Peru had one the worst mortality rates in the world.

Countries with low infection and high mortality were Mexico and Ecuador. The case of Ecuador showed the impact of the early spread of the virus and lack of readiness for the surge of infections. Ecuadorian health systems collapsed, and the lack of treatment resulted in high mortality rates. The case of Mexico showed the denial of government leaders and health policy administrators to admit the seriousness of the pandemic and the undercounting of cases. It was difficult to assess the true impact of cases early in the pandemic, as the official numbers were suspect. The high mortality rate, however, was an undeniable indicator that the situation was worse than the official version.

Countries with high infection and low mortality rates were Uruguay, Panama, Paraguay, and Costa Rica—an interesting mix of countries, as Uruguay is highly urbanized, whereas the others have large rural populations. They all share a small population and geography.

Countries with low infection and low mortality rates have lower levels of urbanization and include a variety of countries in Central America, Cuba, and Bolivia. Lower levels of population density may have deterred the virus's spread. Cuba's particular geography as an island allowed them to have better control of their borders, minimizing the risk of external contagion. In addition, Cuba's greater investments in health infrastructure helped to adequately deal with the cases and to reduce mortality as well as to develop five COVID-19 vaccines that were fully tested and aimed at vaccinating the entire population by the end of 2021.

All countries in the region suffered an economic contraction during the 2020–2021 period. The worst impacts in terms of annual contraction of the GDP were in Venezuela (−30%), Peru (−12.9%), Panama (−11%), and Argentina (−10.9%). Countries that had a lower impact were Nicaragua (−4.0%), Guatemala (−2.5%), Uruguay (−4.5%), and Costa Rica (−4.8%).

In sum, the pandemic of 2020–2021 challenged the region's economic, social, and health systems and compromised recovery over the long term.

Summary

The region's population is in transition to an older population. Some countries in the region have a demographic profile similar to European societies, whereas others are younger. The slowdown of the region's population growth is principally due to falling fertility rates, increased life expectancy, and reduction of overall mortality. With better health services, life expectancy has increased gradually to 75.2 years. With better nutrition and access to basic services, mortality rates have declined from a high of 48 per 1,000 in 1990 to 15 per 1,000 in 2020. Thus, the demographic dividend that partially fueled the economic growth of Latin America has long been subsiding. In the future, Latin America is bound to reach a stage of advanced demographic transition and join the fate of European countries and Japan. By 2030, life expectancy in the region will reach 77 years and 80.5 years by 2050. Birth rates per 1,000 will continue to decrease and reach a low of 11.2 in 2050. The aging of the population will not bode well for Latin America, as the region is not prepared for the challenges of providing healthcare, economic support, and housing for a larger elderly population.

Although the region as a whole is in Stage 3 of demographic transformation, there are significant variations across countries. Uruguay and Chile show advanced stages of transformation with low levels of fertility, high life expectancy, and high levels of urbanization. By contrast, other countries (e.g., Honduras and Guatemala) exhibit younger populations, high levels of fertility, and substantial rural populations.

Latin America has experienced a net outflow of migration. The US is the largest and preferred destination for Latin Americans. The share of immigrants from Latin America into the US has increased from 20% in the 1970s to 50% in 2018 in terms of annual flows. Mexicans are the largest group among Latin Americans immigrating into the US with 11%, Central Americans are second with 8%, and South Americans represent 7%. Intra-regional migration is also on the increase. The greater and more stable the economic opportunities of a country, the more attractive to people from neighboring countries. Recent increases in intra-regional migration emanate from the collapse of the Venezuelan and Haitian societies in 2015–2020. Through 2019, about 5.4 million Venezuelans (19% of its population) decided to leave their country. Of the total, 4.6 million Venezuelans have migrated to other Latin American countries.

Latin America has made substantial progress in education. In 2018, the region's literacy rate was 98.5% greater than the world average of 86.3%. However, public expenditures in Latin America (4%) are behind the world's average of 4.59% of GDP. The learning outcomes of students in the region, compared with those of other regions, also showed that Latin American countries are behind the average for the OECD countries on all subjects.

Latin America has lost its innocence of the assumption of racial and ethnic harmony. The historical effort to achieve racial mixture under the guise of nation-building has resulted in masked racism and discrimination, but the invisibility of racism has been unmasked. The pressure to end violence and brutality against Afro-descendants and Indigenous groups has raised awareness of the plight of these minorities among all levels of society. The current social discourse calls for inclusiveness, justice, dignity, and tolerance. There is hope that the future will bring more equal representation and fair distribution of equal access to opportunities to all groups in Latin America (ECLAC 2020c; Marczak & Engelke 2016).

The region continues its relentless process of urbanization. In contrast to 55% of the world, Latin America is 83% urban. By 2050, it is estimated that 68% of the world and 88% of Latin America will be urbanized. Urbanization in Latin America is related to lower fertility rates, late childbearing age, and an increase of the older population. Six megacities account for 18% of the region's urban population. Mexico City and Sao Paulo, Brazil with 22 million each are among the world's ten largest urban agglomerations. Latin American cities suffer from sprawl, poor transportation systems, and high levels of crime among other failures. This process of unplanned growth has created concentric zones of residential and commercial hubs around the major central core of a Latin American city in what has been referred to as a commercial spine and elite residential sector.

The composition of a typical Latin American household depends on whether the people sharing the same house are related or not. The typical Latin American family is multigenerational, and this type of household accounts for 32% of all households. The more standard household of two-parents and siblings living together accounts for 39% of all households. The empty nest household accounts for 6%, whereas the household with a single parent living with children accounts for 10%. Households of a single person represent 3% of all. The remaining 10% include all other types of household sharing arrangements. Single women raising children in single-parent households in Latin America is a common phenomenon. Variation of household concentrations in Latin American cities is large. In fact, five countries account for 78% of all households in the region (Brazil, Mexico, Colombia, Argentina, and Peru). These five countries comprise the bulk of markets for all types of goods and services.

In 2017, 3% of households in Latin America were in the highest income class with an estimated annual household income at $54,100. The next group comprised middle-income households (high, middle, and low) which represented 46% of the total population with incomes ranging from $22,600 to $8,600. About 45% of households are low income, and 10.5% are considered extremely poor (less than US$1 per week). The total market power of all classes, excluding those in extreme poverty, is estimated at US$2.01 trillion. The 3% of high-income households account for 23.5% of market power. The countries with greater concentration of high-income households are Uruguay, Panama, Chile, Costa Rica, and Brazil.

The health status of the region is mixed. On the positive side, life expectancy has been rising and infant mortality declining. On the negative side, gross mortality for all causes remains high. The gross mortality rate measured by the total number of deaths per year per thousand of the population remains stubbornly high at 6.7% (not including the deaths from the 2020 pandemic). Cardiovascular disease is the number one cause of death in all Latin American countries, except for Peru and Guatemala where it is number two. Stroke (second source of death in Chile, Costa Rica, Cuba, the Dominican Republic, Panama, and Paraguay and third source in Argentina, Bolivia, Brazil, Colombia, and Peru) and lower respiratory disease (number two source in Argentina, Bolivia, Brazil, Honduras, Uruguay, and Venezuela; number one in Peru; and third in Cuba and Ecuador) make up the top three causes of death. Lifestyles of Latin Americans are to a great extent the drivers of diseases including poor diets, sedentary lifestyles, and large intake of calories and alcohol. Other external drivers include poor access to basic services of water and sanitation and the poor environmental conditions of Latin American cities.

The countries with higher investments in health measured as a percent of GDP were Argentina, Brazil, Chile, Uruguay, and Costa Rica. A second tier of countries with high investments comprises Mexico, Cuba, and Panama. On the other end of the scale, countries with low investments in health are the Dominican Republic, Venezuela, and Haiti. The pandemic of 2020–2021 challenged the region's economic, social, and health systems. Paradoxically, countries with better readiness to sustain a health crisis were the most impacted and had higher mortality rates, except for Cuba. The denial of the pandemic from public leaders in Brazil and Mexico translated into a weak public health response to curtail the infections. Brazil became one of the worst cases in the world in terms of total infections and deaths and a source of a virus variance that spread throughout their neighboring countries and the world. Peru had one the worst mortality rates in the world. All countries in the region suffered an economic contraction during the 2020–2021 period from which they are still recovering.

References

Basu, S., McKee, M., Galea, G., & Stuckler, D. (2013). Relationship of soft drink consumption to global overweight, obesity, and diabetes: A cross-national analysis of 75 countries. *American Journal of Public Health.* 103(11), 2071–2077.

Bonilla-Silva, E. (1997). Rethinking racism: Toward a structural interpretation. *American Sociological Review*, 62(3), 465–480.

Brea, J. A. (2003). Population dynamics in Latin America. *Population Bulletin*, 58(1).

Comisión Económica para América Latina y el Caribe - CEPAL. (2018). *Observatorio Demográfico de América Latina 2018: Migración internacional.* https://www.cepal.org/es/publicaciones/44411 -observatorio-demografico-america-latina-2018-migracion-internacional-demographic

Corrales, J. (2019). Welcoming Venezuelans: A scorecard of responses from Latin American countries to the Venezuelan migration. *Americas Quarterly*. https://www.americasquarterly.org/article/responses-to-the-venezuelan-migration-crisis-a-scorecard/

Council on Foreign Relations - CFR. (2019). *Where do Venezuelans Migrants Go?* https://www.cfr.org/in-brief/venezuelan-exodus

Degler, C. (1986). *Neither Black nor White: Slavery and race relations in the United States and Brazil.* Madison, WI: University of Wisconsin Press.

Economic Commission for Latin America and the Caribbean - ECLAC. (2019b). *Statistical yearbook for Latin America and the Caribbean.*

Economic Commission for Latin America and the Caribbean - ECLAC. (2020a). *Social Panorama of Latin America.* https://www.cepal.org/en/publications/46688-social-panorama-latin-america-2020

Economic Commission for Latin America and the Caribbean - ECLAC. (2020b). *Afrodescendants and the matrix of social inequality in Latin America.*

Economic Commission for Latin America and the Caribbean (ECLAC, (2020c). Guaranteeing indigenous people's right in Latin America: Progress in the past decade and remaining challenges.

Economic Commission for Latin America and the Caribbean - ECLAC, (2020d). Education in the time of COVID-19.

Freyre, G. (1951). *Brazil: An interpretation.* New York: Alfred Knopf.

Freyre, G. (1956). *The masters and the slaves: Casa grande e senzala: A study in the development of Brazilian civilization* (2nd ed., English Language ed.). New York: Knopf.

Freyre, G. (1966). *The mansions and the shanties: The making of modern Brazil.* New York: Knopf.

Freyre, G. (1970). *Order and progress: Brazil from monarchy to republic.* New York: Knopf.

Graham, R. (1990). *The idea of race in Latin America, 1870–1940.* Austin: University of Texas Press.

Griffin, E., & Ford, L. (1980). A model of Latin American city structure. *Geographical Review, 70*(4). 397–422.

Global Health Intelligence. (2021). *5 mega trends in Latin America healthcare.* https://globalhealthintelligence.com/5-mega-trends-in-latin-american-healthcare/

Instituto Brasileiro de Geografia e Estatística - IBGE. (2020). *Population census.* Retrieved on February 14, 2021. https://www.ibge.gov.br/en/statistics/social/population/22836-2020-census-censo4.html?=&t=o-que-e

International Monetary Fund - IMF. (2018). *Growing pains- Is Latin America prepared for population aging?* https://www.imf.org/en/Publications/Departmental-Papers-Policy-Papers/Issues/2018/04/16/Growing-Pains-Is-Latin-American-Prepared-for-Population-Aging-45382

Instituto Nacional de Estadística, Geografía e Informática - INEGI. (2021). *Población.* Retrieved on February 14, 2021 https://www.inegi.org.mx/datos/?t=0200

Instituto Nacional de Estadística e Informática - INEI. (2018). *Peru.* Retrieved on February 14, 2021. https://www.inei.gob.pe/media/MenuRecursivo/publicaciones_digitales/Est/Lib1544/00TOMO_01.pdf

Instituto Nacional de Estadística e Informática - INEI. (2021). *Censos de Población y Vivienda.* Chile. Retrieved on February 14, 2021. https://www.ine.cl/estadisticas/sociales/censos-de-poblacion-y-vivienda

International Monetary Fund – IMF (2020). Republica Bolivariana de Venezuela- Country Profile. https://www.imf.org/en/Countries/VEN

John Hopkins. (n.d.). *Coronavirus Resource Center.* Retrieved on June 8, 2021. https://coronavirus.jhu.edu/map.html

Marczak, J., & Engelke, P. (2016). Latin America and the Caribbean 2030: Future scenarios. *Inter-American Development Bank.* https://publications.iadb.org/publications/english/document/Latin-America-and-the-Caribbean-2030-Future-Scenarios.pdf

Marx, A. W. (1998). *Making race and nation: A comparison of the United States, South Africa and Brazil* (1st ed.). New York: Cambridge University Press.

Mead, T. (2004). *A brief history of Brazil.* New York: Checkmark Books.

Migration Data Portal. (2021). *Migration data in South America.* https://migrationdataportal.org/?i=stock_abs_&t=2020&m=2&sm49=5

Migration Policy Institute. (2020). *Venezuelan migrants and refugees in Latin America and the Caribbean: A regional profile.* https://www.migrationpolicy.org/research/venezuelans-latin-america -caribbean-regional-profile

Moraes Silva, G., & Saldivar, E. (2018). Comparing ideologies of racial mixing in Latin America: Brazil and Mexico. *Sociologia & Antropologia, 8*(2), 427–456. https://www.scielo.br/scielo.php?script=sci _arttext&pid=S2238-38752018000200427&lng=en&tlng=en

Muggah, R. (2018). Latin America's cities are ready to take off. But their infrastructure is failing them. *World Economic Forum - WEF.* https://www.weforum.org/agenda/2018/06/latin-america-cities -urbanization-infrastructure-failing-robert-muggah/

New York Times. (n.d.). *Coronavirus world map: Tracking the global outbreak.* Retrieved on April 9, 2021. https://www.nytimes.com/interactive/2021/world/covid-cases.html

Nobles, M. (2000). *Shades of citizenship: Race and the census in modern politics.* Stanford: Stanford University Press.

Organization for Economic Co-operation and Development - OECD. (2020). *Health at glance: Latin America and the Caribbean.* https://www.oecd.org/health/health-at-a-glance-latin-america-and-the -caribbean-2020-6089164f-en.htm

Organization for Economic Co-operation and Development - OECD. (n.d.). *PISA 2018 results.* https:// www.oecd.org/pisa/publications/pisa-2018-results.htm

Pan American Health Organization - PAHO. (2019). *Health trends in the Americas - Core indicators.* https://iris.paho.org/handle/10665.2/51542

Pew Research. (2016). *Afro-Latino: A deeply rooted identity among U.S. Hispanics.* https://www .pewresearch.org/fact-tank/2016/03/01/afro-latino-a-deeply-rooted-identity-among-u-s -hispanics/

Pew Research Center. (2018). *Facts on U.S. immigrants 2018.* https://www.pewresearch.org/hispanic /2020/08/20/facts-on-u-s-immigrants/

Pew Research Center. (2020a). *With millions confined to their homes worldwide, which living arrangements are most common?* https://www.pewresearch.org/fact-tank/2020/03/31/with-billions -confined-to-their-homes-worldwide-which-living-arrangements-are-most-common/

Pew Research Center. (2020b). *Origins of the U.S. immigrant population, 1960–2018.* https://www .pewresearch.org/hispanic/chart/origins-of-the-u-s-immigrant-population-1960-2018/

Population Reference Bureau - PRB. (2020). *World population data sheet.* https://interactives.prb.org /2020-wpds/

Statista (2020). Per capita consumption of carbonated soft drinks in most populated countries worldwide. https://www.statista.com/statistics/505794/cds-per-capita-consumption-in-worlds-top -ten-population-countries/

Socio-Economic Database for Latin America and the Caribbean - SEDLAC. (2021). *Statistics.* https:// www.cedlas.econo.unlp.edu.ar/wp/en/estadisticas/sedlac/estadisticas/

Souza, J., & Sinder, V.(Eds). (2005). *Imagining Brazil.* Lanham: Lexington Books.

Telles, E., Flores, R., & Urrea-Giraldo, F. (2015). Pigmentocracies: Educational inequality, skin color and census ethnoracial identification in eight Latin American countries. *Research in Social Stratification and Mobility, 40,* 39–58.

Telles, E., & Paschell, T. (2014, November). Who is Black, White, or mixed race? How skin color, status, and nation shape racial classification in Latin America. *American Journal of Sociology, 120*(3), 864–907.

Telles, E., & Torche, F. (2019, June). Varieties of indigeneity in the Americas. *Social Forces, 97*(4), 1543–1569.

UNESCO. (2019). *Que se espera que aprendan los estudiantes de América Latina: Análisis curricular del estudio regional.* http://uis.unesco.org.

UNESCO. (2020). *Global education monitoring report 2020: Inclusion and education.* https://en.unesco .org/gem-report/report/2020/inclusion

UNICEF-UNDP. (2020). *Latin America and the Caribbean. Covid-19 and primary and secondary education: The impact of the crisis and public policy implications for Latin America and the Caribbean.* UNDP-LAC C19 PDS No. 20. https://www.latinamerica.undp.org/content/rblac/en/home/library/

crisis_prevention_and_recovery/covid-19-y-educacion-primaria-y-secundaria--repercusiones-de-la-.html

United Nations. (2018a). *World urbanization prospects.* https://population.un.org/wup/

United Nations (2018b), World's cities in 2018. https://www.un.org/en/events/citiesday/assets/pdf/the_worlds_cities_in_2018_data_booklet.pdf

United Nations. (2019a). Volume I: Comprehensive tables and volume II: Demographic profiles. *World population prospects 2019.* https://population.un.org/wpp/Publications/Files/WPP2019_Volume-I_Comprehensive-Tables.pdf

United Nations. (2019b). *2018 revision of world urbanization prospects.* https://www.un.org/development/desa/publications/2018-revision-of-world-urbanization-prospects.html

United Nations. (2019c). *Database household size & composition, 2019.* https://population.un.org/Household/index.html#/countries/840

United Nations, ECLAC. (2020a). *Statistical yearbook for Latin American and the Caribbean.* https://www.cepal.org/en/publications/sy

United Nations, ECLAC. (2020b). https://www.cepal.org/en/topics/redatam/about-redatam

United Nations Population Division. (2020). *International migration 2020 highlights.* https://www.un.org/development/desa/pd/sites/www.un.org.development.desa.pd/files/undesa_pd_2020_international_migration_highlights.pdf

U.S. Congressional Research Service . (2020) *Indigenous people in Latin America: Statistical information.* https://crsreports.congress.gov/product/details?prodcode=R46225

Wade, P. (2010). *Race and ethnicity in Latin America* (2nd ed.). London: Pluto Press.

Wallace, A. (2020). La idea de que América Latina es menos racista que EE.UU. es falsa. *BBC News Mundo.* https://www.bbc.com/mundo/noticias-america-latina-52922526

Wase, P. (2021). Racismos latinoamericanos desde una perspectiva global. *Nueva Sociedad, 292* (Marzo-Abril), 0251-3552.

World Bank. (2015). *Indigenous Latin America in the twenty first century.* https://www.worldbank.org/en/region/lac/brief/indigenous-latin-america-in-the-twenty-first-century-brief-report-page

World Bank (2018). Afro-descendants in Latin America: Towards a framework of inclusion. https://documents1.worldbank.org/curated/en/896461533724334115/pdf/129298-7-8-2018-17-29-37-AfrodescendantsinLatinAmerica.pdf

World Bank (2019). Beyond borders: A look at the Venezuelan exodus. https://documents1.worldbank.org/curated/en/864341554879205879/pdf/Beyond-Borders-A-Look-at-the-Venezuelan-Exodus.pdf

World Bank. (2020a, February). *Pupil-teacher ratio, primary - Latin America & Caribbean.* https://data.worldbank.org/indicator/SE.PRM.ENRL.TC.ZS?locations=ZJ

World Bank. (2020b, September). *Government expenditure on education, total (% of GDP).* https://data.worldbank.org/indicator/SE.XPD.TOTL.GD.ZS

World Bank. (n.d.) Retrieved on January 8, 2021. https://databank.worldbank.org/home.aspx

World Health Organization - WHO. (2020). *World health statistics 2020: Monitoring health for the SDGs.* https://www.who.int/publications/i/item/9789240005105

World Health Organization - WHO. (n.d.). *Indicators.* Retrieved on September 27, 2021. https://www.who.int/data/gho/data/indicators

Worldometers. (2021, September 7). *Covid-19 coronavirus pandemic.* Retrieved on June 8, 2021. https://www.worldometers.info/coronavirus/

World Population Review (2020). https://worldpopulationreview.com/continents/south-america-population

5 The Sociocultural Environment of Latin America

Introduction

Culture is a fundamental aspect of society that shapes a range of individual, group, and organizational behaviors. Culture develops over time and through social interactions among members of a referent group. Latin American cultural values have been cemented by centuries of survival and socialization during colonial, republican, and modern times. Perhaps the most influential factor shaping Latin American long-term values is religion. Latin America has been characterized as conservative in terms of moral values, but the increase of non-religiosity has moved countries into more liberal and tolerant views on moral values associated with issues such as abortion, contraception, divorce, and sexual orientation. Regarding Latin American business culture, the legacy of European colonial heritage has created enduring organizational and decision-making styles characterized by concentration of power, multilevel hierarchical structures, strong networks of relationships, and paternalism.

In this chapter, we explore the manifestation of contemporary Latin American culture in general, and its business culture, in particular. The chapter is organized in six parts. The first part discusses key components of Latin American culture with an emphasis on values, beliefs, and the influence of religion. The second part reviews the historical roots of Latin American business culture and provides a description of it through the perspective of four well-known business cultural frameworks. The next section identifies the idiosyncratic manifestations of national cultures. The fourth section focuses on the influence of cultural norms and values on leadership styles. The fifth section discusses the status and roles of women as leaders in business organizations. The last section focuses on the important role of talent development as a significant source of competitive advantage. We argue that adopting culturally appropriate talent management practices is an essential capability for Latin American organizations wishing to pursue global competitiveness and achieve superior performance.

Latin American Culture

Cultural groups share language, symbols, values, beliefs, and norms. Values are abstract ideas and concepts that tend to be general and long lasting. Beliefs are more specific and reflect ideas or statements that people hold to be true. As such, beliefs can be influenced by others and new information and can be subject to change. Norms are guidelines for behavior or action in particular situations or contexts subject to the approval or disapproval of the referent group. Thus, the complex whole of collective values, beliefs, norms, and behaviors

DOI: 10.4324/9781003182672-7

contributes to the survival and well-being of individuals and groups. We discuss these cultural components next.

Values

Compared to other world regions, Latin America has traditional and moderate self-expression values. These are the dimensions used by the World Values Survey Project, which analyzes cross-cultural variation in the world (Inglehart–Welzel World Cultural Map, 2020). Using a few indicators of values and beliefs, the authors identified two dimensions that reveal variation among world regions. One dimension contrasted traditional versus secular values, capturing the importance of religion, family, authority, and nationalism in societies. Traditional value societies place great importance on religion and family and stand against divorce, abortion, and nationalism. In secular societies, religion has lower importance, and there is greater tolerance of different moral values and more openness to freedom of expression. The other dimension of the cultural map captures the split between survival and self-expression values. Survival values place a premium on economic and physical security. Societies with strong survival values have lower levels of trust and tolerance of outsiders and diversity. Such priorities are attempts to maximize survival and minimize the risks of a highly uncertain world. Thus, these societies emphasize traditional gender roles and adherence to rules and norms. In contrast, self-expression societies focus on personal well-being, human autonomy and choice, and are more open to change, diversity, and participation in social discourse. A shift from survival to self-expression indicates an increase in existential security and human autonomy. This shift requires greater levels of trust and tolerance. Such empowerment in self-expression values strengthens civil society and political freedom and, consequently, greater value is given to democracy.

Based on a mapping of world values, the authors identified eight major cultural groups (see Figure 5.1). In this chart, a horizontal shift from left to right moves a country from survival to self-expression. Such a move seems to be linked to increased standards of well-being associated with increased economic growth and wealth. Having resolved issues of economic and physical security, these societies seem to embrace greater personal self-expression values. A vertical shift moves a country from traditional to secular. Such shifts relate to the dominant religious, philosophical, and political ideas at given times. Once established, the dominant ideas become part of a country's institutions, educational systems, and even media, giving countries their national character. A diagonal move from the origin to the upper right corner reflects the changes that a society may undergo in both dimensions and indicates the impact of modernization on society.

Inglehart and Welzel describe Latin America as a traditional culture and one in transition from survival to self-expression values; such characterization is due to the legacy of colonial rule and the dominant role of the Catholic Church. Within this general description, there is cultural variation within the region. For instance, Uruguay could be part of Catholic Europe and has a similar profile as Poland; Argentina is not far behind and has a similar outlook as Portugal; Chile is grouped with the West and South Asia cultural region, and Brazil is closer to South Africa. In contrast, Nicaragua, Ecuador, Colombia, and Venezuela are the countries with the most traditional cultural values and with similar self-expression values. The country that is most representative of Latin American cultural values is Mexico, as it is in the middle of the region's map. Using information from this project, we analyze the values among Latin American countries starting with the importance of religion in shaping them.

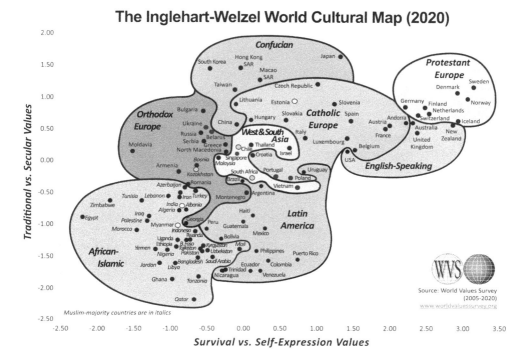

Figure 5.1 The Inglehart–Welzel world values cultural map

Influence of Religion

The Catholic Church has enjoyed a religious monopoly for five centuries since its arrival with Spanish colonizers. Up and until the early 1970s, 90% of Latin Americans identified as Catholic. In more recent estimates, the percentage declaring Catholicism as their primary faith is in the range of 65%–69% depending on the source and year of the estimates (Pew Research, 2014; Rodriguez Cuadros, 2018). In about 50 years, the Catholic Church has sustained a staggering loss of 31%–35% share of its worshipers. This erosion is the result of 1) increasing secularization, 2) the switching of current Catholic members to other faiths, and 3) crisis in the Catholic Church. We explore the drivers of this erosion, and then assess the different impacts of these changes in the region and by country.

1. *Increasing Secularization*: increased levels of urbanization and economic growth have had an impact on lifestyles. With more complex and hurried lifestyles, Latin Americans have gradually reduced the importance of religion as a central driver of family life and activities. With more prosperity, an emphasis on material life and entertainment has left less time for religious practice, particularly among the middle class. Such a change in priorities may explain the increase in secularization in the region with more people asserting that they do not profess a religious faith, particularly a Christian one.
2. *Rise of Evangelical Christians*: some Latin Americans who would like to remain Christian are seeking new ways to express their faith. Such a change in preferences has been matched by an increase in religious options through the presence of Evangelical

churches. (Non-Catholic) Christian churches take many forms of denominations and include the following according to Steingenga and Clearly (2007):

a) Traditional Protestants (Methodist, Presbyterians, Episcopalians, Lutherans)
b) Traditional Pentecostal (Assembly of God, The Church of God)
c) Neo-Pentecostal Preaching Prosperity (Universal Church of the Kingdom of God, Elim Pentecostal Church, El Verbo)
d) New Christians (Mormons, Seventh-Day Adventists, Jehovah's Witnesses).

The emotional appeals and charismatic pastors of these churches have been very effective tools to recruit new members and attract people willing to switch affiliations. This has been particularly effective among lower income Latin Americans with urgent physical and emotional needs or those suffering from poverty, family violence, or addiction. For these people, the conversion experience and rituals used by these churches have been critical to cement their change of faith. They see such revealing experiences as a sign of God to forge a new religious life. As practiced by some churches, the communal expression of such conversion is a powerful experience. Thus, the rise of Evangelical churches is testament to their success in attracting new religious practitioners and Catholics willing to switch affiliations. With an increase in membership, Evangelicals are seizing on opportunities to shape the political process by supporting political parties and candidates that advance their agendas. Brazil's Bolsonaro election in 2018 is one example of such alignment.

3. *Crisis in the Catholic Church*: internal disputes in the Catholic Church have had an impact on its image and connection with Latin American believers. In the early 1960s and because of the Second Vatican Council, several Latin American Catholic Church leaders aligned themselves with social activism and revolutionary movements in the region under what has been called Liberation Theology. With the waning of revolutionary movements in the region, the church retreated to a more conservative position to focus more on Christian morality values, such as opposition to abortion, gay marriage, and divorce, among others. With an emphasis on more traditional values and to a certain extent away from social issues, such as poverty and income inequality, the Catholic Church lost touch with the poor and middle classes. The election of Pope Francis, a Latin American, signals a change in orientation, as he has emphasized a greater missionary role of the church to take care of the more vulnerable sectors of society such as immigrants and victims of armed conflicts. Thus, the Catholic Church may regain a closer association with contemporary issues of Latin America society.

The net impact of these drivers must be understood in relation to larger social and economic changes influencing the religious preferences and affiliations of Latin Americans, such as greater economic growth, increasing wealth, and income inequality. In this context, religion no longer plays a key role in shaping Lain Americans' daily life, with increasing secularism, particularly among middle-class and educated Latin Americans. In addition, the presence of several non-Catholic churches has eroded the historical monopoly of the Catholic Church and resulted in larger and financially solid Evangelical churches that are increasingly exerting their political power and influence.

Table 5.1 shows the results of a poll of religious preferences in Latin America, in particular the reasons for switching church affiliation away from the Catholic Church. The main reason

Table 5.1 Reasons for Leaving the Catholic Church

Reason (... an important reason they are no longer Catholic)	Median %
Seeking personal connection with God	81
Enjoy style of worship at new church	69
Wanted greater emphasis on morality	60
Found church that helps members more	59
Outreach by new church	58
Personal problems	20
Seeking better financial future	14
Marriage to non-Catholic	9

Source: Pew Research Center – Religion in Latin America: Widespread change in a historically Catholic region, 2014.

for such a switch was the search for a better way to connect with God. Other reasons included the attraction of enthusiastic and charismatic style of worship, the greater emphasis on moral values that align with the faithful, and the more aggressive outreach of these other churches.

Religious Affiliation in Latin American Countries

Although erosion of the Catholic Church's influence has been felt across Latin America, the shift has not been the same in all countries. Some countries have been more receptive to Evangelicals, others have experienced a greater level of secularization, and others remain faithful to the Catholic Church. Based on the differential impact, one study revealed three groups: 1) countries that are predominantly Catholic, 2) countries in which the majority of the population is Catholic but with substantial Evangelical participation, and 3) countries with half or less Catholic participation (see Table 5.2). We explore these groups next.

The first group of countries has experienced lower than the region's average erosion of affiliation with the Catholic Church (20% or less). For instance, the erosion of affiliation with the Catholic Church has been only 5% in Paraguay, suggesting that traditional values remain strong in this socially conservative country. The key factors that explain affiliation in this grouping are the lower impact of Evangelical conversions and lower levels of non-religious affiliation (except Argentina). Thus, in this group, the Catholic Church retains a strong grip on society and family values.

The second group includes countries in which the erosion of Catholicism is on average for the region (31%) or greater and where Evangelical Protestantism has made inroads. These countries are mostly in Central America (except Panama) and Brazil. In this group, the rate of Evangelical affiliations ranges from 25% to 41%, rivaling the strength of the Catholic Church. In fact, Brazil has one of the largest Evangelical church memberships outside the US. Pentecostal churches have been particularly well received in Brazil because their worship services include sharing experiences of divine healing, speaking in tongues, and revelations, practices similar to Afro-Brazilian ceremonies. Pentecostals have also been successful in the Dominican Republic and Nicaragua, as have Prosperity Churches in Central American countries in this group. Evangelical churches have aggressively used outreach practices (e.g., high media visibility) driven by the strong competition among the large proliferation of non-Catholic churches in this group. As part of this strategy to achieve dominance, the building of large temples is associated with a strong brand image and economies of scale derived from such an investment. For instance, the Solomon's Temple of the Universal Church of Kingdom

Table 5.2 Religious Affiliation in Latin America

Country	Catholic	Protestant	Unaffiliated	Other	Change in Catholic Affiliation 1970–2014
Predominantly Catholic					
Paraguay	89	7	1	2	−5
Mexico	81	9	7	4	−15
Colombia	79	13	6	2	−16
Ecuador	79	13	5	3	−16
Bolivia	77	16	4	3	−12
Peru	76	17	4	3	−19
Venezuela	73	17	7	4	−20
Argentina	71	15	11	3	−20
Panama	70	19	7	4	−17
Majority Catholic and Strong Evangelical					
Costa Rica	62	25	9	4	−31
Brazil	61	26	8	5	−31
The Dominican Republic	57	23	18	2	−37
El Salvador	50	36	12	3	−43
Guatemala	50	41	6	3	−41
Nicaragua	50	40	7	4	−43
Honduras	46	41	10	2	−47
Catholic and Secular					
Chile	64	17	16	3	−12
Uruguay	42	15	37	6	−21
Region					
Latin America	69	19	8	4	−31

Source: Pew Research Center – Religion in Latin America: Widespread change in a historically Catholic region, 2014.

of God (UCKG) in São Paulo, Brazil, built in 2014, has a capacity for 2,000 in a space which is about the size of five soccer fields. This church uses the appeal of 'stop suffering and misery' and requires followers to make financial contributions to convey that prosperity is within reach (Bazannini & Machado, 2018). With large memberships, the Evangelical churches have achieved significant economic and political clout, with their members supporting political leaders that resonate with their religious beliefs (e.g., Brazil's Bolsonaro).

The third group of countries is small but significant in two aspects. The first aspect is that the level of non-religious affiliation is as large as affiliation with the Catholic Church. In the case of Uruguay, the unaffiliated (37%) and 'other' (5%) category amount to 43%—which rivals that of Catholics (42%). Uruguay has a long tradition of church and government separation and liberalism, which may explain why this country is an outlier in terms of religious affiliation profile. In Chile, the percentage of non-religious and other affiliation is 19%. It is interesting to note that Evangelicals have not been successful in this group of countries. Their participation is low at 15% in Uruguay and 17% in Chile. This group is also characterized by greater economic affluence and modernization and lower poverty levels (Pew Research, 2015).

The diverse range of religious affiliations in Latin America suggests different perspectives on social values, to which we turn next.

Moral Values

Religion is clearly a major force shaping moral values in Latin America. Given the dominant influence of the Catholic Church over more than four centuries, Latin America has been characterized as conservative in terms of moral values. Catholic and Evangelical faiths have sometimes shared this conservative view on social issues but may take different positions on others. The increase of non-religious affiliations, however, may have moved countries toward different morality views. We explore Latin Americans' moral values next using the survey of religious values by the Pew Research Center (2014r) (see Table 5.3).

Abortion raises the dilemma of balancing the protection of the right to life and women's rights over the bodies. Abortion is legal only in Argentina, Cuba, and Uruguay. In other countries, such as Brazil, abortion is allowed under certain circumstances, whereas in El Salvador, abortion is penalized with jail (Reuters, 2020). Opposition to abortion is very strong in Paraguay (95%) and Guatemala (92%). This extreme opposition reveals the impact of the religious profiles of these countries. Paraguay is the country with the highest level of Catholic Church affiliation (see Table 5.2) and Guatemala has the highest level of Evangelical affiliation. Other countries with high opposition to abortion are Central American countries with a strong Evangelical following. Both faiths share a strong opposition to abortion. On the other hand, opposition is weak in Uruguay (43%) and Chile (49%), countries in which the share of secular affiliations is high.

Views on contraception are not like those on abortion, with Catholics and Evangelicals holding different positions on birth control. The majority of Latin Americans seem to be open to the use of birth control; opposition to contraception does not reach 50% in any of the countries in the region, and several countries strongly support birth control (Argentina, Chile, Uruguay, and Venezuela). Support for planned conception is found even in countries in which

Table 5.3 Morality Values in Latin America

Country	Abortion (% oppose legalization)	Contraception (% use is morally wrong)	Divorce (% is morally wrong)	Homosexuality (% is morally wrong)	Gay Marriage (% oppose legality)	Sex Outside Marriage (% is morally wrong)
Argentina	60	10	17	45	40	23
Bolivia	76	26	49	73	67	59
Brazil	77	17	22	61	48	51
Chile	49	8	12	40	42	23
Colombia	73	14	32	67	64	44
Costa Rica	79	—	34	69	61	52
Cuba	—	—	—	—	—	—
The Dominican Republic	86	22	31	83	72	54
Ecuador	79	23	40	78	74	63
El Salvador	89	45	53	86	81	73
Guatemala	92	50	69	91	82	80
Haiti	—	—	—	—	—	—
Honduras	88	47	59	88	83	65
Mexico	67	29	33	57	43	47
Nicaragua	75	26	44	84	77	62
Panama	84	42	55	83	72	56
Paraguay	95	29	29	82	80	48
Peru	75	26	44	73	65	57
Uruguay	43	5	11	34	31	19
Venezuela	86	11	28	70	61	44

Source: Pew Research Center – Religion in Latin America: Widespread change in a historically Catholic region, 2014. Accessed from https://www.pewforum.org/2014/11/13/religion-in-latin-america/

the Catholic Church is very strong (e.g., in Paraguay, only 29% oppose birth control). Yet, opposition is found in countries with high levels of Evangelical affiliation (Central America).

The stand on divorce marks a dividing line between countries with strong Evangelical affiliation and the rest of the region. Central American countries are of the opinion that divorce is morally wrong (Guatemala (69%), Honduras (59%), Panama (55%), and El Salvador (53%)). Less opposition to divorce cuts across a range of other Latin American societies: Brazil is 22%, Colombia 32%, Mexico 33%, and Venezuela 28%. In line with their more secular positions, Uruguay (11%) and Chile (12%) exhibit the lowest opposition to divorce.

Regarding homosexuality and gay marriage, the same Central American countries plus the Dominican Republic, Bolivia, and Ecuador shared the perspective that these sexual preferences are morally wrong. The Evangelical church is strong in these countries. Once again, the more secular countries have a more liberal approach to homosexuality. The opinion on sex outside marriage is mixed across the region with no pattern suggesting either strong opposition or tolerance.

Moral values have gained prominence in recent political contests, prompting a realignment of political preferences. Those with more conservative moral agendas tend to support more conservative right-leaning political parties (Smith & Boas, 2020). Evangelicals in Brazil played an important role in supporting Bolsonaro's ascendance to power and subsequent election and have continued their support of Bolsonaro's embattled position after poorly handling the ravaging impact of the COVID-19 virus. Thus, religion and politics have been closely aligned in Latin America in recent times.

Beliefs

Beliefs are more specific and reflect ideas or statements that people hold to be true. As such, beliefs can be influenced by others, by new information, and are subject to change. Beliefs also depend on other personal factors, such as education, social class, and age. Beliefs may also change with the circumstances. For instance, when the economy is growing, Latin Americans may believe that things are working fine for them. In this section, we explore beliefs regarding democracy, free markets, and science.

Democracy

An enduring and stable democracy is a goal that few countries have achieved. A strong democracy is based on protections of the right to vote and transparent popular elections of the executive and legislative branches. A report on the age of continuous democracies in the world identifies the oldest democracies in the region: Costa Rica (70 years) and Colombia (61 years). This record pales in contrast to the longest democracy in the world: the US (219 years) (Boix, Miller, & Rosato, 2018). The majority of Latin Americans have experienced rapid changes in types of governance from authoritarian dictatorships to short periods of interrupted democratic regimes. With such volatility, it is only reasonable to expect that Latin Americans have become disillusioned with their governments and institutions. Although they may aspire to democratic values, their beliefs reflect their personal experiences with a variety of regimes. Those who have lived long enough yearn for stability and security either under authoritarian or democratic regimes. Table 5.4 shows Latin Americans' support and their degree of satisfaction with different types of governance.

Overall, 48% of Latin Americans support democracy but only 24% are satisfied with it. The countries with the highest level of satisfaction are Costa Rica (63%), Uruguay (61%), Chile (58%), and Colombia (54%). It is not surprising to see Costa Rica and Colombia in

Table 5.4 Preference for Different Types of Governance in Latin America

Country	Support for Democracy 2001	Support for Democracy 2018	Satisfaction with Democracy	Satisfaction Gap 2018	Support for Authoritarian Regime	Indifferent
Argentina	57	58	27	31	14	22
Bolivia	54	53	26	27	12	24
Brazil	30	34	9	25	14	41
Chile	45	58	42	16	23	15
Colombia	36	54	25	29	10	28
Costa Rica	71	63	45	18	11	18
Cuba	—	—	—	—	—	—
The Dominican Republic	—	44	22	22	18	29
Ecuador	40	50	38	12	19	26
El Salvador	25	28	11	17	11	54
Guatemala	33	28	18	10	20	34
Haiti	—	—	—	—	—	—
Honduras	57	34	27	7	10	41
Mexico	46	38	16	22	11	38
Nicaragua	43	51	20	31	10	25
Panama	34	42	21	21	14	34
Paraguay	35	40	24	16	27	23
Peru	62	43	11	32	18	27
Uruguay	79	61	42	19	16	18
Venezuela	57	75	12	63	6	14
Latin America	—	48	24	24	15	28

Source: Latinobarometro, https://www.latinobarometro.org/latContents.jsp

this group, as these societies have experienced longer periods of uninterrupted government transitions. Except for Colombia, this group of countries is mildly satisfied with democracy and exhibits the smallest gaps between support and satisfaction. The country with the largest satisfaction gap in this group is Colombia (29 points). Countries with less support for democracy and low satisfaction with their democratic experience are Central American countries (except Costa Rica), Mexico (38%), and Brazil (34%). These countries also exhibit a high level of indifference to the type of governance in their countries. Countries with mild support for democracy are Peru (43%), Panama (42%), and Paraguay (40%). Peru's satisfaction with democracy is the lowest in the region (11%).

The cases of Nicaragua and Venezuela require special attention. One report singles out Nicaragua and Venezuela as states in democratic breakdown (IDEA, 2019). Venezuela's breakdown started in 1998 with the government of Hugo Chavez and continued with the Maduro administration. A new constitution in 1999 gave the executive large powers and increased authoritarianism, leading to a pseudo-democracy (IDEA, 2019). Support for democracy in Venezuela remains high (75%), but satisfaction with democracy is low (11%), resulting in the largest dissatisfaction gap in the region (63%). For Nicaragua, the gap is 31% (Latinobarometro, 2018).

The Free Market

Since World War II, most economies in the region have followed free-market principles with some degree of government intervention but independent central banks. Therefore, many generations of Latin Americans have experienced free-market conditions and make their

Table 5.5 Views on Free Markets, Inequality, and Science in Latin America

Country	Support for Free Markets %*	Gap between Rich and Poor Is a Major Problem %*	How Fair Is Income Distribution in LA %?**	Support for Human Evolution Theory %*
Argentina	52	60	9	71
Bolivia	64	45	27	44
Brazil	79	61	8	66
Chile	50	66	8	69
Colombia	65	67	14	59
Costa Rica	64	69	19	56
Cuba	—	—	—	—
The Dominican Republic	79	70	17	41
Ecuador	63	45	29	50
El Salvador	61	66	10	46
Guatemala	71	56	17	55
Haiti	—	—	—	—
Honduras	69	59	22	49
Mexico	60	41	12	64
Nicaragua	84	49	23	47
Panama	73	42	16	61
Paraguay	60	75	16	59
Peru	60	49	12	51
Uruguay	59	44	19	74
Venezuela	72	40	8	63

Sources:
*Pew Research Center – Religion in Latin America: Widespread change in a historically Catholic region, 2014. Accessed from https://www.pewforum.org/2014/11/13/religion-in-latin-america/
**World Values Survey https://web.archive.org/web/20131019112321/http://www.worldvaluessurvey.org/wvs/articles/folder_published/article_base_54

everyday life economic decisions based on this assumption. Global and economic crises have introduced short periods of inflationary volatility. Despite these cycles, Latin Americans support free markets rather than controlled economies. High support for market economies is highest in Brazil (79%), the Dominican Republic (79%), and Panama (73%) and lower in Mexico (60%) and Uruguay (59%) (see Table 5.5). It is interesting to note that countries with eroded democracies have high support for free markets: Nicaragua (84%) and Venezuela (72%). These results indicate that, despite attempts to restrict political freedom, people in these countries prefer a free-market system.

Free markets, however, do not guarantee a fair distribution of economic benefits. Despite great efforts and progress to reduce poverty in the region in the past decade, the majority of Latin Americans believe that the gap between the rich and poor is a major problem. For instance, 70% of Dominicans strongly support free markets, but 79% believe that income inequality is a major problem. A similar result was observed in Chile, Costa Rica, and Colombia. Further, only 8%–9% of people in Argentina, Brazil, and Chile believe that income distribution in their societies is fair. As mentioned in Chapter 4, the increase in poverty during the pandemic of 2020 has increased the perception of inequalities in the region (Pew Research, 2014).

Science

We also look at an example of Latin Americans' beliefs on science and its relationship to religiosity. According to one opinion survey, Latin Americans' support of evolution theory is strong in Uruguay (74%), Argentina (71%), Chile (69%), and Brazil (66%). All these countries are relatively affluent, and Uruguay and Chile are largely secular. Countries with lower support for evolution theory are countries where Evangelicals have made great inroads: El Salvador (46%), Honduras (49%), and the Dominican Republic (41%). Thus, it is likely that their views on evolution have been influenced by their religious beliefs (Pew Research, 2014).

Norms and Traditions

Norms are specific guidelines of behaviors subject to the approval or disapproval of the referent group (i.e., prescriptive and proscriptive).

Latin Americans, as a group, share a common set of cultural norms derived from common historical roots and similar development efforts. Latin Americans value personal relationships because these relationships traditionally have been important for advancement in life. Once established, these relationships are maintained and never placed in conflict or in question. Thus, a norm has emerged as a result, referred to as *simpatia*—kindness or empathy to others. Showing empathy to others should reflect an understanding of the individual and the context surrounding the individual. Understanding of others is facilitated if the two individuals also share the same context, which could be economic, social, political, or simply family links. The latter interpretation has also been identified as the tendency for classism or *familism* in Latin American culture (Osland, De Franco, & Osland, 2007).

Relationships are based on *confianza* or trust. One characteristic of *confianza* is the initial effort to gather information on other people to establish common bases of group membership and indicators of trust and loyalty in all situations. Latin Americans are more likely to place greater trust in members of the same group or class (which aligns with the region's collectivist culture). Outsiders are, thus, at a disadvantage in gaining a level of trust necessary to conduct transactions (Osland, De Franco, & Osland, 2007). The intrinsic advantage of trust and loyalty to the group is the expectation of reciprocation. Emphasis on the advancement of the group can clearly lead to nepotism, frequently observed in Latin American organizations.

The outcome of collectivism, classism, and trust is *personalismo* or particularism: the expectation that one is treated differently and receives individualized attention if one belongs to the same group. In some circumstances, Latin Americans expect to be the exception rather than the rule. Such expectations and behaviors are often effective to manage highly bureaucratic systems and organizations in Latin America, particularly the public bureaucracy (Osland, De Franco, & Osland, 2007). This is illustrated by the Brazilian way of seeking alternative channels to find solutions to problems, the so-called *Jeitinho* (Barbosa & Da Matta, 2006).

Paternalism and *power* are two related factors commonly associated with Latin American norms. The roots of paternalism are grounded in the colonial heritage in which members of society expected rulers or *patrones* to take care of them. Paternalism in modern Latin American societies is exercised at all levels, from family to organizations, in which managers and supervisors concentrate and exercise power in decisions. As a result, little input or information from others outside the closed social or business group is shared or incorporated in decision-making. Because they lack influence on important decisions, subordinates in Latin America believe that they should not be held accountable for their performance. Hence, a culture of low accountability permeates Latin American societies (Osland, De Franco, & Osland, 2007).

A legacy of colonialism and the influence of Catholicism—where individuals had little control over the affairs of the state, the economy, or external events—has resulted in a sense of *fatalism,* or resignation and acceptance of faith and destiny. Fatalism makes Latin Americans less confident that they can guide their professional future and advancement based purely on individual efforts. This situation reinforces the lack of accountability mentioned before and increases the perception of uncertainty in general, particularly the outcome of future events that will be determined by destiny (Osland, De Franco, & Osland, 2007).

Other cultural norms that guide interpersonal relationships are respect (*respeto*) to others based on age or education (titles are important), honor, and courage. Finally, Latin Americans are optimists and warm, expressing and revealing their emotions openly.

Latin American Business Culture

Historical Roots of Latin American Business Culture

Latin American business culture is different from that of other regions, but homogeneous within. This assumption is based on the perception that most countries, except for some Caribbean countries, share the same historical and language roots.

A common historical factor is its colonial heritage. Four centuries of colonial rule have exerted a strong influence on Latin American society, particularly in its legal and political systems. Except for British rule in the Caribbean, the rest of the region was either under Spanish or Portuguese rule. The ambitions and empire building approaches of these two colonial masters were different. According to Behrens (2009), Spain imposed its rule through superior military power, centralization, and a hierarchy based on aristocracy. Under this system, courage, honor, and loyalty to the imperial power were highly valued and rewarded. This command and control approach is still prevalent in contemporary economic and political organizations in Spanish-speaking Latin America. For instance, the expansion of multinationals from Spanish-speaking Latin America has been based on a strategy of fully controlled investments and acquisitions.

Behrens (2009) argues that Portugal took a different approach to empire building. As a small European country, Portugal focused on the discovery and exploration of alternative routes to Asia. Thus, colonial Portugal became a merchant empire that, in the process, colonized Brazil, leaving a legacy there that instills values based on trade such as negotiation, collaboration, and flexibility rather than the confrontational and combative tenets of Spanish colonies. As a result, Behrens contends that Brazilians have developed a more mercantile approach to business and a search for global opportunities based on trade rather than the accumulation of power. This colonial legacy has created organizational and decision-making styles characterized by the concentration of power, multilevel hierarchical structures, strong networks of relationships, and paternalism. Yet, insertions into a globalized world have driven Latin American firms to adopt more efficient and effective managerial systems. Next, we examine the region's business culture through the lenses of four cultural frameworks.

Latin American Business Culture under Four Cultural Frameworks

Four organizational cultural frameworks are relevant to contrast Latin American business culture with that of other regions: Hall, Hofstede, GLOBE, and Trompenaars (Hall, 1959; Hofstede, 1980; House, et al., 2004; Trompenaars, 1994). Hall's central focus is to understand the communication aspects of cultures. Hofstede's and GLOBE's frameworks focus on national values and the characteristics of organizational cultures. Trompenaars explores the individual within a culture across several behaviors, decision-making styles, motivations, and aspirations.

Latin American Business Culture According to Hall

Hall's focuses on understanding how individuals within a culture communicate and participate in social interactions. Hall places particular attention on the influence of the context in which the communication takes place. Thus, he describes cultures in terms of the degree of openness to others (individual distance), their idea of compromise and styles of negotiation, and their concept of time (strict or flexible), among others. Based on his study of socialization within cultures, Hall identifies *low-* and *high-context cultures* (Hall, 1959).

Low-context cultures are more explicit and direct. Individuals in these cultures express their intentions clearly, and such understanding does not change with the social context. Low-context cultures tend to behave following explicit rules and norms to guide their behaviors. Written forms of rules and norms avoid misinterpretations or capricious interpretations by individuals. Low-context cultures are monochronistic and adhere to plans, meeting deadlines, and punctuality. For instance, Anglo-Saxon and Germanic cultures are considered low context.

In high-context cultures, the behavior and communication styles of individuals are largely influenced by the specific situation and relationship with others. Thus, individuals will adapt their behavior and intentions to the situation. Take, for instance, the concept of agreement. Individuals may be influenced to agree with others based on the strength of their personal relationships rather than the expectations of the agreement per se. Agreement may be communicated in forms that are only understood by members of the group—such as a handshake or a particular nod of the head. These non-verbal behaviors can be an important part of intra-group communication. Individuals who are not members of the group may miss or misinterpret these signs.

Hall identifies Latin America as high-context societies. As a high-context culture, business communications will be shaped by some of the cultural values that were discussed in the previous section, particularly familism, personalism, respect, and paternalism. Latin Americans are often not direct in their communications with others. They aim to be polite and friendly, avoiding confrontation. Courtesy and goodwill gestures will preface introductions in the search for relationships and trust. Another feature of business communications in Latin America is formality and the use of professional titles as indicators of power relations and need to confer respect. Communications would also emphasize the avoidance of conflict or stress in relationships by offering indirect and implicit messages that are not confrontational, negative, or allow for face-saving outcomes. Time perception in Latin American cultures is flexible, as people tend to be polychronistic (Wardrope, 2005).

Latin America Business Culture According to Hofstede

Hofstede's cultural framework describes organizational cultures in different countries across five dimensions: individualism, power distance, masculine or feminine values, uncertainty avoidance, long-term orientation, and indulgence (Hofstede, 1980, Hofstede et al. 2010).

The first dimension in Hofstede's framework is the level of power sharing in organizations. The lower the distance, the lower the level of participation. In cultures with low power distance, individuals at lower levels are empowered to make decisions by themselves. As mentioned before, Latin America is characterized by power concentrated at the top of the organization and input from subordinates is largely ignored. Table 5.6 supports this observation. Latin America has an average score of 67.8, which indicates high power distance, a result that is like Japan (score of 54) but not as high as China (score of 80). In contrast to Latin

Table 5.6 Hofstede's Values for Selected Latin American Countries

Country	Power (PDI)	Individualism (IDV)	Masculinity (MAS)	Uncertainty Avoidance (UAI)	Long-Term Orientation (LTO)	Indulgence
Argentina	49	46	56	86	20	62
Brazil	69	38	49	76	44	59
Chile	63	23	28	86	31	68
Colombia	67	13	64	80	13	83
Costa Rica	35	15	21	86	—	—
Ecuador	78	8	63	67	—	—
El Salvador	66	19	40	94	20	89
Guatemala	95	6	37	101	—	—
Jamaica	45	39	68	13	—	—
Mexico	81	30	69	82	24	97
Panama	95	11	44	86	—	—
Peru	64	16	42	87	25	46
Uruguay	61	36	38	100	26	53
Venezuela	81	12	73	76	—	—
Latin American Average	68	22	49	80	16	—
US	40	91	62	46	29	68
China	80	20	66	30	118	24
Japan	54	46	95	92	80	42

Source: Geert Hofstede – http://geert-hofstede.com

America, power sharing is more prevalent in the US (score of 40) (Hofstede, 1980, Hofstede et al. 2010).

The second dimension describes the level of individualism or collectivism in a society. In more individualistic societies, organizational decisions are made mostly based on the interests of the individual. In collectivistic societies, individuals make decisions of greater benefit to the community, even if they may be detrimental to their personal welfare. Latin America is a collectivistic society, as indicated by a low average score of 22.3, which is similar to China (score of 20), and more collectivistic than Japan (score of 54) or the highly individualistic US (score of 91). The level of individualism is on the rise in Latin America, but this increase is from a low individualistic base.

The third dimension in Hofstede's framework defines whether predominant values in organizations are driven by masculinity or femininity. Predominantly masculine cultures (a high score on this dimension) are driven by competition, achievement, or success, which are considered masculine values. On the other hand, in feminine societies, being more caring of others and not standing out from the crowd drive decision-making. With an average score of 49.4, Latin America seems to balance both masculine and feminine values. In recent years, Latin America has elected more female presidents than any other world region (Calvano & Marcus-Delgado, 2013). Greater gender equality in politics has not, however, been paralleled in business, although recent studies suggest that this asymmetry is changing, and women in Latin America are gaining influence in business (Martinez-Nadal, 2013). Japan, China, and the US score higher than Latin America with a greater tendency toward masculine values (see Table 5.6).

The fourth dimension of Hofstede's framework is uncertainty avoidance. This dimension describes how individuals behave under situations of ambiguity and poor information. In cultures with low tolerance of ambiguity, individuals' decision-making is aimed at minimizing uncertainty, and these cultures tend to be risk-averters. In cultures with high tolerance, individuals behave in a way that reflects a rational evaluation of alternative options in an uncertain situation. The Latin American cultural value of fatalism may factor in the results for this region. On average, Latin American countries score high in uncertainty avoidance. Individuals in organizations do not cope well with ambiguity and make decisions based more on intuition and emotions rather than a rational evaluation of options. Similar to Latin America, Japan scores high on this dimension (score of 92), but the Japanese are more likely to eliminate emotions from decision-making, instead being overcautious and analyzing any potential risks before making any business decision. In contrast, in China and the US, individuals are more entrepreneurial and risk-takers, and change and innovation are encouraged as ways to reduce business uncertainty (Hofstede, 1980, Hofstede et al. 2010).

The fifth dimension of Hofstede's framework is long-term orientation. In the US, individuals and organizations tend to favor behaviors and decisions that produce immediate results, thus exhibiting a short-term orientation. In contrast, Asian societies prefer long-term horizons and expect outcomes to be realized in the long term. Table 5.6 shows that Brazilians are slightly long-term oriented, but not as much as the Japanese or the Chinese. The rest of the countries in the region are markedly short-term oriented (Hofstede, 1980, Hofstede et al. 2010).

The sixth and most recent dimension is indulgence. This dimension captures the importance that societies place on self-gratification and individual happiness, personal control, freedom of speech, and leisure time. In organizations, this dimension seems to be related to the willingness of their members to voice their opinions and provide feedback. More restrained (less indulgent) societies will be more reserved. As a newer dimension, there are fewer country observations. Among the few Latin American countries with data on this dimension, Mexico, Guatemala, and Costa Rica are the most indulgent. Other countries in the region are more restrained with scores closer to those of the US and Japan (Hofstede et al. 2010).

The results of a comparative analysis of Latin America and other selected countries on five dimensions with complete information appear in Figure 5.2

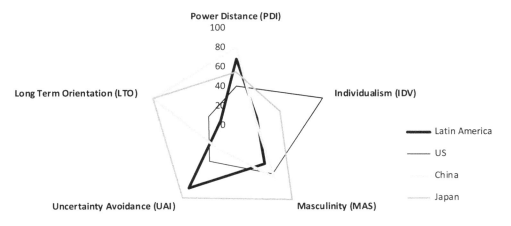

Figure 5.2 Cross-cultural profiles based on Hofstede's value dimensions. Source: Authors' elaboration with data from https://geerthofstede.com

Latin American Business Culture According to Trompenaars

Trompenaars uses seven dimensions to characterize cultures. Some of these dimensions are the same as those already discussed under Hall and Hofstede's frameworks and, therefore, will not be elaborated on fully. The first dimension is universalism or particularism, which describes whether rules and agreements apply to all or depend on the relationship or context (low or high context in Hall's framework). This concept is similar to personalism in Latin America. The second dimension contrasts individualism or collectivism in a culture, a topic already discussed under Hofstede's framework. The third dimension is relationship with the environment and describes whether individuals believe they have control over their environment. The fourth dimension is neutral versus emotional. Emotional cultures express their emotions and thinking to others more freely than neutral ones. The fifth dimension is specific or diffuse relationships. This dimension refers to how much individuals value privacy (e.g., separation of work and private life) and their preference for a more active and public social life. The sixth dimension is related to achievement or ascribed motivation. Societies that reward accomplishments resulting from personal effort exhibit an achievement orientation. Ascription is predominant in societies in which rank, status, or advancement is based on social class, connections, or educational credentials. The seventh and final dimension is time orientation. Sequential cultures see time as chronological and as a valuable resource that should not be wasted; thus, they tend to value punctuality and strict deadlines. Synchronic cultures see the past, present, and future as interconnected, see time as flexible, and are more prone to multitasking (Trompenaars, 1994).

Based on these variables, Trompenaars identifies several cultural clusters, including the Anglo-Saxon, Germanic, Nordic, Latin European, Middle Eastern, and others. Trompenaars's classification indicates that the Latin American cluster has developed its own managerial culture, characterized by particularism, collectivism, external locus of control, emotional, diffuse, ascription, and synchronic (Trompenaars, 1994).

Latin America Business Culture According to GLOBE

The GLOBE study is yet another cross-cultural framework that can be used to contrast Latin American business culture with that of other regions. The GLOBE study, which was designed to examine the relationships between culture and leadership effectiveness, revealed nine cultural dimensions, several of which are the same as the other cultural frameworks reviewed above. These nine dimensions are: uncertainty avoidance, power distance, institutional collectivism, in-group collectivism, gender egalitarianism, future orientation, performance orientation, and humane orientation (House, et al., 2004). For parsimony's sake, this section will comment only on those dimensions that have not been previously discussed.

Institutional collectivism refers to the degree to which collective distribution of resources is rewarded. In-group collectivism refers to the degree to which individuals express pride, loyalty, and cohesiveness in their society. Gender egalitarianism is the degree to which a society minimizes gender differences. Assertiveness is the degree to which individuals are assertive, confrontational, and aggressive in social relationships. Performance orientation refers to how a society rewards individuals for their efforts and excellence. Humane orientation is the degree to which individuals are rewarded for being fair, altruistic, and kind. Uncertainty avoidance is the extent to which society relies on social norms, rules, and procedures to reduce the unpredictability of the future (like Hofstede's uncertainty avoidance dimension, but the scale is reversed in interpretation).

Based on data obtained through more than 17,000 standardized surveys in organizations of 62 countries, the GLOBE study collected data on respondents' perceptions across nine dimensions of cultural values and practices. The results for ten Latin American countries and the region's average are shown in Table 5.7 and Figures 5.3 and 5.4. The cultural value perception measured respondents' views of which values should predominate in an ideal society. Current practices measured respondents' views of which values are practiced in society across the same dimensions. Often, values perception scores were higher than practice values, as aspirations typically run higher than current reality (GLOBE, 2020).

The GLOBE study identified ten cultural clusters. Latin American countries comprise a distinct cluster; the US fits in the Anglo cluster and Japan and China are in the Confucian Asia group (see Table 5.7 for comparison scores for the United States, China, and Japan). The Latin American cluster had high practice scores for in-group collectivism, and low for performance orientation, uncertainty avoidance, future orientation, and institutional collectivism. Therefore, according to GLOBE, in Latin American cultures, individuals tend to take life as it comes, they are not overly worried about results, unpredictability is a fact of life, and there is less concern with institutional collective goals (House et al., 2004).

Next, we elaborate on the results of the GLOBE study for understanding Latin America's business culture vis-à-vis those of the US, China, and Japan, including notable differences in the scores for 'practices' and 'values' which provides a glimpse of expectations for the future of cultural values in the region.

Regarding uncertainty avoidance, the region's average practices score is lower than those of the US and the Asian countries. A lower score suggests that Latin Americans rely more on informal networks, norms, and are less calculating when taking risks than their US and Asian counterparts, who rely more on policies, procedures, and formalities to deal with uncertainty. The value score for this dimension was higher than the practices score, indicating that Latin Americans would prefer more formal and rule-based societies. One would expect that the recent period of macroeconomic stability in the region would help to make the future more predictable in Latin America.

The power distance results support the conclusions of other cultural frameworks that Latin America is a society with substantial power differences and concentration of power. The average practices score for this dimension is the highest among all the comparison countries (see Table 5.7). The expectation that this situation will change is clear not only for Latin America but also for the US, Japan, and China, as noted by the substantially lower scores for values (compared to the score for practices) on this dimension.

Results on institutional collectivism reveal an unexpected finding for Latin America. The region's average practices score was low compared to the other three countries. A low practices score suggests that Latin Americans perceive an environment that is less reliant on institutions for their individual benefit and encourages more individualism. Based on the values scores, however, Latin Americans perceive that their culture will become more collectivistic. This is in contrast to the findings for the U.S, Japan, and China, where lower values scores indicate that these cultures expect their future to be more individualistic.

The analysis of in-group collectivism supports the Latin American cultural trait of familism mentioned earlier in the chapter. Although both China and Latin America score high on this dimension, Latin Americans indicate that a reliance on group relations should be even greater in the future, whereas the Chinese would prefer to diminish it.

Regarding gender egalitarianism, all the regions perceive that their societies have low levels of gender equality with the practice scores for all regions being lower than the mid-range of the scale. Relative to the other countries in the analysis, the Latin American average is

Table 5.7 GLOBE Study Scores for Latin America and Other Selected Countries

	Uncertainty Avoidance		Power Distance		Institutional Collectivism		In-Group Collectivism		Gender Egalitarianism		Assertiveness		Future Orientation		Performance Orientation		Humane Orientation	
	P*	V*	P	V	P	V	P	V	P	V	P	V	P	V	P	V	P	V
Argentina	3.65	4.66	5.64	2.33	3.66	5.32	5.51	6.15	3.49	4.98	4.22	3.25	3.08	5.78	3.65	6.35	3.99	5.58
Bolivia	3.55	4.7	4.51	3.41	4.04	5.1	5.47	6	3.55	4.75	3.79	3.73	3.61	5.63	3.61	6.05	4.05	5.07
Brazil	3.6	4.99	5.33	2.35	3.83	5.62	5.18	5.15	3.31	4.99	4.2	2.91	3.87	5.69	4.04	6.13	3.66	5.68
Colombia	3.57	4.98	5.56	2.04	3.81	5.38	5.73	6.25	3.67	5	4.2	3.43	3.27	5.68	3.94	6.42	3.72	5.61
Costa Rica	3.82	4.58	4.74	2.58	3.93	5.18	5.32	6.08	3.56	4.64	3.75	4.05	3.6	5.2	4.12	5.9	4.39	4.99
Ecuador	3.68	4.67	5.6	2.3	3.9	5.41	5.81	6.17	3.07	4.59	4.09	3.65	3.74	5.94	4.2	6.32	4.65	5.26
El Salvador	3.62	5.32	5.68	2.68	3.71	5.65	5.35	6.52	3.16	4.66	4.62	3.62	3.8	5.98	3.72	6.58	3.71	5.46
Guatemala	3.3	4.88	5.6	2.35	3.7	5.23	5.63	6.14	3.02	4.53	3.89	3.64	3.24	5.91	3.81	6.14	3.89	5.26
Mexico	4.18	5.26	5.22	2.85	4.06	4.92	5.71	5.95	3.64	4.73	4.45	3.79	3.87	5.86	4.1	6.16	3.98	5.1
Venezuela	3.44	5.26	5.4	2.29	3.96	5.39	5.53	6.17	3.62	4.82	4.33	3.33	3.35	5.79	3.32	6.33	4.25	5.31
Latin America Average	3.64	4.93	5.33	2.52	3.86	5.32	5.52	6.06	3.41	4.77	4.15	3.54	3.54	5.75	3.85	6.24	4.03	5.33
US	4.15	4	4.88	2.85	4.2	4.17	4.25	5.77	3.34	5.06	4.55	4.32	4.15	5.31	4.49	6.14	4.17	5.53
China	4.94	5.28	5.04	3.1	4.77	4.56	5.8	5.09	3.05	3.68	3.76	5.44	3.75	4.73	4.45	5.67	4.36	5.32
Japan	4.07	4.33	5.11	2.86	5.19	3.99	4.63	5.26	3.19	4.33	3.59	5.56	4.29	5.25	4.22	5.17	4.3	5.41
GLOBE	4.16	4.62	5.17	2.75	4.25	4.73	5.13	5.66	3.37	4.51	4.14	3.82	3.85	5.49	4.1	5.94	4.09	5.42

Sources: GLOBE 2020: https://globeproject.com; House et al. (2004).

* P = Practices and V = Values.

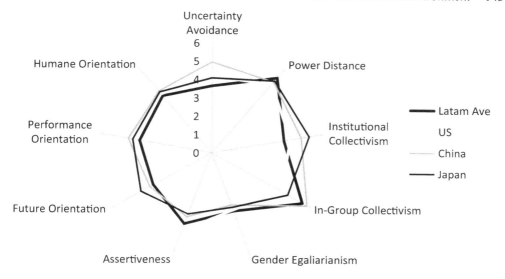

Figure 5.3 Cross-cultural profiles based on GLOBE practices. Source: Authors' elaboration based on data from House et al. (2004), *Culture, leadership and organizations: The GLOBE study of 62 societies*. Thousand Oaks: CA: Sage

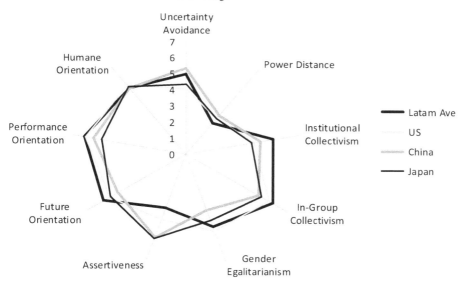

Figure 5.4 Cross-cultural profiles based on GLOBE values. Source: Authors' elaboration based on data from House et al. (2004), *Culture, leadership and organizations: The GLOBE study of 62 societies*. Thousand Oaks: CA: Sage.

higher, an indication of higher achievement in equality. In Latin America, like in the US, there is an expectation that equality should improve in the future.

Both Latin America and the US have higher practices scores on assertiveness than Japan and China, thus, assertiveness seems to be a Western cultural trait. Whereas respondents in Latin America and the US expressed that their societies should have lower levels of assertiveness, the Asian countries anticipated a greater level of assertiveness in the future.

With respect to performance orientation, Latin America scored lower than the other countries in the analysis and the GLOBE average. The current reality is that performance orientation is not part of Latin American business culture, but there is a desire that it be a large component in the future. In fact, the values score for Latin America on this dimension exceeded those of the US, China, and Japan.

Latin America has a low practice score on future orientation, suggesting a greater tendency to live in the moment, consume, and prefer current gratification. This result is congruent with the rise in consumer confidence to be discussed in Chapter 7. A similar result can be observed for China, so this could be a cultural trait of emerging economies. Nevertheless, Latin Americans express that their societies should become more long-term oriented.

On humane orientation, Latin America, the US, Japan, and China have similar mid-range practices scores. In all cases, the future should be better in terms of supporting societies with more interest in the welfare of the individual, increased sensitivity for social issues, and greater social equality.

National Business Cultures in Latin America

In this section, we explore differences in business culture and managerial styles across countries in the region. Some aspects of national business cultures in Latin America remain constant despite the influence of economic reforms and globalization. For instance, in most countries, family business groups are powerful players, with the founding family exerting a great deal of control over decision-making. Yet some studies have concluded that Latin American managerial styles are quite diverse (Lenartowicz & Roth, 2001). Different managerial orientations not only require different business competencies but also cultural mindsets and styles of leadership.

The GLOBE study identified six dimensions of leadership styles for nine countries in Latin America. Three of these dimensions were the effectiveness of a charismatic leader, team orientation, and a participative style. Other dimensions were rewarding fairness and altruism (humane oriented), an emphasis on individualism and independence (autonomy), and emphasis on maintaining safety and security of individuals and groups and saving face (self-protective).

As a group, the Latin American countries in the study exhibit greater charismatic, team orientation, participative, and self-protective managerial styles than the GLOBE's averages (see Table 5.8). On charismatic leadership, Ecuador is the only country with a score higher than that of the US. Most of the Latin American countries in the study have a greater team orientation than the GLOBE as a whole and the US, China, and Japan. Brazil, in particular, scores high on charismatic, team orientation, and participative styles, placing this country apart from the rest of the region. Lenartowicz and Roth (2001) arrived at a similar conclusion in their study of Latin American managerial values. Brazilian business leaders are very successful in building a relationship-based culture, which is particularly effective to manage the diversity of its population. Another study states that the essence of this culture is the unique competency of 'network capillarity,' or the ability to build networks of associates based on empathy and the creation of common value (Parente et al., 2013). Brazilian multinationals have leveraged this competence in their global strategies (Fleury & Fleury, 2010).

Regarding humane orientation, the Latin American cluster of countries had a slightly lower score than the GLOBE's average. The region's humane orientation score was similar to Japan's but much lower than the scores for the US and China. Thus, promoting and caring for the well-being of others in an organization is not as high a priority in Latin America. Finally, the region's managerial style is not characterized by giving people autonomy or fostering individual freedom of decision-making. This result is consistent with the more collectivistic

Table 5.8 GLOBE Study Leadership Scores

Country	Charismatic	Team-Oriented	Participative	Humane-Oriented	Autonomous	Self-Protective
Argentina	5.98	5.99	5.89	4.7	4.55	3.45
Bolivia	6.01	6.1	5.29	4.56	3.92	3.83
Brazil	6.0	6.17	6.06	4.84	2.27	3.49
Colombia	6.04	6.07	5.51	5.05	3.34	3.37
Costa Rica	5.95	5.81	5.54	4.99	3.46	3.55
Ecuador	6.46	6.21	5.51	5.13	3.53	3.62
El Salvador	6.08	5.95	5.4	4.69	3.47	3.43
Guatemala	6.0	5.94	5.45	5.0	3.38	3.77
Mexico	5.66	5.74	4.64	4.72	3.86	3.86
Venezuela	5.72	5.62	4.88	4.85	3.39	3.81
Latin America	5.99	5.96	5.42	4.85	3.51	3.62
GLOBE	5.83	5.76	5.33	4.89	3.85	3.47
US	6.12	5.8	5.93	5.21	3.75	3.15
China	5.56	5.57	5.04	5.19	4.07	3.8
Japan	5.49	5.56	5.07	4.68	3.67	3.6

Source: GLOBE 2020 https://globeproject.com/results/clusters/latin-america?menu=cluster#cluster

nature of Latin America and the emphasis on group decision-making. The exception is Argentina, with a score for the autonomy style that is not only the highest in the region but much higher than the GLOBE's average. According to one study, Argentine business groups have been very effective in adapting to changing economic and political environments and encouraged entrepreneurial and diversification initiatives within their organizations. These efforts may require a great deal of autonomy and risk-taking (Fracchia & Mesquita, 2006). On the other hand, Brazil, again, seems to be different from the rest of the region, as it scores the lowest on this dimension. A preference for charismatic, authoritarian, and paternalistic national and business leaders may blunt the promotion of individualism in Brazil.

The Impact of Culture on Leadership

The ability to recruit, develop, and retain skilled employees and effective leaders is now a source of competitive advantage for domestic and international firms alike. As discussed in Chapter 3, for Latin American companies, acquiring this capability will be essential in their pursuit of global competitiveness. For foreign firms operating in Latin America, the challenge will be understanding the centrality of culture to the practice of talent management in the region and adopting the culturally appropriate practices and leadership styles needed to drive organizational performance. This section highlights the influence of cultural norms and values on the management of organizations in the region, focusing on leadership styles that effectively respond to cultural and competitive realities and best practices for recruiting and growing talent in Latin America.

Leadership Styles and Cultural Values

Understanding leadership in Latin American organizations requires that we first review leadership theories. Table 5.9 summarizes selected leadership theories.

Douglas McGregor's Theory X and Y proposes that leadership and management styles vary according to assumptions about human nature (McGregor, 1960). Theory X is based on

Table 5.9 Selected Leadership Theories

Theory X and Y	*Theory X*: Belief that people are primarily evil and cannot be trusted to self-monitor or self-manage. Assumes people prefer to avoid hard work and require constant supervision and direction.
	Theory Y: Assumes workers are self-motivated and capable of undertaking complex work with little supervision and oversight needed.
Weber's Theory of Leadership	*Charismatic*: Based on devotion to the specific or exemplary character of an individual person.
	Traditional: Based on an established belief in the sanctity of a traditionally ascribed position of authority.
	Rational: Calls for obedience to the legally established impersonal order.
Contingency Model of Leadership	Leaders adapt their behaviors to fit the national culture of their followers, the position of power of the leader, and the task at hand.
Benevolent Paternalistic Leadership	Father figure or patriarch within an organizational hierarchy who commands respect and loyalty from employees in exchange for protection (personal and professional). Benevolent authoritative figure makes decisions on behalf of others for their own good.
Transformational Leadership	Transformational leaders provide vision and inspiration and create the necessary conditions for employees to willingly and enthusiastically contribute to the goals of the organization.

Source: Authors' elaboration.

the belief that people are primarily evil and cannot be trusted to self-monitor or self-manage. Theory X assumes that people dislike work and prefer to avoid it and, thus, require constant supervision and direction. Theory Y has a more optimistic view of human nature. It assumes that work is a natural human process that can provide personal satisfaction and that workers are self-motivated and capable of undertaking complex work with little supervision and oversight. In the context of Latin American organizations, management practices and labor relations are more aligned with Theory X (Page & Wiseman, 1993). Latin Americans have a more pessimistic view of human nature; for instance, there is a strong belief that people cannot be trusted until they earn that trust through actions. This belief is well aligned with the assumptions that underlie Theory X, and leaders who share these assumptions tend to be more controlling and directive. Moreover, the high power distance that characterizes Latin American cultures results in followers being more accepting of autocratic leaders and their perceiving participative leaders—those who adopt leadership style more consistent with Theory Y—as less competent, as subordinates expect their leaders to openly display expertise and power.

Weber's tripartite model of authority (defined as power accepted as legitimate by those subjected to it), identifies three bases for leaders' legitimacy: traditional, rational, and charismatic authority (Weber, 1947). In Latin America, we find both traditional and charismatic leadership styles. Traditional authority, based on established beliefs in the sanctity of a traditionally ascribed position of authority, is consistent with the high degree of masculinity and formality present in the region. Charismatic authority, based on the devotion to the specific or exemplary character of an individual person, is also observed in Latin American organizations, especially when one studies the political history of Latin American populist leaders (*'caudillos'*). This is supported by the GLOBE study findings discussed previously. In many ways, these two bases of legitimacy are intertwined in Latin America, through the predominant preference for a paternalistic leadership style. As Behrens (2010, p. 21) explains, the 'style of charisma acceptable to Latin Americans stems from the notion of paternalism.' Paternalism is defined as, hierarchy within a group, by means of which advancement and protection of subordinates are expected in exchange for loyalty, usually to a father figure, or patriarch, who makes decisions on behalf of others for their good, even if this may be against their wishes...Where patriarchalism rules, its legitimacy has seldom been questioned in organizations. (Behrens, 2010, p. 21)

Exploratory research conducted by Behrens on leadership style preferences in Brazil showed that paternalistic leaders were preferred by most Brazilians (although less so in knowledge-based industries). He further concluded that the tendency of US multinationals in Brazil to appoint subsidiary managers whose style matches the preferred US style of leadership is so ineffective that these managers are rarely able to make the transition to domestic organizations.

The contingency perspective of leadership suggests that effective leaders need to adapt their behaviors to fit the national culture of their followers. Thus, cultural values will have a significant impact on what followers regard as 'good' or 'bad' leadership (Hofstede, 1980; House et al., 2004; Muczyk & Holt, 2008). In Latin American countries, which are characterized by high power distance, followers are comfortable accepting the authority of leaders, as defined by a well-established hierarchy, and there is an expectation of social distance between leaders and followers. Subordinates prefer to depend on others (Lenartowicz & Johnson, 2002) and are more likely to prefer a directive and paternalistic leadership style (Dorfman et al., 1997; Hofstede, 1980; Recht & Wilderom, 1998). Leaders from outside the region may find that overly casual and informal management and more participative or consultative leadership styles do not work as well in Latin American organizations, as followers will have a more traditional perspective of their leaders (i.e., an authority figure, who is not like them and who commands respect, should not be contradicted or told what to do). However, the presence of collectivism alongside high power distance leads to a form of *benevolent paternalism* that has been well documented (Davila & Elvira, 2012; Martinez, 2003; 2005). Moreover, high scores on uncertainty avoidance will lead to followers' expectations that these benevolent but authoritarian leaders provide clear direction and structured processes for followers to do their job effectively (Hofstede, 1980). Abarca, Majluf, and Rodriguez (1998) observed a preference for well-defined rules to guide behavior within organizations in the region.

A high degree of uncertainty avoidance in Latin American cultures is associated with employees' low assertiveness and reluctance to make decisions and accept responsibilities. Research conducted by Abarca, Majluf, and Rodriguez (1998) in the context of Chilean organizations found this to be true; however, they found that low assertiveness and risk aversion diminished among managers with higher levels of education and at higher levels in the organization. High degrees of uncertainty avoidance combined with high degrees of collectivism are also reflected in followers' aversion to conflict and confrontation. This may explain the lower levels of preference for participative or consultative leadership styles (i.e., employees would be reluctant to express their views and opinions when these conflict with those of their superiors). Actions such as pointing out an employee's mistakes in front of others will also be detrimental to the overall organizational climate.

The GLOBE project offered new insights into the culturally contingent nature of leadership in Latin America. As discussed in the previous section, as a group, the nine Latin American countries included in the GLOBE study exhibited a greater preference for charismatic/value-based and team-oriented leadership styles. Participative managerial and self-protective managerial styles were also rated above the GLOBE's averages (see Table 5.8). The study's findings also showed that traits that were universally associated with effective leadership included being trustworthy, collaborative, diplomatic, performance-oriented, skilled administrator, visionary, humane, and team builder. Traits which were seen as hindering effective leadership included being autocratic, self-centered, face-saver, and malevolent, although the intensity of negative perceptions regarding these traits varied by country. Therefore, although in Latin America leaders are not prone to give followers autonomy or to empower them to make decisions, autocratic and self-centered leaders are seen as ineffective. This latter finding is consistent with the well-established preference by Latin Americans for leaders who they see as *benevolent patrones* rather than abusive, autocratic bosses (House et al., 2004; Ogliastri et al., 1999).

Our discussion on leadership styles and culture seems to indicate that a benevolent paternalistic leadership style is preferred and likely to be more effective in Latin America. Benevolent paternalism relies on an unspoken social contract that rules the interactions between managers and employees in today's business organizations. Subordinates expect their managers' protection in exchange for loyalty; thus, there is a sort of dependency-based relationship between leaders and followers. Subordinates expect their managers to take care of their personal and family needs; they also expect to be treated with a minimum level of dignity and respect (Greer & Stephens, 1996). Similarly, managers see the organization as a 'family' for which they need to provide, and any actions that violate this duty will result in employees feeling betrayed. Some researchers have found that this expectation is primarily associated with top-level management and not direct supervisory roles, and employees will often bypass their immediate supervisors and take their problems or concerns to the top (Page & Wiseman, 1993). A corresponding concept of *fraternalism* (brotherhood) has been identified instead for the role expectations of lower level supervisors (d'Iribarne, 2002; Martinez, 2003). Behrens (2010) found that this leadership style may be less predominant in knowledge-based industries. A paternalistic leadership style is also consistent with Latin Americans' expectations for egalitarianism, a balance between what d'Iribarne (2001, p. 28) describes as 'equals that do not cooperate' and 'authority that intimidates.' Attempts by foreign leaders to adopt a more *transactional* leadership style, with its underlying expectation that workers will perform their jobs in exchange for a wage are likely to have disappointing results. Employees in Latin America will not engage with the organization's goals or give their best if they feel the organization, represented by its leaders, does not care about them and their families.

Finally, although Latin Americans seem to gravitate toward charismatic leaders, in today's global organizations, it is more common to find transformational leaders than charismatic ones. Transformational leaders provide vision and inspiration and create the conditions necessary for employees to willingly and enthusiastically contribute to the goals of the organization (Bass & Avolio, 1994). Charismatic leaders appeal to others but tend to be self-centered, while transformational leaders tend to focus on their followers. Over the next few years, it will be interesting to observe whether any changes to leadership style preferences emerge in Latin American organizations. By all accounts, a transition from old to new styles of leadership is already under way in Latin America. For one, some of the largest family businesses in the region are being passed on to a younger generation. This new generation has been educated in some of the best universities in the US and Europe, is fluent in English, and technologically savvy. In the best planned succession cases, they have not only worked abroad outside of the family business but also have spent many years learning their own businesses from the bottom up and are, therefore, extremely knowledgeable about their industries and their national markets. Analysts familiar with the management of family groups in the region expect this new cadre of leaders to be more attuned with the needs of consumers, more aware of social and environmental responsibilities, more willing to embrace modern talent management practices, and more open to internationalization beyond the region. In fact, research on Multilatinas and Global Latinas shows that their visionary, outward thinking leaders are one of these companies' most important success factors (Casanova, 2009; Brenes, 2012; Long, 2013).

Women Leaders in Latin America

Research shows that the presence of women in executive positions and in boards of directors improves organizational performance. Despite gains in the number of women now occupying positions at the top, there is a persistent gender gap across all regions of the world, Latin America is no exception (Artigas, Callegaro, & Novales-Flamarique, 2013; Credit Suisse, 2021; McKinsey & Company, 2010; Moreno, 2013; United Nations, 2010).

Since 2007, McKinsey & Co. has been conducting global surveys on the impact of gender diversity on corporate performance, consistently showing that gender diversity (including having three or more women in C-level positions) is a driver of corporate performance. Their findings also show that gender diversity strengthens organizations' ability to recruit and retain talent and raises productivity and employee morale. Similarly, a study by the European Commission found that 58% of companies with diversity programs reported higher productivity and improved employee motivation, and 62% reported easier recruitment and retention of highly talented people (Desvaux, Devillard-Hoellinger, & Meaney, 2008). Another study found that having at least one woman on the board of directors of a company reduces the chance of bankruptcy by 20% (Women on Boards, 2011). Thus, gender diversity at the top has a positive effect on performance.

Despite the well-documented benefits of gender diversity in organizational leadership, there is a persistent gender gap that needs to be addressed. Culture may help explain gender gaps in leadership positions, but in Latin America, this relationship is not clear cut. For instance, Heller and Gabaldon (2018) looked at the effect of power distance and masculinity on the gender composition of boards in 15 Latin American countries and found mixed results. Our earlier discussion on cultural values shows that Mexico and countries in the Andean region tend to be more masculine, while those in Central America and the Southern Cone are more feminine. One would expect gender inequality to be higher in countries with a more masculine culture. Yet, Heller and Gabaldon's study found gender gaps were present in countries with low and high masculinity scores (the same was true for power distance). Thus, although culture may be a relevant factor, addressing organizational and institutional barriers is perhaps a more viable avenue for closing the existing gender gap in Latin American organizations.

Latin American firms remain reluctant to consider women for governance positions, but there are signs that the region's gender gap is beginning to close. A 2018 study by Grant Thornton found that, on average, 65% of businesses in Latin America had at least one woman in senior management, and 30% of all senior roles were held by women. By 2021, the average percentage of senior roles held by women was 35%, up from 20% in 2017; this was reportedly the best performance over a five-year period for Latin America (Grant Thornton, 2018, 2021). There is also increasing acceptance of women as directors, primarily in the banking and the retail sectors. A 2021 report by Credit Suisse found that in Latin America, 12.7% of board positions are occupied by women. This seems low when compared to Europe (34.4%) and North America (28.6%), but it is certainly an improvement from a decade ago when the percentage of women on boards in the region averaged 6%, ranging from 2% in Chile to 10%

in Colombia (Credit Suisse, 2021; Moreno, 2013). In many cases, the few women who sit on boards of directors of Latin American companies are there because they are members of the family who owns the company, as in the case of FEMSA, a large holding beverage company in Mexico. This is also the case in large family businesses in which a patriarch who is close to retirement age may have daughters rather than sons inherit the reins of the business. Examples of this include Maria Asuncion Aramburuzabala, who took over Grupo Modelo (the maker of Corona) in the 1990s, and Pilar Zabala, the head of Chile's conglomerate Pie de Monte since 2006 (Long, 2013). To the extent that women continue to acquire the same skills and competencies as men (as evidenced by educational achievements) and become more experienced, they are more likely to be considered for these positions. The main benefits of having women in top leadership positions and boards of directors in Latin American firms include strengthening organizational diversity; gaining a better understanding of the marketplace, where women are now more important consumers; balancing men's and women's perspectives in the decision-making process; and developing more open organizational cultures (Moreno, 2013).

Finally, the talent shortages now common in many countries of the world makes the continued gap between men and women in senior management positions untenable; incorporating qualified women into top leadership positions will help fill this talent shortfall (Barsh, Cranston, & Craske, 2008). It could also diversify the pool of leadership and managerial approaches available to Latin American organizations. Past research suggests that women are more likely than men to adopt a transformational leadership style. This may be the result of women adopting a leadership style that allows them to avoid the dangers of gender-incongruent leadership behaviors, whereby women leaders' more communal, relationship-oriented behaviors are seen as more consistent with their traditional gender roles. Women were also more likely than men to use power based on charisma, work record, and contacts (personal power) as opposed to power based on organizational position, title, and the ability to reward and punish (structural power) (Eagly & Carli, 2003; Eagly, Johannesen-Schmidt, & van Engen, 2003; Rosener, 1990). In sum, women's preferred leadership styles can help Latin American organizations effectively compete in the current global environment, which requires companies to place greater emphasis on teamwork, collaboration, and humane-oriented talent management. Furthermore, women's preferred leadership styles are well aligned with the preferred styles of Latin Americans discussed in the previous section.

The incorporation of women across all levels of the organization, but especially in top leadership positions, will help Latin American firms achieve, at a minimum, competitive parity in the global market. Attracting and retaining women leaders will demand that Latin American firms implement clear and deliberate policies aimed at providing skill-building opportunities, social capital building through networking and mentoring, and more flexible working conditions and work-life balance (Artigas, Callegaro, & Novales-Flamarique, 2013; Barsh, Cranston, & Craske, 2008; McKinsey, 2010).

Managing Talent in Latin America

Talent shortages (i.e., skill gaps) have been identified as one of the main challenges facing global leaders, including those in Latin America (Haberer & Kohan, 2007; Ready, Hill, & Conger, 2008; Schwalje, 2011). The main factors driving talent shortages are increased competition, an increasingly aging population, a higher degree of job mobility, and low levels of inclusivity at the top of organizations. The COVID-19 pandemic has exacerbated talent shortages at all levels for most industries. Moreover, today's business organizations require a more sophisticated, globally minded, and technologically savvy manager—this type of manager is in short supply. Latin American firms' ability to recruit and retain talent can become a valuable competitive advantage. This section explores best practices for attracting and developing talent in Latin America.

Research by Davila and Elvira (2005) on work values and human resource management argued that Latin American organizations have adopted hybrid management systems that integrate global and local management practices. Latin American firms increasingly combine the 'old and the new' in the policies and processes that guide their management and development of human capital.

Recruitment and selection practices are influenced by the long-term goals of the organization, local laws, traditional recruitment practices, and cultural differences. As described above, a strong sense of collectivism in the region leads to a preference for those considered members of the in-group. Thus, when there is a job opening, managers will most likely recruit from within their affiliation groups, be it family, friends, university peers, or members of their current employees' families (Flynn, 1994; Gomez & Sanchez, 2005). Selection practices reflect the hybrid management system referenced above. Although skills, merit, and experience are given due weight in the evaluation of an applicant, the applicant's social network and personal characteristics such as gender, age, and physical appearance also play a significant role; this is especially true in the selection of top executives (Abarca, Majluf, & Rodriguez, 1998). Those in the in-group will be more trusted, seen as more reliable, and the availability of more personal information about them may facilitate assessing how an applicant will fit into the organization. In addition, the sense of solidarity and reciprocity that characterizes Latin Americans will impact a manager's decision to choose someone referred by a relative or friend over someone unknown.

Organizational needs for training and development vary by country and are highly dependent on the quality of the country's educational system. Companies operating in Latin America are faced with unskilled and semi-skilled labor pools, and companies are not always able to offer remedial training and education (Davila & Elvira, 2005; Schwalje, 2011). However, companies are recognizing the need for training and have engaged in internal and cooperative training initiatives. The fast pace of technological development and associated work displacement (e.g., automation, artificial intelligence) has raised employees' expectations for reskilling and upskilling. Moreover, developing and maintaining employees' skill sets is fundamental for fostering creativity and innovation (Gonzalez Natal et al., 2021).

Promotions are also influenced by an employee's social network and their personal characteristics, although the influence of these factors is less marked than it is during the selection process (Abarca, Majluf, & Rodriguez, 1998). Promotion, of course, is just shorthand for the more encompassing concept of motivation, a key driver of retention and performance. Maslow's hierarchy of needs theory posits that people's behavior will be motivated by their desire to satisfy lower order needs (e.g., physiological) and will then move up toward the fulfillment of higher order needs (e.g., self-realization) (Maslow, 1970). Given the wide social and economic gaps present in Latin America, one would expect employees to be motivated by lower order needs. This is, in fact, evident in the importance placed by employees on financial compensation and rewards that yield job security, protection for themselves and their families, and a sense of belongingness or affiliation. Lenartowicz and Roth (2001) found that in Brazil, security followed by enjoyment and self-direction were the most important motivators of performance. Yet, Latin Americans are very status conscious; thus, motivators that raise their self-esteem would also have a positive effect on performance. For instance, job titles are very important to individuals to assert their status within the organization, and it is not unusual to see important sounding titles that do not match the level of decision-making power or skills of the title-holder (Flynn, 1994). Perks such as reserved parking spaces, a company phone, and so forth, are highly valued as symbols of higher social standing in the organization.

Herzberg's theory of motivation identified two types of factors: *hygiene* factors, which are considered extrinsic to the job, must be attended to avoid employees' dissatisfaction. *Motivators* are factors which are intrinsic to the employee and are likely to lead to superior performance (Herzberg, 1966). In the context of Latin American organizations, reasonable wages and working conditions would be considered hygiene factors. Similarly, not allowing employees to express their religiosity in the workplace (e.g., crosses, images of the virgin or saints), or publicly criticizing or reprimanding an employee will be deterrents of even minimum levels of performance. Latin American firms seeking superior performance from their employees, however, will need to implement intrinsic motivator factors such as a shared purpose or self-fulfillment.

In terms of the use of positive versus negative reinforcements, Abarca, Majluf, and Rodriguez (1998), found that Chilean managers paid more attention to poor performance, and although they indicated a preference for positive reinforcement, they admitted to using sanctions more frequently than rewards (79% versus 72%). Sanctions were also more formally established than rewards—a practice that has also been observed in the case of Mexican organizations (Kras, 1991).

Performance appraisal and compensation practices, which are intrinsically linked to motivation, must be aligned with employees' cultural values and attitudes. The dislike for conflict and confrontation characteristic of Latin Americans makes performance appraisal impractical and unacceptable to some. The collectivist nature of the culture may lead employees to take an 'everyone is accountable, and thus no one is accountable' position. Power distance also plays a role in performance evaluations. In the case of lower level employees, they may perceive performance appraisals as unfair; because they usually have little control or autonomy over work systems and resources, they may believe that responsibility for performance should fall on upper management. Moreover, employees may see performance appraisals as futile exercises, as they have few expectations of organizational mobility based on merit. Finally, given the high levels of uncertainty avoidance in the region, employees might be reluctant to engage in self-evaluations or accept blame for deficiencies in their performance, as these imply a high professional and financial risk.

The financial rewards and fringe benefits valued by employees are impacted primarily by socioeconomic conditions, labor practices and regulations, and cultural values. In Latin America, a region with wide income differences between the wealthy and the poor, financial compensation is certainly the most important. This can extend beyond salaries to include subsidized or free food, transportation, medical care, and vacation premiums (Flynn, 1994; Gomez & Sanchez, 2005; Greer & Stephens, 1996). Salaries are also important for those in higher positions, as they signal their power and authority to others within and outside the organization. What gives meaning to Latin Americans' work is their need to provide a high quality of life for their families (Davila & Elvira, 2005). Thus, in addition to fair wages, Latin Americans value material and non-material rewards that benefit their families either directly (e.g., educational subsidies for children; health insurance that cover parents) or indirectly (e.g., providing training for the employee that results in promotion possibilities). Moreover, compensation and rewards (e.g., salary increases, vacation time, and promotions) are primarily linked to seniority (Davila & Elvira, 2005). Table 5.10 summarizes the various types of rewards that are valued by employees in Latin American organizations.

Table 5.10 Examples of Rewards Valued by Employees in Latin America

Type of Rewards	Examples
Financial	Fair wages and fringe benefits.
	Especially valued: financial rewards that extend to family (spouse, children, parents). Common benefits include health insurance, school supplies, and educational subsidies.
Security	Position offers a great deal of security in terms of predictable salary, benefits, and future employment.
Affiliation	Social interactions with colleagues.
	Sense of pride of belonging to a well-respected organization.
Status	Rewards that raise the individual's prestige within the group (e.g., promotions, job titles, larger office, reserved parking spaces, use of company car or phone, etc.).
Lifestyle	Work-life balance: time and flexibility to pursue other important aspects of an individual's lifestyle (family, leisure, education, etc.).
Personal Development	Training opportunities related to upskilling and reskilling.
	Horizontal and vertical promotion opportunities.
	Leadership development opportunities.
	Language training.
Well-Being	Resources and systems to prevent burnout and mental health problems.
	Programs to improve physical health (e.g., running clubs, gym memberships).
Authority	Opportunity to manage and direct other people.

Source: Authors' elaboration.

McKinsey's extensive research on talent shortages, especially managerial talent, reveals other best practices that Latin American firms could implement (Guthridge, Komm, & Lawson, 2008; Ready, Hill, & Conger, 2008). These practices include developing a clear company value proposition and brand (i.e., communicating to prospective employees why they should work for your company rather than a competing firm) and offering a good *product* (i.e., jobs that provide meaning, freedom, and opportunities for advancement) as well as a fair *price* (i.e., compensation and lifestyle that meets the needs of employees).

Today's organizations are finding that employees' expectations as to what it means to have a 'good working environment' are evolving. Though the expectation of training and development is not new, expectations about upskilling and reskilling have taken added importance. The fast pace of technology across all industries, results in employees' skills quickly becoming obsolete if not renewed and upgraded, and changes in industries and business models demand learning brand new sets of skills. Allowing employees to improve or replace their skills portfolio also opens opportunities for advancement vertically and horizontally (Gonzalez Natal et al., 2021). Another major change organizations are seeing is the importance employees place on their personal needs, which are also being redefined. For instance, employees may seek to work a reasonable number of work hours vs. working in extreme jobs (Hewlett & Luce, 2006). This is part of a larger trend toward placing greater value on work-life balance, with employees seeking to carve out time for family, fitness, hobbies, or studying. The effects of remote or hybrid work that emerged during the COVID-19 pandemic, and which may become part of a new normal, will require companies to establish clearer boundaries between work and personal time. Related to this is employees' growing concern with their mental and emotional health and their likely preference for working environments that allow them to maintain a healthy lifestyle. Finally, Latin Americans' growing activism reaches into their workplace. Employees, especially the younger generations, expect their employers to be good citizens, to behave in socially and environmentally responsible ways, to pay fair wages, and to support their respective communities. There is more vocal backlash from employees when companies act in ways that run contrary to employees' values (e.g., dumping hazardous waste, supporting a corrupt politician, etc.), and social connectivity means employee discontent can quickly spill over into consumer discontent. Companies that can connect with employees on the causes that matter to them will be more likely to establish a stronger emotional bond with them and, therefore, be better positioned to retain high performing, committed employees (Gonzalez Natal et al., 2021).

Summary

Latin American values have been cemented by centuries of survival and socialization under colonial, republican, and modern times. Perhaps the most influential factor shaping Latin American long-term values is religion. However, the Catholic Church's religious monopoly has been eroded in the past 50 years, a result of 1) their inability to attract new members, 2) the switching of current Catholic members to other faiths, or 3) the increasing levels of secularization. Latin America is still conservative in terms of moral values, but the increase of non-religious affiliations has moved countries into more liberal and tolerant views on abortion, contraception, divorce, and sexual orientation.

Less than half of Latin Americans support democracy, and most are dissatisfied with governments and institutions. A few countries are experiencing democratic breakdowns. Latin Americans strongly support free markets, but the majority believes that the gap between rich and poor is a major problem. Some of Latin Americans' science-related beliefs are aligned with their religious beliefs.

Latin American business culture is rooted in its European colonial heritage. This legacy has created enduring organizational and decision-making styles characterized by concentration of power, rigid hierarchical structures, strong networks of relationships, and paternalism. Yet the differences between Spain and Portugal's colonial approaches led to important distinctions between the business cultures of Brazil and Spanish-speaking Latin America.

Latin Americans are characterized by empathy, familism, particularism, fatalism, and strong relationships. Latin Americans value personal relationships because these relationships have been important for advancement in life. Relationships are based on trust of the same referent group. The intrinsic advantage of trust and loyalty to the group is the expectation that other members will eventually reciprocate.

Four cultural frameworks identify Latin America as a unique business culture. Latin America is described as a high-context culture in which business organizations reflect national cultures characterized by large power distances, collectivism, a tilt toward masculine values, and high uncertainty avoidance. Latin American cultures also have greater tendency toward in-group collectivism, greater gender egalitarianism, and low trust in institutional collectivism.

We also examine leadership styles that are most consistent with Latin American cultural values and are most preferred by followers. As a group, Latin American countries exhibit a preference for charismatic, team-oriented, participative, and self-protective leadership styles. In addition, we find that a benevolent paternalistic style is consistent with followers' preferences, which are shaped by the prevalence of high power distance, masculinity, collectivism, and uncertainty avoidance in the region. Regarding gender diversity in leadership, Latin America lags other regions of the world in the acceptance and presence of women in top positions, although this is slowly changing because of societal and competitive pressures and the adoption of more modern managerial practices.

In terms of motivators, it is important to remember that Latin American workers have an expectation of protection and reciprocity in exchange for loyalty and commitment to the organization's goals. Financial incentives aimed at individual employees alone will not be sufficient. Fringe benefits that extend to families and that provide security and a balanced lifestyle are most valued by employees in Latin America. Therefore, firms in Latin America that adopt best practices aimed at recruiting, retaining, developing, and motivating diverse talent are more likely to position themselves as innovative, competitively agile, and socially responsible; this will, in turn, have a positive effect on organizational performance.

References

Abarca, N., Majluf, N., & Rodriguez, D. (1998). Identifying management in Chile: A behavioral approach. *International Studies of Management and Organizations, 28*(2), 18–37.

Artigas, M., Callegaro, H., & Novales-Flamarique, M. (2013). *Why top management eludes women in Latin America*, 1–7. McKinsey & Co. http://www.mckinsey.com

Barbosa, L., & Da Matta, R. (2006). *O Jeitinho Brasilero: A Arte de Ser Mais Igual Que Os Outros*. Rio Janeiro: Elsevier.

Barsh, J., Cranston, S., & Craske, R. (2008). Centered leadership: How talented women thrive. *The McKinsey Quarterly, 4*, 35–48.

Bass, B. M., & Avolio, B. J. (Eds.). (1994). *Improving organizational effectiveness through transformational leadership*. Thousand Oaks: Sage Publications.

Bazanini, R., & Machado C. (2018). Market as religion: The dynamics of business networks in megachurches. *Brazilian Business Review, 15*, 262–283.

Behrens, A. (2009). *Culture and management in the Americas*. Palo Alto: Stanford University Press.

Behrens, A. (2010). Charisma, paternalism, and business leadership in Latin America. *Thunderbird International Business Review, 52*(1), 21–29.

Boix, C., Miller, M., & Rosato, S. (2018). Dichotomous coding of democracy 1800–2015. *Harvard Dataverse*, V3, UNF:6:dt+jCMIItovQfCIW0PIpOg== [fileUNF]. https://doi.org/10.7910/DVN/FJLMKT

Brenes, E. R. (2012). Latin America's new breed of corporate leaders. *Latin Trade*, (July–August), 14.

Calvano, J., & Marcus-Delgado, J. (2013). *Latin American women rising*. http://www.thedialogue.org/page.cfm?pageID=32 &pubID=3298

Casanova, L. (2009). *Global Latinas: Latin America's emerging multinationals*. London, UK: Palgrave Macmillan.

Credit Suisse. (2021, September 28). *Credit Suisse gender 3000 report shows women hold almost a quarter of board room positions globally*. https://www.credit-suisse.com/about-us-news/en/articles/media-releases/credit-suisse-gender-3000-report-shows-women-hold-almost-a-quart-202109.html

d'Iribarne, P. (2001). Administración y culturas políticas. *Gestión y Política Pública*. 10(1), 5–29, as cited by Elvira, M. M. and Davila, A., Eds. (2005). *Managing Human Resources in Latin America*. London: Routledge.

d'Iribarne, P. (2002). Motivating workers in emerging countries: Universal tools and local applications. *Journal of Organizational Behavior, 23*(3), 243–256.

Davila A., & Elvira, M. M. (2005). Culture and human resource management in Latin America. In Elvira, M. M., & Davila, A. (Eds.), *Managing human resources in Latin America*. London: Routledge.

Davila, A., & Elvira, M. (2012). Humanistic leadership: Lessons from Latin America. *Journal of World Business, 47*, 548–554.

Desvaux, G., Devillard-Hoellinger, S., & Meaney M. C. (2008, September). A business case for women. *The McKinsey Quarterly*. https://internationalwim.org/wp-content/uploads/2020/06/A-business-case-for-women-2008_McKinsey.pdf

Dorfman, P. W., Howell, J. P., Hibino, S., Lee, J. K., Tate, U., & Bautista, A. (1997). Leadership in Western and Asian countries: Commonalities and differences in effective leadership processes across cultures. *Leadership Quarterly, 8*(3), 233–274.

Eagly, A. H., & Carli, L. L. (2003). The female leadership advantage: An evaluation of the evidence. *The Leadership Quarterly, 14*, 807–834.

Eagly, A. H., Johannesen-Schmidt, M. C., & van Engen, M. L. (2003). Transformational, transactional, and laissez-faire leadership styles: A meta-analysis comparing women and men. *Psychological Bulletin, 129*(4), 569–691.

Fleury, A., & Fleury, M. T. (2010). *Brazilian multinationals: Competences and internationalization.* Cambridge, UK: Cambridge Press.

Flynn, G. (1994). HR in Mexico: What you should know. *Personnel Journal, 73*(8), 34–41.

Fracchia, E., & Mesquita, L. F. (2006), Corporate strategies of business groups in the wake of competitive shocks: Lessons from Argentina. *Management Research, 4*(2), 81–98.

Geert Hofstede. (n.d.). *Geert Hofstede globe.* https://geerthofstede.com/hofstedes-globe/

GLOBE 2020. (n.d.). *Latin America.* Retrieved on August 6, 2021. https://globeproject.com/results/clusters/latin-america?menu=cluster#cluster

Gomez, C., & Sanchez, J. I. (2005). Managing HR to build social capital in Latin America within MNCs. In Elvira, M. M., and Davila, A. (Eds.), *Managing human resources in Latin America.* London: Routledge.

Gonzales Natal, D., et al. (2021, February). *Tendencias talento 2021.* Ideas LLYC, Forbes-LLYC. https://ideasplus.llorenteycuenca.com/es/es/tendencias-talento-2021?hsCtaTracking=692ed068-e8e5-4034-a29b-aea1ef6f3896%7C0dc4a6f3-7ce0-403f-be6e-6ee6893cf510

Grant Thornton. (2018). *Women in business: Beyond policy to progress.* www.grantthornton.global/en/insights/women-in-business-2018/

Grant Thornton. (2021). *Women in business 2021: A window of opportunity.* www.grantthornton.global/en/insights/women-in-business-2021/

Greer, C. R., & Stephens, G. K. (1996). Employee relations issues for U.S. companies in Mexico. *California Management Review, 38*(3), 121–145.

Guthridge, M., Komm, A. B., & Lawson, E. (2008). Making talent a strategic priority. *The McKinsey Quarterly, 1*, 49–56.

Haberer, P. R., & Kohan, A. F. (2007). Building global champions in Latin America. *The McKinsey Quarterly*, (Special edition), 1–9.

Hall, E. T. (1959). *The silent language.* New York: Fawcett Publications.

Heller, L., & Gabaldon, P. (2018). Women on boards of directors in Latin America: Building a model. *Academia Revista Latinoamericana de Administración, 31*(1), 43–72.

Herzberg, F. (1966). *Work and the nature of man.* Cleveland: World.

Hewlett, S. A., & Luce, C. B. (2006). Extreme jobs: The dangerous allure of the 70-hour workweek. *Harvard Business Review* (December).

Hofstede, G. (1980). *Culture's consequences: International differences in work-related values.* Thousands Oaks: Sage.

Hofstede, G., Hofstede, G. J., & Minkov, M. (2010). *Cultures and organizations: Software of the minds.* London: McGraw-Hill.

House, R. J., Hanges, P. J., Mansour, M., Dorfman, P. W., & Gupta, V. (Eds.). (2004). *Culture, leadership, and organizations: The GLOBE study of 62 societies.* Thousands Oaks: Sage.

Inglehart, R., & Welzel, C. (2020). *The Inglehart-Welzel world values cultural map.* http://www.worldvaluessurvey.org/

International Institute for Democracy and Electoral Assistance - IDEA. (2019). *The global state of democracy 2019.* https://www.idea.int/publications/catalogue/global-state-of-democracy-2019

Kras, E. S. (1991). *La Administración Mexicana en Transición* [The Mexican Administration in Transition]. Mexico D.F., Mexico: Grupo Editorial Iberoamérica.

Lall, S. (2000). Skills, competitiveness, and policy in developing countries. *QEH Working Paper Series*, Working Paper No. 46.

Latinobarometro. (2018). *Informe 2018*. https://www.latinobarometro.org/latContents.jsp

Lenartowicz, T., & Johnson, J. P. (2002). Comparing managerial values in twelve Latin American countries: An exploratory study. *Management International Review, 42*(3), 279–307.

Lenartowicz, T., & Johnson, J. P. (2003). A cross-national assessment of the values of Latin American managers: Contrasting hues or shades of gray? *Journal of International Business Studies, 34,* 266–281.

Lenartowicz, T., & Roth, K. (2001). Does subculture within a country matter? A cross-cultural study of motivational domains and business performance in Brazil. *Journal of International Business Studies, 32*(2), 305–325.

Long, G. (2013). Dynasties' silent revolution. *Latin Trade.* http://latintrade.com/2013/05/dynasties -silent-revolution.

Martinez, P. G. (2003). Paternalism as a positive form of leader-subordinate exchange: Evidence from Mexico. *Management Research, 1,* 227–242.

Martinez, P. G. (2005). Paternalism as a positive form of leadership in the Latin American context: Leader benevolence, decision-making control, and human resource management practices. In Elvira, M. M., and Davila, A. (Eds.), *Managing human resources in Latin America.* London: Routledge.

Martinez, S. (2013). Women gradually gaining power and influence in Latin America business. *Nearshore Americas.* https://nearshoreamericas.com/women-in-business-latin-america-influence/

Maslow, A. H. (1970). *Motivation and personality.* New York: Harper & Row.

McGregor, D. (1960). *The human side of enterprise.* New York: McGrawHill.

McKinsey & Company. (2010). *McKinsey global survey results: Moving women to the top.* http://www .mckinsey.com

Moreno, A. (2013). Women on board. *Latin Trade.* http://latintrade.com/2013/4/women-on-board

Muczyk, J. P., & Holt, D. T. (2008). Toward a cultural contingency model of leadership. *Journal of Leadership & Organizational Studies, 14*(4), 277–286.

Ogliastri, E., McMillen, C., Altschul, C., Arias, M. E., Bustamante, C., Davila, C., Dorfman, P., Coletta, M. F., Fimmen, C., Ickis, J., & Martinez S. (1999). Cultura y liderazgo organizacional en 10 países de América Latina: El estudio Globe. [Culture and organizational leadership in 10 Latin American countries: The GLOBE study.] *Academia, Revista Latinoamericana de Administración, 22,* 29–57.

Osland, J., De Franco, S., & Oslan, A. (2007). Organizational implications of Latin American culture: Lessons for the expatriate manager. *Economia e Gestao, 7,* 109–120.

Page, N. R., & Wiseman, R. L. (1993). Supervisory behavior and worker satisfaction in the United States, Mexico and Spain. *Journal of Business Communication, 30*(2), 161–181.

Parente, R., Cyrino, A. B., Spohr N., & de Vasconcelos, F. C. (2013). Lessons learned from Brazilian multinationals' internationalization strategies. *Business Horizons, 56,* 453–463.

Pew Research Center. (2014). *Religion in Latin America: Widespread change in a historically Catholic region.* https://www.pewforum.org/2014/11/13/religion-in-latin-america/

Ready, D. A., Hill, L. A., & Conger, J. A. (2008). Winning the race for talent in emerging markets. *Harvard Business Review,* November, 63–70.

Recht, R., & Wilderom, C. (1998). Latin American's dual reintegration. *International Studies of Management & Organization, 28*(2) 3–17.

Reuters (2020). Woman jailed under El Salvador's harsh abortion law walks free from prison. https:// www.reuters.com/article/us-el-salvador-abortion/woman-jailed-under-el-salvadors-harsh -abortion-law-walks-free-from-prison-idUSKCN26E39K

Rodriguez Cuadros, J. D. (2018). The religious shift in Latin America. *Herodote, 171*(4), 119–134.

Rosener, J. B. (1990). Ways women lead. *Harvard Business Review* (November–December), 119–125.

Schwalje, W. A. (2011). The prevalence and impact of skill gaps on Latin America and the Caribbean. *Globalization, Competitiveness, and Governability Journal, 5*(1), 16–30.

Smith, A. E., & Boas, T. C. (2020). Religion, sexuality, politics, and the transformation of Latin American electorates. In *Annual Meeting of the American Political Association,* September 10–13, 2020.

Steingenga, T., & Clearly, E. L. (2007). *Conversion of a continent: Contemporary religious change in Latin America.* New Brunswick: Rutgers University Press.

Trompenaars, F. (1994). *Riding the waves of culture: Understanding cultural diversity in global business.* Burr Ridge: Irwin Professional Publishing.

United Nations. (2010). *The world's women 2010: Trends and statistics.* New York: Department of Economic and Social Affairs, United Nations.

Wardrope, W. (2005). Beyond Hofstede: Cultural applications for communicating with Latin American businesses. In *Proceedings of the 2005 Association for Business Communication*, Irvine, CA.

Weber, M. (1947). *The theory of social and economic organization.* Translated by Talcott Parsons. New York: The Free Press.

Women on Boards. (2011). Department of Business, Innovation, and Skills. https://www.gov.uk/government/publications/women-on-boards-review

6 Business Risks and Uncertainty in Latin America

Introduction

Uncertainty and risks are omnipresent in the world and Latin America with great economic and social consequences for society. The COVID-19 pandemic of 2020 caught the world unprepared and caused devastating human and economic losses. This sad example illustrates the need to assess the likelihood of events that may cause devastating impacts on society and business. It is necessary to develop resilience and adaptive capacity to respond when disasters occur. In this chapter, we explore the nature and types of risks in Latin America as follows. The first section introduces a framework to understand uncertainty and risks and develop scenarios that companies can use to prepare and respond. We use these concepts throughout the chapter. In the following six sections, we identify, define, and assess different types of risks: economic, political, corruption, crime, violence, societal, natural, and climate. In each section, we identify the drivers of risks and provide an assessment of their level across Latin America. We also identify the vulnerability of countries and cities to determine their adaptive capacity and resilience. It is important to note that the level of risks may have dissipated by the time of your reading the chapter, others may have increased in intensity, whereas new risks may have emerged after this publication. Another important characteristic is that risks are interdependent. As you read the analysis of each risk, keep in mind that their sources may be the same, but they manifest in different forms. Furthermore, some risks may feed or amplify others. Also, there is a high degree of heterogeneity of how risks impact each country. For each type of risk, we group countries in terms of their vulnerability to a given risk. Thus, it is important to start with a solid framework to understand risk.

A Framework to Understand Business Risk and Uncertainty

Uncertainty in Latin America is always present and everywhere. Predicting future events is a challenge and requires a better understanding of the nature of uncertainties of a given event and its impact on a business decision. According to experts on the topic, a decision-maker should use all the tools and information available to assess the situation and the nature of uncertainty (Courtney, Kirkland, & Viguerie, 2000; McKinsey Quarterly, 2008). After all these considerations are made, the remaining level of uncertainty is called the residual uncertainty and is the one that is more difficult to assess. The remaining uncertainty can be grouped in four scenarios. The first scenario is identified as a *clear enough future*. This scenario describes a situation of low-level residual uncertainty and a more likely scenario can be identified. Alternative strategies can be easily evaluated with traditional tools such as a discounted cash flow model. Under a second level, several *alternative scenarios* can be identified, but it is

DOI: 10.4324/9781003182672-8

difficult to predict which one would occur. Each scenario may require a different evaluation model and for each model there could be different outcomes. The challenge is to establish the probabilities of each outcome and their associated returns using traditional decision-making analysis. A third level of uncertainty is that of a *range of futures*. Under this situation, some but not all scenarios can be formulated. The uncertainty rests in the risk of not considering a possible scenario that could occur and, therefore, the inability to even identify the outcomes and impacts associated with these unknown scenarios. The challenge under this third level is to consider as many scenarios as are viable and formulate flexible strategies that can be reformulated under evolving unpredictable scenarios. The last level of uncertainty is one of *true ambiguity*, in which the nature of the situation is not well understood, and potential scenarios cannot be identified. At best, one can only identify and monitor favorable or unfavorable indicators through a situation analysis. Decision-makers may be able to gather some insights by analyzing similar events and situations and study strategies that work under those conditions. This level is rare and one in which the uncertainty will resolve overtime with a reduction that moves the situation to a Level 3.

The perception of uncertainty varies with the decision-maker and type of event and is the risk to contemplate. The decision-maker's access to information, familiarity with the event, and resources available to sustain the consequences of a given event are among other factors influencing their perception of risks. Thus, the decision-maker's net risk is the product of their assessment of the likelihood of the event (scenario) times the exposure to them if it takes place (the outcome) and the duration of the exposure (one time or systematic). As described above, this estimation can be precise under a clear future or almost impossible under true ambiguity. A final important concept to introduce is the scope of the risk. The event may impact decision-makers or countries differently or could impact all actors indiscriminately (collective or global risk).

Strategic response depends on the level of uncertainty. *Adapting strategies* work well under a clear enough future (Level 1) and alternative futures (Level 2). These adapter strategies involve a sound analysis of the situation and take the best possible option with no-regrets considerations. When the future is uncertain (Level 3), the recommended strategy is to shape the external environment to favor a positive outcome for the decision-maker. Such *shaper strategies* may, for instance, involve lobbying for favorable legislation or pursuing an innovation strategy that sets a standard for the industry and the firm. These shaper strategies require bold moves and large investments. Strategies for Level 4—true ambiguity—are a challenge. In this situation, firms need to keep all the options open until the uncertainty resolves. This effort requires a stake in all possible plays (reserving the right to play) and monitoring the situation until the uncertainty resolves and a clearer future emerges. In some cases, firms need to invest in capabilities and resources to keep all these options open. No one single player can shape the future and, therefore, such a strategy requires collaboration and credibility leverage among partners and actors (Courtney, Kirkland, & Viguerie, 2000).

With the above introduction of terms and concepts, we proceed to analyze different types of risks in Latin America.

Economic Risks

Current economic prospects and future scenarios present a relatively clear picture of the factors that will drive economic growth and contraction in Latin America over the next few years. In this section, we summarize the economic risks facing Latin America and then assess the level of uncertainty these risks represent for firms doing business in the region.

Understanding of these triggers will facilitate firms' ability to plan for alternative scenarios aligned with Levels 1 and 2 of our previously mentioned uncertainty framework.

Over the next couple of years, the COVID-19 pandemic will continue to be an impending challenge as the global economy recovers. In the short term, how governments in Latin America manage the pandemic and the recovery period post-pandemic will be the number one factor driving economic risk. The region has been one of the hardest hit by the pandemic. By August 2021, COVID-19 had claimed the lives of 1.4 million people in Latin America, with more than 44 million cases reported. Although the region represents only 8.4% of the world's population, by mid-2021, it accounted for about 20% of cases and 30% of deaths in the world (PAHO, 2022; Marsh Specialty, 2021). As discussed in Chapter 1, the pandemic has caused the most severe economic contraction in Latin America over the past century, with many of the gains from the commodity-driven growth of the most recent decades being almost completely wiped out. There are wide disparities across countries in the region regarding handling of the pandemic, including the types of measures put in place to ameliorate damage to the economy and progress on vaccination. In mid-2021, Brazil had the world's second highest number of cases and one of the highest mortality rates. In spite of these alarming numbers, President Bolsonaro continued to downplay the severity of the health crisis, and his government failed to implement an effective response to control the pandemic and drive economic recovery (Marsh Specialty, 2021). Similar scenarios of mismanagement have played out in countries such as Guatemala, Honduras, Mexico, and Venezuela. Countries such as Costa Rica, Chile, and Uruguay implemented a series of measures intended to control the pandemic, from free and accessible testing and increases to hospital capacity to mandatory mask requirements and social distancing measures. Yet even countries that, initially, managed their resources well enough to achieve low incidence of cases and deaths saw their health systems overwhelmed during the new waves caused by variants (PAHO, 2022). In terms of vaccination efforts, there are also significant disparities across the region. By early November 2021, Chile had the highest vaccination rate (87%), with the two largest countries, Brazil and Mexico, trailing at 75% and 68%, respectively. The rate of vaccination was even lower in countries such as Guatemala and Nicaragua, which registered vaccination rates of 30% and 19%, respectively (Our World in Data, 2021).

Governments in the region seeking to manage the pandemic and the recovery post-pandemic have the option of continuing to provide relief through economic subsidies and injections of money into their economies, but this can lead to higher debt risk. Governments with weak revenue and reserve positions and current high debt levels are likely to rely on even more debt in order to finance social support programs and/or to refinance debt payments. The other option is for governments to cut subsidies and social programs, which can lead to deepening recessions and social unrest. Either way, economic risks for countries in the region will trend upward in the short term (CE Noticias Financieras, 2020; PAHO, 2022).

The longer the pandemic wreaks havoc in some countries in the region, the greater the social and economic damage they will have to repair, and likely, the longer their economic recovery will take. It is these asymmetries across the region regarding recovery from the COVID-19 pandemic that will result in different levels of economic risk in the short and medium term. For countries that have been more proactive and effective in managing the pandemic and that have achieved higher vaccination rates, uncertainty falls under Level 1 of our framework. In this case, businesses can use traditional analytical tools to develop clear enough strategic scenarios. For those countries where the pandemic is still far from being controlled and which have a long way to go in achieving wide vaccination coverage, uncertainty will fall under Level 2 of our framework. In the latter case, businesses will need to closely monitor key risk indicators (e.g., unemployment rates, poverty rates, debt levels) and formulate alternative scenarios.

Another important driver of economic risk is social inequality, which has polarized Latin American societies in the past few years. This is evidenced by mass demonstrations and protests that have been triggered in response to certain austerity measures and policy announcements, such as reforms to tax codes and pension systems, price increases to gas and public transportation, and cuts to social programs (Marsh Specialty, 2021; Sheridan, 2019; Ward, 2020). The COVID-19 pandemic has exacerbated social inequality in the region, widening the gap between rich and poor, and reversing years of poverty reduction gains (i.e., more than 22 million people have slid into poverty due to the pandemic). This has been particularly the case among already vulnerable groups (e.g., women, children, those at the base of the socioeconomic pyramid, select racial and ethnic groups) (Marsh Specialty, 2021; Stott, 2021). Therefore, issues like unemployment, food insecurity, and rising costs of energy, healthcare, and housing which impact those at the base of the socioeconomic pyramid most severely will continue to be a lightning rod of social unrest (see the section on societal risks in this chapter for a more detailed discussion). Reducing income gaps and social inequalities will require political action aimed at correcting structural and institutional barriers and policy-making that is consistent and sustained for more than one presidential or legislative period. Government inaction in addressing inequalities that have gone ignored for far too long, even after many years of sustained economic growth—and which have been worsened by the pandemic—is not likely to sit well with Latin Americans, especially the emergent middle class and aspiring lower income class. Political actions that put the burden of recovery on low- and middle-income classes through increased taxes and cuts to social programs will have a similar negative effect. In addition to the risks associated with continued social unrest in the form of strikes, demonstrations, and the like, social inequalities hurt Latin American countries' ability to generate the kinds of productivity gains, innovation, and domestic consumption and investment necessary to reenergize their economies. The risks derived from socioeconomic inequalities are known and easily observable; however, the policy responses to the causes of these socioeconomic inequalities are harder to predict. Addressing the structural problems leading to these inequalities will require political will and governing competency, both of which seem to be currently in short supply across the region. Thus, levels of economic uncertainty due to these inequalities are likely to fall in Levels 2 and 3 of the uncertainty framework.

As already noted, in the short term, as countries in the region emerge from the pandemic, they are likely to adjust current social and economic policies, including elimination of subsidies to individuals and businesses, reduction of social protection programs, increases to interest rates, and the like. Firms, domestic and international, should continue to monitor key macroeconomic indicators that may signal economic or social instability. Long-term factors that may lead to economic instability include low productivity, lack of investments in innovation, poor infrastructure, and high poverty rates. The reversals to income gains caused by the COVID-19 pandemic will need to be recovered to ensure a healthy middle class that can sustain domestic demand. In addition, investments in badly needed infrastructure (e.g., health, education, energy, and transportation) and in innovative capabilities will be necessary for governments and firms in the region to shield themselves from future global economic crises. Economic risks in the region will vary by country depending especially on how each country manages recovery post-pandemic (see Table 6.1 for a summary of economic risks).

Marsh Specialty's World Risk Review platform tracks nine types of risks: contractual agreement repudiation risk; country economic risk; currency inconvertibility and transfer

Table 6.1 Summary of Economic and Political Risks in Latin America

Economic Risks	Risk Level (Low–High) and Uncertainty Level (1–4)	Political Risks	Risk Level (Low–High) and Uncertainty Level (1–4)
Management of COVID-19 pandemic: negative effects on economic growth, business performance, employment, inflation, and public debt.	Medium 1–2	Weakening of democracy: driven primarily by a rise of authoritarianism and growing political extremism. Poor policymaking and lack of real solutions to most pressing problems is also a cause of dissatisfaction with democratic systems.	High 1–2
Ongoing social inequality/ growing poverty rates: exacerbated by COVID-19, recent tax increases, high prices, cuts to social programs, etc.	Medium-High 2–3	Endemic corruption: deters foreign investment, encourages capital flights, lowers productivity of public expenditures, increases business costs.	Medium-High 1–2
Long-term structural risks: low levels of foreign investment, low labor productivity, lack of investments in innovation and infrastructure.	Medium 1–2	Crime and violence: risks derived from organized crime and gangs increase security risks and reduce the region's overall attractiveness and competitiveness. Brain drain, especially vulnerable youth recruited by crime organizations.	High 2–3

Source: Authors' elaboration.

risk; expropriation risk; legal and regulatory risk; sovereign credit risk; strikes, riots, and civil commotion risk; terrorism risk; and war and civil war risk. Marsh rates these risks on a scale of 1–10, with 10 indicating the highest level of risk. Marsh's ratings of country economic risk for select countries in Latin America for 2021 are presented below (Marsh, 2021):

0.0–2.0: No LAC country scored < 2.1
2.1–4.0: Chile, Mexico, Panama, Peru
4.1–6.0: Belize, Bolivia, Brazil, Colombia, Costa Rica, the Dominican Republic, Ecuador, El Salvador, Guatemala, Guyana, Honduras, Nicaragua, Trinidad and Tobago, Paraguay, Uruguay
6.1–8.0: Argentina, Cuba, Haiti, Suriname
8.1–10.0: Venezuela

These estimates of primarily moderate risk and economic-related uncertainty of Levels 1 and 2 of our framework suggest that firms doing business in Latin America should pursue adapter strategies. The 'uncertainty thermometer' developed by Guachamín et al. (2020) identifies some variables that are good predictors of uncertainty and vulnerability, such as inflation, GDP growth rates, FDI flows, debt, poverty gap, and government expenditures on health and education. Businesses are familiar with the process of scanning and analyzing these macroeconomic and social development indicators factors and have the tools necessary to measure and forecast economic scenarios derived from these factors as well as formulate strategic responses to them.

Political Risks

The two primary sources of political risk in the region are the weakening of democracy and endemic corruption. In Chapter 2, we discussed the political environment of the region in detail. Here, we limit ourselves to providing a summary of political risk factors in the short and medium term and assessing these risks within the uncertainty framework presented earlier. In the short term, the 2021–2022 election cycle will determine the types and scope of political risk firms will face. In the medium term, the scope and severity of political risk will depend on various factors, especially, the policies implemented by governments in the region to bring their respective economies out of the pandemic and to address growing societal discontent as well as the actions taken to control corruption and improve governance.

The Weakening of Democracy

The weakening of democracy in the region is being driven primarily by two parallel trends: the rise of authoritarianism and growing political extremism. The democratic landscape in Latin America is decidedly heterogeneous, with some countries demonstrating strong and resilient democracies (e.g., Costa Rica and Uruguay), others sliding away from democracy (e.g., El Salvador and Brazil), and others with open authoritarian regimes in place (e.g., Cuba and Venezuela) (d+i, 2018; International IDEA, 2019, 2021). The *Global State of Democracy 2021* report indicates that the majority of countries in Latin America are considered mid-range performing democracies, with Brazil being considered a backsliding democracy. El Salvador, Guatemala, and Paraguay are deemed weak democracies; Honduras, a hybrid democracy; and Cuba, Nicaragua, and Venezuela totalitarian regimes (International IDEA, 2021). Yet even if the current assessment shows a majority of countries in the region still live in moderately stable democracies, across the region, the tendencies toward more authoritarian regimes seem to be looming and reaching in all directions, from El Salvador on the right side of the political spectrum to Mexico on the left side of the political spectrum. Authoritarian regimes not only influence the openness and dynamism of their economic environments but also may put in jeopardy the fragile gains in democracy and respect of civil liberties made in the past 30 years or so. The history of the region shows that doing away with authoritarian regimes and returning to democracy is an extremely difficult enterprise; thus, any movement in this direction should be considered a high level of political risk.

Even in countries where authoritarianism has not taken hold, we observe high levels of polarization with swings toward extreme left and right positions in the political spectrum, with few opportunities for consensus building and effective governance. The presidential–legislative crises Peru has experienced since 2018 and the 2019–2022 presidential and legislative elections in Argentina are a good example. In Honduras, the November 2021 elections drove Hondurans to the polls (almost 70% participation) even in the midst of the pandemic, to make their voices heard. Xiomara Castro of the Libre Party-led coalition (left-leaning) won the election with 51% of the vote to become the first woman president of Honduras. The incumbent National Party captured 37% of the vote, a clear rejection by Hondurans of the authoritarian aspirations, growing corruption, and poor governance of the National Party (right-leaning) that has ruled Honduras for the past 12 years (CNE, 2021). Xiomara Castro, wife of former president Manuel Zelaya—who had authoritarian aspirations of his own—should take the summary rejection of Juan Orlando Hernandez as a sign that Hondurans are willing to defend their democratic system, weak as it may be. Finally, Chile's second presidential election round was also between candidates who stood on political extremes, with Gabriel Boric representing a left-leaning coalition and the ultra-conservative Jose Antonio Kast representing the right. The election of 35-year-old Gabriel Boric with almost 60% of the vote, however, signaled Chileans ultimate rejection of ultra-conservatism and authoritarianism and a message, especially from women and the younger generations in Chile, that the country must move toward a more inclusive and equitable society (Ramos Miranda & Cambero, 2021; Suarez et al., 2021).

In addition to the extreme swings between left and right that authoritarian aspirations of incumbents lead to, policymaking in countries where the legislative and executive powers hold positions in strong opposition to each other is difficult to say the least. The negative effects of the continuous in-fighting and ensuing lack of progress in addressing the problems afflicting citizens across the region can be seen in the social discontent that has led to recent demonstrations and political turmoil. Democratically elected leaders across the region failed to use the windfalls generated during the commodity boom years to correct structural weaknesses and to build economic systems grounded on strong infrastructure, education, and innovation and a better redistribution of economic gains. Instead, they used those gains to provide cash payments and subsidies that advanced their political goals (e.g., Venezuela). As the revenues from commodities dried up, these same governments were faced with the need to adopt austerity measures and incur debt (Economist Intelligence Unit, 2019). The resulting frustration with the lack of solutions to long-standing problems in the region likely explains the declining ratings that 'democracy as a preferred system of government' receives around the region. Citizens' negative perceptions toward democracy and their increasingly favorable attitudes toward authoritarian regimes (or increasing indifference toward a preferred government system) bode ill for Latin America. In the long term, the danger of weak democratic governments is an even larger number of countries in the region accepting authoritarian leaders that offer 'solutions' to social problems, especially socioeconomic inequalities and crime (Arnson, 2020; International IDEA, 2019, 2021; Sheridan, 2019; Zechmeister & Lupu, 2019). Take the case of Mexico. President Andres Manuel Lopez Obrador (popularly known as AMLO) remains popular (60% approval rating in December 2021), and although the 2021 midterm elections resulted in his party, Morena's-led coalition, losing two-thirds of the lower house, it gained some executive positions across the country (governorships, mayoralties, and seats in local legislatures) (Zissis, 2021). AMLO's popularity, however, is based on personal charisma and populism, and it does not reflect much progress in reducing crime and violence or effectively addressing other problems that continue to ail Mexico. His anti-crime policies have not had much of an effect. In September 2020, two years into his presidency, murders in the country were still around 3,000 per month, about the same level registered during 2018–2019, with drug trade, violence against women, and murdered journalists and political candidates still making headlines regularly. Mexico's economy is struggling, in large part, due to the devastating effects of the current pandemic. The country has the fourth highest number of COVID-19 deaths, and AMLO's government policies have relied on expanding the number of hospital beds, with little testing available, no mandatory lockdowns, and low vaccination rates. This 'blind support' of AMLO, who hails austerity and fighting corruption as his main accomplishments, should be worrisome, especially amid growing accusations of militarization and suspicions of power consolidation aspirations linked to a possible 2022 referendum (Agren & Nuño, 2021; Al Jazeera, 2020).

Corruption

Corruption is not a phenomenon limited to Latin America, all countries to various degrees suffer from corruption. Corruption has some defining characteristics (d+i, 2016):

- It is difficult to define and measure.
- It is, primarily, the result of flaws in a country's institutional environment.
- It is aggravated by national cultural values, behaviors, and attitudes that tolerate and enable it.

There is, nevertheless, some agreement on the negative effects of corruption—the most direct effects of corruption translating into significant economic risks and costs for individuals, organizations, and governments. In Latin America, endemic corruption continues to be a main source of political and economic risks. In 2013, the World Bank estimated that corruption during the 2001–2002 period amounted to 3% of the world's GDP. Economic losses associated with corruption can be observed in Latin American countries. For example, in 2013, the Bank of Mexico estimated that corruption accounted for about 9% of the country's GDP. In 2010, estimates of corruption costs in the State of São Paulo, Brazil, were estimated at between 1.4% and 2.3% of GDP, while Peru estimated that corruption accounted for about 2% of its GDP. In addition, high levels of corruption can deter foreign investors, encourage capital flights, and lower the productivity of public expenditures (d+I, 2016).

Corruption is associated with weak governability and mismanagement of public funds. The resulting poor performance of incumbent regimes due to corruption can, in turn, lead to societal discontent (discussed later in the chapter) and political instability. Citizens across the region are confronted with corruption regularly and at all levels. The widespread perception is that corruption cuts across all governmental institutions and a belief that individuals can take little action in the fight against corruption (Transparency International, 2019). Latin Americans' high awareness of the frequency of corruption scandals and their belief that, even with growing activism, corrupt actions will go unpunished is very much related to their declining trust in democracy and institutions, especially political parties. Corruption perceptions are also present among businesses. About 45% of companies considered corruption a major constraint in their operations, 14% expected to give gifts in order to secure contracts, and 11% expected to give gifts to public officials to 'get things done' (World Bank Enterprise Surveys, n.d.). Corruption in the region has three main characteristics (d+i, 2016):

- Average levels of corruption incidence when compared to other emerging regions such as Asia or Africa.
- Intra-region heterogeneity with some countries having very low levels of corruption and others having disturbingly high levels.
- Modest progress in the fight against corruption but progress, in general, is too slow.

What happened during the 2020–2021 pandemic is a prime example of how corruption aggravated government responses that were already ineffective. Graft has been rampant since the start of the COVID-19 pandemic, including the purchase and provision of low quality personal protective equipment (PPE) for police officers in Peru; overpaying for faulty medical equipment in Bolivia, Honduras, and Mexico; and government officials colluding to grant price-gouging contracts of public hospitals' supplies in Ecuador (Arnson, 2020; Kitroeff & Taj, 2020). See Chapter 2 for additional information on how countries in the region performed on various corruption measures.

From the perspective of managing corruption risk and uncertainty, the question then is, do countries in the region have the capacity to combat corruption? The Capacity to Combat Corruption Index assesses the ability of countries in Latin America to detect, prevent, and punish corruption. The index uses 14 variables grouped in three categories: legal capacity, democracy and political institutions, and civil society and media to determine how effectively countries can combat corruption. Some of these variables include judicial independence and efficiency, access to public information and overall government transparency, quality and enforceability of campaign finance legislation, civil society mobilization against corruption, and quality of the press and investigative journalism. In 2021, the CCI Index evaluated '15 countries, which together represent almost 95% of Latin America's GDP' (Winter & Aalbers, 2021, p. 3). Figure 6.1 below shows their key findings.

Uruguay was the best performer for the second consecutive year; rounding up the top five scorers were Chile, Costa Rica, Peru, and Argentina. The bottom three performers were Guatemala, Bolivia, and Venezuela. About half of the countries saw no changes to their scores from the previous year, while three countries showed large improvements (the Dominican Republic, Ecuador, and Panama), and five showed significant declines (Brazil, Colombia, Mexico, Bolivia, and Guatemala). It is worth noting that the two largest economies in the region—Brazil and Mexico—both saw sharp declines in their ability to combat corruption (−0.45 and −0.30 from the 2020 score, respectively). As mentioned previously and in Chapter 2, the pandemic has dampened the region's ability to continue to make progress in its fight against corruption. Yet, citizens, organizations, and governments must recommit to establishing the institutional environment reforms necessary to reduce corruption. Some key recommendations to move the region's countries in this direction include:

- Providing sufficient funding to anti-corruption and law enforcement agencies and institutions;
- Pushing anti-corruption legislation through the legislative approval process, including passing or strengthening money laundering and campaign financing law; and
- Maintaining the independence of prosecutors and judges to ensure those guilty of corruption charges receive appropriate sanctions (Winter & Aalbers, 2021).

Finally, it is easy to blame public sector officials for corruption, but corruption is a two-way street. The private sector must also confront its roles and responsibilities in fighting corruption, if for no other reasons that economic self-interest. Corruption reduces a country's competitiveness, it raises the costs of operations, it slows down strategy implementation, it can lead to reputational damage, and more. Businesses can be asked to pay bribes and kickbacks, threatened with physical or personal injury through extortion schemes, and forced to give up a business opportunity to avoid breaking the laws of their home and host countries. Thus, the private sector needs to take action to combat corruption alongside the region's governments. Taking care of the 'basics' is a good place to start, including having a code of ethics that guides the behavior of internal actors and external partners, leadership that signals its commitment to anti-corruption efforts, and clear processes that remove ambiguity and, thus, leave little room for employees' and managers' discretion when faced with corruption-related dilemmas. In addition, nurturing a culture of honesty, transparency, and accountability is also key.

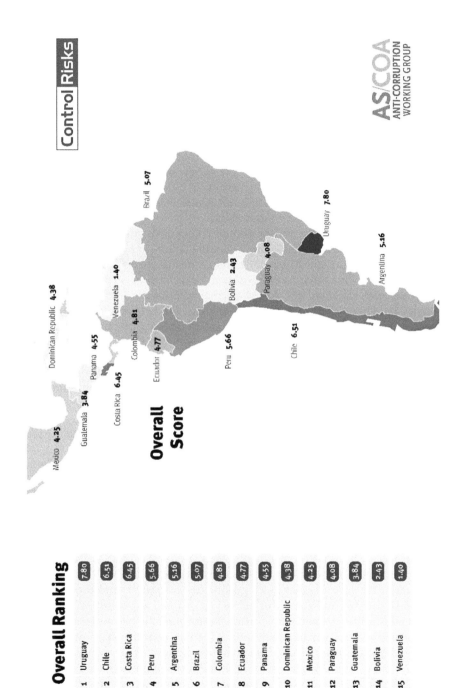

Figure 6.1 Capacity to Combat Corruption Index (2021) Working Group (2021). Source: Winter & Aalbers (2021)

Externally, businesses should support citizens' calls for stronger anti-corruption measures and judicial accountability for bad actors (Venkatesan, 2015).

Although the political risks in the region can be considered high, uncertainty levels fall under Levels 1 and 2 of our framework. The political risks are well known, can be anticipated, and firms can plan strategic responses accordingly. It is the effects (and costs) of these political risks that are more difficult to estimate and measure, thus pointing to a moderate level of uncertainty. For example, businesses operating in countries with leaders that espouse anti-business ideologies (e.g., Pedro Castillo in Peru and Xiomara Castro in Honduras) may be concerned about facing higher levels of political risk. However, these businesses would not find it difficult to anticipate the most likely changes to policies and regulations that such types of administrations may seek to implement. Faced with less business-friendly policies and regulations, companies would need to develop strategic responses to alternative scenarios and then identify and monitor key indicators that would trigger specific responses based on these alternative scenarios. The case of Chile is another example of moderate uncertainty. The process of drafting a new constitution, its approval in 2022, and implementation bring with them some level of uncertainty over the next two to three years. However, businesses can monitor progress in the legislative process and plan for alternative scenarios.

Crime and Violence

Crime and violence in Latin America is as endemic a problem as corruption. Many governments in the region have attempted to reduce the incidence of crime, with limited success. For instance, homicide rates per 100,000 inhabitants in 2015 ranged from 15 in Mexico to 103 in El Salvador; by 2020, the rate for Mexico had increased to 27 but had dropped to 18 in El Salvador. Other countries with high homicide rates also saw significant drops (e.g., Honduras, 60 to 29; Brazil, 29 to 20; and Colombia 26 to 19) (Fonseca & Cruz, 2021). These minor gains, however, have been the result of applying 'band aids' to a problem that needs long-term treatment of its causes.

The rise of transnational crime organizations in the region will be a challenge difficult to overcome. The disbanding of terrorists and paramilitary groups dating back to the 1980s and 1990s gave rise to large groups of well-trained, armed people who were not interested in peace or returning to a quiet life in mainstream society. In many cases, these individuals and groups became partners of or were absorbed by organized crime networks. Over the years, local and regional organized crime networks (which include gangs and drug cartels) have expanded globally, becoming transnational crime organizations (TCOs). These TCOs manage the illicit movement of drugs, arms, minerals, and people; control key strategic territories to ensure free passage for their illicit trade activities; and terrorize local communities via extortion, threats, kidnapping, and other forms of violence. Many of these TCOs have become sophisticated, operating full portfolios of both illicit activities that generate revenue and licit activities used to launder money and gain public legitimacy. In most cases, these crime organizations are well-connected to people in positions of power, from politicians and high-ranking military officials to heads of business organizations (AQ Staff, 2021; Dammert, 2021; Sweigart & Rauls, 2021).

The COVID-19 pandemic has strengthened rather than weakened gangs and TCOs. The closure of schools, particularly in rural areas and low-income communities, is resulting in a larger pool of young people from which gangs can recruit new members (either voluntarily or forcefully). By the end of 2020, 97% of students across the region were still not physically in school. By the end of 2021, many children remained out of physical classrooms, even if some had returned to classes virtually. Children and youth living in rural areas have not benefited from virtual modalities of schooling due to a lack of computers and internet access. In many communities, children's education has been limited to worksheets they complete at home at regular intervals (Otis, 2021). The effects of educational losses to long-term productivity have already been discussed. An equally serious negative effect is the loss of young people, perhaps permanently, to crime and violence. In Colombia, it is estimated that in the first half of 2020, recruitment of young people by gangs was five times the level reported a year earlier. Schools can be safe havens for youth in certain regions of Latin America, providing food, a safe space, and access to caring teachers and administrators that look after them. In the absence of these safe spaces, youth are left at the mercy of gangs that will use recruitment practices such as offering money and guns, or forceful removal under threats of death (Otis, 2021). The increases to unemployment rates caused by the pandemic have left youth—already one of the groups most impacted by unemployment before the pandemic—with even fewer options for legal job opportunities, especially in regions where the economy is largely dominated by drug trafficking. Crime organizations have also proven agile and adaptable, using the pandemic to garner even more control over communities and gain public legitimacy (e.g., providing food, enforcing lockdowns, and delivering services where governments left vacuums), while ramping up their cybercrime practices to counter the effects of lockdowns (Fonseca & Cruz, 2021).

Uncertainty related to the risks derived from increasing crime and violence in Latin America are likely to fall in Levels 2 and 3 of our framework. In this case, companies will need to implement both adapter strategies (based on alternative scenarios developed on the basis of conditions that can be identified and estimated) and shaper strategies (using lobbying, innovation, disruption, and similar strategies to prepare the firm for a range of futures that cannot be fully anticipated). Crime-related uncertainty is likely to fluctuate between Levels 2 and 3 depending on the actions taken by the region's governments to both combat organized crime through law enforcement processes and tackle the root causes of the problem (i.e., social inequality, lack of government attention to the needs of disenfranchised communities, access to legal job opportunities).

Societal Risks

Individuals interacting with others and their habitat can create societal risks. Such interactions are considered risks if they are unpredictable and result in material or personal losses. A clear example of societal risk is a social protest that disrupts the economic and daily activities of a city or a country. Protests may have a structure and agenda or emerge spontaneously; either, however, has the potential to quickly grow in scale and become difficult to control. Protests often have a specific trigger and can produce a rapid mobilization with the support of social media. Although the trigger can be a minor event or policy change, a rapid massive reaction is an indication of built-up discontent, frustration, and anger in society. The scope of protests could be local or national as some are replicated in several cities. When a situation becomes unmanageable for authorities to control or produces a violent backlash from authorities, riots, looting, and widespread damage to private and public property occurs. The cycle of protests could be short lived if the grievances are resolved or become persistent and chronic if these grievances are ignored. Occasionally, social protests lead to major changes and or reversals of the policies or measures that triggered the protests in the first place. As stated above, these events are considered risks because they are uncertain (hard to predict) and have the potential to end in real losses to the economy and affect all citizens. Strikes and riots can disrupt the food supply chain to cities and cause shortages of food, energy, or water. Figure 6.2 provides a visual presentation of the dynamics of social protests in Latin America.

In the short period of 2018–2019, social protests in Latin America reached an unprecedented level of activity (Schifter, 2020). The COVID-19 pandemic of 2020 put a halt to social protests, as all governments mandated lockdowns and restricted public meetings. With some degree of management of the pandemic, social movements returned in 2021. Table 6.2 provides a selective list of social protests in Latin America during such periods. The list does not include the protests related to racial discrimination and violence in the same period, which were discussed earlier in the book (see social protests in Chapter 4). As can be seen in Table 6.2, the triggers of social protests in many Latin American countries were specific issues and policies such as a price increase of metro fares in Chile, gasoline prices in Ecuador, violence against women in Mexico, food shortages in Cuba, or economic austerity policies in Haiti. Other protests were triggered by political developments, such as the removal of corrupt president in Peru, presidential election irregularities in Bolivia, the dismantling of the war crimes commission in Colombia, and the incompetent response of the Brazilian government to the pandemic (Daniels, 2020; Open Democracy, 2020; Phillips et. al, 2021; Wolf, 2020). In most cases, protesters added more endemic and systemic issues to their agenda, such as corruption, political repression, or economic and social inequalities. Many of the groups had cohesive core constituencies such as Indigenous peoples (Price, 2019), women, or students, which allowed them to organize quickly through social media with very effective mobilizations in a very short period. In most cases, governments responded with violence and repression, resulting in injuries and, in some cases, death and missing people. In other cases, social protests led to change. For instance, as a result of social protests in 2019, the Chilean government reversed the decision to increase metro fares (initial agenda), formed a commission to draft a new constitution to replace the one introduced during the dictatorship of Pinochet (broader agenda), and introduced educational reforms for more equal access to education (BBC News, 2020). Yet in other cases, the social protests did not lead to any changes, and the initial enthusiasm of protesters faded out over time, which is the case of the women's movements in Mexico.

Sources of Discontent

Many sources of discontent can build up anger and frustration in Latin America, as shown in Figure 6.2. The main source is the perception of inequality. There are many dimensions of inequality perception, from income and wealth to the perception of inequality of access to education, health services, and housing. All these dimensions translate into the perception of individuals' social class or status as either stagnant or not commensurate to expectations. Other sources of frustration are more tangible, such as unemployment, lack of food, inadequate water supply, or shortages of energy. An additional source of frustration is the perception that democratic systems are not working, whether that means systematic corruption in government, allegations of voting fraud, or lack of representation in the political system by minority populations (Simon, 2019). More recently, a source of anger is the recent migration flow of displaced people from other countries, such as the recent flows of displaced Venezuelans and Haitians, that can burden the ability of recipient cities to accommodate them. For example, Chile has seen violent, xenophobic protests against immigrant settlement camps in northern border cities (Reuters, 2021).

According to country risk experts, the sources of discontent behind civil unrest were numerous and intense in particular countries (Rosales, Selman, Cardenas, & Burford, 2021):

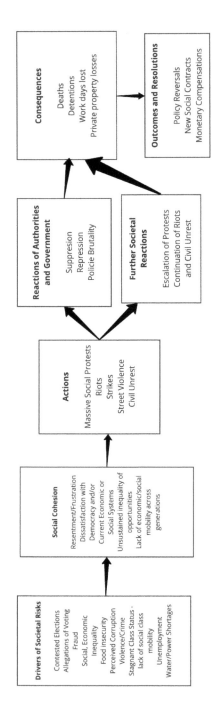

Figure 6.2 Dynamics of societal risk. Source: Authors' Elaboration

Table 6.2 Social Protests in Latin America

Country/Year	Triggers	Arguments/Goals	Scope/Groups	Government Response	Protest Response Consequences	Resolution Outcomes
Haiti 2019–2021	Consumer price increases Rigged presidential election	Corruption, End economic austerity measures Resignation of president	Massive Daily protests	Violent repression	Car burnings, Business closings About 200 protesters and police killed	Massive migration President Moise assassinated New elections called, 2021 earthquake
Ecuador 2019	Gas price increase	IMF economic austerity measures to reduce government deficit	Indigenous communities, Taxi and bus drivers	Excessive police force	Vandalism and looting 11 protesters killed 1,500 injured	Government abandons austerity measures
Bolivia 2019	Presidential election irregularities	Political corruption	Massive Full country	Excessive military force	10 people killed	President Morales fled country, New elections called Clean elections in 2020
Venezuela 2019	Power blackouts	End power blackouts Political repression Coordinated effort to remove President Maduro	Massive Full country Also pro-government groups	Violent repression	Clashes between protesters and security forces	No change
Chile 2019–2021	Metro Price Increase	Consumer price increases Unaffordable education and health	Nationwide 1.2 million in Santiago	Violent repression	Burning metro stations and buses Looting	Minimum wage increase Constitutional referendum
Colombia 2019–2021	Dismantling war crimes commission Overall crime and violence Tax and healthcare reforms	Neoliberal reforms Corruption Implementation of 2016 war crimes agreement Funding social programs	Trade unions Students Environmental activists Indigenous groups	Violent repression	1 protester killed	President Duque withdrew tax plan New president assumed power in 2022 Unresolved

(*Continued*)

Table 6.2 Continued

Country/Year	Triggers	Arguments/Goals	Scope/Groups	Government Response	Protest Response Consequences	Resolution Outcomes
Peru 2020	Corruption	Removal of president Rejection of congress-designated president	Nationwide	Arbitrary detentions	2 protesters died	Congress removed President Vizcarra in 2020 New elections called for in 2021
Mexico 2020	Violence against women	Protection of women rights Police brutality	Feminist groups	Guarded protesters monitoring	Bomb explosion Carried out by protesters	None
Brazil 2021	COVID-19 impact Corruption	Impeachment of president	Anti-government and pro-government		Clashes between anti and pro-government groups	None
Cuba 2021	Food scarcity COVID-19 spikes Power blackouts	Political freedom Economic reforms	Massive Nationwide	Political repression Arrests		None

Source: Compiled by authors based on Human Rights Watch Reports (https://www.hrw.org) and other sources (see References)

- Corruption (Guatemala, Honduras, and Nicaragua).
- Tax increases related to replacing pandemic-related revenue shortfalls (Colombia and Costa Rica).
- Increased incidence of crime, violence, and extortion (Mexico and Haiti).
- Prior consultation of extractive projects or use of water resources (Argentina, Ecuador, and Peru).
- Gender violence (Mexico, Argentina, and Chile).
- Demands for access to COVID-19 vaccines (Argentina, Ecuador, and Peru).
- Voting irregularities and political transitions (Brazil, Chile, Honduras, and Nicaragua).
- Spending cuts and austerity measures (Brazil, Ecuador, Uruguay, and Cuba).
- Job protection against pandemic dismissals (Argentina, Ecuador, and Mexico).
- Police brutality (Brazil, Chile, and Colombia).

The COVID-19 pandemic of 2020 and resulting economic contraction in the region has only aggravated overall dissatisfaction in the region. A recent poll of public sentiment about what worries the world shows Latin Americans are concerned that the region is moving in the wrong direction (Gebrekal & Pearson, 2021). Table 6.3 shows the results of such a poll for six leading Latin American countries, with the world, the US, and Spain included for comparison. In this poll, 89% of Colombians indicated that their country is going in the wrong direction—one of the highest in the world. Colombians have good reasons to think that their country is in the doldrums. About 42.4% of Colombians live below the national poverty line of $90 per month; unemployment was at 15.6% in May 2021; the crime rate in 2021 was the worst in a country where violence has long been endemic; and the country is host to the largest number of Haitian and Venezuelan migrants in the region (Cardenas, 2021, Trading Economics, 2021). Argentineans, Peruvians, and Brazilians followed closely with 80%, 81%, and 79%, respectively. Mexicans are not as pessimistic as their Southern American counterparts. In contrast, respondents from the US, Spain, and the rest of the world were less pessimistic. The main sources of concern vary by country. Health and pandemic worries are greater in Mexico and Peru, but surprisingly not in Brazil despite its high incidence of COVID-19 mortality. Unemployment is worrisome to Argentineans, Colombians, and Mexicans and is on par with Spain. Inequality perception is higher in Colombia and Brazil. Corruption perception is high in Colombia and Peru. Perception of high crime and violence is found in Mexico, Argentina, and Chile. Surprisingly, climate change and environmental threats are not perceived as important concerns and register at a level below that of respondents from the US, Spain, and the rest of the world.

Much of Latin Americans' dissatisfaction and pessimism revolves around the inequality of opportunities and socioeconomic mobility.

Social Mobility

Social mobility is an essential aspiration for those in lower social and economic classes and particularly for those in poverty. The inability to advance in life feeds into frustration, desperation, and anger. As mentioned previously, many of the social protests in Latin America have their roots in such a sense of stagnation. Furthermore, mobility works in both directions, as individuals may experience lower standards of living over time, creating a sense of failure. The case of social protests in Chile in 2019 serves as an example to illustrate this situation. Chile is arguably the most prosperous society in Latin America, with income per capita (adjusted for PPP) increasing from $8,977 in 2000 to $25,974 in 2021 (World Bank

Table 6.3 What Worries the World? Latin America

Country	Global Social Mobility	World Rank	Education				Work			Technology Access	Social Protection	Indus Corrupt
			Health	Access	Quality	Long Life Learning	Opportunities	Wages	Conditions			
Argentina	57.3	51	61	69	38	46	65	47	57	71	60	60
Brazil	52.1	60	62	54	42	38	56	36	61	68	59	45
Chile	60.3	47	72	54	52	53	69	48	57	75	50	73
Colombia	50.3	65	67	49	32	52	59	39	44	64	49	49
Costa Rica	61.6	44	70	69	61	53	62	40	54	75	64	68
Ecuador	53.9	57	64	61	44	53	62	71	35	62	38	54
El Salvador	47.9	68	59	37	33	41	69	49	44	53	39	51
Guatemala	43.5	75	55	30	54	47	51	25	38	51	43	41
Honduras	43.5	74	54	27	44	46	62	30	52	43	28	49
Mexico	52.6	58	61	62	39	45	74	37	47	66	48	47
Panama	51.4	63	61	49	45	45	74	25	50	64	45	57
Paraguay	46.8	69	63	33	39	39	71	38	44	59	32	33
Peru	49.9	66	68	61	38	47	70	38	44	55	29	50
Uruguay	67	30	65	71	59	58	70	38	44	55	29	50
Spain	70	28	90	72	74	57	50	60	71	83	74	70
US	70.4	27	76	67	77	73	83	44	59	90	62	74

Source: IPSOS (2021).

Database, n. d.). Chileans at the poverty level (defined as $3.20 a day adjusted for PPP) were 36% of the population in 2000 and 8.6% in 2017. Despite rising prosperity, many Chileans felt that education and health services were out of reach. The reason is income inequality: Chile is one of the most unequal societies in the world. Despite some improvement from previous high levels—the GINI coefficient has declined from 52.8 in 2000 to 40 in 2017—Chile's income inequality remains very high. In the opinion of Chileans, progress is not happening fast enough (Shifter, 2020). As shown in Table 6.3, 60.3% of Chileans expressed that social mobility is a major issue in their society. Thus, it is not a surprise that two million Chileans went to the streets to protest a metro price increase in 2019. They were already disillusioned from their inability to secure decent levels of health and education for which they blamed the outmoded constitution imposed by the Pinochet dictatorship. Two years later, in 2021, they achieved their goal for change as the country started the process of writing a new constitution which was approved in 2022 (Albertus, 2021).

Drivers of Social Mobility

The World Economic Forum (2020) has developed a Global Social Mobility Index that captures the drivers of current and future social mobility of countries. The index is organized in six dimensions and ten pillars, which are defined as follows:

Health – Ability to provide access to high-quality healthcare
Education – Access: ability to provide access to education
      – Quality: ensure that high quality education is available to all
      – Lifelong learning: assurance that those educational opportunities are available throughout their lives
Technology – Level of technology access and adoption
Work – Opportunities: ability to provide access to employment
      – Fair wages: ability to provide earnings that provide mobility
      – Working conditions: ability to provide secure employment and safe labor conditions
Social Protection – Ability to provide social safety nets such as unemployment benefits and reskilling
Inclusive Institutions – Ability to provide fair and inclusive justice and safeguards against unfair prosecution and incidence of corruption as well as personal violence.

The World Economic Forum advocates the use of the index to introduce policies that prevent the vicious cycle of inherited inequality (parents' education and income) plus less equality of opportunity leading to low social mobility. On the contrary, countries should promote policies and conditions in which citizens may overcome inherited inequalities through access to more equal opportunities that encourage greater social mobility (virtuous cycle).

Table 6.4 shows the rankings and scores of Latin American countries on the Global Social Mobility Index with those of Spain and the US included for comparison purposes. These scores and the relative position of Latin American countries help to explain the nature of discontent in the region. There is a vast discrepancy of opportunity access between the region and countries such as Spain and the US in almost all dimensions except job opportunities in Spain. The index may also provide a reason for why there are few social protests in Uruguay, the Latin American country with the best ranking (35th in the world) in terms of social

Table 6.4 Global Social Mobility Index

Country	Global Social Mobility	World Rank	Health	Education			Work			Technology Access	Social Protection	Inclusive Instit./ Corrupt
				Access	Quality	Long Life Learning	Opportunities	Wages	Conditions			
Argentina	57.3	51	61	69	38	46	65	47	57	71	60	60
Brazil	52.1	60	62	54	42	38	56	36	61	68	59	45
Chile	60.3	47	72	54	52	53	69	48	57	75	50	73
Colombia	50.3	65	67	49	32	52	59	39	44	64	49	49
Costa Rica	61.6	44	70	69	61	53	62	40	54	75	64	68
Ecuador	53.9	57	64	61	44	53	62	71	35	62	38	54
El Salvador	47.9	68	59	37	33	41	69	49	44	53	39	51
Guatemala	43.5	75	55	30	54	47	51	25	38	51	43	41
Honduras	43.5	74	54	27	44	46	62	30	52	43	28	49
Mexico	52.6	58	61	62	39	45	74	37	47	66	48	47
Panama	51.4	63	61	49	45	45	74	25	50	64	45	57
Paraguay	46.8	69	63	33	39	39	71	38	44	59	32	33
Peru	49.9	66	68	61	38	47	70	38	44	55	29	50
Uruguay	67	30	65	71	59	58	70	38	44	55	29	50
Spain	70	28	90	72	74	57	50	60	71	83	74	70
US	70.4	27	76	67	77	73	83	44	59	90	62	74

Source: World Economic Forum (2020) – The Global Social Mobility Report 2020.

mobility. Uruguay offers access to health that is better than the US and on par with Spain. The country also has access to technology on par with Spain and social benefits and inclusiveness that are better than in Spain and the US. A similar case can be made for Costa Rica, with higher levels of access to opportunities relative to other Latin American countries. The reasons for discontent in other Latin American countries are mostly attributed to lower access to quality of education, fair wages, working conditions, and social protections. These conditions were and continue to be aggravated by the COVID-19 pandemic of 2020 that has left many vulnerable to infection and cut off from their main sources of income. Although a return to economic growth may provide some relief to this situation (absolute mobility), more fundamental changes are necessary to change relative mobility and, thus, decrease societal risks of protest and disruption.

Intergenerational Mobility

Economists measure social mobility in terms of intergenerational mobility—the ability of an individual to improve their income or educational achievement vis-à-vis that of their parents. Furthermore, intergenerational mobility can be determined at two levels: (1) absolute mobility—the extent to which living standards of a generation are higher than those of their parents and (2) relative mobility—the extent to which an individual's position is independent to that of their parents (World Bank, 2018). Absolute intergenerational mobility is mostly influenced by economic growth when everyone benefits from prosperity. Relative intergenerational mobility refers to the extent to which one's achievements are affected by the circumstances of one's birth. Stagnant relative mobility (an individual's situation remains the same regardless of factors outside their control) perpetuates inequality across generations and generates dissatisfaction as one experiences no change of status as the rest of society prospers.

Intergenerational mobility can be measured with respect to one's income or educational level relative to that of one's parents. In terms of income, the relationship between a family's income and that of its offspring determines intergenerational income elasticity. (An elasticity of 1 means that all of a child's income is fully dependent on the parents' income and education. Conversely, an elasticity of 0 (zero) means that a child's income or education is independent of that of their parents). Thus, lower intergenerational income elasticity means higher income or educational mobility.

Table 6.5 shows the intergenerational mobility coefficients and elasticity for selected Latin American countries and those of the US, Spain, and Denmark for comparison. These estimates come from a global database of intergenerational mobility among 148 countries, which included a number of Latin American countries (World Bank, 2018). The estimation of income intergenerational coefficients used fewer countries (75) than that of educational mobility, which included a broader cross section of countries (148). As a result, there are only a few (6 countries) estimates of income intergenerational mobility for Latin American countries (6 countries) and a greater number for educational intergenerational mobility (16 countries).

With respect to income, the absolute mobility of the selected Latin American countries was on par or above that of the US, Spain, or Denmark. Greater levels of economic growth from 2000 to 2018 lifted the income of Latin Americans above that of their parents, particularly in Brazil (0.28) and Chile (0.23). Notably however, the relative income mobility of the selected Latin American countries is lower than that of the US, Spain, and Denmark, except for Mexico. As noted above, a higher relative coefficient indicates lower mobility. Such lower relative income mobility indicates that income gains relative to those of one's parents in Latin

Table 6.5 Intergenerational Mobility and Income Inequality in Selected Latin American Countries

Country	Income				Education			Income Inequality	
	Year	Absolute Income Mobility	Relative Income Mobility	Intergenerational Elasticity of Income	Estimation Year	Absolute Educational Mobility	Intergenerational Elasticity of Education	GINI Estimation Year	GINI 2021
Argentina	2014	0.16	0.42	—	2015	0.59	0.34	42	41.4
Bolivia	2008	0.22	0.46	—	2008	0.67	0.43	50.8	42.2
Brazil	2014	0.28	0.56	0.67	2014	0.79	0.35	52.1	53.9
Chile	2009	0.23	0.50	0.67	2013	0.68	0.37	45.8	44.4
Colombia	—	—	—	—	2015	0.72	0.47	52.6	50.4
Costa Rica	—	—	—	—	2015	0.47	0.35	48.4	48
The Dominican Republic	—	—	—	—	2015	0.54	0.34	45.2	43.7
Ecuador	2014	0.18	0.43	0.74	2013	0.59	0.49	46.9	45.4
El Salvador	—	—	—	—	2015	0.44	0.44	40.6	38.6
Guatemala	—	—	—	—	2014	0.49	0.71	48.3	48.3
Honduras	—	—	—	—	2015	0.44	0.57	49.2	52.1
Mexico	2009	0.13	0.24	0.50	2011	0.71	0.40	47.2	36.8
Nicaragua	—	—	—	—	2015	0.43	0.43	46.2	46.2
Panama	—	—	—	—	2008	0.54	0.48	52.7	49.2
Peru	—	—	—	—	2014	0.64	0.39	43.1	42.8
Paraguay	—	—	—	—	2015	0.60	0.40	47.6	46.2
Uruguay	—	—	—	—	2015	0.51	0.45	40.1	39.7
Venezuela	—	—	—	—	2015	0.65	0.33	44.8	39
US	2010	0.14	0.34	0.54	—	0.43	0.33	41.2	41.1
Spain	2010	0.13	0.39	0.42	2015	0.76	0.30	36.2	34.7
Denmark	2010	0.03	0.12	0.14	2014	0.61	0.20	28.4	28.7

Source: World Economic Forum (2020) – The Global Social Mobility Report 2020.

America depend largely on the circumstances of one's birth. This is particularly notable in Brazil (0.56) and Chile (0.50). The intergenerational income mobility elasticity measure is the coefficient (beta) of the regression of the offspring's income with that of their parents—this coefficient provides a more robust way to assess income mobility. As it is indicated in Table 6.3, Latin American individuals' achievement in income depends, to a great extent, on that of their parents in Ecuador (0.74), Brazil (0.67), Chile (0.67), and to a lesser degree in Mexico (0.50).

Whereas absolute income mobility is a reflection of rising prosperity that is broadly shared, educational mobility requires greater effort and investment through much of an individual's lifetime. Early in life, better educated parents tend to provide greater maternal care and better nutrition to their children; they understand the importance of quality education and are more likely to transfer skills that become advantages in the labor market and society. More highly educated parents are also more likely to have higher incomes, which allows them to afford better schools. All these advantages are important later in the labor markets; educated parents may have parental connections and networks that help their offspring to obtain good jobs. Thus, income mobility and educational mobility are strongly positively related (World Bank, 2018). In sum, parental education levels greatly influence opportunities over the lifetime of an individual. This influence is revealed broadly throughout the world and Latin America. The absolute educational mobility coefficients in Table 6.4 are remarkably high for all countries. The cohort of individuals in the study has attained better education than that of their parents whether in Latin America, Spain (0.76), or Denmark (0.61)—but not in the US (0.43). In Latin America, countries that have reached higher educational mobility are Brazil (0.79), Colombia (0.72), and Mexico (0.71). The countries with lower levels of achievement are the Central American countries of El Salvador (0.44) and Honduras (0.44). Higher scores in the elasticity coefficient of educational mobility (an indicator of relative mobility) reveals lower educational mobility; for instance, an individual with less education is more likely to have parents with less education. Such is the case of Guatemala (0.71), Honduras (0.57), and Ecuador (0.49). Countries with higher relative educational mobility are Argentina (0.34), Brazil (0.35), Costa Rica (0.35), and Venezuela (0.33). These countries achieved comparable levels of educational mobility with Spain (0.30) and the US (0.33) but not Denmark (0.12). In sum, Latin America has improved absolute income and educational mobility but still lags in relative mobility. Younger generations have more education than their parents overall, but those born from less educated parents are more likely to remain in the bottom income or educational levels of their generation. Such unfavorable outcomes reflect the inequalities in income and education in the region as explained below.

Economists have established a relationship between intergenerational income mobility and inequality of income measured by the GINI coefficient (Krueger, 2015). Individuals born in a country with lower income inequality are more likely to attain a better economic situation than that of their parents. Conversely, the same individuals born in a country with higher income inequality will have a harder time moving up over their lifetime. A similar relationship can be extended to education. In more blunt terms, a child born of poor and uneducated parents is more likely to remain poor and uneducated. The relationship has been referred to as the Great Gatsby Curve in reference to the character in F. Scott Fitzgerald's novel. Nordic countries have low-income inequality and low intergenerational elasticity, suggesting higher mobility for their people (OECD, 2019). Latin American countries fall in the other extreme of high income inequality and high intergenerational income elasticity. Studies of Latin American countries confirm this relationship and conclude that family background remains a key determinant of one's status and the quality of education (only wealthier families can afford private schools in Latin America) (Ali Brahim & McLeod, 2016; Torche, 2014) and that the upward mobility of individuals with low parental educational background is limited (Neidhofer, 2016). Table 6.3 supports this conclusion. Latin American countries with high GINI coefficients (proxy for income inequality), for instance Brazil (52.1) and Colombia (52.6), have low intergenerational educational mobility (0.35 and 0.47, respectively) and low intergenerational income mobility in Brazil (0.67). The link between income inequality and social mobility may explain the massive protests in both countries.

The pressure and aspiration to achieve decent living standards seems to have reached a boiling point in 2019 with massive street protests; it started, however, earlier in 2015 in what is referred to as the Latin American Spring (Rice, 2020). Protests are the result of a vicious cycle of inequality of opportunities for the younger generation. As described above, income inequality drives unequal access to education, which in turn drives unequal earning opportunities and lower income mobility over the lifetime of a generation (Ferreira & Schoch, 2020). Although the pandemic tamed the protests during the lockdowns of 2020, the level of discontent and frustration remains unresolved, and the societal risk will remain high. As we have reviewed above, it does not take much to trigger these protests (see Table 6.2). Thus, pressure, uncertainty, and the level of societal risk is high, perhaps a Level 3 of a range of future outcomes (see Figure 6.2). Breaking this vicious cycle and reducing social pressure requires broad policy initiatives related to the drivers of social mobility discussed above. The set of policies may be different from one country to another as the relative influence of such drivers varies with country.

Natural and Climate Change Risks

Natural Risks

In the previous section, we discussed human causes or societal risks. Other types of risks are those created by nature. In this section, we focus on natural risks with particular attention to climate change, the nature of climate change in Latin America, and its potential impacts on cities and countries.

Natural risks are naturally occurring events that can be geophysical (earthquakes), hydrological (floods), climatological (drought or forest fires), meteorological (hurricanes), and biological (pandemics) (IFRC, 2021). With a vast land mass and surrounded by oceans and a ring of active volcanoes, Latin America is exposed to all of these risks. To a large extent, these risks are uncontrollable, but human interaction with nature is responsible for the alteration of these natural systems. Furthermore, Latin America is also depleting its rich natural resources, which alter the natural systems (e.g., deforestation of the Amazon); this, in turn, creates hazards (e.g., greenhouse effects, pollution, subsequent warming) which reduce glaciers and water resources for cities and agriculture. With 30% of the world's fresh-water resources, the 20 largest cities in Latin America suffer from water-related stress and risk running out of water entirely (HIS Markit, 2021; Rosales, Selman & Sevilla-Macip, 2021).

Such systemic changes bring serious global impacts to humanity as well as economic activity. At the business level, water challenges in Latin America have resulted in greater control of its use by extractive industries and sparked conflict with local communities. Globally, the confluence of the warm and cold Pacific Ocean currents in northern Peru, known as El Niño and La Niña, create wild climate variations that bring drought to the North American West and heavy rains and floods in Europe.

Facing high risk from natural disasters, it is imperative for Latin American cities to undertake strong disaster planning initiatives. Later in this section, we discuss the resilience of these largest cities and other Latin American cities as it relates to natural disasters.

The Impact of Climate Change on Latin America

Humanity is in a race to control the inexorable warming trends on earth. Current warming is unequivocally the result of human activity. The heat-trapping nature of carbon dioxide and other emitted gases has been demonstrated to increase levels of greenhouse gases and cause the earth to warm. Widespread and rapid changes in the atmosphere, ocean, cryosphere, and biosphere have occurred. As a result, the planet's average surface temperature has risen about 2.12 degrees Fahrenheit or 1.18 degrees Celsius since the late nineteenth century, and the 2016–2020 period has been reported as the warmest on record. Any temperature rise beyond 2 degrees Celsius will have devastating consequences. Yet based on current trends, the earth will warm by 2.7 degrees Celsius by the end of the century (NASA, 2021).

The ocean has absorbed much of this increased heat, resulting in ocean acidification. Other impacts on our planet include shrinking ice sheets, a reduction of the ice mass in Greenland and Antarctica, declining sea ice in the Arctic causing a sea-level rise, retreating glaciers across the world and extreme weather events such as hurricanes, rainfall, storm activity, and record high temperatures (NASA, 2021).

Under the 2015 Paris Agreement (COP 21), the United Nations Framework Convention on Climate Change (UNFCCC) brought together 197 governments and scientists that entered into a legally binding agreement to limit global warming to below 2 degrees C and preferably to 1.5 C compared to pre-industrial levels. The objective of this protocol and its prior versions (Kyoto, 1997) is to stabilize greenhouse gas concentrations in the atmosphere at a level that will prevent dangerous human interference with the climate system, in a time frame which allows ecosystems to adapt naturally and enables sustainable development (UN, 2020).

At its meeting in Glasgow in 2021, the UNFCCC, with more than 200 parties, reached a wide-ranging set of decisions and established a program to define a global goal on adaptation and solutions to the climate crisis already affecting many countries.

In regard to mitigation, the parties collectively agreed to address the persistent gap between emissions levels and targets to ensure that the world continues to advance during the present decade and limit the rise in average temperature to 1.5 degrees Celsius (UN, 2021).

McKinsey Global Institute Report on Global Warming Impacts

As average temperatures rise, acute hazards such as heat waves and floods grow in frequency and intensity. Thus, it is necessary to understand the nature and extent of physical risk from changing climate at regional and local levels. A comprehensive study by the McKinsey Global Institute focused on how climate change affects human life and factors of production and found that the risks of climate change to human beings, physical assets, and natural capital have the following characteristics (MGI, 2020):

- The level of climate risk increases by 2030 and further by 2050, although its impact varies by geographical area. Not every country is impacted equally.
- Climate change is already locked in and, due to inertia, temperatures will continue to increase for decades regardless of the mitigation response.
- The increase in risk is non-linear: as hazards reach thresholds, systems break down, malfunction, and ultimately fail.
- Risks are systemic: impacts are interconnected, creating indirect and 'knock-on' effects on other systems and assets.
- Risks are regressive: less prepared and resilient systems and countries will suffer progressively more.

To assess the magnitude of the risk, the study examines the severity of the hazard, its likeli-hood, and the extent to which the following systems are vulnerable to the hazard. The assess-ment also incorporated the thresholds above which systems fail. For instance, humans may not be able to function at temperatures of 37 degrees Celsius.

Livability and workability. This indicator measures the ability of human beings to work out-doors, where increased temperatures could affect human health. The following three indicators measure the impact:
- The share of the population that lives in areas of lethal heat waves.
- Annual share of effective outdoor working hours affected by extreme heat and humidity.
- Annual demand for water as a share of annual supply.

Food production disruptions from drought, extreme temperatures, or floods; measured by the duration of drought conditions over a decade.

Physical assets and infrastructure services destroyed or damaged by extreme precipitation, flooding, or fires. The impact is measured by the annual share of capital stock at risk of flood damage in climate-exposed locations and the decline in services provided by physical assets such as power services.

Natural capital destruction or changes in natural ecosystems such as glaciers, forests, or oceans; measured by the share of land surface changing climate classification.

Climate research uses scenarios of probable future emissions pathways of atmospheric greenhouse concentrations ranging from a low 2.6% to a high of 8.5% carbon dioxide (CO_2) concentrations. The McKinsey Global Institute (MGI) report focuses on the higher emission scenario and the physical effects of climate change on 105 countries over the next 30 years—2030 and 2050 under the RCP-8 scenario. Under this scenario, global average warming will reach 2.3 degrees Celsius relative to the pre-industrial period by 2050. Such warming will create extreme precipitation, increased frequency and intensity of hurricanes, increased drought conditions, lethal heat wave conditions when temperatures exceed thresholds exceeding the survivability of human beings, and depletion of renewable water supplies with decreased stocks or annual surface water sources.

There are, however, key uncertainties in modeling, which include the emissions pathways and the magnitude of direct and indirect socioeconomic impacts. The amount of risk also depends on the responses that countries may take to adapt to and mitigate these impacts under the United Nations climate change treaties (COP21 and COP26).

Based on these assumptions and modeling, the MGI report analyzed the impacts on 105 countries. The level of impact was gauged in terms of the following levels of risk: no to slight increase, moderate, and high. In a few cases, the report predicted a decrease in risks in which certain countries may exhibit benefits, rather than losses, due to global warming, such as an increase in water resources due to increased rainfall. Based on the patterns of risk, the report clustered the countries in six groups:

- *Significantly hotter and more humid countries.* Characterized by extreme increases in heat and humidity impacts on workability and an increase in water stress.
- *Hotter and more humid countries.* Large potential increases in heat and humidity impacts on workability but does not exceed livability thresholds and water stress decreases.
- *Hotter countries.* Large increase in heat and humidity but is not expected to become so hot or humid to exceed livability thresholds. These countries could become substantially drier and experience water stress.

- *Increased water stress countries.* These countries face a projected reduction in rainfall with a resulting significant increase in water stress and drought frequency.
- *Lower-risk countries.* Low levels of heat and humidity impacts and a decrease in water stress. These countries may, however, see significant biome change, with polar and boreal climates in retreat. Natural capital stock exposure to climate change may also increase.
- *Diverse climate countries.* Countries with differential climate change impacts within their territories.

The results of the MGI (2020) report for the Latin American countries included in the analysis are shown in Table 6.6.

The MGI report does not list any Latin American countries in the group facing the worst impacts of climate change (significantly hotter and humid countries); this group is composed of a number of Asian and African countries.

The second group of most affected countries (hotter and more humid countries) includes Ecuador and Uruguay. Most in this group are closer to the equator. Some estimates indicate that Ecuador has already experienced warming of 1.5 degrees C, with a significant decrease in two of its seven glaciers and a prediction that all will be lost by 2100 (Climate Reality Project, 2021b). Located at a more temperate latitude, the inclusion of Uruguay in this group is puzzling. According to studies, this country will experience average temperature changes of 1.1 degrees Celsius by 2050 and major risks of drought, flooding, heat waves, and storms. With an average elevation of only 383 feet and location among major hydrological resources, Uruguay is predicted to see a significant rise in sea levels on its coastline, all of which will impact its agricultural and food systems (World Bank Climate Knowledge Portal, n.d.).

The majority of Latin American countries in the MGI study are in the hotter group in which temperatures will impact working conditions. Most are in northern latitudes with the exception of Paraguay. The forecasted increase in temperatures will make working under heat and humidity more stressful and slightly stress water resources. Except for Colombia, these countries will have less risk of physical and infrastructure exposure. Cuba is the only country in the group at high risk of loss of natural capital.

Mexico is the only country in the increased water-stress group. Some estimates indicate that the northern part of Mexico may see increases of 3–4 degrees Celsius, while the rest of the country may experience increases of 1.5–2 degrees Celsius (Climate Reality Project, 2021a). The most critical risk for Mexico is the combined impacts of reduced water resources, land rendered unsuitable for growing food, and a population that is still growing at a rapid pace. Mexico is expected to suffer high risks of losses in physical assets, infrastructure, and depletion of natural capital making. This may trigger significant socioeconomic pressures for a country that already struggles with other social problems such as violence and unemployment.

Peru is the only country in the lower risk group. With its complex geography, which includes a long Pacific coastline, the Andes Mountains, and Amazonian forests, Peru will experience a range of warming temperatures and impacts throughout its territory. At the center of the important El Niño/La Niña ocean systems that influence global weather patterns, Peru is estimated to warm by 1 degree Celsius by 2030 and 2 degrees Celsius by 2050, with high variability throughout its territory (Senamhi, 2009). It is already experiencing retreat of its glaciers and increased flooding of Andean villages due to melting ice.

The Southern Cone countries and Brazil are in the diverse climate impact group. They have extensive land mass and diverse climates from tropical Brazil to near-Arctic conditions in Argentina and Chile. Brazil will suffer from heat extremes in working conditions, moderate impacts on food systems, physical assets and infrastructure, and losses of capital and land

Table 6.6 Expected Climate Change Impacts on Latin American Countries

Group	Livability and Workability			Water Stress	Food Systems Under Drought Conditions	Physical Assets/ Infrastructure Flood Exposure	Natural Capital Loss of Land Surface
	Latin American Country	Population Under Lethal Heat Wave	Working Under Extreme Heat and Humidity				
Significantly Hotter and Humid	None	—	—	—	—	—	—
Hotter and More Humid	Ecuador	Slight	High	Decrease	Slight	High	Slight
	Uruguay	Slight	Moderate	Decrease	Slight	High	Slight
Hotter	Colombia	Slight	Moderate	Slight	Slight	High	Moderate
	Cuba	Slight	High	Slight	Slight	Slight	Slight
	Guatemala	Slight	High	Slight	Slight	Decrease	High
	Honduras	Slight	High	Slight	Slight	Slight	Slight
	Nicaragua	Slight	High	Slight	Slight	Slight	Slight
	Paraguay	Slight	High	Slight	High	Moderate	High
	Venezuela	Slight	High	Moderate	Slight	Slight	Slight
Increased Water Stress	Mexico	Slight	Moderate	High	Slight	High	High
Lower Risk	Peru	Slight	Slight	Decrease	Slight	Slight	High
	Argentina	Slight	Moderate	Decrease	Slight	High	High
Diverse Climate Impacts	Brazil	Slight	High	Slight	Moderate	Moderate	Moderate
	Chile	Slight	Slight	High	Slight	Decrease	High

Source: McKinsey Global Institute (2020) – Climate risk and response.

surface (despite continuous Amazon deforestation practice). Argentina is expected to suffer a high loss of physical assets and infrastructure and loss of land surface mostly from sea-level rise. Average temperatures for Argentina are predicted to increase by 1.5 degrees Celsius (the greatest increases in the northern part of the country) under a more drastic RCP 8.5% scenario (see assumptions for the MGI scenarios discussed above). For Chile, temperature increases of 1.4–1.7 degrees Celsius are predicted by 2050, with high water stress in the northern part of the country and loss of natural capital in the southern part of its territory (Reliefweb, 2021). Thus, the impact of global warming in this group does not show a common pattern.

A more comprehensive study of global warming's impact on Latin America provides a more detailed assessment of the level of disasters and economic and human losses already attributed to global warming (CAF, 2014). Table 6.7 summarizes the results from this report. Based on the number of disasters related to global warming, Brazil and Mexico have experienced the greatest number in the region followed by Haiti, Colombia, and Peru. In terms of total economic losses, Brazil, Mexico, Cuba, and Venezuela have the largest impacts. In terms of human losses Venezuela, Honduras, Haiti, Nicaragua, and Colombia have suffered the most. In terms of people affected by global warming events, Brazil and Cuba are the two most affected countries. The economic and human losses clearly have a greater impact on smaller countries. This relative impact is clearly shown by economic loss as a percentage of GDP and the people affected per thousand of population. Economic loss is felt more in the small economies of Honduras, Nicaragua, Haiti, and Cuba. Large countries such as Brazil and Mexico may have more disasters, but their larger economies are less affected than those of smaller countries. The same pattern is found in terms of the share of population affected by global warming events. Countries with lower populations suffer more, as is the case of Cuba, Bolivia, Nicaragua, and Honduras.

Local conditions, geography, and the size of a country's population and economy condition the level and nature of impacts. These local conditions are captured in terms of three aspects of risks: vulnerability, exposure, and sensitivity. Vulnerability is defined as the degree to which a country is susceptible or unable to cope with adverse effects of climate change. Exposure is the nature and degree to which a country is exposed to significant climatic variations, such as droughts, landslides, flooding, and sea-level rise as well precipitation and humidity levels. Sensitivity is a measure of the population's susceptibility to the impacts of climate change. More specifically, the index examines the sensitivity to health, poverty, infrastructure, agriculture, and natural resources. The adaptive capacity index captures the ability of a country to adjust to or even take advantage of events resulting from climate change. Adaptive capacity covers the strength of the economy, government effectiveness, and available natural resources among others. The vulnerability index is a composite indicator based on the three indexes above with the following weights: exposure (50%), sensitivity (25%), and adaptive capacity (25%) (CAF, 2014). These indexes are measured on scale of 1 to 10 with the lowest level (1.0) indicating the highest vulnerability, highest exposure risk, highest sensitivity risk, and lowest adaptive capacity.

As defined above, the sensitivity index measures the degree to which a society exposed to global warming impacts may suffer from those events in terms of hunger, poverty, or food production. For instance, economies that rely more on agricultural production may suffer losses in food supplies. Countries with higher poverty levels or rural populations may also suffer more. Given the diverse profiles of Latin American countries, there is wide variance in sensitivity scores among them. The countries with the highest sensitivity (lower scores) are Haiti, the Dominican Republic, El Salvador, Guatemala, Nicaragua, Honduras, and Cuba. This group of Central American and Caribbean countries has high exposure to global warming events, higher rural populations, and economies that rely on agriculture. On the other extreme, we find countries in the Southern Cone of Latin America with lower sensitivity

Table 6.7 Natural Disasters and Vulnerability

Country	Number of Disasters	Economic Loss US$	Annual Average Loss as % of GDP	Number of Fatalities	Number of People Affected	Annual Average of People Affected per 1,000 Population	Vulnerability	Exposure	Sensitivity	Adaptive Capacity
Argentina	39	8002259	0.067	312	6519328	6.55	6.56	7.32	7.22	6.07
Bolivia	45	4717683	0.666	1049	6340204	24.76	2.48	6.00	4.58	0.8
Brazil	106	13066850	0.022	3982	43453726	9.04	5.77	5.11	6.32	7.88
Chile	30	2317934	0.034	653	1110352	2.63	9.54	8.57	8.04	9.4
Colombia	78	3726513	0.040	4091	9342337	8.06	4.30	5.41	3.72	5.66
Costa Rica	32	1138972	0.097	196	1234612	10.56	7.70	3.7	4.22	9.23
Cuba	49	14044197	0.856	190	12888801	47.67	3.90	1.39	3.15	8.44
The Dominican Republic	39	3734074	0.258	1358	1342128	5.38	1.01	2.28	0.76	2.31
Ecuador	30	1983881	0.095	1066	915104	2.42	3.76	5.82	3.47	4.44
El Salvador	29	3378546	0.572	1031	1003600	6.60	0.79	2.68	0.93	1.44
Guatemala	40	3604904	0.284	2623	4800010	12.93	0.75	1.66	1.38	0.64
Haiti	61	1964353	0.959	7361	3769392	15.22	0.58	2.14	0.22	0.00
Honduras	39	6507194	1.425	15539	3456568	17.79	0.92	2.73	2.43	0.5
Mexico	124	34816774	0.114	3490	13487531	4.59	4.47	3.35	5.32	7.66
Nicaragua	40	3265089	1.222	4075	2740625	18.78	1.19	3.81	2.01	0.13
Panama	29	368307	0.037	145	250887	2.71	5.57	5.26	4.61	6.7
Paraguay	20	40913.8	0.006	29	2421990	14.84	1.58	4.3	3.9	0.94
Peru	66	2842736	0.054	3631	7467837	10.24	4.98	6.69	4.5	5.32
Uruguay	7	403350	0.032	14	152900	1.87	8.33	7.27	8.61	8.18
Venezuela	30	4824776	0.058	30534	659561	0.90	3.64	5.07	6.25	3.62

Sources: Inter-American Development Bank (2000, 2010) – Natural Disasters in Latin America and the Caribbean; Indicators of Disaster Risk and Risk Management.

scores to global warming—Uruguay, Chile, and Argentina. With lower exposure to global warming and more diversified economies, these countries may show greater resilience to the effects of global warming. The remainder of countries fall in the medium or moderate sensitivity levels, with Ecuador, Colombia, and Paraguay on the higher end of this range. Thus, there seems to be a positive correlation between exposure and sensitivity impacts of global warming in Latin America (see Figure 6.3).

Based on the results of the vulnerability index study, the countries most vulnerable to the impact of global warming are Guatemala, Haiti, Honduras, and the Dominican Republic. Among the countries included in the MGI study, Paraguay, Ecuador, and Venezuela are also found to be highly vulnerable. It is interesting that Uruguay, a country at high risk of global warming impact in the MGI study, was not found to be vulnerable in this study.

Figure 6.4 explores the interaction among the vulnerability, exposure, and adaptive capacity indexes. As expected, high vulnerability is positively correlated with exposure but not necessarily with adaptive capacity. Adaptive capacity captures the resilience of a society and economy to recover from the risks of global warming. Countries in the lower left quadrant of Figure 6.4 have higher exposure and higher vulnerability (low scores in both indexes): Haiti, El Salvador, Honduras, the Dominican Republic, and Nicaragua. These countries also have low adaptive capacity (low scores in adaptive capacity on the right y-axis). A number of countries that sit in the middle ground of exposure are very likely to join the group of high vulnerability because of their medium to low adaptive capacity: Bolivia, Ecuador, and Venezuela. On the other hand, Cuba and Mexico, with medium vulnerability scores, have high adaptive capacity and are, therefore, likely to pull away from the high vulnerability group. Another group of countries has medium scores of vulnerability and exposure (Peru, Panama, Brazil, and Argentina). These countries also have medium scores in adaptive capacity and, therefore, will remain as countries with medium impact from global warming. The last group of countries has low vulnerability and exposure and high adaptive capacity (Uruguay, Chile, and Costa Rica). This group has the most robust systems to counter the

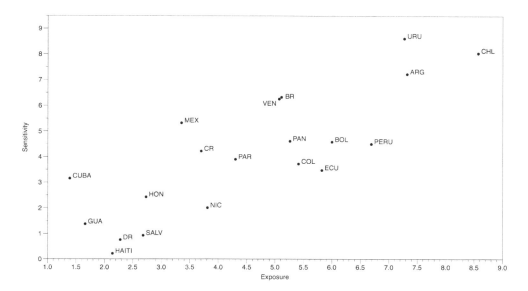

Figure 6.3 Exposure and Sensitivity to climate change in Latin America

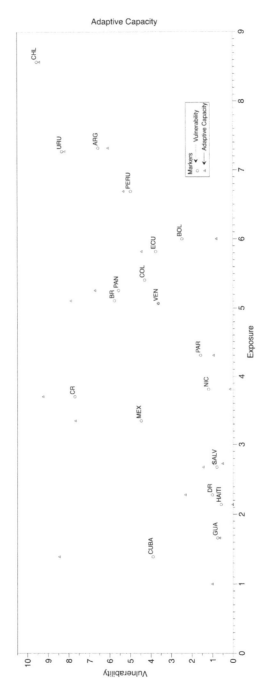

Figure 6.4 Vulnerability, exposure, and adaptability to climate change in Latin America

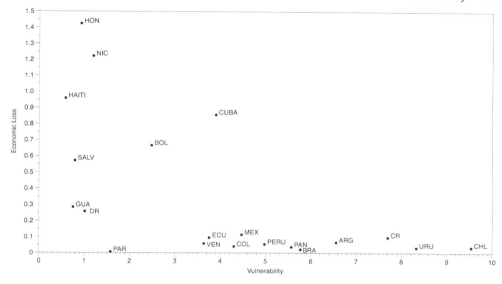

Figure 6.5 Vulnerability and economic loss as percent of GDP

effects of global warming. As such, Uruguay, for example, will be able to cope with extreme heat and humidity conditions as predicted by the MGI assessment reviewed before.

Figure 6.5 shows how the vulnerability index is associated with potential economic losses. Countries with the highest vulnerability and largest impact are Honduras, Nicaragua, Haiti, and Cuba. Countries that are vulnerable but will suffer less economic impact are in the lower left quadrant of Figure 6.5: El Salvador, Bolivia, Guatemala, and the Dominican Republic are high (0.3%–0.8 % of GDP). Venezuela, Ecuador, Colombia, and Mexico have medium vulnerability indexes but low economic impacts from global warming. The remainder of countries have low vulnerability/low economic impacts (lowest right quadrant). No Latin American country was found in the low vulnerability/high economic impact quadrant.

Impact of Global Warming on Latin American Cities

Eighty percent of natural disaster impacts in Latin America are felt in cities, causing substantial human and economic losses (ELLA, 2013). A study published by the global insurance company Swiss Re on the impact of five natural hazards (storms, storm surge, river flood, earthquake, and tsunamis) on 616 cities included 49 Latin American cities (Sundermann, Schelske, & Hausmann, 2014). The study ranked cities in terms of the human impacts by assessing the size of the urban population affected and the impact on the local and national economy by assessing the value of working days lost by the hazard. (See Figure 6.6 for the results of the economic impact of the five natural hazards on the North American, Central American, and South American regions.) Among the top cities affected by all five hazards based on economic loss relative to the national economy are Mexico City, Mexico; San Jose, Costa Rica; Guayaquil, Ecuador; Lima, Peru; Santiago, Chile; Bogota, Colombia; and Buenos Aires, Argentina. In terms of unique natural disasters and in comparison to all 616 cities in the study, San Jose and Lima were first and second in the world in terms of days lost relative to the national economy for earthquakes. For tsunami impact, Guayaquil was ninth in the

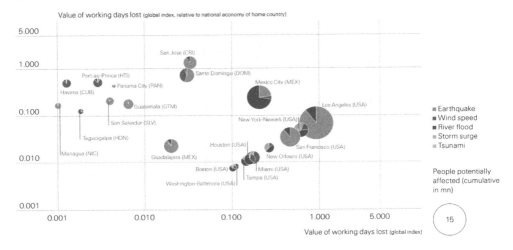

Figure 6.6 Impact of natural disasters in cities in North and South America. Source: Sundermann et al. (2014)

world in terms of people affected and first in terms of working days lost from the event relative to the national economy. In the case of river floods, Mexico City was eighth in the world in terms of people affected, and Havana, Cuba, was tenth in the world for storm surges in terms of working days lost relative to the national economy. Using this last indicator (days lost), Panama City ranked fourth in the world. Finally, Havana (fifth) and Santo Domingo, Dominican Republic (sixth) were among the top ten most affected by a storm.

As discussed above, the sensitivity index captures the degree to which global warming may impact society and infrastructure and how factors such as poverty rates and disadvantaged populations may exacerbate these effects. As discussed in Chapter 5, the majority of the urban poor live in environmentally degraded areas, which will suffer greatly from global warming. An analysis of the vulnerability of 50 cities worldwide to the effects of global warming found that three major Latin American metropolitan areas were in the lower ranks: São Paulo (39), Rio de Janeiro (43), and Mexico City (44). The Corporación Andina de Fomento [Development Bank of Latin America] (CAF) (2014) report on country vulnerability (COVI) mentioned previously also included an assessment of the vulnerability of capital cities. A proxy for the adaptive capacity of cities is provided by another report on the sustainability of 174 cities worldwide (IESE, 2020). The latter report builds an index of sustainability ranging from 0 to 100. The Cities in Motion Index (CIMI) is based on 101 city indicators across nine dimensions (economy, social cohesion, human capital, international projection, technology, urban planning, mobility and transportation, environment, and governance). Table 6.6 provides the results of the CAF and Instituto de Estudios Superiores de la Empresa, Universidad de Navarra [Business School, University of Navarra] (IESE) studies.

According to Table 6.8, the capital cities can be clustered in four groups of vulnerability.

Very High Vulnerability: Guatemala City, Managua, Port-Au-Prince, Santo Domingo.
High Vulnerability: Tegucigalpa, San Salvador (El Salvador), Quito, Bogotá, Panama City.
Moderate Vulnerability: Havana, La Paz, Caracas, Asuncion, San Jose, Mexico City, Montevideo.
Low Vulnerability: Brasilia, Buenos Aires, Lima, Santiago de Chile.

Table 6.8 Vulnerability and Adaptive Capacity of Latin American Cities

Capital City Vulnerability	City	Country	CIVI	COVI	CIMI Rankings										
					Overall	Score	Econ	HumCap	Soc Coh	Envir	Urban Plan	Intl Proj	Tech	Govt	Mobil
Very High	Guatemala City	Guatemala	0.39	0.75	158	33.74	145	160	149	127	149	133	165	138	164
	Managua	Nicaragua	0.39	1.19	—	—	—	—	—	—	—	—	—	—	—
	Port-Au-Prince	Haiti	0.42	0.48	—	—	—	—	—	—	—	—	—	—	—
	Santo Domingo	Dominican Republic	0.55	1.01	137	40.39	120	169	154	44	62	140	155	144	159
High	Tegucigalpa	Honduras	0.63	0.92	—	—	—	—	—	—	—	—	—	—	—
	San Salvador	El Salvador	0.74	0.79	—	—	—	—	—	—	—	—	—	—	—
	Quito	Ecuador	0.90	3.76	142	37.64	164	126	56	97	151	116	157	166	139
	Guayaquil	Ecuador	—	—	164	31.55	165	154	95	124	164	152	161	170	150
	Bogota	Colombia	1.28	4.30	120	45.80	112	110	162	92	155	75	124	43	122
	Medellin	Colombia	—	—	126	43.81	115	132	140	110	141	142	136	99	78
	Cali	Colombia	—	—	145	37.02	118	130	146	118	169	160	143	132	152
	Pan. City	Panama	1.37	5.77	113	47.93	84	145	103	40	50	80	151	149	140
Moderate	Havana	Cuba	2.47	3.90	—	—	—	—	—	—	—	—	—	—	—
	La Paz	Bolivia	2.52	2.48	147	35.88	155	152	126	66	140	150	166	155	154
	Santa Cruz	Bolivia	—	—	150	35.26	152	146	109	20	170	164	164	172	157
	Caracas	Venezuela	2.56	3.64	174	4.15	119	174	101	162	146	132	172	162	130
	Asuncion	Paraguay	2.63	1.58	131	42.34	158	107	75	8	163	161	167	146	135
	San Jose	Costa Rica	3.26	7.70	114	47.56	123	155	112	14	132	101	144	77	144
	Mexico City	Mexico	3.38	4.47	130	42.86	127	67	142	168	63	72	153	92	66
	Montevideo	Uruguay	3.38	8.33	110	50.35	144	133	110	3	118	115	133	174	114
Low	Brasilia	Brazil	3.52	5.77	135	40.92	146	150	155	74	150	124	145	120	62
	São Paulo	Brazil	—	—	123	45.01	137	123	156	102	76	41	139	121	126
	Rio de Janeiro	Brazil	—	—	132	42.26	151	114	164	106	64	69	142	105	155
	Curitiba	Brazil	—	—	138	39.79	156	148	147	52	135	148	148	143	89
	Belo Horizonte	Brazil	—	—	156	33.37	159	141	157	109	159	163	149	154	121
	Salvador	Brazil	—	—	157	33.37	157	137	159	94	145	136	162	153	160
	Buenos Aires	Argentina	3.73	6.66	90	54.71	166	65	139	25	26	31	114	21	123
	Rosario	Argentina	—	—	134	41.70	171	120	82	84	96	144	131	118	146
	Cordoba	Argentina	—	—	139	39	167	127	100	72	147	147	134	130	156
	Lima	Peru	5.51	4.98	155	34.23	143	135	129	147	148	145	163	134	167
	Santiago	Chile	5.70	9.54	68	59.45	103	97	80	29	40	62	94	94	42

Sources: IESE Cities in Motion 2020; CAF 2014.

The very high vulnerability cities (low climate change vulnerability index [CCVI] scores) are capital cities in countries that also are highly vulnerable to global climate (CCVI low scores) in terms of the factors mentioned in the CAF (2014) report. These cities have been exposed to a number of natural disasters already and have not fared well because of their lack of adaptive resources and ability to recover from these disasters. These cities ranked very low across all factors of the sustainability ranking of global cities by the IESE (2020) study. The conclusion that one draws from this analysis is that these cities will continue to suffer devastation from global climate change. Absent the infusion of large levels of capital and human resources, one could predict long-term migration flows from these urban areas.

The next group of capital cities is considered high vulnerability. These cities are also in countries with high vulnerability (low to medium CCVI scores in Table 6.8) and also happen to be in countries classified as hotter (Ecuador) or hot (Colombia, Panama) according to the MGI (2020) study. Climate warming will have a substantial impact on these cities. However, these capitals received much better sustainability scores than those of the first group. Bogotá received good scores on international projection, environment, and governance. Quito, on the other hand, scores well on social cohesion and environment. These strengths may help these cities recover from potential global warming effects. The same strengths cannot be extended to secondary cities in these countries. In the case of Ecuador, Guayaquil is a highly vulnerable city with no recognizable sustainability strengths and is poorly equipped to manage the serious impacts of global warming.

The third group of cities has moderate vulnerability. This group includes a large variety of capital cities across a vast geographic area. With such diversity, there is no single discernable pattern in their sustainability assessments. They range from excellent environment assessments (Montevideo or Asuncion) or relatively good human capital, urban planning, and mobility in Mexico City. It seems that each capital city in this group has developed its own set of strengths and do not have common weaknesses.

Capital cities with lower vulnerability are mostly based in the Southern Cone of Latin America. Both Buenos Aires and Santiago receive good scores in environment, urban planning, international projection, and human capital. Brasilia scores well on environment and mobility. The exception in this group is Lima; its sustainability score places the city at 155 out of 174 ranked. The low vulnerability risk classification of Lima may be explained by the low vulnerability of Peru as a whole (see MGI study). On the other hand, Lima has been identified among the top risks in the world for natural risks such as earthquakes. Thus, we conclude that Lima has a low risk for climate change impact but high risk for other natural disasters and is not prepared to recover from both.

Summary: Many Risks but Also Opportunities

This chapter identifies the various sources of economic, political, societal, and natural risks present in Latin America. The chapter also aims to assess the various levels of uncertainty associated with these risks. The uncertainty framework presented in the introductory section of the chapter, suggests different strategies that companies can use to manage different levels of uncertainty. Although the scope of risks in Latin America is significant and the seriousness of these risks range from moderate to high, most of these risks can be anticipated and estimated, with some exceptions (namely, risks related to crime, violence, and climate change). Thus, uncertainty in the region primarily falls under levels one to three of our framework. This means companies operating in Latin America can, and should, apply sound scanning tool processes, monitoring key indicators of economic, political, social, and natural risk. This would allow them to remain agile and adaptable by identifying trigger points for implementing alternative strategies. Companies can also pursue shaper strategies, especially those grounded in disruptive innovations that may place them in leadership positions in specific sectors or industries.

Our discussion suggests that, in the short term, the main factor driving risk and uncertainty will be the continued management of the health and economic crises caused by the COVID-19 pandemic and the actions taken by governments in the region to help their respective economies recover post-pandemic. In the short and medium term, companies will need to monitor key variables that can be considered triggers of economic, political, societal, and natural risks and uncertainty, such as unemployment, commodity prices, poverty rates, lack of accountability for corruption, impunity for those engaged in crime and violence, and abuses of power by government officials, among others (EIU, 2019).

Companies would be wise to understand the risks they face in the region and prepare to manage these risks and associated uncertainty. Truly visionary companies, however, will see beyond the risk and appreciate the many opportunities the region offers. A post-pandemic Latin America can be one centered on equality and sustainability (CEPAL, 2020). A transformed Latin America would nurture innovations aimed at addressing climate change and social inequality through the nurturing of a dynamic entrepreneurial environment. A transformed Latin America would be fully integrated into the global economy through dynamic and agile value chains. A transformed Latin America would embrace digitalization and automation to improve the region's competitiveness, streamline business operations, and improve the provision of public services to its citizens. A transformed Latin America would strengthen its institutional environment to preserve its democratic systems, combat crime and corruption, and regain the trust of its people.

References

Agren, D., & Nuño, A. (2021, June 4). What do you think of it so far? Voters rate Amlo's Mexico 'transformation.' *The Guardian*. https://www.theguardian.com/world/2021/jun/04/andres-manuel-lopez-obrador-amlo-mexico-midterm-elections

Al Jazeera. (2020). Mexico's 'Teflon' presidency loses some sheen but survives. https://www.aljazeera.com/economy/2020/9/1/mexicos-teflon-presidency-loses-some-sheen-but-survives

Albertus, M. (2021). Chile's constitution is too new for its own good. *Foreign Policy*. Retrieved on October 23, 2021 from https://foreignpolicy.com/2021/05/21/chiles-constitution-is-too-new-for-its-own-good/

Ali Brahim, A., & McLeod, D. (2016). Inequality and mobility: Gatsby in the Americas. *Modern Economy*, 7, 643–655. https://doi.org/10.4236/me.2016.75070

AQ Staff. (2021). The big players. *Americas Quarterly*, 15(1), 32–39.

Arnson, C. J. (2020). Democracy at risk. *Latin Trade* (August/October), 28–29.

BBC News. (2020). Jubilation as Chile votes to rewrite constitution. Retrieved on October 1, 2021 from https://www.bbc.com/news/world-latin-america-54687090

CAF - Corporación Andina de Fomento. (2014). Vulnerability index to climate change in the Latin American and Caribbean region. *Scioteca*. Retrieved on November 5, 2021 from https://scioteca.caf.com/handle/123456789/509

Cardenas, M. (2021, September 30). How to avoid a caudillo in Colombia. *Americas Quarterly*. Retrieved on October 1, 2021 from https://americasquarterly.org/article/how-to-avoid-a-caudillo-in-colombia-and-elsewhere/

CE Noticias Financieras. (2020). 5 economic risks that Latin America will face in 2021. https://digismak.com/5-economic-risks-that-latin-america-will-face-in-2021-and-an-opportunity/

CEPAL-Comisión Económica para América Latina. (2020). *Construir un Nuevo futuro: Una recuperación transformadora con igualdad y sostenibilidad*. https://www.cepal.org/es/

publicaciones/46227-construir-un-nuevo-futuro-recuperacion-transformadora-igualdad
-sostenibilidad
Climate Reality Project. (2021a). How is climate change affecting Mexico? Retrieved on November 27,
2021 from https://www.climaterealityproject.org/blog/how-climate-change-affecting-mexico
Climate Reality Project. (2021b). Glaciers and rivers of Ecuador: Biodiversity under threat. Retrieved on
November 27, 2018 from https://www.climaterealityproject.org/blog/glaciers-and-rivers-ecuador
-biodiversity-under-threat
CNE-Consejo Nacional de Elecciones. (2021). Elecciones Generales de Honduras. 28 de Noviembre
2021: Escrutinio General. https://resultadosgenerales2021.cne.hn/#resultados/PRE/HN
Control Risks and AS/COA Anti-Corruption Working Group. (2021). *The Capacity to Combat
Corruption (CCC) Index 2021*. https://www.as-coa.org/sites/default/files/CCC_Report_2021.pdf
Courtney, H. G., Kirkland, J., & Viguerie, S. P. (2000). Strategy under uncertainty. *McKinsey Quarterly*.
Retrieved on September 7, 2021 from https://www.mckinsey.com/business-functions/strategy-and
-corporate-finance/our-insights/strategy-under-uncertainty
Dammert, L. (2021). When crime and politics meet. *Americas Quarterly*, 15(1), 45–47.
Daniels, J. P. (2020). Latin America's wave of protests was historic-Then the pandemic arrived. *Foregin
Policy*. Retrieved on September 7, 2021 from https://foreignpolicy.com/2020/06/25/latin-america
-protest-pandemic-informal-economy/
d+i Developing Ideas, Llorente & Cuenca. (2018). *América Latina apuesta por más democracia*. Madrid,
Spain.
d+i Developing Ideas, Llorente & Cuenca. (2016). *Corruption: The Achilles heel of Latin American
democracies*. Madrid, Spain.
EIU-Economist Intelligence Unit. (2019). Where next and what next for Latin America? https://www
.eiu.com/public/topical_report.aspx?campaignid=latinamerica2019
ELLA. (2013). Urban disaster risk in management in Latin American cities. Retrieved on November 27,
2021 from https://www.preventionweb.net/files/44804_urbandisasterriskmanagementlatiname.pdf
Ferreira, F., & M. Schoch. (2020). Inequality and social unrest in Latin America: The Tocqueville
paradox revisited. *World Bank Blogs*. Retrieved on September 7, 2021 from https://blogs.worldbank
.org/developmenttalk/inequality-and-social-unrest-latin-america-tocqueville-paradox-revisited
Fonseca, B., & Cruz, J. M. (2021). A mutating virus. *Americas Quarterly*, 15(1), 25–30.
Gebrekal, T., & Pearson, N. (2021). What worries the world? September 2021. IPSOS. Retrieved on
September 7, 2021 from https://www.ipsos.com/en/what-worries-world-september-2021
Guachamín, M., Ramírez-Cifuentes, D., & Delgado, O. (2020). An uncertainty thermometer to
measure the macroeconomic-financial risk in South American countries. *Journal of International
Development*, 32, 854–890. https://doi.org/10.1002/jid.3480
HIS Markit (2021). Water scarcity in Latin America. https://ihsmarkit.com/research-analysis/water
-scarcity-in-latin-america.html
Human Rights Watch. (2021). *World reports*. Retrieved on October 1–24, 2021 from https://www
.hrw.org
IESE. (2020). IESE cities in motion index 2020. Retrieved on November 11, 2021 from https://blog.iese
.edu/cities-challenges-and-management/2020/10/27/iese-cities-in-motion-index-2020/
IFRC. (2021). What is a disaster? Retrieved on November 27 from https://www.ifrc.org/what-disaster
International IDEA. (2019). The global state of democracy 2019. https://doi.org/10.31752/idea.2019.31
International IDEA. (2021). The global state of democracy 2021. https://doi.org/10.31752/idea.2021.91
Inter-American Development Bank (2000). *Natural disasters in Latin America and the Caribbean: An
overview of risk*. Retrieved on January 23, 2021 from https://publications.iadb.org/en/publication/
natural-disasters-latin-america-and-caribbean-overview-risk
Inter-American Development Bank (2010). *Indicators of disaster risk and risk management*. Retrieved
on January 23, 2021 from https://publications.iadb.org/en/publication/11611/indicators-disaster
-risk-and-risk-management-program-latin-america-and-caribbean
Kitroeff, N., & Taj, M. (2020, June 21). Latin America also confronts graft epidemic. *The New York
Times* (East Coast), A:1.

Krueger, A. (2015). The great utility of the Great Gatsby Curve. Brookings. Retrieved on October 23, 2021 from https://www.brookings.edu/blog/social-mobility-memos/2015/05/19/the-great-utility -of-the-great-gatsby-curve/

Marsh Specialty. (2021). *Political risk map 2021: Pandemic recovery complicates risks.* file:///C:/Users/ nwiese/Downloads/Marsh_Political_Risk_Map_2021_Report_update%20(5).pdf

McKinsey Quarterly. (2008). A fresh look at strategy under uncertainty: An interview. December 1. Retrieved on September 4, 2021 from https://www.mckinsey.com/business-functions/strategy-and -corporate-finance/our-insights/a-fresh-look-at-strategy-under-uncertainty-an-interview

MGI - McKinsey Global Institute. (2020). Climate risk and response: Physical hazards and socioeconomic impacts. *McKinsey Sustainability.* Retrieved on November 27, 2021 from https:// www.mckinsey.com/business-functions/sustainability/our-insights/climate-risk-and-response -physical-hazards-and-socioeconomic-impacts

NASA. (2021). Climate change: How do we know? Retrieved on October 27, 2021 from https://climate .nasa.gov/evidence/

Neidhofer, G. (2016). Intergenerational mobility and the rise and fall of inequality: Lessons from Latin America. *Journal Economic Inequality, 17,* 499–520. https://doi.org/10.1007/s10888-019-09415-9

OECD. (2019). Society at glance. Retrieved on October 13, 2021 from https://www.oecd.org/social/ society-at-a-glance-19991290.htm

Open Democracy. (2020). *2019: Protests and disruptive changes in Latin America.* Retrieved on September 7, 2021 from https://www.opendemocracy.net/en/democraciaabierta/2019 -movilizaciones-ciudadanas-y-cambios-disruptivos-en-américa-latina-en/

Otis, J. (2021). School's out. Gangs are thrilled. *Americas Quarterly, 15*(1), 15–23.

Our World in Data (2020). Coronavirus (COVID 19) Vaccinations. https://ourworldindata.org/covid -vaccinations

PAHO- Pan American Health Organization (2022). Core Indicators 2022. https://www.paho.org/en/ evidence-and-intelligence-action-health/core-indicators-2022

Phillips, T., Augustin, E., & Collyns, D. (2021). New wave of volatility: Covid stirs up grievances in Latin America. *The Guardian.* Retrieved on September 7, 2021 from https://www.theguardian.com/world /2021/aug/06/new-wave-volatility-covid-stirs-up-grievances-latin-america

Price, J. (2019). Keystone organization versus clientelism: Understanding protest frequency in Indigenous Southern Mexico. *Comparative Politics, 51*(3), 407–427. https://www.jstor.org/stable /26663937

Ramos Miranda, N. A., & Cambero, F. (2021). Chile election poll shows race tightening as polarized showdown nears. Reuters. https://www.reuters.com/world/americas/chile-election-poll-shows -race-tightening-polarized-showdown-nears-2021-12-14/

Reliefweb. (2021). Climate risk country profile: Chile. Retrieved on November 27, 2021 from https:// reliefweb.int/report/chile/climate-risk-country-profile-chile

Reuters. (2021). Venezuelan migrants in Chile face fiery anti-immigration protests. *NBC News.* Retrieved on October 13, 2021 from https://www.nbcnews.com/news/latino/venezuelan-migrants -chile-face-fiery-anti-immigration-protests-rcna2358

Rice, R. (2020). Too little, too late. *Journal of International Affairs, 73*(2), 137–146. Retrieved on September 7, 2021 from https://jia.sipa.columbia.edu/too-little-too-late-chilean-winter-latin -american-spring

Rosales, A., Selman, C., Cardenas, C., & Burford, V. (2021). Drivers of civil unrest in Latin America. IHS Markit. Retrieved on October 26, 2021 from https://ihsmarkit.com/research-analysis/drivers-of -civil-unrest-in-latin-america.html

Rosales, A., Selman, C., & Sevilla-Macip, J. (2021). Water scarcity in Latin America. IHS Markit. Retrieved on November 21, 2021 from https://ihsmarkit.com/research-analysis/water-scarcity-in -latin-america.htm

Senamhi (2009). https://www.senamhi.gob.pe/usr/cmn/pdf/Resumen_Nacional_Ingles.pdf

Schifter, M. (2020). The rebellion against the elites in Latin America. *The New York Times.* Retrieved on September 7, 2021 from https://www.nytimes.com/2020/01/21/opinion/international-world/latin -america-elites-protests.html

Sheridan, M. B. (2019, October 10). Why political turmoil is erupting across Latin America. *The Washington Post*.

Simon, R. (2019). The changing face of anti-corruption protests in Latin America. Americas Quarterly, February 6. Retrieved on September 7, 2021 from https://americasquarterly.org/article/the-changing-face-of-anti-corruption-protests-in-latin-america/

Stott, M. (2021, March 5). Poverty surge risks setting Latin America back a decade, UN warns. *Financial Times*, 8.

Suarez, K., Romo, R., Regan, H., & Humayun, H. (2021, December 20). Leftist Gabriel Boric, 35, wins Chile's presidential election. *CNN News*. https://cnn.com/2021/12/19/americas/chile-election-gabriel-boric-intl-nk/index.html

Sundermann, L., Schelske O., & Hausmann P. (2014). *Mind the risk–A global ranking of cities under threat from natural disasters*. Zurich: Swiss Re. https://reliefweb.int/sites/reliefweb.int/files/resources/Mind%20the%20risk_A%20global%20ranking%20of%20cities%20under%20threat%20from%20natural%20disasters.pdf

Sweigart, E., & Rauls, L. (2021). Criminal organizations often control territory. *Americas Quarterly*, 15(1), 40–41.

Torche, F. (2014). Intergenerational mobility and inequality: The Latin American case. *Annual Review of Sociology*, 40, 619–642. https://doi.org/10.1146/annurev-soc-071811-145521

Trading Economics. (2021). Colombia unemployment rate. Retrieved on October 1, 2021 from https://tradingeconomics.com/colombia/unemployment-rate

Transparency International. (2019). *Global corruption barometer Latin America & The Caribbean 2019. Citizens' views and experiences of corruption*. https://www.transparency.org/en/gcb/latin-america/latin-america-and-the-caribbean-x-edition-2019

United Nations. (2020). The Paris Agreement: What is the Paris Agreement? Retrieved on November 27, 2021 from https://unfccc.int/process-and-meetings/the-paris-agreement/the-paris-agreement

United Nations. (2021). *COP26 reaches consensus on key actions to address climate change*. Retrieved on November 27, 2021 from https://unfccc.int/news/cop26-reaches-consensus-on-key-actions-to-address-climate-change

Venkatesan, R. (2015). Confronting corruption. *McKinsey Quarterly*. January, 1-9. https://www.mckinsey.com/~/media/McKinsey/Featured%20Insights/Corporate%20Social%20Responsibility/Confronting%20corruption/Confronting%20corruption.pdf

Ward, A. (2020). Chileans want a more equal society. They're about to rewrite their constitution to have it. Vox.com. https://www.vox.com/21534338/chile-constitution-plebiscite-vote-pinochet

Winter, B., & Aalbers, G. (2021). *The capacity to combat corruption (CCC) index*. Control Risks and AS/COA. https://www.controlrisks.com/-/media/corporate/files/campaigns/ccc/ccc_2021_report_english.pdf

Wolf, J. (2020). One year later: The legacy of Latin America's 2019 mass protests. PRIF Blog. Retrieved on September 7, 2021 from https://blog.prif.org/2020/12/17/one-year-later-the-legacy-of-latin-americas-2019-mass-protests/

World Bank. (2018). Fair progress? Economic mobility across generations around the world. Retrieved on September 20, 2021 from https://www.worldbank.org/en/topic/poverty/publication/fair-progress-economic-mobility-across-generations-around-the-world

World Bank Climate Knowledge Portal. (n.d.). Retrieved on September 7, 2021 from https://climateknowledgeportal.worldbank.org

World Economic Forum. (2020). *The global social mobility report of 2020: Equality, opportunity and a new economic imperative*. Retrieved on September 20, 2021 from https://www3.weforum.org/docs/Global_Social_Mobility_Report.pdf

Zechmeister, E. J., & Lupu, N. (Eds.). (2019). *Pulse of democracy*. Nashville: LAPOP.

Zissis, C. (2021, December 1). Approval tracker: Mexico's president AMLO. AS/COA. https://www.as-coa.org/articles/approval-tracker-mexicos-president-amlo

Part 2

Business Strategies for Latin America

7 Marketing Strategies for Latin American Consumer Markets

Introduction

Wander around any major Latin American city and you will see throngs of consumers shopping to their heart's content. Many will be on their smartphones browsing brand name goods or calling up a rideshare service while they listen to music on a streaming app. The Latin American consumer market has grown in size and purchasing power; it has become increasingly segmented, more sophisticated and discerning, and less frugal while remaining distinctive from other world markets. There is increased consumer confidence in the economies of the region driven by individual economic and social progress. As mentioned in Chapters 1 and 4, sustained economic growth, a more dynamic business environment, and key governmental programs have led to many being lifted out of extreme poverty and to a larger middle class that can now more easily afford basic and discretionary goods and services.

The values that characterized consumers at the end of the century have remained ingrained in a generation old enough to remember the economic and political crises of the time. These memories are not necessarily shared by a generation of younger Latin Americans that came of age amidst better economic times and technological advancements. Younger generations espouse different consumer values than their parents; understanding these changes can help us make conjectures about the future of Latin American consumer markets. Additionally, the COVID-19 pandemic has caused a reversal of the economic progress at the base and middle of the economic pyramid. It is too early to predict its long-term effects on Latin American consumers.

The first section of this chapter provides an overview of the size and characteristics of Latin American consumer markets. The next section discusses consumer values that shape Latin American consumers' expectations and behaviors. Next, we discuss various consumer segments in the region and how firms should position their brands to target particular segments. The next three sections discuss pricing, communication, and distribution strategies most appropriate for Latin American consumer markets. The chapter ends with conclusions and key marketing strategy recommendations.

An Overview of the Latin American Consumer Market

Over the past two decades, the Latin American consumer market has grown in size and sophistication. Across the region, the size of the middle class has increased, and poverty has decreased. The liberalization and global insertion of the Latin American economies, increased urbanization, and growing connectivity have resulted in consumer markets that are more cosmopolitan and demanding. Differences in race, ethnicity, social class, and geography point to a variety of consumer markets rich in opportunity and that are complex to navigate. Despite the negative impact of the COVID-19 pandemic, consumer demand remains strong.

DOI: 10.4324/9781003182672-10

In 2020, the total population of Latin America and the Caribbean was estimated at 652 million, representing about 9% of the world's population. Individual country markets range in population size from large ones like Brazil (213 million) to medium-size countries like Ecuador (18 million) to the very small island countries in the Caribbean (World Bank, 2021a). As discussed in Chapter 4, population growth has been declining slowly over time; however, it will continue to increase at an average rate of 0.9%, reaching 800 million by 2050 (United Nations, 2021). There are an estimated 190 million households in Latin America, with an average household size of 3.4 persons, ranging from 2.6 for households in the highest income quintile to 4.4 for households in the lowest income quintile (PRB, 2020).

Latin America is an attractive market in terms of income. In 2019, GDP was US$5.8 trillion and per capita income was US$16,700. The region's economy suffered due to the COVID-19 pandemic, but it has begun to recover. The region's total GDP in 2020 was US$4.8 trillion (about 5% of total world GDP) with an average per capita GNI of US$15,700. The region's average 2021 GDP growth rate was 6.8%, and the estimate for 2022 is 2.5% (World Bank, 2021a). Brazil and Mexico, the two largest markets, represent half of the region's population (32% and 20%, respectively) and GDP (31% and 23%, respectively). These two large countries, along with Argentina, Colombia, Chile, and Peru, account for about 75% of the total regional market in terms of both population and income (referred to as the LAC-6 throughout the book). Table 7.1 summarizes key population and GDP data for selected countries in the region.

Table 7.1 Key Population and GDP Data for Selected Countries

Country	Population (Millions) 2020	GDP (US$ Billions) 2020	GDP p/ Capita (US$) 2020	GNI p/ Capita PPP (US$) 2020	GDP Growth Rate % 2021 (est.)
Argentina	45.38	383.07	8,441.9	20,210	4.9
Bolivia	11.67	36.69	3,143.0	8,250	5.1
Brazil	212.56	1,444.73	6,796.8	14,550	3.2
Chile	19.12	252.94	13,231.7	23,980	5.0
Colombia	50.88	271.35	5,332.8	14,280	5.0
Costa Rica	5.09	61.52	12,076.8	19,840	3.0
Cuba	11.33	103.13 (2019)	9,099.7 (2019)	—	3.0
The Dominican Republic	10.85	78.84	7,268.2	17,060	5.0
Ecuador	17.64	98.81	5,600.4	10,580	1.0
El Salvador	6.49	24.64	3,798.6	8,050	3.5
Guatemala	16.86	77.60	4,603.3	8,690	3.5
Honduras	9.90	23.83	2,405.7	5,050	4.5
Mexico	128.93	1,076.16	8,346.7	18,170	3.8
Nicaragua	6.62	12.62	1,905.3	5,410	1.3
Panama	4.31	52.94	12,269.0	25,010	5.5
Paraguay	7.13	35.61	4,949.7	12,590	3.5
Peru	32.97	202.01	6,126.9	11,490	9.0
Uruguay	3.47	55.71	15,438.4	21,630	4.0
Venezuela	28.44	482.36 (2014)	16,055.6 (2014)	—	-7.0
Total LAC	652.28	4,838.00	15,868.4	15,363	3.7
China	1,402	14,722.84	16,117	17,200	8.5
US	329.48	20,936.60	62,530	66,060	6.3

Sources: ECLAC (2021). *Preliminary overview of the economies of Latin America and the Caribbean 2020.* https://www.cepal.org/en/publications/type/preliminary-overview-economies-latin-america-and-caribbean
World Bank Databank https://data.worldbank.org/
Bureau of Economic Analysis, US Department of Commerce https://www.bea.gov

The region has seen the emergence of a large middle class and a decrease in poverty. According to the World Bank, a middle-class household earns US$13–$70 per day. On this basis, in 2019, the region's middle class represented 40% of the total population. In 2020, the COVID-19 pandemic caused many in the middle class to slip into the vulnerable class (those with incomes between US$5.50–$13) or into poverty (less than US$5.50). About 12 million people across the region fell from the middle class, and about 20 million fell into poverty. The current economic recovery already under way will help some people move back into the middle-income bracket. Those working or operating businesses in the informal market will face a slower recovery (about 50% of the region's workers are in the informal market, 90% of the working poor work in the informal market, and about a third of them are self-employed) (World Bank, 2021b).

A study by Ferreira et al. (2013) found that middle-class families across the region are primarily urban, have heads of households with higher levels of education, are employed in the private sector, and have female members of the household participating in the labor force. In spite of demographic similarities, the values and beliefs held by people in Latin America are still largely determined by nationality. As such, a middle-class person in Colombia is more likely to share values and beliefs with a lower income Colombian than a middle-class person from Mexico. Large and stable middle-class country markets, with more discretionary income are very attractive to marketers.

The segment of the population considered poor (incomes of under US$5.50) or vulnerable (incomes between US$5.50–$13) represents 60% of the region's population (90–100 million households). The needs among lower income consumers continue to be primarily necessities. Half of these consumers' spending goes to food, energy, housing, and transportation and the rest to health, telecommunications, water, clothing, education, and entertainment (Dansk Industry, 2007; TNS, 2010). Yet, the poor remain severely underserved in essential services: less than 25% of poor households have access to adequate sanitation, about 10% do not have access to electricity, and only about 25% have access to the internet at home (World Bank, 2021b). Latin American low-income consumers tend to be family oriented, focused on the present but optimistic about the future, increasingly sophisticated and discriminant, and open to new technology adoption. Low-income consumers like to buy leader brands for specific product categories because of the brand's reputation and reliability. Latin American consumers place importance on social status and keeping face and do not want to be reminded of their income limitations or social class. Furthermore, low-income consumers are dependable borrowers as demonstrated by the high repayment rates of microfinance organizations. In summary, the Latin American low-income market is large in size and purchasing power and—unfortunately—has grown as a result of the COVID-19 pandemic. Its increased urbanization and connectivity have reduced communication and distribution obstacles, creating opportunities in sectors such as financial services, entertainment, and retailing. The lack of attention given to low-income consumers opens opportunities for companies willing to adopt innovative business models that satisfy their needs and constraints.

Higher income levels paired with relatively low rates of inflation over the past two decades have led to the increased purchasing power of Latin American consumers. Table 7.2 summarizes the most important drivers of purchasing power, all of which were discussed in Part I of the book.

By now, it should be evident that there is no such thing as a 'typical' Latin American—the region is socially and culturally diverse; geographically, economically, and politically heterogeneous; and changing at different speeds and to different extents. However, for marketing strategy purposes, it is useful to identify areas of convergence that point to a 'typical Latin

Table 7.2 Purchasing Power Drivers for Latin American Consumer Markets

Economic Drivers	Sociocultural Drivers	Political and Legal Drivers	Technological Drivers
Growing middle class, with greater purchasing power	High levels of urbanization	An enduring return to democracy	Greater connectivity: increased penetration of smart devices and telecommunication technologies
Poverty reduction and social mobility	Insertion of women into workforce	Relative political stability (e.g., absence of armed conflicts)	Improvements to physical infrastructure
Consumer confidence and optimism in the future	Migration flows (into and from the region)	Reduction of regulatory red tape	Access to social networks
Stable macroeconomic indicators (inflation, currency values, debt)	Changes to household composition (e.g., more dual-income households; single-parent households, etc.)	Policymaking supportive of a dynamic business environment	
Economic integration within the region and rest of the world	Values in transition (more tolerant and progressive values coexisting with more traditional and conservative values)	—	—

Source: Authors' elaboration.

American consumer.' Such a profile would include shared characteristics across consumers in the region, such as young but getting older, urban, family-centered, warm, affectionate, traditional, conservative, and religious. This typical consumer is also connected, tech savvy, and more affluent than ever before. Even if we were to accept these commonalities, we must acknowledge differences within and between countries. The many capital cities in the region are undoubtedly key markets, but they do not represent the diversity of peoples and places within their respective countries. Although Spanish is spoken throughout most of Latin America, the largest market in the region—Brazil—is Portuguese-speaking; English and French are also spoken in the Guyanas and several countries in the Caribbean. Bolivia, Paraguay, and Peru have more than one official language, and many Indigenous languages are spoken throughout the region (Guatemala, Bolivia, and Peru have more than 25; Colombia and Mexico have more than 60). Moreover, as discussed in Chapter 4, the region is quite diverse in terms of ethnic and racial composition. For example, Colombia and Brazil have significant population segments of African descendants, Brazil and Peru have large populations of Japanese ancestry, and Central American countries have large communities of people of Middle Eastern descent. Consumer values and behaviors also differ between population groups. For instance, the younger and older generations have diverged in values such as individualism and cultural tolerance. Therefore, while acknowledging some commonalities among Latin American consumers, the high level of heterogeneity of the region's consumer markets makes understanding current perceptions of values among Latin American consumers of critical importance for firms doing business in the region.

Understanding Latin American Consumers' Values

Latin Americans are still considered relatively traditional and conservative. Latin Americans' strong religious beliefs and sense of family duty shape their social norms and individual behaviors. In addition, people in the region have a high level of respect for hierarchy and authority, and favor clearly defined gender roles. Yet, these traditional values now coexist with transitional values of individualism and social tolerance.

Latin American consumers may have changed their lifestyles and consumption in response to the drivers noted above but many remain loyal to their traditions and customs. In fact, Latin Americans value tradition and are more worried about the loss of their cultural identity than other consumers around the world (Powdrill & Hughes, 2012). A new set of consumer values has arisen to resolve the potential contradictions between 'the old and the new' priorities in Latin American societies. In this section, we identify some of these societal contradictions and new and emerging consumer values.

Societal Contradictions

Individualism and Community Contradictions

Latin American consumers face the dilemma of adopting individualistic values while maintaining their commitment to community. This contradiction pits the traditional community-oriented Latin American values of nurturing strong relationships (family, friends, neighbors) and lending solidarity and support to others against the individualistic values of self-reliance and empowerment. Latin American consumers are collectivist-oriented (see Chapter 5), and family is still at the core of Latin American culture. About a third of all households in Latin America are considered multigenerational, and 40% are the traditional nuclear family (Pew Research Center, 2020). Latin Americans rely heavily on family input for purchasing decisions and tend to shop as a family unit.

Latin Americans are increasingly seeking to express their individuality. Smaller households are driving demand for individualized products. As mentioned in Chapter 4, households led by single parents account for 10% of all households; single-person households represent 3% of all, and other household-sharing arrangements represent another 10% of all households (Pew Research Center, 2020). Together, these smaller households account for 25% of all households. Firms will need to offer smaller packages and individual-size products that fit the small consumption footprint and preferences of Latin American consumers living alone or in smaller households. Neighborhood stores open until late hours serve these single-household customers returning from work, evening school, or fitness practice; typically, they dispense their goods through small windows in order to protect themselves from crime and violence.

The growth of individualism in the region has also led to a greater need for personalization and customization (Powdrill & Hughes, 2012), thus increasing demand for products that satisfy consumers' needs of self-esteem and self-realization. Latin Americans are focusing on self-improvement, education, and skill building to realize their own potential as individuals. For many, this need has been driven by fears about the future, especially post-COVID, wherein self-improvement acts as a type of insurance against potential reversals of good fortune, slowdown of the economy, and climate change (LR Foundation, 2022). For others, economic stability and optimism about the future have provided the motivation for self-improvement.

Skepticism and Trust Contradictions

Latin American consumers have become accustomed to living in an environment characterized by crime, corruption, lack of transparency, and distrust of institutions, including business firms. In addition, Latin American consumers are naturally risk averse and dislike uncertainty (see Chapter 5). Given their high level of distrust of people and institutions, Latin Americans value trustworthiness, safety, and authenticity. Building trusting relationships with consumers is essential for achieving growth; this is especially true for firms operating in sectors least trusted by consumers, such as financial services and telecommunications (Llorente & Cuenca, 2018). Companies seeking to appeal to Latin American consumers must identify consumer areas of need where trust and safety are in great demand and develop value propositions that meet those needs. For instance, taxi services are widely used in Latin America, as not everyone owns a car or people want to avoid overcrowded and unsafe public transportation or driving in congested roads (e.g., the three worst world commutes are in Latin American cities!). Safer taxi services connected to mobile apps have gained popularity in Latin American cities, replacing the need to hail a taxi on the street and be involved in a car accident (as many taxis are unregulated and poorly maintained), in a robbery, or assault. These app-based safer taxi and ridesharing services provide a number to call, a description of the car, a profile of the driver, and customer opinions of the service; they also provide assurances that the cars are safe and well maintained. Many offer women-only services (e.g., Lady Driver in Brazil; Voy Contigo in Chile), which offer trusting services to women riders and added safety to women drivers as well. Gaining consumers trust is also important for the safety of online transactions and sharing of information with unauthorized parties. Advertising claims offer another example of the value consumers place on trust. Latin Americans trust people they know the most, with branded websites being the second most trusted source of commercial information. Ads on social networks are trusted by only about a third of Latin American consumers (Nielsen, 2013). This represents a real challenge to business firms as they must strive to gain the trust not just of the individual consumer but also of the groups to which a consumer belongs.

Fast and Easy versus Slow and Complex Contradictions

The days of slow pace and long lunch breaks are gone in Latin America. The fast pace of modern life places a demand on time and efficiency. In the midst of such a hurried and stressful lifestyle, Latin Americans still believe it is important to pause and take a deep breath between tasks. Latin American culture thrives on socialization and, thus, breaking up the day to catch up with family and friends is still seen as a priority. A casual walk in a Latin American city reveals cafes and restaurants filled with customers at all hours of the day and well into the late evening. These short breaks provide the energy people need to move to the next task in the day. In this environment, Latin American consumers concerned with time saving and efficiency compensate for 'time lost' on social activities by 'saving time' in other less important transactions such as banking, government services, and house chores. Consumers will delegate these tasks to others (e.g., hiring home cleaning services) or make them online during off-work hours (e.g., mobile banking). App-based delivery services such as those provided by Brazil's iFood and the popular Rappi have also gained adepts among urban consumers who wish to avoid wasting time driving or being stuck in traffic just to pick up a meal or groceries (Guzman & Mackinson, 2020). Finding an equilibrium between a hurried life and leisure time is key to managing the complex requirements of modern life in urban Latin America

(TNS, 2010). Therefore, urban consumers especially will increasingly opt for marketers that offer them convenience and efficiency.

Passivism and Activism Contradictions

Latin Americans can be fatalistic, pessimistic, and deterministic, believing there is not much they can do to change society or their personal life. This deterministic attitude means they feel the deck is stacked against them, so they resign themselves to a future of which they have little control. This is in sharp contrast to the new (or renewed) sense of empowerment and optimism that can be observed in the region among the younger generations. Growing individualism, sustained economic prosperity, and access to new communication technologies have given Latin Americans a sense of empowerment of their influence on society as well as more control over their personal lives. The social protests that have occurred across the region over the past three years or so are a testament to this sense of empowerment. Social tolerance is also on the rise, and there are more people willing to change both social norms and laws that prevent them or others from living full lives (e.g., recognition and protection of LGBTQ+ individuals). Most of the region has decriminalized same-sex sexual acts between consenting adults. In some countries, LGBTQ+ individuals are constitutionally protected (i.e., Bolivia, Cuba, Ecuador, and Mexico). Since 2010, other countries have passed laws prohibiting discrimination based on sexual orientation and protections of the rights of LGBTQ+ individuals. Mexico City passed a law in 2009 allowing gay and lesbian couples to marry and to adopt children. Argentina became the first Latin American country to legalize same-sex marriage in 2010. Marriage equality laws have also been adopted in Brazil and Uruguay (2013), Colombia (2016), Ecuador (2019), Costa Rica (2020), and Chile (2021) (Planas, 2013; Farrell, 2021). A more tolerant and inclusive society will have an impact on consumer markets, from opening up market opportunities in niche segments to changing the types of communication messages that consumers consider socially acceptable.

Social awareness about environmental sustainability has also become widespread throughout the region, and activism in this area has been instrumental in raising expectations for policymaking and corporate action. As their economies have relied on intense exploitation of natural resources for economic growth, Latin Americans have become worried about the degradation of their rich natural resources. Some Latin American governments and entrepreneurs have introduced greener collaborative services such as public bicycling systems or car sharing in an effort to reduce pollution and the use of oil resources (examples of carsharing services include Argentina's *Carpoolear*, Chile's *Nos Fuimos*, Colombia's *Ilikko*, and Brazil's *BlaBlaCar*). High rates of smartphone usage and broadband penetration enables Latin American consumers to use these services. In fact, the carsharing and ridesharing industry in Latin America is worth almost a billion dollars, making the region the world's second-largest market for shared mobility (Maya, 2019). Latin American consumers are gradually being converted to the idea that they can make a positive impact on their natural environment via their purchasing choices. This empowerment goes beyond consumption to larger issues such as less tolerance of corruption, unethical behavior, environmental degradation, and social injustice.

As Latin American consumers seek to resolve these contradictions, new consumer priorities and values have emerged. The new Latin American consumers are more individualistic; better informed; cautious with their money; have higher expectations of convenience and efficiency as well as environmental and social responsibility; and are more concerned with issues such as health, education, and personal safety. Some of these issues and values are more important than others, which suggests that Latin American consumers will prioritize and attempt not to compromise on important values. Other values are peripheral, and consumers may be more flexible in finding a consumption solution. We identify core and peripheral consumer values next.

Core Consumer Values

Emerging 'Me' Identity

Individualism, empowerment, and modernism create pressure to seek a strong identity. As consumers are embedded in their local and national milieu, Latin American consumer individualism has generated a variety of 'local identities' which are characterized by the most immediate environment first (the city), their country second, and their passion for a local activity (soccer, music, or food) third. Take the archetypal Buenos Aires *porteño*, who is a mix of a strong self-image, Argentine pride, fierce loyalties to their favorite soccer team, and a passion for beef or tango. The Rio de Janeiro *carioca* is casual and relaxed and places a high priority on an aesthetic lifestyle that reflects the beauty of the city and its inhabitants. Cariocas are passionate about soccer, music, food, and physical fitness. The *chilango*, a name used for residents of Mexico City, celebrates the cachet of being at the center of the country's political power and cultural dynamism. The chilango cultural identity is manifested in its particular style of speech (jargon), trendy fashion style, food consumption, music, and vivid entertainment (e.g., masked luchadores).

Relying solely on these so-called archetypes, however, risks making decisions based on misguided stereotypes and misses the rich and complex layers of identity of Latin American consumers. These layers of identity are shaped by personal characteristics and experiences as well as contextual variables and relationships. Thus, it is difficult to generalize about the 'identity of Latin American consumers' at the regional, sub-regional, or national level. Gaining a deeper and nuanced understanding of individuals' 'me identities' at each level must be a strategic imperative for marketers interested in reaching Latin American consumers effectively. Netflix and Amazon Prime Video, for instance, have succeeded in the region by recognizing that Latin Americans want to see their own stories and narratives on screen, told from various perspectives (and in their own languages). Both companies have adopted localization strategies that combine a variety of global and regional content with locally produced content—primarily in Brazil, Mexico, and Colombia, but also in Argentina and Chile (EBANX, 2021).

Affordability and Liquidity

After suffering the impact of economic recessions and the economic shocks of the ongoing COVID-19 pandemic, Latin American consumers are careful stewards of their money, placing a high value on both affordability of products and ability to use cash over credit. Larger incomes and better information result in a more optimistic view of the future; the opposite scenario results in a pessimistic attitude and cautious consumption. Regardless of how optimistic or pessimistic Latin American consumers are, they constantly search for value-adding and multifunctional products, are sensitive to the cost-benefits of alternative options, and are not swayed by loyalty to brands based on familiarity or emotional attachments (Balvé, 2012). The lack of trust in financial institutions paired with limited access to credit and unstable income sources (especially for those who work in the informal sector) lead to a preference for cash transactions, and, although this is changing, cash is still the preferred method of payment. Thus, marketers targeting consumers in the region will need to consider cash-based options for high-priced items such as layaway or payment plans.

Easy, Convenient, and Fast

Latin American urban consumers are attaching greater value to time and simplicity to cope with the demands of busy lifestyles. Due to these constraints, consumers are concerned about wasting time and demand faster and simpler solutions. For instance, payment with cash is simple, transparent, and yields savings in terms of discounts from the full price because vendors prefer cash. Payment with credit cards can also be fast and convenient but carries the risk of overspending and has additional fees attached. As such, it is limited to more affluent consumers. Electronic payments and use of smartphone technologies to finalize transactions is still in its infancy but offers great promise to meet the time pressures of Latin American consumers. These pressures and the low cost of labor and transportation have also created a delivery economy where almost everything can be delivered to wherever the customer is. The COVID-19 pandemic has accelerated the use and acceptance of online ordering and payments and of deliveries of at-home services. Amazon, Rappi, iFood, Uber Eats, among others, have all experienced newfound popularity since the start of the pandemic and are likely to remain successful in the future

Honesty, Trust, and Authenticity

Latin American consumers have reached their limit of tolerance for corruption and dishonest behavior. They can easily distinguish fake or pirated products from authentic products. They are demanding greater transparency in transactions, and search for product offerings they consider genuine and honest. They have also become more vocal about 'telling the truth' about their experiences with brands and vendors, relying on social media to openly praise or criticize products with which they engage.

Health, Safety, and Security

Concern with personal health has made the Latin American consumer more aware of the quality of what they eat and consume. For instance, obesity is on the rise, primarily due to the proliferation of fast-food restaurants and consumption of soft-drinks and pre-packaged foods. Latin Americans are turning to healthier living impacting the demand for gym memberships, diet products, and health supplements. Latin American consumers are also dealing with high volatility and uncertainty and seek to release the related stress through consumption behaviors that increase their well-being (e.g., spa treatments, yoga, vacations). Within a climate of violence, safety and security concerns are becoming important considerations in shopping behavior as well. Latin American consumers are increasingly taking safety and security of the retail environment into consideration, choosing to shop in stores that offer well-lit parking and private security, for instance. As mentioned, delivery services prevent the risks of on-site shopping, especially late at night. In sum, marketers may enhance their appeal by providing protection from safety risks.

Empowerment

Consumer empowerment and the realization that their consumption practices can make a difference have given Latin American consumers a sense of mission. This energy and activism have become another important value for Latin American consumers. The promise of more responsible and collaborative consumption emerging from this priority is a positive sign for the region. Consumers are likely to respond well to brands that share their personal mission of 'changing the world,' which may be reflected through a company's treatment of their employees, consumers, or society at large.

In 2016, Arcos Dorados, the master franchisee for McDonald's in the region, embarked on a series of initiatives to become more socially and environmentally responsible. Consumers' need for empowerment will translate into greater affinity to McDonald's if the company can show it can 'do some good.' Some of the initiatives Arcos Dorados has undertaken include the elimination of plastic straws and lids; responsible sourcing of inputs (e.g., eggs, beef, coffee, fish, palm oil); recycling and reusing waste in its restaurants, not just packaging, but used oil (turned into biofuel), and water from its air conditioned units (used to flush toilets and water gardens); and integrating solar energy, LED lighting, and low-energy consumption equipment in its restaurants. Arcos Dorados has also relaxed uniform dress and appearance rules for its employees, allowing them to show up to work with long hair, tattoos, and piercings. It offers training to help workers advance their careers as chefs and technicians, for example. The result has been 'a happier workforce, lower turnover rates and better customer service' (Newbery, 2020, p. 32). The company is making progress on its social and environmental goals, and it has adopted a 'lead by example with honesty and transparency' approach hoping its customers will believe their efforts are genuine, based not on what they say, but on what they do (Newbery, 2020).

Social Connectivity

Latin Americans are extremely social in nature. Large families and a variety of social group affiliations require good connectivity. Digital technology and social media have allowed Latin Americans to establish and nurture large webs of connections. A later section on communication strategies focuses on the value of social connectivity among consumers in the region.

Peripheral Consumer Values

Other values relevant to consumers in Latin America are peripheral to their consumption preferences. Among these values are quality, prestige, uniqueness, novelty, consumption experience, and globalism. Some of these consumer values may become important to particular market segments (e.g., novelty to younger consumers) or unique consumption situations (e.g., consumption experience when on vacation). Affluent consumers may also care more about prestige and uniqueness, while quality may be more important to consumers in middle- and low-income brackets. Some consumers are interested in experiential purchases, including occasional indulgences and small luxuries (Borges, 2018). Another layer of variation is regional differences within a country. These regional differences will influence which peripheral values are given more relevance during specific purchasing situations.

Recent trends in the food and beverages sector illustrate the ways in which core and peripheral values impact consumption preferences and behavior. The concerns for health and empowerment have translated into Latin American consumers' growing consumption of vegetarian and vegetable-based protein alternatives. Though consumption of vegetarian foods is still very low, there has been an explosion of products to meet the needs of vegetarian, vegan, and flexitarian consumers. Consumers are seeking to reduce their consumption of meat and other animal-based products due to health, environmental, and ethical concerns (Wolf & Mackinson, 2020). Concerns for health are also evident in the beverages category. For instance, US company Jugos Caribe introduced healthy bottled juices to the Dominican Republic; in Central America, Colombian company Quala S.A., known for its energy drink Vive 100, has introduced Saviloe, a fortified aloe vera-based beverage, and JugosYa, a brand of affordable, healthy, tasty offerings based on traditional flavors such as jamaica, horchata, and coconut (Krol, 2019). The recent growth in the consumption of traditional and ancient grains (e.g., quinoa) is a result of consumers' desire to be healthier, support their local economies, and connect to their cultural roots. Throughout the region, quinoa can be found in everything from cereal and cookies to chocolate and burgers (Chehtman, 2020a). Recent changes to lifestyles caused by the COVID-19 pandemic have reinforced consumers' preferences for convenience, health, empowerment, and value for money. As people began to work and study from home, consumers had less need for on-the-go foods (e.g., cereal bars) and more need for foods that could be used to prepare meals at home. The rise in the use of e-commerce for at-home delivery of groceries is in line with consumers' growing need for 'easy, convenient, and fast.' Other foods with health benefits, especially those associated with improved immunity (fresh produce, vitamin fortified foods, organic food, etc.) have also gained in popularity. In addition, consumers have shown a desire to support local farmers and local food producers to contribute to their local communities (i.e., adding emotional and social value to their purchases). Finally, the economic crisis caused by the pandemic has led to consumers' seeking value options, such as lower priced, but high-quality, private-branded products and discount retailers (Chehtman, 2020b; Llorente y Cuenca, 2019).

Segmenting the Latin American Consumer Market

A region of more than 650 million people spanning a wide range of geographies, demographics, and economic realities should be approached through a careful segmentation process. Using demographic and geographic variables is perhaps the easiest way to segment the region's market, but, as noted previously, psychographic segmentation may be equally important. In most cases, marketers will need to use multiple segmentation variables to identify consumer groups that share specific values, lifestyles, and consumption behaviors. Below, we discuss examples of age, gender, and geographic-based segmentation.

Age-Based Segmentation

Latin America is a young but aging market, where 25% of the population is under 15 years of age, and two-thirds of the population (about 440 million) are 15–64 years of age. Yet, the over 65 segment has almost doubled in size in the past 20 years, from about 5% in 1990 to 9% in 2020 (PRB, 2020). Children and young people tend to be important influencers of family purchases. Many in the 'young consumer segment,' which encompasses people under 35 years of age, are also part of the 'digital consumer segment,' constituting an important target market. The young, digital consumer tends to be urban, more affluent, tech savvy, and active on social media, primarily via smartphones. If captured, children and young people have longer lifetime value as consumers; thus, the younger Latin American consumer segment represents an attractive market for toys, educational products, apparel, footwear, tourism, online entertainment, and more. The older population segment is a prime segment for nutrition, healthcare, and entertainment services sectors, among others.

Gender-Based Segmentation

The insertion of Latin American women into the workforce has resulted in increased financial independence, with women now able to make more purchasing decisions on their own for themselves and for their households. Yet women who are mothers still carry the burden of family obligations, resulting in high levels of stress and time constraints. Women who find themselves living hurried, time-starved, multitasking lives would find goods and services that streamline family living extremely appealing, from digital solutions (e.g., robo vacuums and online grocery shopping) to everyday conveniences (e.g., frozen foods). One-stop retailers are also likely to see increased traffic from women working outside the home. For women leading single-parent households, especially those from low- and middle-income groups, products need not only to provide time-saving benefits but do so at reasonable prices.

Geographic-Based Segmentation

Latin America's high level of geographic fragmentation has a direct impact on the growth and composition of consumer markets in the region. Geography impacts climate and health, agricultural yields, labor productivity, exposure to natural disasters, and access to markets. These geographic differences result in differing patterns of development across the region, with coastal cities for example, typically registering higher economic growth and more trade and foreign direct investment activity than inland zones. The economic vitality of some regions results in larger consumer markets with greater purchasing power, who are likely to have more access to communication and distribution channels. Moreover, different geographic zones are likely to develop their own social customs and cultural idiosyncrasies, which, in turn, shapes consumers' expectations and buying behaviors.

Gallup, Gaviria, and Lora (2003, p. 11) define geographical fragmentation as 'the probability that two individuals taken at random do not live in similar ecozones.' Based on this definition, they found that Latin America was the most fragmented region in the world, particularly Ecuador, Colombia, and Peru. They identified seven geographical zones, including tropical highlands, lowland Pacific coast, lowland Atlantic coast, Amazon, temperate Southern Cone, Mexican-US border, and highland and dry Southern Cone. This geographic fragmentation can lead to economic and social distinctions among consumers from different zones, which translate into different consumer needs, tastes, and preferences.

In addition to using geographic ecozones to segment consumer markets, level of urbanization can be a useful geographic segmentation variable. Latin America is the most urbanized region in the world with more than 80% of the population living in cities (see Chapter 4). According to the United Nations Habitat 2020, there are 215 cities with more than 300,000 inhabitants in Latin America, representing about half of the region's population. The urban population is expected to grow at a declining average rate of 1.06% between 2020 and 2035 (0.7% less than the average growth registered in the period 2000–2020), adding another 53 million people to large metropolitan areas by 2035. The region is home to several megacities, with six metropolitan areas exceeding ten million inhabitants (São Paulo, México City, Buenos Aires, Río de Janeiro, Bogotá, and Lima), and 68 cities that have between one and ten million people. Brazil and Mexico account for almost half of all the largest cities in the region (61 in Brazil and 54 in Mexico). A 2011 McKinsey Global Institute report estimated that the ten largest cities alone accounted for about 50% of the region's GDP, and by 2025, the 200 largest cities in the region would have generated US$3.8 trillion in GDP growth and would boast a US$23,000 per capita income. The most significant growth is expected to happen in mid-size cities, those between 200,000 and 10 million people (Cadena et al., 2011). By far, the most important metropolitan areas in the region are São Paulo (22 million people and 30% of Brazil's GDP) and Mexico City (22 million people and 15% of Mexico's GDP) (Figure 7.1).

The benefits of urbanization are related to the agglomeration effects associated with urban centers. The larger markets and higher population density of primary and secondary cities will appeal to firms seeking economies of scale, enhanced productivity, and more efficient distribution. As these metropolitan areas exceed their capacity, a B2B market strengthened

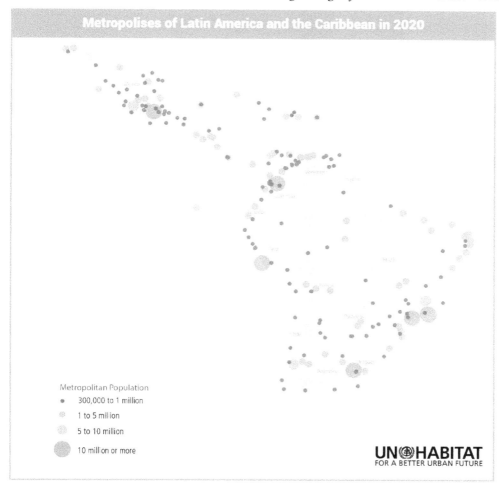

Figure 7.1 Urbanization in Latin America. United Nations-Habitat (2020). *Global State of Metropolis 2020–Population Data Booklet*. https://unhabitat.org/global-state-of-metropolis-2020-%E2 %80%93-population-data-booklet#:~:text=In%202020%20there%20are%201934,third %20of%20the%20global%20population

by local governments' demand for construction, transportation, and public services will open new opportunities.

Increased urbanization and decaying cities' infrastructures in Latin America are also shaping consumer values in the region. The growth of cities means traffic congestion, longer commutes, and less protection against urban violence. Such a hostile environment for shopping increases demand for convenient and time-saving goods and services and fosters a reliance on trusted neighborhood providers. Convenience stores and home delivery services have evolved to supply consumers with almost anything imaginable. Time and simplicity of consumption have also emerged as top priorities. Yet, urban centers across the region differ in terms of economic and social performance: Monterrey, Mexico is home to a strong technology cluster and has the lowest share of people living in poverty in the region; Curitiba,

Brazil has shaped itself as an example of sustainable living. These intra-country differences will further shape consumers' values and behaviors.

Building a Relevant Brand in Latin America

Building a strong brand is a core element of a Latin American marketing strategy. The challenge is to build brands that resonate with Latin Americans' values and help consumers to achieve their personal goals. Marketing messages should also reassure Latin American consumers of the brand's commitment to serve their needs in the long term. A good start for a firm operating in the region is to build a brand strategy that integrates some, if not all, of the consumer priorities reviewed previously to meet specific consumer needs in the market category in which the brand participates. To summarize, these values are:

1. Strong identity, optimism, and confidence
2. Trust, transparency, honesty, and authenticity
3. Easy, convenient, and fast
4. Value-to-price and liquidity
5. Safety and security
6. Empowerment to tackle large social issues
7. Connectivity

A Brand Architecture for Latin America

A brand strategy for Latin America will be a carefully coordinated effort to develop the brand architecture needed to deliver on these consumer priorities, creating economic value, relevance, and resonance for the Latin American consumer. This architecture (based on Keller, 2012) is deconstructed into several brand-building block efforts shown in Figure 7.2.

The first building block is *brand salience*. This effort establishes the brand identity and initiates engagement with the Latin American consumer. A well-orchestrated communications strategy is the best approach to establish salience. The second building block is *brand meaning*. The effort here is to establish credibility and showcase the benefits of the marketing offer. Building brand meaning involves (1) appealing to the rational side of the Latin American consumer by communicating and demonstrating the product's benefits (e.g., convenience, safety) and (2) creating a brand personality that appeals to the emotional side of the Latin American consumer. The latter includes highlighting the heritage and character of the brand as well as generating positive feelings about the brand based on associations with specific consumer values (e.g., authenticity, social connectivity).

The third building block moves the consumer to make the *brand the preferred choice*. This is accomplished through brand comparisons with alternative choices that demonstrate the superiority of the brand's functional performance and relevance to important consumer priorities as well as clearly demonstrating the price-to-value ratio. This part of the strategy communicates the firm's capabilities and competencies that support the brand's performance. A second component of this building block is the effort to seek a positive emotional response and connection with the Latin American consumer that may lead to brand loyalty and alignment with their personal lifestyles.

The final building block is *brand resonance*. Here, the effort is to address the more altruistic aspirations and the large social and environmental concerns of Latin American consumers. This effort particularly addresses Latin American consumers' lack of trust as well as

Brand Objectives at Each Stage

Intense, Active Loyalty

Positive, Accessible Reactions

Strong, Favorable & Unique Brand Associations

Deep, Broad Brand Awareness

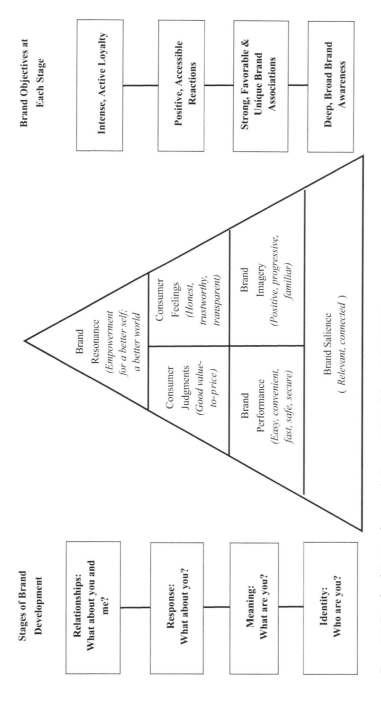

Brand Resonance
(Empowerment for a better self; a better world)

Consumer Feelings
(Honest, trustworthy, transparent)

Brand Imagery
(Positive, progressive, familiar)

Consumer Judgments
(Good value-to-price)

Brand Performance
(Easy, convenient, fast, safe, secure)

Brand Salience
(Relevant, connected)

Stages of Brand Development

Relationships: What about you and me?

Response: What about you?

Meaning: What are you?

Identity: Who are you?

Figure 7.2 Brand architecture framework. Source: Adapted from Keller (2012)

their concerns about the environment and social justice. Figure 7.3 briefly describes Brazilian Natura & Co.'s brand-building strategy.

Establishing an integrated brand strategy in Latin America is a challenging feat. For non-Latin American multinationals, a Latin American brand strategy is typically an extension of their global brand strategy that is localized to the region or a specific country while keeping some integrity of the global brand identity (e.g., Starbucks, Netflix). For Latin American firms, their brand strategies could extend beyond the firm's country of origin without losing their national identity. For instance, the Corona (beer) and Televisa (TV/film entertainment) brands are recognized and established in many countries in Latin America, but consumers associate these brands with their Mexican roots. Itau (financial services, Brazil) and Mercado Libre (online marketplace, Argentina) are also examples of brands that have expanded their reach to other countries in the region and beyond but which consumers still associate with their countries of origin. Strong Latin American national brands, on the other hand, tend to focus on gaining the trust of consumers within their country: BCP (financial services) in Peru and Bodega Aurrera (retailing) in Mexico are good examples of this branding strategy.

Brands that resonate the most with Latin American consumers become icons in their marketplaces, as consumers show their admiration and appreciation in many different ways. Kantar's report of the BrandZ 50 most valuable brands in Latin America reflects the successful strategies adopted by brands from across the region (Kantar, 2020). BrandZ's Most Valuable Brands Index is composed of five sub-indices:

Brand Purpose: consumers care about more than goods and services—they are seeking brands that have a positive impact on consumers and society.
Innovation: innovation can lead to long-term relationships with customers. Innovative brands set trends and are responsive to market factors. Innovation extends beyond technology adoption and may involve new services, new channels, and portfolio diversification.
Communication: gaining visibility through a consistent and distinctive message that resonates with consumers and clearly communicates the brand's purpose. Messages must also be conveyed through the right channels.
Brand Experience: how a person interacts with the brand at every touchpoint. It is not limited to the moment of purchase but extends to the consumers' experience before and after purchase.
Love: emotional connection between the brand and consumers. It is developed through investments in purpose, innovation, and consumer experience; it allows brands to build and maintain a long-term relationship with consumers.

The index uses an average score of 100. A score above 100 on the total index or any of the sub-indices indicates a brand is particularly strong (above average) on that metric. Scores below 100 indicate areas of weakness. The 2020 findings are summarized in Table 7.3 and Figure 7.4. About a third of the top 50 brands are in consumer goods categories (beer, food and dairy, and personal care). Financial institutions, retail, and services each represented about 20% of brands in the top 50. Although Latin American brand average scores for all five sub-indices were all above 100, Latin American brands average scores fell short of those of comparison groups (i.e., global, United States, and China). Latin American brands' strongest performance was in the area of brand purpose (this was also the metric with the smallest gap among the comparison groups). The region's brands have work ahead in the areas of innovation, communication, and consumer experience. To the extent that improvements to these three areas are achieved, the love metric will also be strengthened.

Natura & Co is a Brazilian based firm founded in 1969 that encompasses four brands: Natura, Avon, The Body Shop and Aēsop. The company is the largest B-Corp in the world, operating in over 100 countries with over 35,000 employees, 7.7 million consultants, and 2021 net revenues of over US$7.5 billion.

The firm's stated purpose is, "To nurture beauty and relationships for a better way of living and doing business." Natura & Co has demonstrated a commitment to an ethical approach to business, grounded on cooperation, co-creation, and collaboration to drive positive social and environmental change, including gender equity, environmental sustainability, and empowerment of their sourcing communities.

The logo of their flag ship brand, Natura is *'Bem estar bem'* (well-being/being well). Natura & Co.'s extensive product portfolio emphasizes cruelty free, vegan and/or botanical products that have been socially and environmentally sourced, The company also supports relevant global causes such as campaigns against gender violence and breast cancer.

RESONANCE

Building a more socially and environmentally just world

FEELINGS

Caring for oneself while helping others

JUDGMENTS

*High quality
Affordable
Responsible*

BRAND PERSONALITY

Clean, natural, caring, community oriented

BRAND PERFORMANCE

High quality, innovative, natural products to meet personal care and aesthetic needs

BRAND SALIENCE

Relevant to women; those interested in sustainability and social justice

Figure 7.3 Natura & Co.'s brand building Source: Elaborated by the authors based on information from various sources, including: The company's website: https://www.naturaeco.com/. Eccles, R. G., Serafeim,G., & Heffernan, J. (2011). *Natura Cosméticos*, S.A. Harvard Business School Case 412–052. Select youtube videos: https://www.youtube.com/watch?v=vpY1j1XBb54 / https://www.youtube.com/watch?v=xdIctBWLYlM https://www.youtube.com/watch?app=desktop&v=AM8ipyIIaiU

Table 7.3 BrandZ Top 25 Most Valuable Latin American Brands

Rank	Brand	Category	Brand Value 2020 (US$ Billion)
1	Bradesco	Financial Institutions	9.47
2	Itaú Unibanco	Financial Institutions	8.39
3	Corona	Beer	7.53
4	Skol	Beer	7.25
5	Telcel	Communication Providers	5.48
6	Bodega Aurrera	Retail	5.42
7	Falabella	Retail	5.19
8	Brahma	Beer	3.78
9	Globo	TV Stations	3.62
10	Aguila	Beer	3.52
11	Grupo Modelo	Beer	3.27
12	Sodimac	Retail	3.18
13	Lider	Retail	3.16
14	Banco de Chile	Financial Institutions	3.13
15	Claro	Communication Providers	3.08
16	Televisa	Communication Providers	2.76
17	Copec	Energy	2.70
18	Antartica	Beer	2.67
19	Mercado Libre	E-Commerce	2.48
20	Bimbo	Food and Dairy	2.43
21	Liverpool	Retail	2.42
22	Telmex	Communication Providers	2.41
23	Banorte	Financial Institutions	2.37
24	Magazine Luiza	Retail	2.29
25	Cemex	Industry (Cement)	2.05

Source: Kantar (2020). *BrandZ Top 50 most valuable Latin American brands 2020.*

The value consumers in the region assign to 'brand purpose' is worth emphasizing. In 2020, HSR Specialist Researchers conducted a study in Brazil based on more than 18,000 interviews of consumers across all income levels and product categories to create a ranking of the 'most transformative brands' in the country. The purpose of the study was to identify brands that have been most successful at strengthening the value of their brands by developing relevance in the minds of consumers, especially during a time of crisis. The metrics used for ranking brands assessed a brand's relevance, visibility, and power of voice, using attributes such as actions aimed at society, investments in the safety of consumers, preparedness to offer solutions to clients in times of crisis, search for innovation in times of crisis, and fair and ethical behavior (LABS, 2020). The three most transformative brands for Brazilian consumers were Magazine Luiza (241/300), Netflix (233/300), and iFood (171/300). (Other brands in the top ten included Natura, Ambev (now merged into AB InBev), Nestle, O Boticario, and Mercado Libre.) How have the top three brands become so relevant to Brazilian consumers and come to be perceived as transformative? Magazine Luiza (Magalu) is a good example of what a brand should be. It has consistently, even before the pandemic, remained relevant to all stakeholders, with a history of solidarity, social engagement (e.g., campaigns against domestic violence), and innovation (i.e., it has become one of the region's most valuable and fastest growing retailers because of organic innovations and acquisitions of technology-based companies). Thus, actions taken by Magalu during the pandemic were seen as genuine and authentic, as they were in line with the image the brand has spent years creating. For

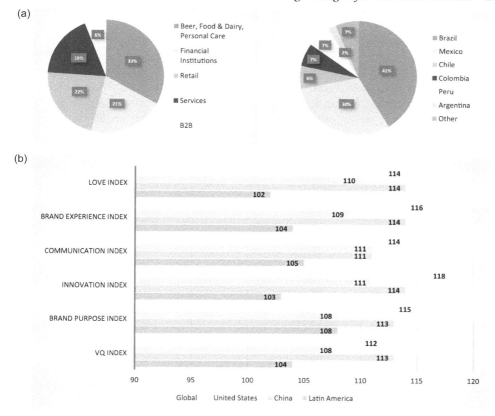

Figure 7.4 BrandZ Top 50 Latin American Brands (2020). (a) distribution of top 50 brands by sector and country; (b) comparison of top 50 Latin American brands to other global brands. Source: Kantar. (2020). BrandZ Top 50 most valuable Latin American Brands 2020. https://www.kantar.com/campaigns/brandz/latin-america

instance, it allowed small retailers and freelancers to use its e-commerce platforms for free and provided assistance to those who had little prior experience operating in digital environments. Netflix has become popular among younger consumers who appreciate the brand's communication approach on social networks through a persona that is infused with irony, humor, transparency, and caring for consumers. During the pandemic, Netflix adjusted the quality of its transmissions to avoid overloading internet networks, thus preserving a satisfactory experience for viewers while 'sharing' the infrastructure with other carriers and users. Finally, iFood has been particularly effective at communicating with consumers quickly and constantly during the pandemic, keeping them informed about safety and sanitation protocols to keep customers and drivers safe. It has also shown solidarity with small restaurants through its Assistance Fund and encouraged consumption from neighborhood eateries. For all three brands, a community-oriented purpose, agile innovations, a great consumer experience, and clear communications have resulted in high levels of love for the brands.

Building a brand that resonates with Latin American consumers' values cannot be accomplished without a marketing mix that is supported by the other three Ps of the marketing mix: pricing, promotion, and placement. In the next sections, we highlight important considerations and trends related to each of these marketing mix elements.

Pricing Strategies for Latin American Consumer Markets

As noted above, affordability and liquidity are important consumer values for Latin Americans. The economic slowdown of the past five years and the economic crisis of the last two generated by the COVID-19 pandemic makes affordability and liquidity more important than ever. Latin American consumers seek value offerings: quality products that meet their needs while being affordable and accessible. Our focus in this section, however, is not on price setting per se but, rather, on the payment mechanisms that may enable consumers to purchase goods and services. We discuss financial inclusion in the region, focusing especially on access to debit and credit cards. We then summarize innovations in the payment space that are driving the growth of e-commerce in the region.

Financial Inclusion in Latin America

The low levels of financial inclusion prevalent in Latin America continue to stall economic growth and competitiveness for consumers, businesses, and governments in the region. Latin America is a predominantly cash-based economy. There are various reasons for this. The percentage of people over 15 years of age with a financial institution account is estimated at just over 50% (EBANX, n.d.). Among the unbanked, low-income individuals and those in rural areas are particularly excluded from access to financial services and the market in general. The large size of the informal sector is also a factor (i.e., consumers and informal businesses can minimize their tax responsibilities by conducting business on a cash-only basis).

Access to credit has been one of the major drivers of consumer growth in the region, allowing consumers to buy high-ticket items they would not be able to afford otherwise. Beginning in the early 2000s, the availability of store credit, bank-issued credit cards, and other forms of lending soared throughout the region. In Brazil, for instance, the number of credit cards issued between 2002 and 2006 grew 91% to 79 million; mortgage lending rose to 26.5% between 2005 and 2007, and consumer loans expanded eight times from 2002 to 2012 (Chester et. al., 2010; Price, 2013). Regarding credit card ownership, in 1990, only 3% of Latin American households had a credit card (Price, 2013). In 2017, the region's average credit card ownership among those 15 years or older was 19%. There are wide variations in credit card ownership among countries (see Figure 7.5), with Uruguay (41%), Chile (30%), and Brazil (27%) occupying the top three spots, and Honduras, Nicaragua, and El Salvador registering credit card penetration rates in the single digits (5%–6%) (World Bank, 2021c). Improved access to credit cards has positively impacted the purchasing power of consumers, especially the emerging middle class; yet there is still significant room to expand access, not just of credit cards but also of bank credit (e.g., mortgages, credit lines).

The COVID-19 pandemic accelerated the necessity of purchasing goods and services online, and in the process, it has been a major catalyst for financial inclusion in the region. The number of digital buyers in Latin America grew from 127 million in 2016 to 156 million in 2019 (25% of the population), with e-commerce sales reaching US$73 billion in 2019 (EBANX, n.d.; UNCTAD, 2020). The pandemic forced Latin American consumers to embrace e-commerce. It is estimated that at the start of 2020, just around half of Latin Americans shopped online; by the end of that year, 80% of Latin Americans had shopped online (Lehr, 2020). Yet in an environment where Latin American consumers, especially those at the bottom of the socioeconomic pyramid, experience financial exclusion, how do consumers access goods and services online without a credit card? An explosion of alternative forms of payment provides the answer (see Figure 7.6). The financial services sector in

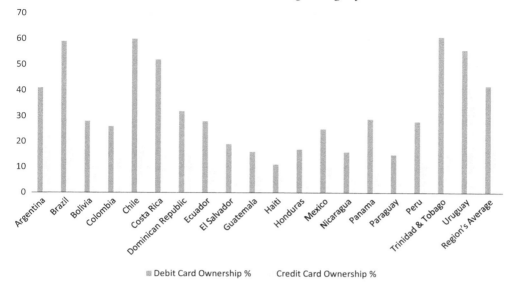

Figure 7.5 Access to debit and credit cards in select Latin American countries. Source: Authors' elaboration with data from UNCTAD. (2020). *The UNCTAD B2C E-Commerce Index 2020: Spotlight on Latin America and the Caribbean: UNCTAD technical notes on ICT for development, No. 17.*

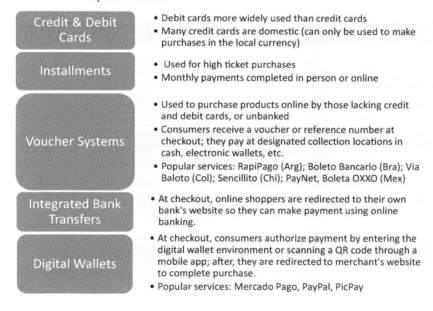

Credit & Debit Cards	• Debit cards more widely used than credit cards • Many credit cards are domestic (can only be used to make purchases in the local currency)
Installments	• Used for high ticket purchases • Monthly payments completed in person or online
Voucher Systems	• Used to purchase products online by those lacking credit and debit cards, or unbanked • Consumers receive a voucher or reference number at checkout; they pay at designated collection locations in cash, electronic wallets, etc. • Popular services: RapiPago (Arg); Boleto Bancario (Bra); Via Baloto (Col); Sencillito (Chi); PayNet, Boleta OXXO (Mex)
Integrated Bank Transfers	• At checkout, online shoppers are redirected to their own bank's website so they can make payment using online banking.
Digital Wallets	• At checkout, consumers authorize payment by entering the digital wallet environment or scanning a QR code through a mobile app; after, they are redirected to merchant's website to complete purchase. • Popular services: Mercado Pago, PayPal, PicPay

Figure 7.6 Alternative forms of payment in Latin America

Latin America, led by financial technology (fintechs), has introduced digital innovations aimed at payment facilitation (*Americas Market Intelligence*, 2018). According to fintechs, such as Uala and Movie, the need to have access to a prepaid debit card drove most of the growth in new account openings in 2020—a method that is likely to remain popular in the next few years. In addition to prepaid debit cards, a range of innovative payment solutions were facilitated by high levels of internet penetration and the wide adoption of smartphones (more on this in the next section on communication strategies). One of the most common payment methods in the region is the use of vouchers that can be paid at designated locations to complete online purchases. Consumers receive a voucher or reference number at checkout, then complete their transactions at kiosks, stores, and other locations where authorized collection agents receive payment in cash, money transfers, bank transfers, electronic wallet payments, and more. This method of payment is popular because it is user-friendly, accessible, convenient, and low-tech. For example, Via Baloto is used and trusted by 85% of Colombians who can buy online and pay with cash at more than 13,000 stores across the country. Boleta OXXO, a similar service, is used by 35% of Mexican online shoppers. The use of digital wallets and instant payment systems are also on the rise. Pix in Brazil and Yape in Peru are good examples. Instant payments Pix launched at the end of 2020, and within one week, the number of transactions had reached the equivalent of 90% the average number of weekly debit card transactions in Brazil (about three million). In volume, it represented only a small percentage of total transactions (about 1%), but their penetration and volume have grown since. By the end of 2021, Pix was used by 60% of Brazilians, with 107 million registered users and more than 300 million registered keys, surpassing credit card ownership in Brazil (25%). More than US$700 billion dollars had been transferred in 2021 alone, and the service is being lauded as one of the most successful examples of financial inclusion. In Peru, Yape, which launched in 2017, had reached more than five million users in a three-year period—about half of the country's banked population. However, Peru has one of the lowest levels of banking penetration and the highest levels of cash usage in the region. Thus, Yape, prompted by new competition in 2020, allowed consumers to open accounts without having a bank account. All Peruvian consumers can now use their national ID to set up a Yape account that they can recharge through various means (including having a friend send money over Yape to recharge the account, with the customer then paying back their friend with cash). As a result, by the end of 2020, Yape had grown seven times its original size (Lehr, 2020; Notini, 2022). The pandemic has also resulted in a reduction in the use of cash throughout the region—60% of consumers reduced cash usage by at least 20% in 2020—with credit card, debit card, and digital payments (including contactless) gaining favor (*Latin America Online*, 2021).

In summary, the examples above showed the various ways to create added value by facilitating consumer purchases through the integration of multiple payment options that meet consumers' needs for simplicity and accessibility. We found that the pandemic accelerated the levels of bankarization, increasing availability and adoption of debit and credit cards as well as driving disruptive innovations in financial services and payment-enabling technologies and services to support both consumers and businesses.

Communication Strategies for Latin American Consumer Markets

The growing adoption of information and communication technologies in Latin America has made it cheaper and easier for consumers to access product and market information. Today, Latin American consumers are more informed, demanding, and sophisticated.

Wireless telephony has experienced a boom in Latin America. Cell phone penetration and mobile subscriptions have been growing steadily over time (Powdrill & Hughes, 2012). In 2020, there were 437 million unique mobile subscribers in the region (69% penetration rate), and this number is expected to reach 485 million by 2025 (73% penetration rate). Half of all new subscribers will come from the two largest markets: Brazil and Mexico. There will also be growth opportunities in underdeveloped markets (e.g., Central America). Smartphone connections were estimated at 500 million in 2021 (74% adoption rate). By 2025, it will grow by 100 million new connections to reach an adoption rate of 80%. SIM connections have now exceeded the 100% penetration rate, with 644 million connections in 2020 and an estimated 730 million (111%) connections by 2025. This all translates into an 81% penetration rate of mobile internet users (GSMA, 2020, 2021). Although voice communication remains an important service, the bulk of the growth is occurring in non-voice communication and data-based services (e.g., instant messaging, e-mail, and social media). In fact, Latin America has the highest rates of digital application engagement in the world across all categories of application uses—communication, information, entertainment, and financial/commerce. Mobile data usage in the region averaged 4.7 GB per subscriber per month in 2019 and is expected to grow fivefold by 2025 (GSMA, 2020).

Internet users in Latin America represent about 10% of the world's users, but the region's average rate of internet users grew from about 50% in 2010 to 75% in 2021 or about 500 million users. This is lower than Europe's 89% penetration rate but higher than Asia's 64% rate. There are intra-regional differences in internet usage rates: South American countries have the highest penetration rates (average of 79%), with Central American countries in the middle (62%), and Caribbean countries lagging behind (51%). Differences among countries range from Chile's 92% penetration rate to Haiti's 18% rate. Brazil and Mexico account for half of the internet users in the region, with Brazil being the largest market (160 million users) (Internet World Stats, 2021). Physical infrastructure improvements, a more competitive landscape of providers, and significant investments have driven improved affordability and better access. For instance, mobile operators are expected to invest more than US$73 billion in their networks between 2020 and 2025, partially related to increasing access to 5G services (GSMA, 2021). Latin Americans also seem to prefer the convenience of multiple functionalities, favoring providers that allow access to various services and platforms through bundled offerings. (See Table 7.4 for a summary of connectivity indicators for select countries in the region.)

Table 7.4 Connectivity of Latin American Consumers

Country	Mobile Broadband Subscriptions per100 People	Internet Users % of Adult Population	Mobile Cellular Subscriptions Per 100 Pop.
Argentina	80.7	79.3	132.1
Bolivia	79.9	43.8	100.8
Brazil	88.1	67.5	98.8
Chile	91.6	82.3	134.4
Colombia	52.3	62.3	121.9
Costa Rica	97.2	74.1	169.9
The Dominican Republic	60.8	74.8	84.1
Ecuador	54.7	57.3	92.3
El Salvador	55.8	33.8	146.9
Guatemala	16.5	65.0	118.7
Honduras	32.1	31.7	79.2
Mexico	70.0	65.8	93
Nicaragua	29.6	27.9	115.1
Panama	70.3	57.9	130.1
Paraguay	57.7	65.0	107.0
Peru	65.7	52.5	123.8
Uruguay	123.8	68.3	149.9
Venezuela	54.5	72.0	71.8

Sources: WEF Global Competitiveness Report, 2019; http://infralatam.info/en/home/

Media Penetration

In Latin America, traditional media coexists and increasingly competes with newer media. Free TV, out-of-home (media that reaches consumers while in transit or waiting such as outdoor advertising), and radio are the key universal media channels. These traditional media channels have always been popular forms of reaching Latin American consumers. Watching TV is a favorite pastime of Latin Americans. Increasingly, TV viewing is happening via pay-TV or streamed services (OTT). Pay-TV is still limited by affordability, but penetration continues to grow. In 2018, the largest pay-TV markets in Latin America were Mexico and Brazil, with 19.3 and 17.8 million pay-TV households, respectively. One of the factors driving this growth is pay-TV operators' control over HD channels, which continues to attract subscribers (Raucci, 2019). Subscription of video-on-demand services is the main component of the OTT sector, but further growth is limited by low broadband penetration in households, slow broadband speeds, and low credit card penetration. Currently, most OTT streaming happens via smartphones, but improvements to infrastructure, network capacity, and payment mechanisms should create additional growth opportunities (Raucci, 2019). Radio is also important, particularly for Latin Americans on the go during the day who listen to radio stations for the latest news and music entertainment. These days, consumers frequently listen to radio stations via the internet on their phones. They have also added media to their listening options that give them access not only to music but also to educational and entertaining programming, primarily in the form of podcasts via streaming platforms (e.g., Spotify). Print is the medium with the least reach, as even newspapers and magazines have now moved to online formats, allowing readers to access news, stories, etc. on their electronic devices.

As mentioned before, connectivity in the region is on the rise. The internet has become an important communication channel for marketers given Latin American consumers' preference for online and streamed media (Torres Dwyer, 2018). Consumers are exposed to advertisements when watching videos on YouTube, listening to music on Spotify, or streaming a Netflix movie. They also use the internet to search information about products, compare products and prices, search for deals, read consumer reviews, or post complaints.

Latin Americans are active social media users, with about 85% of the population (550 million) engaging with social media in 2019 (Carrasquilla, 2019). The most popular social media sites are WhatsApp, Facebook, YouTube, Instagram, and Twitter. WhatsApp is used by about 65% of people in the region (of WhatsApp's total number of users, about a quarter are in Latin America). The app is popular because it allows Latin Americans to connect with others, domestically and internationally, for free. Increasingly, Latin Americans are relying on WhatsApp to communicate with companies as well (83% of users). Facebook is used by about 60% of people in the region, and although the site has come under scrutiny lately for its lack of willingness to curtail misinformation and hate speech, it continues to connect Latin Americans seeking entertainment, news, and product information (especially from micro and small businesses). YouTube's penetration is about 40%, and it is used primarily for music and video sharing and, most recently, for educational purposes (access to free classes on every topic imaginable). Instagram and Twitter are less popular in Latin America than in other world regions (23% and 12% penetration rates, respectively), but both are gaining followers. About 80% of Instagram accounts follow a business, and the platform is used regularly for advertising either through ads or through connections with influencers. Many businesses (including informal ones) use it as a way to communicate with current and potential customers. It is particularly popular with millennials and Gen Z consumers. Twitter is used primarily for those interested in news, particularly political news, as the platform has been popular among Latin American presidents and other politicians. Most news outlets also have a presence on Twitter. In addition to following news about celebrities and famous athletes, Latin Americans use Twitter to share their views on companies and products—both negative and positive (Carrasquilla, 2019). In terms of country differences in social media usage, Brazil is the leader, ranking as the third largest social media market worldwide, contributing 10% of all global time spent on social media. Mexico is the second-largest social media user in the region, followed by Argentina and Colombia. In Mexico, Facebook is the most popular social media platform (used by 81% of the population), and the country leads the region in Snapchat users. In Argentina, 90% of adults 18–34 years of age post something on social media every hour. In Colombia, Facebook and WhatsApp are the most popular sites, with 90% of the country's internet users having an account on these platforms (Carrasquilla, 2019).

Social media is, therefore, an important communication channel for marketers in the region, as the information shared through the various platforms influence consumer attitudes, beliefs, and behaviors. This is especially the case among Latin America's digital consumers, who tend to be younger, more affluent, urban, tech savvy, and well connected (Adhikary, 2018; Evans, 2017). Digital consumers in Latin America also tend to be more accepting of targeted advertisements and do not consider this practice an invasion of privacy. These consumers are motivated to shop online by time and money savings, but, to reach them effectively, targeted promotions, easy navigation (especially in mobile devices), and a rewarding customer experience are a must (Evans, 2017).

Reaching Latin American consumers through the array of traditional and new media requires a financial commitment by firms. In the next section, we analyze patterns of advertising expenditures to identify effective ways to build connections with consumers.

Allocating Promotional Expenditures

The COVID-19 pandemic changed the digital habits of Latin American consumers in ways that are likely to endure into the future. The acceleration in the use of digital communication and retail distribution channels has reduced some of the lack of familiarity, perceived risk, and distrust that many consumers have when interacting with marketers in a virtual space. This means advertisers will need to create content that works in virtual environments: easy to see/hear, enjoy, and access. Communication and distribution are now two sides of the same coin, and they must work in unison in order to deliver seamless, satisfying experiences to consumers across all touchpoints. Marketers in Latin America will need to focus on three tasks:

1. Designing advertising and promotional messages that stand out among competing messages, capture consumers' fleeting attention, and connect with them at an emotional level;
2. Producing digital content that is high quality and versatile; and
3. Placing advertising and promotional content on digital and non-digital media (an omni-media strategy, if you will).

Design, production, and placement of advertising content, now more than ever, must be based on data-driven insights of the consumer's consumption experience.

The total ad spending in Latin America in 2021 was US$27 billion, almost double the total ad spend in 2010 (US$14 billion) (Guttmann, 2021b). The breakdown of advertising

expenditures reveals how companies in Latin America split their communications investments across media channels, providing insights on the most important media touchpoints
for Latin American consumers. Geographically, Brazil represents, by far, the largest advertising market in the region, capturing 60% of all ad spending. Mexico (18%) and Colombia
(6%) round up the top three ad markets. In Brazil, traditional media is still dominant, and in
2020, advertising on free TV stations accounted for almost 80% of all ad spending. Brazilians
also respond well to ads placed on TV, with almost half searching for additional information
after seeing a product advertised on TV. Brazil is also an extremely innovative and creative
ad market, ranking third in the world after the United States and the United Kingdom. Yet,
with one of the largest online populations in the world, digital ad spending is growing at a fast
rate—it is expected to grow 10% during 2020–2025, compared to a compound annual growth
rate (CAGR) for traditional advertising of 2.3% for the same period. In 2021, digital ad spending in Brazil reached US$4.4 billion (Guttmann, 2021a; Statista Research Department, 2021).
Also worth noting is Argentina. Before the pandemic, Argentina was the smallest ad market
among the LAC-6, but the fastest growing in the region, growing 20% from 2017 to 2018,
and another 30% in 2019 (Guttmann, 2021a). (See Figure 7.7 for additional information on
advertising spending patterns.)

Traditional media—TV, newspapers, magazines, radio, and outdoor—still capture the
majority of ad dollars in the region. TV advertising—the most invested media, representing
about 50% of the total region's ad spending—is seeing a slow decrease in ad dollar capture,
from US$14.7 billion in 2019 to US$12.5 billion in 2020 (Guttmann, 2021a). Newspaper advertising accounts for about 5% of total ad spending in the region, while magazine ads account
for less than 1%. Although traditional media remains important for marketers, digital ads and
online media channels will offer the most potential and attract the most ad dollars in the near
future. Internet advertising spending grew from US$1.1 billion in 2011 to US$11 billion in
2021 (Statista Research Department, 2021). As reported by Kantar (2020), when asked where
they expected changes to their ad budgets for the following year, Mexico's marketers ranked
online video, social networks, podcasts, advanced TV, and online displays as the top five media
where they expected to allocate more advertising dollars. At the other extreme, they expected
budget allocations to drop for traditional radio and TV, cinema, newspapers, and magazines
(Kantar, 2020). Digital displays and social networks are also important media channels in
Brazil, as are search engines, which are trusted by Brazilian consumers more than traditional
media (Navarro, 2022). It should be noted that the COVID-19 pandemic caused advertising
expenditures to fall in most countries of the region, as firms chose a conservative spending
approach. In Mexico, advertising revenues across all media dropped 22% in 2020 compared
to the previous year. The losses in advertising revenue were most significant in print (−54%),
outdoor (−39%), and TV (−29%). In Peru, advertising revenue saw a 16% contraction in 2020
across all media, with print (−43%) and outdoor advertising (−39%) suffering the most. Even
TV (which saw its audience soar) and digital media experienced contractions (−8% and −5%,
respectively). As the region's economies began to emerge from the pandemic, both countries
began to see a recovery in advertising revenues (estimated 2021 recovery of 15% in Mexico; a
recovery of 19% in 2021 and estimated +11% in 2022 for Peru) (Redaccion Adlatina, 2020a,
2020b, 2022). Other regional markets also showed signs of recovery in ad spending (2021 estimates of +33% for Argentina, and +8% for Chile (Redacción Adlatina, 2020c, 2020d).

In sum, communicating with Latin American consumers requires a mix of traditional
and new media approaches. Although TV, outdoor, and radio advertising are still important, the growth and innovation in advertising in the future will be in the digital and online
channels, with social media ads, digital displays, and mobile advertising leading the way.

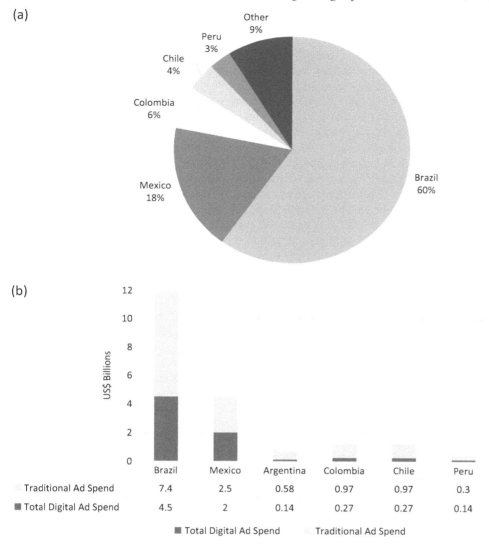

(a)

(b)

	Brazil	Mexico	Argentina	Colombia	Chile	Peru
Traditional Ad Spend	7.4	2.5	0.58	0.97	0.97	0.3
Total Digital Ad Spend	4.5	2	0.14	0.27	0.27	0.14

■ Total Digital Ad Spend   Traditional Ad Spend

Figure 7.7 Advertising spending patterns in Latin America (2020). Elaborated by authors with data from Statista (Guttmann, 2021a & 2021b)

For marketers seeking to position themselves in Latin America, Brazil remains the most important ad market, both in traditional and online media channels. The remaining LAC-6 countries, Mexico, Colombia, Chile, Peru, and Argentina, in that order, are the next most important ad markets.

Omnichannel Strategies for Latin America

In this section, we focus on the last P of the marketing mix: placement. We first provide an overview of the retailing environment in the region—including the growth of e-commerce—and then discuss the strategic imperative of adopting omnichannel strategies for effectively reaching consumers in Latin America.

Retailing in Latin America

Traditional retailing, especially through mom-and-pop stores and open markets, has been the main distribution channel through which Latin Americans fulfill their consumer needs. In the last decade, 'modern retailing' options (e.g., hypermarkets, supermarkets, convenience stores, and online retailers) have gained considerable ground over traditional retailers. In Chapter 8, we provided a brief overview of the competitive environment in the retailing sector; here, we expand on that discussion by reviewing some of the drivers of retailing activity, retailing trends, and the adoption of omnichannel strategies by sellers seeking to reach Latin American consumers effectively.

Retailing in Latin America is composed of a mix of traditional and modern retailers and retailing platforms, which are continuously evolving and expanding to match the evolving lifestyles, values, and pressures of Latin American consumers. New retail technology has also opened up alternative channels not only to shop but also to engage consumers before, during, and after their shopping visit. The COVID-19 pandemic has accelerated the adoption of technologies by retailers and consumers alike, pointing to significant growth in online and mobile channels in the years to come. As the region is largely urbanized, most of the modern retail expansion has taken place in the largest metropolitan areas, but it is now gradually reaching secondary and tertiary cities in most countries in the region. In the midst of these changes, traditional places such as small mom-and-pop stores located close to home in people's neighborhoods and open markets offering fresh food products and artisanal goods are still vibrant and viable.

The Latin American region has been one of the most attractive retail markets in the world because of a combination of factors that propel an expansion of retail investments and growth. Favorable factors fueling retail development over the past decade were the large concentration of urban middle-class consumers, increasing real disposable income, relatively low inflation, expansion of consumer credit, improved consumer confidence, and large untapped markets in low-income peripheral zones of the main metropolitan areas as well as in secondary and tertiary metropolitan areas.

The 2013 A.T. Kearney Global Retail Development Index (GRDI), ranking the top 30 retail world markets based on indicators of market attractiveness, market saturation, country risk, and time pressure (urgency to enter), ranked 7 Latin American markets in the top 30 global retail development markets. That year, Brazil, Chile, and Uruguay, respectively, ranked as the number 1, 2, and 3 most attractive retail markets in the world. The second tier of Latin American retail markets included Peru (12), Colombia (18), Mexico (21), and Panama (22). The 2013 analysis noted that retail growth in the region was being fueled by major domestic and foreign retailers (e.g., Walmart, Cencosud) adding stores, expanding current stores, and improving technology, and by new retailers (especially luxury brands) entering the region (A.T. Kearney, 2013). The 2015 GRDI, ranked eight Latin American markets in the top 30 global retail development markets. Three were in the top ten: Uruguay (2), Chile (3), and Brazil (8); the rest of the countries included Peru (16), Panama (19) Colombia (20), Costa Rica (28), and Mexico (29). The end of the commodities boom for Latin America in 2015 saw most of their economies begin to slow down with a resulting drop in consumer confidence and optimism. Yet the still growing middle class and the lack of saturation in second and third tier cities was continuing to fuel retail development, but the economic slowdown was reflected in the type of retail activity observed, with apparel and consumer goods sales increasing, and sales of durables decreasing. The region also saw some steady increases in e-commerce (35% increase in Mexico, for instance), leading to local players' implementation of multichannel approaches (A.T. Kearney, 2015). By 2017, 6 Latin American countries were in the top 30, but only 2 were in the top 10 (Peru was 9th and Colombia, 10th). The other four countries included in the 2017 GRDI ranking were the Dominican Republic, Paraguay, Bolivia, and Brazil. While Brazil dropped to 29 that year, driven primarily by the economic and political crises the country was experiencing, Peru continued to be a strong performer. The country's retail environment, however, was maturing, with more consolidations in grocery and pharmacy retailers, a higher presence of foreign luxury brands, and an expansion of convenience stores offering ready-to-eat meals and convenient hours and locations to time-starved urban consumers. In Colombia, growth was being driven by low and middle-income consumers offering 'opportunities for value-oriented discount retailers, private labels, and local product offerings' (p. 19). E-commerce represents another area of growth opportunities for retailers across the region. In Colombia, e-commerce represented 1% of retail sales but grew 22% from the previous year. Logistics infrastructure and credit continued to be the main barriers to growing the online retail channel (A.T. Kearney, 2017). Latin America has continued to be an attractive region for retail investment and development. The GRDI ranking for 2019 included six Latin American countries and one in the top ten (Colombia). In 2021, 6 out of 35 countries in the ranking were from Latin America, with only 1 in the top 10 (the Dominican Republic) (A.T. Kearney, 2019, 2021).

The Global Retail Development Index identifies windows of opportunity for retail investment and development in emerging markets. The index advances a model whereby a country retail market develops in four stages: opening, peaking, maturing/declining, and closing.

According to A.T. Kearney, this process used to take 10–15 years, but the digitization of retailing is causing an acceleration of this process, whereby countries move from the opening to the declining stage in a shorter period (see Table 7.5).

The GRDI reports illuminate the development of retail markets in Latin America. In 2013, Mexico was the more mature market in the region, having opened up around 2003, and closing in 2016 (it ranked at 29/30 in 2015. Mexico did not appear in the 2017 ranking). Brazil's retail market opened up in 2005 and peaked in 2013. As Brazilian consumers continue seeking out more modern retail formats, this country's retail market continued to mature through 2019 (Brazil did not make an appearance in the 2021 ranking). Chile is

Table 7.5 Latin American Countries Ranked in the Global Retail Development Index (2013–2021)

GRDI 2013	GRDI 2015	GRDI 2017	GRDI 2019	GRDI 2021
1 – Brazil (69.5)	2 – Uruguay (65.1)	9 – Peru (54.0)	10 – Colombia (51.1)	10 – The Dominican Republic (51.4)
2 – Chile (67.1)	3 – Chile (62.3)	10 – Colombia (53.6)	13 – Peru (50.0)	23 – Bolivia (45.2)
3 – Uruguay (66.5)	8 – Brazil (57.9)	13 – The Dominican Republic (51.7)	14 – The Dominican Republic (47.0)	25 – Guatemala (44.1)
12 – Peru (56.5)	16 – Peru (50.8)	19 – Paraguay (45.7)	16 – Brazil (46.6)	27 – Peru (43.8)
18 – Colombia (52.1)	19 – Panama (49.1)	28 – Bolivia (39.6)	21 – Paraguay (44.5)	28 – Colombia (43.7)
21 – Mexico (49.2)	20 – Colombia (49.0)	29 – Brazil (39.3)	29 – Guatemala (36.9)	30 – Paraguay (42.3)
22 – Panama (48.7)	28 – Costa Rica (45.0)	—	—	—
—	29 – Mexico (44.4)	—	—	—

Source: A.T. Kearney's Global Development Retail Index (2013, 2015, 2017, 2019, 2021).

another country that went through these stages, opening around 1998 and closing around 2016. These three markets are now considered well developed and more sophisticated, with a broad availability of modern retailing options and high levels of online retailing, but they are now considered saturated and offer less opportunities for retail investment and development. Other Latin American countries have continued to advance through the four stages noted, some maturing (e.g., Peru, Colombia), others peaking (e.g., the Dominican Republic, Guatemala, Paraguay), and some opening up (e.g., Bolivia). With such a number of attractive retail markets, the retail industry is not only expanding in reach and number of outlets but also in its innovative retailing approaches. Thus, Latin American consumers are enjoying and continuing to demand improved retail services.

Early in the chapter, we identified several consumer priorities or values. These priorities translate into expectations about their off-and-online shopping environments. Table 7.6 shows the translation of these values into shopping expectations.

The search for *strong identity* and confidence opens a realm of purchasing possibilities and expectations. With more discretionary income and confidence, Latin American consumers expect to have a good and satisfactory purchase experience. They feel entitled to having the option to buy from any vendor they choose. This gained confidence translates into expectations of respect, attention and assistance from vendors, and some degree of buying comfort (i.e., not feeling pressured). Latin American shoppers will pay attention to cues such as the store ambiance, location, and the behavior of the staff to determine whether there is an affiliation with their perceived social status. The second value of *trust, transparency, honesty, and authenti*city translates into vendor trust. A history of satisfactory experiences will develop trust in a retailer, especially regarding its promotions and prices. The third consumer value of *simplicity, convenience, and speed* translates into a shopping strategy that favors practicality and efficiency. Convenient access to the store's location (e.g., proximity to public transportation, parking), store hours, and delivery services are, thus, important considerations. The consumer priority of *value-to-price and liquidity* correlate with affordability and buying risk. Consumers will carefully weigh what they are getting for the price, typically spending within the confines of their budget and level of liquidity (i.e., access to cash or credit). The majority of Latin American consumers will spread their purchases in payment installments that match their cash flows and cycles of income. For these reasons, Latin American consumers consider store-based customer credit and payment flexibility even for the most common purchases. Having liquidity and cash on hand can also bring price discounts from retailers that try to reduce their credit financing costs. The value placed on *safety and security* also affects shopping considerations. The store's location, cleanliness, and presence of private security guards are also safety cues that will lead to positive associations with a retailer. The consumer value of *empowerment* relates to the shift of control to shoppers who now feel they can exercise their buying power to contribute to society, such as choosing retailers that prove their commitment to social goals through specific actions. Retail practices that encourage sustainable consumption, such as returnable bottles or reduced packaging, the availability of environmentally friendly products, and the support of small producers can all reassure consumers. Finally, increased connectivity through technology has made an impact on both retailers and consumers. Modern retailers in Latin America are investing in technology to offer a better experience, lower costs, and attract shoppers. Retail credit cards, store loyalty programs, and scanning technology are giving Latin American retailers a wealth of information about their customers. In turn, consumers can use their mobile phones to access retailer-based promotions, access information about products, or order online from their preferred retailer.

Table 7.6 Consumer Values and Shopping Expectations

Purchasing Proximity	Consumer Values	Shopping Values	Value Description	Expected Shopping Benefits
Emotional Proximity	Identity, optimism, and confidence (social inclusion)	Purchase experience: Do I belong here?	You deserve a good experience and to be treated well.	Respect, attention, assistance, buying comfort Store ambiance Affiliation with staff and shopping customers
	Trust, transparency, honesty, and authenticity	Vendor trust	Do I trust this retailer?	Satisfactory history of purchasing experiences Credibility of promotions and prices
	Empowerment	Make a difference	Live a better life	Environmentally friendly product choices Recycling options Store support of neighborhood
Rational Proximity	Value-to-price and liquidity	Affordability	Can I afford to buy this item? Do not make a buying mistake	Product quality Credit availability Purchase plans tailored to income possibilities Price discounts with cash purchases
	Safety and security	Protect yourself and assets	Do not be exposed to personal risks	Product quality Store location Store cleanliness and hygiene Use of security guards Delivery services
Transaction Proximity	Simple, convenient, and fast	Practicality and efficiency	Use my shopping time efficiently	Familiarity with store layout or services Assortment and Product Mix Store location and proximity to other stores and public transportation Store hours Delivery services
	Connectivity	Engaged at all stages	Be informed and leverage your technology	Take control and plan your purchases

Source: Authors' elaboration.

Retail Strategies in Latin America

A retail strategy in Latin America needs to address the shopping values explained above. For such a strategy, retailers must start with a value proposition that captures their positioning and differentiation strategy to attract target customers to their store. Ideally, such a value proposition will allow the retailer to close any gap between their offering and customers' expectations. In Table 7.7, we cluster the Latin American shopper expectations in three dimensions of distance between the retailers and the customer: *rational, emotional, and transactional proximities*. Based on their expertise, technology and resources, retailers will identify how many and which of these proximity gaps they would like to close and how (format strategy). For instance,

Table 7.7 Retail Strategies and Consumer Values

Purchasing Proximity	Shopping Values	Customer Shopping Benefits	Retail Strategy	Strategic Components
Emotional Proximity	Purchase experience	Respect, attention, assistance, and buying comfort Store ambiance Affiliation with staff and shopping customers	Excellence in customer service and shopping climate	Store value image: nice and trendy Comfortable ambiance Staff attitude Staff profile recruited from same social experience or neighborhood
	Vendor trust	Satisfactory history of purchasing experiences Credibility of promotions and prices	Value proposition	Customer experience guarantees Extended product warranties Returns policies
	Make a difference	Environmentally friendly product choices Recycling options Store support of neighborhoods	Social and environmental policies and practices	Community involvement Environmental practices (e.g., product portfolio, operations)
Rational Proximity	Affordability	Product quality Credit availability Purchase plans tailor to income possibilities Price discounts with cash purchases	Retail format and value positioning	Product mix and assortment Store size Price and quality positioning Private labels offerings Promotion and cash discounts Retail credit availability Loyalty and rewards programs
	Purchase protection: yourself and assets	Product quality Store location Store cleanliness and hygiene Personal safety Shopping from home	Cleanliness and customer safety	Product handling and display Extended warranties Return policies Use of security guards Delivery services
Transaction Proximity	Practicality and efficiency	Familiarity with store layout or services Product mix Store location and proximity to other stores and public transportation Store hours Delivery services	Convenience: bring the store to the customer	Location Extended hours Shopping services Ordering and delivery services Self-service and payment
	Engaged at all stages	Take control and plan your purchases	Use of retail IT	Engagement strategy before, during and after shopping Online shopping Shopping assistance Services connectivity

Walmart in Latin America has been successful in closing the rational and transaction proximity gaps with a replication of its global value proposition of 'save money, live better' with its traditional large discount store formats; it has also gotten closer to the customer through its small neighborhood and express store formats (e.g., Bodega Aurrera). Walmart has continued to enhance its transaction proximity through the expansion of its Latin America unit with a strong physical and e-commerce presence concentrated in Mexico, Central America, and Chile (see Chapter 8) (Euromonitor International 2020; Internet Retailer, 2013).

Therefore, delivering on customers' expectations will require implementing a retail strategy that aligns the value proposition with other strategic decisions regarding retail format, service level, store ambiance, product mix, store size, retail credit, locations, and use of retail technology, among others.

As part of their strategy, Latin American retailers need to choose between targeted strategies or a mass-market approach. A targeted strategy is more effective, as retailers may develop a more focused strategy and offer benefits that their target segments value the most. At the core of this targeted strategy is understanding how a consumer leverages their buying power to satisfy their shopping priorities; the latter will be based on the trade-offs they make between the diverse benefits they expect from their shopping experience. These trade-offs depend on the purchase category and urgency as well as the type of customer. For instance, Latin American consumers prefer to purchase food in small quantities and from small vendors where they can choose the freshness of the product and bargain the price. This shopping strategy favors the small independent neighborhood store. For more durable and hard goods, consumers likely prefer a more organized retailer among the variety of modern retail formats. Affluent Latin American consumers may prefer to patronize stores based on location, perception of quality of the products and services, and store ambiance. Low-income consumers may look at affordability, credit availability, and payment flexibility. For instance, two retailers of durables that focused on the low-income shopper with success are Casas Bahia in Brazil and Elektra in Mexico. Both retailers focus on a narrow category of home appliances at a low cost. As appliances are high-ticket items for low-income consumers, these retailers offer retail credit that allows low payments over a long period of time and a sound collection system for resolving payment issues (Booz & Co, 2006).

E-commerce in Latin America

E-commerce has traditionally accounted for a small percentage of the retail market in Latin America. In 2017, 92% of retail sales in the region were still taking place in physical stores (Goñi, 2018). Yet e-commerce has been gaining ground. Store-based sales steadily decreased at a rate of about 4% in the five-year period 2012–2017, while internet sales grew at a rate of 12% yearly during the same period (Goñi, 2018). It is estimated that, in 2019, 21% of Latin Americans shopped online, representing about 6% of the total number of online shoppers worldwide (UNCTAD, 2020). The COVID-19 pandemic only accelerated the upward trend on online shopping. In 2020, online retail sales in the region reached US$85 billion (up from US$73 billion in 2019). In 2020, Brazil registered 7.3 million first-time online shoppers, an increase of almost 50%; in Argentina, the number of new online buyers was equivalent to 30% the online shopping base in 2019; and in Mexico, 37% of online shoppers were first-time customers. Mercado Libre, the largest online marketplace in the region, saw their sales increase by more than 100% in both dollar value and number of orders (UNCTAD, 2020). The six largest e-commerce markets in the region are Brazil, Mexico, Argentina, Chile, Colombia, and Peru. Together, these six countries comprise 75% of the region's population, but account for more than 90% of the region's online shoppers and B2C online sales, with Brazil and Mexico accounting for about 60% of the online market (UNCTAD, 2020).

Excluding the significant impact the pandemic has had on retailing, growth of e-commerce in Latin America over the past decade has been driven by a multitude of factors, including shifting consumer needs and values, higher incomes, improved access to the internet, higher credit card penetration, innovations in payment mechanisms, and increasing competition among e-commerce sellers. New services that rely on online channels have also gained in popularity, driving additional growth. For example, online subscription services that allow consumers to order products they need on a regular basis (e.g., grocery items) or curated selections of products based on seasonality or personal preferences (e.g., fresh produce, wine). In 2017, 38% of Latin Americans surveyed by Euromonitor International indicated they use or have used this type of service (Goñi, 2018). In early 2021, Amazon began offering in Brazil its recurring shopping program (*Programe e Poupe* or Subscribe and Save), which allows users to schedule deliveries in advance of products they buy regularly, with a 10% discount on the amount of all orders, plus free shipping starting with the second delivery (EBANX, 2021). Finally, the presence of e-commerce sites has enhanced consumers' access and choices. The five largest online sellers in the region are: (1) Mercado Libre, based in Argentina but present in 18 LAC countries, has more than 40 million active customers; (2) B2W in Brazil is the country's largest online store and a marketplace hosting almost 50,000 sellers; (3) Casas Bahia is a Brazilian furniture and appliance retail chain with its own online store; (4) Dafiti is an online seller operating in Argentina, Brazil, Chile, and Colombia with about six million active customers; and (5) Amazon, the largest non-Latin based e-commerce site in the region. Together, the four largest LAC-based e-commerce retailers accounted for about a third of all merchandise value in 2019; this represented US$21 billion in sales, an 11.5% growth rate compared to 2018 (UNCTAD, 2020).

Online distribution channels, even post-pandemic, can offer real value to Latin American consumers. Consumers who live in areas with little access to transportation, high crime, or in rural zones, would benefit from being able to shop online and have goods delivered either at home or in central locations. Safety and convenience are highly valued by Latin American consumers, and marketers have an opportunity to satisfy these needs through e-commerce options. This is true for almost all types of consumers, but it is especially appealing to younger, tech-savvy, urban consumers who are not only permanently connected to their electronic devices but face time pressures and traffic congestion in their everyday lives. E-commerce and other hybrid retailing modalities that are influenced by (e.g., searching for product information online, receiving discount codes online to be used in-store) or initiated in online channels (e.g., ordering online, picking up in store) are the new reality in the region. Aided by innovative payments systems and new online media options, marketers will need to implement omnichannel strategies that give consumers the seamless, engaging, multi-touchpoint shopping experience they expect.

Omnichannel Strategies

Omnichannel marketing integrates and coordinates several organizations and platforms into a unified channel network aimed at giving consumers a consistent experience across multiple touchpoints. An omnichannel strategy can include physical channels, such as stores, vending machines, and digital channels (websites, online marketplaces). In Latin America, omnichannel strategies are no longer a choice but an imperative. As our discussion in this chapter has shown, consumers in the region value ease, speed, and convenience, affordability, and a pleasant shopping experience; marketers who either stick to single channels or uncoordinated multiple channels (see Figure 7.8) will not achieve the level of consumer responsiveness that omnichannel adopters will.

Our earlier discussion on developing brands that respond to consumers' priorities in order to build resonance suggest that adopting an omnichannel strategy would support this type of brand-building efforts. Coordination across distribution channels results in consumers having a seamless experience and a clear and relentlessly consistent message about the brand. Omnichannel strategies that are well designed and implemented will also capture massive amounts of consumer, market, vendor, and partner data which can be mined for valuable insights that can further advance the firm's strategic goals. Data analytics allow a firm not only to track traditional sales data but also to use data to understand its customers intimately (when and how they interact with the brand at each possible touchpoint).

Omnichannel strategies should offer Latin American consumers a seamless shopping experience between offline and online spaces (e.g., ordering online, picking up in store; ordering in the store, having product delivered to home; etc.). Such a strategy would also integrate consumer service, communication, and payment via physical and digital means, connecting with consumers at every possible touchpoint in brick-and-mortar stores, and through websites, mobile apps, social media, digital outdoor displays, and more. For example, in Chile, Walmart's Pickup program allows customers to shop online or via an app and pick up at physical store locations without leaving the comfort of their car and at no additional cost; customers can also pick up products from lockers at select locations. Expanding traditional channels to reach consumers where it is most convenient for them to shop is also part of an omnichannel strategy. For instance, Walmart will be extending access to grocery products via vending machines located in metro stations in Santiago, where consumers can buy not just beverages and food, but cleaning supplies and personal care products, among others (Buchanan, 2018, Walmart Chile, 2021). In short, the convenience, flexibility, safety, and choice companies can offer consumers through an omnichannel strategy align well with the consumer values and expectations of Latin American consumers.

Figure 7.8 Multichannel vs. omnichannel strategies. Source: Elaborated by author

Summary

The Latin American consumer market has grown in size and purchasing power; it has also become increasingly segmented, more sophisticated and discerning, and less frugal while remaining distinctive from other markets around the world. This evolution is the result of increased consumer confidence in the economies of the region and individual economic and social progress. Many consumers have been lifted from extreme poverty, and consumers at the middle and top of the pyramid have also experienced increased affluence and gains from long periods of economic stability, effective government programs, and expanding business opportunities. Social mobility led to the emergence of a larger middle class that will continue to drive domestic market demand. The COVID-19 pandemic reversed some of these economic gains from years past, but the region is already on the road to recovery, and the consumer market will offer renewed potential in the years to come.

Latin American consumers are more urban, educated, tech savvy, and socially and environmentally aware, and they are ready to express their values, beliefs, and personalities through their purchases. Latin American consumers are confident and pleased with their lifestyles and, consequently, are more discerning and demanding. Their rational side makes them more focused on value, convenience, and time saving and seeking an efficient shopping experience. On the emotional side, Latin American consumers look for honesty, transparency, and relevance in terms of making a contribution to the environment and society.

In reaching Latin American consumers, firms need to develop brands that resonate well with their values and priorities. Brand-building efforts should focus on creating salience using a mix of traditional and modern media while delivering offerings with functional, emotional, and social benefits at affordable prices. Furthermore, brands should be grounded on a clear purpose that reflects society's priorities and be perceived as honest, transparent, and authentic.

Advances in digital communication technologies and high levels of internet penetration and smartphone ownership have radically changed the consumer market environment in Latin America. The COVID-19 pandemic has accelerated the digitalization of media, distribution channels, and forms of payment, creating opportunities for product and process innovations. Firms will need to adopt omnimedia strategies that do not abandon traditional media (especially TV) but prioritize digital and online media, particularly social media advertising, mobile advertising, and digital displays. Firms' communication strategies must also be integrated with omnichannel strategies that provide consumers with a seamless shopping experience across offline and online channels. Although traditional and modern store retailing still dominates the market, the growth of e-commerce is unstoppable. Retailers in Latin America that adopt omnichannel strategies aimed at increasing choice, convenience, and safety will enhance the consumer experience at all touchpoints and cement consumer loyalty. Finally, firms must focus not only on affordability of products but also on payment facilitation. Current trends indicate the future of payments in Latin America will be digital, instant, and contactless. The emergence of alternative payment mechanisms, in addition to cash, debit cards, and credit cards, will further drive growth in e-commerce.

References

Adhikary, S. (2018). *Social media is a key platform for reaching Brazilian consumers.* Euromonitor International. https://blog.euromonitor.com/social-media-platform-brazilian-consumers/

Americas Market Intelligence. (2018). *Latin America cards & payments trends whitepaper.* https://americasmi.com/wp-content/uploads/2018/08/latin-america-cards-and-payments-trendsfinal.pdf

AT Kearney. (2013). *The 2013 global retail development index. Global retailers: Cautiously aggressive or aggressively cautious?* https://www.kearney.com/documents/20152/5004989/GRDI_2013.pdf/b8699270-39fc-535d-55c5-0c14baa66b95?t=1608467443000

AT Kearney. (2015). *The 2015 global retail development index. Global retail expansion: An unstoppable force.* https://www.kearney.com/documents/20152/5004989/GRDI_2015.pdf/aa5f3909-9f68-23ae-c9db-347b662fe583?t=1608467445000

AT Kearney. (2017). *The 2017 global retail development index: The age of focus.* https://www.kearney.com/global-retail-development-index/2017

AT Kearney. (2019). *The 2019 global retail development index: A mix of new consumers and old traditions.* https://www.kearney.com/global-retail-development-index/2019

AT Kearney. (2021). *The 2021 global retail development index: Leapfrogging into the future of retail.* https://www.kearney.com/global-retail-development-index/2021

Balvé, M. (2012). Breaking through the boundaries. *Research World.* http://rwconnect.esomar.org/breaking-through-the-boundaries/

Booz&Co. (2006). *Successful retail innovation in emerging markets: Latin American companies translate smart ideas into profitable businesses.* http://www.booz.com/media/file/SuccessfulRetail InnovationinEmergingMarkets.pdf

Borges, M. (2018). *Middle-class retreat and retailers in Latin America.* Euromonitor International. https://blog.euromonitor.com/middle-class-retreat-and-retailers-in-latin-america/

Buchanan, D. (2018). E-commerce in Latin America: Shop till you drop. *Latin Trade, 26*(3), 14–15.

Cadena, A., Remes, J., Manyika, J., Dobbs, R., Roxburgh, C., Elstrodt, H.-P., Chaia, A., & Restrepo, A. (2011, August 1), *Building globally competitive cities: The key to Latin American growth.* McKinsey Global Institute. https://www.mckinsey.com/featured-insights/urbanization/building-competitive-cities-key-to-latin-american-growth

Carrasquilla, A. (2019). *A marketer's handbook to social media usage in Latin America.* Colibri Content. https://colibricontent.com/social-media-latin-america/

Chehtman, A. (2020a). *Opportunities and challenges for ancient grains in Latin America.* Euromonitor International. https://www.euromonitor.com/article/opportunities-and-challenges-for-ancient-grains-in-latin-america

Chehtman, A. (2020b). *Packaged food in Latin America: Opportunities for a new normal.* Euromonitor International. https://blog.euromonitor.com/packaged-food-in-latin-america-opportunities-for-a-new-normal/

Chester, F., Fox, Z., Gervaz, J., Reise, N., & Valls, A. (2010). The Brazilian consumer: Opportunities and challenges, in first-hand perspectives on the global economy. *Knowledge @Wharton-Lauder Global Business Insight Report 2010.*

Dansk Industry. (2007). *Working with the bottom of the pyramid: Success in low-income markets.* Copenhagen, Denmark: Confederation of Danish Industries.

ECLAC (2021). *Preliminary overview of the economies of Latin America and the Caribbean* 2020. https://www.cepal.org/en/publications/type/preliminary-overview-economies-latin-america-and-caribbean

EBANX. (2021). *How the world's biggest brands are succeeding in Latin America.* https://blog.ebanx.com/en/how-brands-are-succeeding-in-latin-american-market/

EBANX. (n.d.). *Latin America: Payments and market.* https://business.ebanx.com/en/resources/latin-america-payments-and-market

Euromonitor International. (2020). *Passport Walmart Inc. in retailing.* https://www-portal-euromonitor-com.proxygw.wrlc.org/portal/analysis/tab

Evans, M. (2017). 3 things you need to know about Latin American digital consumers. *Forbes.* https://www.forbes.com/sites/michelleevans1/2017/08/10/3-things-you-need-to-know-about-latin-american-digital-consumers/#116c59a2e5aa

Farrell, G. (2021). The state of LGBTQ+ rights in Latin America. *Weekly Asado.* https://www.wilsoncenter.org/blog-post/state-lgbtq-rights-latin-america-0

Ferreira, F. H. G., Messina, J., Rigolini, J., Lopez-Calva, L.-F., Hugo, M. A., & Vakis, R. (2013). *Economic mobility and the rise of the Latin American middle class.* Washington, DC: IBRD/The World Bank.

Gallup, J. L., Gaviria, A., & Lora, E. (2003). *Is geography destiny? Lessons from Latin America.* Washington, DC: Stanford University Press/The World Bank.

Goñi, P. (2018). *Shopping reinvented and retailers in Latin America.* Euromonitor International. https://www.euromonitor.com/article/shopping-reinvented-latin-america

GSMA. (2020). *Latin America, Q1 2020. Covid-19 puts network resilience at the forefront.* https://www.gsma.com/latinamerica/wp-content/uploads/2020/06/Region-in-Focus-Latin-America-Q1-2020-1.pdf

GSMA. (2021). *The mobile economy: Latin America 2021.* https://www.gsma.com/mobileeconomy/wp-content/uploads/2021/11/GSMA_ME_LATAM_2021.pdf

Guttmann, A. (2021a). *Advertising industry in Latin America-Statistics & facts.* Statista. https://www.statista.com/topics/1499/advertising-in-latin-america/#dossierKeyfigures

Guttmann, A. (2021b). *Latin America: Advertising spending 2010–2024.* Statista. https://www.statista.com/statistics/429025/advertising-expenditure-in-latin-america/

Guzman, R., & Mackinson, D. (2020). *Foodservice delivery in Latin America: The search for growth.* Euromonitor International. https://go.euromonitor.com/white-paper-cf-2020-foodservicedeliveryinlatam.html

Internet World Stats. (2021). http://www.internetworldstats.com/stats2.htm

Internet Retailer. (2013). *WalMart Latin America hires new CEO.* http://www.internetretailer.com/2013/01/11/walmart-latin-america-hires-new-ceo

Kantar. (2020). *BrandZ top 50 most valuable Latin American brands 2020.* https://www.kantar.com/campaigns/brandz/latin-america

Keller, K. (2012). *Strategic brand management: Building, measuring, and managing brand equity.* 4th edition,Upper Saddle River: NJ: Prentice Hall.

Krol, C. (2019, October 8). *Central American beverage trends in 2019.* Euromonitor International. https://blog.euromonitor.com/central-american-beverage-trends-in-2019/

LABS. (2020). *Magazine Luiza, Netflix and iFood are the most transformative brands during the pandemic, study shows.* https://labsnews.com/en/notes/magazine-luiza-netflix-and-ifood-are-the-most-transformative-brands-during-the-pandemic/

Lehr, L. (2020). *Latam payments: Top 20 lessons learned.* Americas Market Intelligence. https://americasmi.com/insights/latam-payments-top-2020-lessons-learned/

Llorente y Cuenca. (2018). *The new Latin American consumer: A question of trust. A regional Analysis of six economic sectors.* IDEAS LLYC. https://ideasen.llorenteycuenca.com/2018/07/27/the-new-latin-american-consumer-a-question-of-trust/

Llorente y Cuenca. (2019). *Latin American discount stores and future challenges for own brands.* IDEAS LLYC. https://ideasen.llorenteycuenca.com/2019/12/26/latin-american-discount-stores-and-future-challenges-for-own-brands/

LR Foundation (2022). *World Risk Poll 2021: A changed world? Perceptions and experiences of risk in the COVID age.* London: UK. https://wrp.lrfoundation.org.uk/LRF_2021_report_risk-in-the-covid-age_online_version.pdf

Maya, A. (2019). *Ridesharing and carsharing are growing in Latin America.* Geotab. https://www.geotab.com/blog/ridesharing-in-latin-america/

Navarro, J. G. (2022, February 7). Trust in media in Brazil 2011-2021. *Statista.* https://www.statista.com/statistics/695784/media-trust-brazil/

Newbery, C. (2020). McDonald's beefs up sustainability in Latin America. *Latin Trade, 28*(1), 32–33.

Nielsen. (2013). *Global ad spend: 1H global ad spend increases 2.8%, led by Latin America and Asia Pacific.* https://www.nielsen.com/us/en/insights/article/2013/global-ad-spend-1h-global-ad-spend-increases-2-8-led-by-latin-am/

Notini, J. P. (2022). *The future of payments in Latin America is instant. EBANX.* https://blog.ebanx.com/en/the-future-of-payments-in-latin-america-is-instant/

Pew Research Center. (2020). *With millions confined to their homes worldwide, which living arrangements are most common?* https://www.pewresearch.org/fact-tank/2020/03/31/with-billions-confined-to-their-homes-worldwide-which-living-arrangements-are-most-common/

Planas, R. (2013). 6 most LGBT-friendly countries in Latin America. *The Huffington Post.* http://www
.huffingtonpost.com/2013/06/03/lgbt-friendly-latin-america_n_3378373.html

Powdrill, G., & Hughes, C. (2012). *The coming decade for Latin America: Belleza del Sur.* The Futures
Company. https://wppstream.com/-/media/sharedwpp/readingroom/consumer%20insights/the
_futures_company_coming_decade_latin_america_dec12.pdf

PRB-Population Reference Bureau. (2020). *World population data sheet.* https://interactives.prb.org
/2020-wpds/

Price, J. (2013). Credit is king. *Latin Trade, 21*(1), 14. http://latintrade.com/2013/02/credit-is-king

Raucci, C. (2019). *Regional focus: Latin America.* IBC. https://www.ibc.org/trends/regional-foucs-latin
-america/3660.article

Redacción Adlatina. (2020a, June 19). En Perú se espera una recuperación de ventas publicitarias de más
del 7% en 2021. https://www.adlatina.com/publicidad/en-per%C3%BA-se-espera-una-recuperaci
%C3%B3n-de-ventas-publicitarias-de-m%C3%A1s-del-7-en-2021#:~:text=El%20confinamiento
%20en%20Per%C3%BA%20ha,todos%20los%20formatos%20de%20medios%E2%80%9D.

Redacción Adlatina. (2020b, June 18). Los ingresos publicitarios en México crecerán un 15% en 2021.
https://www.adlatina.com/publicidad/los-ingresos-publicitarios-en-m%C3%A9xico-crecer%C3
%A1n-un-15-en-2021

Redacción Adlatina. (2020c, June 24). Se prevé que en 2021 la inversión en digital en la Argentina
tenga una fuerte recuperación, con un repunte del 43%. https://www.adlatina.com/publicidad/se
-prev%C3%A9-que-en-2021-la-inversi%C3%B3n-en-digital-en-la-argentina-tenga-una-fuerte
-recuperaci%C3%B3n-con-un-repunte-del-43

Redacción Adlatina. (2020d, June 23). La industria publicitaria chilena repuntará un 8% en 2021. https://
www.adlatina.com/publicidad/la-industria-publicitaria-chilena-repuntar%C3%A1-un-8-en-2021

Redacción Adlatina. (2022, June 22). Magna prevé que el mercado publicitario en Perú crecerá 11%
este año. https://www.adlatina.com/publicidad/magna-preve-que-el-mercado-publicitario-en-peru
-crecera-11-este-ano

Statista Research Department. (2021, December 10). *Latin America: Digital advertising spending 2010–
2024.* https://www.statista.com/statistics/237967/online-advertising-spending-in-latin america/

TNS Discover. (2010). *Changing consumers in Latin America.*

Torres Dwyer, D. (2018, May 28). *Latin America: Challenges and opportunities for retail and consumer
goods.* LSInternational. https://ls-international.com/challenges-opportunities-retail-consumer
-goods-latin-america/

UNCTAD. (2020). *The UNCTAD B2C E-commerce index 2020: Spotlight on Latin America and the
Caribbean: UNCTAD technical notes on ICT for development, No. 17.* https://unctad.org/system/
files/official-document/tn_unctad_ict4d17_en.pdf

United Nations. (2021). *World population prospects 2019.* https://population.un.org/wpp/Graphs/
Probabilistic/POP/TOT/904

United Nations-Habitat. (2020). *Global state of metropolis 2020 – Population data booklet.* https://
unhabitat.org/sites/default/files/2020/09/gsm-population-data-booklet-2020_3.pdf

Wolf, A., & Mackinson, D. (2020). *Vida saludable en América Latina: Alimentación a base de productos
vegetal y proteínas alternativas.* Euromonitor International. https://www.euromonitor.com/
article/vida-saludable-en-america-latina-alimentacion-a-base-de-productos-vegetal-y-proteinas
-alternativas

World Bank. (2021a). *Latin America and Caribbean. World Bank online database.* https://data
.worldbank.org/indicator/SP.POP.TOTL?locations=ZJ

World Bank. (2021b). *Pandemic crisis fuels decline of middle class in Latin America and the Caribbean.*
https://www.worldbank.org/en/news/press-release/2021/06/24/pandemic-crisis-fuels-decline-of
-middle-class-LAC.print

World Bank. (2021c). *Financial inclusion databank.* https://databank.worldbank.org/source/global
-financial-inclusion

8 Corporate Strategies for Firms from Outside the Region

Introduction

Multinationals assess the importance of opportunities in Latin America in relation to opportunities in other emerging markets. Based on this assessment, they allocate resources to build their presence in the region. These companies also identify key country markets in which to concentrate their efforts and investments and adapt their global strategies to Latin American managerial styles. This chapter presents a framework to formulate such a strategy for multinational companies from outside the region.

The chapter focuses on several aspects of formulating a regional strategy for multinational companies (MNCs) from outside the region. The first section discusses the challenges for strategy formulation in regional markets and elaborates on the advantages and disadvantages of MNCs in Latin America. The next section introduces a framework for a regional strategy for MNCs and describes a path of regional expansion for these companies. The following section describes the extent of replication and adaptation of MNCs in the region. The chapter ends with a case study of a regional strategy for the premier global retailer Walmart.

MNCs' Challenges and Competitive Advantages in Latin America

As we have discussed in Chapters 4, 5, and 7, Latin America has vast differences in buying power, consumer markets, culture, and managerial styles. Different countries in the region also present unique vulnerabilities and risks, as discussed in Chapter 6. These differences present challenges to the formulation of a regional strategy. At the same time, despite the differences mentioned, Latin American countries share a number of similarities. Their core markets are based on robust vibrant middle-class markets with affordability as the key factor for success. These similarities present MNCs with a similar set of market opportunities and challenges.

To understand the strategy of MNCs from outside the region, we need to identify first their strengths and weaknesses as competitors in Latin American markets. In formulating their regional strategies, MNCs will leverage their advantages and try to compensate for their disadvantages. MNCs possess strong global brands, innovative products, and proven production processes. With a global presence, MNCs enjoy large economies of scale that bring a strong cost advantage in local markets. With a presence in different types of economies, MNCs also benefit from the ability to leverage the different comparative advantages of the countries in which they operate. This flexibility to leverage advantages gained in different world locations is also known as *arbitrage*. Furthermore, MNCs in Latin America bring to bear a wealth of resources and technology from their global parent corporations and the subsidiaries in other parts of the world.

DOI: 10.4324/9781003182672-11

On the other hand, MNCs suffer from a number of competitive disadvantages. For one, MNCs tend to have higher costs of operation than local competitors. They lack the deep understanding of the business culture that local companies have. Initially, MNCs will not have access to local supply networks, and they may be driven to build their own at a high cost of development. In the relationship-driven cultures of Latin America, MNCs may also need to invest (at a cost) in building strong relationships with business and government.

MNC Regional Strategy in Latin America

Attracted by the mineral and natural resources of the region, non-regional MNCs have a decades-long presence in Latin America. Incipient domestic consumer markets, particularly those in consumer retail and goods, attracted other early pioneer MNCs. More recently, MNCs in high technology and more advanced manufacturing have entered the region, attracted by qualified labor and proximity to major markets such as the US to either compete with or complement their Asian manufacturing operations.

Traditional Strategy

Historically, the strategy of MNCs can be described in three stages: initial penetration, regional market expansion, and consolidation. In the first stage, MNCs target two or three large regional markets and focus on premium market segments only. A second stage is the gradual expansion into other market segments as well as deeper penetration of the initial country markets. Several strategies are utilized to carry out expansion. Acquisitions of local companies and brands allow MNCs to expand their offerings to other market segments. Expansion to secondary and tertiary market segments within a country is another expansion strategy. In the third stage of consolidation, MNCs reassess their competitive situation and, if necessary, withdraw from uncompetitive market situations; they also focus on rationalizing production, marketing, and financial activities. Thus, production may occur in one or two countries to serve the regional markets—manufacturing facilities in Brazil may supply Southern Cone markets, whereas Mexico would be the supplier for northern areas.

One important characteristic of the traditional MNC regional strategy is its focus on global brands aimed at affluent market segments. Aiming at the top of the market allowed MNCs to fully leverage their advantages and nullify any competitive threat from local companies. Global and premium brands were a good fit with the tastes of more affluent and cosmopolitan customers.

One disadvantage of this strategy is the narrow customer base of the affluent market segment. MNCs lacked the products or distribution to enter other attractive market segments. Another disadvantage of the traditional strategy is that the initial premium price strategy was eventually challenged by local competitors who learned quickly how to develop their own versions of premium brands at a lower cost. In most cases, MNCs were forced to lower their prices, and a price war evolved as even discount products entered into the fray. The only way out of this vicious circle of price erosion was either the introduction of more innovative products in the premium segment or rapid expansion to mass markets.

This phenomenon triggered a reassessment of regional strategy, which evolved to focus on larger mass markets as well as consolidation to a few country markets in the region. As was discussed in Chapter 7, the emergence of middle classes has led to the creation of large mass markets. This increase has been dramatic in Brazil and Mexico but also in mid-size countries such as Argentina, Chile, Colombia, and Peru. In many countries, these consumers have migrated from the bottom of the pyramid and have no experience with or taste for the global premium brands of MNCs.

This expansion strategy requires either extensive adaptation or innovation in mature markets that respond to new consumer realities. As pandemic lockdowns have reduced or closed indoor dining, restaurants and fast-food chains have focused on increasing the takeout and drive-thru business, which has remained robust. Burger King, for instance, is introducing in Latin America smaller, touchless stores where customers can access digital menus and place their orders at drive-thru or walk-up areas through apps. A suspended kitchen with a conveyor belt delivers the orders to designated solar powered canopies to or coded lockers that customers can open scanning QR codes. Another version of this innovation features stores with tall glass walls where customers can see the kitchen and preparation areas while they wait (Beckett & Littman, 2020). Clearly, this innovation captures the power of mobile applications, new scanning technologies, and customer separation under pandemic protocols. Such a strategy will also appeal to all customers, whether they are the affluent driving their cars or those focused on affordability and utilizing the walk-in options. Therefore, the new strategy has focused on improving efficiency and lowering costs through automation and smaller scale stores. The downside of this strategy is that personnel are reduced, and jobs are lost, delivering further blows to economies that are struggling to recover from the effects of the pandemic.

Adapting products to market trends is another example of a modified expansion strategy. Nestle Latin America is focused on formulating more nutritional products for the region. They have added iron, calcium, and vitamins to their Nido milk powder brand for low-income consumers throughout Latin America. A worldwide leader in infant formula for decades, Nestle is innovating in this mature mass market with the introduction of its Nido One Plus organic powdered milk. This new product is made from milk produced by organically certified farms and fortified with vitamins A, C, D, and iron, selenium, and zinc. The organic dairy food and beverage market is growing strongly in Latin America—the $2.56 billion market has increased 70% in 2019 relative to 2018 alone and is estimated to reach $4 billion by 2023 (Statista 2021a). As Latin Americans have become more health conscious and aware of natural food alternatives, Nestle is increasing investments in the organic food market through acquisition of brands and companies already with strong market recognition in this market niche. The company acquired Terrafertil in 2018, a company with strong followers in seven Andean countries that works with hundreds of farmers in Colombia, Ecuador, Mexico, and Chile (Nestle, 2018). Latin America is an important region for Nestle which contributes to 9.2 CHF (Swiss francs) or 12.3% of their total revenues of 74.8 CHF billion in 2020 not including the Nespresso business, which is a separate entity (Nestle, 2021).

These two examples show the importance of mass markets in gaining and maintaining market leadership. Doing so requires that companies continue to innovate, monitor market trends and changing macroeconomic and social conditions, and remain open to strategic acquisitions.

An Evolving Regional Strategy: Strategic Divestment from the Region

The worldwide economic contraction of 2020 is challenging the conventional wisdom of long-term building of a regional strategy. For some MNCs such as Telefónica of Spain, it took 40 years to achieve a footprint of operations in almost 18 countries and a full business portfolio of telecommunications products and services across consumer and business markets. As a result of the shock and other economic and competitive pressures, MNCs are redrawing the business map of the region (Casanova, 2020). Such realignment may bring new players to fill the space left by traditional MNCs, such as ambitious Latin American or Asian MNCs without a presence in the region.

Today's presence of non-Latin American MNCs in the region reflects waves of investments and decisions to have an established footprint. Their impact is large in terms of revenues, assets, and employees. As Table 8.1 shows, a number of these MNCs are among the largest 200 companies in Latin America and range across many sectors: telecommunications, retail, consumer foods and beverages, consumer electronics, automotive, agriculture, mining, energy generation, diversified manufacturing, and electronics. They come from diversified home countries in the United States, Europe, and Asia. After years of building assets and resources, many of them experienced a large economic contraction in 2020 due to the pandemic lockdowns. The automotive sector, in particular, witnessed a large contraction in sales. This brought readjustments to those with a large regional footprint and forced them to adopt a more focused strategy. MNCs in natural resources-based sectors, such as mining or agricultural commodities, did not suffer as much and continued to generate revenues at the same pace as in the past. Notably, since the first edition of this book, several MNCs have exited from this group and drastically reduced their presence through divesting from some or all of their Latin American assets. Examples of MNCs listed in our first book edition that are not in this list are Caterpillar (US) and GN Fenosa rebranded as Naturgy (Natural Gas, Spain). For instance, GN Fenosa divested from the important Chilean market in 2020 by selling their energy distribution assets to China's state-owned energy conglomerate SGID (Enerdata 2020).

The largest non-Latin American MNC, Walmart Latin America, had revenues of US$109 billion in 2020—about 21% of its worldwide revenues in 2020 of $523.96 billion (see Table 8.1) (Walmart Inc., 2021). Almost 76.6% of Walmart's Latin American presence comes from its operations in Mexico and Central America. This large sub-market percentage is the result of Walmart's divestment of its Brazilian subsidiary in 2019 and Argentina in 2020, leaving the company with a South American presence only in Chile. These realignments reflect a reassessment of priorities and competitive position by Walmart. An opposite strategy has been that of Telefónica of Spain, which announced a reformulation of its worldwide strategy with a focus on large markets: Spain, Brazil, the UK, and Germany. Telefónica will gradually divest from the rest of Latin America. With 30 years of investing and building assets in the region, the pull out will take years to conclude. Drivers of Telefónica's reconfiguration and more focused strategy are the changing macroeconomic conditions in Latin America, greater competitive pressure, insufficient scale of smaller markets, volatility of currencies, and the need to reduce its corporate debt (Thomson, 2019; Casanova, 2020). To execute its exit strategy, Telefónica has grouped its 17 Spanish-speaking operations under a new autonomously managed unit with the charge of gradually divesting its assets. In 2019, Telefónica sold its Costa Rican, Panamanian, and Nicaraguan assets to the rising Liberty Latin America, a spun-off unit of the British-Dutch-US MNC Global Liberty. Liberty Latin America plans to buy Telefónica's operations in Colombia and Ecuador (Donkin, 2020). Telefónica has also exited its own mobile network in Mexico and is using AT&T's network to sell value-added mobile services in that country (Thomson, 2019). As European and US MNCs reduce their presence in Latin America, they are replaced by either Latin (Multilatinas) or Asian MNCs which are not yet large enough to rank among the top 200 companies in the region. This is the case for Chinese MNCs, which in 2020, had $7 billion in mergers and acquisitions (M&As) deals in Latin America (Devonshire, 2021). Most of these acquisitions are in sectors in which Chinese companies have experience in other parts of the world, namely mining,

Table 8.1 Non-Latin American MNCs among the 500 Largest Companies in the Region in 2020

Industry	Company/Home Country	National Company/Country/(Rank)	2020 Revenues in $ Millions	2019 Revenues in $ Millions	Employees	Business/Subsidiaries/Brands
Telecommunications	Telefónica Spain	Latin America	15,340 Euros*	19,690*	—	Argentina, Mexico, Peru, Ecuador, Venezuela, and Uruguay; Sold Costa Rica and El Salvador Operations in 2020
		Telefonica Brasil (49)	8,445	11,240	34,000	Fixed, mobile, internet, TV Vivo Brand
	AT&T US	AT&T Mexico (178)	3,106	3,258	—	Wireless 19 million subscribers
Retail	Walmart US	Walmart Mexico (7)	29,035	26,890	—	—
		Bodega Aurrera (31)	12,215	11,976	—	—
		Sam's Club Mexico (61)	7,486	6,976	—	—
		Walmart Mexico – Central America (6)	35,437	34,218	—	Costa Rica, Guatemala, El Salvador, Honduras, and Nicaragua
		Walmart Brazil	7,928	8,008	—	20% equity share on rebranded stores under the Big and Big Bompreco, Maxxi and kept Sam's Club
		Walmart Chile (50)	8,302	7,914	—	Lider, Lider Express, Super Bodega aCuenta, Lider.cl Central Mayorista
		Walmart Hypermercados Lider Chile (94)	5,396	5,144	—	—
		Walmart Argentina (123)	4,021	3,351	—	—
	Carrefour France	Carrefour-Brazil (18)	14,658	15,555	—	—
	Costco US	Costco Mexico (193)	2,802	2,645	12,000	—
	Intercorp Canada	Inretail-Peru (128)	3,949	3,911	44,658	Supermercados Peruanos (Plaza Vea, Vivanda, Makro, and Mass) Pharmacies (Inkafarm, Mifarma) Retail malls (Real Plaza) Presence in Ecuador and Bolivia

Sector	Firm (HQ)	Operation			Employees	Notes
Consumer Goods	Kellogg US	Kellogg Mexico (20)	13,770	13,578	31,000	—
	Ambev Belgium/Brazil	Ambev Brazil (35)	11,432	13,205	29,296	Operates in 14 Latin American countries
	Pepsico US	Pepsico Mexico (119)	4,259	4,269	43,163	—
	Unilever Netherlands	Unilever Latin America	—	—	9,000	11 countries Businesses: Beauty and Personal Care Food and Refreshments Home Care 40 global brands
		Unilever Brazil (91)	5,629	5,117		—
	Nestle	Nestle Mexico (155)	3,408	3,269	—	—
		Nestle Brazil (156)	3,400	3,740	—	—
Consumer Electronics	Samsung South Korea (ROK)	Samsung Brazil (85)	5,864	5,923	—	—
		Samsung Mexico	4,040	4,020	9,000	—
	LG Electronics South Korea	LG Electronics Mexico (104)	4,865	5,406	—	—
	General Electric US	GE Brazil (140)	3,737	3,775	—	—
	Electrolux Sweden	Electrolux Latin America	38,219 Sek	38,954	11,551	Latin America accounts for 14% of global revenues
		Electrolux Brazil	2,759	3,058	—	Operates in Brazil, Argentina, and Chile
Automotive	Stellantis Fiat (Italy) and Peugot SA (France)	Fiat Brazil (84)	5,827	7,757	—	—
	Volkswagen Germany	VW Mexico (51)	11,750	8,224	14,695	Argentina, Brazil (M), Bolivia, Chile, Ecuador, Mexico (M), Paraguay, Peru, Uruguay, Venezuela, Central America, and Caribbean
		VW Brazil (118)	4,281	5,786	—	

(Continued)

Table 8.1 Continued

Industry	Company/Home Country	National Company/Country/(Rank)	2020 Revenues in $ Millions	2019 Revenues in $ Millions	Employees	Business/Subsidiaries/Brands
	Toyota Japan	Toyota Mexico (86)	5,807	8,093	12,000	—
		Toyota Brazil (139)	3,745	5,061	—	—
	Kia	Kia Mexico (87)	5,736	7,511	7,437	—
	Fiat Chrysler Automotive US/Italy	FCA Mexico (27)	12,629	18,041	—	Seven car assembly plants
	Ford Motor Company	FMC Mexico (45)	8,669	8,416	10,197	—
	General Motors US	GM Mexico (12)	21,033	23,338	21,744	—
		GM Brazil (162)	3,319	4,384	—	—
	Nissan	Nissan Mexico (39)	9,612	17,622	17,000	—
	Honda Japan	Honda Mexico (73)	6,312	9,294	8,000	—
	Renault France	Renault Brazil (204)	2,679	3,539	—	—
Agricultural Commodities	Cargill US	Cargill Brazil (34)	11,952	—	—	—
	Louis Dreyfus Netherlands/France	LDC Brazil (76)	6,187	5,290	—	—
Mining	Anglo American England	Anglo American Chile (66)	7,176	5,840	4,000	Also in Peru, Brazil, and Colombia
		Anglo American Brazil (180)	3,074	2,313	2,500	
	BHP Billiton (57.5%) Rio Tinto (30%) Australian and JECO (12.5%)-Japan	Escondida Chile (58)	7,651	7,120	—	Copper, Fluor

Industry	Parent	Subsidiary				Description
Energy	Enel Spa (Italy) Parent Endesa (WHO) (Spain)	Enel Americas	14,300	—	15,411	Generation and distribution: Argentina, Brazil, Chile, Colombia, and Peru. Wind and hydro in Costa Rica, Guatemala, Panama, and Mexico. Transmission: border of Argentina and Brazil.
	Iberdrola Spain	Enel Brazil (67)	8,427	—	—	—
		Neoenergia Brazil (74)	6,264	7,227	—	Generation (hydro and thermo), transmission and distribution
		Iberdrola Mexico (163)	3,311	2,908	1,314	Generation and distribution green hydrogen
Diversified Manufacturing	BASF Germany	BASF Latin America	—	3,802 Euros	7,486	Operates in Argentina, Brazil, Chile, Peru, Colombia, Ecuador, Venezuela, and Mexico. Regional revenues include Brazil and Argentina
		BASF Brazil (134)	3,804	3,216	—	Chemicals, automotive coatings, construction supplies, agricultural supplies, paper, plastics, pharmaceuticals
		BASF Argentina	436	—	—	—
Electronics	Cisco US	Cisco Mexico (82)	5,961	6,228	680	Networking hardware, telecom equipment, software
	Hewlett Packard US	HP Brazil	2,684	2,675	—	Technology and office equipment

Sources: America Economia (2021) and Annual Reports.

oil, energy, and infrastructure. The US-based Sempra MNC has been divesting from Latin America and sold its energy assets in Chile and Peru to Chinese MNCs. In Chile, Sempra sold its Chilquinta Energía subsidiary, the third largest energy distributor in Chile, to Chinese energy MNC SGCC (Enerdata, 2020). The Chinese MNC is also acquiring key companies providing construction, infrastructure, and power transmission services to Chilquinta, suggesting a vertical integration strategy (Sempra, 2021). SGCC is not new to Latin America; they have been operating in Brazil since 2010 in power generation, distribution, and transmission and have 23 concession companies in 14 different states and joint ventures to operate transmission lines (Zhou, 2019). In Peru, Sempra sold its Luz del Sur energy generation business to China Yangtze Power International (Sempra, 2020). Sempra is now focusing its Latin America strategy on a single country: Mexico.

Two other MNCs with long-term presence in Latin America are the chemical- and petrochemical-based German MNC BASF and Sweden's Electrolux. BASF has established a wide regional footprint of production units and research and development centers in South America and Mexico. In 2019, the South America region contributed Euros 3.8 billion to the corporate total of Euros 59.3 billion and had 5,957 employees. With headquarters in São Paulo, Brazil, the South American operation is organized under a matrix of 13 business and three sub-regional clusters: Brazil; Northwest (Chile, Peru, Colombia, Venezuela, Ecuador, and Guyana); and South (Argentina, Bolivia, Paraguay, and Uruguay). In this region, BASF operates 14 production plants and 42 agricultural centers, two of them with global mandates. BASF's Mexico operations are part of the North America unit with the United States and Canada. As an example of how resources are distributed in this region, the number of employees across these sub-regional units is as follows: 69.7% in Brazil, 19.2% in the South unit, and 11.1% in the Northwest unit. Brazil is clearly the main market for BASF (BASF, 2021).

The Swedish MNC Electrolux also has a long-established presence in the market for household appliances, room air conditioners, floor care products, water heaters, heat pumps, and other small domestic appliances. In Latin America, Electrolux markets its products under the Electrolux and Frigidaire global brands and national brands such as Continental in Brazil, Mademsa in Chile, and Gafa in Argentina. In the difficult year of 2020, demand for household appliances dropped worldwide, with the pandemic impacting revenues to all companies. Electrolux was not an exception, and sales dropped from Swedish Krona (SEK) 19.6 in 2019 to SEK 16.9 billion in 2020. Despite this drop in global demand, Latin America had experienced strong market demand driven by online sales and high-end products particularly in Brazil. In 2020, the Latin American region contributed 15% of the global revenues of Electrolux's total corporate sales of SEK 115.9 billion. Latin America is one of four regional business units along with Europe (40% of sales); North America (33%); Asia Pacific, Middle East, and Africa (13%) (Electrolux, 2021).

A Regional Strategy Formulation Framework

A regional strategy is embedded within a MNC's global strategy and organization. In this section, we discuss the regional strategy only. The main assumption is that the MNC has a presence in two or more country markets in Latin America.

Within this global strategy, a new regional strategy has four essential components (Lasserre & Schutte, 2006). The first component is regional ambition, which requires the determination of the strategic importance of the Latin America region in the global business portfolio of the MNC. A second component is strategic thrust, which is the identification of regional targets of opportunities. The third component is building the infrastructure and assets of the

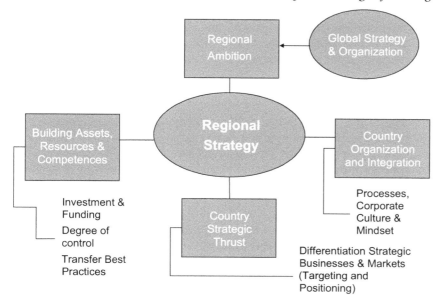

Figure 8.1 Regional strategy framework. Source: Adapted from Lasserre & Schutte (2006)

regional strategy. The final component focuses on the operational aspects and, in particular, the regional mindset that provides the personality of the firm in the region. These components are visualized in Figure 8.1. We elaborate on these four components next.

Regional Ambition

Regional ambition has two components. One part is shaping the regional vision. This part of the strategy is to visualize the role of the region in the future of the company. This aspect of ambition entails deciding whether the company wants to be an important player in the region. If so, what is the level of assets and resources that must be dedicated to this region to become a viable player? Finally, as there will be risks and challenges, ambition should address how the company will attempt to minimize them.

The second part of ambition is very straightforward. This aspect defines more specifically the importance of the region as a market and/or platform of production. This component will define more precisely the level of importance within the global corporate realm. For instance, a company may designate Mexico as one of the top five sources of global revenues and profits in the future.

A second element of regional ambition is strategic importance based on the range of opportunities that a region offers. These opportunities range from domestic market demand, natural resources, and/or cost-effective service or manufacturing platforms. Latin America offers all these opportunities. Large countries such as Brazil and Mexico offer a mix of opportunities, as they offer large internal markets and are endowed in rich natural resources. For example, Brazil and Mexico are manufacturing bases for General Motors, Ford, Volkswagen, and Fiat. Smaller countries, such as Costa Rica and Uruguay, offer educated and bilingual labor forces at competitive costs for a range of service outsourcing. Panama offers very efficient logistics services and financial services. Thus, an MNC has to formulate a regional strategy that integrates the diversity of comparative and competitive advantages that Latin American countries offer and identify each country's contribution to the overall regional strategy and, in some cases, to the global strategy.

Concept of Proportionality

The strategic importance of a region can be used for important corporate decisions such as resource allocation. Using a simple example based on regional market size, we illustrate in Figure 8.2 the concept of proportionality. The horizontal axis measures the contribution of the region to an economic indicator. For instance, if we were to use population as our base of comparison, Latin America's share of the world's population is about 10%. For Asia, the share is about 50%. If we were to use the share of GDP, Asia accounts for 26% of the world's GDP and Latin America 6%.

In the vertical axis of Figure 8.2, you have the region's contribution to the MNC's global revenues. For instance, assume that Asia represents 30% of MNC global revenues. If Asia accounts for 50% of the world's population, we may argue that Asia is underrepresented in the global business portfolio of an MNC. If Latin America contributes to 10% of global revenues, the region is on target in realizing its potential using the same population base. The best alignment of a region's performance is the diagonal line in Figure 8.2, which assumes equal representation.

A further example illustrates, numerically, how to estimate regional representation (see Figure 8.3). In this example, the world's GDP is depicted on the right column and MNC sales by region in the left column. In this example, the region is North America, which comprises the United States, Canada, and Mexico. Thus, the example shows that the home market economy, for instance the United States, generates 5% of the world's GDP. The rest of the region, Canada and Mexico, accounts for 17% of the world's GDP. The region then constitutes 32% of the world's GDP. The rest of the world accounts for

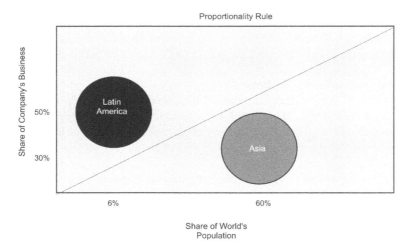

Figure 8.2 Concept of proportionality

Global Corporate Sales by Region	Base: World GDP = 100%
For each one (1) unit sold in the home market;	Home market = 5%
5.4 (27/5) units are sold in the rest of the region	Rest of Region = 27%
6.4 (32/5) in the home region, and	Region = 32%
12 (68/5) units to the rest of the world	Rest of the World = 68%

Figure 8.3 An example of proportionality

68% of the total world's GDP. Applying the rule of proportionality to the firm, we would expect that for any one unit of sales in the home market, the firm should sell 5.4 units in North America and 12 in the rest of the world.

Regional Strategic Thrust

A second component of regional strategy is regional strategic thrust. To develop thrust, the MNC identifies key strategic country markets, businesses, and particular market segments. The MNC also identifies countries to access the strategic resources to support a regional strategy. Finally, the MNC formulates a strategy of differentiation from competitors in those key country markets.

The key regional markets in Latin America should offer the largest business market opportunities in the region. More likely than not, these markets are Brazil and Mexico. A third market among the top three regional opportunities should be a medium-size market such as Argentina or Chile. A second tier of regional markets comprises countries with good potential but not as matured. Examples of these second-tier markets are Colombia, Peru, Uruguay, or Central America.

Another aspect of formulating strategic thrust is a strategy for regional market development beyond the first tier of opportunities. MNCs with a long presence in Latin America have already achieved good penetration of the primary markets in the first-tier countries and even the second-tier group. These companies have already achieved a strong presence in the largest urban concentrations with populations of one million or more. These companies are now expanding into secondary and tertiary cities in the first and second tier markets. The third level consists of mostly rural areas and small cities of 100,000 inhabitants or less. Brazil has 15 cities with populations over one million inhabitants and 213 cities with more than 100,000 but less than one million inhabitants (World Population Review, 2021a). Similarly, Mexico has 12 cities with one million or more inhabitants and 122 cities with 100,000 or more but less than one million (World Population Review 2021b). The strategic thrust for the three levels of market potential within a country may need to be adapted to reflect differences in consumer sophistication, buying power, and local competition.

Building Assets, Resources, and Competencies

A third component of regional strategy is building the regional infrastructure of assets, resources, and competencies. Building such infrastructure requires financial resources as well as physical infrastructure. In addition to physical assets, firms also must assemble human resources and build social capital in the region.

Take for instance the Latin American regional strategy for Chevron. This giant oil MNC has built an infrastructure network for their downstream exploration and production operations in countries with oil reserves in the region, namely Argentina, Brazil, Mexico, and Venezuela. The company also operates a network of upstream operations with refinery, petrochemical, and marketing assets, which include retail stations in the Caribbean under the Chevron and/or Texaco brands and Texaco Food Mart convenience stores (Chevron 2021).

Organization and Integration

The final component of regional strategy is organization and integration. There are two parts to organization and integration. On the one hand, the firm has to develop policies, processes, and systems to function effectively and integrate the region with global operations. In addition to the organization and integration aspects, another aspect of regional strategy is nurturing a regional cultural mindset. A lot has been written about the need to have a global mindset to operate successfully in today's globalized world (Gupta & Govindarajan, 2002). The same is true at the regional level. As part of regional strategy, MNCs provide a regional culture imprint to their operations in terms of imbuing their staff and decision-making with a Latin American personality.

Regional Strategy Replication and Adaptation

Over time, MNCs transfer and adapt their advantages and competencies to different regions and cultures. This experience provides MNCs with advantages of transferability and replication. In this section, we discuss how MNCs have replicated and adapted their strategies to the particular context of Latin American markets. We identify particular adaptation strategies and explain their effectiveness in particular market contexts.

An example of replication is Danone's regional strategy for bottled water. The Bonafont bottled water brand has its origin in Mexico where Danone acquired the locally owned brand and transformed it into a national brand leader. In 2013, Bonafont commanded about 30.8% market share of the Mexican bottled water market (Euromonitor International, 2021b). In Mexico, Bonafont initially targeted the female consumer segment with an appeal to lose weight, drink 'light water' frequently, and keep hydrated. Clever advertising showing the svelte silhouette of a female athlete promotes a fashionable image in this country. Changes in society with respect to gender roles and identification have inspired Danone to become more inclusive and aim for a broader brand identification and tagline aimed not just at women or men. Its product mission captures such change:

> At Bonafont, we know that Mexico is a country with great gender inequality. We can find these differences in the workplace, where women are in disadvantage simply for being women. That is why we made the largest alliance in our history with UN Women, and committed to support equal opportunities for men and women. Bonafont has always promoted women in many aspects, and we want to invite everyone to do the same, so that we can live in a country free of prejudice and stereotypes, and so that we can co-create a greater Mexico without gender inequality. Mexico can go even further

if we join this cause. We are the first brand to make an alliance with UN Women! (Danone 2021)

In 2008, Danone replicated the Mexican strategy with the introduction of the Bonafont brand in the US (Hispanic PRwire 2008). They aimed to target Americans familiar with the brand while visiting Mexico and the broad Hispanic market segment. In Brazil, Bonafont targeted primarily the urban areas of southern Brazil, where Bonafont has achieved 20% of the important São Paulo market in 2013. The targeting and positioning strategy used in Mexico remains the same: women seeking to maintain social status and physical attractiveness. The brand differentiation in Brazil, however, is different. Advertising messages for Bonafont in Brazil emphasize its low sodium content, lower than rival competitive brands, and its role in the reduction of bloating, associated with water intake (Danone Brazil, 2021). In Argentina and Uruguay, Danone uses a different strategy altogether. After acquiring the local water brands Villavicencio and Villa del Sur in Argentina and Salus in Uruguay, Danone has kept the local brand identities and marketing (Danone Argentina and Uruguay, 2021).

A Case of a Global MNC's Regional Strategy

Walmart in Latin America

Giant global retailer Walmart offers a good case analysis of an evolving global and regional strategy. Like many other MNCs, after building a large global and regional footprint over 30 years, this company has started a process of divesting from unprofitable countries and ventures and focusing more on the US home market and a few others where it can be competitive and profitable. This process started a few years ago and has only accelerated because of the competitive inroads made by non-traditional brick-and-mortar and online retailers, which in recent years have grown to be global giants themselves. Another aspect that makes this case interesting is the devastating impact of the coronavirus pandemic on the retail industry, particularly in 2020. In the US, alone, a daunting 5,994 retailers closed and exited the industry. This major disruption has sparked a rethinking of strategies to effectively respond to the decline in demand in (non-essential) stores and changed consumption patterns under lockdowns and new health restrictions. Clear winners (food and grocery stores) and losers (apparel retailers) have emerged. The pandemic also disrupted global supply chains creating scarcities and supply driven inflation. Product availability supplanted price/value considerations for consumers. Walmart is one of the winners from this process and is emerging as a stronger and more formidable rival than ever before; in this context, it is interesting to analyze its global and regional strategy. We will briefly outline the global retail market, focusing on the sub-markets where Walmart operates and competes. We follow with a more in-depth analysis of Walmart's current presence in Latin America and end with a summary of how the global and regional strategies are closely intertwined (Walmart, 2021a).

The Global Retail Market

The global retail market is estimated at $20.30 trillion in 2020, reflecting an overall 3% decline from 2019 and a compound annual growth rate (CAGR) of −1 %. However, the global market is expected to rebound and reach $29.361 trillion in 2025 for a CAGR of 7.7% and $39.93 trillion in 2030 (R&M, 2021).

The global market is broken down as follows:

Region	2020 Market Size in $ Trillions	%
Asia Pacific	7.15	35
North America	5.88	29
Western Europe	3.85	19
Latin America	1.66	8
Rest of the World	1.76	9
Total	25	100

Source: Authors' elaboration from several sources (Research & Markets, 2021).

The Asia Pacific market is clearly the largest with the colossal markets of China ($6.05 trillion) and India ($1.2 trillion) (Jingjing, 2021; Statista, 2021b). The North America market is dominated by the US ($5.6 trillion) as compared to Canada ($0.44 trillion) and Mexico ($0.24 trillion). Western Europe was hard hit by the pandemic and suffered a contraction of 17% in 2020 with sales of $3.85 trillion (Trading Economics, 2021). For the purposes of this book, we place several world regions into a single 'Rest of the World' group at $1.76 trillion (Middle East, Africa, Eastern Europe, Russia) because of the lack of retail sales data for these regions. In this context, the Latin American market, excluding Mexico, is last at $1.66 trillion or 8%, a proportion that is less than this region's global share of population (about 10%) (Euromonitor International, 2021a).

The e-commerce or non-store market benefited from the pandemic's impact and grew 27.6% worldwide to reach $4.2 trillion. China was the giant e-commerce market with $2.779 trillion or a whopping 66% of the total global e-commerce market (Ceurvels, 2020; Practical Ecommerce, 2021). The second largest e-commerce market was the US with $843 billion or online growth of 9.1% of which Amazon alone took a 39% market share (Finance Online, 2021).

Although the Asia Pacific e-commerce market is the largest, there are some indications that it is maturing and not growing as quickly as that of other regions. According to some estimates, the e-commerce market in Latin America reached $85 billion in 2020 and, according to others, is at $89.7 billion (Ceurvels, 2020; Euromonitor International, 2021a). Thus, the region's share of the global e-commerce market ranges from 1.8% to 2.3%. In 2020, Latin America's e-commerce sales grew by 63.3% from the previous year making this region the fastest growing in e-commerce sales followed only by North America. Argentina is the fastest growing market in the region with a 79% growth (see the table below) (Ceurvels, 2020).

Region	% Change in e-commerce Sales
Latin America	36.7
North America	31.8
Central and Eastern Europe	29.1
Asia Pacific	26.4
Western Europe	26.3
Middle East and Africa	19.8
Worldwide	27.6

Source: Ceurvels, 2020.

Although the global retail market includes all types of products, to align with the retail areas where Walmart operates, we focus on retail sales in the following product categories: fast moving consumer goods with a short shelf life that are frequently purchased and consumed rapidly (FMCG), soft line goods (apparel and accessories, linens), and hardline and leisure goods (hardware, electronics, sporting goods, health and beauty, and furniture). With respect to the channel, the major distinction is between brick-and-mortar or store-based retail and online or non-store based. We

Table 8.2 2020 Global Retail Sales—Narrow Categories (FMCG)

Region	Stored Based		Non-store Based	
	Sales $ Billion	%	Sales $ Billion	%
Asia Pacific	4,652	37	1,308.9	44.4
Australia	216.1	1.6	32.1	1.0
Eastern Europe	665.3	5.1	85.6	2.8
Latin America	672.7	5.2	89.7	3.1
Middle-East Africa	971.6	7.4	30.36	1.0
North America	2,779.3	22.1	963.0	32.7
Western Europe	2,507.9	21.6	442.5	15.0
World	12,528.9	100.0	2,952.3	100

Source: Euromonitor International 2021.

now examine the global retail market of this narrower view of global and retail sales that better applies to Walmart. Table 8.2 shows the breakdown of the global and regional store and non-store FMCG retail markets for 2020. As shown in Table 8.2, the Asia Pacific retail market is the most dominant both in store and non-store with 37% and 44.4% market shares, respectively, followed by North America. Latin America accounts for 5.2% of global store-based retail sales and 3.1% of non-store retail sales; the shares for the region are lower under this narrower definition of global retail sales. The region is comparable to the Eastern European retail market in store-based sales and slightly larger in non-store retail sales (Euromonitor International, 2021a).

We conclude that:

- The region's share of the global retail market is 8% and from 1.8 to 2.3% of the online market.
- Latin America is the fastest growing regional online market and Argentina is the fastest growing country market.
- The region's share of the narrowed FMCG global retail market is 5.2% and 3.1% for non-store-based retail sales.
- The Latin American retail market is equivalent to that of Eastern Europe in total sales but lags in term of spending per capita as follows:

Region	Store-Based Retail Sales $ Billions	Non-store Retail Sales $ Billion	Population Million	Store Sales Per Capita $	Non-store Sales Per Capita $
Latin America	672. 7	89.6	653	1030	140
Eastern Europe	666.5	85.6	292	2270	290

Source: Authors' elaboration from public sources.

The Competitive Landscape

Using the narrowed definition of retail, we now focus on competition. First, we analyze overall competition at the global and regional level (Latin America). We then focus on competition by product (e.g., food, apparel, or electronics) and channel (brick and mortar, online). Table 8.3 shows the ten largest retailers in the world; Walmart is the largest global retailer

Table 8.3 Top Global Retailers in 2020

Company	Home Country	Revenues $ Millions	Revenue Growth %	Online Sales Growth	Online Sales as % of Total	Profit Margin %	Return on Assets %	Compound Annual Growth 2014–19 %	# Countries in Operation	% of Revenue from International Operations	# of stores
Walmart Inc	US	523,964	1.9	79	11	2.9	6.4	1.5	27	23.2	10,500
Amazon	US	158,439	13.0	50	92	4.1	5.1	17.7	17	31.0	
Costco	US	152,703	7.9	40	6	2.4	8.2	6.3	12	26.8	829
Schwarz Group	Germany	126,124	8.6	—	—	—	—	7.4	33	66.0	12,500
The Kroger Co.	US	121,539	1.0	116	8	1.2	3.3	2.3	1	0.0	2,742
Walgreens	US	115,994	4.8	—	—	2.9	5.9	8.7	9	9.9	13,449
The Home Depot	US	110,225	1.9	80	20	10.2	21.9	5.8	3	8.1	2,300
Aldi Einkauf GmbH	Germany	106,326	5.6	—	—	—	—	6.4	19	68.9	11,235
Tesco PLC	UK	81,347	1.4	77	12	1.5	1.9	0.8	8	18.38	4,673

Source: Deloitte 2021a.

by far. The second largest retailer (Amazon) is one-third the size of Walmart in total revenues. US-based retailers dominate the list followed by two German-based retailers (Schwarz and Aldi) and one UK-based (Tesco). The list also includes an online company (Amazon), an indication of how e-commerce companies are reaching the size of the largest traditional retailers. As for the type of products, the top ten include food retailers (Kroger, Aldi, Tesco), pharmacies (Walgreens, CVS) and home improvement (Home Depot). By format, the top ten include warehouse stores (Costco) and direct retail (all others). Such a variety of different types of global retail companies suggests that no one retail strategy is dominant across all products, channels, and formats. Global retailers are in the process of formulating a dominant omnichannel strategy that integrates channels, products, and formats—a daunting task.

On the operational side, the majority of retailers operate internationally, with the exception of the primarily domestic Kroger group and CVS. The German Schwarz group is the most international, operating in 33 countries and deriving 66% of sales from overseas. According to Table 8.3, in 2019, Walmart operated in 27 countries and had 23.2% international sales. In terms of performance, Walmart struggles to keep up with the top performers in the group. By far, Amazon records the largest sales growth of this group with 17.7 compound annual growth rate (CAGR) compared to Walmart's tepid 1.5%. The most profitable is Home Depot with 10.2% margins, whereas the rest operate under very narrow margins including Walmart's 1.9%. It is perhaps the higher margin that allows Home Depot to achieve the best return on assets of 21.9%. This is the competitive landscape in which Walmart must compete, where its major strength is scale (10,500 stores); among the global top ten retailers, Schwarz (12,500 stores) and Aldi (11,235 stores) have similar scale (Deloitte, 2021a).

An analysis of the top 250 largest global retailers by their regional home base provides a view of the strength of competition in those regions (see Table 8.4) (Deloitte, 2021a). Europe and North America have the highest representation among the top 250 largest global retailers with Asia Pacific a close third. Latin America contributes 11 retail companies to this group, while the Middle East and Africa have the lowest number of retailers. In terms of the total revenues by region, North America-based retailers' account for 47% of the total revenues of the largest 250 companies. Latin America-based retailers' account for only 2% of the total. From a perspective other than size, Latin American companies had the second largest CAGR growth (8.8%) in the period 2015–2019 which is double that of North America (4.5%) and the second-best profit margins (3.2%) of all regions. On return on assets, Latin America places a distant fourth (2.5%) with North America being the best performer at 6.3%, suggesting that North American retailers are more effectively generating revenues and profits from their investments despite the lower margins. We can see such differentiation in the average retail sales in each region. In North America, average retail sales are $28.577 billion, whereas

Table 8.4 Financial Performance of Top 250 Global Retailers in 2019

Region	Companies	Total Revenues $ Billions	% of Revenues	CAGR %	Profit Margin %	Return on Assets %	Average Retail Revenue ($ Millions)
North America	80	2,284	47	4.5	3.6	6.3	28,557
Western Europe	87	1,617	33	4.9	2.9	3.2	18,593
Asia Pacific	63	786.3	16	6	2.7	3.1	12,482
Latin America	11	90.6	2	8.8	3.2	2.5	8,235
Africa-Middle East	9	68.2	2	9.3	−3.3	−3.8	7,576

Source: Deloitte 2021a.

in Latin America, they are $8.235 billion. Once again, in terms of scale, Latin America is small in comparison with retail companies operating in North America and Europe but close to those in Asian Pacific (Deloitte, 2021a).

Walmart competes directly with some of these giant companies and indirectly with others. A view of competition by product line provides another way to define Walmart's competitive space. Based on whether more than half of total revenues are derived from apparel, FMCG, or hard lines, a company is classified under those product groups. If these product lines account for less than half of the revenue, a retailer has a mixed or diversified product portfolio. The following chart allows a better assessment of where Walmart competes and its closest competitors among the top 250 largest global retailers.

	Apparel and Accessories	Fast Moving Consumer Goods	Hardline and Leisure Goods	Mix or Diversified
Lead Companies	Macy's (US) TJ Maxx (US) H&M (Sweden) LVMH (France) Zara (Spain)	Walmart (US) Costco (US) Schwarz (Germany) Kroger (US) Walgreens (US)	Amazon (US) Home Depot (US) Lowe's (US) Best Buy (US)	Target (US) Lotte Shopping (ROK) Alibaba (PRC) Liberty Qurate-QVC (US)
CAGR % 2014–2019	6.2	4.1	8.7	2.4
Profit Margin %	6.9	2.0	4.4	2.8
Return on Assets %	6.3	3.1	6.1	2.6

Source: Deloitte, 2021a.

Clearly, Walmart has a base in the FMCG group but straddles lines to other groups, thus, competing with other retail giants. Another important aspect of the competitive space is the revenues and profitability of retailers in these groups. Based on the analysis of the top 250 global retail companies, apparel and accessories retailers perform well on all performance indicators. As mentioned before, the hardline (hard goods) have experienced the fastest revenue growth and decent returns on assets. The mixed or diversified retailers are the worst performers. Walmart is positioned in the FMCG group along with Costco, Schwarz, Kroger, and Walgreens. The performance indicators for this group are not stellar, with narrow profit margins and return on assets. Under those conditions, these companies focus on efficiencies and are constantly reevaluating their business and assets to remain profitable.

Latin America's Competitive Space

The analysis of Latin American companies among the 250 largest retailers in the world provides a view of the competitive market space in this region (see Table 8.5). In Latin America as of 2021, Walmart operates in Mexico, Central America, and Chile after divesting from Brazil in 2019 and Argentina in 2020. In terms of size, Walmart dwarfs all its Latin American competitors. Its Mexican and Central America operation, Walmex, is its largest international subsidiary with $34.7 billion in revenues and 2,703 stores in six countries. The closest Latin American retailer, Cencosud, generates half of those revenues with $12.89 billion and 1,545 stores in five countries. Other large Latin American retailers come from Mexico and Brazil. The Mexican retailers include Grupo Coppel, Grupo Soriana, and Grupo Comercial Chedraui.

Table 8.5 Latin America's Top Retailers

Company	Country	Revenues $ Millions	Dominant Format	Countries	CAGR %	Net Profit Margin %	# Stores
Walmex	Mexico and Central America	34,720 34,900 (D&B)	Hypercenters Supermarkets Discount	6	5.18	8.1	2,703
D&S (Walmart)	Chile	1,970	Hypermarkets Discount	1	7.16*	5.86**	382
Cencosud	Chile	12,895	Hypercenters Supermarkets	5	−2.6	3.0	1,545
Grupo Coppel	Mexico	9,650	Department Stores	2	16.7	—	1,561
Organizacion Soriana	Mexico	8,088	Hypermarkets	1	8.9	2.1	824
Grupo Comercial Chedraui	Mexico	6,667	Hypermarkets Supercenters Discount Groceries	2	12.7	1.2	487
Via Varejo	Brazil	6,496	Electronics Home Appliances	1	—	1.9	1,000
Magazine Luiza	Brazil	5,016	Department Stores	1	15.2	4.6	880
Lojas Americanas	Brazil	4,728	Department Stores	1	2.9	3.1	1,945
Raia Drogasil	Brazil	4,660	Drugstore Pharmacy	1	20.0	3.2	2400

Sources: Deloitte (2021a) and companies annual reports.
* 2012–2016.
**2016.

Soriana and Chedraui compete directly with Walmart with a combination of hypermarket, supercenters, and supermarkets, whereas Coppel is a more distant competitor with a department store format. The Brazilian retailers are large by Latin American standards and have built sizable Brazilian retail footprints mostly in apparel, electronics, and drugstores; these are not the categories where Walmart operates. In Chile, Walmart's subsidiary is the market leader with almost 30% market share. Chile has been a bright spot for Walmart since its acquisition of D&S in 2009 (Sucre o Sale, 2021) but it is relatively small ($1.9 billion in sales) compared to Chile's more internationally diversified Cencosud with US$12.89 billion in sales—the second market leader in the FMCG group in this country (USDA, 2020). One distinct advantage that a few Latin American retailers have with respect to Walmart is their strong sales growth. Grupo Coppel, Magazine Luiza, and Raia Drogasil registered CAGR rates of 15% or more during the 2014–2019 period. In addition, Magazine Luiza is achieving above normal profits for retail operations with a margin of 4.6%. Altogether, Walmart has established two solid bases to operate in Mexico and Chile with a formidable scale advantage in the former (Deloitte, 2021a).

Impact of the COVID-19 Pandemic on Global Retailers

2020 was a business year to remember for everyone, and retailers in particular. The pandemic was a perfect storm impacting policymakers and regulators, consumers, retailers, producers, and supply chains all at once. Policymakers instituted lockdowns and social distancing and closed non-essential establishments. With reduced consumer mobility and in-store shopping, consumers increased home consumption and turned to online shopping. Travel restrictions reduced mobility within and across borders and slashed travel demand. The mobility of workers was also reduced, impacting the production of material goods and creating remote working environments. Global supply conditions were disrupted, creating shortages of goods and increasing supply costs; retailers passed on the increased costs which, in turn, pushed up price inflation.

The perfect storm did not affect all countries, consumers, and retailers equally. We already mentioned steep retail casualties, with 5,994 closing in the US alone in 2020 and US clothing retailers experiencing a 29% decrease in sales. European retail suffered a contraction of 19% and clothing retailers a decline of 24% in sales in 2020 (COFACE, 2021). The loser retail categories included apparel and accessories, cosmetics, luxury goods, and travel-related retailing (duty-free stores at airports for instance). As home consumption increased, a number of retail product categories experienced strong demand, such as food and groceries, home improvements, household goods, health and personal care, and home-based leisure and entertainment. The impact on countries was also uneven. Some countries were more lax in terms of pandemic restrictions. The reduced cross border travel restrictions produced greater demand for home products in countries that typically send large numbers of visitors abroad. Northern European countries, for instance, benefited from strong home demand as people traveled less or not at all during 2020. In Latin America, Brazil experienced an increase in retail sales of about 5% despite being devastated by the pandemic, while Mexico had a contraction of 10% (COFACE, 2021).

Retailers' Responses to Market Trends

Confronted with such market shaping trends, retailers reassessed their priorities and implemented initiatives for a quick response to these threats and opportunities in anticipation of a recovery beyond 2020 (KPMG, 2021; Deloitte, 2021b). Among many, the following initiatives were most notable:

1. Become an online platform or leverage one. A retail platform is an ecosystem of producers, retailers, supply chain participants, and last mile delivery partners. These platforms are referred to as omnichannels, in which a consumer experiences a seamless shopping process across any device, location, and delivery (Mckinsey, 2021). A retailer such as Amazon becomes a shopping platform through an online aggregation (products, retailers, delivery partners) strategy. A retailer such as Walmart or Costco has developed a brick-and-mortar platform with some online retail options. Other retailers leverage these platforms and participate in their ecosystems or develop their own channel. Omnichannel participants were very quick to react to shifting consumer demand during the pandemic. Omnichannel leaders have developed a set of competencies to manage such complex systems such as data analytics and delivery systems (see Chapter 7).
2. Digital acceleration. One of the most important competencies in the future of retail is e-commerce. The surge of pandemic digital demand has unmasked the limitations of some retailer's resources and capabilities such as bandwidth and delivery systems. In such a crowded online market space, retailers need to differentiate by creating value other than price and address connectivity and convenience, anticipating demand, online security, and privacy.
3. Purpose and intention. With the turbulent and muddy political process both before and during the pandemic, consumers are voting with their hearts and convictions. Many retailers were caught up in politically driven boycotts as a result of either the political views of their shareholders or top managers. Consumers also boycotted brands for their impact on the environment, their manufacturing or sourcing activities (e.g., child labor), or lack of transparency and pressured retailers to drop them from their offerings. Retailers have been pressed to examine political and social considerations and, in some cases, have chosen to distance themselves from the views of their main shareholders.
4. Supply chain resiliency. Supply chain disruption is arguably the most important driver of retailers' initiatives. Rethinking an overall supply chain is not a minor task, as it involves so many moving parts. Retailers are looking at improvements in warehouse management, order fulfillment, inventory management, and last-mile deliveries just to mention some of their initiatives with the goal of building resilience (flexibility in dealing with future disruptions).
5. Consumer safety. The pandemic was one but not the only factor to consider in addressing consumer anxiety for personal safety and security. Looting and riots led to a perception that in-person shopping was not safe. Retailers quickly learned to manage retail hours, in-store protection and security, sanitation, and checkouts. The challenge for retailers was to build the trust of consumers with respect to safety.
6. Cost pressures. With already narrow margins, retailers are pressed to look at cost efficiencies and maintain those margins. Every aspect of the business of retailing is being examined for efficiency improvements, and technology seems to be the answer. From automated shelf stocking to floor cleaning driven by robots, retailers are investing in labor-saving or data analytic technologies that allow them to maintain and improve their margins.

It is under these pressures and post-pandemic concerns that we now analyze Walmart's strategic response and focus on their Latin American strategy.

Table 8.6 Walmart Financial Performance 2016–2020

	2016	2017	2018	2019	2020
Total Revenues $ Billions	482.1	485.8	500.3	514.4	523.9
Annual Revenue Growth	(0.7)	0.8	3.0	2.8	1.9
Gross Profit Margin %	20.3	21.2	21.5	21.0	20.9
Operating Income $ Billion	24.1	22.7	20.6	21.9	20.5
Income as % Revenues	4.0	4.3	4.1	4.25	3.91
Number of Stores					
Walmart US	4,574	4,672	4,761	4,769	4,756
Walmart Intl	6,299	6,363	6,360	5,993	6,146
Sam's Club	655	660	597	599	596
Total	11,528	11,695	11,718	11,361	11,501

Source: Walmart Annual Reports.

Walmart's Strategy Realignment

In response to market pressures and the drive to maintain profit margins, Walmart has focused its overall strategy on improving efficiency and concentrating on a few quality growth markets. The pandemic has only accelerated those trends and resulted in its more aggressive strategy to become a retail platform. As a result, Walmart store expansions have slowed both in the US and abroad. In the US, Walmart is investing in remodeling stores, converting less profitable store formats (large mass merchandising outlets) to more profitable ones (hypermarkets), and closing unprofitable Sam's Club locations. Abroad, Walmart is exiting unprofitable and low-growth countries. In a short two year period, Walmart sold its business in Brazil (2019), Argentina (2020), and Japan (2020) and retained its only remaining European operation in the UK (Asda) in 2021 (Walmart, 2021b; Wilson 2021). Walmart intends to keep its more profitable markets in Latin America and China. In a push to reduce costs under pressures of wage and benefit increases, the company is investing heavily in automation of low-level store tasks using robots. Its strategy to become a retail platform continues to improve as it expands its grocery offerings and invests in its e-commerce business. All these initiatives can be observed through the lens of Walmart's financial operations and store footprints. We start with its overall financial performance during the 2016–2020 period (see Table 8.6).

Walmart's total consolidated sales have consistently grown every year after a dip in 2016. Sales growth in 2018 and 2019 were robust and in the devastating 2020 year, it managed to score a 1.9% annual growth to reach $523.9 billion. Its gross profit margin has remained steady at about 20%, yielding operating incomes of about $20 billion and resulting in net profit margins of more than or close to 4%. Overall store units increased during 2016–2018 but started to decline in 2018 (11,718) to reach 11,501 in 2020. (This last number includes 92 stores in Argentina, which were sold in that year but included in the 2020 annual report. Thus, the net stores after the sale should be 11,409). If the UK divestiture is approved, the store count will be further reduced by its 613 stores there for a net of 10,596, a target retail footprint that aligns with that of comparable global retailers such as France's Carrefour (10,103) and Germany's Lidi (10,000) and Aldi (10,366) (Walmart, 2021a; Deloitte, 2021a).

Walmart operates three distinct businesses: US grocery and mass merchandising; international grocery and mass merchandising; and its Sam's Club outlets (domestic and international). Table 8.7 shows the contributions of these units to total corporate performance. The US retail operation accounts for 65% of total sales and has performed well in 2018 (3.5%) and 2019 (4.1%); like most traditional retailers, it suffered a decline from those rates but managed to attain 2.8% annual growth. The US unit delivers strong and consistent profit margins above 5%, suggesting that all of Walmart's initiatives mentioned above are paying off. The US accounts for 41.3% of total worldwide stores in 2020. The international unit contributed 23% of corporate sales and generated smaller annual sales growth of 1.7% in 2018 and 2.3% in 2019 and a loss of −0.6% in 2020. One may conclude that the pandemic had a more serious impact on Walmart's international stores. Net income as a percent of sales of international operations is as robust as that of the US and, even under a decrease in sales in 2020, this profit margin turned positive at 2.8% in 2020. The number of international stores is 53.4% of total stores. Walmart's international business generates smaller revenues per store than the US. The third unit is Sam's Club, which includes both the domestic and international operations. Sam's Clubs contribute to 11.2% of corporate sales. This unit's sales growth performance is uneven—3.2% growth in 2018 with a decrease of −2.3% in the pre-pandemic 2019 and modest growth of 1.6% in 2020. Its operating margin is a modest 2.8% and is certainly not as large as the other two business units. The number of Sam's Club units has been steady at 599, which represents 5.2% of total stores (Walmart, 2021a).

Based on the above review of financial performance, it is clear that the US retail unit is the jewel in the crown of Walmart's empire. The international business for Walmart is important

Table 8.7 Walmart Financial Performance of Three Business Units 2018–2020

Business Unit	2018	2019	2020
Walmart US			
Revenues	318.4	331.6	341.0
% of Total Walmart Revenues	63	64.4	65
Annual Revenue Growth	3.5	4.1	2.8
Operating Income	16.9	17.4	17.3
Op. Income as % of Revenues	5.3	5.2	5.1
Stores	4,761	4,769	4,756
Walmart International			
Revenues	118.0	120.8	120.1
% of Total Walmart Revenues	23.5	23.4	23
Annual Revenue Growth	1.7	2.3	(0.6)
Operating Income	5.2	4.8	3.4
Op. Income as % of Revenues	4.4	4.0	2.8
Stores	6,360	5,993	6,146
Sam's Club			
Revenues	59.2	57.8	58.7
% of Total Walmart Revenues	11.8	11.2	11.2
Annual Revenue Growth	3.2	(2.3)	1.6
Operating Income	0.915	1.52	1.64
Op. Income as % of Revenues	1.5	2.6	2.8
Units	597	599	599

Source: Walmart (2021a) – 2020 Annual Report.

Table 8.8 Walmart Stores Distribution in 2020

US

Format	Stores	%
Supercenters	3,571	66.7
Discount Stores	376	7.0
Neighborhood small stores	809	15.1
Sam's Club	599	11.2
Total US	5,355	

International

	Stores	Wholesale	Others	
Africa	351			
Argentina*	92			
Canada	408			
Central America	836			
Chile	362	5		
China	412	26		
India		28		
Japan*	333			
Mexico	2,408	163		
UK*	613		18	
Total International	5,815	313	18	6,144

Source: Walmart 2021a Annual Report.
* Sold in 2020.

to the extent of its 25% contribution to total revenues. Within that 25%, the Latin America businesses are a very important contributor. To assess its contribution, we turn to analyze the distribution of retail units by business and country. Table 8.8 provides such information.

Walmart's concentration strategy in a few high growth international markets has proceeded at a rapid pace. With departures from Brazil, Argentina, and the sale of equity shares of its business in Japan and the UK, Walmart's international stores declined from a total of 5,815 in 2020 to 4,777 in 2021. This leaves four international markets in Walmart's international portfolio: Canada, China, Latin America, and Africa. Based on store count, Latin America accounts for 75.4% of these stores, of which 66% are in Mexico, 23% in Central America, and 20% in Chile. As a separate business, Sam's Club has a presence in Mexico (160 outlets), Brazil (27 outlets), and China (15 outlets). This membership business has room to grow internationally; by retaining the Sam's Club unit in Brazil and divesting from other Walmart businesses, the company realizes such potential. We now analyze Walmart's strategy in Latin America through examining its operations in Mexico, Central America, and Chile (Euromonitor International, 2020).

Walmart's Latin America Strategy

As mentioned previously, as of 2021, after reducing its Latin America portfolio, Walmart's presence in the region currently accounts for 75.4% of all of its stores outside the US. Walmart entered Brazil in 1995 and expanded its presence organically and through acquisitions. In 2018, Walmart sold 80% of its Brazil's ownership in 471 stores to local investment company Advent International that has since been renamed Grupo Big. At that time, the Brazilian subsidiary generated $6.8 billion in revenue but consistently recorded losses (Mercopress, 2018); the underperforming subsidiary was plagued with labor problems, underperforming stores in poor locations, and intense competition from other global (Carrefour and Makro) and domestic retailers. In 2021, France's Carrefour acquired Grupo Big stores from Advent International and the remaining 20% equity share from Walmart and became the largest grocery and mass merchandiser in Brazil. Such an investment signifies Carrefour's assessment of the large market potential of this country (Retail Insight Network, 2021). Two years later, in 2020, Walmart divested fully from its Argentina business and sold its 107 stores to Grupo Narvaez, an Argentine retail company that operates in Argentina, Uruguay, and Ecuador. Walmart entered Argentina in 1995 and operated under the Walmart and Changomas banners. The brand targeted middle-class consumers through super centers (31 stores) and supermarkets (6). The Changomas brand appealed to lower class consumers with hypermarkets (51 stores), supermarkets (9), and small format stores under the Changomas Express (10 stores). Walmart generated just over $1 billion in 2018 in Argentina (Euromonitor International, 2020). Walmart's sale of its Brazilian and Argentine business was part of its effort to exit underperforming international business operations and focus on those with better profit potential. We now turn to a discussion of its strategies in its remaining markets of Mexico, Central America, and Chile.

Walmart in Mexico and Central America

Walmart's first international investment was in Mexico in 1991 through a joint venture and subsequent full acquisition of Mexican retailer Cifra in 1997. The Mexican retailer built a successful network mostly aimed at middle- to low-income consumers under the Bodega Aurrera brand mass merchandise discounters and the Superama brand for supermarkets. After the acquisition, Walmart also invested in its own brand of hypermarkets and Sam's Clubs. In addition, Walmart diversified into other specialized businesses with pharmacies, apparel stores (Suburbia), and Banco Walmart with 260 branches located inside Bodega Aurrera outlets. Later in 2014, Walmart sold the banking unit to Mexico's Grupo Financiero Inbursa and the Suburbia stores to Mexico's El Puerto. In 2021, Walmart Mexico generated $34.75 billion (Companies Market Cap, 2021; Walmart, 2021d) and its portfolio of stores was as follows (Dunn & Bradstreet, 2021):

Bodega Aurrera discounter: 516 stores
Mi Bodega discounters: 355 stores
Bodega Aurrera Express: 1,719 stores
Medimart pharmacies: 10 stores
Suburbia apparel: 114 stores
Superama supermarkets: 95 stores
Walmart hypermarkets: 256 stores
Walmart Sam's Clubs: 160 stores
Walmart.com.mx: online shopping

With a solid base in Mexico, Walmart expanded into Central America, where it operates in Costa Rica (230 stores), El Salvador (88 stores), Guatemala (217 stores), and Honduras (82 stores), operating under its own and other retail banners. Some of the other banners are unique to a given country, whereas others are used across other Central American countries as follows:

Retail Brand	Channel Format	Costa Rica	Guatemala	El Salvador	Honduras	Nicaragua
Walmart	Hypermarket	⊠	⊠	⊠	⊠	⊠
Paiz	Supermarket		⊠		⊠	
La Despensa de Don Juan	Supermarket			⊠		
Mas x Menos	Supermarket	⊠				
La Union	Supermarket					⊠
Despensa Familiar	Discount		⊠	⊠	⊠	
Maxi Despensa	Discount		⊠	⊠	⊠	
Pali	Discount	⊠				⊠

Source: Euromonitor (2020).

Walmart's strategy in Central America is a good lesson to understand how to combine global, sub-regional, and national retail brands. Customers will patronize and have the same shopping experience in Walmart's stores throughout Mexico and Central America. Walmart also used local retail brands in Costa Rica (Mas x Menos), El Salvador (La Despensa de Don Juan), and Nicaragua (La Union). Within Central America, Walmart groups countries in geographic proximity and with more migrant flows and uses the same sub-regional retail banner. For instance, Costa Rica and Nicaragua are in one market for the Pali discount stores, and Guatemala, El Salvador, and Honduras are another group for La Despensa Familiar discount stores. There is a large population of migrant workers from Nicaragua in Costa Rica who may recognize the same retail brand in both countries. Most migrants from Guatemala, El Salvador, and Honduras may travel to Mexico for shopping. It is clear that Walmart uses differentiated retail strategies based on the shopping differences among Central American countries as well as that between Central America and Mexico.

Walmart in Chile

Walmart entered Chile in 2009 with the acquisition of the grocery chain Distribucion y Servicio (D&S) and used its Lider and Ekono retail brands. After an infusion of capital to upgrade and reconvert stores to the Lider brand, Walmart is the leading grocery retailer with 42-market share and 382 Lider stores, generating $1.97 billion (Dunn & Bradstreet, 2021). Walmart Chile has the following distribution of stores by brand and format (Walmart, 2021c):

Lider Hypermarkets: 97 stores
Express de Lider Supermarkets: 153 stores
Lider.cl: e-ccommerce
Ekono Discount: 2 stores
Bodega aCuenta Discount: 119 stores
aCuenta.cl: e-commerce
Central Mayorista – Wholesale: 11 stores

Walmart has invested aggressively in its e- commerce business, as Chile has high internet penetration, and its omnichannel offers pick-up stations across all of its brands, including the aCuenta discount brand. These innovations and investments have received industry recognition (Walmart Chile, 2021b).

In summarizing the case of Walmart in Latin America, we offer the following lessons learned:

- The economic impact of the pandemic has accelerated the search for value, safety, and ethical choices that are relevant to consumers.
- A permanent shift to expanding e-commerce worldwide and in Latin America.
- Omnichannel strategies are becoming predominant as consumers become accustomed to blending digital and physical experiences.
- Latin America is an important component of its international business strategy.
- Walmart has clearly recognized countries and markets where further presence and investments may not improve underperforming operations: Brazil, Argentina, the UK, and Japan.
- The Latin America strategy rests in two sub-regions: North America (Mexico and Central America) and Chile.
- These two regions have different market characteristics and competitive challenges. The Walmart brand equity is valued and recognized in the North American market but not in Chile where it uses a local brand: Lider.
- The pandemic has driven and accelerated e-commerce and omnichannel initiatives in both sub-regions.
- Mexico and Chile have high internet penetration, and their consumers use online shopping and store pick-up intensively.
- Initiatives that are used in the home market are replicated quickly and with success in these two sub-regional markets.

Summary

Latin America has attracted many MNCs interested in participating in the growing domestic markets in the region. The rich and abundant natural resources and skilled labor pools and proximity to the US market are attractive to MNCs.

These MNCs bring a wealth of resources and advantages to the region. They also integrate their global value supply chains to either receive inputs or serve the domestic markets.

Non-Latin American MNCs entered the region with expectations of replicating their competencies and adapting their strategies to achieve greater market penetration. Given the diversity of market opportunities and resource advantages that the region offers, MNCs focus on key country markets to sustain their viability. In most cases, this multicountry strategy includes the largest economies of Brazil or Mexico and a few additional country markets.

The MNCs' strategy for Latin America is highly integrated with their global strategy but with substantial adaptations to the local market conditions. This regional strategy has four components: (1) regional ambition; (2) regional strategic thrust; (3) building assets, resources, and competencies; and (4) a regional organization and culture.

Regional ambition is the effort to assess the strategic importance and contribution of Latin America to the MNC's global strategy and performance. Based on the concept of proportionality, Latin America's importance and contribution range from 6% to 10% of a given indicator, whether revenues or assets. Such assessment may impact the strategic decisions of resource allocation and investments. MNCs may decide to focus more on other emerging regions such as Asia and underperform in Latin America discussed in this chapter. On the other hand, the case of Walmart illustrates an equal representation of Latin America in this MNC global business portfolio in terms of number of outlets.

Regional strategic thrust focuses on leveraging the MNCs' advantages in the region. Global brands, marketing competencies, and technology advantages are bases for differentiation. Walmart is a good example of the ability to penetrate, grow, and maintain markets where efficiency and innovation lead to strong cost position and price advantages and abandoning those where these drivers do not lead to market leadership.

Building strategic resources and assets can be accomplished in many ways. Some MNCs such as Electrolux and BASF have invested in manufacturing and distribution assets across the region and time. Others such as Walmart have built organically and through acquisitions.

Non-Latin American MNCs organize their Latin American activities by grouping countries in a particular way. Brazil is sometimes a separate organization, as are the Southern Cone and the Andean countries. Mexico and Central America are combined to form a third unit. The Caribbean becomes a fourth unit.

Organizational and marketing adaptations are common in the implementation of regional strategies in Latin America. Adaptation to address local preferences is important in markets where national culture is strong. MNCs have found similarities across regional markets and replicated successful business models from one market to another, such as the case of Danone's bottled water by Bonafont in Mexico and Brazil.

Despite their overwhelming advantages, MNCs face strong competition from national companies. Given the strong market fundamentals of the region, one would expect that MNCs would deepen their efforts to be more aggressive and innovative in the future.

References

BASF. (2021). *2020 annual report*. Retrieved on December 1, 2021 from https://www.google.com/url?sa=t&rct=j&q=&esrc=s&source=web&cd=&ved=2ahUKEwikh4655MP0AhUHG80KHaPsDq0QFnoECAsQAQ&url=https%3A%2F%2Fwww.basf.com%2Fglobal%2Fdocuments%2Fen%2Fnews-and-media%2Fpublications%2Freports%2F2021%2FBASF_in_South_America_Report_2020.pdf&usg=AOvVaw0uVqsNvWpuiCv0H8Fo7zf0

Beckett, E., & Littman, J. (2020). *How 5 mega chains are designing restaurants for a digital future*. Retrieved on November 30, 2021 from https://www.restaurantdive.com/news/how-5-mega-chains-are-designing-restaurants-for-a-digital-future/589162/

Casanova, L. (2020, March 31). After 30 years of Telefonicas expansion in Latin America. *Latin Trade*. Retrieved on November 30, 2021 from https://latintrade.com/2020/03/31/after-30-years-of-telefonicas-expansion-in-latin-america-what-now/

Ceurvels, M. (2020). Latin America will be the fastest growing retail ecommerce market this year. *Insider Intelligence: eMarketer*. Retrieved on December 6, 2021 from https://www.emarketer.com/content/latin-america-will-fastest-growing-retail-ecommerce-market-this-year

Chevron. (2021). *Chevron corporate sites*. Retrieved on December 14, 2021 from https://www.chevron.com/-/media/chevron/annual-report/2020/documents/2020-Annual-Report.pdf

COFACE. (2021). *Has the global retail sector returned to normal?* Retrieved on December 9, 2021 from https://www.coface.com/News-Publications/News/Has-the-global-retail-sector-returned-to-normal

Companies Market Cap. (2021). *Walmex*. Retrieved on December 7, 2021 from https://companiesmarketcap.com/walmex/revenue/

Danone. (2021). *Bonafont*. Retrieved on December 14, 2021 from https://www.danone.com/brands/waters/bonafont.html

Danone Argentina. (2021). *Aguas*. Retrieved on December 14, 2021 from https://www.danone.com/brands/waters/villa-del-sur.html

Danone Brazil. (2021). *Aguas*. Retrieved on December 14, 2021 from https://corporate.danone.com.br/aguas

Danone Uruguay. (2021). *Aguas*. Retrieved on December 14, 2021 from https://www.danone.com/brands/waters/salus.html

Deloitte. (2021a). *Global powers of retailing in 2021*. Retrieved on December 5, 2021 from https://www2.deloitte.com/ru/en/pages/consumer-business/articles/global-powers-of-retailing.html

Deloitte. (2021b). *2021 retail industry outlook*. Retrieved on December 9, 2021 from https://www2.deloitte.com/us/en/pages/consumer-business/articles/retail-distribution-industry-outlook.html

Devonshire-Ellis, C. (2021). *Chinese companies hunting in Latin America for belt and road M&A*. Retrieved on December 2, 2021 from https://www.silkroadbriefing.com/news/2020/12/30/chinese-companies-hunting-in-latin-america-for-belt-and-road-ma/

Donkin, C. (2020). *Liberty Latin America targets Telefonica units*. Retrieved on November 30, 2021 from https://www.mobileworldlive.com/featured-content/top-three/liberty-latin-america-targets-telefonica-units

Dunn & Bradstreet. (2021). *Walmart Chile SA*. Retrieved on December 7, 2021 from https://www.dnb.com/business-directory/company-profiles.walmart_chile_sa.f71d51ff8869965ce8895802b9355356.html

Electrolux. (2021). *2020 annual report*. Retrieved on December 1, 2021 from https://www.electroluxgroup.com/en/electrolux-publishes-2020-annual-report-32367/

Enerdata. (2020). *Naturgy sells Chilean power distributor CGE to China's state grid*. Retrieved on November 30, 2021 from https://www.enerdata.net/publications/daily-energy-news/naturgy-sells-chilean-power-distributor-cge-chinas-state-grid.html

Euromonitor International. (2020). *Passport Walmart Inc in retailing*. Retrieved on December 15, 2021 from https://www-portal-euromonitor-com.proxygw.wrlc.org/portal/analysis/tab

Euromonitor International. (2021a). *Retailing global industry overview*. Retrieved on December 15, 2021 from https://www-portal-euromonitor-com.proxygw.wrlc.org/portal/analysis/tab#

Euromonitor International. (2021b). *Bottled water in Mexico*. Retrieved on December 15 from https://www-portal-euromonitor-com.proxygw.wrlc.org/portal/analysis/related

Gupta, A. K., & Govindarajan, V. (2002). Cultivating a global mindset. *Academy of Management, 16*, 116–126.

Hispanic PRwire. (2008). *Bonafont arrives in the United States*. Retrieved on December 14, 2021 from https://hispanicprwire.com/en/bonafonttm-llega-a-los-estados-unidos/

Jingjing, M. (2021). China's retail sales dip 3.9% in 2020 amid pandemic; positive growth expected in 2021. *Global Times*. https://www.globaltimes.cn/page/202101/1213126.shtml

KPMG. (2021). *Global retail trends 2020*. Retrieved on December 9, 2021 from https://home.kpmg/xx/en/home/insights/2020/05/global-retail-trends-2020-preparing-for-new-reality.html

Lasserre, P., & Schutte, H. (2006). *Strategies for Asia Pacific: Meeting new challenges*. New York: Palgrave-McMillan.

McKinsey. (2021). *Retail's need for speed: Unlocking value in omnichannel delivery*. Retrieved on December 9, 2021 from https://www.mckinsey.com/industries/retail/our-insights/retails-need-for-speed-unlocking-value-in-omnichannel-delivery

Mercopress. (2018). *Walmart leaving Brazil after 22 years: 80% takeover by advent*. Retrieved on December 12 from https://en.mercopress.com/2018/06/05/walmart-leaving-brazil-after-22-years-80-takeover-by-advent

Nestle. (2018). *Nestle acquires majority interest in Latin American company Terrafil*. Retrieved on November 30, 2021 from https://www.nestle.com/media/news/nestle-acquires-majority-interest-in-terrafertil

Nestle. (2021). *Nestle sharpens geographic focus, creates zones north America and greater China*. Retrieved on November 30, 2021 from https://www.yahoo.com/now/nestl-sharpens-geographic-focus-creates-063000027.html

Practical Commerce. (2021). *Charts: Ecommerce share of global retail sales*. Retrieved on December 6, 2021 from https://www.practicalecommerce.com/charts-ecommerce-share-of-global-retail-sales

R&M-Research and Markets. (2021). *Global retail market report 2021-2030: Market is expected to reach $29361.95 billion in 2025ata CAGR of 7%*. Retrieved on December 6, 2021 from https://www

.prnewswire.com/news-releases/global-retail-market-report-2021-2030-market-is-expected-to-reach-29361-95-billion-in-2025-at-a-cagr-of-7-301232417.html

Retail Insight Network. (2021). *Carrefour Brazil to buy Grupo Big from Advent International, Walmart.* Retrieved on December 12, 2021 from https://www.retail-insight-network.com/news/carrefour-brazil-grupo-big-walmart/

Sempra. (2020). *Sempra Energy completes $3.59 billion divestiture of Luz del Sur in Peru.* Retrieved on December 2, 2021 from https://www.sempra.com/sempra-energy-completes-359-billion-divestiture-luz-del-sur-peru

Sempra. (2021). *Sempra energy and state grid international development target to close sale of Chilquinta Energia in Chile.* Retrieved on December 2, 2021 from https://www.sempra.com/sempra-energy-and-state-grid-international-development-target-close-sale-chilquinta-energia-chile

Statista. (2021a). *Organic dairy food and beverages market value in Latin America.* Retrieved on November 30, 2021 from https://www.statista.com/statistics/800210/organic-dairy-food-drinks-market-value-latin-america/

Statista. (2021b). *Retail market worldwide- statistics and facts.* Retrieved on December 6, 2021 from https://www.statista.com/topics/5922/retail-market-worldwide/

Sucre o Sale. (2021). *In Chile, Walmart adapts to local tastes to…* Retrieved on December 7, 2021 from https://sucreosale.com/index.php/2021/03/21/in-chile-wal-mart-adapts-to-local-tastes-to/

Trading Economics. (2021). *Euro area retail sales.* Retrieved on December 16, 2021 from https://tradingeconomics.com/euro-area/retail-sales-annual

Thomson, S. (2019). *Telefonica plans operational spin-off of Latin American units in major restructure.* Retrieved on November 30, 2021 from https://www.digitaltveurope.com/2019/11/28/telefonica-plans-operational-spin-off-of-latin-american-units-in-major-restructure/

USDA - U.S. Department of Agriculture. (2020). *Retail foods: Chile.* Retrieved on December 12, 2021 from https://apps.fas.usda.gov/newgainapi/api/Report/DownloadReportByFileName?fileName=Retail%20Foods_Santiago_Chile_06-30-2020

Walmart Chile. (2021). *Walmart Chile fortalece estrategia omnicanal y lanza plataforma de ecommerce en supermercados Acuenta.* Retrieved on December 13, 2021 from https://www.walmartchile.cl/walmart-chile-fortalece-estrategia-omnicanal-y-lanza-plataforma-de-ecommerce-en-supermercados-acuenta/

Walmart Inc. (2021a). *2020 annual report.* Retrieved on November 30, 2021 from https://corporate.walmart.com/media-library/document/2020-walmart-annual-report/_proxyDocument?id=00000171-a3ea-dfc0-af71-b3fea8490000

Walmart Inc. (2021b). *KKR and Rakuten complete Seiyu share purchase from Walmart.* Retrieved on December 10, 2021 from https://corporate.walmart.com/newsroom/2021/03/01/kkr-and-rakuten-complete-seiyu-share-purchase-from-walmart

Walmart Inc. (2021c). *Chile.* Retrieved on December 13, 2021 from https://corporate.walmart.com/about/chile

Walmart Inc. (2021d). *Mexico.* Retrieved on December 7, 2021 from https://corporate.walmart.com/our-story/our-business/international/walmart-mexico

Wilson, M. (2021). Walmart completes sale of Asda. *Chain Storage Age: The Business of Retail.* Retrieved on December 10, 2021 from https://chainstoreage.com/walmart-completes-sale-asda

World Population Review. (2021a). *Brazil.* Retrieved on December 14, 2021 from https://worldpopulationreview.com/countries/cities/brazil

World Population Review. (2021b). *Mexico.* Retrieved on December 14, 2021 from https://worldpopulationreview.com/countries/cities/mexico.

Zhou, M. (2019). State Grid helps Brazil harness power. *China Daily.* Retrieved on December 2, 2021 from https://www.chinadaily.com.cn/a/201911/14/WS5dcc8604a310cf3e35577345.html

9 Strategic Approaches of Multilatinas and Global Latinas

Introduction

For the past 30 years, multinational companies from emerging economies have entered the world market and made their mark. Among them, we find a group of global companies from Latin America that spans all sectors, from consumer goods to industrial goods to commodities. This chapter looks at the rise of the *Multilatinas*—Latin American-based firms that expanded to other countries in the region—and of the *Global Latinas*—Latin American-based firms that have a presence in at least one other world region outside Latin America.

The chapter is divided into five sections. The first section provides a historical overview of the emergence of Multilatinas and Global Latinas. The second section describes the motivations and drivers of Latin American firms' internationalization, including country- and firm-specific factors that help explain their ability to develop competitive advantages in global markets. The next section identifies Multilatinas and Global Latinas, highlighting country of origin, sector/industry, and scope of globalization. The fourth section discusses the various strategic approaches they have undertaken and key factors of their success. The final section analyzes the competitiveness of Multilatinas and Global Latinas at present and draws some conclusions about their prospects into the near future.

The Emergence of Multilatinas and Global Latinas

The last three decades in Latin America were characterized by significant economic reforms that created the perfect backdrop for the emergence of Latin American firms with a regional and global orientation.

For much of the twentieth century (1930s–1970s), Latin American countries adopted an economic policy of import substitution. In order to encourage national self-sufficiency through the consumption of locally produced goods, the region's governments supported domestic producers through protectionist trade policies and subsidies. The economic growth of the 1960s and 1970s, which included large investments in infrastructure and industrialization of the region's national economies, were financed by private and public loans. The oil crisis and economic recession of the second half of the 1970s, however, precipitated a debt crisis in Latin America and a corresponding collapse of the region's economies characterized by high inflation, a drop in purchasing power, and capital flights, among others. The aftermath of the debt crisis that started in 1982 and lasted through 1990 has become known as Latin America's *lost decade*. Many of the countries that could not repay their foreign debts resorted to the International Monetary Fund (IMF) in an attempt to resolve their debt

DOI: 10.4324/9781003182672-12

crisis (Mexico, Argentina, and Brazil were among them). The IMF loans were accompanied by strict austerity measures that limited government spending and required that structural reforms aimed at introducing free-market-like competition (and the elimination of protectionist policies) be implemented within the Latin American economies. Latin American countries, at the time, had little choice but to comply with the demands of the IMF and the imperatives of the so-called *Washington Consensus*. These structural reforms brought the region's economies more in line with the economies of the developed world, and Latin America began a process of economic reintegration and expansion. The region's experience during the early 1990s to 2000s (i.e., *the golden decade*) gradually demonstrated that trade and investment liberalization could provide the means to promote economic growth and poverty reduction (Casanova, 2009; Cuervo-Cazurra, 2019; Santiso, 2013).

The evolution of the Latin American economies during these past 50 years or so had profound implications for firms in Latin America (see Figure 9.1 for an overview of the historical evolution of Multilatinas and Global Latinas). In the 1970s, several Latin American firms joined a modest wave of South–South investment (investment from an emerging economy into another emerging economy) that had been triggered by healthy levels of economic growth in many developing countries. The early Multilatinas came into existence during this early period. In most cases, these firms sought out natural markets that shared cultural affinity or geographic proximity (Casanova, 2009; Cuervo-Cazurra, 2008, 2019). The economic stagnation of the lost decade put a stop to these outward investments. Later, the economic transformation of the 1990s, as a result of economic liberalization policies, led to opportunities for expansion and internationalization of Latin American firms. During this period, there was an increase in the number of Multilatinas and the emergence of Global Latinas—Latin American firms which pursued growth beyond their regional markets. In the face of increased foreign competition and the loss of government protection, the reinvention and internationalization of Latin American firms during this period was a strategic response to both ensure survival and strengthen their positions. Firms unable to adapt either closed or were acquired by more competitive domestic or foreign firms. Others devised survival strategies in such a way that national champions were created. Some of these national champions subsequently became regional champions and eventually developed into global champions (Casanova, 2009; Casanova et al., 2009; Cuervo-Cazurra, 2019; Santiso, 2008). In the next section, we discuss drivers and motivations of internationalization in greater depth.

The Internationalization of Latin American Firms

As mentioned earlier, the reduction or elimination of government protections and the influx of foreign multinationals into their own domestic markets that began in the 1990s forced Latin American firms—especially the large, family-owned conglomerates that dominated the region at the time—to focus on innovation and cost efficiencies to more effectively compete in this highly competitive environment. The new competitive pressures led some firms in Latin America to develop unique competitive advantages that facilitated their expansion into new regional and global markets. For many Multilatinas, even limited regional exposure gave them the confidence and experience needed for broader international expansion, often leading to the creation of more significant core competencies that could be implemented on a broader, global scale. This gave rise to the development of the Global Latinas. (Throughout this chapter, we use the term *Latin American multinationals* when referring to both, Multilatinas and Global Latinas.)

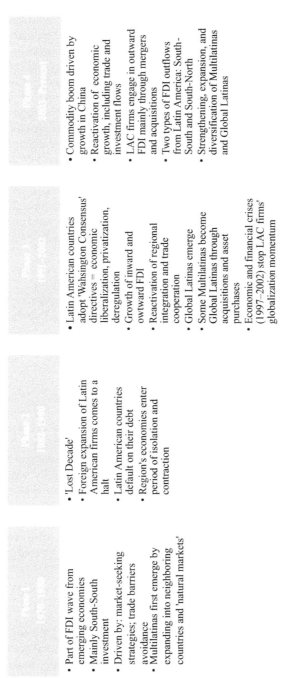

- Part of FDI wave from emerging economies
- Mainly South-South investment
- Driven by: market-seeking strategies; trade barriers avoidance
- Multilatinas first emerge by expanding into neighboring countries and 'natural markets'

- 'Lost Decade'
- Foreign expansion of Latin American firms comes to a halt
- Latin American countries default on their debt
- Region's economies enter period of isolation and contraction

- Latin American countries adopt 'Wahsington Consensus' directives = economic liberalization, privatization, deregulation
- Growth of inward and outward FDI
- Reactivation of regional integration and trade cooperation
- Global Latinas emerge
- Some Multilatinas become Global Latinas through acquisitions and asset purchases
- Economic and financial crises (1997–2002) stop LAC firms' globalization momentum

- Commodity boom driven by growth in China
- Reactivation of economic growth, including trade and investment flows
- LAC firms engage in outward FDI mainly through mergers and acquisitions
- Two types of FDI outflows from Latin America: South-South and South-North
- Strengthening, expansion, and diversification of Multilatinas and Global Latinas

Figure 9.1 A historical overview of the emergence of Multilatinas and Global Latinas. Source: Authors' elaboration with information from Aguiar et al. (2018), Casanova (2009), Cuervo-Cazurra (2019), and Martinez et al. (2003)

Drivers of Internationalization

The international expansion of emerging market firms into the global scene has attracted renewed research focus on their characteristics, motivations, and strategic approaches. The global expansion activities of Asian firms first caught (and held) researchers' attention. When emerging market firms began their international expansion in earnest, research focused on their need to overcome their *liability of foreignness*, defined as a series of costs associated with operating in unfamiliar environments, managing administrative and cultural differences, and coordinating business activities over geographical distances, among others (Zaheer, 1995). These views led to a discussion among business and academic communities on the challenges facing emerging market multinationals. They were often viewed as weaker competitors with weak national institutional environments that could not easily rival developed market multinationals in the global arena. The first decade of the twenty-first century showed that emerging market multinationals could achieve global leadership status in many industries and did so often in a relatively short time frame. Research on Latin American multinationals became a subject of research starting in the early 2000s. We now draw on some of that research to better understand the country- and firm-specific factors that have driven Latin American firms' internationalization from the 1990s to the present.

Country-Specific Advantages

The internationalization of Latin American firms was driven by country-specific factors (e.g., challenging national environments, economic prosperity, commodities boom) that allowed them to develop the resources and capabilities needed to venture outside their domestic markets. The most important of these enabling factors are summarized below.

Challenging National Environments

It is true that, for many years, the largest, most dominant firms in the region benefited from some level of government protection from competition. Still, all firms in the region have learned to operate in national environments riddled with red tape and corruption; high operating costs related to infrastructure inefficiencies, tariff and non-tariff trade barriers, and underdeveloped capital markets; and political and economic volatility. Latin American firms have had to thrive in relatively small domestic markets—with some exceptions—with price-sensitive consumers. This challenging business environment has led Latin American firms to develop distinctive competitive capabilities, resiliency, and a long-term orientation (Haberer & Kohan, 2007). They have, in turn, been able to leverage these competitive advantages in other markets, sometimes closer to home and other times in geographically and culturally distant markets.

Economic Prosperity

The region's economic prosperity since the early 1990s, and especially during the 2003–2007 period, contributed to economic growth and stability and the emergence of a larger middle class. The latter has been a crucial driver. The presence of a middle class can result in more demanding consumers that pressure local firms to innovate to more readily meet their needs. The resulting product, process, and business model innovations can then be transferred to other locations where the local consumer base may not have pressured the firm to innovate but may be equally interested in purchasing the firm's innovative offerings. A growing and dynamic domestic market also results in revenue growth, which provides the financial stability firms need to internationalize.

Globalization

Two aspects of globalization are especially important in understanding the rise of Latin American multinationals. First, the region's growing participation in trade and economic integration agreements reduced entry barriers for Latin American firms, which took advantage of export opportunities and of locating operations in countries with which there were existing relationships. Second, globalization brought to Latin America more and more varied competition. The pressure to compete for customers, which had not existed prior to the opening of the region's economies in the 1980s, forced Latin American firms to innovate, seek cost efficiencies at home and abroad, strengthen their branding and supply chain management capabilities, pursue new markets to counter the risks at home, and find the best talent and technology. Thus, firms from the region pursued global opportunities that offer the resources, efficiency, markets, and assets they needed.

Global Commodities Boom

The rise of Latin American multinationals somewhat paralleled an era characterized by growing global demand and rising prices for commodities. Latin American countries' natural-resource riches meant firms from these countries were especially positioned to capitalize on the commodities boom that spanned the period 2000–2014. The increasing global demand for natural resources (e.g., oil, gas, iron, copper, lithium, etc.) and food products (e.g., soy, meat, etc.), fueled by the growth being experienced in the world's emerging economies, especially China and India, opened opportunities for Latin American firms' international expansion, first through exports and then through acquisitions and joint ventures (Blita International, 2018; Santiso, 2008).

Innovative Capabilities

Latin America has made great strides in education, particularly regarding technology and engineering education. The readily available talent pool, and at significantly lower cost than one might find in developed countries, has likely contributed to improved firm-level innovation capabilities. The research and development (R&D) capacity of the region has also improved, with more private organizations and governments investing in R&D through the establishment of research labs, innovation parks, incubators, and more.

Knowledge Spillovers

Latin America's low labor costs, abundance of natural resources, and growing domestic markets attracted many foreign multinational firms into the region. The presence of large foreign multinationals has led to knowledge spillovers as a result of industry clusters created in Latin American markets or of collaborations and partnerships between foreign multinationals and Latin American firms. These dynamics led to greater sharing of technological and management know-how, thus allowing Latin American firms to acquire the organizational capabilities needed to enter and operate in foreign environments.

Firm-specific Advantages

Internationalization of Latin American firms was also the result of firm-specific characteristics and capabilities, such as the nature of family ownership and their broad scope diversification.

Family Ownership

As mentioned in Chapter 3 and in the opening to this chapter, many of the Latin American multinationals have been family-owned or controlled for multiple generations. These family-owned firms are fully embedded in their local environments. Their leaders, who are typically members of the owning or controlling family, know their companies inside and out, and they have deep experience in their markets and industries and strong social networks. These firms tend to be managed somewhat conservatively and with very little reliance on debt financing. The result of these ownership and management characteristics, is that, when opportunities abroad arose, large Latin American firms had the leadership and resources to expand, and they did.

Diversification through Organic Growth and Acquisitions

Large Latin American firms use geographic and sector diversification as a risk management strategy. Diversification protects them from economic or sector downturns, currency fluctuations, and capital restrictions, among others. In many cases, their diversification has been organic and has taken place over many decades. In addition, during periods of economic crisis (i.e., the lost decade of 1982–1990, the lost half-decade 1997–2002, and the global financial crisis 2008–2010), many foreign multinationals exited the region. Large, well-positioned Latin American business groups snatched up assets from the departing multinationals at bargain prices. The facilities and technology acquired strengthened their positions, allowing them to expand first regionally and then globally (Casanova, 2009; Ramirez, 2015).

Technology Adoption

Technology development and adoption has been an important internationalization driver for firms in the region. Latin American firms' technological developments have led to new core competencies that can be applicable in global markets. For example, several of Brazil's large resource extraction firms (e.g., Vale, Petrobras) now have a presence in Africa where they have undertaken horizontal foreign direct investments that involve leveraging their technological know-how in the host countries. Several countries in Latin America have also become a new haven for technological developments in the services sector, from Brazilian Banco Itau Unibanco's tech-based banking model to tech startups in sectors such as retailing, logistics, and financial services (e.g., Rappi, Nubank).

Motivations for Internationalization

International business theory suggests that there are four main motivations behind foreign investment behavior: market-seeking, efficiency-seeking, resources-seeking, and strategic asset- seeking (Dunning, 1993).

Market-Seeking Motivations

Firms may seek new markets abroad in order to increase their sales and revenues or to expand the reach of their brands, for example. Many Latin American firms seek out natural markets, such as neighboring countries or countries with cultural ties (e.g., Spain, Portugal, the United States). Mexico's Bimbo has expanded abroad, motivated by the need to grow its consumer base. The large Hispanic population in the United States offered Bimbo access to an important diaspora that was geographically nearby. In addition, the cultural and geographic proximity of other countries in Central and South America offered Bimbo an opportunity to internationalize without having to overcome significant entry barriers.

Efficiency-Seeking Motivations

Although Latin American firms themselves rarely go abroad looking for low-cost resources, many of them have become suppliers or manufacturing contractors to large multinationals from developed countries seeking to lower their labor and other production costs. Their integration into global value chains, in response to efficiency-seeking behaviors on the part of developed country multinationals, has allowed Latin American firms to internationalize without 'leaving home.' Many of the family-owned business groups in Mexico and the Central American countries, for instance, have become actively involved in global supply chains of textiles, apparel, autos and auto parts, and electronics. In many cases, these local firms have built state of the art manufacturing facilities in industrial parks and free-trade zones dispersed across the region. Latin American firms that pursue global expansion for efficiency reasons are typically looking to achieve economies of scale that may allow them to develop barriers to entry for competitors operating with higher cost structures.

Resource-Seeking Motivations

Most countries in Latin America are rich in natural resources and have large pools of labor (skilled and not skilled); thus, firms in the region have access to these valuable resources. So why seek resources abroad? For commodity-focused firms (e.g., oil, gas, mineral extraction), seeking access to new resources is necessary. Brazilian state-owned oil producer Petrobras and mining giant Vale have both expanded abroad seeking new oil and mineral reserves (Casanova, 2009). In addition, Latin American firms may look to global markets for resources such as technology and capital which may be in lower supply or be of lower quality in their respective home markets.

Strategic Asset-Seeking Motivations

Emerging market firms may lack the assets necessary to compete globally. Assets can be tangible (e.g., facilities) and intangible (e.g., well-established brands). Investments that help them secure access to much needed assets are an important internationalization motivation of Latin American firms. For example, Colombian multinationals Grupo Orbis, Colombina, and Grupo Exito have expanded their international presence through asset acquisition. In 2014, Grupo Orbis, a chemical and paints producer, acquired two chemical firms in Brazil to strengthen its presence in that country. In 2015, sweets and ice cream producer Colombina acquired Spanish firm Fiesta's equipment, machinery, and brands to strengthen its position in the European market. The same year, Grupo Exito followed suit, acquiring assets (e.g., retailing chains) in Brazil, Mexico, and Argentina to expand its reach in the region (El Tiempo, 2015; Ramirez, 2015).

Of course, there are firms that may have multiple motivations to expand internationally. Take Mexico's Cemex. Over the years, Cemex has made a series of international acquisitions to secure access to both resources and assets. These acquisitions have also resulted in scale-driven efficiencies and an expansion of Cemex's market base (e.g., Latin America, Europe, Asia, and Africa).

Multilatinas and Global Latinas: Who Are They?

Who are the Multilatinas and Global Latinas? This section identifies some of the largest and more prominent Multilatinas and Global Latinas. There is no single, complete list of Multilatinas and Global Latinas, and even the use of those terms varies with some sources using the term Multilatinas to refer to Latin American multinationals in general, whether or not their reach is global. Deloitte Consulting (2014, 2015) conducted two studies to identify the key characteristics and success factors of Multilatinas and Global Latinas and to identify important differences between them. A summary comparison based on Deloitte's findings is presented in Figure 9.2.

We rely on various listings of international Latin American firms to identify the most prominent among the region's multinationals while providing a basic description of them in terms of country of origin, industry, and size. We also highlight the case of state-owned Latin American multinationals. The four main sources that inform this section are (a) *America Economia's 2021 Multilatinas Ranking,* (b) the *Boston Consulting Group's (BCG) 2018 list of Multilatinas,* (c) *Latin Trade's 2021 Top 500 Largest Latin American Firms,* and (d) *Forbes' 2021 Global 2000.* Each of these sources uses different variables to categorize and rank firms, including total assets, market value, number of countries and regions in which they operate, percentage of sales from outside the home country, and percentage of employees located abroad. Table 9.1 presents a compilation of the most prominent Latin American multinationals.

Since first emerging onto the regional and global stage, the geographic and industry scope of Latin American multinationals' reach has expanded, and the list of home countries from which they originate has grown. Highlights from each of the rankings mentioned above provide some key insights about the countries and industries in which Latin American multinationals are concentrated and their performance in the global market.

According to America Economia's 2021 Multilatinas Ranking, the top 100 Multilatinas are concentrated in three countries: Mexico (30), Brazil (28), and Chile (23). As a group, these firms generate over half of their sales outside their home countries, and more than one-third of their employees are located abroad (over one million employees total). The firms in the America Economia's ranking represent a wide array of industries: food and beverages, auto/auto parts, airlines, telecommunications, shipping, steel, energy, petrochemicals, cement, and construction/engineering. The top five firms in the 2021 ranking are, in order: Orbia, Bimbo, Cemex, Vale, and America Movil. Except for Brazilian mining company Vale, all other firms in the top five are from Mexico. Number one, Orbia, is a multisector holding group with activities in industrial goods (e.g., irrigation equipment, pipes, plastics, resins), construction, and data communications. The company's operations expand across 41 countries in all regions of the globe except for Oceania and the Middle East. More than 80% of the company's sales and employees are from outside Mexico. Food manufacturer Bimbo operates in 33 countries and generates almost 70% of its sales from abroad, while cement

Global Latinas

- **Similarities:**
  - Access to top talent and high quality education in countries of origin
  - Top players in home country
  - Internationalization through acquisitions
  - Access to home country stock market to secure expansion funding

- **Differences:**
  - Market /sector leader
  - Main growth strategy: Cost efficiency; economies of scale
  - International expansion: Less organic growth; more use of M&As and strategic alliances that allow bridging geographic and cultural distance of foreign markets
  - Broad access to global capital markets: Growth through debt and equity
  - Diversified ownership: Less family influence and more accountability to shareholders; more mature and professional governance structures and practices; more independent directors

Multilatinas

- **Similarities:**
  - Access to top talent and high quality education in countries of origin
  - Top players in home country
  - Internationalization through acquisitions
  - Access to home country stock market to secure expansion funding

- **Differences:**
  - Among top three market/sector players
  - Growth through multiple strategies: Cost efficiency; vertical integration; portfolio diversification; economies of scope
  - International expansion: Less use of M&As and strategic alliances; more organic growth/greenfield enabled by greater relevance of assets and capabilities in similar/affinity foreign markets
  - Limited access to global capital markets: Growth through debt
  - Family ownership: More family influence in decision making; more immature governance structures and practices; less independent directors
  - May not be able or willing to become global

Figure 9.2 A comparison between Multilatinas and Global Latinas. Source: Authors' elaboration with information from Deloitte Consulting (2014, 2015)

Table 9.1 Multilatinas and Global Latinas

Company	Sector	Revenue 2021 US$ Billions
Brazil		
Vale	Mining	41.4
Grupo JBS	Food	53.2
Itau Unibanco	Financial Service	37.2
Cosan	Bioenergy	2.5
Marfrig	Food and Beverage	13.3
Embraer	Automotive	3.4
Braskem	Chemicals	11.5
Gerdau	Mining and Metals	8.1
Tupy	Automotive	0.8
Suzano Papel E Celulose	Agriculture	6.2
Mexico		
Orbia Advance Corp.	Multisector	6.4
Arca Continental	Food and Beverage	9.1
Cemex	Mining and Metals	12.8
America Movil	Media and Telecoms	52.3
Nemak	Automotive	3.5
Televisa	Other	5
Gruma	Food and Beverage	4.8
Grupo Elektra	Consumer Goods and Retail	6.1
Femsa	Food and Beverage	26.1
PEMEX	Energy	61.7
Argentina		
Arcor	Food and Beverage	1.2
Despegar.com	Travel Services	0.3
Globant	Technology	1
Mercado Libre	Consumer Goods and Retail	4.9
Ternium	Mining and Metals	8.5
Tenaris Argentina	Manufacturing (Industrial)	6.5
Arcos Dorados	Food and Beverage	2
YPF	Energy	4.5
Telecom Argentina	Media and Telecoms	2.4
Pan American Energy	Energy	1.3
Chile		
Cencosud	Consumer Goods and Retail	12.9
Falabella	Retail	10.8
Enel	Energy	10.5
Antofagasta Minerals	Energy	5.2
Celulosa Arauco y Constitución	Agriculture	4.4
Banco de Crédito e Inversiones	Finance	3.1
Compañia Cervecerias Unidas	Beverages	2.6
Concha y Toro	Wine	0.97
Empresas Copec	Energy	12
ENTEL-Empresa Nacional de Telecommunicaciones	Telecoms	2.7
Colombia		
Bancolombia	Finance	10.5
Ecopetrol	Energy	13.9
Empresa de Energía de Bogotá	Energy	1.4
Grupo Aval	Finance	9.2
Grupo Nutresa	Food Processing	3.1
Cementos Argos	Energy	2.5
Alpina	Automobiles	0.82
Quala	Food Processing	0.27
Empresa Publicas de Medellin	Energy	5.9
Terpel	Energy	5

(*Continued*)

Table 9.1 Continued

Company	Sector	Revenue 2021 US$ Billions
Peru		
Ajegroup	Beverages	9.6
Alicorp	Food and Beverages	2.8
Inretail Perú	Consumer Goods and Retail	3.8
Petroperú	Energy	3.4
Ferreycorp	Consumer Goods and Retail	1.2
Leche Gloria	Food and Beverages	1.3
Aceros Arequipa	Mining and Metal	1.1
Unión Andina de Cementos	Mining and Metal	0.91

Source: Authors' elaboration with information from the following sources: The Latin Trade 500 (2021); America Economia (2021a); Forbes Global 2000 (2021).

producer Cemex operates in 19 countries and generates 80% of its sales from outside Mexico. In terms of total volume of foreign sales, the top three firms are (1) Brazilian Group JBS, a food producer with operations in 15 countries and a customer reach in almost 100 countries (US$ 40.8 billion; 77% of total sales); (2) Mexican telecom America Movil (US$37.2 billion; 72%); and (3) Brazilian mining company Vale (US$36.7 billion; 92%) (America Economia, 2021a, 2021b).

The Boston Consulting Group's (BCG) 2006 list of *Global Challengers* (multinationals from emerging economies) included a total of 18 Latin American companies; in 2007, it included 22. In 2009, BCG published a list of 100 Latin American companies with either regional or global reach. That list was dominated by firms from Brazil (34) and Mexico (28), with the rest of firms being from Chile (21), Argentina (7), Colombia (5), Peru (3), El Salvador (1) and Venezuela (1). BCG's most recent 2018 list of Multilatinas included firms from Mexico (28), Brazil (26), Chile (18), Colombia (11), Argentina (9), Peru (5), and Costa Rica, El Salvador, and Panama (1 each) (see Figure 9.3). These numbers show a slight improvement in Mexico's position compared to Brazil's, and the emergence of Multilatinas from the smaller Central American countries. Multilatinas from Colombia deserve special mention. Although they represented only about 10% of all multinationals in the BCG list (and a similar percentage in the America Economia's Multilatinas Ranking), firms from Colombia have been pursuing internationalization opportunities consistently over the past two decades. Colombian multinationals operate across Latin America, in the United States, Europe, and Asia. They have pursued global expansion primarily through mergers and acquisitions (Grupo Sura, Grupo Nutresa, Cementos Argos, Grupo Aval, Bancolombia, and Grupo Carvajal are behind some of the most important foreign acquisitions). Motivations behind the internationalization of Colombian firms include capitalizing on new opportunities brought about by the growth and integration of the national and global economies, seeking new markets to counter domestic market saturation and risk diversification (Aguiar et al., 2018; El Tiempo, 2015).

The Latin Trade list of the largest 500 firms in Latin America reveals some characteristics and patterns in line with our discussion thus far. There are key sectors from which the largest Latin American multinationals come with the most dominant being oil and gas, mining, retailing, telecommunication, and food and beverages. These large global companies also show some geographic concentration in terms of countries of origin, with the majority coming from the LAC-6, especially Brazil and Mexico.

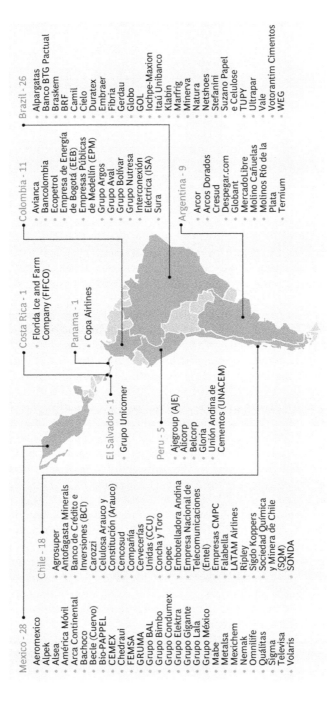

Figure 9.3 The 2018 BCG Multilatinas. Source: Aguiar et al. (2018)

The 2021 Forbes Global 2000 ranks the largest public companies in the world. The 2021 list includes a total of 37 Latin American multinationals. Fifteen firms are from Brazil and ten are from Mexico. The remaining Latin American firms in the list come from Chile (5), Colombia (3), Argentina (2), and Peru and Venezuela (1 each). Compare this to China's multinationals, 292 of which made the list, including the number one ranking, and a total of four in the top ten. Thus, although many Latin American firms have transformed into Multilatinas and Global Latinas, there is plenty of opportunity for them to continue to grow and internationalize.

Regardless of the ranking or list used to identify Latin American multinationals, or the variables used to generate these rankings, it is clear that Multilatinas and Global Latinas are concentrated in the LAC-6 but not limited to them. Brazil, Mexico, and Chile are the most prolific producers on international firms in the region, but Latin American multinationals can also be found in Colombia, Argentina, Peru, and some of the Central American countries. As may be expected, Latin American multinationals' characteristics and strategies vary by their country of origin. For instance, Chilean multinationals are more likely to be Multilatinas, with their international expansion concentrated in other parts of the region. Some of the most well known include retailers Cencosud and Falabella. Unlike their Chilean counterparts, Brazilian firms are generally Global Latinas. They tend to have a wide geographic presence, often in several world regions, and tend to be concentrated in a few key sectors: mining, energy, construction, agriculture, and consumer packaged goods (e.g., Vale and Petrobras, two of the largest Brazilian Global Latinas are present in most world regions).

Latin American multinationals also represent a diverse mix of sectors, including natural-resource extraction, airplane manufacturing, airlines, shipping, chemicals, energy, cement, pulp and paper, telecommunications, food and beverages, and financial services, among others. This industry variety makes it difficult to draw conclusions about Latin American multinationals, but the following section attempts to identify some of the factors that account for their growth and success as well as some of the strategies they have pursued.

Strategic Approaches of Multilatinas and Global Latinas

Competitive Strengths and Weaknesses

Understanding the experiences of Multilatinas and Global Latinas demands a look at both their competitive strengths and weaknesses. Key success factors associated with Latin American multinationals are visionary leadership, family ownership and control, innovation, and a leading market position in their home markets. We briefly discuss each of these strengths below.

Leadership

Latin American multinationals are led by a new cadre of men and women with a vision to conquer the world (Casanova, 2009). In the large, multinational business groups, many leaders are the third or fourth generation of their families to have run their businesses. As such, they know their own companies and industries well and can leverage their knowledge and experience to respond in an agile manner to threats in the external environment. As mentioned in Chapter 5, these leaders tend to be younger, highly educated, and tech savvy. They anticipate a long tenure as head of their companies and, thus, can focus on long-term goals while assuming some well-measured risks.

Family Ownership

The fact that many of the largest and most successful Latin American multinationals are owned or controlled by family groups suggest that this type of ownership can be a source of competitive strengths. These firms can take a long-term orientation to their strategic planning (Aguilera et al., 2019), have coherent goals and values, and, in many cases, the social capital of the family can be leveraged for business opportunities.

Innovation

The success of Multilatinas and Global Latinas can typically be traced back to some type or form of innovations. Innovations of Latin American multinationals include product, process, management, and business model innovations. They are also known for reverse innovation, frugal innovation, and social innovation. The last three, in particular, give them unique advantages over multinationals from more developed countries. For example, Latin American multinationals have had to find ways to serve low- and middle-income consumers with high-value offerings (i.e., reasonable quality at low prices) while remaining profitable. This has led many firms in the region to pursue frugal and social innovations in order to achieve product and operational excellence (Casanova, 2009; Deloitte, 2015; Martinez et al., 2003; Nettesheim et al., 2016).

Leading Position in Their Home Market

The leadership position enjoyed by many Multilatinas and Global Latinas in their home markets gives them the resources, protection, and time they need to venture abroad. In the process of becoming national leaders these companies developed exceptional customer orientation, learning and operational capabilities as well as agility and flexibility that they are then able to deploy in other markets (Blita International, 2018; Deloitte, 2015; Martinez et al., 2003).

Latin American multinationals lag behind other multinationals primarily because of three competitive weaknesses: lack of brand recognition, family involvement in governance, and low levels of investments in research and development.

Lack of Brand Recognition

Most Latin American multinationals have brands that are completely unknown, which hinders their ability to enter regional and global markets (Casanova, 2009; ABConomics, 2011). Many Multilatinas and Global Latinas choose to enter foreign markets with acquired brands (e.g., Bimbo); others invest heavily in redefining and reinventing their brands, so they can deploy them in foreign markets (e.g., Chilean Viña Concha y Toro and Brazilian Natura Cosmeticos).

Family Involvement in Governance

As discussed above, there are many advantages Latin American multinationals derive from family ownership. However, family involvement in governance can be detrimental if it prevents them from adopting more formalized corporate governance processes or from obtaining external financing due to lack of transparency, for instance (Deloitte, 2015).

Low Levels of Research and Development Spending

Innovation is a major success factor, and one that has been leveraged successfully by many of the Multilatinas and Global Latinas (e.g., Embraer, Cemex, Politec, Tenaris, Mercado Libre, Itau Unibanco, etc.) (Santiso, 2008). However, these technological leaders are the exception. Latin American multinationals will need to invest much more in research and development if they are to meet the competitive challenges of the future.

Preferred Strategies of Multilatinas and Global Latinas

Latin American multinationals have achieved regional and global expansion through a variety of strategies; here, we discuss some of the most common ones (Casanova, 2009; Fleury & Fleury, 2011; Velez-Ocampo, Gonzalez-Perez, & Sin, 2021).

Global Integration

Latin American multinationals that pursue this strategy establish global organizations that seek to leverage economies of scale to achieve efficiency throughout the value chain. These firms are heavy users of technology for operational efficiency and rely on acquisitions and joint ventures to capture the skills, assets, and synergies needed to accelerate growth. In many cases, their internationalization process starts by entering natural markets (other emerging economies, neighboring countries, culturally similar markets) before expanding to less familiar markets. Many are domestic and regional leaders that engage in learning and capability building before becoming full-fledged global integrators. Mexican firms Cemex, America Movil, and Grupo Bimbo are examples of global integrators.

Global Sourcing

These firms internationalize primarily for resource-seeking motives. Many are in the commodities and industrial sectors and seek to ensure access to a steady supply of resources or to low-cost or high-quality inputs. Thus, global expansion is seen as both necessary for growth and risk reduction. These firms engage in internationalization through acquisitions and joint ventures and rely on their operational, logistical, and relational expertise to establish a global sourcing base. Brazilian firms Petrobras and Vale are examples of global sourcers.

Global Marketing

Some Latin American multinationals have established a regional or global presence through innovative and diversified product portfolios, strong branding, broad distribution, and innovative processes for handling customer service functions (e.g., ordering, payment, fulfillment, etc.). These companies build brands that resonate with consumers, continually add value through their marketing mix, and seek to redefine the image of their brands in the global stage (with some choosing to disguise their country of origin for market advantage). Global marketers are adept at using niche or multisegment targeting strategies. Many of these brands are in consumer goods sectors (food and beverages, telecommunications). Argentinian Tenaris, Brazilian Natura Cosmetics, Chilean winemaker Concha y Toro, and Mexican Grupo Modelo are all examples of global marketers.

Brazilian Multinationals

The number of Brazilian multinationals has been rising since the early 2000s. According to Fleury and Fleury (2011), Brazilian multinationals emerged as direct competitors of foreign MNCs' subsidiaries, gradually evolving first into national champions and then into regional and global players. During the economic transformation and privatization of the early 1990s, many Brazilian companies were unable to adapt; those that developed the management competencies necessary to survive and thrive eventually built their own identity, managerial styles, and business models. The Brazilian government has also played an important role in the emergence of global champions through policies focused on two areas, improving access to capital and supporting national champions (Finchelstein, 2017). As is the case in other Latin American countries, many Brazilian multinationals are owned by family groups and are adept at managing in turbulent environments, though cautious in their approach to risk taking. Thus, Brazilian firms' internationalization process was sustained over several years and accomplished mainly through acquisitions in culturally and geographically near markets. Today, many Brazilian multinationals occupy global leadership positions in their industries, such as Embraer (aircraft manufacturing), Vale do Rio Doce (mining), and Gerdau (steel) (Fleury & Fleury, 2011). Brazilian multinationals have internationalized motivated by resource and efficiency-seeking motives (e.g., Petrobras, Vale) as well as market (e.g., Natura) and strategic asset-seeking motives.

Over time, Brazilian multinationals developed their own *Brazilian way* of doing business. This is characterized by a highly creative and innovative attitude toward problem solving that yields agility and flexibility. At the national level, Brazil has emerged as a new hotbed of innovation, and Brazilian multinationals are at the center of this innovative ecosystem. Brazilian multinationals are gaining important global positions in a wide range of sectors, from green energy to financial services technology. These leadership positions are the result of product, process, and business model innovations. Other types of innovations typical of Brazilian multinationals include reverse innovation, social innovation, and frugal innovation. It is interesting to note that many Brazilian global leaders have been adept at pursuing complementary types of innovations that enhance the value of their offerings and protect them from competition. Natura Cosmeticos and Nubank, for instance, have reached their successful global positions by implementing frugal, product, process, and social innovations (Cahen, Casanova, & Miroux, 2021; Casanova, 2009; Casanova, 2019a; Santiso, 2013).

Mexican Multinationals

Huesca-Dorantes et al.'s (2018) study of 13 Mexican multinationals provides some insights into the characteristics, internationalization processes, and key success factors of Mexican Multilatinas and Global Latinas. First, Mexican multinationals were largely controlled by family-owned business groups (10 out the 13 studied) that were highly diversified. Three of the 13 firms studied were former state-owned enterprises or had been related to them: America Movil—telecom, Grupo Mexico—copper mining, and Grupo Financiero Banorte—banking. One of the most interesting findings from their study were the differences among Mexican multinationals based on where they were headquartered. The study identified two groups of firms, those based in Monterrey (northern industrial region of Mexico) and those based in Mexico City. The authors found that the Mexican multinationals based in Monterrey (e.g., Grupo Alfa, FEMSA, Cemex) were politically aligned with the more conservative political party in Mexico (PAN), tended to exhibit an antagonistic attitude toward the government, and kept close ties with the local business elite, allying themselves as a unified group when necessary. The Mexican MNCs headquartered in Mexico City (e.g., Grupo Carso, Grupo Televisa, Grupo Bimbo) tended to be more closely affiliated with the center-left PRI party, which ruled Mexico for more than 70 years during the twentieth century. These companies keep closer ties to the government and the political elite in Mexico City, using these connections for competitive advantage.

In terms of their internationalization strategies, most had adopted incremental regional strategies, expanding first into other countries in Central and South America and later into other regions of the world. The Mexican multinationals also enjoyed preferential access to the US market through their participation in the region's free-trade agreement (USMCA, formerly NAFTA). Most of the Mexican multinationals had internationalized via mergers and acquisitions, as well as strategic alliances. They seemed particularly adept at acquiring assets at low prices during times of economic crisis. Finally, their motivations for internationalization ranged from resource-seeking investments (e.g., Grupo Mexico, mining); efficiency-seeking (e.g., Cemex, cement); market-seeking (e.g., FEMSA, food and beverages), and asset-seeking (e.g., Grupo Bimbo, food/baked goods). Finally, some Mexican multinationals that expanded beyond the Americas sought to improve their organizational capabilities through exposure to global competition (e.g., Cemex, Grupo Bimbo). In most cases, these Mexican multinationals have shared a key competence: their ability to innovate, whether in product (America Movil), process (Grupo Bimbo), or business model innovation (Cemex) (Cahen, Casanova, & Miroux, 2021; Huesca-Dorantes et al., 2018; Lessard & Lucea, 2009).

State-owned Global Latinas

There are a number of important Latin American multinationals that are also state-owned enterprises (SOEs). State-owned Global Latinas are primarily concentrated in the oil industry and other natural-resource extraction. They can be fully state-owned or partially state-owned, with some even trading as public companies. Their internationalization has been motivated primarily by the need to secure new resources and to achieve scale-based efficiencies (see Table 9.2 for a list of the most important state-owned Global Latinas).

Table 9.2 Top State-Owned Latin American Multinationals

Company	Sector	Revenue		
		2021 $US Millions	*% Change 2020–2021*	*% Change 2019–2020*
Petrobras, Brazil	Energy	51.1	−2.4	−30.2
PEMEX, Mexico	Energy	61.7	28.7	−35.6
Banco do Brasil, Brazil	Financial Services	16.9	0.1	−1.8
Codelco, Chile	Mining	14.5	2.5	10.0
Ecopetrol, Colombia	Energy	13.9	−3.5	−33.8
Eletrobras, Brazil	Energy	6.2	9.9	−18.7
ENAP, Chile	Energy	5.6	14.29	−35.9
Petroperú, Peru	Energy	3.4	10.3	−33.4

Sources: Latin Trade's Top 500 (2021); Forbes Global 2000 (2021).

State-owned enterprises, especially those that have become global, represent an important source of income for their home country governments. Petroleos Mexicanos (PEMEX) contributes about a third of the Mexican government's budget, because it pays more than 90% of its profits in taxes. This revenue-generating role, however, can conflict with the need to manage these firms as businesses. PEMEX, for instance, has sometimes been unable to allocate sufficient funding for sorely needed investments in exploration and expansion of its extraction capacity.

Companies that are wholly owned by the state receive the benefits of government protection, subsidies, and other types of preferential treatment. In some cases, governmental support can translate into a strong innovative capacity. However, this protection from competition may also reduce their competitiveness, especially if they lack the visionary and non-political leadership necessary to achieve high levels of performance. A benefit enjoyed by state-owned firms with only partial state ownership (e.g., Petrobras) is their ability to access international capital markets to fund expansion. On the other hand, these companies have to be more concerned with short-term shareholder expectations which may deter long-term investments. Governments may also see the lack of full control as curtailing their ability to use revenues generated by a state-owned company for investments in public goods or development initiatives, which their citizens expect.

Multilatinas and Global Latinas: Into the Future

As you probably gathered from reading this chapter, there is a relatively small group of Latin American firms that stand out as the most successful Multilatinas and Global Latinas. Granted, the ones we use in the chapter as examples are not the only Latin American multinationals. Yet during the past decade, there has been a decline of outward investment from Latin America, with the outflows being concentrated in Brazil and Mexico, who represent 31% and 27%, respectively, of the accumulated outward FDI stock. Chile (20%) and Colombia (9%) contribute another third. Outward investment is also concentrated in terms of the firms doing the investing. In Mexico, two firms accounted for more than half of all greenfield investments from Mexico during the period 2009–2017: America Movil (45%) and Cemex (11%). Investments from Brazil are less concentrated than in Mexico; however, Vale alone accounted for almost a quarter of all greenfield investments during the same period noted above. Concentration among a handful of firms is also observable in Chile, where three companies (LATAM, Falabella, and Siglo Koppers Group) accounted for a third of all greenfield investments between 2009 and 2017 (Casanova, 2019b).

This downward trend in outward investment from the region does not bode well for the future of Multilatinas and Global Latinas and other national champions that may aspire to expand globally. The COVID-19 pandemic is also likely to have a negative effect on outward investments in the short term. One of Latin American multinationals' core competencies is their ability to manage uncertainty and crisis; these competencies have proved valuable during the past couple of years. Nonetheless, as Latin American firms continue to compete for resources and customers with multinationals from both developed and emerging economies, they will need to sharpen existing capabilities and acquire new ones. Creating and deploying new capabilities will be a necessity. Among the most critical capabilities they will need to acquire and deploy to compete globally are innovation development, technology adoption, talent management, and supply chain management (Ramirez, 2019). In addition, ethical, transparent, humane, and responsible leadership can give Multilatinas and Global Latinas the edge they need to compete successfully in the *new normal* (Forbes & LLYC, 2021).

Summary

Multilatinas—Latin American-based firms that have expanded to other countries in the region—and *Global Latinas*—Latin American-based firms that have a presence in at least one other world region outside Latin America—have gained importance and attention in the past few years. The pro-market reforms of the 1980s and 1990s led to the development of the Multilatinas and the Global Latinas, but the firms accelerated their international expansion in the past two decades. These firms play a vital role in their respective economies (boosting employment, expanding the knowledge base, generating export-based tax revenue, etc.), but they also enhance the region's competitiveness.

The internationalization of Latin American firms was driven primarily by external factors. The economic transformation that began in the 1990s, forced Latin American firms, especially family-owned, national market leaders to pursue growth beyond their national borders to counter competition from foreign multinationals and the loss of government protection. Firms may have initially internationalized as a survival strategy, but many found that they could thrive and lead in regional and global markets—many have.

Mexico and Brazil, followed by Chile and Colombia tend to produce the largest number of Latin American multinationals. Multilatinas and Global Latinas span all sectors but are especially present in energy, financial services, retailing, telecommunications, and food and beverages. Some Multilatinas and Global Latinas are leaders regionally or globally in their respective sectors.

Key success factors that characterize Multilatinas and Global Latinas include visionary leadership, family ownership that lends continuity and a long-term orientation, innovation, and operational (e.g., cost efficient operations, supply chain management), marketing (e.g., branding, distribution), and management (talent management, financial management) capabilities. Their main strategic weaknesses include lack of brand recognition outside their home markets, family ownership that may hinder their access to global financing, and low levels of R&D spending.

Based on their primary strategies, Multilatinas and Global Latinas can be global integrators, firms that seek efficiency and scale and have the ability to create and manage highly integrated global operations; global sourcers, firms that expand abroad in search of resources; or global marketers, firms that focus on product innovation and diversification, brand building, and customer service excellence. The common thread across Multilatinas' and Global Latinas' strategic approaches regionally and globally is innovation: these firms have succeeded by developing product, process, management, and business model innovations. They have also pursued reverse, frugal, and social innovations to build operational and market advantages.

The world post-pandemic will likely bring new challenges for all firms, including Latin American multinationals. Consolidating their presence in global markets in the presence of intense competition for resources and customers will require Multilatinas and Global Latinas to develop and deploy existing and new capabilities, primarily those related to innovation development, technology adoption, talent management, and supply chain management.

References

ABConomics. (2011, June 12). *At home and abroad: The rise of Global Latinas.* https://abconomics .wordpress.com/2011/06/12/at-home-and-abroad-the-rise-of-global-latinas/

Aguiar, M., Azevedo, D., Becerra, J., Leon, E., Gomes, N., Rivera, R., de T'Serclaes, J.-W., Ukon, M., & Valle, J. (2018, March). *Why Multilatinas hold the key to Latin America's economic future*. The Boston Consulting Group. https://www.bcg.com/publications/2018/why-multilatinas-hold-key -latin-america-economic-future

Aguilera, R. V., Crespi-Cladera, R., & Kabbach de Castro, L. R. (2019). Corporate governance in Latin America: Towards shareholder democracy. *AIB Insights, Special Issue on Latin America*, *19*(2), 13–17.

America Economia. (2021a, December 14). *Estos son los resultados del Ranking Multilatinas 2021*. https://www.americaeconomia.com/negocios-industrias/multilatinas/estos-son-los-resultados-del -ranking-multilatinas-2021

America Economia. (2021b, December 16). *Ranking Multilatinas 2021: La globalización no se detiene*. https://www.americaeconomia.com/negocios-industrias/multilatinas/ranking-multilatinas-2021 -la-globalizacion-no-se-detiene

Blita International. (2019). *5 Keys to the success of Multilatina companies in Latin America*. https:// www.blita.com/news/5-keys-success-of-multilatina-companies-in-latin-america

Cahen, F., Casanova, L., & Miroux, A. (2021). *Innovation from emerging markets: From copycats to leaders*. Cambridge, UK: Cambridge University Press.

Casanova, L. (2009). *Global Latinas: Latin America's emerging multinationals*. Hampshire, UK: Palgrave Macmillan.

Casanova, L. (2019a). Natura alcanza la mayoría de edad en la escena global. *Latin Trade* (Second Quarter), 16.

Casanova, L. (2019b). Are Latin American companies too focused on domestic markets? *Latin Trade* (Third Quarter), 16.

Casanova, L., Golstein, A., Almeida, A., Fraser, M., Molina, R., Hoeber, H., & Arruda, C. (2009). *From Multilatinas to Global Latinas: The new Latin American multinationals*. https://publications.iadb .org/publications/english/document/Multilatinas-to-Global-Latinas-The-New-Latin-American -Multinationals.pdf

Cuervo-Cazurra, A. (2008). The multinationalization of developing country MNEs: The case of Multilatinas. *Journal of International Management*, *14*, 138–154.

Cuervo-Cazurra, A. (2019). Multilatinas and international business studies. *AIB Insights*, Special Issue on *Latin America*, *19*(2), 3–7.

Deloitte. (2014). *Latin America rising: How Latin American companies become global leaders*. https:// www2.deloitte.com/content/dam/Deloitte/global/Documents/Strategy/dttl-latin%20america -rising-english.pdf

Deloitte. (2015). *Becoming a Multilatina: Key factors to regionalizing in Latin America*. https://www2 .deloitte.com/content/dam/Deloitte/us/Documents/strategy/us-cons-becoming-a-multilatina.pdf

Dunning, J. H. (1993). *Multinational enterprises and the global economy*. New York, NY: Addison-Wesley.

ECLAC-United Nation's Economic Commission on Latin America and the Caribbean. (2012). *Foreign direct investment in Latin America and the Caribbean*. http://www.eclac.org/publicaciones/ xml/4 /49844/ForeignDirectInvestment2012.pdf

El Tiempo. (2015, September 15). *Las causas para que las multilatinas del pais aceleren expansion*. https://www.eltiempo.com/archivo/documento/CMS-16374798

Finchelstein, D. (2017). The role of the state in the internationalization of Latin American firms. *Journal of World Business*, *52*(4), 578–590.

Fleury, A., & Fleury, M. T. (2011). *Brazilian multinationals: Competences for internationalization*. Cambridge, UK: Cambridge University Press.

Forbes (2021). *The Global 2000*. https://www.forbes.com/lists/global2000/#5a1cb3645ac0

Forbes & LLYC. (2021, September). *Multilatinas: Bajo la nueva normalidad*. https://ideas .llorenteycuenca.com/2021/09/multilatinas-bajo-la-nueva-normalidad/

Haberer, P. R., & Kohan, A. F. (2007). Building global champions in Latin America. *The McKinsey Quarterly. Special edition: Shaping a new agenda for Latin America*, 1-9

Huesca-Dorantes, J. L., Michailova, S., & Stringer, C. (2018). Aztec multilatinas: Characteristics and strategies of Mexican multinationals. *Review of International Business*, *28*(1), 2–18.

Lessard, D. R., Lucea, R., & Vives, L. (2013). Building your company's capabilities through global expansion. *MIT Sloan Management Review, 54*(2), 61–67.

Martinez, A., De Souza, I., & Liu, F. (2003). Multinationals vs. Multilatinas: Latin America's great race. *Strategy + Business, 32*, 1–12.

Nettesheim, C., Fæste, L., Khanna, D., Waltermann, B., & Ullrich, P. (2016, February). *Transformation in emerging markets: From growth to competitiveness.* The Boston Consulting Group. https://web -assets.bcg.com/img-src/BCG-Transformation-in-Emerging-Markets-Feb-2016_tcm9-145373.pdf

Ramirez, D. (2015). Multilatinas, ready for 2016. *Latin Trade* (November–December), 22–26.

Ramirez, D. (2019). The Multilatina of the future. *Latin Trade* (Third Quarter), 13–15.

Santiso, J. (2008). La emergencia de las Multilatinas. *Revista de la CEPAL, 95*, 7–30.

Santiso, J. (2013). *The decade of the Multilatinas.* Cambridge, UK: Cambridge University Press.

The Latin Trade 500 (2021). *Latin Trade* (September / November), 40–52. https://latintrade.com /2021/09/30/the-latin-trade-500-the-annual-ranking-of-the-largest-non-financial-latin-american -companies/

Velez-Ocampo, J., Gonzalez-Perez, M. A., & Sin, K. (2021). Jaguar firms: Tropic dwellers, camouflage masters, and solitary predators. *Management and Organization Review, 17*(5), 885–917. https://doi .org/10.1017/mor.2021.24

Zaheer, S. (1995). Overcoming the liability of foreignness. *Academy of Management Journal, 38*, 341–363.

10 The Entrepreneurial Environment in Latin America

Introduction

Promotion of and access to entrepreneurial opportunities are incorporated into the United Nations' Sustainable Development Goals (SDGs). SDG 4.4 seeks to increase the number of youth and adults who have relevant skills, including technical and vocational, for employment and entrepreneurship. SDG 8.3 seeks to promote development-oriented policies that support productive activities, job creation, entrepreneurship, creativity, and innovation and encourage the formalization and growth of micro, small-, and medium-size enterprises (MSMEs). New ventures and MSMEs are considered main drivers of innovation, employment, income generation, poverty eradication, and social inclusion. This chapter starts by providing a brief discussion of factors that facilitate or hinder innovation in Latin America. The second and third sections provide an overview of the state of entrepreneurship in Latin America, rates of entrepreneurial activity, and insights on attitudes toward entrepreneurship in the region, followed by an analysis of the entrepreneurial ecosystem in select countries and in the region. The next section covers specific types of entrepreneurs in the region, including technology, women, and social entrepreneurs. The chapter concludes with a summary assessment of the strategic opportunities and challenges faced by small- and medium-size businesses (SMEs) in Latin America.

Innovation in Latin America

A country's innovative capacity can either support or hinder its firms' abilities to become world competitors. In Chapter 3, 'innovation capability' was identified as the weakest Global Competitiveness Index pillar for all Latin American countries (Schwab, 2019). Innovation capability captures the diversity and collaborative nature of a country's talent base, the country's investments in research and development (R&D), and consumers' level of sophistication. Low performance in innovation capability is echoed in the 2021 Global Innovation Index, with all Latin American countries ranking low compared to other regions. None of the Latin American countries made it into the top 50, compared to Asia, where five countries made it into the top 15; only four Latin American countries (Chile, Mexico, Costa Rica, and Brazil) made it into the top 60 (Dutta et al., 2021). Public and private sector initiatives seeking to enhance the innovation capability of countries in the region should target human capital development, R&D investments in science and other knowledge-based technologies, and product and market-oriented innovations.

Latin American growth and transformation from the early 2000s up to 2015 led to the development of 'pockets of innovation.' Business-friendly, vibrant, and resilient environments

DOI: 10.4324/9781003182672-13

emerged in São Paulo, Brazil; Guadalajara, Mexico; Bogotá and Medellin in Colombia; Santiago de Chile and San Jose, Costa Rica. These regional clusters became technological hubs in banking, aeronautics, and information technology (Casanova et al., 2019; de Miranda Oliveira et al., 2019). Friendlier business ecosystems propelled Latin American firms from imitators of innovation to innovation leaders of new products and business models that span R&D-based, low-cost, frugal, and social and environmental innovations (Casanova et al., 2019). As discussed in Chapter 9, Multilatinas, Global Latinas, and state-owned enterprises developed innovation capabilities central to their domestic growth and internationalization strategies. Yet, innovation has not been restricted to large firms in Latin America. In this chapter, we focus on new and small ventures, discussing entrepreneurial firms first, and SMEs later.

A country's innovative capability is directly linked to the entrepreneurial attitudes and behaviors of its people and the resulting entrepreneurial activity in the country. Countries will differ in the types of innovative entrepreneurial ventures they are likely to nurture. While in some countries government policies and private sector initiatives may promote technology-oriented entrepreneurs, in others, the emphasis may be on social entrepreneurs or in entrepreneurship by vulnerable or disadvantaged segments of the population (e.g., Indigenous groups, women, low-income youth). Some countries focus on entrepreneurship in agriculture, tourism, health, or telecommunications. The types of innovative entrepreneurial ventures in a country will also be dependent on the ratio of necessity-driven versus opportunity-driven entrepreneurs. The opportunity-driven entrepreneur—the scalable startup type—typically aims to grow their business into a large operation and/or be bought out. This is often feasible because there is a novel idea or excitingly innovative product, process, or business model behind the new venture, enabling it to grow into a large domestic or international business with significant core competencies and market share. These types of entrepreneurial ventures require significant infusions of capital to scale up and transform from a small startup into a mature, established business. This is in contrast to necessity-driven entrepreneurs who tend to be much less innovative and scalable, without taking away the value of their ingenuity and risk-taking. Necessity-driven entrepreneurs may or may not be interested in growth, and they are more likely to operate in the informal sector. The entrepreneurial heartbeat of necessity-driven entrepreneurs is clearly discernible in Latin America. Street vendors, open-air marketplaces, and micro and small shops are common, as is finding a skilled person in one's neighborhood that can perform any type of activity (e.g., catering, tailoring, etc.) working out of their homes. These are self-employed entrepreneurs striving to make a living by developing a business that can be used to support their families but who may not be actively pursuing growth opportunities or seeking outside investors.

Innovation and new business formation can have a significant impact on a nation's growth and development leading to employment, productivity, and wealth creation (Anchorena & Ronconi, 2012; Castellani & Lora, 2013; King & Levine, 1993; Schmitz, 1989; Schumpeter, 1934; Wennekers & Thurik, 1999). Entrepreneurship has also been identified as a key mechanism of wealth creation and redistribution that can lead to poverty reduction and expansion of the middle class. Institutionalized support for entrepreneurship can have positive long-term effects, such as improvements to education and talent development, stronger innovative capabilities, and greater inclusivity. Therefore, the important role of entrepreneurship in nurturing creativity and innovation must be supported by strong national business ecosystems (Bosma, et al., 2020; Bosma et al., 2021; Larroulet & Couyoumdjian, 2009; Montealegre, 2012).

The importance of innovation and new business formation leads to the question of what conditions, policies, and institutions spur entrepreneurial activity? In the next two sections, we describe the state of entrepreneurship in Latin America, focusing on attitudes toward entrepreneurship and related behaviors. We also assess the effects of the COVID-19 pandemic on entrepreneurial intentions and activity. Next, we discuss the main factors that support or hinder entrepreneurship in the region and draw conclusions regarding government policies necessary to improve the region's entrepreneurial ecosystems.

The State of Entrepreneurship in Latin America

The Global Entrepreneurship Monitor (GEM) collects data on entrepreneurship for 50 countries. Their studies allow comparison of entrepreneurship in Latin American countries against other regions over time. The GEM annual reports describe the level of entrepreneurial activity based on two dimensions:

1. Entrepreneurial attitudes, perceptions, and expectations of individuals based on a survey of at least 2,000 adults (18–64) in each country; and
2. The national context conditions that impact entrepreneurship based on a survey of at least 36 national experts (see GEM's conceptual framework in Figure 10.1).

Here, we report findings from the 2019/2020 report, which includes Brazil, Colombia, Chile, Ecuador, Guatemala, Mexico, and Panama, and the 2020/2021 report, which includes the same countries plus Guatemala and Uruguay and only entrepreneurial conditions for Mexico and Panama. The 2019/2020 report provides data on entrepreneurial attitudes and activity pre-COVID-19, while the 2020/2021 report provides insights on potential changes to entrepreneurial attitudes and activity as a result of the pandemic (Bosma et al., 2020; 2021).

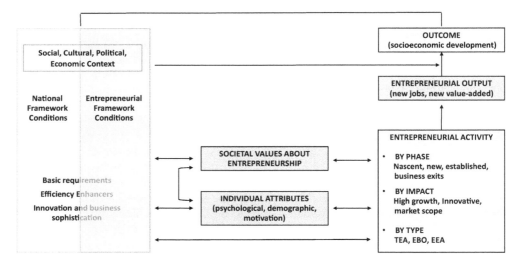

Figure 10.1 Global Entrepreneurship Monitor's conceptual framework. Source: Bosma et al. (2021)

Attitudes and Perceptions toward Entrepreneurship

As entrepreneurship and innovation are individual experiences, it is important to understand the individuals engaged in these activities (Cromie, 1994; Dodd & Anderson, 2007). Findings from the 2019/2020 and 2020/2021 GEM reports indicate that entrepreneurship is well regarded in Latin America (see Table 10.1 for entrepreneurial attitudes and perceptions among adults in eight Latin American countries). A large percentage of adults surveyed in Colombia (58% and 53%), Guatemala (79% and 94%), Panama (66% and 67%), and Uruguay (64% and 65%) agreed that successful entrepreneurs are given a high social status in their respective countries and that entrepreneurship is considered a good career choice. The 2019/2020 GEM report showed that personal affiliation with someone who has started a business is high in the region (~70% of adults in Chile, Colombia, and Guatemala and 45%–50% of adults in the rest of the countries). Perceptions of good opportunities to start a business ranged from 45% to 70% of adults surveyed, and perceptions of having the skills and knowledge needed to start a business were reported by more than 65% of adults surveyed. The intention to start a business ranged from 30%–58% of respondents in most Latin American countries with only 16% of adults in Mexico indicating so. Individuals' perceptions of the ease of starting a business, however, were some of the lowest compared to other regions, ranging from 33% to 57%, with adults in Ecuador and Panama perceiving the least amount of barriers and those in Chile and Colombia perceiving the most barriers. As for other constraints to entrepreneurial activity, six in ten adults in Chile and half of surveyed adults in Mexico reported they would not start a business due to a fear of failure. For all other Latin American countries in the study, between 33% and 41% of adults reported fear of failure as a deterrent to entrepreneurship. Mexico presented the most interesting set of findings: high percentages of adults reported perceived opportunities of (63%) and capabilities for (71%) entrepreneurship and only about half of respondents reported fear of failure as a deterrent or perceived difficulties in starting a business; yet less than one in five Mexicans indicated an intention to start a business within three years. In summary, the 2019/2020 GEM report indicated that Latin Americans perceive rich opportunities for entrepreneurship in the region and feel confident that they have the capabilities needed to pursue these opportunities. Some are deterred by fear of failure, while most are deterred by significant barriers, particularly lack of access to financing and government policies related to taxes and bureaucratic procedures and regulations to start a business (Bosma et al., 2020).

The GEM 2020/2021 report reveals some differences in attitudes toward entrepreneurship across Latin American countries compared to 2019/2020. Some of these changes may be due to the effects of the COVID-19 pandemic (see Table 10.1). The countries with the higher perceived entrepreneurial opportunities were Guatemala (63%), Brazil (57%), and Colombia (48%). Compared to 2019/2020, the percentage of adults that perceived entrepreneurial opportunities increased significantly in Brazil (from 46% to 57%) and marginally in Colombia (47% to 48%). It decreased in Chile, Guatemala, and Panama. In 2020/2021, perceived entrepreneurial capabilities decreased for all countries compared to the previous year, revealing some lost confidence in individuals' ability to succeed, perhaps due to the uncertainty caused by the pandemic. Still, for all countries in the region, around two in three adults agreed that they have the skills and knowledge needed to start a new business. Findings for Brazil yielded some interesting insights: entrepreneurial intentions increased significantly, from 30% to 53%, as did the perception of ease when starting a business (41% from 39%); yet the fear of failure as an obstacle also increased (from 36% to 43%). Thus, while Brazilians saw more entrepreneurial opportunities—even in the midst of the COVID-19 pandemic—and

Table 10.1 GEM 2019/2020 and 2020/2021—Entrepreneurial Attitudes and Perceptions in Eight Latin American Countries

	Perceived Opportunities		Perceived Capabilities		Entrepreneurial Intentions		Fear of Failure Rate		Perceived Ease of Starting a Business	
	% of Adults (2019/2020 %)	Rank/43	% of Adults (2019/2020 %)	Rank/43	% of Adults (2019/2020 %)	Rank/43	% of Adults (2019/2020 %)	Rank/43	% of Adults (2019/2020 %)	Rank/43
Brazil*	57.3 (46.4)	15=	67.8 (62.0)	12	52.7 (30.2)	6	43.4 (35.6)	19	41.4 (39.4)	32
Chile	46.7 (47.6)	26	71.7 (75.5)	10	50.6 (57.6)	8	46.3 (58.1)	15	46.1 (32.9)	29
Colombia	47.9 (46.7)	22	64.8 (72.4)	15	33.9 (35.5)	14	39.5 (32.7)	31	33.2 (36.0)	36=
Guatemala	62.7 (67.3)	10	74.4 (77.4)	8	49.7 (52.2)	9	40.0 (39.6)	29	48.8 (46.6)	27
Panama	47.2 (53.4)	24=	72.7 (72.9)	9	46.1 (40.8)	12	39.8 (40.8)	30	55.9 (57.2)	21
Uruguay*	47.3	23	65.6	13	33.0	15	48.8	9	39.4	33
Ecuador** (2019/2020: rank/50)	(55.9)	20	(78.3)	3	(42.5)	7	(35.1)	=39	55.3	19
Mexico** (2019/2020: rank/50)	(62.8)	15	(70.7)	11	(16.3)	28	(47.7)	12	(50.9)	23
United States***	48.6	21	64.0	17	12.5	29	41.2	27=	68.6	11

Source: Global Entrepreneurship Monitor (2020/2021 and 2019/2020 reports) (Bosma et al., 2020 & 2021).

= Indicates this rank is shared with other countries in the study.

*Uruguay was not included in the 2019/2020 report.

**Ecuador was not included in the 2020/2021 report. Mexico did not participate in the Adult Population Survey for 2020/2021.

***United States percentages and ranks are included for comparison purposes only.

perceived less constraints in starting a business, they cited fear of failure as a deterrent. Chile also offers an interesting case. Compared to 2019/2020, only about half of Chileans continued to perceive entrepreneurial opportunities (47% vs. 48%); they perceived themselves as less capable (72% vs 76%) and were less intent on starting a business within three years (51% vs. 58%), perhaps indicating lower levels of confidence related to the uncertainty caused by the pandemic. A higher percentage of Chileans perceived that starting a business was easy (41% vs. 39%), and less of them cited fear of failure as a deterrent to entrepreneurial endeavors (46% vs. 58%). Compared to all other countries included in the study, Latin American countries ranked high on perceived capabilities and entrepreneurial intentions but ranked lower on perceived ease of starting a business and fear of failure as a deterrent to start a business (see Table 10.1). Governments in the region would do well to streamline regulations and processes related to starting a business so that individuals who perceive entrepreneurial opportunities and feel confident in their ability to do so can, in fact, pursue them.

Entrepreneurial Activity

The GEM data identifies differences on levels and types of entrepreneurial activity prevalent in Latin America. Tables 10.2a–10.2c summarize key measures of entrepreneurial activity in the region:

- Table 10.2a highlights *total early-stage entrepreneurial activity* (TEA) (the percentage of adults who are actively engaged in starting a new business—the *nascent entrepreneur*—plus those owning and managing a business that has been active for up to 3.5 years—the *new business owner*).
- Table 10.2b summarizes *established business ownership* (EBO) rates (percentage of adults owning and managing an established business, defined as businesses that have paid wages for 3.5 years or more).
- Table 10.2c shows *entrepreneurial employee activity* (EEA) (employed workers who engage in entrepreneurship, such as developing or launching new goods or services or setting up a new business unit or subsidiary).

In general, all Latin American countries have consistently high levels of TEA compared to other regions. As was the case for 2019/2020, the 2020/2021 report shows that at least one

Table 10.2a Entrepreneurial Activity in Latin America by Type: (a) Total Early-Stage Entrepreneurial Activity (TEA)

Country	% Adults (18–64)	Total Early-Stage Entrepreneurial Activity (TEA)					
		Rank/43	Female/Male TEA	% Female	Rank/43	% Male	Rank/43
Brazil (20–21)	23.4	7	0.83	21.3	8	25.6	7
Chile (20–21)	25.9	6	0.74	22.1	6	29.9	5
Colombia (20–21)	31.1	4	0.94	30.2	3	32.2	3
Guatemala (20–21)	28.3	5	0.81	25.5	5	31.3	4
Panama (20–21)	32.4	3	0.82	29.1	4	35.6	2
Uruguay (20–21)	21	9	0.84	20.1	10	23.8	9
Ecuador (19–20)	36.2	2	—	33.6	—	38.8	—
Mexico (19–20)	13	19	—	12.4	—	13.6	—

Table 10.2b Entrepreneurial Activity in Latin America by Type: (b) Established Business Ownership (EBO)

	Established Business Ownership (EBO)			
	% Adults	Rank/43	% Female	% Male
Brazil (20–21)	8.7	13	5.4	12
Chile (20–21)	6.1	25=	5.1	7.1
Colombia (20–21)	5.5	30	5.3	5.6
Guatemala (20–21)	12.3	6	9.7	15.1
Panama (20–21)	4.1	38=	2.6	5.5
Uruguay (20–21)	5.1	32=	3.2	7.1
Ecuador (19–20)	14.7	4	11.1	18.3
Mexico (19–20)	1.8	48	1.4	2.3

Table 10.2c Entrepreneurial Activity in Latin America by Type: (c) Entrepreneurial Employee Activity (EEA)

	Entrepreneurial Employee Activity			
	% Adults (18–64)	Rank/43	% Female	% Male
Brazil (20–21)	4.5	15	3.6	5.5
Chile (20–21)	3.2	18	1.3	5.1
Colombia (20–21)	2.1	22	1.4	2.7
Guatemala (20–21)	1.1	28=	0.4	1.8
Panama (20–21)	2.7	19	1.5	3.9
Uruguay (20–21)	0.2	41=	0.1	0.2
Ecuador (19–20)	1.3	33	0.7	1.9
Mexico (19–20)	0.2	47=	0.1	0.2

= Indicates this rank is shared with other countries in the study.
Source: GEM – Global Entrepreneurship Monitor, 2020/2021 and 2019/2020 Global Reports. (Bosma et al., 2020 & 2021)

in five adults reported starting or running a business, and in Colombia and Panama, at least one in three adults reported doing so. From the countries included in both studies, Colombia and Panama both increased their TEA rates by more than 30%, Brazil kept its TEA rate steady, while Chile's TEA rate decreased by more than a quarter. The trend in Chile's TEA rate seems consistent with other measures that indicate lower levels of confidence in Chile among the adults surveyed. An examination of the rates of TEA for countries with different levels of income shows Latin America's high rate of entrepreneurial activity. Among middle-income countries, the three Latin American countries in that group—Brazil, Guatemala, and Colombia—reported the highest levels of TEA; the same was true for the high-income group, in which Uruguay, Chile, and Panama also reported the highest percentages of TEA among all high-income countries.

As for established businesses, compared to 2019, the percentages of adults running an established business (businesses 42 months or older) dropped for four of the countries included in both studies (Brazil, Chile, Guatemala, and Panama) and increased for Colombia (4.3% to 5.5%). Guatemala and Brazil had the highest percentages of established business ownership (12.3% and 8.7%, respectively). Finally, the percentages of EEA were relatively low for all countries in Latin America compared to other regions of the world (rankings fell between 15 for Brazil and 41 for Uruguay out of 43 countries in the study). Compared to 2019, the percentage of adults reporting EEA increased in 2020 for Brazil, Colombia, and

Panama, while decreasing in Chile and Guatemala. The low rates of EEA for Latin American countries seem aligned with GEM's findings that EEA rates are typically higher in high-income economies. Latin American governments should provide incentives for firms to engage in R&D, encourage more collaboration between industry and academia, and improve access to and quality of entrepreneurial education in order to increase entrepreneurial activity by individuals, whether as part of their employment or through independent ventures (GEM Staff, n.d.).

In terms of the type of industry where entrepreneurial activity is occurring, GEM identifies four categories: extractive (including agriculture), transformative (including manufacturing and transportation), business services (including professional services and information and communications technology), and consumer services (including retail, hospitality, and personal services). The percentage of TEA in the extractive sector is small for all Latin American countries, ranging from 1.0% in Colombia to 6.9% in Uruguay, likely a result of the high barriers to entry in this sector. The transformative sector is one of the largest worldwide; across the six Latin American countries, it represented between 22% and 28% of all TEA. The 2020/2021 GEM report found that no country had less than half of its early-stage entrepreneurial activity in either the business or consumer services sector; and for three-quarters of the 43 countries in the study, these two sectors represented over 60% of all new businesses. In Latin America, consumer services represented between 50% and 67% of all TEA in the region. Business services, on the other hand, represented between 6.3% (Guatemala) and 20% (Chile) of TEA. This aligns with GEM's findings that business services are more common in developed economies, while consumer services are more common in low-income countries because of lower entry barriers. Consumer services were some of the hardest hit by the pandemic; thus, the region's overall entrepreneurial activity suffered (see Figure 10.2).

Next, we summarize findings on early-stage entrepreneurial activity by age, gender, and education level for the six Latin American countries in the GEM study (Bosma et al., 2021).

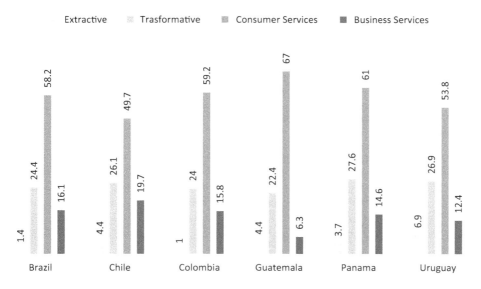

Figure 10.2 TEA by sector

The relationship between age and entrepreneurial activity yields mixed results (see Figure 10.3). Although younger people may have more energy, drive, and ambition and have 'less to lose' by embarking on entrepreneurial ventures and may be more technology savvy, they may lack financial resources, experiences, and broad social networks. Older people, on the other hand, may have more resources and experience, but they may have more responsibilities and commitments, and entrepreneurial ventures may represent a higher risk for them. For all countries in the GEM study, entrepreneurial activity seems to increase with age and then decline. Latin America was not the exception: in three of the Latin American countries (Brazil, Colombia, and Uruguay), the percentage of adults starting new businesses was highest for the group 25–34 years of age; in Chile and Panama, it was highest among the 35–44-year-olds. The lowest percentages of TEA for all countries from the region were observed among the 55–64 age group (12.6 to 20.8%).

In terms of gender, the ratio of female to male TEA in the region ranges from 0.74 in Chile to 0.94 in Colombia. Between 24% (Uruguay) and 36% (Panama) of males are involved in early-stage entrepreneurial activity, while between 20% (Uruguay) and 30% (Guatemala) of females report starting or running a new business. Regarding established business owners, the ratios of female to male are much lower, ranging from 0.45 (Uruguay and Brazil) to 0.72 (Chile), with Colombia being the only country out of the six with a female/male EBO ratio similar to that seen for TEA (0.95). The percentage of males reporting running an established business ranged from 5.5% (Panama) to 15.1% (Guatemala), while the percentage of females running an established business ranged from 2.6% (Panama) to 9.7% (Guatemala).

Finally, the GEM reports that, globally, TEA among graduates (i.e., those who have completed at least a post-secondary degree) tends to be higher than among non-graduates. This is the case in Latin America as well, except for Brazil, where non-graduates are slightly more likely to start a new business than graduates. Thus, in Latin America, entrepreneurs tend to be younger (25–44), male, and educated.

The GEM report also provides information on the outcomes and impact of entrepreneurs in terms of job creation and export sales (see Table 10.3). On the basis of entrepreneurs planning to hire six or more employees within five years, countries in Latin America ranked high compared to other regions in the world (ranks were between 1 for Colombia and 13 for Uruguay). In Brazil, the percentage of adults reporting an intention to hire rose significantly from 2% in 2019 to 8% in 2020. Chile, on the other hand, ranked 8/43 on the expectation to hire, but that rate dropped from 13% to 9% in 2020.

Effects of the COVID Pandemic on Entrepreneurial Attitudes, Perceptions, and Activity

Our discussions in Chapters 3 and 6 highlight some of the national and business environment conditions that may hinder the competitiveness of businesses in Latin America as well as the levels and types of risk and uncertainty prevalent in the region. Although it may seem counterintuitive, it has been argued that uncertainty spurs innovation and entrepreneurship—that is, difficulties and uncertainties in the marketplace may lead to the development of innovative goods or services as well as new business models that can ultimately yield competitive advantages (Ernst & Young, 2013; Porter, 1990). Currently, the main source of short-term uncertainty is the ongoing COVID-19 pandemic. The GEM 2020/2021 report tried to determine the effects of the COVID-19 pandemic on entrepreneurial attitudes, perceptions, expectations, and activity (Bosma et al., 2021). We highlight some of their most interesting findings below.

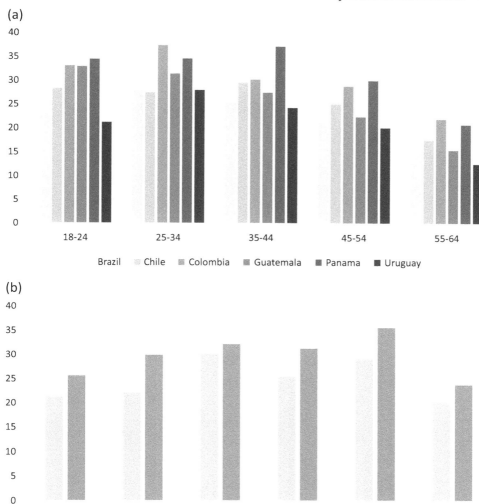

Figure 10.3 (a, b) TEA by age and gender (%) Source: Bosma et al., 2021

In Latin America and Caribbean countries, except for Uruguay, more than 50% of adults knew someone who had started a business because of the pandemic. This was a much higher percentage than the less than 10% of adults reported in the Europe and North America group, for example. In addition to cultural differences, it is likely that lower incomes and the absence of social support systems (e.g., unemployment benefits) may explain the higher rates of entrepreneurship observed in low- and middle-income countries where people may turn to self-employment for economic survival. Comparing the percentages of those who know someone who has started a business versus those who know someone who has stopped a business, only two of the Latin American countries—Panama and Colombia—have higher proportions of adults knowing someone who had started a business than knowing someone

Table 10.3 Outcomes and Impact of Entrepreneurial Activity in Latin America

Countries	Entrepreneurship Outputs and Impact									
	Job Creation Expectations (Plan to Hire 6+)*		International (25%+ Revenue from Abroad)		National Scope for Customers and New Products and Processes		Global Scope for Customers and New Products and Processes		Industry (% TEA in Business Services)	
	% Adults	Rank/43	% Adults	Rank/43	% Adults	Rank/43	% Adults	Rank/43	% Adults	Rank/43
Brazil*	8.4	9	0.3	35=	1.1	24=	0.1	30=	16.1	26
Chile	9.2	8	0.4	31=	2.6	9	0.3	21=	19.7	21=
Colombia	16.8	1	2.2	7=	5.1	4	1.3	1=	15.8	27=
Guatemala	6.3	10	0.5	28=	0.9	27=	0.1	30=	6.3	36
Panama	13.9	3	2.1	10	7	2	1.1	5	14.6	30
Uruguay	4.6	13=	0.4	31=	1.8	16=	0.2	26=	12.4	32
Ecuador* (2019/2020; Rank/50)	8.6	3=	0.7	29=	1.2	32=	0.1	34=	8.1	41
Mexico (2019/2020; Rank/50)	3	21	0.5	35=	0.7	39	0.1	34	6	44

Source: Global Entrepreneurship Monitor – GEM, 2019/2020 and 2020/2021 Global Reports. (Bosma et al., 2020 & 2021)
*Unless otherwise noted, the data reported is from the GEM 2020/2021 report.
**Data for Ecuador and Mexico from the 2019–2020 GEM report is included here to provide a broader perspective on entrepreneurial differences among countries in the region.

who had stopped a business because of the pandemic. The contrast between regions can be best observed by the ratio of these two percentages. For all countries in the Latin America and Caribbean region, the ratio ranged from 0.9 to 1.2, indicating the percentages of adults knowing 'stoppers' and 'starters' were very similar. Meanwhile, about 75% of countries in the Europe and North America region had a ratio of more than two to one (i.e., more adults were likely to know a 'stopper' than a 'starter'). Regarding intentions to start a business within three years, those being influenced by the pandemic ranged from a low of 35% in Brazil to a high of 64% in Panama. For established business owners, the perceived new growth opportunities because of the pandemic varied from 35% among Chileans to 51% among Panamanians.

Although the full effects of the COVID-19 pandemic are still unknown, we can make some conjectures. As the analysis on entrepreneurial activity above shows, the mass displacement of workers will likely lead to an increase in necessity-driven entrepreneurial activity by those seeking a source of income. The business closures have also led to opportunity-driven entrepreneurship, as individuals and firms find creative and innovative solutions to the provision of products demanded by both consumers and businesses. Entrepreneurial activity and innovation in areas such as marketing communications, commerce, product development, and logistics is likely to take place, led by both independent entrepreneurs and those employed by firms seeking to survive and thrive during and after the pandemic.

In the next section, we explore the entrepreneurial ecosystem in Latin America and highlight key conditions in the national contexts that drive or hinder entrepreneurial activity.

The Entrepreneurial Ecosystem in Latin America

Contextual conditions can either nurture entrepreneurs or hinder them. The GEM's Entrepreneurial Framework Conditions (EFCs) incorporate nine factors to assess the entrepreneurial environment of countries. These conditions are measured through a National Expert Survey (NES) of at least 36 carefully selected national experts (four per EFC) for each country. The nine EFCs are (Bosma et al., 2021, p. 76):

1. *Access to entrepreneurial finance.* Sufficient funds are available to new startups, from informal investment and bank loans to government grants and venture capital.
2. *Government policies*
   2.1 *Government policy: support and relevance.* Government policies promote entrepreneurship and support those starting a new business venture.
   2.2 *Government policy: taxes and bureaucracy.* Business taxes and fees are affordable for the new enterprise. Rules and regulations are easy to manage without undue burden on the new business.
3. *Government entrepreneurship programs.* Quality support programs are available to the new entrepreneur at local, regional, and national levels.
4. *Entrepreneurial education*
   4.1 *Entrepreneurial education at school.* Schools introduce ideas of entrepreneurship and instill students with entrepreneurial values such as enquiry, opportunity recognition, and creativity.
   4.2 *Entrepreneurial education post-school.* Colleges, universities, and business schools offer effective courses in entrepreneurial subjects alongside practical training in how to start a business.

5. *Research and development transfer.* Research findings, including from universities and research centers, can readily be translated into commercial ventures.
6. *Commercial and professional infrastructure.* There are sufficient affordable professional services such as lawyers and accountants to support the new venture within a framework of property rights.
7. *Ease of entry*
   7.1 *Ease of entry: market dynamics.* Free, open, and growing markets where no large businesses control entry or prices.
   7.2 *Ease of entry: market burdens and regulations.* Regulations that facilitate entry.
8. *Physical infrastructure.* Adequate physical infrastructure, internet access and speed, and the cost and availability of physical spaces are adequate and accessible to entrepreneurs.
9. *Social and cultural norms.* Degree to which national culture encourages and celebrates entrepreneurship through the provision of role models, mentors, and support for risk-taking.

Latin America's entrepreneurial ecosystem is weak. None of the seven Latin American countries in the GEM 2020/2021 study rated above 7.5 (on an 11-point scale) for any entrepreneurial framework condition. At the regional level, the weakest performance for the region was in entrepreneurial education at school, access to financing for entrepreneurs, and government policy: taxes and bureaucracy (regional averages of 2.6, 3.6, and 3.6, respectively). The region performed best in the EFCs of physical infrastructure, post-school entrepreneurial education, and cultural and social norms (regional averages of 6.6, 5.4, and 5.2, respectively). At the country level, Colombia performed the best among the middle-income countries, and Uruguay performed the best among the high-income countries. Colombia's strengths were in post-school entrepreneurial education, physical infrastructure, and cultural and social norms, in that order. Uruguay's strongest EFCs were physical infrastructure, post-school entrepreneurial education, and governmental entrepreneurship programs, in that order. Among middle-income countries, Guatemala had the weakest entrepreneurial conditions, especially in the areas of entrepreneurial education at school, government policy: support and relevance, and government entrepreneurship programs, in that order. Among the high-income countries, Panama's context was the weakest, particularly on entrepreneurial education at school, R&D transfer, and access to entrepreneurial financing. Although none of the countries in the region offers a context overly attractive or supportive of entrepreneurship, they all have strengths and weaknesses. The region offers adequate and accessible physical infrastructure (roads, internet access, physical spaces), cultural receptiveness and support of entrepreneurship, and practical entrepreneurship training by higher education institutions. The region must improve its offerings of entrepreneurial education at the primary and secondary levels to instill basic skills in opportunity recognition and creativity, reduce rules and regulations that make it difficult to start and run businesses, and increase access to financing. It should be noted that the regulatory and institutional weaknesses observed in the entrepreneurial ecosystem of Latin America likely explain, at least in part, the high levels of informality in the region. Entrepreneurs may start informal businesses as a way to circumvent the inefficiencies and corruption of the region's regulatory environments. This, in turn, will likely motivate entrepreneurs to limit their growth in order to avoid attracting the attention of regulatory enforcers, thus, condemning these ventures to narrow product and market scopes, low productivity, minimal job creation, and low revenues and profits. Governments should encourage the formation of opportunity-driven, scalable entrepreneurial ventures that flourish as formal business entities. Thus, there is an urgent need to improve the business regulatory environment in the region (Larroulet & Couyoumdjian, 2009).

Compared to 2019, the country-level measures seem to indicate some of these improvements are taking place. In 2020, Brazil saw a decrease to its score on 'access to financing,' and its score for 'government policy: taxes and bureaucracy' remained low (2.4, 44/45); however, the country improved its 'ease of entry: market dynamics' (5.8 to 6.6, 6/45), 'ease of entry: burdens and regulations' (3.9 to 4.1), and 'social and cultural norms' (3.7 to 4.8). In the case of Colombia, the country improved many of its EFCs, a true accomplishment given the difficulties 2020 presented. Gains in the areas of 'entrepreneurial financing' and 'government entrepreneurship programs' were minor, but gains to 'entrepreneurial education at school and post-school' were more significant (3.1 to 3.6 and 5.3 to 6.6, respectively). Worthwhile improvements were also noted in 'social and cultural norms' (4.7 to 5.6) and both 'ease of entry' scores, indicating the domestic market was both more receptive to new products and services and less constrained by regulations. Guatemala also saw some improvements to its EFCs. As the country's scores are quite low relative to other GEM countries, any improvements are seen as positive developments. Guatemala registered small increases to its scores of 'access to entrepreneurial financing,' 'government policy: support and relevance,' and 'government entrepreneurship programs.' More significant improvements were seen in 'R&D transfers' (2.6 to 3.4), 'social and cultural norms' (4.5 to 5.2), and 'ease of entry: market burdens and regulations' (3.2 to 3.7). Additional easing of regulations for entrepreneurs, including reducing taxes and bureaucracy, will strengthen Guatemala's entrepreneurial environment. Finally, Panama saw marked improvements to 'access to financing,' 'government policy: taxes and bureaucracy,' 'commercial and professional infrastructure,' and 'social and cultural norms.' The most significant gains were to the EFCs of 'government policy: support and relevance' (2.6 to 3.7), and 'government entrepreneurship programs' (4.0 to 4.5). The improvements to the three government-related measures and more favorable 'social and cultural norms' condition may suggest increasing support of entrepreneurs in Panama.

Sadly, the 2020/2021 GEM study also showed some reversals in entrepreneurial conditions. Mexico saw a sharp decline in its EFCs scores, especially in the three government-related conditions: 'government policy: support and relevance' (from 4.0 to 2.6, 43/45), 'government policy: taxes and bureaucracy' (from 3.7 to 3.2, 33/45), and 'government entrepreneurship programs' (from 4.4 to 3.4, 38/45). Scores for 'ease of entry: market burdens and regulations,' 'physical infrastructure,' and 'social and cultural norms' also dropped significantly from 2019. Chile also experienced declines across most of its EFCs, particularly 'access to financing' (3.8 to 3.3, 41/45), 'ease of entry: market burdens and regulations' (3.9 to 3.4, 37/45), and all three 'government-related conditions.' These declines are likely reflected in the gap between the experts' assessments of Chile's governmental and entrepreneurial responses to the pandemic discussed below (Bosma et al., 2020; 2021).

Uruguay's performance based on the 2020/2021 GEM report showed that Uruguay outscored all other countries in the region in several of the EFCs. The country performed exceptionally well on 'physical infrastructure' (7.5, and highest in the region), 'entrepreneurial education post-school' (6.6, same as Colombia and second overall among all GEM countries), 'government entrepreneurship programs' (6.4, highest in the region and second among all GEM countries), and 'government policy: support and relevance' (4.9, highest in the region and thirteenth overall) (Bosma et al., 2021).

The region scored moderately well in two other conditions: 'commercial and professional infrastructure' and 'ease of entry: market dynamics.' This indicates entrepreneurs have access to sufficient and affordable professional services to support new business formation and to markets that are open and growing. Maintaining the latter will be especially challenging in the years to come due to the negative effects of the pandemic. Some have suggested that the presence of a large middle class drives entrepreneurial activity; this idea seems in line with the EFC of 'ease of entry: market dynamics.' As Castellani and Lora (2013) state, middle-class individuals have the resources and values to postpone gratification and, thus are more likely to invest in innovative ventures that may yield benefits in the long term. Given the growth of Latin America's middle class, one could assume that this has led to increases in entrepreneurship in the region and, in turn, economic growth. Although the presence of a middle class alone is not sufficient to drive entrepreneurship and growth (Anchorena & Ronconi, 2012), it is, nonetheless, an important factor. As discussed in Part I of the book, the pandemic has pushed many in Latin America into poverty, and at this time, it is difficult to predict what the medium-term effects of this economic sliding will be on the size and dynamism of regional markets.

See Figures 10.4a, b for a summary of framework conditions for middle-income and high-income Latin American countries in the GEM studies.

Finally, in 2018, the GEM introduced the *National Entrepreneurship Context Index* (NECI). This is a single measure that summarizes the average state of a country's entrepreneurial environment. The NECI score is the mean of a country's EFC scores, and it is measured on an 11-point Likert scale from 0 to 10, where a score of 5.0 is considered as 'just sufficient.' None of the Latin American countries in the 2020/2021 study received a score of 5 or higher, with Uruguay scoring the highest (4.88) and Guatemala the lowest (3.97). The region has a long way to go in creating the type of ecosystems needed for new businesses to be created and for established businesses to grow and flourish. Moreover, the devastating effects of the COVID-19 pandemic on the region's economies behooves policymakers to take aggressive action to correct the structural barriers currently faced by entrepreneurs. According to the experts' assessments, the regional governments' responses have been dismal when compared to those of entrepreneurs. Responses by the region's governments received scores ranging from 2.86 (Mexico) to 6.38 (Uruguay), versus entrepreneurs' responses, which received ratings ranging from 6.84 (Uruguay) to 7.54 (Guatemala). It is worth noting that in some of the countries where governments' responses to the pandemic were the most deficient, entrepreneurial responses were scored highly (Mexico, 2.86 vs. 6.86; Guatemala, 3.60 vs. 7.54; and Brazil, 3.88 vs. 7.44). The gaps between governmental (G) and entrepreneurial (E) responses to the pandemic are most obvious when one looks at rankings on both these measures. For instance, Chile's governmental response ranked 23/45 vs. the country's entrepreneurial response, which ranked 9/45. Similar gaps were observed for Brazil (G-33 vs. E-6), Guatemala (G-36 vs. E-3), Mexico (G-43 vs. E-12), and Panama (G-25 vs. E-2). One exception was Uruguay, where both the responses by governments and entrepreneurs received similar scores (6.38 and 6.84, and ranks of 10/45 and 13/45, respectively). Thus, where governments have failed, entrepreneurs across the region have continued to step up to meet the challenges of the pandemic, demonstrating high levels of resiliency and innovative capabilities.

In summary, Latin Americas' entrepreneurs face barriers of insufficient financing and burdensome and inefficient regulatory systems and lack of entrepreneurial education injected into school curricula. The entrepreneurial ecosystems in the region are strongest in terms of offering sufficient and accessible physical and commercial infrastructure, access to entrepreneurial training, and cultural acceptance and support of entrepreneurs. The countries offer various levels of governmental support programs for entrepreneurs and open and growing markets—though this may have shrunk due to the pandemic. Many countries showed improvements to their entrepreneurial environment in 2020, even amidst the economic

(a)

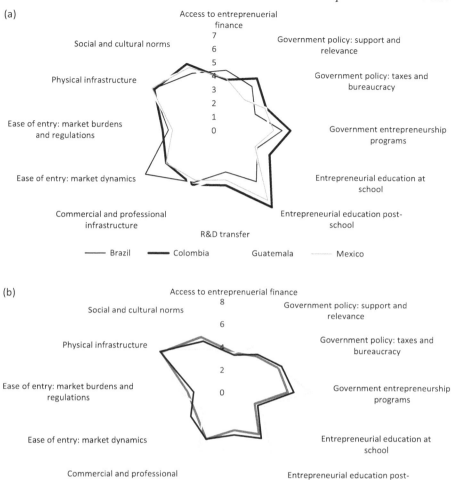

Figure 10.4 (a, b) Environmental framework conditions for select Latin American countries. (a) Middle income countries. (b) High income countries

and social challenges the COVID-19 pandemic entailed. There is ample room for additional improvements to the entrepreneurial environment if the region is to leverage entrepreneurship and innovation to raise its overall competitiveness vis-à-vis other regions.

Hotbeds of Entrepreneurship

Tech Entrepreneurs

Latin America still has a long way to go to nurture and support innovation to the levels necessary to drive productivity and competitiveness. Yet it is also true that innovation is receiving increasing attention (and funding) from both the public and private sectors. One type of entrepreneur that is highly coveted by the region's national governments and investors is the 'tech entrepreneur.' Technology startups thrive in fast-paced, rapidly changing, and highly uncertain environments, and Latin America's highly volatile economic environment is a hotbed for technological entrepreneurs from home and from the rest of the world. We focus our attention on these two types of entrepreneurs next, with particular attention given to high performing tech entrepreneurs.

Home-Grown Tech Entrepreneurs in Latin America

The new tech entrepreneurs in Latin America are highly educated and highly skilled. Many, for example, are engineers or computer science professionals who have pursued graduate education in business at local, American, or European institutions. In addition, many have worked abroad for international companies before pursuing an entrepreneurial venture. The tech entrepreneurs who study outside of Latin America generally do so with two motivations in mind: to broaden their exposure to a more entrepreneurially focused curriculum than might be available closer to home and/or to establish a broader network of contacts that might be leveraged when establishing a business venture post-graduation.

Universities in the United States—as in other countries—are actively seeking to attract this highly skilled, highly educated Latin American talent pool through coursework, international alumni outreach programs, and online communities. Columbia University, for example, offers coursework in a special program called Entrepreneurship and Competitiveness in Latin America (ECLA). The ECLA Program is an executive program for entrepreneurial leaders of medium-sized companies who seek specialized training to expand their business beyond borders and compete in changing environments. This one-year certificate program targets Latin American entrepreneurs that wish to fine-tune their entrepreneurial skills and training (The ECLA Program, n.d.). The University of Pennsylvania's Wharton School sponsors entrepreneur networking events in Latin America as part of its Global Alumni Forums. An online community was launched in spring 2013 in Cambridge, Massachusetts specifically targeting Latin American entrepreneurs and professionals interested in business and/or economic development in Latin America (Knowledge at Wharton, 2013). There is clearly an effort underway to harness the tech talent in Latin America and link it to universities or other entrepreneurial communities in the United States and Europe.

Attracting World Entrepreneurs to Latin America

Looking for a few good tech startups! That is the message that is implicitly heard time and time again from Latin American governments seeking foreign investors from the high-tech sector. Where local tech entrepreneurs are scarce, or simply where 'more is preferable,' government recruitment programs have been implemented to attract them. Startup Chile is among the region's most highly publicized programs aimed at attracting tech entrepreneurs.

In 2010, Chile began a program known as Start-Up Chile aimed at attracting tech startups to Chile through a highly competitive process, enticing them with seed money, office space, one-year temporary visas, and facilitation of introductions with key business contacts and networks within the country. Since its inception, Start-Up Chile had high expectations as the goal was not simply to attract innovative tech startups and talent from the world over, but rather to transform Chile into the innovation and entrepreneurship hub of Latin America. Start-Up Chile sought to capitalize upon one of Silicon Valley's weaknesses—immigration constraints—to entice international entrepreneurs to Chile. Three years after the program's inception, the organization had worked with more than 1,300 entrepreneurs and 700 projects from 65 countries. Start-Up Chile has adapted overtime, expanding and changing its programs to align with its goals. By 2020, Start-Up Chile entrepreneurs had raised over $2 billion in capital and had generated a similar amount in global sales. The program boasts 5,000 alumni from 85 countries and a portfolio of more than 2,000 startups valued at more than $5 billion (Start-Up Chile, n.d.).

This program has garnered so much media attention that Brazil, Colombia, and Mexico have sought to replicate its mission. While these countries have embraced Start-Up Chile's ideals, the tactics used by each of these countries to attract entrepreneurs have been adapted to local needs and local political realities. Brazil is not as willing as Chile to use government funds to support non-Brazilian entrepreneurs. Brazil, instead, has opted to strengthen its venture capital industry. Colombia, like Chile, is jockeying to become Latin America's next innovation hub and, as a result, has invested in venture capital, established local accelerators, promoted role models and mentoring among entrepreneurs, created co-working spaces, and used government funds as seed money for laudable entrepreneurial initiatives. The establishment of various accelerators and incubators[1] (see Table 10.4) has helped Latin America to become a hotbed for tech startups.

In addition, access to financing has led to an explosion of tech startups in Latin America. Venture capital invested in the region grew from US$2.2 billion in 2017 to US$13.1 billion in 2021. Brazil has captured most of this growth, accounting for 77% of the total number of startups (more than 17,000) and 70% of the investments into the region in 2021 alone. Mexico occupies second place, accounting for 8% of startups in the region (more than 1,800) and 13% of investment. Chile takes the third place in the number of startups (5%; more than 1,100), while Colombia takes third place in terms of investment share (7%). The ten startups that attracted the most investment in the period 2015–2021 raised a total of US$14 billion, about 40% of the US$36 billion total raised by Latin American startups during that period. Seven of these ten were Brazilian (including Nubank, CG Bank, Stone and Loft), one was Colombian (Rappi), one was Argentinian (Mercado Libre), and one was Mexican (Kavak) (Pompeo, 2021).

One of the most interesting events occurring in the region is the emergence of so-called unicorns—tech startups that are not publicly listed that have reached a value of at least US$1 billion. The first unicorn in Latin America was Mercado Libre (the Argentinian firm that has become the largest e-commerce platform in Latin America), which reached this status in 2007. It was joined in 2015 by Decolar (a Brazil-based firm that has become the largest online travel agency in Latin America). Until 2017, these were the only two unicorns in the region. In 2021, the number of unicorns in Latin America jumped to 34. Brazil has the largest number of unicorns (60%), followed by Argentina (17%), and Mexico (11%) (Pompeo, 2021). More recently, other mythological creatures have emerged, namely decacorns and hectacorns—high-tech startups valued at more than US$10 billion (e.g., Canva) and over US$100 billion (e.g., TikTok), respectively in the private investment market. In Latin America, only Brazilian fintech Nubank has reached the status of a decacorn, reaching US$30 billion in value in 2019. A few Latin American unicorns that are starting to approach the US$10 billion mark include Mexican Kavak (US$8.7 billion), Colombian Rappi (US$5.3 billion), and Brazilian firms QuintoAndar and CGBank (both valued at US$5 billion) (Park, 2021).

The main reason for the sharp growth in the number of unicorns is the increasing infusion of foreign capital into Latin America. Of the 15 top investors in the region, 12 are from outside the region. Japanese-based Softbank, for instance, is the top investor, with 13 startups in its portfolio; Tiger Global and Endeavor—both from the United States—have 11 and 10 unicorns in their portfolios, respectively. The growth of unicorns during 2021 was also

Table 10.4 Incubators and Accelerators of Tech Startups in Latin America

Name of Accelerator/ Incubator	Country	Main Mission/Activities	Impact (Measures of Impact)
NXTP Labs	Argentina (based); Chile, Colombia, Mexico, and Uruguay	Focuses on B2B companies (pre-seed and seed-stages), particularly e-commerce, fintech, and data-driven businesses	130+ investments 6 unicorns in portfolio
Start-Up Chile	Chile	Provides funding for high potential entrepreneurs from all over the world willing to base their firms in Chile	Other countries have followed Chile's lead and made their own publicly funded accelerator programs
500 Startups LatAm	Mexico	Most active early-stage investment fund	170+ companies
Parallel18	Puerto Rico	Inclusive and innovative entrepreneurship	US$189 million revenue generated by their startups
ACE	Brazil	Helping startups attain global reach	450+ startups have gone through their program
Acelera MGTI	Brazil	Supports tech startups and startups with a global vision	Alumni include Moip, Midhaz, and Contentools
Wayra	Argentina, Brazil, Chile, Colombia, Mexico, Peru, and Venezuela	Functions as an accelerator and incubator Portfolio of services: funding, consulting, networking, connections to Europe	Invested in 800 startups, helped drive the creation of more than 10,000 high-skilled jobs, and helped generate €285 million in revenues with entrepreneurs
SociaLab	Argentina, Chile, Colombia, Mexico, Uruguay, and Brazil	Supports early-stage entrepreneurs that are solving social problems in innovative and internationally sustainable fashions	Worked with more than 40 organizations, US$842,000 in seed capital, created more than 10,000 impact solutions all in 2020
Ruta N	Colombia	Focuses on developing projects in the science, technology, and innovation fields	As of 2019, Ruta N has helped to create 3,000 new jobs and has welcomed more than 150 local and international businesses
Innpulsa	Colombia	Initiative of Colombia government, works with a range of fields	In its first 4 years, used US$161.6 million to support entrepreneurship and innovation
CUBO Itau	Brazil	Creates solutions to build major market innovation in the tech field	The revenue of Cubo startups reached BRL US$4.4 billion in 2020, a growth of 1.552% over the previous year
SUM-Start-up Mexico	Mexico	To position Mexico as the bridge of innovation and economic engine between Latin America and the most developed markets	Worked with hundreds of startups/companies, creating many jobs

Source: Elaborated by the authors with information from corporate websites.

Table 10.5 Unicorns (and Other Horned Creatures) in Latin America

Name	Country	Description of Industry/Sector/ Products/Technologies	Highlights (e.g., value, revenues, market share, geographic scope, etc. – Based on 2021 data)
Nubank	Brazil	Fintech: online banking	$41.5 billion valuation in 2021; $1.06 billion in revenue in first 9 months of 2021
Rappi	Colombia	On demand delivery app	$5.25 billion valuation in 2021; $220 million revenue in 2018
Despegar	Argentina	Traveltech: travel agency	$722.02 million market cap
iFood	Brazil	Foodtech: ordering and delivery app	More than 80% market share
99	Brazil	Mobility: e-hailing app	Merged with Didi in 2018 to expand in Latin American market
PagSeguro	Brazil	Fintech: online payment platform	$9.41 billion market cap
Ascenty	Brazil	Deeptech: data center firm	Largest provider of Data Center services in Latin America
Stone Pagamentos	Brazil	Fintech: payment solutions company	$5.97 billion market cap
Gympass	Brazil	Healthtech: fitness discovery platform	$2.92 billion valuation
Loggi	Brazil	Logtech: same day delivery app	$1 billion valuation
Quinto Andar	Brazil	Real estate: online marketplace for residential rentals	5 visits every minute, $5.1 billion valuation
Ebanx	Brazil	Fintech: payment processor for international companies in Brazil	In 15 Latin American countries, more than $1 billion valuation
Wildlife Studios	Brazil	Mobile gaming company	More than 2 billion downloads, $1.3 billion valuation
Prisma Medios de Pago	Argentina	Fintech: payment company	More than 60 issuers in Latin American countries, more than 7 million collecting entities and service companies, more than 600 million company and business users
Loft	Brazil	Real estate: marketplace for real estate	$2.2 billion valuation
VTEX	Brazil	Retailtech: e-commerce platform	Operates in more than 32 countries with more than 2,500 online stores, $1.88 billion market cap
C6 Bank	Brazil	Fintech: full service online bank	Latin America's largest independent investment bank with 7 million clients
Kavak	Mexico	Mobility: online marketplace for cars	$8.7 billion valuation

(Continued)

Table 10.5 Continued

Name	Country	Description of Industry/Sector/ Products/Technologies	Highlights (e.g., value, revenues, market share, geographic scope, etc. – Based on 2021 data)
MadeiraMadeira	Brazil	Online marketplace specializing in home products	$1 billion valuation
Creditas	Brazil	Fintech: online collateral loan platform	Offices in three countries, $1.75 billion valuation
Hotmart	Brazil	Edtech: platform for the distribution of digital products	More than 29 million users in 188 countries, more than 200 languages, more than $1 billion valuation
Mercado Bitcoin	Brazil	Fintech: cryptocurrency exchange	More than 3 million customers, $2.1 billion valuation
Unico	Brazil	Deeptech: provides digital identity protection solutions	More than $1 billion valuation
Nuvemshop	Brazil	Retailtech: online retailer	90,000 clients, $3.1 billion valuation
Clip	Mexico	Fintech: allows businesses to easily accept all electronic payments methods	$2 billion valuation
Bitso	Mexico	Fintech: cryptocurrency exchange	More than 3 million users, more than 27 million trading transactions, $2.2 billion valuation
NotCo	Chile	Foodtech: produces plant-based foods	$1.5 billion valuation
Cornershop	Chile	Logtech: grocery delivery	More than $3 billion valuation
Mural	Argentina	Adtech: digital workspace for teams to collaborate virtually	Trusted by more than 90% of Fortune 100 companies, more than $2 billion valuation; tripled annual recurring during past 2 years
Ualá	Argentina	Fintech: personal finance management app	Issued 2 million cards, $2.45 billion valuation
dLocal	Uruguay	Fintech: cross border payments	Operates in three regions, $1.2 billion valuation
Kio Networks	Mexico	Deeptech, IT services	$1 billion valuation in 2021
Mercado Libre	Argentina	Operates online marketplaces	$66.09 billion market cap (June, 2021); $6.27 million revenue for past 12 months
Arco Educação	Brazil	Edtech	$1.1 billion valuation; net revenue of R$256.3m in 2021 for second quarter
Gymtech	Brazil	Healthtech	$1 billion valuation

Sources: Elaborated by authors with information from corporate websites, plus the following: LABS-Latin America Business Stories (2021); Lima (2021); Pompeo (2021); Yahoo Finance.

driven by high levels of mergers and acquisitions, primarily of Brazilian firms (84% of all startups acquired in the region since 2018 were Brazilian). In 2020, a total of 200 startups were acquired; by August 2021, 195 startups had already been acquired. While investments into startups are led by foreign investors, mergers and acquisitions of startups are led by Latin American firms, mainly Brazilian ones (eight of the ten biggest buyers in 2021 were Brazilian companies). Among the most important acquirers of startups were Brazilian mega-retailer Magazine Luiza, which has acquired 25 startups; Brazilian software management company Linx, with 17 acquisitions; and Brazilian IT service management company Locaweb, with 16 acquisitions. About a quarter of all acquired startups were retail techs, 15% were fintechs, and 13% were food techs (Pompeo, 2021).

Finally, corporate venture capital (CVC) has also played a role in the growth of startups in the region, particularly foodtechs. Argentina, Brazil, Chile, Colombia, and Mexico have the largest numbers of foodtech companies in the region, with Brazil commanding the sector (123 foodtechs out of 323 for the region). The sector has raised more than US$1.7 billion in the last decade, 64% of which was raised between 2020 and 2021. As an example, Frubana, a Colombian platform that supplies small restaurants, raised US$25 million in 2020 (America Economia, 2021a). The need to satisfy the demand for food products for the large and growing Latin American consumer market may explain some of the attraction of foodtechs. Latin America is also a major world producer of agricultural products that is being seriously impacted by climate change; transforming agricultural and food production into more sustainable sectors will require innovation and technology adoption. Moreover, the COVID-19 pandemic has accelerated the adoption of technologies in the sector. Technology adoption can help entrepreneurs in the food sector eliminate or reduce inefficiencies, optimize the use of resources, and strengthen connections along the value chain aimed at both reducing costs and improving quality of products. The three main types of foodtechs are logistics and data management (22%), sales (17%), and organic, natural, and healthy food products (16%). The three main categories of foodtechs in terms of growth (i.e., number of employees, revenues, and profits) are logistics and data management, sales, and transportation and distribution. Finally, the percentage of foodtechs that have internationalized is only 26%, but, in some countries, the percentages are much higher (49% in Argentina and 52% in Chile), indicating high levels of growth in both domestic and international markets. This dynamic and competitive landscape makes access to capital critically important. CVC has filled some of this financing need. Large corporations such as Bimbo, Coca Cola, and AB InBev have all invested in foodtech startups in Latin America, particularly those in logistics and data management and transportation and distribution (America Economia, 2021a).

The environment for the emergence of unicorns is more favorable in some countries than others. Nurturing environments have led to successful unicorns such as Uala, Aleph, Mural, and Tiendanube in Argentina; Kavak and Clip in Mexico; and Norco in Chile. Brazil is the most attractive startup market in the region for several reasons. First, Brazil is the largest market in terms of population and GDP, which increases the potential success and scalability of B2C startups (America Economia, 2021b). This is reflected in the country's GEM score for 'ease of entry: market dynamics' of 6.6, the highest in Latin American (Bosma et al., 2021). Second, over the past several decades, Brazil has gradually established a business-friendly environment for entrepreneurs in general, and tech startups in particular. This mature ecosystem includes regulatory frameworks, technology parks, incubators and accelerators, sources of financing, and collaboration initiatives between research universities, government, and companies (de Miranda Oliveira, et al, 2019). Peru and Ecuador lack startups with the potential to become unicorns, primarily due to lack of access to financing, low levels of government support, and low levels of innovation. There are also insufficient support organizations and programs such as incubators, accelerators, and mentoring and training programs in the latter countries. The scarcity of venture capital, especially seed capital and early-stage funding, is also a major obstacle for tech startups in the region. This impacts the ability of 'soonicorns' (i.e., Latin American firms founded after 2012 with a valuation of over US$100 million or which raised over US$20 million in their last investment round) to raise the capital needed to become unicorns (America Economia, 2021b). See Table 10.5 for a list of the most important unicorns in Latin America.

It is undeniable that tech entrepreneurship has grown significantly in Latin America, with tech hubs emerging in São Paulo, Santiago de Chile, and Mexico City. Nevertheless, tech entrepreneurship in the region faces some barriers, mainly talent shortages and lack of access to financing. Not only is entrepreneurial education lacking (as discussed earlier in this chapter), but Latin America's education systems, in general, lag behind those of other developed and emerging countries. As mentioned in Chapter 4, the OECD's PISA tests (2018) showed that, in spite of some minor improvements, students from participating Latin American countries (Argentina, Brazil, Chile, Colombia, Costa Rica, the Dominican Republic, Mexico, Panama, Peru, and Uruguay) are two to three years behind in reading, mathematics, and science relative to a student from an OECD country. This gap grows for students from more disadvantaged backgrounds (Di Gropello et al., 2019). The educational systems in the region are mired by issues such as lax regulations controlling the quality of educational offerings, poor access to educational technology, and a disconnect between curricula and the needs of the job market. This is compounded by the social inequalities that limit access to educational opportunities, especially among low-income youth, women, and other socially marginalized groups. This puts Latin America's youth at a significant disadvantage vis-à-vis talent from other regions of the world and makes it extremely difficult for tech entrepreneurs in the region to hire the talent they need to grow their businesses. As discussed in Chapter 4, Latin America is an aging region past its 'demographic bonus.' Investments in human capital that focus on high-level skill building, by both public and private sectors, will be the best way to raise productivity and improve competitiveness in the region. In addition, there is a need to diversify the talent pool by improving the inclusivity of educational systems across the region, especially in STEM fields. In this sense, tech startups themselves can contribute to human capital development by offering digital solutions aimed at closing the education and skill gaps that exist in the region (Costa Checa, 2019).

Women Entrepreneurs in Latin America

Women entrepreneurs are valuable agents of economic growth and development, contributing to poverty reduction, job creation, social empowerment, and quality of life improvements for themselves and their families. In this section, we summarize key descriptors of women entrepreneurship in Latin America and briefly discuss barriers for Latin American women entrepreneurs and initiatives to remove them.

The Mastercard Index of Women Entrepreneurs (MIWE) tracks the working and business environments of 58 countries to assess how successfully each country is advancing women entrepreneurialism in comparison to other countries. The MIWE uses 12 indicators and 25 sub-indicators to rank each economy according to its performance over the past year along three components:

- *Component A—women's advancement outcomes*: women entrepreneurial activity rate (F/M), women labor force participation (F/M), women business leaders (F as a % of Total), and women professionals & technical workers (F%T).
- *Component B—knowledge assets & financial access* (that allow women to transit, survive, and thrive): support for SMEs, women borrowing/saving for business (F/M); women financial inclusion (F/M), and women tertiary education enrollment.
- *Component C—entrepreneurial supporting conditions* (that strengthen the continued role and progress of women): ease of doing business, cultural perceptions of entrepreneurs, quality of governance, and entrepreneurial supporting factors.

These indicators correspond to our earlier discussion on the factors that drive or inhibit entrepreneurial activity in a country, including institutionalism, access to financing, human capital development, presence of role models and networks, and government-led support. The index aggregates data for these various indicators to provide an 'overall grade' on how well a country is performing on its ability to advance women's progress in business, in general, and entrepreneurship, in particular. In most cases, changes in a country's performance will reflect the effects of gender-focused policies and investments implemented by the country.

According to the 2020 MIWE, a score of 60–70 indicates an economy is successful in advancing women entrepreneurship. Seven of nine Latin American countries included in the study scored 60 or higher, consistent with the GEM 2020/2021 findings showing six Latin American countries ranked in the top ten in percentage of female adults engaged in TEA activity. Colombia is the top performer in the region (66.2), ranking 14th among the 58 economies included in the MIWE. The country climbed ten positions from 2019. This was driven by a moderate female entrepreneurial activity rate (21% of working-age women are entrepreneurs) and very high representation of women business leaders (57% F/T) and women professionals and technical workers (54% F/T). Chile and Argentina round the top three positions among Latin American countries. Argentina, Brazil, and Mexico also improved their scores and positions. Chile, Costa Rica, Ecuador, Peru, and Uruguay all dropped positions relative to 2019, although all the countries, save Ecuador, saw improvements to their scores (see Table 10.6).

Brazil and Mexico, the two largest economies in the region, performed in the middle of the pack (62.4 and 62.1, respectively). Both countries improved their scores and rankings from 2019, but both still have work to do removing barriers that hinder women's advancement in business. Brazil, for example, had a low level of financial inclusion before the

Table 10.6 Women Entrepreneurship in Latin America

Country	MIWE Score 2020	MIWE Score 2019	% Change from 2019 to 2020	2020 Rank/58	Rank 2019	Change in Ranking from 2019
Colombia	66.3	62.7	5.8	14	24	10
Chile	63.4	62.7	1.1	27	23	− 4
Argentina	62.9	60.0	4.8	29	35	6
Brazil	62.4	59.1	5.6	32	37	5
Mexico	62.1	58.9	5.5	34	38	4
Uruguay	61.3	60.4	1.5	35	31	− 4
Costa Rica	60.9	60.5	0.7	36	30	− 6
Peru	59.7	59.5	0.3	39	36	− 3
Ecuador	58.0	58.1	−0.3	41	40	− 1

Source: Mastercard Index of Women Entrepreneurship – 2020.

COVID-19 pandemic, with only 67% of women having a bank account, compared to more than 90% of all women in countries such as Australia, Japan, and Switzerland. The pandemic may have a positive effect, increasing financial inclusion for all Brazilians, including women. Caixa (Brazil's government-owned bank) reported receiving 11 million new requests from informal workers in a span of two days to open bank accounts needed to receive government emergency assistance funds during the pandemic. Access to smartphones and internet connections should also facilitate digital banking (Mastercard Index, 2020). In the case of Mexico, the country needs to improve the entrepreneurial support conditions for women, including ease of doing business, support of SMEs, and women's ability to save and borrow for business purposes.

Effects of the COVID-19 Pandemic on Women Entrepreneurs in Latin America

Although the COVID-19 pandemic has had some positive effects on entrepreneurial activity in Latin America (see our discussion above on innovation and tech entrepreneurs), it has had a devastating effect on women entrepreneurs in the region. According to MIWE, women were disproportionately more vulnerable to the disruptions caused by the pandemic, with more than 50% of companies led by women in Brazil, Argentina, Ecuador, and Uruguay being negatively affected by the pandemic (Mastercard Index, 2020; Zanini Graca, 2021). The GEM 2020/2021 data showed that the Latin America and Caribbean region registered the highest levels of business closures among all participating regions (8.5% women-owned and 7.1% men-owned ventures). Although the pandemic was the main reason for business exit in 2020 for all entrepreneurs across all regions, Latin American women entrepreneurs were the most impacted (57.5% of women vs. 48.4% of men). This disproportionate impact on women entrepreneurs may be explained by (1) the sectors most affected by the pandemic are those with more women workers and entrepreneurs: tourism and hospitality, retail, food services, and entertainment and recreation services and (2) women were disadvantaged by pre-existing gender gaps, such as inferior digital and technical skills, financial exclusion, disproportionate burden of household and family duties, and overrepresentation in the informal sector (Mastercard Index, 2020).

Nevertheless, the pandemic also generated opportunities for women entrepreneurs globally, including in Latin America. The MIWE report indicated that some women adapted by tapping into new business opportunities or changing their business models to better respond to changes in consumer needs and behaviors.

> We can see this as 42% have shifted to a digital business model, 37% are developing an area of business to meet local or global needs, and 34% have identified new business opportunities since the pandemic. The desire to transform and be nimble has strengthened women business owners' resilience, and will certainly be needed in helping their economies on the path to recovery.
>
> (Mastercard Index, 2020, p. 7)

This is consistent with the GEM 2020/2021 finding that entrepreneurial intention among Latin American women entrepreneurs improved, especially in Brazil, Chile, and Colombia and that women had better growth expectations than men for both early-stage entrepreneurial activity and established businesses. There is, therefore, positive indications that women entrepreneurs in the region have adopted an optimistic attitude though a conservative approach to entrepreneurship, collaborating with others in their ecosystems, and adopting more agile, technology-based business models in order to survive and thrive during and after the pandemic.

Barriers to Women Entrepreneurship

The proportion of women entrepreneurs in Latin America is high compared to other regions. In 2020, the six Latin American countries in the GEM study reported that between 20% and 30% of all female adults were engaged in TEA activity, and between 3% and 10% were established business owners (Bosma et al., 2021). These figures are encouraging, but barriers remain. Past research on women entrepreneurship in Latin America has identified lack of access to financing sources, biases and stereotypes that disadvantage women in the institutional environment, poor access to information and networks, and challenges in balancing family responsibilities and work life as some of the factors that prevent women from starting and developing businesses. The national entrepreneurial context thus constrains women's ability to capitalize on opportunities and grow their businesses (e.g., Aidis et al., 2015; Avolio Alecchi, 2020; Baughn et al., 2006; Boitano, 2017; Heller, 2010; World Bank, 2010; ILO, 2019; Terjesen & Amoros, 2010; Welter, 2011). Here, we focus on three key barriers to women entrepreneurship: limited access to financing and credit, lack of mentoring and networking opportunities, and the asymmetric distribution of paid/unpaid work.

Access to Financing and Credit

Access to financing and credit has been consistently noted as one of the main barriers to women entrepreneurs in Latin America (Heller, 2010, ILO 2019). Overall, funding for women's entrepreneurial ventures in the region is extremely limited, with only 20% of the funding needed being provided by financial institutions. A study commissioned by the IDB's Multilateral Investment Fund showed that 70% of high-growth women entrepreneurs and 84% of low-growth women entrepreneurs finance their early-stage entrepreneurial ventures through savings and funds from family and friends, compared to 62% of high-growth male entrepreneurs (Ernst & Young, 2014). Moreover, according to the GEM 2018/2019 report, lack of profits and funding problems was responsible for 56% of business closures among women entrepreneurs in the region (Zanini Graca, 2021). Reporting on the lack of women's financial inclusion in relation to the challenges derived from the pandemic, the Mastercard Index for Women Entrepreneurs (2020, p. 39) noted that 'For women business owners seeking loans to pay workers' salaries or to boost reserves for rental payments, the challenge of lower credit scores due to low wages or credit standing is disqualifying them from obtaining loans.' Yet there are signs that the situation is improving, with women increasingly being able to access financing sources ranging from seed capital and investment funds for early-stage entrepreneurial ventures (e.g., NXTP Labs, Sercotec's Capital Abeja Emprende) to crowdfunding and microloans (e.g., Pro Mujer). Policies and initiatives aimed at increasing financial inclusion of women is an important first step, but in order to close the existing financing gap, banks and investors will need to remove any other perceptual and structural barriers that prevent women entrepreneurs from obtaining the loans and investments needed to start and scale up their ventures.

Mentoring and Networking

Another challenge cited by women entrepreneurs in Latin America is the lack of access to role models and networks that could provide support and advice to would-be entrepreneurs. Mentors can share their own experiences and networks and can help coach entrepreneurs during the early stages of venture formation. Networks are essential for making connections to financing sources and potential supply chain partners, as well as tapping into talent pools and gaining market information. In many cases, networks also provide access to education and training and customizable services. Progress on this front is observed throughout the region, with new initiatives such as Pro Mujer's 'Mujeres de Cambio' (Women Changemakers), which offers mentoring, networking, and training for women entrepreneurs, and IDB Lab's initiatives WeXchange and WISE. For instance, WISE (Women in STEM Entrepreneurship), which first launched in 2018, provided mentoring resources for more than 1,500 women founders of science- and tech-based startups in its first three years of operation. (See Table 10.7 for a summary of accelerators, incubators, and other support programs for women entrepreneurs in Latin America.)

Table 10.7 Accelerators and Other Support Programs for Women Entrepreneurs in Latin America

Name of Organization	Country	Mission/Activities	Impact
NXTP Labs-Mujer Emprendedora	Argentina	Fostering Argentina's women entrepreneurship	Accelerated 59 female startups and invested in 27
WeXchange – IDB Lab	All of Latin America	Early-stage ventures, mentorship, business networking, funding through venture idea competitions	Organizes annual forums across Latin America
WISE-Women in STEM Entrepreneurship (partnership of the IDB Lab and IAE Business School)	Argentina, Peru, Colombia, and Ecuador	Supporting women in STEM	Has provided mentoring resources to more than 1,500 women who founded science and tech-based startups
Laboratoria	Peru	Trains women computer engineers	More than 2,000 graduates, more than 800 contracting companies, 2.7x average salary increase
Start-Up Chile, Female Founder Factor	Chile	Looking for female founders with high-impact ventures as part of gender parity program	$10 million Chilean pesos available for participants
Sebrae Delas	Brazil	Helps small businesses to compete on equal footing with larger companies	700 service centers throughout the country, experts in every field to help
Capital Abeja	Chile	Dedicated to supporting small and micro-businesses, as well as entrepreneurs	$200,000 CLP to $500,000 CLP available for business management actions and $2,800,000 CLP to $3,300,000 CLP for investments

Sources: Elaborated by the authors with information from corporate websites, plus the following: Lestch (2020).

Distribution of Paid and Unpaid Work

Finally, the undue burden carried by Latin American women of unpaid work related to family responsibilities is a major barrier to women's entrepreneurial activities (Figure 10.5 shows these proportions for select countries in the region). Mexico, Peru, and Chile registered the highest number of total paid and unpaid work hours for women (65, 62, and 62, respectively). Not only do the total hours of paid and unpaid work tend to be higher for women, but their unpaid hours are also higher. The average number of unpaid work hours per week for women ranged from 22 in Brazil to 43 in Mexico. Compared to men's work hours, women's unpaid work hours were between 1.5 and 6 times those worked by men, with Guatemala being at the high end (6 for men vs. 36 for women) and Cuba at the low end (20 for men vs. 35 for women). The burden of unpaid work constrains women's ability to work outside the home: women's paid work hours did not exceed 23 hours for any of the countries in Figure 10.5, suggesting most women likely work in part-time positions (ECLAC, n.d.; ILO, 2019). These time limitations will impact self-employed women as well, curtailing their ability to pursue high-growth, scalable entrepreneurial opportunities. Government policies and regulations can play an important role in rebalancing family and work responsibilities among men and women. For example, paid parental leave that requires fathers to take a portion of the total leave allowed for the family, and thus assume some of the early child rearing responsibilities, could have a positive effect on speeding up women's return to work, whether as an employee or as a business owner.

Removing the abovementioned barriers has driven the recent growth and success of women tech entrepreneurs. Some examples of female founders of tech startups include Mexico's healthtech Unima and online payment platform Conekta; Peru's Laboratoria, which provides computer science training and placement for women; and Ecuador's Kushki, a digital payment platform (Lestch, 2020). The rise of female STEM entrepreneurs in the region can be explained by the confluence of several factors: the emergence of incubators and accelerators focused on supporting women, mentoring, and networking initiatives by both public and private organizations, more financing options, and government support programs. For instance, it was reported that a 2018 survey of 50 startups selected for accelerator programs found 28% of them had female founders. NXTP Labs, one of the most active accelerator programs in the region, has accelerated 59 startups with female entrepreneurs and invested in 27 (Lestch, 2020). Similarly, IDB Lab's WeXchange initiative offers women STEM entrepreneurs in Latin America opportunities to connect with mentors and investors, access to training, and the opportunity to receive seed funding through a pitch competition. One example is Mexican healthcare startup Unima, which had successfully raised US$2.5 million in venture capital and grants by 2020, allowing the firm to scale up its operations (Letsch, 2020). Finally, Start-Up Chile has a commitment to gender parity, whereby women are expected to lead half of the startups in each of the accelerator's cohorts (Start-Up Chile, n.d.).

Social Entrepreneurs

Social entrepreneurs establish ventures dedicated to solving social and environmental challenges by applying business principles (Tan, Williams, & Tan, 2005). Social entrepreneurial ventures take the form of altruistic businesses that aim to benefit a segment of society via innovation (Tan et al., 2005) or enterprises that apply for-profit models to create shared value for the company and for a segment of society (Porter & Kramer, 2011; Porter, 2012). In Latin

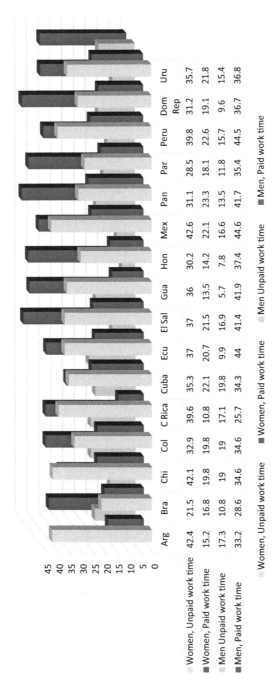

Figure 10.5 Distribution of paid and unpaid work* for select countries in Latin America and The Caribbean (2019). *Average time spent on paid and unpaid work of the population aged 15 and over, by sex, by country for 2019 (Average hours per week). Source: Adapted from United Nations-ECLAC, Gender Equality Observatory for LatinAmerica and the Caribbean. https://oig.cepal.org/en/indicators/total-work-time . Source: United Nations-ECLAC, Gender Equality Observatory for Latin America and the Caribbean. https://oig.cepal.org/en/indicators/total-work-time

America, social entrepreneurs have embraced these ventures to solve its more pressing social and environmental problems. The GEM 2020/2021 study found that at least half of all adults in the Latin American countries surveyed by GEM, with the exception of Uruguay, indicated that 'making a difference in the world' was a main motivation for starting a business. Guatemala had the largest percentage with this main motivation (76%, ranked 2/43), the other four LAC countries ranged from 58%–67%. Countries in the region, with the exception of Uruguay, ranked in the top 10 of the 43 countries in the GEM study (Bosma et al., 2021). Tech startups are leading the way (Palma, 2019). For instance, Brazilian startup Home Agent enables women to work from at-home contact centers, allowing women—who make up 90% of the company's workforce—to customize their schedules, so they can balance work and family responsibilities. Ecovec, another Brazilian startup, uses GPS-enabled traps to monitor and predict epidemic outbreaks. In Mexico, SalaUno offers easy access to cataract surgery at subsidized costs, thus providing an option to the thousands facing blindness due to a lack of healthcare access.

Programs that support social entrepreneurship in Latin America are flourishing. Agora Partnerships, for instance, aims to accelerate the success of early-stage impact entrepreneurs through consulting and capability building, facilitating partnership formation, strengthening the entrepreneurial ecosystem, and inclusive financing. Agora Partnerships has supported women's agricultural cooperatives, employment for marginalized youth in Nicaragua, and post-disaster relief in Haiti. As one of the first impact investors in Latin America, Agora has pioneered financial instruments to support social entrepreneurs in the region (Agora Partnerships, 2021). Ashoka, a global non-governmental organization (NGO) with nearly 3,000 members worldwide, has a strong presence in Latin America, including in Central America, Brazil, and Argentina. Ashoka provides support services, a global network of business and social contacts, and startup financing to entrepreneurial ventures with a social impact component. Finally, state-sponsored programs, such as Brazil's BNDES angel fund, Start-Up Chile, and Mexico's Fund of Funds, also provide support and funding to social entrepreneurs.

Many for-profit businesses in Latin America have also implemented business models with a triple-bottom approach (financial, human, environmental), so-called 3P businesses (profits, people, planet). Many of these businesses are focused on having a positive impact on reducing the effects of climate change and/or serving the needs of vulnerable and underserved populations. For instance, CEMEX's Patrimonio Hoy initiative offers home building solutions to low-income families in Mexico, Colombia, Costa Rica, Nicaragua, and the Dominican Republic. Other examples are Nutrivida in Costa Rica (nutritional food), Natura in Brazil (environmentally sustainable personal care products), Tecnosol in Central America (alternative energy), Mejoramiento Integral Asistido-MIA in Mexico (low-income housing), Frogtek in Mexico (information technology to support small retailers), and Pixza in Mexico (restaurant supporting homeless youth).

Despite the strong presence of social ventures in the region, Latin American countries still lack the kind of entrepreneurial ecosystems needed to encourage the formation of more socially oriented ventures. For instance, governments should (a) modernize the archaic tax and business regulatory systems that create disincentives for the formation of social enterprises by allowing B-Corp incorporation, currently available only in Argentina, Brazil, Chile, Colombia, Ecuador, Mexico, Paraguay, Peru, and Uruguay; (b) invest in human capital development aimed at enhancing entrepreneurial and technical skills early in life, especially among marginalized communities; and (c) open access to seed financing via grants, subsidies, targeted promotion programs, and collaborations with private investors.

Entrepreneurial startups eventually grow into SMEs. Opportunity-based and high-impact entrepreneurs, in particular, are likely to seek growth, domestically and internationally, as soon as they are able. The next section describes some key characteristics of SMEs in Latin America, identifies barriers to SMEs' growth and internationalization, and examines some initiatives aimed at improving the business environment for SMEs in the region.

Small- and Medium-Size Businesses in Latin America

A Profile of SMEs in Latin America

The SMEs (or PYMES in Spanish) are important economic actors in Latin America. Variables used to classify SMEs include number of employees, revenue, and assets (Ferraz & Ramos, 2018). SMEs comprise the bulk of the private sector, both formal and informal (ILO, 2016). There are an estimated 1.5 million SMEs in Latin America, representing 90% of all private sector firms and 60%–70% of formal employment. According to the Inter-American Development Bank (IDB, n.d.), accounting for microenterprises would add another 26 million firms to this total, with the majority of microenterprises operating in the informal market. Despite their large numbers, SMEs' contribution of 25% to the total region's GDP is relatively low (ILO, 2016), suggesting there is significant potential to enhance their growth and performance. Most Latin American SMEs are concentrated in the domestic market, particularly in small-scale agriculture and services (e.g., wholesale and retail trade, food, hospitality). In terms of their internationalization, only about 10% of all SMEs in Latin America export part of their production, a low percentage when compared to Europe, where about 40% of SMEs are exporters (CEPAL, n.d.; Ferraz & Ramos, 2018; Francis et al., 2013; OECD/CAF, 2019; Veiga, 2021).

Barriers to Growth for Latin America's SMEs

At the heart of SMEs' growth challenges is a lack of access to adequate financing. SMEs need options to finance their growth; otherwise, they are exposed to economic shocks, constrained in making capital investments and adopting new technologies, and unable to purchase inventory and make timely payments to suppliers or employees. In 2017, the financing gap for Latin American SMEs was estimated to be US$1.2 trillion, the second largest in the world, behind the East Asia region (IDB, n.d.; IFC, n.d.). In Argentina and Peru, 78% and 45% of all SMEs face growth constraints due to lack of access to financing (Abumohor, 2020). The ITC (2019) estimates that closing the financing gap for SMEs in developing countries would have a positive effect in helping them to achieve many of the SDGs directly related to economic growth and innovation (SDGs 8 and 9).

Access to credit is also limited. MSMEs in the region receive only 12% of total credit, about half the share received by their counterparts in OECD countries. Only 17% of the region's SMEs use bank credit to finance short-term working capital needs (versus 29% of large companies), and only 22% use it for fixed asset financing (versus 34% of larger companies) (IDB, n.d.). CEPAL showed that, in Costa Rica, 70%–73% of SMEs financing came from personal savings, about 11% came from personal and business credit/loans, and 4% from suppliers' credit. In Mexico, 30% of small businesses and 40% of medium-size businesses had external financing, primarily from banks. In Brazil, 52% of SMEs relied on suppliers' credit, and at least 20% of them indicated not accessing any form of external financing. A small percentage relied on loans from family and friends (14%) or informal lenders (3%) (Ferraz & Ramos, 2018). Given the size of the informal sector in Latin America, the financing gap is likely to be much larger than official figures suggest. Requirements and interest rates imposed by banking institutions can make accessing credit restrictive, slow, and expensive for SMEs. A 2018 study by BSLatAm comparing the levels of banking and financial services adoption in eight Latin American countries showed that MSMEs lagged behind large firms significantly, with banking rates ranging from 15% to 65% for MSMEs versus 75%–95% for larger firms. Closing this gap will require broadening available financing options (e.g., accelerators, crowdfunding platforms, fintechs), capacity building programs that prepare SMEs to secure credit and attract investment, and reforming the financial services sector in areas such as access, inclusivity, and transparency (Abumohor, 2020; Veiga, 2021;Vega, 2020).

Other main challenges of Latin America's SMEs are limited access to business contacts and networks, weak technical and managerial skills, and low levels of technology adoption and innovation. Various programs have been implemented that aim to enhance the growth and competitiveness of SMEs in the region and increase their efficiency and efficacy in order to realize their full potential (e.g., job creation, sustainable production, consumer innovations, wealth accumulation). Governmental policies have focused on streamlining and modernizing regulatory and administrative procedures, providing business training and trade assistance, and creating spaces for collaboration with other economic actors (i.e., larger firms, non-profits, academic institutions, and government) (OECD/CAF, 2019). More programs supporting SME development are clearly needed. Some examples include:

- Brazil's Ministry for Micro and Small Enterprises' *To Think Simple (Pensar Simples)* initiative, launched in the early 2010s, has sought to reduce the time and number of procedures required to open and close a business by creating an electronic portal and one-stop shop (America Economia, 2013a).
- The European Union launched a US$5 million, five-year program (2009–2013) to help internationalize 1,200 SMEs in Guatemala. These SMEs were in sectors such as, artisanal crafts, agro-products, home decoration, energy, infrastructure, and information technology (América Economía, 2013b).
- National Export Promotion Organisms, such as PRO ECUADOR, PROESA (El Salvador), and PROMPERU focus on assisting SMEs' internationalization through training and education, export assistance, networking, online commerce facilitation, financing, and more (Frohmann et al., 2016).
- Programs sponsored by the Inter-American Development Bank (IDB), the Central American Bank of Economic Integration (BCIE for its Spanish initials), and the International Finance Corporation (IFC). In 2020, the IDB approved a US$150 million line of credit to support the recovery of Panamanian SMEs affected by the COVID-19 pandemic to strengthen the country's agricultural and food processing sectors. In 2021, the BCIE and IFC also made a US$100 million line of credit available to SMEs from the Northern Triangle (Guatemala, El Salvador, and Honduras) to support the recovery and reactivation of SMEs, particularly those in the agricultural, renewable energy, tourism and hospitality, construction, and communication sectors. The funds will aid SMEs by providing working capital and funding for skill building and business process improvements (Central America Data, 2021a, 2021b).

Strategies Pursued by Latin America's SMEs

SMEs have strategic choices to make to stay relevant in the competitive landscape of the region; they may specialize in a niche market through a customized product offering, internationalize, and/or insert themselves into a global value chain. We discussed niche marketers, including SMEs, in Chapter 7 and briefly discuss SMEs' insertion into global value chains in Chapters 3 and 11. We focus next on the internationalization of SMEs as a potential growth strategy. We close the section with an overview of strategic responses by Latin American SMEs to the COVID-19 pandemic.

Internationalization of Latin America's SMEs

Internationalization is a process by which SMEs can access new foreign markets and/or inputs from foreign suppliers. The easiest way for SMEs to internationalize is through international trade. In 2010–2015, only 1% of Latin American firms were exporters (Park et al., 2019). According to CEPAL (n.d.), during the 2008–2014 period, about 90% of Latin American exporting firms were SMEs. These SME exporters accounted for a quarter of employment of all exporters and 6% of the region's total export value. In contrast, the European Union SME exporters generate 47% of total export value. The OECD/CAF (2019) estimates that about half of all firms that begin exporting abandon the activity within a year, and only around 62% of SMEs that export one year remain exporters the following year (versus 85% of large firms) (Frohmann et al., 2016; Veiga, 2021). The very low percentage of Latin American firms engaged in exporting (less than 1%), the low percentage of export sales value generated by Latin Americas' SMEs (6%), and the low staying power of SMEs in the export sector (62%) suggest there are significant obstacles and limitations to their internationalization.

Barriers to the internationalization of Latin American SMEs include lack of technical knowledge (e.g., exporting documentation and logistics), cultural constraints (e.g., language barriers, lack of understanding of foreign consumers), insufficient financing to meet escalating costs, lack of access to business contacts abroad, and weak innovative capabilities (i.e., adapting business models, processes, and offerings to meet international requirements and demand) (EU-LAC Foundation, 2017; Frohmann et al., 2016; Veiga, 2021). Digitalization and the adoption of information technologies have the potential to help SMEs overcome these multiple barriers to internationalization (Veiga, 2021). Incorporation of the following digital tools may allow internationalizing SMEs:

a) Easier and faster communication with customers and suppliers abroad through the use of communication platforms and applications (Microsoft Teams, Zoom, etc.).

b) Implementation of lower cost marketing strategies, effective branding, and communication strategies through the use of data analytics, social media platforms, and virtual B2B and B2C marketplaces (Alibaba, Amazon, Mercado Libre, etc.).

c) Access to market information through the leverage of data analytics, online research software, artificial intelligence, and machine learning technologies that enable SMEs to learn customers' needs and preferences, test ideas, and anticipate and/or respond to consumer complaints, etc.

d) Adoption of electronic payment systems that are secure and easy for consumers to access, regardless of geographic location.

e) Access to global financing sources, especially those offered by fintechs and crowdsourcing platforms.

f) Use of electronic tools for business transactions that do not require the parties involved to be physically present (electronic documents, electronic signatures, etc.).

SMEs Responses to the COVID-19 Pandemic

Most recently, the COVID-19 pandemic has pushed SMEs in Latin America to transform their business models, develop new products and services, and adopt technology-based operational processes. The lockdowns, extended quarantines, and economic fallout of the pandemic has hurt Latin American SMEs. CEPAL (2020) estimated that by the end of 2020, 2.7 million businesses (about 20% of the total for the region) and 8.5 million jobs (8% of the region's total) would be lost in Latin America because of the pandemic. For MSMEs, the percentage of business closures and jobs lost were estimated at about 21%, 7%, and 3%, respectively. Comparatively, business closures and job losses among large firms were estimated at less than 1% (0.6%). Most SMEs did not have the financial reserves, liquidity, or credit access needed to survive—even in cases in which governments tried to provide some relief. For those that have managed to stay in business, flexibility, adaptation, and innovation have been key. An example of this is the digitalization of operations and services. It is estimated that only 3% of SMEs were selling online before the pandemic, but by mid-2021, about a third of all SMEs had changed their commercial models, offering online sales via social networks and virtual market platforms and adopting apps that allowed for no-contact delivery of services (Sanchez, 2021; Veiga, 2021). SMEs should continue to embrace digitalization and automation in at least four areas: financial management, human resources management, customer service, and analytics. The potential benefits include better financial planning and resource allocation, stronger data management security, more accurate market information, and higher utilization of self-managed internal services, among others. Adoption of new technologies could also lead to cost reductions, new product development, and access to new markets (Sanchez, 2021; Veiga, 2021).

Summary

There is no doubt that the entrepreneurial climate in Latin America is being transformed, yet there is much work that remains to be done before entrepreneurs and small business owners in Latin America can experience a high level of public and private sector support. One example of Latin America's accomplishment is the availability of venture capital and other sources of financing. Although more investors are betting on the region and banking institutions are more open to lending to entrepreneurs and small business owners, sources of capital remain woefully insufficient to support both early-stage entrepreneurs and small businesses seeking to scale up.

Policymakers must continue to build strong institutions that support entrepreneurs and SMEs as well as promote innovation across all sectors of their economies. Streamlining of regulatory procedures and more favorable regulation and taxation policies that can enhance the entrepreneurial environment should be implemented. National economic policies that create spaces and incentives for collaboration between entrepreneurs, scientists, larger businesses, and government are also needed to spur higher levels of information and knowledge dissemination and innovative capacity building. This may require a renewed commitment to new and improved physical infrastructure (e.g., transportation and logistics, internet access).

Entrepreneurial skills can be developed through education in the sciences and technology but also via business skills and management training. Training in management and business skills for entrepreneurs should be broadly accessible and not just limited to certain demographic groups. Educators at all levels might also play a role in this regard by championing curricular reforms that promote critical thinking, creativity, and technical skills.

Finally, the private and public sectors must strengthen their commitment to social and economic inclusion. The business ecosystems in the region must be open and accessible to all entrepreneurs, regardless of gender, socioeconomic status, or level of education. The diversity of talent in the region must be fully leveraged if the region is to not only enhance its productivity and competitiveness but also find viable solutions to its social, economic, and environmental challenges.

Note

1 Business incubators are typically shared physical spaces where entrepreneurs can develop and grow ideas, many offer mentoring and networking. Business accelerators help startups 'gain speed' by setting timeframes for testing ideas, developing working plans, etc. Many provide funding, mentoring, and connections to business partners and funding sources (Mercer, 2021)

References

Abumohor, A. (2020). How fintechs can build trust with SMEs in Latin America. Crowdfund Insider. www.crowdfundinsider.com/2020/03/159239-how-fintechs-can-build-trust-with-smes-in-latin -america/

Agora Partnerships. (2021). Official website. https://agora2030.org/

Aidis, R., Weeks, J., & Anacker, K. (2015). The global women entrepreneur leaders scorecard 2015: From awareness to action. Dell Technologies. Executive Report. www.dell.com/learn/us/en/vn/ corporate_secure_en/documents_2015-gwel-scorecard-executive-summary.pdf

América Economía. (2013a). Ministro apuesta por reducir de 180 a 5 días la apertura de pymes en Brasil. http://www.americaeconomia.com/node/103705

América Economía. (2013b). UE contribuyó a internacionalización de 1200 Pymes de Guatemala. September 13. www.americaeconomia.com/ node/100932

América Economía. (2021a). Foodtechs Latinoamericanas despiertan el apetito del capital de riesgo: Levantan más de US$ 1.000 millones en el último año. https://www.americaeconomia.com/negocios -industrias/foodtechs-latinoamericanas-despiertan-el-apetito-del-capital-de-riesgo-levantan

América Economía. (2021b). Emprendimiento en Peru y Ecuador: Ecosistemas que aún no logran convertir startups en unicornios. https://www.americaeconomia.com/negocios-industrias/ emprendimiento-en-peru-y-ecuador-ecosistemas-que-aun-no-logran-convertir

Anchorena, J., & Ronconi, L. (2012). *Entrepreneurship, entrepreneurial values and public policy in Argentina*. Inter-American Development Bank. Working Paper Series No. 316.

Avolio Alecchi, B. (2020). Toward realizing the potential of Latin America's women entrepreneurs: An analysis of barriers and challenges. *Latin America Research Review*, 55(3), 496–514. https://doi.org /10.25222.larr.108

Baughn, C. C., Chua, B., & Neupert, K. E. (2006). The normative context for women's participation in entrepreneurship: A multicountry study. *Entrepreneurship Theory and Practice*, 30(5), 687–708. https://doi.org/10.1111/j.1540-6520.2006.00142.x

Boitano, A. (2017). La etnia y el género en relatos de mujeres profesionales e intelectuales mapuche: Tradición y emancipación. *Latin American Research Review*, 52(5), 735–748. https://doi.org/10 .25222/larr.239

Bosma, N., Hill S., Ionescu-Somers, A., Kelley, D., Levie, J., & Tarnawa, A. (2020). *The global entrepreneurship monitor 2019/2020 global report*. London, UK: Global Entrepreneurship Research Association. https://www.gemconsortium.org/report/gem-2019-2020-global-report

Bosma, N., Hill, S., Ionescu-Somers, A., Kelley, D., Guerrero, M., & Schott, T. (2021). *The global entrepreneurship monitor 2020/2021 global report*. London, UK: Global Entrepreneurship Research Association. https://www.gemconsortium.org/report/gem-20202021-global-report

Casanova, L., Cahen, F., Miroux, A., et al. (2019). Innovation in emerging markets: The case of Latin America. *AIB Insights, 19*(2), 8–12.

Castellani, F., & Lora, E. (2013). *Is entrepreneurship a channel of social mobility in Latin America?* Inter-American Development Bank. Working Paper Series No. 425.

Central America Data. (2021a). Panamá: $150 millones para PyMEs. https://www.centralamericadata .com/es/article/home/Panam_150_millones_para_PyMEs

Central America Data. (2021b). Avalan $100 millones para PyMEs del Triangulo Norte. https:// www.centralamericadata.com/es/article/home/Avalan_100_millones_para_PyMEs_del_Tringulo _Norte

CEPAL. (2020). *Mipymes y el COVID-19*. https://www.cepal.org/es/euromipyme/mipymes-covid-19

CEPAL. (n.d.). Acerca de Microempresas y Pymes. https://www.cepal.org/es/temas/pymes/acerca -microempresas-pymes

Costa Checa, M. (2019). Latin America is a growing tech hub. But it needs to invest in its talent. *Fortune.* https://fortune.com/2019/09/24/latin-america-invest-tech-talent/

Cromie, S. (1994). Entrepreneurship: The role of the individual in small business development. *IBAR, 15*, 62–76.

de Miranda Oliveira, M., Cahen, F. R., & Borini, F. M. (Eds.). (2019). *Startups and innovation ecosystems in emerging markets*. Cham: Palgrave Macmillan. https://doi.org/10.1007/978-3-030-10865-6_1

Di Gropello, E., Vargas, M. J., & Yanez Pagans, M. (2019, December 6). What are the main lessons from the latest results from PISA 2018 for Latin America? *World Bank Blog.* https://blogs.worldbank.org /latinamerica/what-are-the-main-results-pisa-2018-latin-america

Dodd, S. D., & Anderson, A. R. (2007). Mumpsimus and the mything of the individualistic entrepreneur. *International Small Business Journal, 25*(4), 341–360.

Dutta, S., Lanvin, B., Rivera León, L., & Wunsch-Vincent, S. (Edit.). (2021). *Global innovation index 2021: Tracking innovation through the COVID-19 crisis*. 14th ed. Geneva: WIPO-World Intellectual Property Organization. https://www.wipo.int/edocs/pubdocs/en/wipo_pub_gii_2021.pdf

ECLA Program - Entrepreneurship and Competitiveness in Latin America Program. (n.d.). Columbia Business School. https://www8.gsb.columbia.edu/ecp/latin-america?nid=49=38

Ernst & Young. (2013). *Entrepreneurship and innovation: The path to growth in Latin America.* DocPlayer. https://docplayer.net/13403700-Entrepreneurship-and-innovation-the-path-to-growth -in-latin-america.html

Ernst & Young. (2014). *WEGrow unlocking the growth potential of women entrepreneurs in Latin America and the Caribbean*. Ernst Young and the Multilateral Investment Fund of the Inter-American Development Bank. https://financialallianceforwomen.org/download/wegrow-unlocking -the-growth-potential-of-women-entrepreneurs-in-latin-america-and-the-caribbean/

EU-LAC Foundation. (2017). The internationalization of Latin American SMEs and their projection in Europe. https://eulacfoundation.org/en/system/files/eu_lac_smes.pdf

Ferraz, J. C., & Ramos, L. (2018). *Inclusión financiera para la inserción productiva de las empresas de menor tamaño en América Latina: Innovaciones, factores determinantes y prácticas de las instituciones financieras de desarrollo*. LC/TS.2018/22. Santiago: Naciones Unidas-CEPAL. https:// repositorio.cepal.org/handle/11362/43427

Francis, D. C., Rodriguez Meza, J. L., & Judy Yang, J. (2013). *Mapping enterprises in Latin America and the Caribbean*. The World Bank Group, Latin America and the Caribbean Series, Note No. 1. https://www.enterprisesurveys.org/content/dam/enterprisesurveys/documents/research/Mapping -Enterprises-LAC-Note.pdf

Frohmann, A., Mulder, N., Olmos, X., & Urmeneta, R. (2016). *Internacionalizacion de las pymes: Innovación para exportar*. LC/W.719. Santiago: Naciones Unidas-CEPAL. https://repositorio.cepal .org/bitstream/handle/11362/40737/1/S1600442_es.pdf

GEM Staff. (n. d.). *Entrepreneurial employee activity is a major contributor to business development and innovation*. Global Entrepreneurship Monitor. https://gemconsortium.org/news/Entrepreneurial %20Employee%20Activity%20is%20a%20major%20contributor%20to%20business %20development%20and%20innovation

Heller, L. (2010). *Mujeres emprendedoras en América Latina y el Caribe: Realidades, obstáculos y desafíos.* Serie Mujer y Desarrollo No. 93. Santiago de Chile: Naciones Unidas, Comisión Económica para América Latina y el Caribe. http://www.cepal.org/es/publicaciones/5818-mujeres-emprendedoras-america-latina-caribe-realidades-obstaculos-desafios

IDB-Inter-American Development Bank. (n.d.). Micro, small, and medium size enterprises. https://idbinvest.org/en/solutions/advisory-services/micro-small-and-medium-sized-enterprises

IFC-International Finance Corporation SME Finance Forum. (n.d.). *MSME finance gap.* www.smefinanceforum.org/data-sites/msme-finance-gap

ILO-International Labor Organization. (2016). *Formalization of SMEs in supply chains in Latin America: What role for multinational enterprises?* Geneva, Switzerland: ILO Publications.

ILO-International Labor Organization. (2019). *2019 labour overview: Latin America and the Caribbean.* https://www.ilo.org/caribbean/information-resources/publications/WCMS_735507/lang--en/index.htm

International Trade Centre. (2019). *SME competitiveness outlook 2019: Big money for small business–Financing the sustainable development goals.* Geneva: ITC.

King, R., & Levine, R. (1993). Finance, entrepreneurship, and growth. *Journal of Monetary Economics, 32,* 513–542.

Knowledge at Wharton. (2013). Entrepreneurs in Latin America: A new mindset among a "rising tide." Wharton University of Pennsylvania. https://knowledge.wharton.upenn.edu/article/entrepreneurs-in-latin-america-a-new-mindset-among-a-rising-tide/

Larroulet, C., & Couyoumdjian, J. P. (2009). Entrepreneurship and growth: A Latin American paradox? *The Independent Review, 14*(1), 81–100.

Lestch, C. (2020). Latin America is the new hub for female STEM entrepreneurs. *The Story Exchange.* https://thestoryexchange.org/incubators-accelerating-female-stem-entrepreneurs-latin-america/

Lima, A. (2021). Colombian startup unicorn Rappi: Why the company wants to be the first Latin American super app. *LABS-Latin American Business Stories.* https://labsnews.com/en/articles/business/colombian-startup-unicorn-rappi-super-app/

The Mastercard Index of Women Entrepreneurs 2020 Report. (2020). https://www.mastercard.com/news/media/1ulpy5at/ma_miwe-report-2020.pdf

Mercer, L. (2021). The Latin American startup movement gaining momentum. Nomad Capitalist. https://nomadcapitalist.com/entrepreneurs/latin-american-startup-movement-gaining-momentum-030/

Montealegre, O. (2012). Innovation rising: A snapshot of entrepreneurship in Latin America. *Diplomatic Courier.* https://www.diplomaticourier.com/posts/innovation-rising-a-snapshot-of-entrepreneurship-in-latin-america

OECD/CAF. (2019). *SME policy index: Latin America and the Caribbean 2019-policies for competitive SMEs in the Pacific Alliance and participating South American countries.* Paris: OECD Publishing. https://doi.org/10.1787/d9e1e5f0-en

Palma, J. L. (2019). How Latin American entrepreneurs are changing the region, one business at a time. *Crunchbase News.* https://news.crunchbase.com/news/how-latin-american-entrepreneurs-are-changing-the-region-one-business-at-a-time/

Park, H., Urmeneta, R., & Mulder, N. (2019). *El desempeño de empresas exportadoras según su tamaño: Una guía de indicadores y resultados.* LC/TS.2019/41. Santiago: CEPAL. https://repositorio.cepal.org/bitstream/handle/11362/44664/1/S1900418_es.pdf

Park, S. (2021). Caballos con múltiples cuernos: ¿Qué son los decacornios y hectacornios? *America Economia.* https://www.americaeconomia.com/multilatinas/caballos-con-multiples-cuernos-que-son-los-decacornios-y-hectacornios

Pompeo, C. (2021, October 4). Latin America goes from 2 to 34 unicorns in four years, says Sling Hub. LABS. https://labsnews.com/en/articles/business/latin-america-goes-from-2-to-34-unicorns-in-four-years-says-sling-hub/

Porter, M. E. (1990). *The competitive advantage of nations.* New York: Free Press.

Porter, M. E. (2012). Interview at the world economic forum. Davos, Switzerland. http://www.huffingtonpost.com/2012/09/13/solo-sessions-2012-michael-porter_n_1878421.html

Porter, M. E., & Kramer, M. R. (2011). Creating shared value. *Harvard Business Review* (January–February).

Sanchez, K. (2021). Es el momento de las Pymes Centroamericanas. *Forbes Centroamerica*. https://forbescentroamerica.com/2021/08/04/es-el-momento-de-las-pymes-centroamericanas/

Schmitz, J. (1989). Imitation, entrepreneurship, and long-run growth. *Journal of Political Economy, 97,* 721–739.

Schumpeter, J. (1934). *The theory of economic development: An inquiry into profits, capital, credit, interests, and the business cycle.* Cambridge, MA: Harvard University Press.

Schwab, K. (Ed.). (2019). *The global competitiveness report 2019.* World Economic Forum. www.weforum.org/gcr

Start-up Chile. (n.d.). Official website. https://startupchile.org

Tan, W.-L., Williams, J., & Tan, T.-M. (2005). Defining the 'social' in 'social entrepreneurship': Altruism and entrepreneurship. *International Entrepreneurship and Management Journal, 1,* 353–365.

Terjesen, S., & Amorós, J. E. (2010). Female entrepreneurship in Latin America and the Caribbean: Characteristics, drivers and relationship to economic development. *European Journal of Development Research, 22*(3), 313–330. https://doi.org/10.1057/ejdr.2010.13

Vega, M. (2020). SMEs: A motor of sustainable growth and development. HechoxNosotros. https://www.hechoxnosotros.org/post/smes-a-motor-of-sustainable-growth-and-development

Veiga, L. (2021). *Hacia una infraestructura digital para la internacionalización de las pequeñas y medianas empresas.* LC/TS.2021/33. Santiago: Naciones Unidas-CEPAL. https://www.cepal.org/es/publicaciones/46793-infraestructura-digital-la-internacionalizacion-pequenas-medianas-empresas

Wennekers, S., & Thurik, R. (1999). Linking entrepreneurship and growth. *Small Business Economics, 13,* 27–56.

Welter, F. (2011). Contextualizing entrepreneurship: Conceptual challenges and ways forward. *Entrepreneurship Theory and Practice, 35*(1), 165–184. https://doi.org/10.1111/j.1540-6520.2010.00427.x

World Bank (2010). *Women, Business and the Law 2010: Measuring Legal Gender Parity for Entrepreneurs and Workers in 128 Economies.* Washington, DC.: World Bank. https://openknowledge.worldbank.org/handle/10986/20190 License: CC BY 3.0 IGO.

Zanini Graca, P. (2021). Female entrepreneurship in Latin America. *International Policy Digest.* https://intpolicydigest.org/female-entrepreneurship-in-latin-america/

11 Global and Regional Value Chains in Latin America

Introduction

Global value chains (GVCs) are the engines of the global economy. Their emergence has been driven by a combination of increased fragmentation and dispersion of production as many countries have upgraded their capabilities and invested in supporting infrastructure that has lowered transportation and communication costs. GVCs move products and services across borders in a synchronized fashion and orchestration of resources, activities, and logistic operations in a marvel of efficiency. Multinational companies (MNCs) have been the driving force with their ability to organize and coordinate supplier development efforts (World Bank, 2021a). Over the years, they have built mechanisms and rules that govern their performance. Hundreds of actors across borders participate in the production and services delivered by GVCs. As the name suggests, value is created and built upon by their participants in different locations and geographies. The configuration of these value chains represents a balancing act of firms searching for the most efficient locations to combine resources, materials, and other inputs with the capabilities that transform these inputs into intermediate and final products and services. In an ideal world of free trade and exchanges, these configurations would reflect the optimization that combines resources no matter their location. As this is not the case, trading and transaction costs, among other factors, shape the less-than-optimal configurations that exist today.

Latin America has been largely at the edges of GVCs, mostly supplying raw materials and commodities based on its natural resources. The efficiencies of this organized mechanism delivered the products and services that the world consumes until the pandemic of 2020 disrupted GVCs. Across the world, government responses to limit the impact of the pandemic closed borders and the smooth operations of GVCs and created shortages of goods everywhere. Such disruption pressed companies to reassess operating models based on single supply sources centered on China and made Latin America, and particularly Mexico, an attractive supplier base for the US and European markets (World Bank 2021b).

In this chapter, we review Latin America's participation in GVCs and regional value chains. The chapter is organized in four parts. The first part introduces basic concepts of value chains. The second part analyzes Latin American participation in GVCs. The third part focuses on regional value chains and sectoral differences. The last section focuses on the multinational firm's perspective and logic to configure value chains and assess the attractiveness of Latin American countries based on MNC's considerations. We conclude the chapter with an assessment of Latin America's potential for deeper participation in global value chains.

DOI: 10.4324/9781003182672-14

Global Value Chains

Value chains are the activities that turn raw materials into finished products; they add value through simple and complex processes that involve labor, tools, and equipment. In GVCs, these activities are dispersed among different participants across multiple countries. Their participation is based on factor costs, expertise, and capacity to deliver the intermediate and finished products and services (Park et al., 2013).

The Concept of the Smiling Face

Michael Porter first introduced the concept of value chain activities as a source of the competitive advantages of firms (Porter, 1985). The author makes the argument that the competitive advantage of firms lies in their ability to create value (by exceeding the costs of producing such activities) across five primary activities: inbound logistics, operations, outbound logistics, marketing and sales, and post-sale services. The disaggregation of the firm's activities defined the concept of value chain. The author emphasized that competitive advantage emanates from achieving maximum efficiency in all processes involved in these activities in what is known as the operating model (Porter, 1985). The firm's business model captures and delivers this value to the market in a way that generates revenue and profits. With advances of technology and fragmentation of markets and industry players, the lines between business and operating models are blurring (World Economic Forum, 2020). Customers can participate in the creation of value of the products they consume. The fragmentation of production has added many more activities to the value chain, such as design and research and development (R&D). Value added is not linear, and products and components go back for value added creation by different entities until its final form. Value and products can be reconfigured and customized in many different ways and offered through different platforms, leading to increased supplier and production fragmentation and flexibility (World Economic Forum, 2020). Thus, a value chain is a constellation of participants that form networks on their own and create their own set of relationships and links: for instance, the supplier's suppliers create a hierarchy of suppliers that is referred to as Tier 1 suppliers, Tier 2 suppliers, and so on. Similarly, value chain customers of the final product can be arranged in tiers reflecting the many intermediaries in distribution before reaching the final customer. Thus, a more integral definition of a value chain is the network of firms and processing plants with common goals of participating in the exchange of inputs and intermediate products on a repeated basis through informal arrangements and contracts to deliver a final product or service to the market (Lin et al., 2019; USITC, 2019.

Figure 11.1 provides a contemporary interpretation of these primary activities in the context of today's complex world—the smiling face of the value chain (Stollinger, 2021). As Figure 11.1 shows, downstream activities of the value chain add more value than those upstream and closer to the market (marketing and demand management). High value-added activities such as R&D and design are more likely to be located in countries with abundant resources and support systems for innovative activities. Firms and countries participate in these activities by trading their value with others in the chain. When countries or firms export or transfer their value to other participants which, in turn, add more value, they are participating forward (forward integration) in the value chain. Their exported value is embodied in the value of the product or service exported by the third participant to others. For instance, the cotton fiber exported by a country may be processed into a yarn and exported as a fabric

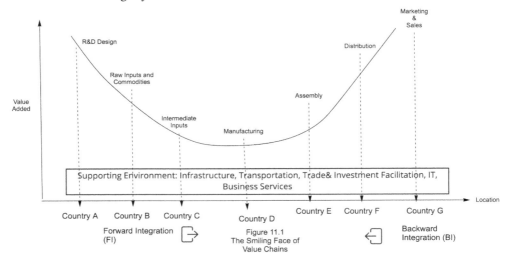

Figure 11.1 The smiling face of value chains

by another country. The fabric exports embody some value added by the exporter of cotton fibers. A country may use the fabric to cut and sew garments that are, in turn, exported. This latter country is said to have a backward participation (backward integration) in the value chain, as it uses the value of others in making a final product.

Management of the inputs and components needed at each stage is referred to as supply chain management or logistics. This function is either coordinated by a lead firm or delegated to specialized firms that procure materials, inputs, intermediate products, and production capacity as well as the assembly of a final product, inventory, and distribution to the market. Both the value added and supply chain activities are embedded in an environment that facilitates the linkages of value chain activities such as transportation, communication, certification, documentation, education, training, and many others. The efficiency, capacity, and accessibility of the supporting infrastructure will either facilitate or hinder the flows of the value chain (Jones et al., 2020).

When those activities take place across borders, the value chain is either global or regional. The location of the different activities of a value chain is based on the comparative and competitive advantages of countries and firms. Activities that are labor intensive may be more efficiently performed in labor abundant countries. For instance, Central American countries produce garments from imported fabric and yarns manufactured in the United States or Asia. Those garments are exported to the US market, given its proximity (low transportation costs) and preferential trade agreements. The value added in Central America is related to the production (sewing and stitching) of garments such as a T-shirt (see Figure 11.2) (Frederick et al., 2014).

Governance, Configurations, and Types of Value Chains

The governance of the chain determines who, what, where, and how value is added through these activities and processes. GVCs distribute the tasks in terms of expertise and efficiency requirements and when their intermediate inputs at any stage can be easily traded across

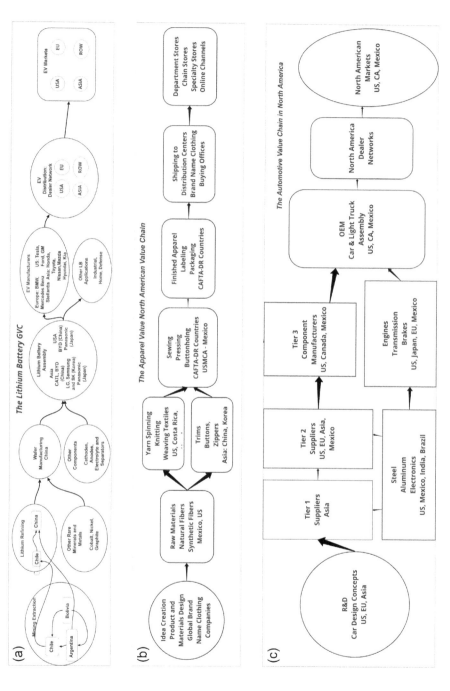

Figure 11.2 Examples of global and regional value chains in Latin America

borders. Other value chains are regional when trade agreements provide tariff protection and incentives for production and distribution within the confines of the agreement—for instance the European Union and the United States–Mexico–Canada Agreement (USMCA). At the national level, value chains are replicated or developed entirely for the production and delivery of product or services domestically.

Firms that control or own these assets and ideas, or unique processes controlling those activities exercise more value chain control. Power based on R&D and design create what is known as *supplier driven value chains*–for instance, pharmaceutical companies exercise high levels of control in their value chains through their drug formulations and patents. Power based on market control derived from brand equity or retail operations create what is known as *buyer driven value chains*. Walmart's value chain is a good example of buyer-driven chains. A few companies may have control of both ends of the value chain—supplier and buyer— such as Apple. In any of these cases, MNCs exercise their control by taking a leadership role in how the value chain is governed. Three types of value chain governance are market-based (participants have the same power), collaborative networks (control and power shared by buyers and sellers in the value chain), and vertically integrated hierarchy (the firm owns and controls all activities). In turn, collaborative networks can be modular (lead firm delegates power to a turn-key sub-contractor that secures all materials, equipment, labor, and processes to produce a module under the lead firm specification), relational (network of suppliers linked by trust relations work with the lead firm), captive (lead firm exercises a strong degree of control over small and captive suppliers) (Gereffi et al., 2005, Gereffi 2014).

Value Chain Configurations

Some value chains are simple and involve few participants and countries—garments, for instance—while others involve multicountry participants producing parts and components from a range of materials and processes that are assembled into the final product, such as automobiles. Thus, every value chain has a unique configuration and governance depending on the complexity of the product or service. Not all configurations follow the linear process described in Figure 11.1. The linear process depicted in Figure 11.1 assumes an incremental value added in what is known as a snake value chain. Another configuration is called a spider value chain. Under this arrangement, parts, components, and intermediate goods are produced by many suppliers in different countries and transported to single facilities for assembly into the final product that is distributed to final markets (Baldwin & Venables, 2010). In some cases, there is modularity of production networks. Each module forms a node in the value chain with its own network of suppliers and producers. Modules are then moved to a central assembly operation for market distribution. The example of the mobile telecom industry is an example of how this industry is organized in specialized modular platforms with vertical geographic concentration (Thun et al., 2021). These modules are interconnected, based on standard interfaces, and relate to a particular smartphone function (processing and storage, user interface, display, network connectivity, memory). For instance, Korea (ROK) specializes in memory and displays. Within this country, the dominant player with expertise and production capabilities is Samsung. For processors, US-based Qualcomm is the designated supplier. The design of all of these modules and processors is done by UK-based ARM. Using these standard modules, different companies assemble under different brand names. The companies in a given module create their own constellation of participants and together innovate and advance their capabilities which, in turn, push the frontier smartphone capabilities.

Types of Value Chains

The comparative advantages of countries and the competitive advantage of their firms provide home to clusters of specialization in one or more of the activities' value chains. The collective efficiencies of these clusters are based not only on the internal efficiencies of participants but also the externalities providing the supporting service. Thus, the competitive advantage of these clusters is the joint effort of their collective efficiency and the external economies derived from the supporting environment. Clusters derive their own governance mechanisms to acquire inputs, specialized skilled resources, machinery, and the rapid dissemination of information through formal associations or community organizations. Cluster formation may be organic (historically) or could be the result of national and local government economic development initiatives.

Value chains around clusters can be identified by the product and value added creation process. The following is a synthesis of several value chains (Antras, 2020; Lund et al., 2019).

- Resource intensive: agriculture, mining, energy, and basic metals.
- Limited manufacturing: furniture, garments, textiles, footwear.
- Advanced manufacturing: automotive, machinery, aerospace, electronics.
- Labor intensive services: business process outsourcing (BPO), software, healthcare.
- Innovation and R&D intensive: robots, pharmaceuticals, electric vehicles (EVs).
- Knowledge intensive services: financial intermediation, IT, professional.

Countries may participate in several value chains in which they can leverage their comparative advantages. As a result, clusters emerge around particular geographies because of proximity, regional integration, and in terms of trust and relational assets (World Bank 2020c). The concentration of clusters and value chains generate ecosystems of hubs and nodes such as in East Asia. We now turn our attention to Latin American participation in global and regional value chains.

Latin America's Participation in Global Value Chains

MNCs and national firms choose to participate in value chains at any level (global, regional, or national) or a given stage. Large MNCs have the resources and market power to organize and coordinate complex GVCs across different geographies. Organized networks of suppliers also secure contracts with MNCs. National companies participate in GVCs by providing competitive skills and processes that add value at some stage of the value chain. Countries encourage and facilitate their national firms to participate in these value chains by providing a supportive environment of resources, finances, training, and information. Governments also facilitate the efficient movement of materials and inputs by investing in modern and efficient infrastructure and lower transaction costs, such as tariffs; efficient communication networks; and the facilitation of documentation, taxation, standards, and procedures that govern cross-border trade and manufacturing processes within their borders.

Based on its abundance of natural resources and agriculture, Latin America's participation in value chains has been as a provider of raw materials and basic commodities, with limited capacity as a manufacturing or service provider (Blyde, 2014). Clusters of specialization at each stage have developed in certain countries with participation in GVCs (see Table 11.1)

Table 11.1 Latin America Value Chain Clusters

Agriculture	Light Manufacturing	Advanced Manufacturing	Labor Intensive Services
Salmon – Puerto Mont, Chile Mangoes – Petrolina, Brazil Avocados – Michoacan, Mexico; O'Higgins, Chile Raspberries – Maule, Chile Grapes – Peru; Chile Melons – Rio Grande do Norte, Brazil Apples – Santa Catarina, Brazil Wine – Mendoza, Argentina; Colchagua, Chile Horticultural – Antioquia, Colombia; Sugar – Valle del Cauca, Colombia	Undergarments (Hanes Underwear) – El Salvador Apparel (Ralph Lauren, Levi Strauss) – Nicaragua Furniture – Puebla, Mexico Metal working – Espirito Santo, Brazil Footwear – Leon, Mexico	Automotives – Puebla, Hermosillo, Guanajato, Mexico Small Aircraft – Sao Jose dos Campos, Brazil; Queretaro, Mexico Medical Devices – Instruments, Disposables, and Therapeutics (J&J, Baxter, GE Healthcare) – Baja California, Mexico; Costa Rica; Dominican Republic Microelectronics, Bio-fuels – Minas Gerais, Brazil	BPO – San Jose, Costa Rica ICT Software – Guadalajara, Monterrey, Mexico

Source: Authors elaboration from public sources

Take, for instance, the case of the GVC for lithium batteries in electrical vehicles, aviation, and national defense. The stages of the value chain are: (1) mining and extraction of lithium, (2) materials purification and refinement and processed material and cell manufacturing, (3) pack manufacturing, (4) use in a final product (car, airplane, or defense vehicle), and (5) recycling and reuse (see Figure 12.2 for a visual representation of the lithium battery value chain). Lithium accounts for 33% of the components in batteries that also include nickel, cobalt, and manganese among others. Latin America is central to this value chain with 58% of world reserves in just three countries: Chile, Argentina, and Bolivia. Other Latin American countries with significant lithium reserves are Brazil and Mexico. Mexico is currently developing lithium deposit extraction (Berg, 2021). Mining and extraction in Argentina have already started with large projects undertaken by Canadian and Australian mining giants with contracts with BMW, Toyota, and battery manufacturers in ROK and China. Other countries with major reserves are Australia (22%), China (7%), the United States (3.5%), and Canada (2.5%). Extraction is mostly done in Australia (60%), Chile (19%), China (9%), and Argentina (7%). Lithium refining and purification is even more concentrated in China (60%), Chile (30%), and Argentina (10%). Cell manufacturing is concentrated in China (42%), Japan (33%), and ROK (15%). Battery manufacturing with imported cells from China is done closer to the markets for final products that incorporate them (car manufacturers, industry and home applications, defense). With global production and demand for EVs taking off, access to a supply of critical inputs is a limiting factor (White House, 2021).

Latin America's increased participation as a key supplier of lithium does not come free of environmental impacts. Most of the lithium deposits in Chile are in the fragile desert of Atacama, in northern Chile. Extraction is water intensive, taking 500,000 million liters of water for 1 ton of lithium that creates a brine that, once evaporated, produces the rich concentrate ready for refining but leaves chemicals used in the evaporation process. Water is scarce in northern Chile, and the processing pools have undesirable environmental impacts (The Guardian, 2021; Berg, 2021). The irony is that lithium-producing countries experience environmental degradation for participating in a value chain that creates EVs, which benefits the world by reducing pollution. There are trade-offs of increased participation in GVCs for Latin American countries.

The ease of trade flows in inputs, components, and intermediate products is a critical aspect of GVC participation. A study of GVCs by the Organisation for Economic Co-operation and Development (OECD, 2012) found that trade facilitation and logistics performance, quality of infrastructure and institutions, intellectual property protection, and quality of electricity supply were the most important determinants of participation in GVCs (Cadestin et al., 2016). Another study by the World Bank found that the key determinants of GVC participation were factor endowments, geographical location, political stability, tariffs, foreign direct investment, and domestic industrial capacity (Fernandes et al., 2020). The indicators for ease of trading across borders as well as the quality of enforcing contract and judicial processes in the World Bank Doing Business Indicators can be used to assess some of these determinants in Latin America (World Bank, 2020a, 2020b). Table 11.2 summarizes these indicators for selected countries and those of East Asia, China, and the US for comparison.

Latin America is not competitive with the standards set by China and the US in all respects. The region is competitive with East Asia in almost all indicators except in terms of the costs of exporting ($516.3 in Latin America vs. $381.1 in East Asia) and importing ($628.4 vs. $422.8). Within the region, Mexico, El Salvador, the Dominican Republic, and Panama are the best performers in trading across borders, particularly in more time efficiency and costs to export and import. El Salvador offers the lowest costs to export and import, making this country a good candidate for companies looking for applications that involve bringing inputs from elsewhere, adding value in the country, and reexporting the finished product, such as garments. Countries with the worst trading conditions are Uruguay, Colombia, and Honduras. These countries suffer from expensive and time inefficient trading. In terms of enforcing contracts, Latin American countries are not the best in comparison with China or the US. The best performers are Ecuador and Brazil. If trade disputes may arise, Argentina offers the region's best quality of judicial processes; the worst are Bolivia, Nicaragua, Ecuador, Guatemala, and the Dominican Republic.

Other factors that contribute to GVC participation are the quality of infrastructure, connectivity, and skills of the workforce (see Chapter 3). Using the Global Competitiveness Index (World Economic Forum, 2019c), we can assess the performance of Latin American countries vis-à-vis selective competitors. Table 11.3 provides such information.

The overall quality of infrastructure in Brazil (65.5) and Chile (56.6) is comparable to that of China (68.9). Chile achieves better road quality ratings than China (4.6), which is closer to that of the US (5.5). As far as train, port, and airport efficiency, Panama (4.8, 5.9, and 5.7, respectively) is the best performer in Latin America, with ratings above China (4.5, 4.6, and 4.5, respectively) and very comparable to the US (5.2, 5.8, and 5.6, respectively). In terms of trade openness—a slightly different concept from the trading efficiency concept discussed

Table 11.2 Doing Business across Borders in Latin America

Country	Trading Across Borders Overall Score (0–100 best)	Export				Import				Enforcing Contracts (0–100 best)	Quality of Judicial Processes (0–18 best)
		Border Compliance Time	Border Compliance Cost US$	Documentary Compliance Hours	Documentary Compliance US$	Border Compliance Hours	Border Compliance US$	Documentary Compliance Hours	Documentary Compliance US$		
Mexico	82.1	20	400	8	60	44	450	18	100	67	10.1
Brazil	69.9	49	862	12	226	30	375	24	107	64.1	13.1
Costa Rica	77.6	20	450	24	80	80	500	26	75	55.2	9.5
Argentina	67.1	21	150	25	60	60	906	166	120	57.5	12.5
El Salvador	89.8	24	128	9	50	36	128	13	67	51.9	8
Colombia	62.7	112	630	48	90	112	545	64	50	34.3	9
Uruguay	58.4	96	1038	24	231	6	500	48	285	56.3	8
Chile	73	60	290	24	50	54	290	36	50	54	10
Guatemala	77.2	36	310	48	105	72	405	32	37	34.5	6
The Dominican Republic	83.5	16	488	10	15	24	579	14	40	50.6	6.5
Panama	85.5	24	270	6	60	24	490	6	50	49	8
Peru	71.3	48	630	24	50	72	700	48	80	59.1	9.5
Honduras	64.3	198	601	48	80	96	483	72	70	44.2	7.5
Paraguay	65.1	120	815	24	120	24	500	36	135	61.6	10.5
Ecuador	71.2	96	560	24	60	24	250	120	75	57.5	6.5
Nicaragua	77	72	240	48	47	72	400	16	86	58.6	6.5
Bolivia	71.6	48	65	144	25	114	315	72	30	55.6	6
Latin America	69.1	55.3	516.3	35.7	100.3	55.6	628.4	43.2	107.3	53.5	8.8
East Asia	71.6	57.5	381.1	55.6	109.4	68.4	422.8	53.7	108.4	53.0	8.1
China	86.5	18	249	8	70	37	230	11	75	80.9	16.5
US	92	2	175	2	60	2	175	8	100	73.4	15

Source: World Bank (2020a, 2020b) https://www.doingbusiness.org/en/doingbusiness

Table 11.3 Logistic Support to Value Chains in Latin America

Country	Infrastructure					Trade Openness				
	Overall (0–100)	Roads Quality (1–7 best)	Trains Efficiency (1–7 best)	Airport Efficiency (1–7 best)	Seaport Efficiency (1–7 best)	Overall (0–100)	Non-tariff Barriers (1–7 best)	Weighted Tariff 2019 (%)	Tariff Complexity (1–7 best)	Border Clearing Efficiency (1–7 best)
Argentina	47.7	3.6	2.7	4.4	3.9	51.1	4	7.3	6.6	2.4
Bolivia	34.4	3.5	2.6	3.6	—	50.8	4	4.7	6	2.3
Brazil	**65.5**	3.0	2.5	4.4	3.2	46.7	3.4	8.0	6.6	2.4
Chile	56.6	**5.2**	3.2	4.9	4.9	**76.3**	**5.2**	**0.4**	7	3.3
Colombia	43.8	3.4	1.7	4.5	4.1	59.7	3.9	2.9	6.4	2.6
Costa Rica	49.4	3.0	—	4.8	3.9	64.5	4.0	1.6	6.5	2.6
The Dominican Republic	61	4.7	—	5.1	4.9	60.6	4.3	4.2	6.5	2.4
Ecuador	52.8	4.9	—	4.9	4.5	44.5	3.3	8.1	4.9	**2.8**
El Salvador	45.3	4.2	—	4.5	3.4	61.2	4.1	2.0	6.4	2.3
Guatemala	37.2	2.4	—	4.1	3.9	63.5	4.3	1.4	6.7	2.2
Honduras	43.1	4.1	—	4.3	4.4	62.2	4.1	3.4	6.6	2.2
Mexico	57.4	4.5	3.3	4.4	4.3	64.8	4.7	1.2	6.3	**2.8**
Nicaragua	40.3	4.2	—	3.7	3.2	63.7	4.0	1.9	6.6	2.5
Panama	57.8	4.5	**4.8**	**5.9**	**5.7**	66.3	4.5	5.4	6.7	2.6
Paraguay	42.1	2.6	—	3.5	3.5	62.2	4.5	5.0	6.7	2.6
Peru	42.4	3.2	2.9	4.3	3.8	66.5	4.3	0.7	6.0	2.5
Uruguay	44.2	3.7	1.2	5.1	4.8	58.0	4.5	5.3	6.7	2.5
Venezuela	24.7	2.6	1.5	2.2	2.1	43.3	3.3	10.2	6.6	1.8
China	68.9	4.6	4.5	4.6	4.5	57.6	4.5	2.5	6.4	3.3
US	79.6	5.5	5.2	5.8	5.6	67.0	4.9	13.8*	3.7	3.8

Country	Skills of Workforce					ICT Adoption						R&D (0–100)
	Overall (0–100)	Vocational Training Quality (1–7 best)	Skill Sets of Graduates (1–7 best)	Digital Skills (1–7 best)	Ease of Finding Skilled Workers (1–7 best)	Overall (0–100)	Mobile Cellular Subscriptions per 100 Pop	Mobile Broadband Subscriptions per 100 Pop	Fixed Broadband Internet Subscriptions per 100	Fiber Internet Subscriptions per 100	% of Population with Internet Access	
Argentina	53.2	4.8	4.2	4.0	4.2	58.0	132.1	80.7	19.1	0.5	79.3	35.3
Bolivia	41.0	3.6	3.5	3.2	3.7	51.4	100.8	79.9	4.4	1.3	43.8	19
Brazil	39.4	3.3	3.2	3.1	3.4	58.1	98.8	88.1	14.9	1.6	67.5	**54.3**
Chile	**59.2**	4.9	4.6	4.3	**4.9**	**63.1**	134.4	91.6	17.4	**2.2**	**82.3**	35.8
Colombia	51.7	4.5	4.3	3.8	4.3	49.9	121.9	52.3	13.4	1.4	62.3	28.2
Costa Rica	**63.0**	**5.0**	4.9	4.9	4.8	60.0	**169.9**	**97.2**	16.6	0.4	74.1	—

(Continued)

Table 11.2 Continued

Country	Skills of Workforce					ICT Adoption						R&D (0–100)
	Overall (0–100)	Vocational Training Quality (1–7 best)	Skill Sets of Graduates (1–7 best)	Digital Skills (1–7 best)	Ease of Finding Skilled Workers (1–7 best)	Overall (0–100)	Mobile Cellular Subscriptions per 100 Pop	Mobile Broadband Subscriptions per 100 Pop	Fixed Broadband Internet Subscriptions per 100	Fiber Internet Subscriptions per 100	% of Population with Internet Access	
The Dominican Republic	48.8	3.9	3.8	3.6	4.1	51.8	84.1	60.8	7.5	1.3	74.8	19.3
Ecuador	49.4	4.2	4.1	3.8	4.2	47.6	92.3	54.7	11.4	1.6	57.3	23.6
El Salvador	42.5	3.7	3.6	3.2	3.8	40.6	146.9	55.8	7.7	0.2	33.8	16.4
Guatemala	51.1	4.5	4.1	3.3	4.2	37.7	118.7	16.5	3.1	0.1	65.0	16.8
Honduras	49.1	3.9	4.0	3.6	4.0	30.2	79.2	32.1	3.7	0.0	31.7	15.5
Mexico	50.3	4.2	4.1	3.8	4.2	55.0	93	70	14.6	2.5	65.8	38.3
Nicaragua	37.5	3.1	3.3	3.2	3.3	35.9	115.1	29.6	3.0	–	27.9	17.0
Panama	44.8	3.7	3.8	3.5	3.6	50.1	130.1	70.3	10.8	0.5	57.9	21.8
Paraguay	36.8	3.1	3.1	2.9	3.2	45.7	107.0	57.7	4.6	0.2	65.0	17.4
Peru	42.1	3.8	3.5	3.4	3.6	45.7	123.8	65.7	7.3	0.0	52.5	22.3
Uruguay	53.6	4.6	4.3	4.3	4.1	79.7	149.9	123.8	28.3	18.8	68.3	27.4
Venezuela	46.1	4.3	4.2	3.6	3.4	46.7	71.8	54.5	8.7	0.0	72.0	22.0
China	59.4	4.5	4.5	4.7	4.6	78.5	115.0	95.4	28.5	23.9	54.3	79.5
US	63.0	5.0	4.9	4.9	4.8	74.3	123.7	142.5	35.6	4.2	87.3	95.7

Source: World Economic Forum (2019a) Global Competitive Report.
*In 2018, it was 1.59.

above—Chile is by far the most open country in the region with the lowest weighted average tariff of 0.4%, low non-tariff barriers, and trading simplicity. Mexico and Ecuador are the most efficient countries in clearing borders.

Other factors that are important are workforce skills. In that respect, Costa Rica's workforce (63.0) is more competitive than China's (59.4) and comparable to that of the US (63.0). Costa Rica gathers the best scores on vocational training in terms of graduates' skill sets and is second only to Chile in the ease of finding skilled workers. Costa Rica's distinction has been very attractive to a diverse number of companies in the software, information and communications technology (ICT) industries, and medical sectors, and a number of MNCs in these sectors have a presence there (Vmware, IBM, HP, Microsoft, Experian) (Hewitt and Monge-Gonzalez , 2010; Dempsey, 2019). Relative to China, Costa Rica has the added advantage of lower transportation costs and proximity to the US (same time zone and short air transportation). Chile also ranks high on the quality of workforce skills. Chile has been successful in developing their own high-technology sector, particularly in the software industry, IT services, BPO, and data centers for such companies as Oracle, Microsoft, Huwei, Citigroup, and Equifax. For instance, the subsidiary of the large Indian MNC Tata Group, Tata Consultancy Services (TCS), provides IT and BPO services for Latin American clients out of its Chilean base (Invest Chile, 2021). Chile (63.1) ranks first in technology infrastructure (ICT) and has the largest internet penetration in the region (82.3%). Costa Rica has deeper mobile cellular penetration (169.9 per 100 population) and broadband mobile subscriptions (97.2 per 100 population). Fixed and fiber internet subscriptions are much higher in the small country of Uruguay. Finally, Brazil is the best country in the region for R&D activities. In conclusion, based on infrastructure, connectivity, trade costs, and R&D, Costa Rica, Chile, and Brazil offer the best conditions for GVC participation.

Regional Integration and Global Value Chains

Trade and regional integration agreements boost cross-border trading in global and regional value chains, as they smooth the flows of cross-border production through reduction or elimination of tariffs and non-tariff restrictions and harmonized standards. There are hundreds of bilateral and multilateral trade agreements between Latin American countries and the rest of the world. There are also a few regional market integration agreements that should also facilitate further integration. In this section, we examine the extent to which these agreements shape the participation of Latin America in GVCs and create regional value chains.

The Free Trade Agreement between the US and Central American countries and the Dominican Republic (CAFTA-DR), which went into effect in 2006, has certainly spurred investments and trade flows among the participants for many years and has been the driver of the sub-region's integration with North American GVCs (USTRa and USTRb, 2021). Trade between the US and CAFTA-DR countries rose from $34.8 billion prior to the agreement in 2005 to $56.1 billion in 2021, an average of 38.7% per year (US Census Bureau, 2021). The US has turned a $1.18 billion trade deficit position in 2005 into a $6.62 billion surplus in 2021, mostly because of US exports of intermediate goods that are later returned to the US as imports of finished goods.

Beyond trade agreements, the region has a number of advanced market integration mechanisms that further spur the creation of regional value chains. We turn our attention to two of those vehicles: The US–Canada–Mexico integration (USMCA) and MERCOSUR–South America.

Countries' participation in value chains is measured by their contribution of value to the different value chain activities (see Figure 11.1 the smiling face of value chains). As mentioned above, supplier countries are linked to value chains by their level of forward integration (FI) and countries involved in the later stages of the value chain by their level of backward integration (BI).

In review, FI is the extent (percent) to which foreign inputs are used for a third country's exports. BI is the extent (percent) to which a country's exports (e.g., electrical vehicles) incorporate value added from importer countries (e.g., China's wafers) (Cadestin et al., 2016). The two indicators are added to assess full participation in value chains (GVC Participation Ratio = FI + BI). In an international study of GVCs by the OECD, Chile was the Latin American country with the largest GVC Participation ratio (52%), followed by Mexico (47%), Costa Rica (45%), Colombia (38%), Brazil (35%), and Argentina (30%). It should be noted that not all Latin American countries are members of OECD. When the overall participation is disaggregated into FI and BI, Mexico (32%) and Costa Rica (28%) had the highest BI and Chile (32%), Colombia (30%), and Brazil (24%) exhibit higher FI (Cadestin et al., 2016). These results show that Mexico and Costa Rica are positioned in the upstream stages of GVCs with greater activities in manufacturing and assembling of intermediate or end products. Chile, Colombia, and Brazil mostly participate by providing basic inputs for further processing of value chains. Although such differential specialization is based on comparative advantages, geographic distance also plays an important role. Mexico and Costa Rica benefit from proximity to the large US market.

A more recent study, which included a larger representation of Latin American countries, examined backward participation in GVCs. In this study, Mexico is, again, the top Latin American country in terms of BI with 42%, followed by Honduras at 32% and Nicaragua, Costa Rica, and Dominican Republic at 22%. Countries in the study with lower levels of participation in GVCs were Chile (14%), Brazil (12%), Argentina (11%), and Peru (12%). Countries with the lowest BI were Venezuela (10%), Ecuador (10%), and Colombia (7%). These results seem to suggest that Mexico and Central America have greater backward linkages with GVCs and South American countries are mostly suppliers of natural-resource-based commodities.

Regional Value Chains in Latin America

Although 'global value chain' suggests a global footprint, most value chains are regional. For physical products, proximity to manufacturing centers is an important determinant because of transportation costs. The emphasis on 'just in time' processes demands the availability of parts and components closer to assembly operations, such as automobiles. Proximity to the market and consumers is also an important consideration because of ease and familiarity of connectivity. Although services can be efficiently rendered anywhere in the world, the effective delivery of the service sometimes requires proximity to the market in terms of language and cultural affinity. As mentioned before, preferential trade agreements and market integration mechanisms shape the regional configurations of value chains. Their rules of origin (ROOs) and market access incentives promote the creation of value chains embedded in the geographical footprint of those agreements. We turn our attention to two sub-regional footprints in Latin America: North and South America.

North American Value Chains

The US economy is the central node for regional value chains in North America. The landmark USCAM and CAFTA-DR trade and integration agreements have reoriented the production of many of the economic sectors in this region (USITA, 2021; USTR, 2021b). These agreements have also been influential in the investments of large MNCs to create and expand production capacity to serve markets within the region and the rest of the world. As discussed in Chapter 8, Walmart is an example of an MNC that has successfully built a strong North American footprint of markets and supply networks in Mexico and Central America.

One of the most important considerations in those agreements is the definition of rules of origin (ROOs). ROOs are the criteria that define the national source of a material, component, or final product (WTO, 2021). ROOs establish the criteria by which inputs imported from non-member countries can be incorporated into a product and have it (the manufactured product) qualified for duty-free benefits under the agreement. For instance, under the USMCA, a product must have at least 70%–75% of regional content to qualify for the trade benefits (USTR, 2021a). Under this rule, an auto part made with 75% Mexican content can enter the US duty free. This part can be incorporated in cars assembled in the US and exported to Canada and back to Mexico duty free. Similarly, a US auto part can be used in an assembly operation in Mexico, resulting in Mexican cars exported to the US tariff-free under the agreement. Automobile companies from all over the world have established a strong production and assembly capacity in the US, Canada, and Mexico. The combined North American market produced 16.8 million passenger cars in 2019, of which 10.9 million were produced in the US, 3.9 million in Mexico, and 1.9 million in Canada. About 97% of US vehicle or parts imports from Mexico and 70% from Canada were duty free (USITA, 2021). With lower wages and costs, Mexico has a substantial advantage in manufacturing costs vis-à-vis the US and Canada (see Table 11.4). This cost advantage remains substantial after transportation costs are added for a Mexican car to be delivered in the US market. Furthermore, Mexico holds a cost advantage in third markets (Europe) as a result of a trade agreement with the European Union. The following example shows an estimation of Mexico's cost advantage in car manufacturing vis-à-vis an equivalent car produced in the US for US and European markets (US Congressional Research Service, 2021).

Table 11.4 Mexico Cost Advantage on Export Car Markets Based on a Generic $25,000 Car

	Differential between a US and Mexican car production for delivery in the U.S. market	Differential between a US and Mexican car production for delivery in the European market
Assembly labor costs	$600 less in Mexico	
Parts	$1,500 less in Mexico	
Transportation to market	$900 more for Mexico to ship a car to the US	$300 more for a Mexican car to be shipped to Europe than a US equivalent car to Europe
Tariffs	None	$2500 EU tariff on US made cars. No tariff on Mexican cars.
Total cost advantage	$1,200 in favor of a Mexican produced car in the US	$4300 in favor of a Mexican car delivered to the EU market

Source: US Congressional Research Service (2017)

The examples above show that value added in the North American automobile value chain is distributed at different stages and in all three countries (see Figure 11.2). By one estimate, 74% of all the parts used by vehicle assemblers in Mexico are imported from the US. Mexico adds one-third of the value into a finished car. The other two-thirds is value imported from the U S and other countries. It is estimated that 38% of the value of a Mexican car exported to the US is the value of US parts returning to the US. In contrast, the value of US parts in a Mexican made car exported to Europe is 18% (De Gortari, 2018).

Over the years, Mexico has become the sixth-largest producer and fourth-largest exporter of vehicles in the world. About 80% of Mexico's production is of mid-size vehicles and light- and heavy-duty trucks and engines. As mentioned above, its production is mostly destined for the North American markets, with 89% of its production exported. In 2021, a number of the largest car manufacturers had established plants in Mexico including Audi, Baic Group, BMW, Stellantis (Fiat and Peugeot), Ford, General Motors, Honda, Kia, Mazda, Nissan, Toyota, and Volkswagen. Several heavy truck manufacturers have also established plants in Mexico such as Cummins, Detroit Diesel Allison, Daimler, Mack Trucks, Scania, Volvo, Hino, Isuzu, and Mercedes Benz among others (USTR, 2021). After reaching a peak of 3.9 million vehicles produced in 2017, the 2021 estimated production is 3.38 million. The internal market size is estimated at 1 million vehicles in 2021, served by local production and imports (Mexico Now, 2021). Auto parts are also an important sector of the North American value chain. Several MNCs have established operations in Mexico to be close to the car assembly and manufacturing plants. A large percentage of auto parts, however, are imported from the US and other countries (Badillo Reguera & Rozo Bernal, 2019).

Mexico has been relatively successful with its BI (the percent of foreign value added in the exports of a country) into the North American vehicle value chain with the production of small- and medium-size cars. As it deepens its involvement, Mexico seeks to produce vehicles demanding greater levels of skilled labor and more complex production technologies and market diversification beyond North America. One example of this transition to higher value chains is Audi, a unit of the Volkswagen group. The company opened its manufacturing facility in Puebla in 2016 with the mandate to produce 150,000 Audi Q5 SUVs for global markets, including the US, Europe, and China. In 2019, it began production of its Q5 TFS1, a premium hybrid SUV. Puebla is centrally located in Mexico with access to rail for transportation to the efficient Mexican ports in the Atlantic (Veracruz) for shipments to Europe and the Lazaro Cardenas Pacific coast of Mexico for exports to China. Exports to the US are moved by road. Audi's Mexico plant exports 95% of its output. The plant uses the most up to date technology with almost 80% automation (robots) and 5,200 people. Radio-frequency identification (RFID) technology is used to track every vehicle flow to manage its assembly line with real-time data. Audi has already achieved 62.5% USMCA's ROOs content and plans to achieve 75% in 2023 to reach free-trade benefits for exports to the US. The plant reuses the wastewater through an extensive reprocessing method (Johns, 2020). Audi is not alone in showing confidence in Mexico as a platform for global car manufacturing. In 2019, BMW opened its first Mexican manufacturing plant in San Luis de Potosi. The location is also in Central Mexico with rail and road connections to the Veracruz and Lazaro Cardenas ports in addition to Mexico's city airport. The Mexican plant is a twin model of its US plant in Spartanburg, South Carolina, with a capacity to produce 175,000 units, with an initial focus on its 3 Series sedan. The factory brings 90% of its parts from North America and 10% from outside the region. BMW uses about 400 suppliers in North America, with 180 based in Mexico. The plant is co-located in an industrial park with many of its suppliers for its Just in Time (JIT) process. Most of the parts arrive by ship or road with small electronic components arriving by air into Mexico City. JIT supplies are transported by trucks parked next to the plant as warehouses on wheels. Inventories and cars are tracked digitally, which allows BMW to shift sources and modes of transportation if delays occur at any time, such as those caused by the 2020 pandemic. BMW plans to ship 60% of its output to the US, 20% to Europe, and eventually to 30 markets worldwide. In the future, BMW's Mexico plant will lead the introduction of a new car for the first time anywhere in the BMW system—a designation that speaks to the promising future of Mexico in the automotive GVC (Perry, 2020).

Although Audi and BMW are moving Mexico to the frontier of automotive manufacturing, the country remains an important participant of the regional North American value chain. In addition to the automotive sectors, Mexico has achieved a more modest integration in the manufacturing of electronics, consumer goods, and services for North American markets. A greater presence in other sectoral value chains gives Mexico the ability to upgrade its labor skills and resources to become a more diversified producer of goods and services. The country is already attracting investments seeking to relocate to Mexico from distant operations in East Asia and China (O'Neil, 2021; Lopez, 2020).

South American Value Chains

South American participation in global value chains is mostly in terms of providing natural resources and commodities and is in early stages of transformation to value added. Distance to the main production hubs in Asia, Europe, and North America is one of the reasons for the lower level of integration with GVCs. Distance within the region is another reason for low integration among them. For instance, the distance between a major production hub in Sao Paulo, Brazil, and Santiago, Chile, is 1,600 miles and will take 43 hours by road to connect.

Despite the difficult distance, South American countries have made efforts to integrate under a wide variety of trade and market integration agreements among themselves and the rest of the world. Southern Cone countries have established highly structured rules to trade and integrate under the MERCOSUR customs union (Argentina, Brazil, Paraguay, and Uruguay were founding members, and Venezuela joined later). Andean countries have also formed a free trade area under the Andean Community (Colombia, Ecuador, Peru, and Bolivia). Chile has decided to go it alone and to participate with these groups as an associate member with limited benefits. These groups, as a block, have entered into trade agreements with other groups (the European Union). Several South American countries (Colombia, Chile, and Peru) have joined efforts with Canada and Mexico to create a group (Pacific Alliance) with the goal to engage Asian economies under the larger Trans-Pacific Partnership group. Chile has forged a myriad of bilateral agreements with other Latin American countries and with the world. The goal of all these agreements is to maximize market access, although, for the most part, these efforts have not been that effective in the economic development of the region and the need for cooperation to address the devastating impacts of the 2020 pandemic (World Bank, 2019; Garcia, 2020).

In general, studies of South American value chains conclude that intra-regional value added integration is not large and only accounts for 14% of total trade within the region (Amar & Landau, 2019). The authors conclude that the major countries contributing value added are Brazil, Argentina, and Chile. Brazil contributes to the generation of value added in refined petroleum products, automobiles and auto parts, metals, and chemical products. Argentina contributes largely in value added in agricultural, oil and gas refining, food products, and automotive parts. Chile contributes value added in mining, wood and paper production, chemicals, food and beverages, and air transportation. The majority of the value added (62%) takes place within MERCOSUR with most of it between Brazil and Argentina. Value added among non-MERCOSUR countries is more concentrated in certain activities and not as broad as in MERCOSUR.

For instance, Peru imports Ecuadorian, Colombian, and Venezuelan oil that it later exports as refined gasoline or petroleum with some of those exports going back to the sourcing countries. Chile's extensive mining activities are energy intensive, which Chile partially supplies but also uses energy imported from Bolivia, Peru, and Argentina in the production of copper and other minerals that it exports to the rest of the world. In general, the study concludes that, relative to the total exports of these countries, the traded value added is very small as is the use of imported value added from outside the sub-region. In contrast to the cases of Mexico or Central America reviewed above, South America is a seller of value added (forward linkages) with a small percent of imported inputs from the rest of the world. Next, we analyze the disaggregation of the value added exchanges among South American countries and the rest of the world.

As mentioned before, the degree of integration in value chains is measured by the degree of FI (the percent of the exports of one country that is used by the importer in its exports to other countries) and BI (the percent of foreign value added in the exports of a country). The total of the two is an indication of the level of value chain integration. The ratio of BI/FI indicates the position of a country in the value chain. A ratio that is greater than 1 indicates that a country's position is the last stage of transformation or generation of value. A lower ratio suggests that exports from a country are further processed before they become part of a final product. Table 11.5 summarizes these indicators and includes Mexico for comparison. The values for these tables come from the large GVC integration database (RIVA, n.d.).

For all South American countries, except for Ecuador, the FI indicator is greater than the BI indicator, supporting the conclusion that the sub-region, as a whole, is a supplier of value added. Mexico, in contrast, is a net buyer of value added, mostly from the US. The country with the highest level of integration is Chile, with a total index of (34.6%) followed by Bolivia, Peru, and Brazil. The ratio of BI/FI is less than 1.0 in all South America (except for Ecuador), which places them in early stages of the value chain. Venezuela has the lowest value chain integration ratio (0.25), whereas the ratio for Mexico, 5.45, puts this country closer to the production of final goods for the market.

Table 11.6 disaggregates the FI value in terms of the destination of the exchange: other South American countries and the US, Mexico, China, the European Union, and the Asia Pacific region. As China is part of the Asia Pacific region, there is some double counting in

Table 11.5 Value Chain Integration in Latin America

Country	Market/Trade Agreement Group	Forward Integration (FI)	Backward Integration (BI)	Total Integration (FI+BI)	Ratio of BI/FI
Argentina	MERCOSUR	15.0	8	23	0.47
Brazil		20.4	10.7	31.1	0.52
Paraguay		14.7	11.3	26.0	0.76
Uruguay		17.2	9.6	26.8	0.55
Venezuela		19.5	5	24.5	0.25
Chile	PA, TPP	21.7	12.9	34.6	0.59
Peru	AC	24.9	7.2	32.1	0.29
Colombia	Pacific Alliance	22.1	8.2	30.3	0.37
Ecuador	TPP	11.6	11.7	23.3	1.08
Bolivia	AC	19.3	13.0	32.3	0.67
Mexico	USMCA, PA, TPP	7.1	38.7	45.8	5.45

Source: RIVA (n.d) https://riva.negotiatetrade.org/#/gvc-links
AC – Andean Community
PA – Pacific Alliance
TPP – Trans-Pacific Partnership
USMCA – United States–Mexico–Canada Agreement

Table 11.6 Destination of Forward Integration in South America and Mexico

Country	Arg	Bra	Par	Uru	Ven	Chile	Peru	Col	Ecu	Bol	Mex	Asia Pacific	EU	US	China
Argentina	—	0.92	0.59	0.53	—	2.74	0.53	—	—	—	—	3.2	3.9	—	0.61
Brazil	0.24	—	—	—	—	—	—	—	—	—	0.75	6.7	6.4	1.06	2.35
Paraguay	0.80	2.19	—	0.29	—	0.50	—	—	—	—	—	—	—	—	—
Uruguay	0.34	2.04	—	—	—	—	—	—	—	—	0.67	2.7	3.9	0.40	1.08
Venezuela	—	—	—	—	—	—	—	—	—	—	—	8.0	3.0	5.92	3.7
Chile	—	0.55	—	—	—	—	—	—	—	—	—	12.5	5.8	0.63	4.53
Peru	—	—	—	—	—	0.63	—	—	—	—	—	11.7	7.5	0.97	5.9
Colombia	—	0.65	—	—	—	2.20	0.59	0.16	—	—	—	12.5	5.8	2.56	0.84
Ecuador	—	—	—	—	—	—	—	—	—	—	—	2.5	1.4	3.43	0.48
Bolivia	1.31	2.39	—	—	—	—	—	—	—	—	—	6.4	4.4	1.03	0.8
Mexico	—	—	—	—	—	—	—	—	—	—	—	0.9	1.6	3.00	0.17

Source: RIVA https://riva.negotiatetrade.org/#/gvc-links

the value for this group. Taking Argentina as an example, Table 11.6 shows that Argentina exports contribute to 0.92% of the value of Brazilian exports (to any region) and 0.59% of those of Paraguay, 0.53% of Uruguay, 2.74% of Chile, and 0.53% of Peru. Outside the region, Argentinian exports contribute to 3.2% of Asian Pacific exports to the world, 3.9% of those of Europe, and 0.61% of those of China. This example shows that Argentinean inputs are found within MERCOSUR, other South American countries, and the rest of the world. Within the region, Chile is the largest user of Argentinean inputs; Asian economies are the largest users outside the region. It is interesting to note that Argentinean inputs do not have an impact on Mexican or US exports. In contrast to Argentina, Brazilian value exports have much less impact in the region, but they are particularly relevant in China (they contribute to 2.35% of China's exports, which is huge given the size of the Chinese export machinery). Uruguay has a relatively substantial global FI with European Union exports (3.9%).

Countries outside the MERCOSUR group have limited or non-existent forward value chain integration with MERCOSUR; their FI is with the rest of the world. Chile's highest level of integration is with the Asian Pacific (12.5 % of Chilean value added is incorporated in the exports of this region to the world), 5.8% to European Union exports, and 4.53% to Chinese exports. Colombia, Peru, and Bolivia also show a good level of integration with the rest of the world. Among the Andean countries, Ecuadorian value added is incorporated in the exports of Chile, Colombia, and Peru, mostly in terms of petroleum. All of the South American countries, except Argentina and Paraguay, have some degree of integration with the US value added chain. Brazil is the only South American country with some degree of FI with Mexico.

Backward integration among South American value chains shows how their economies use intermediate inputs from within the region in the transformation of value of products and services that are consumed internally or exported (see Table 11.7). Once again, this exchange is more intense among MERCOSUR members which trade cars, agricultural products and inputs, food and beverages, metals, steel and iron from Brazil, and transportation services. For instance, Paraguay buys tobacco from members, which is then processed and exported to the world as cigars. Uruguay buys leather from members and exports shoes to the world. Perhaps, the largest exchange within MERCOSUR happens in the automotive sector in which Brazil and Argentina exchange parts and cars.

We use the case of the 2017 trade of parts and cars between Argentina and Brazil in 2017 to illustrate the disaggregation of the value added exchange.

- Brazil exported $1.37 billion in cars and parts to Argentina. It exported a total of 10.13 billion cars to the world.
- Argentina exported $2.7 billion in cars and parts to Brazil. It exported a total of $6.88 billion in cars to the world.
- 13.6% of the value added in intermediate output produced in Argentina was consumed in Brazil.
- 22.06% of the value added in intermediate output produced in Brazil was consumed in Argentina.
- 40.90% of the value added in finished cars produced in Argentina was consumed in Brazil.
- 60.64% of the value added in finished cars produced in Brazil was consumed in Argentina.
- 5.49% of Argentine value added was used in Brazilian automotive exports to the world.
- 2.82% of Brazilian value added was used in Argentine automotive exports to the world.
- 0.88% of Argentine value added and transformed in Brazil was reexported back to Argentina.

Table 11.7 Backward Integration in South America and Mexico

Country	Source														
	Arg	Bra	Par	Uru	Ven	Chile	Peru	Col	Ecu	Bol	Mex	Asia Pacific	EU	US	China
Argentina	–	1.24	0.16	–	–	–	–	–	–	0.15	–	1.9	1.5	1.14	0.96
Brazil	–	–	–	–	–	–	–	–	–	–	–	2.9	2.4	1.56	1.04
Paraguay	–	–	–	–	–	–	–	–	–	0.15	–	2.7	1.0	0.75	1.56
Uruguay	–	–	–	–	–	–	0.20	–	–	–	–	1.7	1.9	1.25	0.85
Venezuela	–	0.08	–	–	–	0.18	0.27	–	–	–	0.11	0.5	0.5	1.31	0.27
Chile	2.29	1.18	–	–	–	–	0.24	0.30	0.48	–	–	2.2	2.1	2.13	1.12
Peru	–	–	–	–	–	0.16	–	0.15	0.21	–	–	2.0	1.1	1.39	1.07
Colombia	0.33	0.23	–	–	–	–	–	–	–	–	–	1.7	1.78	–	0.72
Ecuador	0.96	0.44	–	–	–	–	0.45	0.44	–	0.26	–	2.5	1.4	2.4	1.22
Bolivia	1.32	1.89	–	–	–	–	1.02	–	–	–	–	2.8	2.1	2.19	1.69
Mexico	–	0.52	–	–	–	–	–	–	–	–	–	11.3	3.2	16.78	4.82

Source: RIVA (n.d.) https://riva.negotiatetrade.org/#gvc-links

- 1.34% of Brazilian value added and transformed in Argentina was reexported back to Brazil.
- The rest was double counting (parts going back and forth, which happens frequently in the automotive industry).

The above example shows a symmetrical exchange of value added in parts and components between Argentina and Brazil, which is incorporated in cars for their domestic consumption and exports. In contrast, the value exchanged between the US and Mexico is asymmetrical—Mexico is a net importer of US value added.

Beyond MERCOSUR, the Andean countries are buyers of value added in food and beverages from MERCOSUR members, mostly Brazil and Argentina. Chile and Peru trade value added in natural resources and mining products. As these two countries have well-developed mining sectors, this exchange may be complementary inputs and services that they both need for their exports to the world. All South American countries have BI with suppliers from the Asian Pacific region, Europe, China, and the US. China's inputs are used in the value transformation of all countries in South America. Brazil and Venezuela have a small degree of BI with Mexico.

To conclude, the value chain configurations in the northern and southern regions of Latin America are different. As shown in Figure 11.2, the lithium battery case places Latin American countries as suppliers of raw and refining inputs that are processed by China in wafers that are used in the assembly of lithium batteries that supply energy to electric cars, principally in advanced markets in the US, Europe, and Japan. These car manufacturers participate in the early stages of the value chain with design and specifications for batteries. The North American GVC features Mexico as an assembler of imported components from the US and Canada and, to a lesser extent, from other regions (Europe). Cars assembled in Mexico end up in North America with some small share going to Europe. The Southern Cone automotive value chain is the integration of Brazilian and Argentinean automotive national industries where parts manufactured from local raw inputs (steel, aluminum, rubber, and plastic) are incorporated into the production of cars for local consumption and exports to the rest of the world. In the case of garments, Central American countries contribute to the sewing and stitching of imported yarns and textiles from the rest of the world for exports, mainly to the U.S., under preferential trade agreements.

Firm Perspective on Value Chain Configurations

A firms' decision to participate in value chains is based on internal factors (efficiency or profits for example) or external factors (distance, regulations, transportation). Value chain configurations and participants are constantly adapting to changing conditions, as unanticipated events, such as the pandemic, may impact any of its parts or members or stop the flow of goods and services (Qiang et al., 2021; World Economic Forum, 2019a, World Economic Forum, 2019b; World Economic Forum, 2021).

As discussed before, large MNCs have enough market power and possess the technological and financial resources to take a leading role in global and regional value chains. In some cases, they exercise this power based on their R&D and innovation capabilities, such as the case of Tesla in lithium batteries. Large Chinese mining companies, such as Ganfeng and Zinging, invest in lithium extraction in Chile and Argentina, which is further refined in China and used in the production of lithium batteries by China's mining MNC, CATL, which has one-third of the world capacity (Keen & Erickson, 2021). CATL has long-time contracts to supply lithium batteries to Tesla, GM, Volkswagen, and BMW (Bradsher & Forsythe, 2021). Automotive manufacturers decide how many EVs to produce based on their anticipation of demand and, based on these forecasts, enter short- and long-term contracts that specify the prices and terms of their commitments to buy lithium batteries. Thus, a GVC is the aggregation of all of these operational decisions made by their participants.

At the most strategic level, these large MNCs make decisions related to their business and operating models (World Economic Forum, 2020). At the operating level, MNCs may look at how value is created in the value chain. That is, they address the questions of what value (product or service), how value is created (the transformation process), where is value created (geographic location), and by whom (the participants of the value chain). In making decisions of how to participate or organize value chains, these companies have to determine whether it is better to own or contract any or all of the activities of the value chain as well as the degree of sharing information and technology on the design, manufacturing, and/or logistic activities. Based on their assessments, these companies identify ideal configurations or extracting, manufacturing, and distribution hubs. At the business model level, MNCs determine how to capture the value created. This decision is based on their assessment of how to monetize their capabilities and resources and how those generate streams of revenue. These strategic considerations were discussed in Chapter 8. In this chapter, we focus on the operating decisions.

The operating decisions depend on the complexity of products and markets. For simple, mature, and standard products, the decisions are based on costs, availability, and efficiency of production. For complex and innovative products in complex markets, decisions are based on protection of technology and proprietary knowledge and ability to serve markets. In both situations, value chain decisions involve cost and risk trade-offs of production costs, transaction costs, supply risks, and preservation of market power considerations. Firms consider whether to outsourcing is more efficient than producing. In outsourcing, firms may also consider the advantages and disadvantages of distant (offshoring) or closer supply sources (near-shoring). When transportation and tariff costs favor countries in proximity to end markets, companies may prefer near-shoring suppliers. We assess the conditions of Latin American countries in delivering these conditions next.

A study by A.T. Kearney in 2018 included several Latin America countries with world-wide production capabilities (World Economic Forum, 2018). The study introduces the concept of structure of production and scale capacity to undertake production tasks. Countries with large and more complex structures offer a base to support complex value chains. Complexity is captured by the mix and uniqueness of products manufactured in a country, and it is an indication of the knowledge and sophistication of capabilities embedded in the human and technological resources of countries (Atlas of Economic Complexity, 2022). Scale is assessed by the sheer volume of manufacturing output in a country and its significance to a country's economy measured by the manufacturing value added as percent of gross domestic product (GDP). The structure of production for Latin American countries, and the US and China as referent countries, is given in Table 11.8 measured on a scale of 1 (worst) to 10 (best). Figure 11.3 provides a visual of the production structure of these countries.

Based on the results of the study, Mexico is the only country in Latin America relatively close to the structure of production of the US and China. As such, it is the only country with a strong consideration as a manufacturing base for MNCs. Latin American countries with greater complexity and scale are Brazil and Argentina. Costa Rica offers complexity but with a lower scale than the previous countries. Colombia, Chile, and El Salvador are also options

Table 11.8 Structure of Production in Latin America, US, and China

Country	Structure			Production Drivers						
	Overall	Complexity	Scale	Overall	Technology Innovation	Human Capital	Trade and Investment	Institutions	Sustainability	Demand
Mexico	6.74	7.16	6.11	5.04	4.51	4.45	6.25	4.15	5.88	5.85
Brazil	5.22	5.33	5.05	5.03	4.49	4.42	5.27	4.51	7.55	6.1
Costa Rica	4.97	5.61	4.01	4.9	3.87	5.67	4.19	5.87	6.94	4.23
Argentina	4.91	4.71	5.2	4.25	3.78	4.94	3.15	4.16	5.84	4.99
El Salvador	4.81	5.1	4.36	3.55	2.64	3.45	4.03	3.63	6.53	3.14
Colombia	4.61	4.94	4.12	4.53	4.01	4.6	3.89	4.6	7.53	4.91
Uruguay	4.52	5.44	3.14	4.75	4.46	4.84	3.57	6.36	6.68	3.77
Chile	4.18	4.47	3.76	5.6	4.36	5.32	6.02	6.91	6.87	4.89
Guatemala	4.05	3.75	4.5	3.71	2.89	4.02	3.53	3.2	6.94	4.24
The Dominican Republic	3.99	4.03	3.95	4.02	3.49	4.29	3.85	4.22	6	3.65
Panama	3.82	5.27	1.64	4.89	3.91	4.9	5.6	4.95	7.6	4.26
Peru	3.67	3.12	4.49	4.18	3.34	4.24	3.96	4.32	6.27	4.61
Honduras	3.43	3.32	3.59	3.61	2.69	3.73	4.32	3.19	6.76	3.26
Paraguay	3.24	3.71	2.54	3.84	3.02	3.99	4.46	3.7	6.05	3.37
Ecuador	2.85	2.42	3.5	3.66	3.55	4	3.16	3.57	4.69	3.8
China	8.25	7.08	10.0	6.14	5.74	5.57	7.21	4.88	5.52	7.93
US	7.78	8.58	6.59	8.16	8.52	7.91	7.73	8.55	6.69	8.54

Source: World Economic Forum: Readiness for the future of production report 2018
https://www.weforum.org/reports/readiness-for-the-future-of-production-report-2018
Scale: 1 = worst; 10 = best.

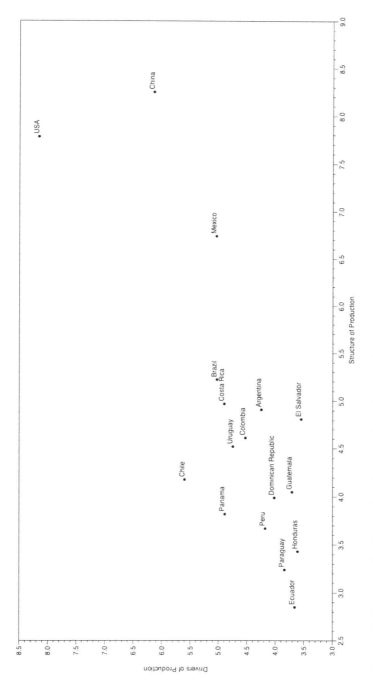

Figure 11.3 Frontiers of readiness of production in Latin America, the US, and China

for manufacturing bases. The rest of Latin American countries in the study have neither the scale nor complexity to be considered.

The Kearney study identifies the drivers of production: technology and innovation, human capital, trade and investment conditions, quality of institutions, sustainable resources (use of natural resources and alternative energies), and demand environment (sophistication of the consumer and availability of foreign or local suppliers to satisfy demand). Considering all factors, Chile provides the highest support of production (overall rating of 5.6) followed by Brazil (5.03) and Mexico (5.04). None of these countries comes close to the US (8.16) and China (6.14). Mexico offers the best combination of technology, innovation, and demand conditions, which could be important for MNCs seeking advanced research bases and greater flexibility in investing, moving products, and services. For MNCs requiring high quality of human resources, Costa Rica and Chile are the highest in human capital. These countries and Uruguay offer solid institutional bases, which exceed China's (4.88). All Latin American countries have solid performance on the sustainable use of natural resources, even better than those of the US and China in this respect.

In conclusion, Mexico has greater capacity to diversify into a greater number of value chains given its strengths. Mexico's proximity to the US market provides it with great potential for near-shore production. Brazil offers the scale and complexity but lags in terms of human capital, institutions, and does not provide an environment supportive of trade and investment facilitation. Costa Rica and Chile compensate for their lack of scale with solid human resources and quality of institutions, and they are supportive of trade and investments. Costa Rica has the additional advantages of greater production complexity (5.61) and proximity to the US market. The remainder of the Latin American countries lack the conditions for efficient production.

Summary

MNCs have carefully built complex supply networks over the years guided by costs and risk considerations. Latin America has been on the edges of these GVCs, mostly supplying raw materials and commodities. The COVID-19 pandemic of 2020 has disrupted the fragility of these efficient arrangements and questioned the logic of the single-supplier operating model, in many cases centered in China. These same MNCs are reevaluating their operating models, and Latin America could be favored in this realignment to create alternative supplier bases. Mexico, in particular, could be a winner of this rebalancing (O'Neil, 2021). It will take some time to build or expand supplier networks in Latin America given the shortcomings of the region in supply chain conditions reviewed in this chapter. A few countries are better prepared for these conditions based on their adequate pools of skilled labor, technological and innovation readiness, more open and friendly trade and investment climates, and quality of institutions. Countries that are closer to the frontier of production readiness based on their production readiness (production complexity and scale factors) are Mexico, Chile, Costa Rica, Colombia, Uruguay, and Panama. Other factors, such as geography (distance to markets) and ability to learn and adopt new technologies related to these relocation efforts will determine the early winners.

As we reviewed in this chapter, the backward and forward linkages to GVCs are different in North America and South America. North American countries leverage their lower labor costs, proximity, and trade agreements to participate in downstream production activities destined to the US market. These countries add value by the assembly of imported inputs. Mexico has developed value chains in automotive, machinery, and electronics; Central

American countries in garment value chains; Costa Rica in high-tech products and services; and the Dominican Republic in medical devices. In contrast, South American countries operate in backward linkages to GVCs and export raw and refined inputs to other countries that transform them into intermediate and final products. There is limited integration of South American countries in value added of these raw inputs, with Brazil and Argentina being the exception in the exchanges of automotive products.

Latin America contributes a number of advantages to current and future value chains. The most important contribution is the supply of basic inputs used across many economic activities, which include mining (copper, iron, bauxite, lithium, nickel, and manganese among others). Latin America is a large contributor of energy (gas and oil), agricultural products (grains, fruits, beef, pork, and seafood), and natural resources (wood, rubber). Manufacturing costs in Mexico ($4,439) are lower than China ($6,675) and are competitive with Southeast Asian rivals such as Vietnam ($4,066). Adding transportation, tariff and other advantages, PricewaterhouseCoopers (PwC) estimates that companies can save 23% in sourcing from Mexico vis-à-vis China (PwC, 2020). Near shore advantages lower logistic costs (transportation—truck versus ship) and shorter lead times (transit time from China to the US).

Latin America has a number of shortcomings to support efficient value chains; the most important is that it does not have the extensive density of supplier networks available in East Asia and Eastern Europe. As reviewed above, infrastructure is poor and the efficiency to move inputs across borders is below the standard of other countries. Institutional quality to enforce contracts and judicial quality is uneven. Some countries provide robust protections, such as Uruguay and Costa Rica, but the rest are below par. Corruption and bribery in the region also affect the costs of trading and moving products across borders. Addressing these disadvantages may take some time, and as the economies of the region have been devastated by the pandemic, governments may not have the resources to upgrade roads, ports, and airports for quite some time.

In conclusion, Latin America faces challenges and opportunities to improve and upgrade its participation in GVCs and to develop more regional ones (World Bank, 2020d). The region must improve its competencies, invest in the efficiency of processes supporting value chains, and use more advanced technologies that support complex tasks to produce more complex products (Pietrobelli & Rabellotti, 2006; Taglioni & Winkler, 2016). An upgrade of supply chain capabilities will allow Latin American countries to support a greater diversity of supply chains. A few initiatives may promise more immediate results. Latin America already has myriad trade agreements and market integration vehicles, but these are determined by geography or individual country initiatives. A better effort of trade integration to support regional participation in GVCs is needed. What is lacking are agreements around the integration of value chain activities in which countries specialize in particular production tasks and contribute with materials and inputs accordingly. Improving cross-border integration may attract enough firms to create sizable clusters of critical mass to supply GVCs.

References

Amar, A., & Landau, M. T. (2019). Cadenas regionales de valor en America del Sur. CEPAL. Retrieved on January 4, 2022 from https://www.cepal.org/es/publicaciones/45002-cadenas-regionales-valor-america-sur

Antras, P. (2020). Conceptual aspects of global value chains. *World Bank Policy Research Paper 9114*. Retrieved on December 30, 2021 from https://openknowledge.worldbank.org/handle/10986/33228

Atlas of Economic Complexity. (2022). The Atlas of Economic Complexity by the Growth Lab at Harvard University. Retrieved on January 8, 2022 from https://atlas.cid.harvard.edu

Badillo Reguera, J., & Rozo Bernal, C. A. (2019). Mexico in the global value chain of the automotive industry. SCIELO. Retrieved on January 16, 2022 from http://www.scielo.org.mx/scielo.php?script=sci_arttext&pid=S1665-952X2019000300121

Baldwin, R., & Venables, A. J. (2010). Spiders and snakes: Offshoring and agglomeration in the global economy. *Journal of International Economics*, *92*(2), 245–254. https://doi.org/10.1016/j.jinteco.2013.02.005

Berg, R. C. (2021). South America's lithium triangle: Opportunities for the Biden administration. Center for Strategic & International Studies. Retrieved on January 4, 2022 from https://www.csis.org/analysis/south-americas-lithium-triangle-opportunities-biden-administration

Blyde, J. S. (2014). *Synchronized factories: Latin America and the Caribbean in the era of global chains*. Springer Publishers. https://doi.org/10.1007/978-3-319-09991-0

Bradsher, K., & Forsythe, M. (2021, December 22). Why a Chinese company dominates electric car batteries. New York Times. Retrieved on January 9, 2022 from https://www.nytimes.com/2021/12/22/business/china-catl-electric-car-batteries.html

Cadestin, C., Gourdon, J., & Kowalski, P. (2016). Participation in global value chains in Latin America. Retrieved on January 4, 2022 from https://www.oecd-ilibrary.org/docserver/5jlpq80ts8f2-en.pdf?expires=1641401129&id=id&accname=guest&checksum=D4CF4429D4CD9298DEE337F71E58075B

De Gortari, A. (2018). How much of your car is made in Mexico? Econofact. Retrieved on January 6, 2022 from https://econofact.org/how-much-of-your-car-is-made-in-mexico

Dempsey, C. (2019). How Costa Rica reinvented itself as the tech epicenter of Central America. Nearshore Americas. Retrieved on January 4, 2022 from https://nearshoreamericas.com/how-costa-rica-reinvented-itself-as-the-tech-epicenter-of-central-america/

Fernandes, A., Kee, H. L., & Winkler, D. (2020). *Determinants of global value chain participation: Cross-country evidence*. World Bank Policy Research Working Paper 9197. Retrieved on December 30, 2021 from https://openknowledge.worldbank.org/handle/10986/33519

Frederick, S., Bair, J., & Gereffi, G. (2014). Nicaragua and the apparel value chain in the Americas. Retrieved on January 16, 2022 from https://gvcc.duke.edu/wp-content/uploads/2014-03-25a_DukeCGGC_Nicaragua_apparel_report.pdf

Garcia, P. M. (2020). Deeper integration of Latin America against COVID-19. Beyond Borders. Retrieved on January 16, 2022 from https://blogs.iadb.org/integration-trade/en/integration-against-covid-19/

Gerefy, G. (2014). Global value chains in a Post-Washington consensus world. *Review of International Political Economy*, *21*(1), 9–37. https://doi.org/10.1080/09692290.2012.756414

Gerefy, G., Humphrey, J., & Sturgeon, T. (2005). The governance of global value chains. *Review of International Political Economy*, *12*(1), 78–104.

Hewitt, J., & Monge-Gonzalez, R. (2010). Innovation, R&D, and productivity in the Costa Rican ICT Sector: A case study. IDB. Retrieved on January 16, 2022 from https://publications.iadb.org/en/publication/innovation-rd-and-productivity-costa-rican-ict-sector-case-study

Invest Chile. (2021). Global services and technology industry in Chile. Retrieved on January 4, 2022 from https://investchile.gob.cl/wp-content/uploads/2021/05/globalservices-e-book-eng-vf.pdf?_ga=2.58491053.688337718.1641337215-1182344538.1641337215

Johns, V. (2020). Audi's future-proof factory in Mexico. Automotive Logistics Digital. Retrieved in January 6, 2022 from https://automotivelogistics.h5mag.com/al_fvl_summer_2020/audi_s_future-proof_factory_in_mexico

Jones, L., Demirkaya, M., & Bethman, E. (2020). Global value chains: Overview and issues for congress. United States Congressional Research Service. Retrieved on December 30, 2021 from https://sgp.fas.org/crs/row/R46641.pdf

Keen, K., & Erickson, C. (2021). China mining companies sweep up lithium supplies in acquisitions. S&P Global Market Intelligence. Retrieved on January 9, 2022 from https://www.spglobal.com/marketintelligence/en/news-insights/latest-news-headlines/china-mining-battery-companies-sweep-up-lithium-supplies-in-acquisition-blitz-67205411

Lin, J., Demirkaya, M., & Bethmann, E. (2019). Global value chain analysis: Concepts and approaches. *Journal of International Commerce and Economics* (April). Retrieved on January 3, 2022 from https://www.usitc.gov/publications/332/journals/concepts_approaches_in_gvc_research_final _april_18.pdf

Lopez, E. (2020). As supply chains cut costs, El Paso, Texas, takes on a new role. *Supply Chain Dive*. Retrieved on January 16, 2022 from https://www.supplychaindive.com/news/el-paso-texas-DHL -border-logistics-trade/588614/

Lund, S., Manyika, J., Woetzel, J., Bughin, J., Krishnan, M., Seong, J., & Muir, M. (2019). Globalization in transition: The future of trade and value chains. *McKinsey Global Institute*. Retrieved on December 30, 2021 from https://www.mckinsey.com/featured-insights/innovation-and-growth/globalization -in-transition-the-future-of-trade-and-value-chains

Mexico Now. (2021). Mexico's automotive industry closed 2021 with 1 million new cars sold. Retrieved on January 6, 2022 from https://mexico-now.com/mexicos-automotive-industry-closed-2021-with -1-million-new-cars-sold/

OECD. (2012). Mapping global value chains. Retrieved on December 30, 2021 from https://www.oecd .org/dac/aft/MappingGlobalValueChains_web_usb.pdf

O'Neil, S. K. (2021). U.S. should look south for better supply chains. Retrieved on January 10, 2022 from https://www.cfr.org/article/us-should-look-south-better-supply-chains

Park A., Nayyar, G., & Low, P. (2013). Supply chain perspectives and issues: A literature review. *World Trade Organization*. Retrieved on January 3, 2022 from https://www.wto.org/english/res_e/ publications_e/aid4tradesupplychain13_e.htm

Perry, J. (2020). A new home in Mexico. *Automotive Logistics Digital*. Retrieved on January 6, 2022 from https://automotivelogistics.h5mag.com/al_fvl_spring_2020/bmw_mexico

Pietrobelli, C., & Rabellotti, R. (2006). Upgrading to compete: Global value chains, clusters, and SMEs in Latin America (eds). *IDB*. Retrieved on December 30, 2021 from https://publications.iadb.org/ publications/english/document/Upgrading-to-Compete-Global-Value-Chains-Clusters-and-SMEs -in-Latin-America.pdf

Porter, M. (1985). *Competitive advantage: Creating and sustaining superior performance*. New York: Free Press.

PwC. (2020). Beyond China: US manufacturers are sizing up new and cost-efficient global footprints. Retrieved on January 10, 2022 from https://www.pwc.com/us/en/services/consulting/fit-for-growth /library/supply-chain-resiliency.html

Qiang, C. Z., Liu, Y., & Steenbergen, V. (2021). An investment perspective on global value chains. Washington, DC: World Bank. https://openknowledge.worldbank.org/handle/10986/35526

RIVA. (n.d.). Regional integration and value chain analyzer. Retrieved on January 9, 2022 from https:// riva.negotiatetrade.org/#/gvc-links

Stollinger, R. (2021). Testing the smile curve: Functional specialization and value creation in GVCs. *Structural Change and Economic Dynamics*, 56(March), 93–116. https://doi.org/10.1016/j.strueco .2020.10.002

Taglioni, D., & Winkler, D. (2016). *Making global value chains work for development*. Trade and Development. Washington, DC: World Bank. https://openknowledge.worldbank.org/handle/10986 /24426

The Guardian. (2021). The rush to go electric comes with a hidden cost: Destructive lithium mining. Retrieved on January 3, 2022 from https://www.theguardian.com/commentisfree/2021/jun/14/ electric-cost-lithium-mining-decarbonasation-salt-flats-chile

Thun, E., Taglioni, D., Sturgeon, T., and Dallas, M. P. (2021). Why policy makers should pay attention to the concept of massive modularity: The example of the mobile telecom industry. Retrieved on January 23, 2022 from https://blogs.worldbank.org/developmenttalk/why-policy-makers-should -pay-attention-concept-massive-modularity-example-mobile

United States Census Bureau. (2021). Trade in goods with the CAFTA-DR. Retrieved on January 4, 2022 from https://www.census.gov/foreign-trade/balance/c0017.html

United States Congressional Research Service. (2017). NAFTA and motor vehicle trade. Retrieved on January 6, 2022 from https://sgp.fas.org/crs/row/R44907.pdf

United States Congressional Research Service. (2021). USMCA: Motor vehicle provisions and issues. Retrieved on January 6, 2022 from https://crsreports.congress.gov/product/pdf/IF/IF11387

United States International Trade Administration (USITA). (2021). Mexico country commercial 20Guide: Automotive industry. Retrieved on January 6, 2022 from https://www.trade.gov/country -commercial-guides/mexico-automotive-industry

United States International Trade Commission (USITC). (2019). Global value chain analysis: Concepts and approaches. Retrieved on December 30, 2021 from https://www.usitc.gov/publications/332/journals/concepts_approaches_in_gvc_research_final_april_18.pdf

United States International Trade Representative (USTR). (2021a). USCAM-Chapter 4, rules of origin. Retrieved on January 6, 2022 from https://ustr.gov/sites/default/files/files/agreements/FTA/USMCA/Text/04-Rules-of-Origin.pdf

United States International Trade Representative (USTR). (2021b). CAFTA-DR. Retrieved on January 4, 2022 from https://ustr.gov/trade-agreements/free-trade-agreements/cafta-dr -dominican-republic-central-america-fta/final-text

White House. (2021). Building resilient supply chains, revitalizing American manufacturing, and fostering broad-based growth. Retrieved on January 4, 2022 from https://www.whitehouse.gov/wp-content/uploads/2021/06/100-day-supply-chain-review-report.pdf?utm_source=sfmc%E2%80%8B&utm_medium=email%E2%80%8B&utm_campaign=20210610_Global_Manufacturing_Economic_Update_June_Members

World Bank. (2019). Trade integration as a pathway to development? Retrieved on January 16, 2022 from https://openknowledge.worldbank.org/bitstream/handle/10986/32518/9781464815164.pdf

World Bank. (2020a). Doing business 2020. Retrieved on December 30, 2021 from https://openknowledge.worldbank.org/bitstream/handle/10986/32436/9781464814402.pdf

World Bank. (2020b). Doing business 2020: Latin America and The Caribbean. Retrieved on December 30, 2021 from https://www.doingbusiness.org/content/dam/doingBusiness/media/Profiles/Regional/DB2020/LAC.pdf

World Bank. (2020c). *World development report: Trading for development in the age of global value chains.* Retrieved on December 30, 2021 from https://www.worldbank.org/en/publication/wdr2020

World Bank. (2021a). Foreign direct investments and global value chains. Retrieved on December 15, 2021 from https://elibrary-worldbank-org.proxygw.wrlc.org/doi/epdf/10.1596/978-1-4648 -1683-3_ch1

World Bank. (2021b). Global chains at the time of Covid. Retrieved on December 15, 2021 from https://elibrary-worldbank-org.proxygw.wrlc.org/doi/epdf/10.1596/978-1-4648-1683-3_ch5

World Economic Forum. (2018). Readiness for the future of production. Retrieved on December 30, 2021 from https://www.weforum.org/reports/readiness-for-the-future-of-production-report -2018

World Economic Forum. (2019a). *Global competitiveness report.* Retrieved on December 30, 2021 from https://www3.weforum.org/docs/WEF_TheGlobalCompetitivenessReport2019.pdf

World Economic Forum. (2019b). Shaping the sustainability of production systems. Retrieved on December 30, 2021 from https://www.weforum.org/whitepapers/future-of-manufacturing-and -production-report

World Economic Forum. (2019c). Reshaping global value: Technology, climate, trade- global value chains under pressure. Retrieved on December 30, 2021 from https://www3.weforum.org/docs/WEF_Reshaping_Global_Value_Report.pdf

World Economic Forum. (2020). Winning the race for survival: How advanced manufacturing technologies are driving business-model innovation. Retrieved on January 2, 2022 from https://www.weforum.org/reports/towards-a-new-normal-new-design-rules-for-advanced-manufacturing -business-models

World Economic Forum. (2021). The resilience compass: Navigating global value chain disruption in age of uncertainty. Retrieved on December 30, 2021 from https://www3.weforum.org/docs/WEF_Navigating_Global_Value_Chains_Disruptions_2021.pdf

WTO–World Trade Organization. (2021). Rules of origin. Retrieved on January 6, 2022 from https://www.wto.org/english/tratop_e/roi_e/roi_info_e.htm

12 Strategic Opportunities and Risks in Latin America

A Summary

Introduction

A market of more than 600 million people and a region characterized by dramatic and constant social, economic, and political changes, Latin America presents significant opportunities and challenges for domestic and global businesses alike. Latin America is a mosaic of countries with distinct cultures and political economies rather than a monolithic region. This book aims to:

- Provide a comprehensive overview of the business environment in Latin America.
- Identify the major drivers of market opportunities and risks in Latin America.
- Assess the characteristics and behaviors of Latin American consumers and the implications for marketing strategies in the region.
- Determine the most relevant business drivers and critical success factors for effective strategies in Latin American markets for companies from within and outside the region.
- Assess effective managerial and leadership practices for the region.
- Provide an educated prognosis of the future of the business environment in Latin America.

The book is, therefore, grounded on strategic thinking and focuses on assessing opportunities and risks in the region. Other important strategic themes guiding our discussion include country and firm competitiveness, competencies and skill building, resilience, adaptation, integration, and collaboration. The analysis also approaches business opportunities and risks from a triple bottom results perspective, paying attention to economic, social, and environmental concerns. Finally, innovation is a running theme throughout the book, from identifying key product, process, and management innovations undertaken by foreign and domestic companies to highlighting innovative entrepreneurial activity in the region.

The Business Environment in Latin America

The Economic Environment

In our first edition (Robles, Wiese, & Torres-Baumgarten, 2015), we questioned the degree to which the growth that the region had experienced during the first decade of the twenty-first century was sustainable. At the time, the region had successfully emerged from the 2008 recession, with growth similar or higher than before the financial collapse. By 2014, however, concerns for the sustainability of such economic growth into the future loomed, due in part to an overreliance on natural resource exports, realignment of countries in the region into two

DOI: 10.4324/9781003182672-15

geographic clusters, continued social inequalities, and increasing warnings about irreversible climate change. In the second decade of the twenty-first century, those concerns have been exacerbated by the health and economic crises that enveloped the globe with the spread of the coronavirus in 2020 and beyond.

Countries in the region continue to share a legacy of issues that include poor educational and health systems, income inequality, weak infrastructure, a large informal sector, corruption, and obsolete legal and regulatory frameworks. The onset of the COVID-19 pandemic in early 2020 brought with it an economic collapse that only made evident these institutional voids and inefficiencies and accentuated the economic, political, and social problems that had been brewing in the region for several years.

At the present juncture, Latin American economies will need to imagine and adopt new models of development that are human centered, addressing not only stark social inequalities but also the real threats of climate change. Public and private investments in the region, domestic and foreign, should seek to close the economic, social, and environmental gaps that the 'old models' produced. Each country is likely to forge its own path to reignite their economies for the next decade, but any reengineering effort will also require deeper integration within the region and with the rest of the world.

The Political and Legal Environment

Latin America has come a long way in adopting democracy as the predominant governmental system in the region; yet the region's democracies remain fragile. The failure of national governments in enacting and implementing the kinds of policies and development programs needed to eradicate poverty, reduce inequality, and move the region out of its current economic growth slump is driving the democratic fatigue currently afflicting Latin American citizens. Lack of progress controlling crime and corruption round-up the list of citizens' frustrations with their current governments. Weak governance and institutional voids have led to a lack of trust in major political institutions (e.g., all branches of government, the police, electoral systems), increasing protests and demonstrations by segments of the population most affected (e.g., those in lower and middle-income brackets, vulnerable minorities). In the midst of growing citizen discontent and anger, populist and autocratic leaders are making a comeback and succeeding in their efforts to entrench themselves in positions of power.

The near future points to ongoing instability, citizen discontent, and democratic backsliding. Yet there are reasons for optimism. Civilian protests and demonstrations, uninterrupted transitions of power via democratic processes, lower tolerance for corruption, and greater activism across the region are all positive signs. Latin Americans may have taken a few steps back on the road to solidifying democracy and achieving stability, but they are unlikely to renounce their hard-won civil rights and political freedoms to give way to the dictatorial aspirations of a handful of politicians.

On the legal front, Latin America has made little progress over the past five years to establish a regulatory environment that encourages investment and productivity while protecting consumers, minority investors, and other stakeholders. Red tape and inefficient systems of taxation and business registration continue to shape the business environment, one of the worst in the world. The COVID-19 pandemic led to the streamlining and digitalization of some business-related processes, but these small improvements will need to be not only made permanent but also greatly expanded to make a real difference in the formation and operational conditions of businesses.

The Competitive Environment

The competitive landscape in Latin America has evolved significantly over the past few decades. Formerly protected markets, which were dominated by a few large family groups and state-owned enterprises, have been replaced by open markets and more diverse and dynamic competition. Although large family-controlled domestic conglomerates still play a dominant role, there is now a stronger presence of multinational corporations from developed and emerging economies and a more vibrant small- and medium-size business sector.

The main drivers of competitiveness in Latin America are its relative macroeconomic stability, a relatively healthy labor market, and a stable (though less than inclusive) financial system. The main barriers to competitiveness for countries in the region are weak institutional environments, inadequate infrastructure, low and slow information and communications technology (ICT) adoption, and lack of innovation capabilities.

Though the region's competitiveness has significant room for improvement, Latin America has been successful in integrating itself into global value chains, albeit through different mechanisms and geographic hubs. While countries like Mexico have specialized in manufacturing of consumer and industrial goods, countries like Peru and Chile have specialized as suppliers of raw materials and intermediate goods. Others, such as Panama and countries in the Caribbean sub-region, have specialized in logistics and other supporting services. The structure of global value chains may evolve after the world recovers from the COVID-19 pandemic, and Latin American countries must seek opportunities to deepen and diversify their forward and backward linkages in these global chains.

As Latin America emerges from the current health and economic crisis, countries in the region must seize the opportunity to rebuild and transform their economies through substantial investments in infrastructure, skill building, and research and development. There are also clear opportunities to generate real gains to productivity by closing inequality gaps, promoting inclusivity, and addressing climate change. Integrating solutions to these challenges into policies and programs aimed at increasing economic output has the potential to create a virtuous cycle of growth, productivity, and human development.

Demographic Transitions and Population Dynamics

The region's population is in transition to a highly urbanized, older population. By 2050, it is estimated that 88% of Latin America will be urbanized, and life expectancy will reach 80.5 years. The slowdown of the region's population growth is mainly due to falling fertility rates, increased life expectancy, and a reduction of mortality rates, all of which have been driven by the economic growth and changing social dynamics of the past few decades. Increased urbanization is also correlated to lower fertility rates and an aging population. Although the region, as a whole, is in a mature stage of demographic transformation, there are significant variations in the population dynamics across countries. Some countries in the region have a demographic profile similar to European societies, aging and largely urban (e.g., Uruguay and Chile), whereas others exhibit younger, more rural populations (e.g., Honduras and Guatemala). Increased urbanization and aging of the population does not bode well for Latin America. First, the demographic dividend that fueled, in part, the economic growth of the region has long been subsiding. Second, the region is ill-prepared for the challenges of providing health care, economic support, and housing for the elderly. Third, Latin American cities suffer from sprawl, poor transportation systems, and high levels of crime. Therefore, managing these challenges will require public and private efforts aimed at better urban planning and enhanced social services.

Latin America has experienced a net outflow of migration. The US is the largest and preferred destination for Latin Americans by far, with Mexicans and Central Americans being the largest groups of immigrants into the US. Intra-regional migration is also on the increase, with people in the region migrating to neighboring countries that offer growing and more stable economic opportunities. In addition, recent increases in intra-regional migration emanate from the collapse of the Venezuelan and Haitian societies in 2015–2020.

Latin America has lost its innocence of the assumption of racial and ethnic harmony. The historical effort to achieve racial mixture under the guise of nation building, which had resulted in masked racism and discrimination, has recently been unmasked. The rejection and pressure to end the violence and brutality against Afro-descendants and Indigenous groups by police or drug traffickers through street protests and more militant groups has raised awareness of the plight of these minorities among all levels of society. The current social discourse calls for inclusiveness, justice, dignity, and tolerance, and there is hope across the region for more equal representation and fair distribution of equal access to opportunities for all groups in the not so distant future.

Other demographic characteristics and trends in the region include:

- A more educated population, with almost universal literacy and school attendance. Yet the region's public expenditures in education and learning outcomes continue to lag behind the averages for Organization for Economic Cooperation and Development (OECD) countries.
- Multigenerational families and households. The more standard household of two-parents and siblings living together accounts for almost half of all households, but single women raising children in single-parent households is also a common phenomenon.
- Marked differences in income. Middle-income households account for about half of the region's population, but an almost equal percentage still falls under poverty levels.
- Increased access to health services and improved nutrition, but an increase in cardiovascular diseases and diabetes. The lifestyles of Latin Americans (e.g., poor diets, sedentary lifestyles, and large intake of calories and alcohol) are the main drivers of health problems in the region. Other drivers include lack of access to basic services of water and sanitation and poor environmental conditions in major urban centers.

The Sociocultural Environment

Latin American values have been cemented by centuries of survival and socialization under colonial, republican, and modern times. Perhaps the most influential factor shaping Latin American long-term values is religion. The Catholic Church's religious monopoly for five centuries, however, has sustained a staggering loss of worshipers. The increases in non-religious affiliations and secularization among large segments of the region's population have moved countries towards more liberal and tolerant views on moral values related to abortion, contraception, divorce, and sexual preferences.

Latin Americans are a high-context culture characterized by empathy, Familism, particularism, and fatalism. Latin American cultures value large power distances, high uncertainty avoidance, and in-group collectivism. The region exhibits low levels of institutional collectivism and gender egalitarianism with a tilt toward masculine values.

Latin American business culture is rooted in its European colonial heritage. This legacy has created organizational and decision-making styles characterized by concentration of power, multilevel hierarchical structures, strong networks of relationships, and paternalism. Latin Americans value personal relationships because these relationships traditionally have been important for advancement in life. Relationships are based on trust of the same referent group and the expectation of loyalty and reciprocity among members of the in-group.

In terms of leadership preferences in organizational settings, charismatic leadership, team-oriented, participatory, and self-protective styles seemed to be preferred. Another prevalent leadership style is benevolent paternalism, which is consistent with the prevalence of high power distance, masculinity, collectivism, and uncertainty avoidance in the region. Also worth noting is the region's slow progress regarding gender inclusivity in top leadership positions, even in the face of the increasing talent shortages facing today's organizations.

Business Strategies for Latin America

Marketing Strategies for Latin American Consumer Markets

The Latin American consumer market has grown in size and purchasing power; it has also become increasingly segmented, more sophisticated and discerning, and less frugal while remaining distinctive from other markets around the world. Social mobility led to the emergence of a larger middle class and reduction of poverty across the region. Many consumers at the base of the pyramid have been lifted from extreme poverty by economic growth and governmental programs. Consumers at the middle and top of the pyramid have experienced increased affluence and gains from long periods of economic stability and expanding business opportunities. The COVID-19 pandemic reversed some of these economic gains, but as the region recovers, the consumer market will offer renewed potential in the years to come.

Latin American consumers are mostly urban, educated, technologically connected, more socially and environmentally aware, and ready to express their values, beliefs, and personalities through their purchases. They are also confident and pleased with their lifestyles and, consequently, are more discerning and demanding. Their rational side makes them more focused on value, convenience, and time-saving and efficiency seeking. On the emotional side, Latin American consumers look for honesty, transparency, authenticity, and relevance (e.g., making a contribution to the environment and society). To reach this market, firms need to develop brands that resonate well with Latin Americans consumers' values and priorities. Brand building efforts should focus on creating salience by delivering offerings with functional, emotional, and social benefits at affordable prices.

Advances in digital communication technologies and high levels of internet penetration and smartphone ownership have radically changed the consumer market environment in Latin America. The COVID-19 pandemic has accelerated the digitalization of media, distribution channels, and forms of payment, creating opportunities for product and process innovations. Firms will need to adopt omnimedia strategies that do not abandon traditional media (especially TV) but that prioritize digital and online media. Communication strategies must also be integrated with omnichannel strategies that provide consumers with a seamless shopping experience across offline and online channels. Although traditional and modern store retailing still dominate the market, the growth of e-commerce is unstoppable. Retailers in Latin America, large and small, that adopt omnichannel strategies aimed at increasing choice, convenience, and safety will enhance the consumer experience at all touchpoints and cement consumer loyalty. Finally, firms must focus not only on affordability of products but also on payment facilitation. Current trends indicate the future of payments in Latin America will be digital, instant, and contactless. The emergence of alternative payment mechanisms, in addition to cash, debit cards, and credit cards, will further drive growth in e-commerce.

Corporate Strategies for Firms from Outside the Region

Latin America has attracted many multinationals interested in participating in the growing domestic markets in the region or those that are attracted to the region's rich and abundant natural resources, skilled labor pools, and proximity to the US market. These multinationals bring a wealth of resources and advantages to the region. They also integrate their global value supply chains to either receive inputs or serve the domestic markets.

Non-Latin American multinationals' strategy for Latin America is highly integrated with their global strategy but with substantial adaptations to local market conditions. Given the diversity of market opportunities and resource advantages that the region offers, multinationals may implement multicountry or sub-regional strategies. This regional strategy has four components: (1) regional ambition; (2) regional strategic thrust; (3) building assets, resources, and competencies; and (4) a regional organization and culture. *Regional ambition* is the effort to assess the strategic importance and contribution of Latin America to the multinational's global strategy and performance. Such assessment may impact the strategic decisions of resource allocation and investments. *Regional strategic thrust* focuses on leveraging the multinationals' advantages in the region (e.g., global brands, marketing competencies, technology advantages). *Building strategic assets, resources, and competencies* can be accomplished in many different ways such as greenfield investments in manufacturing and distribution assets or through mergers and acquisitions. *Regional organization and culture* results in various structural and geographic configurations, such as organizing around key countries (e.g., Brazil or Mexico) or by sub-region (e.g., Southern Cone, Central America, etc.). Adaptation of regional strategies to address local preferences is important in markets where national culture is strong. Multinationals operating in Latin America have found similarities across regional markets and replicated successful business models from one market to another. Despite their overwhelming advantages, multinational companies face strong competition from national companies and will need to continually refine their regional strategies to sustain their long-term viability.

Strategic Approaches of Multilatinas and Global Latinas

During the past three decades, firms native to Latin America successfully internationalized to other countries in the region (*Multilatinas*) and to other regions across the globe (*Global Latinas*). The internationalization of Latin American firms was driven primarily by external factors. The economic transformation that began in the 1990s forced Latin American firms, especially family-owned, national market leaders, to pursue growth beyond their national borders to counter competition from foreign multinationals and the loss of government protection. Firms may have initially internationalized as a survival strategy, but many found that they could thrive and lead in regional and global markets.

Multilatinas and Global Latinas play a vital role in their respective economies (e.g., boosting employment, expanding the knowledge base, generating export-based tax revenue, etc.), and they also enhance the region's competitiveness. They are mostly privately owned, many by large family-owned or family-controlled conglomerates, yet a few are wholly or partially owned by the state. Mexico and Brazil, followed by Chile and Colombia, tend to produce the largest number of Latin American multinationals. Multilatinas and Global

Latinas span all sectors but are especially present in energy, financial services, retailing, telecommunications, and food and beverages, with some being considered regional or global leaders in their respective sectors.

Key success factors that characterize Multilatinas and Global Latinas include visionary leadership, family-ownership that lends continuity and a long-term orientation, and innovation as well as operational (e.g., cost efficient operations, supply chain management), marketing (e.g., branding, distribution), and management (e.g., talent management, financial management) capabilities. Their main strategic weaknesses include lack of brand recognition outside their home markets, family-ownership that may hinder their access to global financing, and low levels of research and development spending.

Based on their primary strategies, Multilatinas and Global Latinas can be *global integrators*, firms that seek efficiency and scale, and have the ability to create and manage highly integrated global operations; *global sourcers*, firms that expand abroad in search of resources; or *global marketers*, firms that focus on product innovation and diversification, brand building, and customer service excellence. The common thread across Multilatinas and Global Latinas' strategic approaches regionally and globally is innovation. These firms have succeeded by developing product, process, management, and business model innovations. They have also pursued reverse, frugal, and social innovations that have led to operational and market advantages.

The Entrepreneurial Environment in Latin America

There is no doubt that the entrepreneurial climate in Latin America is being transformed. More business-friendly, vibrant, and resilient ecosystems throughout the region now support entrepreneurs and small- and medium-size businesses (SMEs) in all sectors. Technological hubs are also present in some countries (e.g., Brazil, Colombia, Chile) and sectors (e.g., financial services, information technology, alternative energy, aeronautics). Still, much work remains to be done before entrepreneurs in Latin America can boast the levels of support from the private and public sectors observed in developed countries. One example of Latin America's accomplishments—and of the work that remains—is the availability of venture capital and other sources of financing. Although more investors are betting on the region and banking institutions are more open to lending to entrepreneurs and small-business owners, sources of capital remain woefully insufficient to support both early-stage entrepreneurs and small businesses seeking to scale up.

A country's innovative capability is directly linked to the entrepreneurial attitudes and behaviors of its people and the resulting entrepreneurial activity in the country. New ventures and small- and medium-size enterprises are considered main drivers of employment, income generation, poverty eradication, and social inclusion. Countries may differ on the types of entrepreneurial ventures they choose to support. While in some countries, government policies and private sector initiatives may promote technology-oriented entrepreneurs, in others, the emphasis may be on social entrepreneurs or entrepreneurship by vulnerable or disadvantaged segments of the population (e.g., Indigenous groups, women, low-income youth, etc.). Some countries may also differ on the sectors toward which investment and supporting resources are channeled, such as agriculture, tourism, health, and telecommunications, among others.

Policymakers must continue their push to build strong institutions that support entrepreneurs and small- and medium-size businesses as well as promote innovation across all sectors of their economies. For instance, streamlining of regulatory procedures and more favorable regulations and taxation policies can enhance the entrepreneurial environment.

National economic policies that create spaces and incentives for collaboration between entrepreneurs, scientists, educational institutions, larger businesses, and government are also needed to spur higher levels of knowledge dissemination and innovative capacity building. This may require a renewed commitment to new and improved physical infrastructure (e.g., transportation and logistics, internet access). Another important area for improvement is education. Entrepreneurial skills can be developed through education in the sciences and technology as well as business skills and management training. Educators at all levels might also play a role in this regard by championing curricular reforms that promote critical thinking, creativity, and technical skills.

Finally, the private and public sectors must strengthen their commitment to social and economic inclusion. The business ecosystems in the region must be open and accessible to all entrepreneurs, regardless of gender, socioeconomic status, or level of education. The diversity of talent in the region must be fully leveraged if the region is to not only enhance its productivity and competitiveness but also find viable solutions to its social, economic, and environmental challenges.

Global and Regional Value Chains

Global value chains (GVCs) are the engines of the global economy. Their emergence has been driven by a combination of increased fragmentation and dispersion of sourcing and production as countries around the world have upgraded their capabilities and invested in supporting infrastructure that have lowered transportation and communication costs. As the name suggests, value is created and built upon by a wide range of participants located in different geographies. Multinational firms have carefully built complex value networks over the years guided by costs and risk considerations. Latin America has been largely at the edges of GVCs, mostly supplying raw materials and commodities based on its abundant natural resources.

Across the world, government responses to limit the impact of the COVID-19 pandemic included business and border closures, which disrupted GVCs, creating shortages of goods everywhere. Such disruption pressed companies to reassess operating models based on single-supply sources centered on China and made Latin America, and particularly Mexico, an attractive supplier base for the US and European markets. It will take some time to build or expand supplier networks in Latin America given the shortcomings of the region in supply chain conditions. A few countries are better prepared, having adequate pools of skilled labor, technological and innovation readiness, more open and friendly trade and investment climates, and a stronger institutional environment. Countries that are closer to the frontier of production readiness include Mexico, Chile, Costa Rica, Colombia, Uruguay, and Panama. Other factors, such as geographic distance to markets and ability to learn and adopt new technologies related to these relocation efforts, will determine the early winners.

The backward and forward linkages to global value chains are different in North America and South America. North American countries leverage their lower labor costs, geographic proximity, and trade agreements to participate in downstream production activities destined to the US market. These countries add value primarily through the assembly of imported inputs. For example, Mexico has developed value chains in automotive, machinery, and electronics; Central American countries in apparel and electronic component value chains; and the Dominican Republic in medical devices. In contrast, South American countries operate in backward linkages to global value chains through their exports of raw and refined inputs to other countries that transform them into intermediate and final products. There is limited integration of South American countries in value added of these raw inputs, with Brazil and Argentina being the exception in the exchanges of automotive products.

Latin America faces challenges and opportunities to improve and upgrade its participation in GVCs and to develop more regional ones. The region must improve its competencies, invest in the efficiency of processes supporting value chains, and use more advanced technologies that support complex tasks to produce more complex products. An upgrade of supply chain capabilities will allow Latin American countries to support a greater diversity of supply chains and improving cross-border integration may attract enough firms to create clusters of critical mass to support regional participation in GVCs.

Strategic Opportunities and Risks in Latin America

This section presents a summary of the main strategic risks and opportunities facing firms doing business in Latin America. We begin with a discussion of the main drivers of potential risks and challenges to business in the region at present and into the future, namely: health pandemics, social inequality, authoritarianism, corruption, and climate change (see Table 12.1). There is no clear resolution to these risks because they continue to evolve even as we write. Nevertheless, a better understanding of the scope, severity, and potential consequences of these drivers in the region gives firms an opportunity to adopt risk-minimization strategies aimed at developing greater resiliency, agility, and flexibility. We focus our analysis on the business impacts of these driving factors with an emphasis on effects on consumer markets, the talent pool, and value chains.

Business Risks and Uncertainty

High uncertainty and risks are omnipresent in the region, and their economic and social consequences for society are paramount. The 2020 health pandemic caught the world unprepared and caused devastating human and economic losses. This sad example illustrates the need to assess the vulnerability of countries and firms and determine their adaptive capacity and resilience to health and other sources of risks. It is clear that risks manifest in different forms, and their intensity is amplified by their interdependent nature. Moreover, there is a high degree of heterogeneity on how different sources of risks impact specific countries, industries, and firms.

The framework we use for assessing risks and uncertainty identifies four levels of uncertainty as well as strategies that companies can use to manage these levels of uncertainty (see Chapter 6).

- *First level—clear enough future.* This level describes a situation of low levels of uncertainty in which a more likely scenario can be identified, and alternative strategies can be easily evaluated using traditional analytical tools.
- *Second level—alternative scenarios.* Under this level, several alternative scenarios can be identified, but it is difficult to predict which one would occur. Thus, each scenario may require a different evaluation model, and for each model, there could be different outcomes. The challenge is to establish the probabilities of each outcome and their associated returns using traditional decision-making analysis.
- *Third level—range of futures.* Under this situation, some but not all scenarios can be formulated. The uncertainty rests in the risk of not considering a possible scenario that could occur and, therefore, the inability to even identify the outcomes and impacts

Table 12.1 Summary of Opportunities and Risks in Latin America

Source of Opportunity/ Risk (Chapter)	Drivers		Opportunities	Sample Countries	Risks/Challenges	Sample Countries
	Broad	*Specific*				
Economic Environment (Chapters 1 and 3)	Growth/Contraction	Recovery post-COVID-19	– Increase in consumer market demand – Increase in commodity exports – E-commerce expansion	Chile, Brazil	– Unemployment – Lower purchasing power among hardest hit consumer segments – Social instability	Honduras, Mexico, Peru
		High inflation	Increasing demand for high-value products, especially by low-income consumers	Brazil, Chile, Colombia, Mexico, Peru	– Higher interest rates – Lower purchasing power – Social unrest – Contraction of consumer demand	Brazil, Chile, Colombia, Mexico, Peru
	Economic Inequality	Inequality of opportunity: – Frustrated aspirations of young and minority population groups – Reversal of poverty reduction gains	– Private sector initiatives that create equal access to jobs and venture formation – Increasing demand for high-value products – Branding and positioning that centers equity and opportunity, especially for disadvantaged groups	Uruguay, Chile	– Losses in purchasing power and contraction of consumer markets due to low intergenerational mobility and stagnant middle class – Contraction of talent pools	Brazil, Central America, Mexico

	Trend	Sub-trends	Opportunities	Countries	Risks	Countries
	Business and Investment Climate	– Market-friendly policies – Improvements to infrastructure – Greater (and more inclusive) access to financing	– Opportunities for trade and investment in all sectors (natural resource extraction, agriculture, manufacturing, and services) – Lower transaction and operation costs – New venture formation	Argentina, Brazil, Chile, Costa Rica, Panama, Uruguay	The business environment in select countries remains closed and unattractive	Cuba, Nicaragua, Venezuela
Political Environment (Chapter 2)	Anti-democratic Trends	– Authoritarian and populists regimes – Contested and polarized elections – Violent repression	– Private sector initiatives that fulfill citizens' needs for efficiency, trust, transparency, equity – Branding and positioning strategies grounded in pro-democracy principles		– Social unrest – Political instability	Brazil, Cuba, El Salvador, Nicaragua, Venezuela
Institutional Environment (Chapters 2, 3, and 4)	Increased Transparency and Accountability	– Decrease in corruption – More efficient and effective public management	– More equal playing field – Lower cost of doing business	Chile, the Dominican Republic, Paraguay, Uruguay		
	Weakening of Institutions	– Governmental actions against basic freedoms (i.e., speech, press, association) – Ongoing impunity and corruption			– Governmental failure – Social unrest – Less attractive environment for FDI and trade – Higher cost of doing business	Brazil, El Salvador, Honduras, Mexico, Peru

(Continued)

Table 12.1 Continued

Source of Opportunity/ Risk (Chapter)	Drivers		Opportunities	Sample Countries	Risks/Challenges	Sample Countries
	Broad	*Specific*				
	Internal Conflicts & Failed States	Migration (inter- and intra-regional migration)	– Brain gain: receiving countries' absorption of new talent pool (young, educated) – Consumer segments with unique needs	Argentina, Chile, Colombia, Peru	Countries experiencing outmigration: – Brain drain – Contraction of consumer markets and productive capacity – Loss of FDI Economic and social strain on receiving cities/ countries	Haiti, Nicaragua, Venezuela, Brazil, Chile, Colombia, Costa Rica, Peru
Regulatory Environment (Chapter 2)	Removal of Obstacles to Competitiveness	– Streamlining and digitalization of bureaucracy – Improved trade facilitation	– Increased productivity – Lower transaction costs – More friendly business environment for domestic and foreign investors – Greater integration to global value chains		Greater exploitation of natural resources leading to further environmental degradation and social conflicts	Bolivia, Brazil, Ecuador, Peru
		High Informality			Low social protection for informal business = economic and social instability	
Demographics (Chapter 4)	Demographic Transformation	Younger population	Large pool of young, skilled workers	Central America, the Dominican Republic, Paraguay		

Trend		Opportunities	Countries	Risks	Countries
Aging population		– Increasing demand for products and business models aimed at older consumer segment – Higher demand for digitalization and automation		– Lower productivity – Talent shortages – Higher social costs	Chile, Costa Rica, Cuba, Uruguay
Urbanization	Increasing urbanization rates	Increasing demand for products and business models that meet needs of urban consumers: time-saving, convenient	Argentina, Chile, Uruguay		
	Insufficient and deteriorating infrastructure	– Consumer demand for reliable and affordable basic services – Remote work		Collapse of cities = social and economic instability	
Changing Family Structures	Multigenerational, single-parent, and single-person households	Increasing demand for goods/services to meet the needs of non-traditional households			
Racial/Ethnic Minority Populations (e.g., Indigenous, Afro-descendants)	– Conflictive race relations – Discrimination / unequal access to social and economic opportunities – Increased social awareness – Individual empowerment	– Racial/ethnically defined consumer markets of substantial size and unmet needs – Larger talent pools (through better policies and programs)	Brazil, Colombia, the Dominican Republic, Mexico, Panama, Peru	Ongoing discrimination leading to: – Smaller consumer markets – Unemployment – Brain drain Continued police violence directed at these groups	Bolivia, Guatemala, Mexico, Peru

(Continued)

Table 12.1 Continued

Source of Opportunity/ Risk (Chapter)	Drivers — Broad	Drivers — Specific	Opportunities	Sample Countries	Risks/Challenges	Sample Countries
National Violence (Chapters 4 and 5)	Transnational Crime	Stronger criminal organizations			– Lack of security for investments and business operations – Social and economic instability	El Salvador, Honduras, Mexico
		Street violence	High demand for safety and security products		– Human and material losses – Low consumer confidence	Brazil, Colombia, Peru
Natural Environment (Chapters 3 and 6)	Global Climate Change	– Decline in availability and quality of water – Unhealthy temperatures – Loss of habitats – Greater exposure to natural disasters (earthquakes, floods, hurricanes, etc.)	– Public and private investments in environmentally friendly and resilient infrastructure – Increased demand for environmentally friendly products and technology	Brazil, Chile, Costa Rica	– Human, economic and material losses – Food scarcity and insecurity = social and economic instability – Higher operational costs due to water and energy shortages – Higher insurance costs	Central America, the Dominican Republic, Peru
	Natural Resources Demand		Increasing global and regional demand for: – Biofuel production – Sustainable food products – Metals and minerals	Argentina, Bolivia, Brazil, Chile, Peru	Environmental degradation and contamination	Central America, Ecuador, Peru

Energy Needs	– Increasing cost of oil – Concerns over climate change – Insufficient or deteriorating energy grids – Unequal access to energy resources	– Public and private investments in energy production and infrastructure (especially alternative) – Increasing global and regional demand for alternative and off-grid energy resources	Bolivia, Brazil, Ecuador, Peru, Venezuela	– Air pollution leading to health problems – Higher operational costs – Contraction of consumer demand for high energy-need products	Brazil, Mexico
Health (Chapters 3 and 4) Health Systems Preparedness	– Low investments in public health (human and physical infrastructure) – Unequal access to health services	– Public and private investments in human and physical health infrastructure – Demand for pharmaceuticals and medical equipment – E-health services		– Mortality – Collapse of health systems – Higher cost of managing chronic health conditions – Unemployment	Honduras, Peru, Venezuela
Infectious Diseases & Pandemics (COVID-19 Pandemic)	– Unequal access to health services – Lack of social protection nets – Informality (jobs and businesses)	– Public and private investments in human and physical health infrastructures – Demand for pharmaceuticals and medical equipment		– Mortality – Unemployment – Economic contraction	Brazil, Mexico, Peru
Population Resilience	– Poor nutrition – Lifestyles (obesity, alcohol consumption) – Access to water and sanitation – Poor living/housing conditions	– Production and manufacture of food products – Demand for health- and fitness- related products and services – Public and private investments in water sanitation, and housing infrastructure		– Mortality – Higher cost of health services – Low productivity	Central America, Haiti, Mexico, Peru

(Continued)

Table 12.1 Continued

Source of Opportunity/ Risk (Chapter)	Drivers		Opportunities	Sample Countries	Risks/Challenges	Sample Countries
	Broad	*Specific*				
Socio-Cultural Environment (Chapters 4, 5, and 7)	Changing Cultural Values	– Individual empowerment (primarily among women and racial/ ethnic minorities) – Increased social acceptance and tolerance	– Expansion of labor pools at all levels, especially for top leadership positions Inclusive policies and strategies that promote entrepreneurial opportunities – Marketing strategies targeted at racial minorities, LGBTQ+ communities, other minority groups		Unwillingness to implement changes to policies and practices may lead to: – Difficulties attracting and retaining talent – Consumer backlash	
	Changing Religious Preferences and Affiliations	Rise of evangelism and secularism	– Demand for more inclusive products – Recruiting and retaining younger talent whose preferences may lean liberal			
	Less Tolerance for Corruption		– Lower transaction and operating costs – Business strategies and practices built on honesty, trust, and authenticity		Polarized society along the conservative/liberal spectrum Backlash against companies/products that lean to the extreme left or right	Brazil, Central America, Chile, Uruguay

Driver	Trend	Opportunities	Countries	Risks	Countries
Social Mobility	Income and educational mobility	– Higher demand for consumer products that appeal to middle-income consumers (e.g., education, health, housing, entertainment, and travel, etc.) – Larger and more educated talent pool	Argentina, Brazil, Colombia, Mexico Uruguay	– Low mobility leads to social unrest and protests – Economic, human, assets losses	Chile, Central America, Colombia, Paraguay, Peru
Innovation (Chapter 7 and 10)	Adoption of Disruptive Technologies Increased Connectivity	– Increased digitalization (business applications, automation, digital/online services) – E-commerce – Online payment systems – New venture formation – Easier access to consumers with an expanded portfolio of marketing communication tools		– Labor Displacement – Digital Divide – Cybersecurity	
Labor Force / Talent Pools (Chapters 5 and 10)	Higher public expenditures in education Increased Education and Employability	– Larger pools of educated and technology savvy workers – Tech hubs – Practical retraining of displaced workers	Argentina, Brazil, Chile, Costa Rica Cuba, Mexico, Uruguay	– Knowledge skill gaps (i.e., countries with lower expenditures in education and literacy rates) – Unequal access to economic opportunities – Lower consumer demand among less educated consumer segments	Central America, the Dominican Republic, Haiti, Paraguay

(Continued)

Table 12.1 Continued

Source of Opportunity/ Risk (Chapter)	Drivers		Opportunities	Sample Countries	Risks/Challenges	Sample Countries
	Broad	*Specific*				
	Remote Working		Outsourcing (manufacturing and business processes)	Chile, Costa Rica, Uruguay	Contraction of consumer spending due to slow post-COVID-19 recovery	Central America
Consumer Markets (Chapters 1, 3, and 7)	Sustained Economic Growth	– Social mobility – Higher purchasing power – More sophisticated and demanding consumers	– Larger consumer markets – Higher purchasing power – Demand for technology-based and non-discretionary products	Argentina, Chile, Colombia, Brazil		
	Competition	Open and more deregulated markets = more and more diversified domestic and foreign competition	– Demand for high-value offerings – Demand for innovative products and business models		– Greater competitive rivalry = higher costs – Higher pressures for efficiency and responsiveness	
	Retailing Trends	– Higher purchasing power driven by economic growth and social mobility – Broad adoption of technology – Better infrastructure	– Increasing demand for all retailing models (specialized, discount, luxury, etc.) – Expansion of e-commerce and omnichannels – Increasing demand for digital and alternative payment systems and technologies			

Supply Chains (Chapter 11)					
Global Supply Chains	Resource intensive supply chains	- Private investments in agricultural sector/food production - Growth of mining sector (including rare minerals)	Argentina, Bolivia, Brazil, Chile, Paraguay	- Food insecurity - Environmental degradation - Social conflicts and reputational losses if managed irresponsibly	Argentina, Bolivia, Brazil, Central America, Chile, Haiti, Peru
	Labor intensive supply chains	Private investments in apparel, call centers	Central America, the Dominican Republic	- Increasing cost of labor - Social backlash and reputational losses if managed unethically	Central America, Mexico
	Knowledge intensive supply chains	Private investments in tech hubs	Chile, Brazil, Mexico, Uruguay		
	Global demand for energy resources	Public and private investments in the oil and gas sector	Argentina, Bolivia, Brazil, Colombia, Ecuador, Mexico, Venezuela	Environmental degradation	
Near-Shoring	- Increasing transportation costs - Overreliance on China as a sole sourcing location - Higher consumers' expectations for responsiveness	Private investments in key sectors/supply chains: automotive, medical devices, and apparel	Mexico, Costa Rica, the Dominican Republic		

Source: Authors' elaboration.

associated with these unknown scenarios. The challenge under this third level is to consider as many viable scenarios and formulate flexible strategies that can be reformulated under evolving unpredictable scenarios.

- *Fourth level—true ambiguity.* The nature of the situation is not well understood, and potential scenarios cannot be identified. At best, one can only identify and monitor favorable or unfavorable indicators through a situation analysis. Decision-makers may be able to gather some insights by analyzing similar events and situations and study strategies that work under those conditions.

The various sources and levels of uncertainty emanate from the economic, political, regulatory, societal, competitive, and natural environments in Latin America. The level of uncertainty in the region falls primarily under Levels 1–3 of our framework above. The seriousness of risks in Latin America ranges from moderate to high, most of these risks can be anticipated and estimated, with some exceptions (e.g., risks related to climate change). This means companies operating in Latin America can, and should, monitor key indicators of economic, political, social, and natural risk on an ongoing basis. This would allow them to remain agile and adaptable by identifying trigger points for implementing alternative strategies. Companies can also pursue shaper strategies, especially those grounded in disruptive innovations that may place them in leadership positions in specific sectors or industries.

In the short term, the main factor driving risk and uncertainty will be the continued management of the health and economic crises caused by the COVID-19 pandemic and the actions taken by governments in the region to help their respective economies recover post-pandemic. In the short- and medium-term, companies will need to monitor key variables that can be considered triggers of economic, political, societal, and natural risks and uncertainty, such as unemployment, commodity prices, poverty rates and income gaps, deteriorating infrastructure, lack of accountability for corruption, impunity for those engaged in crime and violence, and abuses of power by government officials, among others.

Strategic Opportunities in Latin America

Companies would be wise to understand the risks they face in the region and prepare to manage these risks and associated uncertainty. Truly visionary companies, however, will see beyond the risks and appreciate the many opportunities Latin America offers (see Table 12.1).

The most important strategic opportunities in the region are in the areas in which the region is currently experiencing growing consumer markets, significant supply gaps, or deteriorating conditions. Here is a sample of key opportunities in the region:

- Technological solutions to environmental pollution and degradation—water supply, sanitation, alternative energy, waste management, organic and sustainable food production (agriculture, fishing, etc.), natural disaster prevention, habitat restoration.
- Infrastructure—all areas of infrastructure in the region are either insufficient, deteriorating, or outdated, including roads, communication systems, ports, and public health and educational facilities.
- Products and services for poorly served but growing consumer segments such as, the elderly, racial/ethnic minorities, LGBTQ+ communities, and consumers in rural and low-income urban areas.
- Health, both services and manufacturing—fitness and nutrition, chronic illness management, pandemic preparedness, pharmaceuticals, medical devices.

- Education, especially in science and technology.
- Financial services—greater and more inclusive access to venture capital by entrepreneurs and small- and medium-size businesses and payment facilitation.
- Digital services—e-commerce facilitation, payment systems, logistics, business processes, etc.
- Natural resource extraction, including oil, gas, metals, and minerals.
- Supply chain management and logistics, including deepening, diversifying, and furthering integration of Latin American firms into GVCs through both backward and forward linkages.

Concluding Thoughts

The vision for a post-pandemic Latin America should be one centered on equality and sustainability through economic, institutional, and social transformations. A transformed Latin America will seek to strengthen its institutional environment to preserve its democratic systems, combat crime and corruption, and regain the trust of its people. A transformed Latin America will nurture innovations aimed at addressing climate change and social inequality through a supportive, vibrant, and inclusive entrepreneurial environment. A transformed Latin America will be fully integrated into the global economy through dynamic and agile value chains. A transformed Latin America will embrace digitalization and automation to improve the region's competitiveness, streamline business operations, and improve the provision of public services to its citizens.

Finally, firms wishing to succeed in Latin America should aspire to be leaders in their respective industries by pursuing social and environmental goals alongside financial outcomes. Firms operating in the region, regardless of origin or size, should build competitive advantages that allow them to respond to the pressures of climate change, social inequalities, and unexpected events (e.g., health pandemics) through the adoption and adaptation of strategies and managerial practices that meet local conditions, build resilient value chains; and adopt human-centered organizational structures and processes. In addition, transformative innovations at the product, process, and managerial levels will be a prerequisite for firms to remain viable in the long-term. Finally, coping with volatility and uncertainty must be a key strategic consideration for companies operating in the region. A focus on risk analysis and risk management will be an essential key success factor. Recent events show that all world regions are vulnerable to pandemics, environmental catastrophes, and social and political crises. The preparedness and resilience of different companies and countries may ameliorate the impact of these negative macro events.

Index

Milton Keynes UK
Ingram Content Group UK Ltd.
UKHW031122031224
451949UK00020B/375

9 781032 022772